President Carter 1978

Timely Reports to Keep
Journalists, Scholars and the Public
Abreast of Developing Issues, Events and Trends

April 1979

CONGRESSIONAL QUARTERLY
1414 22ND STREET, N.W., WASHINGTON, D.C. 20037

58820

Congressional Quarterly Inc.

Congressional Quarterly Inc., an editorial research service and publishing company, serves clients in the fields of news, education, business and government. It combines specific coverage of Congress, government and politics by Congressional Quarterly with the more general subject range of an affiliated service, Editorial Research Reports.

Congressional Quarterly was founded in 1945 by Henrietta and Nelson Poynter. Its basic periodical publication was and still is the CQ *Weekly Report,* mailed to clients every Saturday. A cumulative index is published quarterly.

The CQ *Almanac,* a compendium of legislation for one session of Congress, is published every spring. *Congress and the Nation* is published every four years as a record of government for one presidential term.

Congressional Quarterly also publishes paperback books on public affairs. These include the twice-yearly *Guide to Current American Government* and such recent titles as *The Middle East: U.S. Policy, Israel, Oil and the Arabs, Third Edition; Energy Policy;* and *Urban America: Policies and Problems; Taxes, Jobs and Inflation.*

CQ Direct Research is a consulting service that performs contract research and maintains a reference library and query desk for the convenience of clients.

Editorial Research Reports covers subjects beyond the specialized scope of Congressional Quarterly. It publishes reference material on foreign affairs, business, education, cultural affairs, national security, science and other topics of news interest. Service to clients includes a 6,000-word report four times a month bound and indexed semiannually. Editorial Research Reports publishes paperback books in its fields of coverage. Founded in 1923, the service merged with Congressional Quarterly in 1956.

Editor: John L. Moore

Contributors: Irwin B. Arieff, Alan Berlow, Christopher R. Conte, Ann Cooper, Harrison H. Donnelly, Martin Donsky, Alan Ehrenhalt, John Felton, Mark Gruenberg, Barry M. Hager, Diane Huffman, Larry Light, Bob Livernash, David M. Maxfield, Warden Moxley, Ann Pelham, David R. Tarr, Pat Towell, Elizabeth Wehr.

Production Manager: I. D. Fuller. **Assistant Production Manager:** Maceo Mayo.

Book Department Editor: Patricia Ann O'Connor.

Photos: cover, White House; pp. 2, 69, Wide World Photos.

Library of Congress Cataloging in Publication Data

Congressional Quarterly, Inc.
President Carter, 1978.

Includes index.
1. United States — Politics and government — 1977-
2. United States — Foreign relations — 1977-   3. United States —
Economic policy — 1971-   4. Carter, Jimmy, 1924-   I. Title.
E872.C66   1979   973.926'092'4   79-12319
ISBN 0-87187-147-5

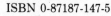

Table of Contents

Editor's Note

President Carter 1978 provides researchers with an overview of Jimmy Carter's second year in the White House. This volume, the tenth in Congressional Quarterly's *Presidency* series, contains summaries of White House and congressional action in all major legislative fields, as well as details on congressional action on Carter's legislative proposals and his executive and judicial nominations.

New this year are articles providing supplementary background on Carter decisions concerning the B-1 bomber, inflation, federal regulation of business, and other issues confronting his presidency.

The documents section of this book contains the texts of Carter's key messages to Congress and major statements during the year, including television addresses and notable speeches. Also included are the transcripts of Carter's presidential news conferences. An index to the texts contained in *President Carter 1978* may be found at the end of the documents section.

Introduction

Presidency 1978: Foreign Policy Triumphs
Helped Carter Weather Domestic Reverses

A string of foreign policy triumphs — from the Panama Canal treaties to the Middle East summit to the recognition of the Peoples' Republic of China — carried Jimmy Carter through 1978.

The accomplishments were not full-blown by year's end — no Middle East agreement had been reached — but the overall tone was positive, successfully overshadowing a mixed record on domestic issues.

A high point came on Sept. 17, when Carter stood before a joint session of Congress and described what was then a remarkable breakthrough on the Middle East reached at Camp David.

With Anwar Sadat of Egypt and Menachem Begin of Israel grinning from the gallery at their new friend, the legislators warmly and enthusiastically applauded the president.

The moment capped the gradual emergence of a more confident Carter, comfortable with the presidency and educated by early mistakes and misjudgments. The months-long decline in public ratings of the Carter presidency was finally halted.

Unresolved Problems. But problems loomed for Carter in the final months of 1978 that would pose major tests of his presidency in 1979:

● The Dec. 17 deadline for a Middle East settlement, set at the Camp David summit, came and went as dickering continued. Quick resolution of the long-festering feud seemed less and less likely.

● Negotiations with the Soviet Union on the arms control treaty spilled into the new year despite last-minute efforts by Secretary of State Cyrus Vance at a Geneva meeting. Once the strategic arms limitation treaty (SALT) was written, the administration still faced a difficult job in selling the treaty to two-thirds of the Senate.

● The formal recognition of the People's Republic of China was hailed by many U.S. leaders, but the effect of the move on U.S. relations with Taiwan drew harsh criticism from many in Congress.

● Inflation, once a lower priority for Carter than reducing unemployment, did not slow and was expected to be about 8 percent in 1978. In October, recognizing inflation as "our most serious domestic problem," Carter proposed voluntary wage and price controls for 1979. He asked Congress to give tax credits to workers in case inflation continued at a high rate and their wage control agreements backfired.

About a week later, Carter announced a series of anti-inflation moves to prop up the value of the dollar on foreign exchange markets and to tighten credit in the United States. But the dollar was still far from healthy at the end of 1978, and some economists predicted the anti-inflation efforts would cause an economic slowdown and perhaps a recession by mid-1979.

Legislative Record. The apparent success at Camp David, announced in the midst of the last, hectic weeks of the congressional session, seemed to spill over into legislative activity, though even Carter himself tried to minimize the connection. The independent-minded 95th Congress, in those last weeks, gave Carter victories on Civil Service reform, airline deregulation and natural gas pricing. Two vetoes — on defense spending and water projects — were sustained.

These accomplishments muted the painful defeat of other key domestic proposals during the year — labor law reform, a consumer protection agency and a Department of Education.

Perhaps his most stinging loss was the rejection of the hospital cost control bill that was to have been the showpiece of the Carter administration anti-inflation effort.

Floundering on other issues was avoided when, after a mid-year reassessment, Carter decided not to push for radical tax reform or for his welfare proposals, which were in trouble in Congress. Another result of the reassessment was that national health insurance legislation, promised for months in advance, was not sent to Congress.

Fiscal Conservatism. Though a "balanced federal budget" was an early Carter promise, his fiscal conservatism became a more and more prominent part of the administration's policies during 1978. Carter and his economic advisers said that reduced government spending was a central element in the fight against inflation. A central argument for his two vetoes, for example, was that the rejected programs were budget-busters.

As a practical political matter, this litany of fiscal restraint was in tune with the mood explicitly expressed by California voters when they approved Proposition 13's property tax cuts, and believed to exist in many other parts of the country. Many members of Congress, too, appreciated Carter's sensitivity to larger government spending, but the emphasis on budget cutting was seen by critics as an unfortunate shift away from the Democratic Party's tradition of enacting programs that did things for people.

But Carter, when he sought passage of his packages of urban aid and welfare reforms, for example, found that Democrats in Congress were already questioning that tradition. Their lack of enthusiasm for Carter's proposals defied the notion that a Democratic president and a Democratic Congress could reach agreements not possible when Republicans held one of these branches.

Ironically, as this alliance of Democrats was eroding on domestic issues, Republicans were playing a surprisingly large role in Carter's foreign policy successes.

The Other Camp David Summit. As 1978 began, the energies of the White House were focused on getting the Senate to pass the Panama Canal treaties. But this well-organized effort did nothing to hide the painful sight of congressional committees slowly ripping apart and rewriting Carter initiatives, including tax reform and hospital cost controls. Though the administration spoke with one voice on the canal, the official "line" on other issues was often unclear as Cabinet officers endorsed positions independently of the White House. Political columnists were complaining that Carter wasn't "presidential," and, by April, a majority of those surveyed in public opinion polls did not approve of how he was handling his job.

Carter's top aides decided a "stock taking" was necessary and, with the president, retreated to Camp David the weekend of April 13.

The result, according to insiders, was the following:

● Setting of priorities, with a focus on one issue at a time, instead of juggling several goals at once.

● Better control over Cabinet officials, with less tolerance of public dissent.

● More sophisticated lobbying of both Congress and interest groups. Anne Wexler, an undersecretary of commerce and longtime Washington political operative, was added to the White House staff to concentrate on this area. The meeting prompted the decision to bring media consultant Gerald Rafshoon onto the White House staff.

● Improving relations with Democratic Party leaders.

"If a few pieces fall into place in the next three months, we'll look better in the fall than we do in the spring," a White House aide told *The New York Times* April 13.

A few days later, a major piece "fell into place" when the Senate approved one of the Panama Canal treaties.

President Carter shakes hands with President Anwar Sadat of Egypt, left, and Prime Minister Menachem Begin of Israel after announcing the Middle East peace agreement reached at Camp David.

Personnel Troubles

In 1977, attention to Carter's programs was distracted by charges that close friend and budget chief Bert Lance had mismanaged his bank's funds. Though the troubles of aides in 1978 were a less serious problem, Carter was still bothered by poor publicity.

Dr. Peter Bourne, the president's assistant for health affairs, admitted July 19 that he had written an assistant a prescription for a controlled drug using a false name. He resigned the next day.

But Bourne was quoted by *The New York Times* as saying there was a "high incidence" of marijuana use and some use of cocaine among White House staffers. He later denied making the statement, but the impression remained of drug use close to the White House.

United Nations Ambassador Andrew Young was outspoken on many issues throughout 1978. Demands for his resignation reached a peak in July when he said there were "hundreds, perhaps even thousands, of political prisoners in the U.S." Carter gently rebuked Young in private, but then publicly declared his full faith in the ambassador.

Another touchy situation for Carter resulted from the dismissal of Robert T. Griffin as deputy administrator of the General Services Administration.

GSA chief Jay Solomon, eager to carry out Carter's directive to clean up the scandal-ridden agency, wanted to replace the veteran Griffin because the two men did not get along. But Griffin was a close friend of House Speaker Thomas P. O'Neill Jr., D-Mass., who was very upset at Griffin's firing. Carter, seeking to mollify O'Neill, a key ingredient to success on the Hill, gave Griffin a $50,000 White House job with few visible duties. That satisfied O'Neill, but demonstrated that Carter could not entirely free himself from political gamesmanship.

Foreign Policy

The victory on the canal treaty was one of three major legislative wins on foreign policy for the administration. Along with the Camp David summit on the Middle East and the recognition of the People's Republic of China on Dec. 15, these accomplishments gave Carter an impressive record on foreign affairs.

Panama Canal. The lengthy fight over the canal treaty drew well-financed opposition from a coalition of conservative organizations, who charged the treaty was a "giveaway" of the canal. But the administration's lobbying effort was given crucial support from both Senate Majority Leader Robert C. Byrd of West Virginia and Minority Leader Howard H. Baker Jr. of Tennessee.

After 38 days of often repetitive debate, a carefully crafted coalition of 68 "yes" votes gave final approval to the agreement. The first treaty, ratified March 16, guaranteed the neutrality of the canal and gave both the United States and Panama the permanent right to defend the canal. The second treaty, ratified April 18, gave Panama "full responsibility" for running the canal as of Dec. 31, 1999.

Jet Fighters. Less than a month after his Panama Canal victory, Carter again convinced the Senate to endorse his position on a controversial foreign policy issue: the sale of $4.8 billion worth of jet fighters to Israel, Egypt and Saudi Arabia.

The strong Israeli lobby vigorously opposed the sale of warplanes to Arab states, but Carter insisted that the sales were a necessary part of the new "evenhanded" American policy in the Mideast.

But the arms sales did not prevent the Saudis later in the year from going along with other Arab states in criticizing Egypt's efforts to make peace with Israel. In addition, the sales didn't keep the Saudis from accepting a decision by the Organization of Petroleum Exporting Countries (OPEC) to increase oil prices by 14.5 percent in 1979, even though Saudia Arabia preferred a smaller hike.

Turkish Arms Embargo. Another foreign policy victory came on a close House vote in August to end the U.S. arms embargo against Turkey. The president won the vote 208-205, with key support from Republicans.

Defense

Carter argued that a $2 billion nuclear-powered aircraft carrier was too expensive and unnecessary when he vetoed the fiscal 1979 defense weapons procurement bill. The president said the Navy carrier would divert money from other important weapons programs. Though the Aug. 17 veto caused grumbling among Armed Services Committee members in both houses, the effort to override failed even to win a majority in the House, much less the two-thirds required.

Carter won another weapons battle earlier, in February, when the House reversed a December 1977 vote and killed the B-1 bomber program.

But some of the most crucial defense issues — the strategic arms limitation treaty with the Soviet Union and withdrawal of troops from Korea, for example — were left for debate in 1979 or later.

Public Works

Carter and Congress had a major fight in 1977 over his efforts to stop dams and other water projects that he considered environmentally and economically unsound. But, in 1978, Congress restored funding for projects cut the previous year, and the bickering began anew.

This time, though, Carter carried out his threat to veto the public works appropriations bill, arguing that the projects were too expensive. Despite efforts by Democratic leaders to override the veto, the Oct. 5 House vote was 53 votes short of the two-thirds needed to override.

Economy

On Jan. 21, the administration submitted a tax package to Congress that called for a net $24.5 billion tax cut, tighter restrictions on deductions for business expenses and financial activity abroad and a crackdown on tax shelters. But the major reforms were scrapped by the House, and most of the remaining revisions died in the Senate and in the conference committee.

A tax cut — of $18.7 billion — was passed, but it was aimed primarily at easing the tax burden on middle- and upper-income groups. Instead of stimulating the economy, as Carter had originally hoped, the cut would simply ease the reductions in take-home pay that were to start in January 1979 when an increase in Social Security taxes was scheduled.

In the end, the president's proposal to reduce business deductions for expenses such as the "three martini" lunch was stripped down to a prohibition on deductions for business entertainment facilities such as yachts and hunting lodges.

Congress also completely reversed the direction Carter had wanted to take on capital gains taxes. The president had campaigned on a promise to try to eliminate the special tax break given to income resulting from the sale of stock or real estate.

But the legislators, under pressure from business lobbyists and hoping to mollify middle income homeowners, voted to cut capital gains taxes by more than $2 billion. A timely veto threat convinced the conference committee to moderate some of the more generous tax breaks in the Senate bill.

Both houses also passed legislation giving parents tax credits to offset tuition costs, but Carter threatened to veto the bill and the measure died.

Hospital Cost Controls

One of the most disappointing defeats for Carter in 1978 was Congress' rejection of his plans for controlling soaring hospital costs.

Carter in 1977 proposed strict limits on hospital revenues, but soon found that lobbyists for doctors, hospitals and other medical groups had a great deal of sway with Congress. The hospitals said federal controls were unnecessary and took voluntary steps to prove their point.

Just before Congress adjourned, the administration managed to nudge a weakened version of the legislation through the Senate, but failed in the House.

National health insurance played a key role in a highly publicized split between Carter and Sen. Edward M. Kennedy, D-Mass.

In July, Kennedy angrily denounced Carter's unwillingness to immediately push for national health insurance, which the senator said was necessary to help keep health costs down.

At the Democratic Party's midterm conference in Memphis, Kennedy continued his call for health insurance with an emotional speech that drew an enthusiastic ovation from participants.

By the end of 1978, Carter's aides were working on a plan to link hospital cost controls with catastrophic health insurance.

Energy

In April 1977, Carter introduced his energy policy, saying its efforts to deal with coming energy shortages were the "moral equivalent of war."

Nearly 18 months later, on the last day of the session, Congress passed a five-part energy package vastly different from the measure Carter said was necessary for the nation's survival.

Carter, in an effort to cut consumption, sought to raise gasoline taxes, tax domestic oil to raise its price to world petroleum levels and revamp electricity rate-making procedures.

But Congress thought it more important to encourage energy production than to discourage use and rejected the key elements of Carter's program.

Nevertheless, the president saw passage of the bill as a victory. "We have declared to ourselves and the world our intent to control our use of energy and thereby control our own destiny as a nation," he said.

For most of 1978, the measure was bogged down in the conference committee trying to resolve differences over the natural gas pricing section.

But an on-again, off-again compromise, nursed by Carter, Energy Secretary James R. Schlesinger and top aides, was finally passed by the Senate Sept. 27, and then by the House Oct. 15.

Civil Service Reform

The administration had unexpected success in redeeming Carter's campaign pledge to shake up the federal bureaucracy.

The key to his effort was reform of the Civil Service system, which the administration submitted to Congress March 2. Despite resistance from the labor unions that represented most of the 2.1 million federal employees, Carter won many points, including more freedom for managers to fire incompetent workers.

Labor

In the weeks following the death of Sen. Hubert H. Humphrey in January, there was talk that Congress would quickly enact the Humphrey-Hawkins "full employment" bill as a memorial to the popular Minnesota senator. Carter endorsed the proposal, which set a goal of reducing unemployment to 4 percent by 1983, as an important part of his legislative program.

The House passed the bill in March, but it was stalled for months in a Senate panel. There senators tacked on an amendment calling for a zero percent inflation rate by 1983.

The final version, worked out in the closing hours of Congress, called for unemployment to be reduced to 4 percent by 1983, with inflation cut to 3 percent by 1983 and to zero by 1988. Carter quickly signed the measure, even though it contained no real mandates or promises of federal action to meet the ambitious goals.

Another measure supported by organized labor was labor law reform, which Carter adopted as one of his major legislative goals. But the bill, strongly opposed by the Chamber of Commerce and other business and industry groups, was talked to death in June by a Senate filibuster.

Consumer Protection

Another defeat for Carter was congressional rejection of his proposal for a consumer protection agency. Business lobbyists again showed their strength as they argued against the agency and additional federal regulations. ∎

Carter vs. Congress: Institutional Conflict

The submission of President Carter's budget, tax and economic proposals to Congress in early 1978 created new conflicts between the executive and legislative branch even before old ones from 1977, particularly involving energy, had been resolved.

Even though both branches were controlled by the same political party, there was little reason to believe that 1978 would be much more harmonious than was 1977. It wasn't.

This stemmed partly from political and policy disagreements, but also in important part from an institutional conflict that has its roots in the history of the last 30 or so years and has precedents throughout America's history. It is a conflict that Jimmy Carter had no role in making and can do relatively little to prevent.

In effect, it is a conflict that results from the pendulum of power in national affairs swinging back from the gross imbalance that in recent decades had much favored the executive.

Crises Cause Imbalance

The constitutional provision for separate and competing executive and legislative branches sets up a continuing struggle for power. During times of great crisis, the executive branch usually becomes predominant because of its ability to mobilize and direct national energies. But there is always a reaction, and when the crisis atmosphere passes, a resurgence of congressional power usually occurs.

This oscillation has characterized presidential-congressional relations throughout American history. In the years 1973-77, the constitutional struggle was partly masked by the simultaneous battle between a Democratic Congress and a Republican President. Many Democrats argued that once their party took over control of the White House, relations would become relatively free of the conflict and rancor that characterized the Nixon-Ford years. But now that a Democratic President faces a Democratic Congress, the extent of the institutional differences between the White House and Congress—in both foreign and domestic policy—is becoming clearer.

The struggle is complicated, and sometimes hidden, by many other factors. In President Carter's case, for example, the complexity and controversial nature of some of the issues he has addressed—energy, welfare, the Panama Canal treaties—have inevitably slowed the congressional process and created strong opposition.

Moreover, there has been a lack of consensus in the nation on solutions to many problems or, in some areas, on the nature or even the existence of problems. This has been reflected in congressional inaction on a number of important Carter proposals.

For example, a September 1977 Gallup Poll showed Americans closely divided on the President's handling of

the energy situation, with 44 per cent approving and 39 per cent disapproving. Other polls have showed Americans doubt there really is an energy crisis. A November 1977 Harris survey revealed an even split—43 to 43—in the percentage of Americans supporting and opposing the sharp raise in Social Security taxes to bolster the financing of the Social Security system. Polls also have revealed much disagreement among Americans about returning control of the Panama Canal to Panama.

Finally, the fact that Carter ran behind almost all Democratic winners in 1976 House and Senate races means that these members of Congress owe him very little politically. Combined with the decline of party organizations and the trend toward each candidate running on his or her own, Carter has less leverage to exert for his legislative program than would a President who led the ticket. Nor did his coming to the presidency from the outside, never having had to deal directly with Congress, help him in his relations with that body.

Redressing the Balance

But along with all these immediate problems runs the theme of redressing the balance between the executive and legislative branches.

The newest era of congressional assertiveness began as a reaction to the Vietnam War, with congressional criticism and opposition slowly building from the Senate Foreign Relations Committee hearings in 1966 through the adoption in 1973 of the congressional ban on using appropriated funds for U.S. combat activities in Indochina. Although the

1973 action came after the Vietnam peace agreement, it nevertheless represented not only a revulsion against the war, but a determination to circumscribe the President's ability to reignite American participation in it.

The 1973 ban was but one of a series of congressional initiatives that sought to assert congressional authority after the long period of presidential ascendancy during the New Deal, World War II and the Cold War that followed. Looked at in perspective, the actions taken by the 93rd and 94th Congresses present an almost breathtaking array of controversial measures designed to bring the presidency to heel and enable Congress to have what it considers its proper say in running the government.

Nixon Challenges

At the beginning of 1973, a newly re-elected President Nixon laid down a serious challenge to congressional authority by refusing to spend some appropriated money, refusing to let certain members of his administration appear before congressional committees, and refusing to stop the bombing of Indochina despite protests from both houses that it was illegal.

The ban on Indochina combat activities was the congressional response to the immediate issue of the Indochina bombing, but Congress did not stop there. It dealt Nixon—and the presidency—a stunning setback in November 1973 by voting to override his veto of legislation—the War Powers Act—limiting the President's powers to commit U.S. forces abroad without congressional approval.

In addition to certain reporting requirements, the law set a 60 day limit on any presidential commitment of U.S. troops abroad without specific congressional authorization. The commitment could be extended for another 30 days if necessary for the safe withdrawal of troops. Unauthorized commitments could be terminated prior to the 60 day deadline through congressional passage of a concurrent resolution, a measure which does not require the President's signature to take effect. This action was a far cry from the Tonkin Gulf Resolution of 1964, in which Congress resolved that they approved and supported "the determination of the President, as Commander in Chief, to take all necessary measures to repel any armed attack against the forces of the U.S. and to prevent further aggression."

Underscoring the institutional nature of the struggle over the war powers bill, 25 Senate Republicans out of 40 voting were in favor of overriding Nixon's veto. In the House, 86 Republicans, close to half the party's membership, voted to override the veto, while 103 voted to sustain.

Spending Controls

In 1974, Congress responded to presidential impoundment of funds and, at the same time, attempted to deal with long-standing internal problems with its own handling of the federal budget. Although the federal budget had grown substantially since New Deal days of the 1930s, Congress had not established an effective overall control of appropriations.

Congress in 1974 voted to remove language in existing law that had been cited as justification for presidential impoundments. In addition, it set up procedures to keep Congress informed of impoundment actions and to force the release of impounded funds.

Moreover, the impoundment provisions were but a small part of the overall budget reform. The budget reform act required Congress before acting on appropriations and spending measures to adopt a budget resolution setting target figures for total appropriations, total spending and appropriate tax and debt levels. The measure also created new House and Senate Budget Committees as well as a Congressional Budget Office to analyze budget options. The new congressional budget procedure provided the framework for Congress to reassert its influence over government spending. Both parties agreed that Congress needed this new power, with the measure passing the Senate 75-0 and the House 401-6.

Emergencies, Impeachment

During the 94th Congress in 1975-76 one additional piece of legislation was added to the list of measures Congress passed in order to redress the power imbalance that had tilted in favor of the executive branch. The new measure provided for congressional oversight and review of national emergencies declared by the President. In addition, the bill formally terminated four existing states of emergency, dating back to 1933, that remained technically in force although the relevant crises had passed.

The legislation was born of a concern in Congress that, to expedite

dramatic action in times of emergency, it had granted the President extraordinary powers largely unchecked by Congress. To correct the situation, Congress provided for automatic congressional review, every six months, of all future national emergencies—with termination possible through congressional resolution—and congressional review and accountability of all presidential actions taken under emergency powers.

Finally, the use of impeachment process—the ultimate in congressional power over the executive—against President Nixon, demonstrated Congress' determination to assert its role in the federal government.

Constraints on the Future

Although there has been no overt struggle between Carter and Congress similar to that between Nixon and Congress, Carter—and his successors—must conduct the presidency under the constraints enacted by the 93rd and 94th Congresses.

As a result of the budget reforms, for example, Congress now has the tools to examine and alter the President's budget as a whole. Before, Congress never acted on the budget as an entity, and as a result no effective overall budget policy direction came from the legislative branch.

Also, Carter and Congress have not had to test the effectiveness of the war powers or national emergency legislation. But their constraints on executive action must be an integral part of national security planning. And the executive must not just take the specifics of the new laws into consideration.

The psychological momentum of congressional assertiveness creates a climate in which executive actions can quickly come under closer scrutiny. Also, Congress often will write into bills extremely detailed instructions on policy that bind executive action tightly. An example occurred in the 1975 action by Congress in imposing a ban on arms shipments to Turkey to try to force settlement of the Cyprus dispute. Secretary of State Henry A. Kissinger claimed the action circumscribed his efforts to negotiate a settlement with Turkey and exacerbated Turkish-American relations.

Historical Power Transitions

Previous transitions from a strong presidency to an assertive Congress provided some of the most dramatic events in American political history. The most famous occurred when Andrew Johnson succeeded Abraham Lincoln as President in 1865.

To fight the Civil War, Lincoln had exercised wider powers than any other President up to that time. He proclaimed martial law, suspended *habeas corpus*, spent public money without congressional appropriations, seized property, emancipated the slaves, and imposed a plan of reconstruction. All this was done in the name of solving a national crisis, when the normal lengthy ritual of congressional compromise and consensus was inadequate for the times. Quick and decisive executive action was needed and Congress consented, often by omission, to Lincoln's actions.

But after the immediate crisis had passed with the ending of the war, Congress rebounded with a vengeance. To be sure, the political struggle was aggravated by the personalities and immediate issues involved. And congressional determination to take back its prerogatives from an executive grown strong in a time of national emergency soon combined with violent policy disagreements. This combustible mix resulted eventually in a near-successful attempt to impeach and remove Johnson from office. Johnson's defiance of the Tenure of Office Act, which forbid the President from removing civil officers (appointed with the consent of the Senate) without approval of the Senate, was the immediate cause of the impeachment.

Johnson was saved from removal by one vote in the Senate, but the presidency went into a decline from which it did not recover for a generation. Between the Civil War and the turn of the century, Congress played a co-equal if not dominant role in the federal government. Congressional barons and committees were generally able to work their will on federal policy, often in a negative way, by refusing to pass legislation they disliked.

Early 1900s

But new crises in the early 1900s led to a renewal of activist and assertive Presidents who demanded and got congressional action. Abuses connected with the new industrial economy that had grown up after the Civil War had created an increasing demand for remedial legislation. The populist and progressive movements reflected this discontent and produced a series of reforms, most of which were put into effect during the first third of the 20th century.

Theodore Roosevelt, the first of the new activist Presidents, pushed vigorously for conservation, consumer safety, and railroad regulation legislation.

Roosevelt still did not tackle the congressional barons on the hottest issue of the day—the tariff. That was left to his successor, William Howard Taft, who proposed a downward revision. But he had to settle for little real change.

The era's second activist President, Woodrow Wilson, carried out additional reforms, including a lower tariff, the establishment of the Federal Reserve system, and a new antitrust law. With World War I, presidential powers grew to an extent not reached since Civil War days. The executive branch was empowered to control the nation's production, allocate food and fuel supplies, direct the nation's railroads, and coordinate and consolidate government departments.

At the end of the war, Wilson sought to shape the peace, with a League of Nations to be the centerpiece of a new world order. Dramatizing his leadership role, Wilson attended the Versailles Peace Conference.

But with the end of the war and the return of peace, the presidential-congressional conflict flared up once again. Republicans captured control of both houses of Congress in the 1918 elections, which aggravated the struggle. The great symbolic issue on which the clash came was the ratification of the Versailles Treaty containing the League of Nations. Wilson refused to compromise enough to gain the two-thirds margin needed in the Senate.

After Wilson

The League struggle broke the image of a strong, domineering presidency. Wilson was succeeded by Warren G. Harding of Ohio, a weak President selected by party bosses and congressional leaders. The 1920s, with its reaction against the reformism and internationalism of earlier decades, saw a series of Presidents little interested in disturbing the status quo and a Congress closely circumscribing whatever presidential initiatives were tried.

With the advent of the next major crisis in American history, the Great Depression, the presidency once again assumed vast powers. Moreover, the depression was only the first in a long series of crises. It was followed by World War II, the breakdown of the postwar peace into the Cold War, the Korean War, the Vietnam War. Congress went along with most presidential actions in foreign policy, allowing decisions over peace and war to be largely centralized in the presidency.

But finally, the pendulum began to swing back once again. The thawing of the Cold War, the split between the Soviet Union and China, the decision to withdraw from the Vietnam War, all reduced the tension, anxiety, and crisis atmosphere of the Cold War era. This in turn gave Congress a chance to reassert its powers without being accused of crippling an executive trying to grapple with a major crisis.

In many ways, Carter came to the presidency in a period analogous to that surrounding the accession of Presidents Ulysses S. Grant in 1869 and Harding in 1921.

The country was tired of activist Presidents and activist policies. Worn out by war and its aftermath, sick of the political feuding between Congress and President and skeptical of any further government initiatives, the American people wanted to be free to pursue their private interests.

The result in each case was an era of economic growth and prosperity, weak Presidents, and a disinterest in foreign affairs.

The eras climaxed with the outburst of a new set of crises, all of which had been developing below the surface for years before they broke. The great economic booms of both periods created conditions which led to demands for federal initiatives. In the 1900s, the demands were for legislation to curb abuses created by the growth of the industrial system, such as breaking up trusts and monopolies and promoting conservation and public health. In the 1930s, the demands centered around combating conditions created when the bubble of 1920s prosperity burst.

In an era of nuclear weapons, emerging nations, and a potential energy crisis, it is problematical how long the current era of congressional assertiveness can last. If the nation finds itself in the midst of an immediate crisis, demands for presidential action should quickly mount, and the balance begin to swing back to the executive again. ∎

White House Lobby Gets Its Act Together

In early 1978 stories about the Carter administration's congressional lobbying efforts often drew snickers and groans. But by year's end less talk of White House clumsiness and naivete was being heard on Capitol Hill.

Jimmy Carter's liaison operation with Congress was coming of age, according to members, staffers and other observers questioned by Congressional Quarterly. If true, that was good news for the president because White House lobbyists faced immense challenges in the 96th Congress.

The inflation-wary administration was preparing to push a budget through Congress that was austere on social programs and generous on defense spending. Opposition from liberal, labor, urban and minority groups was expected. At the same time, Carter expected to be seeking ratification of a Strategic Arms Limitation Treaty (SALT) in the teeth of possibly intense conservative resistance.

A Job for Frank Moore

The man in charge of selling Carter's programs to Congress is Frank B. Moore, assistant to the president for congressional liaison.

Soft-spoken, even-tempered, with a paunch and a slightly rumpled look, Moore hardly fits the glib and suave stereotype of a lobbyist. The sole counterpoint to his unassuming style lies next to his desk: a bright red University of Georgia throw rug bearing the picture of a pugnacious bulldog and the rallying cry, "Go you hairy dogs."

A loyalist who had been with Carter since he was an obscure southern governor, Moore was new to Washington when the administration took office. He quickly proved himself ill-prepared to steer a complex legislative agenda through Congress.

Moore's lobbying operation had significant problems for a year-and-a-half as the White House's relationship with Congress and especially its Democratic leadership went through a series of rough spots, near-disasters and unpleasant episodes.

Problems ranged from Moore's frequent failure to return members' telephone calls to complete communications breakdowns between the White House and Democratic leaders. Last summer, relations with House Speaker Thomas P. O'Neill Jr., D-Mass., were nearly destroyed because of a lack of consultation when Carter fired an O'Neill crony from the General Services Administration. For a time, O'Neill had Moore banned from his office.

Not unexpectedly, there were a number of early predictions Moore would not last. But he has confounded those pessimistic forecasts, and Moore's Capitol Hill lobbying efforts have markedly improved, demonstrating both Carter's confidence in his head lobbyist and the administration's ability to learn from its mistakes.

Painful Lessons

All those painful lessons that Moore and his lobbyists learned in their long struggle to enact an energy package and the Panama Canal treaties in the 95th Congress prompted some fundamental changes in the staff's operation.

Phone calls are now returned promptly, power centers are consulted regularly and pressure is applied more deftly. The results are demonstrable: Carter was able to get a number of his major proposals through Congress late in 1978.

The improvements may generally be traced to a late-1977 review of Moore's lobbying operation by Vice President Mondale, a 12-year Senate veteran, and an April 1978 conference at Camp David with Carter and senior advisers.

The size of the lobbying staff was increased from four to seven. Several Washington veterans were added, and the clerical and support staff was doubled. Tighter controls were put on lobbyists from the various government departments.

A mid-1978 alteration in White House policy proved particularly helpful for Moore's work with Congress: The number of presidential priority bills was slashed in half, from about 60 to 30, allowing more resources to be concentrated on issues like civil service reform and airline deregulation. The White House was expected to focus its legislative sights on an even smaller shopping list in 1979.

"We had too much on our platter," said Leslie C. Francis, who coordinates the different elements in Moore's office and looks after relations with departmental lobbyists.

In this smaller 1978 agenda, several bills were targeted for what Moore's people called "task force treatment." The task force concept first was used by the administration in February when it persuaded Congress not to continue the

---

'What began as a comedy of errors has definitely matured. Now people on the Hill are more willing to work with Frank Moore.'

—Professor Robert L. Peabody

B-1 bomber, which the president found unnecessary and overly expensive. Energy, the Panama Canal accords, Mideast arm sales, civil service reform and sustaining the public works veto were issues for which task forces were mobilized.

In a task force, a senior staffer is put in charge of seeing that all the White House's resources are utilized. Hubert L. Harris Jr., assistant director of the Office of Management and Budget, will head the budget task force in 1979 and top aide Hamilton Jordan will lead the one for SALT.

The lobbyists enlisted for a task force, both from Moore's office and the departments, are coordinated by Francis. Lobbying procedures conform to those employed by past administrations. The lobbyists identify the undecided members, who are then divided up for personal

White House Liaison History

Presidents have had their own lobbyists on the Hill for only the past 25 years. Before, congressional relations were handled on an ad hoc basis, with administration officials or allies in Congress tapped to guide bills into law.

The first formal liaison office appeared under President Eisenhower and was headed by a retired general, Wilton B. Persons, and later by Bryce N. Harlow, once staff director of the House Armed Services Committee.

Compared to the liaison operation under the Kennedy and Johnson administrations, however, the Eisenhower lobbying office was a somnambulistic affair. The reason: The go-slow Eisenhower legislative agenda was smaller than that of his successors. Also, the opposition Democrats controlled Congress for most of Eisenhower's tenure.

Under Kennedy, the liaison office took the form that persists to this day. The chief Kennedy lobbyist, former congressional staffer Lawrence F. O'Brien (now commissioner of the National Basketball Association), expanded the staff to push through a number of far-reaching government programs. O'Brien maintained a close relationship with the Democratic leadership and tightly controlled the departmental lobbyists.

Even though O'Brien stayed on as office chief after Kennedy's death, the lobbying staff acquired a new head, President Johnson. Because of his many years in Congress, Johnson oversaw his liaison office on an almost-daily basis. During important votes, he kept in close phone contact with his lobbyists, directing strategy.

When O'Brien moved on to become postmaster general in 1965, he kept his congressional relations post, too, but the day-to-day White House lobbying was conducted in the Senate by Mike Manatos, a former Hill aide, and in the House by Harold Barefoot Sanders Jr., a Texas lawyer and politician.

President Nixon brought back Harlow, who had become a lobbyist for Procter and Gamble, for a short stint as liaison head. Harlow briefly tried to cut the office back to its size under Eisenhower, but found that to be was unrealistic because Congress had since become used to relying on it for services.

With Harlow's return to P&G, William E. Timmons, who had been administrative assistant to then-Sen. Bill Brock, R-Tenn., took over and found himself in the middle of a growing conflict between the Democratic Congress and the Republican White House. Provoked by the passions of the Vietnam War, the animosity was sharpened by the disdain that key presidential advisers H. R. Haldeman and John Ehrlichman felt for Capitol Hill.

When President Ford took over, Timmons left to start his own Washington lobbying firm, Timmons and Co., and Max L. Friedersdorf became top lobbyist. A 25-year veteran of the House, Ford initially promised a harmonious partnership with Congress. But these intentions foundered on partisan difference over economic policy. Ford ended up vetoing 66 bills, leaving his lobbyists the unhappy task of rounding up the votes to sustain.

contacts. The most difficult to convince are brought in for a talk with the president.

"Task forces serve as a clearing house," said Francis. "They minimize mixed signals. They're a forum to check things, like rumors, and to follow up and see that assignments are carried out."

Other improvements include the hiring of Atlanta public relations man Gerald Rafshoon and Connecticut political activist Anne Wexler, even though they are not part of Moore's office.

Rafshoon's assignment was to improve Carter's image of weakness, which had diminished the president's clout with Congress. Wexler's task was to mobilize behind the president's programs special interest groups, which in turn put pressure on Congress.

Another Camp David-inspired change beneficial to Moore was the shift of Tim Kraft from handling the president's appointments to dispensing patronage — a role that had been performed haphazardly by Jordan, Carter's free-wheeling chief assistant. When a legislator wants to get a federal job for a friend, he now can rely on better service.

Since the early part of the administration, Moore has reshuffled his organization and modeled it after the most successful presidential lobbying effort of all time, that of Lawrence F. O'Brien, who handled congressional liaison for Presidents Kennedy and Johnson.

The task force concept was a hallmark of the O'Brien liaison office. Other O'Brien techniques adopted by Moore include dividing coverage of the House by his lobbyists on a geographical basis, servicing of lawmakers' needs, closely coordinating departmental lobbyists and having the president personally intervene when rounding up votes on crucial issues.

New Committee Lineups

Two years ago, Moore's office was too busy getting itself organized to worry much about the shape of the new Congress. But this time, he and his staff have spent a lot of time consulting with the Democratic leadership over committee assignment changes resulting from the 1978 election.

"We had 18 or 19 votes on Ways and Means last time and there [were] five vacancies this time," said William H. Cable, Moore's principal lobbyist in the House. "We want[ed] these vacancies to be filled with pro-Jimmy Carter people. Committee assignments are important. We lost hospital cost containment in 1978 in the Commerce Committee by one vote."

The administration's reaction to the outcome of the committee selection process was that the overall situation should not change much.

The House Ways and Means Committee appeared to register a net gain in potential Carter supporters, but the make-up of the Commerce Committee was not hailed at the White House.

"We didn't improve our lot," said Cable. "We may have lost a couple of votes there on cost containment."

Evidencing the seriousness with which Moore looks upon the task ahead are his plans to have his own troops lobby on the subcommittee level, especially on the Appropriations Committee — something White House liaison staffers seldom do.

He also intends to beef up his staff by temporarily detailing four departmental lobbyists to the White House for help with the budget struggle. They are: Christopher L. Davis and Robert M. Meyer from the Office of Management and Budget, Gael Sullivan from the Commerce De-

The White House Lobbying Team

DIRECTOR

Frank B. Moore, 43, is a Georgia native who served as Carter's executive secretary from 1972-74 when Carter was governor. He also was the governor's liaison to the state legislature and to municipal governments. In the presidential campaign, Moore was first finance director and, later, southern states coordinator. He is a graduate of the University of Georgia with a bachelor's degree in business administration.

SENATE

Danny C. Tate, 34, the chief Senate lobbyist, is another Georgia native. Tate was legislative assistant to Sen. Herman E. Talmadge, D-Ga., for seven years. He holds a bachelor's degree from Emory University and a law degree from the University of Georgia.

Robert Thomson, 35, comes from Washington state. He worked as a private attorney specializing in campaign finance laws and was a counsel to the Democratic Senate Campaign Committee. He graduated from the University of Washington with a bachelor's degree and from the Georgetown University Law Center.

HOUSE

William H. Cable, 33, the head House lobbyist and an Illinois native, was a congressional staffer for almost a dozen years before joining Moore's team. He received a law degree from George Washington University in 1970, and later served as staff counsel for the House Education and Labor Committee and staff director of the Committee on House Administration. He also served on the staffs of the commissions that drafted House reforms for the last two Congresses.

James C. Free, 31, was campaign chairman for Carter in the 1976 Tennessee primary and handled Alabama, Mississippi and Tennessee in the general election. A Tennessean, he served as chief clerk of that state's House of Representatives for four years, and previously held college administrative jobs for three years. Free holds a bachelor's degree from Middle Tennessee State University and a master's in public administration from the University of Tennessee.

Valerie Pinson, 48, joined Carter's transition staff in December 1976. Before that she was a lobbyist for the National Association of Counties, worked on the staff of Sen. Thomas J. Dodd, D-Conn. (1953-71), and in the Johnson White House on equal employment opportunities. She held several positions with the Office of Economic Opportunity and served as Rep. Yvonne Brathwaite Burke's, D-Calif. (1973-1978), administrative assistant. Born in upstate New York, she earned her bachelor's degree at Howard University.

Terrence D. Straub, 33, was congressional affairs director at the Office of Management and Budget before shifting to Moore's staff in June 1978. He directed Carter's Indiana primary effort and helped organize 16 states in the November election. He was born in Indiana, graduated from Indiana University, and was legislative assistant to Indiana's secretary of state from 1970-72. He ran unsuccessfully for Congress in 1970.

FOREIGN AFFAIRS

Robert Beckel, 30, served on the State Department's lobbying staff before his transfer to the White House in January 1978. A New Yorker who graduated from Wagner College, he once had his own political consulting firm and was director of the liberal National Committee for an Effective Congress. Technically, Beckel is a House lobbyist, but he specializes in foreign affairs and he swings over to the Senate for votes on those issues.

ADMINISTRATIVE SUPPORT

Leslie C. Francis, 35, a Californian, is Moore's assistant in charge of coordinating the office's internal operations and its relations with the departmental lobbyists. A San Jose State University graduate, he worked as an organizer and director for two teachers unions before becoming administrative assistant to Rep. Norman Y. Mineta, D-Calif. He worked on the 1976 Carter campaign, first in the Pennsylvania primary then moving on to more general duties.

partment and Sargent Carlton from the Interior Department.

Tell-Tale Style

One sign of the congressional relations operation's maturity is that it has developed a fairly consistent style — in contrast to 1977 when Hill people complained they never knew what would come out of the Carter White House next.

These characteristics are apparent:

● The administration will engage in political horsetrading — despite its expressed disdain for the practice — if a major bill is involved.

By all accounts, the White House blitzed fence-sitting House members with patronage enticements and other blandishments to gain their votes during the fight over sustaining Carter's veto of the public works bill in 1978.

Rep. Samuel L. Devine, R-Ohio, was one of several Republicans who said the president had offered to cease campaigning for Democrats in their home districts in return for a vote upholding the veto.

● The White House will continue to work through the Democratic leadership.

Cable contacts House Speaker Thomas P. O'Neill's office at least once a day. "And four times or more when they have a bill they're interested in," said Gary Hymel, the Speaker's executive assistant. In the House, administration lobbyists are based in the Speaker's office.

The White House's Senate lobbying team also consults frequently with Democratic leaders of the upper house.

Every Tuesday, House and Senate leaders meet with Carter. The president has had O'Neill and his wife over socially on several occasions — unlike the early days of the administration, when the Speaker and his family were assigned obscure seats at the inaugural ball.

The leadership is a superb source of intelligence, Moore's lobbyists have found. Its vote counts often are the most reliable. When the administration early on tried to count votes itself, it had difficulty spotting which supporters were shaky.

So valuable does Carter consider his ties with O'Neill and Senate Majority Leader Robert C. Byrd, D-W.Va., that the president took pains to make up with them when he went against the leadership on the public works question. "Don't gloat," he reportedly told Moore after the House upheld his veto of the water projects.

GOP Support

● Republicans are largely ignored unless their votes are needed on major issues.

Under both Presidents Nixon and Ford, the leadership of both parties was invited to regular meetings. This obviously was because the GOP presidents had more need to call upon the majority held by the opposition party. Carter seldom has to go outside his own party.

"Nobody ever walked through this door and asked what the minority on Ways and Means wanted," commented Rep. Barber B. Conable, N.Y., ranking Republican on that important House committee. "And it isn't as though I were bitterly hostile toward the president," he noted. "I supported him on [the B-1 bomber] and civil service."

Although Moore denies that he uses the Republicans only on "the tough things," he and his lobbyists admit that the GOP gets far less attention than the Democrats.

"Sure we spend more time with Democrats," said Cable. "You tend to go to people who do things for you. If you strike out 90 percent of the time with some people, it's not worth it."

To the extent that Republicans are consulted by the White House, the Senate minority leader fares far better than his House counterpart. That, said Moore, is because the administration gets more backing from Senate Republicans than from those in the House. According to a Congressional Quarterly study, House Republicans backed Carter on only 36 percent of all roll-call votes in 1978, while Senate Republicans were behind him 41 percent of the time. House Democrats supported the president at a level of 60 percent and Senate Democrats 66 percent. *(Presidential support, p. 13)*

An aide to House Minority Leader John J. Rhodes, R-Ariz., said White House "consultation with us has been almost nil." But the White House keeps in touch with Senate Minority Leader Howard H. Baker Jr., R-Tenn., "once every three weeks," said a Baker staffer. Baker has supported the president on key foreign policy votes like the Panama Canal treaties.

"It's different with the Senate," said Moore. "Their rules tend to make them more of a bipartisan body. On domestic issues in the House, we're lucky to get 10 or 12 Republican votes."

Also, he acknowledged, the personalities of Baker and Rhodes are a factor in the treatment they receive from the administration. The more outgoing, politically ambitious Baker is flexible on some issues, while the dour, ideologically conservative Rhodes seldom departs from traditional GOP doctrine, observers noted.

In 1978, the bulk of the support the administration received from Republicans came on issues affecting foreign policy (Panama, Mideast warplane sales, ending the Turkish arms embargo) and economy in government (civil service reform, public works veto). The reason for the pro-Carter foreign policy votes, students of Congress say, is that the Republicans have an internationalist element that habitually backs a president on such matters. And guarding the public till has long been a Republican tenet.

The White House is likely to look for Republican help when it attempts to hold the line on social spending in 1979 as part of its anti-inflation drive. "Conservative Republicans are a logical area of support," pointed out Rep. John B. Anderson, R-Ill. "The only thing that might militate against that is that we're getting closer to 1980 and the partisan atmosphere will be charged."

● The White House stays away from internal issues in Congress and other emotional questions that won't pay political dividends.

The government ethics bill, which affected the executive as well as the legislative branch, got virtually no administration lobbying, although Carter favored it and signed it. Ethics is a sensitive topic in Congress — one the administration believed was best avoided. During the two years the measure was being considered, several lawmakers were accused of improprieties, three were reprimanded by the House, two were indicted and another convicted.

Although Carter is on the record as favoring public financing of congressional campaigns — a controversial proposal on the Hill — his lobbyists reportedly will not push the issue this year.

Similarly, Moore's team stayed clear of the 1977 battle over common-site picketing, a pro-labor bill that Carter at least had said he supported, but that the administration sensed was not popular with the public.

Abortion, regarded as a no-win issue in the White House, was another subject on which the administration was neutral. Despite the opposition Carter expressed toward abortion in his 1976 campaign, his lobbyists kept their distance when amendments cropped up aimed at curbing federally financed abortions.

"When abortion would come up, they'd find us in the House restaurant," said Moore.

Slow Start

Those surveyed agreed that the White House Office for Congressional Liaison has come a long way in learning how to navigate the treacherous shoals in Congress and to avoid the past mistakes.

The bloopers committed at the outset of the administration stemmed partly from the inexperience of Moore, who had been Carter's lobbyist in the Georgia legislature, and of many other administration people.

Another cause of the early errors was that "we were undermanned," according to Danny C. Tate, Moore's lieutenant in the Senate. Owing to Carter's initial desire to pare the size of the presidential staff, which he felt had grown too large under his predecessors, the White House liaison office began with only four lobbyists aside from Moore. Eventually it was able to expand to seven.

Foul-ups will occur in the chaotic start-up of any administration, regardless of who is in power. "You always get a lot of [complaining] in the beginning," said Tom C. Korologos, a lobbyist with the Ford administration.

"Everybody's calling at once," he said.

Early Errors

Democratic representatives and senators, eager to make points on pet legislative projects and to receive patronage they had missed during eight years of Republican rule, besieged Moore with phone calls almost as soon as Carter was elected. Many calls were not returned, earning Moore a bad reputation among some Hill Democrats even before the inauguration.

Carter's disdain for the "wheeling and dealing" of Washington scored him points during the campaign. But it caused him problems once he moved into the White House. Many observers said that one of the reasons the energy package took nearly two years to be enacted was because it was drafted in secret by the administration with no Hill consultation.

Carter's relations with Congress, and especially with the Democratic leadership, were rocky for almost a year and a half. The incidents followed a predictable sequence: First came a usually uncalculated rebuff by Carter or his staff, then a public outcry from the damaged person, the administration's scurrying to make amends and, finally, a grudging acceptance of an apology.

Ill-tutored in the mechanics of working with Congress, the administration found itself often upsetting such potent figures in Congress as House Ways and Means Committee Chairman Al Ullman, D-Ore., and Senate Budget Committee Chairman Edmund S. Muskie, D-Maine. These two, stalwart backers of Carter's 1977 plan to offer a $50 tax rebate were never even consulted when the White House decided suddenly to withdraw the idea.

O'Neill, although assiduously courted by the administration, was for a time the chronic recipient of unintended White House slights. Two prominent Republicans from O'Neill's home state were elevated to important positions by Carter in 1977 without checking with the Speaker — former Pittsfield, Mass., Mayor Evan S. Dobelle was made chief of protocol, and former Cabinet member Elliot L. Richardson was named ambassador to the Law of the Sea Conference. (Dobelle later switched parties and now is treasurer of the Democratic National Committee.)

Carter's ouster of Robert T. Griffin, an O'Neill protegé, from the No. 2 spot at the troubled General Services Administration caused the Speaker to ban Moore from his office. The breach was healed only after yet another quickly called conciliation meeting. Griffin was given a White House job to appease O'Neill.

Reassessment

"Those horror stories of the early days had some merit," said Rep. Morris K. Udall, D-Ariz. "But the Carter staff proved in 1978 that they had learned the Hill."

By the end of its first year, the administration realized it had problems. A review of the Hill liaison effort, headed by the vice president was begun in November 1977, resulting in the decision to enlarge Moore's staff.

Robert Beckel, who had gained Washington experience as head of the liberal National Committee for an Effective Congress and as a State Department lobbyist, joined the staff in January 1978. Six months later, the team was rounded out with the addition of Terrence D. Straub, who had worked for the Democratic National Committee and in the Carter campaign.

Perhaps the most important personnel action in Moore's office occurred before the Mondale review, in June 1977, when Cable, a highly respected House staffer, was named to direct the House lobbying. He replaced Frederick T. Merrill Jr., a one-time aide for the reform-oriented House Democratic Study Group who had raised the hackles of some old-guard representatives. Merrill was shifted to the Department of Energy's lobbying staff.

Cable draws widespread praise from House members and aides. Typical is the assessment of Hymel, O'Neill's influential aide: "Bill Cable is known for his impeccable trustworthiness."

Moore's task also was helped when Carter chose to invite more members of Congress to the White House for personal meetings and entertainment. The president himself grew bolder in his approach to members during meetings.

"In the last six or eight months [of the 95th Congress], he became his own finest congressional liaison person," remarked Rep. Richard Bolling, D-Mo. "He moved from proposing and letting Congress dispose to knowing his priorities and how to get them through."

"The more you saw [Carter], the more you came to appreciate him," said former Rep. Paul G. Rogers, D-Fla.

The changes have impressed not only members of Congress who must work with the White House, but also those who study the workings of Capitol Hill.

"What began as a comedy of errors has definitely matured," said Robert L. Peabody, a Johns Hopkins University scholar who studies Congress. "Now people on the Hill are more willing to work with Frank Moore." ∎

Voting Support for Carter Remained Low During 1978 For Democratic President

President Carter's congressional support in 1978 showed a slight improvement, but still lagged behind the success record a president usually enjoys when his own party controls Capitol Hill.

The Democratic dominated Congress supported Carter on 78.3 percent of the votes on which he indicated a clear position. That was a small rise from the 75.4 percent success rate he posted in 1977, when relations between the newcomer from Georgia, who had run against Washington, and Congress got off to a poor start.

For the second year, Carter's performance in Congress fell in the middle range. Since 1953, the highest support score was 93 percent, received by Lyndon B. Johnson in 1965, and the lowest was 50.6 percent, by Richard M. Nixon in 1973.

Congressional Quarterly selected the votes using the same method it has employed every year since 1953, when it started analyzing presidential support. *(Ground rules, box, p. 15)*

By mid-1978, the administration had acquired a measure of sophistication in dealing with Congress and was able to rack up several significant legislative victories — passage of an energy bill by both houses, revisions in the Civil Service system, approval of a Panama Canal agreement. Carter even got the House to sustain his veto of the sacrosanct water projects bill, which he deemed inflationary.

But the White House still suffered its share of defeats, especially at the beginning of the year.

Carter Support Below Predecessors'

Carter's rating paled in comparison with those of his two Democratic predecessors during their second years in office. John F. Kennedy had an 85.4 percent score in 1962 and Johnson 93 percent in 1965. Republican Dwight D. Eisenhower, who had a GOP Congress in 1954, got his way with legislation on 82.8 percent of the votes that year.

In fact, Carter's tally was only a little better than the second-year record of Nixon, a Republican who had a 77 percent success rating from a Democratic Congress in 1970.

To be sure, Carter generally did better than Gerald R. Ford. He also outpaced Eisenhower's record from 1955 onward, when the Democrats made a comeback in Congress, and was significantly better than the performance of the post-Watergate Nixon.

The Carter support score was based on 151 votes in the Senate and 112 in the House. His position was defeated in the Senate 23 times and in the House 34 times.

He appeared to have greater support in the Senate, which backed him with 84.8 percent, than in the House where his victory level was 69.4 percent. However the difference reflects the large number of Senate votes taken

on proposed changes in the Panama Canal treaties. The Senate support figure was inflated by the 55 votes taken on this single issue, which pro-treaty forces — and President Carter — won each time.

Administration lobbyists and supporters in the Senate beat down virtually all the amendments that would have revised the treaties and probably required renegotiation with Panama — an event that many observers feared would kill the long-sought transfer of the canal to that nation.

Carter's Defeats

Carter suffered losses on a broad range of issues, encompassing such areas as economic policy and federal public works. One of his most significant defeats in early 1978 was the House's surprise rejection of the proposed consumer protection agency.

Several of the president's defeats concerned legislation he later ended up vetoing. The House, for instance, tacked on money to the weapons procurement bill for a fifth nuclear aircraft carrier, over Carter's opposition. Terming the carrier unnecessary, he vetoed the entire procurement measure.

Carter also vetoed a bill limiting his authority to allow generally cheaper foreign beef into the country — legislation he failed to stop on the floor. The long list of water projects passed over strenuous White House objections drew a veto as well.

Among the first presidential losses in the Senate were two out of three votes that sought to couple waterway user

---

Success Rates

Following are the annual percentages of presidential victories since 1953 on congressional votes where the Presidents took clear-cut positions:

Eisenhower			1967	79.0
1953	89.0%		1968	75.0
1954	82.8			
1955	75.0		**Nixon**	
1956	70.0		1969	74.0%
1957	68.0		1970	77.0
1958	76.0		1971	75.0
1959	52.0		1972	66.0
1960	65.0		1973	50.6
			1974	59.6
Kennedy				
1961	81.0%			
1962	85.4		**Ford**	
1963	87.1		1974	58.2%
			1975	61.0
			1976	53.8
Johnson				
1964	88.0%		**Carter**	
1965	93.0		1977	75.4%
1966	79.0		1978	78.3

fees, which Carter favored, with water project authorizations, which he did not.

In addition, Congress went against Carter by ignoring his objections to limiting veterans preference for government jobs and authorizing sugar import quotas to keep up domestic prices for the commodity. It brushed aside his desire to curb special tax benefits for business.

Party Differences

As usual, the president attracted more support from his own party than from the opposition.

In the Senate, the average Democrat was behind Carter 66 percent of the time, with the GOP supporting him, on the average, only 41 percent of the time. Democrats opposed him just 23 percent of the time, while the Republicans went against him on 46 percent of the votes. (Absentees make up the remainder of the percentage points.)

In the House, Carter was backed by the average Democrat on 60 percent of the votes and by the average Republican on 36 percent. Democrats opposed him 29 percent of the time and Republicans, 53 percent.

Regional Differences

Members from the West and the South were Carter's most consistent opponents, with the bulk of his support coming from the East and the Midwest.

In the 1976 election, Carter did poorly in the West, a problem that he did not help by his effort to revise federal water project policy. The fact that, for the second year, members from the traditionally conservative South gave the southern president little help suggested the president could face additional re-election problems in 1980 if the low support reflects voter discontent in that region.

In the Senate, the average eastern senator supported Carter 77 percent of the time, midwestern senators 70 percent and western senators 66 percent. Southern Democratic senators were in the Carter column on just 53 percent of the votes.

The geographical pattern held true for Republican senators. His support was 64 percent from the East and 44 from the Midwest, yet a mere 29 percent from the West and 28 from the South.

The same regional variations held sway in the House, although Carter's support figures were a bit lower across-the-board.

The president's most diehard opposition, according to the tabulations, came from the South. Southern Democrats in the Senate deserted him 34 percent of the time and in the House 40 percent. Southern Republican senators went against Carter 56 percent of the time and southern House members 63 percent. Indeed, southern opposition to Carter grew in 1978, as compared to the year before.

Individual Support Scores

Carter's biggest supporters among individual senators were Democrats Alan Cranston of California, Paul S. Sarbanes of Maryland, John Glenn of Ohio and Patrick J. Leahy of Vermont — all at 87 percent. Among Republicans, his best backers were Jacob K. Javits of New York (86 percent), Robert T. Stafford of Vermont (81), Charles H. Percy of Illinois (79) and Clifford P. Case of New Jersey (79).

In the House, Carter's chief Democratic allies were clustered in the mid-80's percentile range. The top scorer was Democrat Paul Simon of Illinois (88 percent), followed by Gerry E. Studds of Massachusetts (87). Another consis-

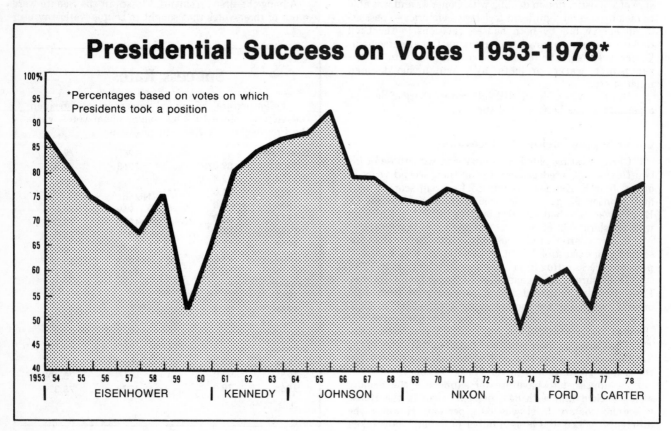

Presidential Success on Votes 1953-1978*

*Percentages based on votes on which Presidents took a position

Ground Rules for CQ Presidential Support-Opposition

Presidential Issues—CQ tries to determine what the President personally, as distinct from other administration officials, does and does not want in the way of legislative action by analyzing his messages to Congress, press conference remarks and other public statements and documents.

Borderline Cases—By the time an issue reaches a vote, it may differ from the original form on which the President expressed himself. In such cases, CQ analyzes the measure to determine whether, on balance, the features favored by the President outweigh those he opposed or vice versa. Only then is the vote classified.

Some Votes Excluded—Occasionally, important measures are so extensively amended on the floor that it is impossible to characterize final passage as a victory or defeat for the President.

Procedural Votes—Votes on motions to recommit, to reconsider or to table often are key tests that govern the legislative outcome. Such votes are necessarily included in the presidential support tabulations.

Appropriations—Generally, votes on passage of appropriation bills are not included in the tabulation, since it is rarely possible to determine the President's position on the overall revisions Congress almost invariably makes in the sums allowed. Votes on amendments to cut or increase specific funds requested in the President's budget, however, are included.

Failures to Vote—In tabulating the support or opposition scores of members on the selected presidential-issue votes, CQ counts only "yea" and "nay" votes on the ground that only these affect the outcome. Most failures to vote reflect absences because of illness or official business. Failures to vote lower both support and opposition scores equally.

Weighting—All presidential-issue votes have equal statistical weight in the analysis.

Changed Positions—Presidential support is determined by the position of the President at the time of a vote, even though that position may be different from an earlier position, or may have been reversed after the vote was taken.

tent Democratic backer was John Brademas of Indiana, the majority whip (85). Carter's best Republican supporter in the House was, for the second year in a row, Silvio O. Conte of Massachusetts (80 percent), with second place going to Millicent Fenwick of New Jersey (77).

Individual Opposition Scores

In the Senate, Carter's leading opponents were Republicans Paul Laxalt of Nevada and Jake Garn of Utah (both 82 percent) and Clifford P. Hansen of Wyoming (79). Among Democratic senators, the biggest anti-Carter voter was James O. Eastland of Mississippi (54 percent), with Edward Zorinsky of Nebraska (53) and Dennis DeConcini of Arizona (48) coming next.

Independent Harry F. Byrd Jr. of Virginia, who caucuses with the Democrats, opposed the president on 68 percent of the votes.

In the House, the leading Carter opponents were Republicans Robert E. Bauman of Maryland and James M. Collins of Texas, who voted against his positions 79 percent of the time. Leading the list of Democrats against Carter was David E. Satterfield III of Virginia (78 percent), followed by Dan Daniel of the same state (75 percent).

State Rankings

By state, Carter's highest Senate support in 1978 came from eastern and midwestern states. Another characteristic of these states was that their two senators were liberals, whether Democratic or Republican. Backing on the average was most consistent from Ohio, 85 percent; Vermont, 84; Iowa, 82; New Jersey, 82; Rhode Island, 82; New York, 81; and Illinois, 80.

Opposition was centered in the Senate in states with conservative senators who mostly were Republican: Utah, 78 percent; Virginia, 70; Wyoming, 70; Nevada, 63; Nebraska, 61; and New Mexico, 60.

House delegations with two or more members that averaged the most faithful support of the president were: Wisconsin, 71 percent; Hawaii, 69; Massachusetts, 66; Iowa, 63; New Jersey, 63; New York, 62; and Rhode Island, 62.

Opposition in the House ran the highest in: Idaho, 70 percent; Virginia, 60; Oklahoma, 55; Louisiana, 54; Mississippi, 54; South Dakota, 54; and Utah, 54.

New Approach to Hill

Both Carter's legislative program and his public esteem, as measured in the polls, were faring so badly in the beginning of 1978 that he called a conclave of his staff at Camp David on April 16-17. Out of that grew a new effort to coordinate activities better and focus on which of the many items on the agenda deserved the strongest emphasis.

The White House congressional liaison effort was bolstered by the addition of three lobbyists to its force of four, as well as by an augmented support staff. Several of the new lobbyists had Hill experience, which helped close the breach that had developed between many in Congress and the administration.

Average Scores

Following are composites of Democratic and Republican scores for 1978 and 1977:

	1978		1977	
	Dem.	Rep.	Dem.	Rep.
	SUPPORT			
Senate	66%	41%	70%	52%
House	60	36	63	42
	OPPOSITION			
Senate	23	46	21	38
House	29	53	28	50

<table>
<tr><td colspan="9">**REPUBLICANS**</td></tr>
<tr><td>Senate</td><td>26</td><td>(28)</td><td>59</td><td>(45)</td><td>56</td><td>(44)</td><td>43</td><td>(35)</td></tr>
<tr><td>House</td><td>45</td><td>(40)</td><td>55</td><td>(54)</td><td>63</td><td>(57)</td><td>51</td><td>(50)</td></tr>
</table>

1978 Presidential Position Votes

Following is a list of all Senate and House recorded votes in 1978 on which President Carter took a position. The votes, listed by CQ vote number, appear in the 1978 CQ *Almanac.*

Senate Votes (151)

Presidential Victories (128) — 24, 25, 26, 30, 34, 35, 36, 37, 38, 39, 40, 41, 42, 43, 44, 45, 46, 47, 48, 49, 50, 51, 52, 53, 54, 55, 56, 57, 58, 63, 64, 65, 66, 67, 68, 73, 74, 75, 76, 77, 79, 80, 81, 82, 83, 86, 87, 88, 89, 90, 91, 92, 93, 94, 95, 96, 97, 98, 116, 119, 120, 125, 127, 141, 142, 143, 144, 156, 157, 161, 169, 196, 197, 204, 207, 212, 214, 215, 223, 240, 254, 267, 305, 307, 313, 314, 320, 346, 347, 361, 363, 374, 378, 381, 385, 386, 388, 389, 390, 404, 407, 416, 418, 420, 421, 422, 432, 433, 435, 436, 437, 438, 446, 451, 455, 457, 462, 463, 472, 475, 476, 480, 482, 491, 501, 508, 511, 512

Presidential Defeats (23) — 85, 149, 151, 153, 170, 180, 185, 224, 264, 319, 380, 406, 419, 427, 449, 453, 458, 459, 470, 479, 484, 485, 515.

House Votes (112)

Presidential Victories (78) — 11, 12, 36, 42, 43, 57, 58, 61, 78, 120, 135, 141, 160, 176, 180, 181, 182, 183, 210, 216, 278, 285, 286, 290, 297, 318, 371, 466, 469, 519, 532, 548, 549, 550, 555, 559, 560, 563, 564, 565, 566, 587, 601, 609, 612, 613, 614, 615, 620, 634, 639, 642, 643, 646, 647, 648, 654, 662, 676, 687, 719, 723, 746, 751, 760, 766, 771, 774, 783, 786, 792, 794, 799, 805, 824, 826, 827.

Presidential Defeats (34) — 41, 88, 156, 315, 317, 338, 377, 400, 448, 474, 480, 556, 561, 567, 569, 575, 600, 611, 640, 653, 657, 658, 675, 720, 755, 784, 785, 791, 798, 801, 802, 817, 831, 833.

Regional Averages

SUPPORT

Regional presidential support scores for 1978; scores for 1977 are in parentheses:

	East		West		South		Midwest	
DEMOCRATS								
Senate	77%	(77)	66%	(69)	53%	(64)	70%	(71)
House	66	(69)	62	(66)	47	(53)	68	(69)
REPUBLICANS								
Senate	64	(63)	29	(46)	28	(44)	44	(55)
House	45	(51)	29	(35)	28	(36)	37	(42)

OPPOSITION

Regional presidential opposition scores for 1978; scores for 1977 are in parentheses:

	East		West		South		Midwest	
DEMOCRATS								
Senate	14%	(17)	22%	(19)	34%	(26)	17%	(20)
House	24	(21)	24	(25)	40	(38)	23	(23)

High Scorers - Support

Highest individual scorers in presidential support — those who voted for the president's position most often in 1978:

SENATE

Democrats		Republicans	
Cranston (Calif.)	87%	Javits (N.Y.)	86%
Sarbanes (Md.)	87	Stafford (Vt.)	81
Glenn (Ohio)	87	Percy (Ill.)	79
Leahy (Vt.)	87	Case (N.J.)	79
Culver (Iowa)	85	Chafee (R.I.)	78
Williams (N.J.)	85	Danforth (Mo.)	74
Pell (R.I.)	85	Heinz (Pa.)	71
Nelson (Wis.)	85		

HOUSE

Democrats		Republicans	
Simon (Ill.)	88%	Conte (Mass.)	80%
Studds (Mass.)	87	Fenwick (N.J.)	77
Hamilton (Ind.)	86	Green (N.Y.)	74
Brodhead (Mich.)	86	Whalen (Ohio)	73
Kastenmeier (Wis.)	86	Steers (Md.)	72
Obey (Wis.)	86	McCloskey (Calif.)	71
Brademas (Ind.)	85	Marks (Pa.)	71
Fisher (Va.)	85	Pritchard (Wash.)	64
Reuss (Wis.)	85		

High Scorers - Opposition

Highest individual scorers in Carter opposition — those who voted most often against the president's position in 1978:

SENATE

Democrats		Republicans	
Byrd (Va.) *	68%	Laxalt (Nev.)	82%
Eastland (Miss.)	54	Garn (Utah)	82
Zorinsky (Neb.)	53	Hansen (Wyo.)	79
DeConcini (Ariz.)	48	Hatch (Utah)	75
Nunn (Ga.)	46	Scott (Va.)	72
Stennis (Miss.)	46	Schmitt (N.M.)	70
Cannon (Nev.)	44	Curtis (Neb.)	69
Ford (Ky.)	42	Helms (N.C.)	68

* Elected as an independent, but caucuses with Democrats

HOUSE

Democrats		Republicans	
Satterfield (Va.)	78%	Bauman (Md.)	79%
Daniel, D. (Va.)	75	Collins (Tex.)	79
McDonald (Ga.)	72	Holt (Md.)	77
Stump (Ariz.)	65	Daniel, R. (Va.)	77
Montgomery (Miss.)	65	Kelly (Fla.)	76
Hall (Texas)	64	Robinson (Va.)	76
Burleson (Texas)	64	Taylor (Mo.)	74

	1	2	3	4
ALABAMA				
Allen, M.[1]	22†	29†	22*	29*
Sparkman	68	10	69	13
ALASKA				
Gravel	67	13	66	14
Stevens	28	64	37	54
ARIZONA				
DeConcini	44	48	53	38
Goldwater	14	62	21	54
ARKANSAS				
Bumpers	70	17	69	17
Hodges	74	18	74*	18*
CALIFORNIA				
Cranston	87	13	84	14
Hayakawa	54	36	50	42
COLORADO				
Hart	84	9	80	15
Haskell	43	7	46	12
CONNECTICUT				
Ribicoff	81	9	79	12
Weicker	66	18	64	22
DELAWARE				
Biden	71	17	73	16
Roth	32	62	42	54
FLORIDA				
Chiles	66	30	67	28
Stone	64	32	68	30
GEORGIA				
Nunn	52	46	60	38
Talmadge	51	38	57	35
HAWAII				
Inouye	72	11	71	10
Matsunaga	82	14	82	15
IDAHO				
Church	76	19	73	18
McClure	18	60	27	56
ILLINOIS				
Stevenson	81	14	82	11
Percy	79	11	73	14
INDIANA				
Bayh	74	14	73	16
Lugar	35	64	40	59

	1	2	3	4
IOWA				
Clark	79	9	80	13
Culver	85	7	82	12
KANSAS				
Dole	32	65	40	57
Pearson	63	11	64	15
KENTUCKY				
Ford	49	42	58	33
Huddleston	68	17	70	16
LOUISIANA				
Johnston	34	38	46	33
Long	57	32	58	32
MAINE				
Hathaway	69	7	70	12
Muskie	80	11	79	10
MARYLAND				
Sarbanes	87	12	85	14
Mathias	66	10	65	13
MASSACHUSETTS				
Kennedy	80	12	79	14
Brooke	41	40	53	34
MICHIGAN				
Riegle	74	17	69	20
Griffin	30	46	38	39
MINNESOTA				
Anderson	46	10	58	11
Humphrey, M.[2]	74†	10†	74*	10*
MISSISSIPPI				
Eastland	20	54	35	43
Stennis	31	46	40	40
MISSOURI				
Eagleton	76	13	78	13
Danforth	74	24	69	26
MONTANA				
Melcher	53	40	60	34
Hatfield, P.	54	28	54*	28*
NEBRASKA				
Zorinsky	45	53	53	46
Curtis	15	69	26	62
NEVADA				
Cannon	46	44	54	35
Laxalt	11	82	20	69

	1	2	3	4
NEW HAMPSHIRE				
Durkin	78	18	75	20
McIntyre	59	16	64	16
NEW JERSEY				
Williams	85	11	83	12
Case	79	12	77	15
NEW MEXICO				
Domenici	25	50	37	46
Schmitt	26	70	32*	65*
NEW YORK				
Moynihan	75	16	75	16
Javits	86	9	79	14
NORTH CAROLINA				
Morgan	64	27	61	28
Helms	20	68	28	62
NORTH DAKOTA				
Burdick	54	39	62	34
Young	25	55	36	46
OHIO				
Glenn	87	11	86	13
Metzenbaum	83	16	82	18
OKLAHOMA				
Bartlett	24	62	23	53
Bellmon	44	41	47	41
OREGON				
Hatfield	62	18	64	22
Packwood	53	33	54	34
PENNSYLVANIA				
Heinz	71	24	65	29
Schweiker	36	58	45	50
RHODE ISLAND				
Pell	85	7	82	11
Chafee	78	13	70	18
SOUTH CAROLINA				
Hollings	66	23	66	26
Thurmond	30	61	39	53
SOUTH DAKOTA				
Abourezk	38	9	38	14
McGovern	68	11	65	15
TENNESSEE				
Sasser	63	30	67	27
Baker	53	27	54	30

- KEY -

† Not eligible for all recorded votes in 1978.

* Not eligible for all recorded votes in 95th Congress.

	1	2	3	4
TEXAS				
Bentsen	60	28	61	29
Tower	15	62	24	59
UTAH				
Garn	15	82	26	70
Hatch	19	75	27	65
VERMONT				
Leahy	87	10	84	13
Stafford	81	11	77	15
VIRGINIA				
Byrd, H.[3]	31	68	41	57
Scott	11	72	21	64
WASHINGTON				
Jackson	80	19	79	21
Magnuson	72	23	73	22
WEST VIRGINIA				
Byrd, R.	82	15	83	15
Randolph	54	35	62	30
WISCONSIN				
Nelson	85	13	81	17
Proxmire	74	26	70	30
WYOMING				
Hansen	19	79	28	69
Wallop	30	61	36	56

Democrats   *Republicans*

1. Sen. Maryon P. Allen (D Ala.) sworn in June 12, 1978 succeeding her husband, James B. Allen (D) who died June 1, 1978. His presidential support score for 1978 was 14 percent; opposition was 86 percent. For the 95th Congress his support score was 39 percent; opposition was 61 percent.

2. Sen. Muriel Humphrey (D Minn.) sworn in Feb. 6, 1978 succeeding her husband, Hubert H. Humphrey (D) who died Jan. 13, 1978. He was not eligible for any presidential-issue votes in 1978.

3. Sen. Byrd (Va.) elected as an independent.

Presidential Support and Opposition: Senate

1. Carter Support Score, 1978. Percentage of 151 Carter-issue roll calls in 1978 on which senator voted "yea" or "nay" *in agreement* with the President's position. Failures to vote lower both Support and Opposition scores.

2. Carter Opposition Score, 1978. Percentage of 151 Carter-issue roll calls in 1978 on which senator voted "yea" or "nay" *in disagreement* with the President's position. Failures to vote lower both Support and Opposition scores.

3. Carter Support Score, 95th Congress. Percentage of 239 Carter-issue roll calls in 1977 and 1978 on which senator voted "yea" or "nay" *in agreement* with the President's position. Failures to vote lower both Support and Opposition scores.

4. Carter Opposition Score, 95th Congress. Percentage of 239 Carter-issue roll calls in 1977 and 1978 on which senator voted "yea" or "nay" *in disagreement* with the President's position. Failures to vote lower both Support and Opposition scores.

Presidential Support and Opposition: House

1. Carter Support Score, 1978. Percentage of 112 Carter-issue recorded votes in 1978 on which representative voted "yea" or "nay" *in agreement* with the President's position. Failures to vote lower both Support and Opposition scores.

2. Carter Opposition Score, 1978. Percentage of 112 Carter-issue recorded votes in 1978 on which representative voted "yea" or "nay" *in disagreement* with the President's position. Failures to votes lower both Support and Opposition scores.

3. Carter Support Score, 95th Congress. Percentage of 191 Carter-issue roll calls in 1977 and 1978 on which representative voted "yea" or "nay" *in agreement* with the President's position. Failures to vote lower both Support and Opposition scores.

4. Carter Opposition Score, 95th Congress. Percentage of 191 Carter-issue roll calls in 1977 and 1978 on which representative voted "yea" or "nay" *in disagreement* with the President's position. Failures to vote lower both Support and Opposition scores.

1. *Rep. William M. Ketchum (R Calif.) died June 24, 1978.*
2. *Rep. Ralph H. Metcalfe (D Ill.) died Oct. 10, 1978.*
3. *Rep. Goodloe E. Byron (D Md.) died Oct. 11, 1978.*
4. *Rep. Thomas P. O'Neill Jr. (D Mass.), as Speaker, votes at his own discretion.*
5. *Rep. S. William Green (R N.Y.) sworn in Feb. 21, 1978 to succeed Edward I. Koch (D) who resigned Dec. 31, 1977.*
6. *Rep. Robert Garcia (D N.Y.) sworn in Feb. 21, 1978 to succeed Herman Badillo (D) who resigned Dec. 31, 1977.*
7. *Rep. Clifford Allen (D Tenn.) died June 18, 1978.*

- KEY -

† Not eligible for all recorded votes in 1978.
* Not eligible for all recorded votes in 95th Congress.

	1	2	3	4
ALABAMA				
1 Edwards	38	61	39	54
2 Dickinson	21	62	26	59
3 Nichols	32	59	37	53
4 Bevill	45	52	49	48
5 Flippo	44	52	43	37
6 Buchanan	43	52	50	47
7 Flowers	34	28	46	29
ALASKA				
AL Young	13	44	24	41
ARIZONA				
1 Rhodes	32	49	36	48
2 Udall	71	15	72	16
3 Stump	20	65	24	63
4 Rudd	13	61	21	62
ARKANSAS				
1 Alexander	57	26	58	29
2 Tucker	47	21	55	23
3 Hammerschmidt	25	71	30	65
4 Thornton	41	23	49	27
CALIFORNIA				
1 Johnson	68	31	64	28
2 Clausen	33	63	37	57
3 Moss	55	10	56	15
4 Leggett	60	17	61	19
5 Burton, J.	63	21	65	20
6 Burton, P.	71	17	72	16
7 Miller	48	12	57	16
8 Dellums	76	17	75	16
9 Stark	75	13	71	17
10 Edwards	79	14	81	15
11 Ryan	64	27	66	23
12 McCloskey	71	20	66	21
13 Mineta	81	19	80	19
14 McFall	70	21	71	24
15 Sisk	28	25	40	26
16 Panetta	68	28	68	28
17 Krebs	71	29	71	28
18 Ketchum [1]	23†	74†	28*	61*
19 Lagomarsino	32	68	36	64
20 Goldwater	29	60	30	57
21 Corman	80	16	78	15
22 Moorhead	29	65	29	65
23 Beilenson	76	12	72	16
24 Waxman	75	14	74	17
25 Roybal	77	21	75	20
26 Rousselot	22	73	23	71
27 Dornan	26	63	28	62
28 Burke	22	9	36	15
29 Hawkins	63	15	61	16
30 Danielson	77	17	75	20
31 Wilson, C.H.	29	32	39	30
32 Anderson	63	36	63	35
33 Clawson	18	51	20	57
34 Hannaford	64	31	67	30
35 Lloyd	62†	36†	63*	34*
36 Brown	76	13	73	14
37 Pettis	28	36	31	39
38 Patterson	76	17	70	18
39 Wiggins	29	32	34	36
40 Badham	19	55	24	56
41 Wilson, B.	35	57	38	51
42 Van Deerlin	72	17	68	20
43 Burgener	33	59	34	57
COLORADO				
1 Schroeder	68	27	66	30
2 Wirth	71	21	71	22
3 Evans	58	21	66	20
4 Johnson	36	52	38	50

	1	2	3	4
5 Armstrong	15	47	21	53
CONNECTICUT				
1 Cotter	66	21	62	18
2 Dodd	71	23	72	20
3 Giaimo	70	18	71	15
4 McKinney	60	27	53	20
5 Sarasin	28	20	37	27
6 Moffett	71	20	75	19
DELAWARE				
AL Evans	39	57	46	50
FLORIDA				
1 Sikes	38	42	42	41
2 Fuqua	41	42	45	39
3 Bennett	48	52	53	47
4 Chappell	25	52	30	49
5 Kelly	23	76	27	71
6 Young	31	68	37	60
7 Gibbons	56	20	60	21
8 Ireland	39	44	49	38
9 Frey	13	38	23	39
10 Bafalis	29	70	34*	64*
11 Rogers	70	26	68	28
12 Burke	28	47	30	51
13 Lehman	63	13	68	15
14 Pepper	67	17	65	18
15 Fascell	78	13	78	15
GEORGIA				
1 Ginn	53	46	58	40
2 Mathis	31	45	39	42
3 Brinkley	43	54	48	48
4 Levitas	58	41	61	39
5 Fowler	70	25	71*	25*
6 Flynt	26	50	30	55
7 McDonald	14	72	18	73
8 Evans	44	46	49	41
9 Jenkins	44	34	47	34
10 Barnard	40	46	45	42
HAWAII				
1 Heftel	69	28	69	26
2 Akaka	70	27	69	25
IDAHO				
1 Symms	13	71	17	69
2 Hansen, G.	13	69	18	70
ILLINOIS				
1 Metcalfe [2]	63†	14†	60*	14*
2 Murphy	64	26	66	25
3 Russo	57	37	60	32
4 Derwinski	47	50	46	52
5 Fary	66	21	70	22
6 Hyde	43	54	45	53
7 Collins	54	14	57	17
8 Rostenkowski	71	21	71	20
9 Yates	81	16	79	18
10 Mikva	61	10	65	13
11 Annunzio	68	26	71	25
12 Crane	9	60	15	62
13 McClory	46	50	46	50
14 Erlenborn	43	46	42	49
15 Corcoran	38	54	39	56
16 Anderson	54	24	53	28
17 O'Brien	41	53	43*	51*
18 Michel	42	56	43	51
19 Railsback	51	38	51	37
20 Findley	61	31	54	39
21 Madigan	44	48	48	43
22 Shipley	24	9	34	20
23 Price	74	24	67	25
24 Simon	88	7	82	14
INDIANA				
1 Benjamin	62	38	61	39
2 Fithian	64	33	63	30
3 Brademas	85	13	82	13
4 Quayle	43	47	39	50
5 Hillis	33	52	40	48
6 Evans	45	52	48	46
7 Myers, J.	29	67	31	63
8 Cornwell	56	25	61	24
9 Hamilton	86	14	80	18
10 Sharp	80	20	77	23
11 Jacobs	62	31	61	35
IOWA				
1 Leach	56	43	54*	46*
2 Blouin	73	16	73	20
3 Grassley	30	70	32	68
4 Smith	71	27	67	27
5 Harkin	69	28	65	28
6 Bedell	79	20	73*	21*

Democrats **Republicans**

Member	1	2	3	4
KANSAS				
1 Sebelius	33	59	33	56
2 Keys	70	24	72	24
3 Winn	34	56	38	52
4 Glickman	65	34	65	34
5 Skubitz	37	45	39	47
KENTUCKY				
1 Hubbard	46	49	49	47
2 Natcher	66	34	65	35
3 Mazzoli	66	26	68	25
4 Snyder	28	69	32	63
5 Carter	38	57	42	52
6 Breckinridge	52	30	55	32
7 Perkins	69	28	71	26
LOUISIANA				
1 Livingston	30	67	32*	65*
2 Boggs	64	32	61	32
3 Treen	30	61	32	61
4 Waggonner	31	61	29	63
5 Huckaby	28	52	36	52
6 Moore	31	69	35	65
7 Breaux	25	54	31	50
8 Long	59	34	59	34
MAINE				
1 Emery	43	49	50	45
2 Cohen	39	37	51	34
MARYLAND				
1 Bauman	20	79	23	76
2 Long	62	36	65	32
3 Mikulski	78	21	77	21
4 Holt	21	77	25	69
5 Spellman	67	22	72	22
6 Byron [3]	39†	48†	45*	44*
7 Mitchell	72	18	72	19
8 Steers	72	27	68	27
MASSACHUSETTS				
1 Conte	80	20	77	23
2 Boland	70	16	66	17
3 Early	69	29	67	26
4 Drinan	74	22	74	24
5 Tsongas	37	8	54	11
6 Harrington	46	7	55	11
7 Markey	79	18	77	20
8 O'Neill [4]				
9 Moakley	74	21	73	22
10 Heckler	58	26	60	27
11 Burke	54	29	52	24
12 Studds	87	13	83	17
MICHIGAN				
1 Conyers	49	11	53	16
2 Pursell	58	35	54	38
3 Brown	41	50	42	51
4 Stockman	35	53	38	47
5 Sawyer	38	50	41	43
6 Carr	75	23	74	25
7 Kildee	75	25	74	26
8 Traxler	66	25	62	26
9 Vander Jagt	32	57	36	51
10 Cederberg	40	56	39	53
11 Ruppe	40	31	39	34
12 Bonior	79	15	79	18
13 Diggs	42	8	49	10
14 Nedzi	76	19	77	20
15 Ford	69	15	66	14
16 Dingell	63	25	66	24
17 Brodhead	86	13	83	16
18 Blanchard	80	17	79	19
19 Broomfield	36	50	42	48
MINNESOTA				
1 Quie	19	21	31	28
2 Hagedorn	22	62	30	60
3 Frenzel	52	43	49	40
4 Vento	76	17	78	18
5 Fraser	54	8	62	10
6 Nolan	70	21	71	19
7 Stangeland	27	70	31*	63*
8 Oberstar	75	25	74	26
MISSISSIPPI				
1 Whitten	40	48	42	48
2 Bowen	38	61	44	54
3 Montgomery	30	65	31	61
4 Cochran	13	30	19	45
5 Lott	29	66	30	65
MISSOURI				
1 Clay	70	13	63	13
2 Young	54	43	60	37
3 Gephardt	74	26	73	27
4 Skelton	48	41	54	38
5 Bolling	74	8	71	10
6 Coleman	32	65	37	61
7 Taylor	26	74	27	71
8 Ichord	30	62	33	58
9 Volkmer	59	40	62	36
10 Burlison	73	24	75	21
MONTANA				
1 Baucus	52	26	58	27
2 Marlenee	25	65	29	62
NEBRASKA				
1 Thone	21	39	30	45
2 Cavanaugh	71	25	73	23
3 Smith	29	59	35	58
NEVADA				
AL Santini	46	45	46	39
NEW HAMPSHIRE				
1 D'Amours	61	37	65	34
2 Cleveland	31	58	35	54
NEW JERSEY				
1 Florio	66	29	62	26
2 Hughes	71	27	68	29
3 Howard	71	13	75	12
4 Thompson	72	13	72	13
5 Fenwick	77	21	72	27
6 Forsythe	42	50	42	44
7 Maguire	74	18	73	19
8 Roe	63	31	54	26
9 Hollenbeck	56	29	57	31
10 Rodino	31	7	50	13
11 Minish	70	27	71	25
12 Rinaldo	55	40	59	38
13 Meyner	75	20	73	20
14 LeFante	47	15	57	17
15 Patten	79	20	78	20
NEW MEXICO				
1 Lujan	18	53	25	52
2 Runnels	24	52	26	53
NEW YORK				
1 Pike	63	29	65	28
2 Downey	76	20	77	18
3 Ambro	62	37	68	30
4 Lent	41	55	43	49
5 Wydler	34	58	36	54
6 Wolff	61	34	62	29
7 Addabbo	68	25	67	23
8 Rosenthal	76	16	75	16
9 Delaney	63	24	70	20
10 Biaggi	57	31	61	27
11 Scheuer	73	20	76	18
12 Chisholm	74	18	71	19
13 Solarz	79	13	80	14
14 Richmond	63	14	68	15
15 Zeferetti	46	34	54	27
16 Holtzman	77	22	75	24
17 Murphy	57	24	57	20
18 Green [5]	74†	25†	74*	25*
19 Rangel	79	12	77	17
20 Weiss	79	17	77	19
21 Garcia [6]	66†	15†	66*	15*
22 Bingham	80	14	82	14
23 Caputo	28	31	40	34
24 Ottinger	79	18	78	19
25 Fish	50	41	50	39
26 Gilman	54	46	58	41
27 McHugh	84	15	79	17
28 Stratton	54	39	58	36
29 Pattison	81	14	80	16
30 McEwen	34	58	36	50
31 Mitchell	45	49	49	46
32 Hanley	67	27	70	25
33 Walsh	33	57	39	51
34 Horton	49	43	51	40
35 Conable	51	32	48	38
36 LaFalce	81	13	77	16
37 Nowak	78	21	75	24
38 Kemp	33	53	34	54
39 Lundine	73	18	71	21
NORTH CAROLINA				
1 Jones	42	48	49	42
2 Fountain	41	54	47	50
3 Whitley	38	52	47	46
4 Andrews	58	35	59	35
5 Neal	66	31	66	29
6 Preyer	75	21	75	21
7 Rose	63	33	62	27
8 Hefner	56	44	59	40
9 Martin	35	60	39	57
10 Broyhill	34	63	38	58
11 Gudger	46	47	54	42
NORTH DAKOTA				
AL Andrews	35	60	38	55
OHIO				
1 Gradison	48	48	47	45
2 Luken	45	46	51	39
3 Whalen	73	8	71	12
4 Guyer	32	55	35	55
5 Latta	29	66	31	62
6 Harsha	29	67	35	58
7 Brown	34	50	36	52
8 Kindness	22	69	27	66
9 Ashley	79	12	79	12
10 Miller	31	68	33	66
11 Stanton	49	47	53	45
12 Devine	24	71	27	69
13 Pease	79	17	76	20
14 Seiberling	82	14	81	14
15 Wylie	47	48	51	47
16 Regula	46	54	49	51
17 Ashbrook	16	73	21	70
18 Applegate	46	46	54	40
19 Carney	56	26	59	24
20 Oakar	60	28	62	30
21 Stokes	76	15	76	17
22 Vanik	79	18	72	18
23 Mottl	36	51	44	46
OKLAHOMA				
1 Jones	52	46	47	50
2 Risenhoover	22	48	30	48
3 Watkins	34	62	37	58
4 Steed	47	44	50	41
5 Edwards	22	71	25	71
6 English	35	63	35	64
OREGON				
1 AuCoin	59	27	59	29
2 Ullman	64	24	69	21
3 Duncan	56	29	57	31
4 Weaver	65	23	66	24
PENNSYLVANIA				
1 Myers, M.	67	29	66	27
2 Nix	57	13	65	16
3 Lederer	71	27	69	26
4 Eilberg	62	24	65	25
5 Schulze	24	64	35	57
6 Yatron	51	45	54	40
7 Edgar	76	21	75	19
8 Kostmayer	74	26	75	25
9 Shuster	22	73	29	68
10 McDade	42	41	51	37
11 Flood	65	23	65	27
12 Murtha	59	40	62	36
13 Coughlin	51	45	52	43
14 Moorhead	82	13	80	16
15 Rooney	69	23	67	26
16 Walker	29	71	32	65
17 Ertel	51	48	59	40
18 Walgren	70	24	69	24
19 Goodling, W.	36	54	38	53
20 Gaydos	57	40	62	34
21 Dent	26	23	24	18
22 Murphy	47	51	57	41
23 Ammerman	42	15	57	18
24 Marks	71	29	69	28
25 Myers, G.	46	52	51	47
RHODE ISLAND				
1 St Germain	65	25	62	21
2 Beard	59	33	62	31
SOUTH CAROLINA				
1 Davis	42	54	48	47
2 Spence	30	68	33	65
3 Derrick	56	33	57	32
4 Mann	58	30	52	36
5 Holland	53	32	48	29
6 Jenrette	51	35	54	32
SOUTH DAKOTA				
1 Pressler	29	46	34	47
2 Abdnor	27	61	30	59
TENNESSEE				
1 Quillen	31	54	32	50
2 Duncan	32	66	40	59
3 Lloyd	37	46	46	45
4 Gore	68	28	72	26
5 Allen [7]	69†	17†	62*	30*
6 Beard	28	64	29	60
7 Jones	40	48	50	41
8 Ford	66	17	69	18
TEXAS				
1 Hall	34	64	32	64
2 Wilson, C.	54	35	52	34
3 Collins	19	79	23	75
4 Roberts	30	54	33	55
5 Mattox	65	29	65	31
6 Teague	4	3	4	7
7 Archer	28	69	29	68
8 Eckhardt	76	13	75	15
9 Brooks	54	39	53	38
10 Pickle	54	41	52	42
11 Poage	32	60	28	57
12 Wright	68	22	72	20
13 Hightower	41	53	45	50
14 Young	25	17	35	29
15 de la Garza	36	56	39	56
16 White	35	54	42	51
17 Burleson	30	64	29	66
18 Jordan	79	11	76	16
19 Mahon	58	37	52	43
20 Gonzalez	56	39	53	35
21 Krueger	15	19	27	28
22 Gammage	31	50	32	48
23 Kazen	38	55	39	55
24 Milford	35	30	32	39
UTAH				
1 McKay	47	45	50	40
2 Marriott	27	64	29	62
VERMONT				
AL Jeffords	60	33	63	30
VIRGINIA				
1 Trible	31	66	36	61
2 Whitehurst	34	62	34	59
3 Satterfield	22	78	25	75
4 Daniel	23	77	26	73
5 Daniel	22	75	27	71
6 Butler	31	63	34	63
7 Robinson	23	76	26	73
8 Harris	77	23	77	23
9 Wampler	28	65	31	61
10 Fisher	85	13	81	17
WASHINGTON				
1 Pritchard	64	29	60	31
2 Meeds	64	9	67	15
3 Bonker	71	16	68	19
4 McCormack	55	39	58	35
5 Foley	64	30	67	28
6 Dicks	69	24	68	24
7 Cunningham	23	71	23*	67*
WEST VIRGINIA				
1 Mollohan	56	42	59	38
2 Staggers	65	29	64	25
3 Slack	43	48	48	46
4 Rahall	62	29	64	28
WISCONSIN				
1 Aspin	81	12	76	15
2 Kastenmeier	86	14	82	18
3 Baldus	81	17	75	19
4 Zablocki	73	27	71	29
5 Reuss	85	11	80	16
6 Steiger	49	36	48	38
7 Obey	86	14	81	17
8 Cornell	77	22	76	23
9 Kasten	21	29	30	38
WYOMING				
AL Roncalio	56	20	58	23

Democrats **Republicans**

Economic Policy

When President Carter sent his fiscal year 1979 budget to Congress, in January 1978, he probably gave the best indication to date of the course of his presidency. A year earlier, the newly elected president had just a few short weeks in which to make his imprint on the federal budget, and while he had proposed significant changes in the program recommended by his predecessor, Gerald R. Ford, he told the nation to wait a year to see a full statement of his budget priorities.

The 1979 budget was thus anticipated more eagerly than most — especially by the various constituencies that had made up the Democratic coalition. Weary after eight years of Republican rule, they had high hopes for a renewal of the Democratic commitment to social programs.

Carter, although he won the presidency without the endorsement of the Democratic establishment, owed much to those groups. But he also had made a campaign commitment to give expression to another sentiment that was sweeping the land — one born of frustration with Vietnam and Watergate — which insisted, in Carter's words, on a more efficient, competent government.

The Economy in 1978

The state of the economy in 1978 gave Carter reasons both for good cheer and for concern. It had recovered doggedly from the worst recession since the 1930s — in the process outstripping the recovery of the other industrialized Western nations. But that performance was clouded by several persistent problems. Despite the strong recovery, unemployment stayed at high levels. Business confidence seemed as yet not fully restored, with the result that new investment was at discouragingly low levels. That gave rise to concerns that the economy would be unable to continue the strong expansion. Inflation appeared to be stuck at a level of 6 percent or higher. Finally, there were indications that the economic recovery was about to run out of steam, even though joblessness was still far above levels traditionally acceptable to Democratic administrations.

Trying to balance the various competing forces represented by his presidency, Carter proposed a budget which he proudly asserted was "lean and tight" but still "compassionate" enough to meet the social needs of the nation. It included a call for a substantial tax cut, which Carter said was necessary to continue the economic recovery and help reduce unemployment.

The promised tax cut and other social program proposals seemed to be in keeping with the traditional Democratic philosophy. The tax cut was consistent with the approach of past Democratic administrations in aiming more relief at lower income groups while at the same time proposing tax "reforms" which would close "loopholes" that benefit the well-to-do.

The budget also included an ambitious proposal to reform the welfare system. Later, under pressure from urban groups, Carter sent Congress a new package designed to help the nation's deteriorating cities to rebuild. He also said he would work to develop other prized liberal programs — including national health insurance.

Taxpayer's Revolt

While some Democrats continued to doubt Carter's liberal credentials, developments through 1978 appeared to suggest that a conservative trend was even stronger than the president had believed.

One of the first indications came from California, where voters June 6 overwhelmingly approved Proposition 13, a state constitutional amendment sharply limiting property taxes. While the meaning of the vote was subject to debate, it appeared to reflect a fairly widespread belief that government spending had grown too rapidly — at least given the results that government was achieving.

The "taxpayer's revolt," as it was dubbed, had a distinctly middle class flavor as it was expressed in Congress. A surprisingly large number of lawmakers denounced Carter's tax proposals on the grounds that they failed to recognize that the time had come to help the "middle class," rather than lower income people. That political view came armed with an economic theory. It asserted that the economy's ills could be traced to a tax system which put too great a burden on "working, productive" people — in the process sapping their initiative to work, save and invest. The result, according to the new theory, was that the economy produced below its capacity — thus causing unemployment — while at the same time suffering inflation because of the resulting shortage of goods and the low labor productivity caused by insufficient business investment.

Whatever the merits of that argument — liberals denounced it as the old "trickle down theory," and its following among economists was relatively small — it proved very persuasive to an inflation-besieged middle class. The result was that Carter's tax proposal was significantly skewed — most notably by a large cut in capital gains taxes — so that it did relatively more for the well-to-do than any tax bill in recent memory.

In the meantime, the welfare reform proposals floundered, the urban policy was picked apart, and national health insurance was postponed. Growing increasingly concerned about inflation as unemployment dipped and the rise in prices appeared to accelerate — and as an election drew near — Congress chipped away at the budget and scaled back the size of the tax cut. But while strong sentiment to cut spending was expressed in many ways — probably most notably in a series of across-the-board spending cuts added to major appropriations bills on the floor of the House and Senate — most of the congressional reduction in Carter's proposed deficit resulted from scaling back the tax cut and from spending re-estimates based on the inability of various agencies to spend money as rapidly as they had anticipated.

Further Economic Developments

As the year went on, the economy performed in ways not entirely anticipated. Most surprisingly, employment rose much more than expected. That, combined with a new surge of inflation, served to shift the attention of economic policy-makers away from the feared downturn and back to inflation.

Other forces were forcing the administration to take steps to combat inflation. Among them was pressure on the dollar in international money markets. Explanations for the dollar's woes — which caused considerable concern among other Western nations, who feared the increased competitiveness of American products — were varied. Some blamed the United States' tremendous trade deficit, which they said created a glut of dollars abroad. The deficit was caused partly by the nation's continuing heavy dependence on imported oil and partly by the fact that more restrictive fiscal and monetary policies in other nations kept their economies from generating purchasing power for American imports to match the renewed purchases of foreign goods in the revived American economy. The result was that the American hunger for foreign imports far outstripped the market for American products in the other industrialized Western nations. In addition, it was undeniable that American industry had lost some of its competitive superiority relative to the nations of Western Europe and Japan.

But clearly another part of the problem was the relatively high inflation rate in this country, which threatened holders of dollars with a continuing loss of purchasing power.

Carter Inflation Strategy

Early in the year, Carter acknowledged that inflation was a vexsome problem, but his economic policy focused more on the dangers of an economic downturn. The unexpected increase in employment, coupled with a sharp rise in prices, prompted Carter in April to make a stronger commitment to fight inflation. Repeating a promise not to resort to wage-price controls — a bogeyman that frightened the business community, whose confidence Carter was very eager to win both for political and economic reasons — the president renewed a request that business and labor voluntarily keep wage and price increases below the rate for the previous two years. He also acknowledged that government should take the lead in making sacrifices that would help slow inflation, promising further fiscal restraint and citing a number of proposals before Congress that would help bring down prices in specific sectors.

'Guidelines' and the Rescue of the Dollar

By October, Carter's tax reforms were long since moribund. A tax cut was assured, but in its details it bore almost no resemblance to what Carter had proposed. Welfare reform was essentially dead for the year. Parts of the urban program were enacted, but others stood no chance of being approved. Some of the programs Carter had promised as related to his inflation fight — such as an energy program and airline deregulation — had been at least in part achieved. But others — including hospital cost control — were lost. All in all, the record of the 95th Congress gave little cheer to those concerned about inflation.

Pressured by other Western nations, and by domestic political realities as well, Carter strengthened his anti-inflation stance further on Oct. 24 by calling for wage and

Carter on Inflation

President Carter's Oct. 24, 1978, statement that inflation was "our most serious domestic problem" and that the nation "must face a time of national austerity" marked a complete turnabout from his position in the early days of his presidency. Then, he argued that the government should concentrate on reducing the unemployment rate and that inflation would take care of itself.

The following excerpts from various statements Carter made on inflation indicate how his position evolved:

Dec. 3, 1976, press conference: "I have no intention of asking the Congress to give me standby wage and price controls and have no intention of imposing wage and price controls in the next four years. I believe that the primary threat in these next four years is with continued unemployment, and I believe that with strong leadership, with my appealing to both industry and business on the one hand, and labor on the other, to show constraints, that an adequate mutual responsibility will be assumed and unnecessary increases of prices and wages can be avoided."

Feb. 23, 1977, press conference: "Well, I think rigid guidelines are a mistake. If we said that, for instance, no price increase or no wage increase could exceed 6 percent, this would be too restrictive. It would be contrary to my own philosophy of government."

March 24, 1977, press conference: "My own guess is that the inflationary pressures will continue at about the level that they have historically the last couple of years, around 6 or a little bit better percent."

April 15, 1977, press conference: "More and more in the last few months it has become obvious that inflationary pressures are building up. We have not been willing to control inflation by deliberately dampening the economy nor holding down employment. I have become convinced that the government by itself can't do it. We can take the lead. We can hold down unnecessary expenditures, work toward a balanced budget by the end of this administration."

April 11, 1978 speech: "[Inflation] has become embedded in the very tissue of our economy. It has resisted the most severe recession in a generation. It persists because all of us — business and labor, farmers and consumers — are caught on a treadmill that none can stop alone. I expect industry and labor to keep price, wage and salary increases significantly below the average rate for the last two years."

Oct. 24, 1978, speech: "Inflation has . . . been a serious problem for me ever since I became president. We have tried to control it, but we have not been successful. If there is one thing I have learned beyond any doubt, it is that there is no single solution for inflation. We must face a time of national austerity. Hard choices are necessary if we want to avoid consequences that are even worse."

price "guidelines." He pledged to back up those "voluntary" standards with as much moral suasion and indirect pressure as possible. In addition, he proposed that the next Congress consider linking the tax system to the inflation fight by establishing a system of tax rebates that would go to workers in companies which adhered to the wage guidelines. The rebates would be paid in the event that inflation exceeded the minimum rate to which the government appeared to be resigned for the short run — by then 7 percent.

The new program included a pledge from the Carter administration for even greater budget stringency — a promise that appeared consistent with the spirit of the "taxpayer's revolt," but which raised new questions about how well Carter could hold together the Democratic coalition.

Those doubts were further amplified in the wake of the "Stage II" anti-inflation announcement. Labor expressed strong doubts about the new program, and AFL-CIO President George Meany issued a call for mandatory wage-price controls. But more immediately, the value of the dollar plummeted on international markets after Carter's new inflation address — a sign that foreign currency traders were very skeptical about the new program.

The dollar's new fall prompted the Carter administration to take sudden and fairly drastic action. The decision to intervene on a massive scale in foreign currency trading in order to prop up the dollar, coordinated with Federal Reserve Board action to raise interest rates sharply, sent the dollar rebounding. The immediate crisis, which had threatened seriously to destabilize the international monetary system, force an increase in world oil prices (which are based on the dollar), flood other Western nations with ever-cheaper American imports and set off renewed inflation in the United States, was alleviated.

Risk of Recession

But the shift in American economic policy evidenced by a more restrictive fiscal and monetary policy gave rise to warnings that the nation could tip into a recession in 1979. The administration denied that was a danger, but there were indications that a recession would be an acceptable price policy-makers would pay to help wring out inflation — provided the downturn was sufficiently mild and short-lived.

The year ended in a state of uncertainty similar to the one in which it began, with businessmen and politicians looking to the administration's fiscal 1980 budget with the same degree of eagerness they had felt about the previous one. All questioned the degree to which the administration would risk recession to hold down the federal deficit — and what domestic priorities it would be willing to sacrifice.

Beyond that were broader questions — questions about whether a relatively mild anti-inflation program could halt the rapid rise of wages and prices, whether Carter could apply the economic brakes and still hold the Democratic coalition that elected him, and — most fundamentally — whether the economy could still afford to complete the liberal agenda with programs such as national health insurance. ∎

Urban Aid: 'A Time of Austerity'

Presidential adviser Anne Wexler did not mince words when she appeared before a late 1978 conference of city planners and urban deveopment officials in Washington.

"Let me be frank," she declared. "The president is committed to dealing with inflation. It will be a time of austerity in the federal budget."

Her message was clear. With inflation the chief domestic concern, the Carter administration would not be seeking any major new spending for urban programs when the 96th Congress convened.

"There will not be a lot of new money for urban aid during the next few years," Wexler added in a subsequent interview.

Overall, administration officials were signaling that curbing inflation and strengthening the economy would have the most beneficial impact on urban areas across the country.

President Carter himself emphasized that point in a speech to the annual conference of the National League of Cities in St. Louis Nov. 27. "The future of our cities is at stake in our fight against inflation," the president said.

That did not mean that the Carter administration would not seek urban-oriented legislation in 1979. Although new spending would not be part of the package, the administration was expected to offer several proposals.

Development Bank

It appeared likely that the administration again would push for the creation of a National Development Bank to stimulate private enterprise in "distressed" urban and rural areas through packages of grants, loans and subsidies.

The development bank, an idea debated for more than a decade by urban advocates, government officials and academicians, was touted by many early in 1978 as the "centerpiece" of the president's urban policy, although adminstration officials didn't push that view themselves.

But Congress reacted coolly to the proposal, and the administration, plagued by sharp internal disagreements over control and direction of the bank, did not press for the legislation. As a result, Congress adjourned without taking action on the measure. (High-ranking administration officials now concede that the bank bill was hastily and poorly drafted.)

Revised Proposal

Although a new effort was expected to be made on behalf of the bank, the actual proposal may be quite different from the plan submitted in the 95th Congress.

In a 1978 panel discussion at the same conference of planners who heard Wexler, Ralph Schlosstein, an urban policy adviser on the White House Domestic Council, outlined some of the issues White House officials were grappling with. For example, he said, they were wondering precisely how strong incentives must be to attract new industry and manufacturing to the inner city. Further, he asked, can the administration design a bank proposal that

will require review by a minimum number of congressional committees?

Attractive Option

During the 95th Congress, several committees sought jurisdiction over the bank proposal, with at least two subcommittees of the House Banking Committee angling to control the measure.

The more committees involved in the bank, Schlosstein told the planners, the "more likely [the proposal] will bog down."

Schlosstein did not provide many clues as to what specific direction the administration intended to take. But he indicated that heavy emphasis will be placed on some loan-grant mechanism to stimulate private sector activity in economically declining inner cities and rural areas. With the desire to reduce federal spending, the use of loan guarantees, as opposed to actual appropriations, is an attractive option.

"This administration will make a very strong commitment to economic development in the cities in the fiscal 1980 budget," Schlosstein pledged.

Status Uncertain

It was uncertain, though, whether the administration would push for congressional action on other major urban measures left over from the 95th Congress — including a "labor-intensive" public works program for the hard-core unemployed, supplemental fiscal aid to cities with long-term financial problems, and grants to states to stimulate state activity in urban revitalization.

"All of those are being looked at," Wexler said, adding that no final decisions had been made.

The failure to win approval of the supplemental aid bill was particularly disconcerting both to the administration and urban interest groups. "The biggest loss," is the way the U.S. Conference of Mayors recently described it. Regardless of what the administration decided, the conference and other lobbyists for local governments planned to seek enactment in 1979.

There was some speculation that the administration would place major emphasis only on the development bank and welfare reform as its major urban-oriented programs in

"There will not be a lot of new money for urban aid during the next few years."

—Presidential adviser
Anne Wexler

1979. Welfare reform would include fiscal relief for the states, which would substantially reduce the financial burden for many highly urbanized states and counties.

Some indication that welfare reform will be on the agenda in 1979 came from Sen. Daniel Patrick Moynihan, D-N.Y., a leading welfare reform advocate in Congress. Moynihan said he had been assured by Stuart E. Eizenstat, Carter's chief domestic adviser, that the administration would offer a less costly welfare measure to Congress in 1979. The expected price tag, according to congressional sources, would be no more than $6 billion or $7 billion above current costs. The administration's original welfare reform bill, which carried a price tag of about $20 billion, floundered in the 95th Congress.

Public works spending for urban areas also may receive scrutiny in 1979 as part of congressional examination of the various programs run by the Economic Development Administration (EDA). EDA's authorization expires in 1979, and congressional committees in the House and Senate are planning extensive hearings. In the past, EDA has been rural-oriented, but the Carter administration has sought to channel more funds to urban areas, and may seek greater "targeting" of EDA funds to the cities in 1979. EDA, a part of the Department of Commerce, was last reauthorized in 1976.

Legislative Tally

The development bank, public works proposal, incentive grants to states and fiscal aid to distressed cities were considered the most important legislative proposals in the urban package outlined by the president last March. Citing the lack of congressional action on those bills, many analysts have concluded that Carter's urban program was a

Carter's 1978 Urban Program...

Following is a listing of various bills considered part of the Carter administration's urban program, and how each fared on Capitol Hill in 1978:

● **Public Works.** A three-year, $3 billion program of labor-intensive public works projects to rehabilitate and renovate public facilities (HR 12933, S 3186). Considered in subcommittees in both the House and Senate, but stiff resistance, particularily in the Senate. led backers to put off consideration until 1979.

● **Employer Tax Credits.** Tax credits for employers who hire low-income, unemployed youths. The administration initially proposed that the credit be up to $2,000 per employee for the first year of employment, and up to $1,500 for the second year. Passed, after alteration by tax-writing committees. The final version of the tax bill (HR 13511) included a "targeted jobs credit" of up to $3,000 per employee for the first year of employment, and $1,500 per employee for the second year.

● **Development Bank.** A National Development Bank, to be run on an inter-agency basis by a board composed of the secretaries of the Departments of Housing and Urban Development (HUD), Commerce and the Treasury, to guarantee loans totaling $11 billion during fiscal 1979-81 to businesses located in both urban or rural "distressed areas" (HR 13230, S 3233). No action.

● **Investment Tax.** A special tax credit for companies investing in "distressed areas" of 5 percent above the 10 percent investment tax credit allowed on the purchase of new machinery and equipment. The administration also proposed extending the credit to rehabilitation of existing plants and equipment. The tax bill included an expansion of the credit for building rehabilitation, but the 5 percent "differential" was rejected.

● **Fiscal Assistance.** A new aid program for cities with long-term financial problems, to replace the countercyclical revenue sharing program enacted by Congress in 1976 (HR 2852). Passed by Senate, after various changes, including reduction in cost to $500 million for fiscal 1979 from initial $1 billion. Rule granted by House Rules Committee Oct. 14, but never called up for floor action.

● **Welfare Reform.** Carter also proposed a change in the fiscal relief portion of the administration's welfare reform bill to allow immediate financial aid to the states. As initially drafted, the reform bill would not provide relief to states until 1981. The administration's welfare reform bill was the subject of lengthy hearings in both the House and Senate, and a special House subcommittee approved a slightly revised version. But no further action was taken. In its final accounting of urban legislation, the administration did not list welfare reform.

● **Housing Loans.** An increase of $150 million for fiscal 1979 for low-interest housing rehabilitation loans under the so-called Section 312 program. Congress approved an increase in the authorization of $150 million and in the actual appropriation of $120 million. The authorization was included in the fiscal 1979 housing bill (S 3084).

● **Social Services.** An increase of $150 million in the ceiling for Title XX social service grants. Congress approved a larger increase, raising the ceiling to $2.9 billion from $2.5 billion for fiscal 1979 only. The increase was included as part of HR 13511.

● **Volunteers.** A $40 million neighborhood volunteer corps, to be run by ACTION, to create a pool of professionals such as lawyers, architects, planners and others with specialized skills available to help neighborhood renewal programs. Passed by the Senate after the authorization was scaled down, but never considered by the House. Proposal was included in reauthorization legislation for ACTION (HR 11922, S 2617). Measure will be considered in 1979.

major disappointment during his second year in office.

But Congress did pass almost all of the grant proposals sought by the administration. Two tax provisions the president wanted also were enacted, although changes were made in both. The administration, in its tally of legislative successes and failures, said it won approval of 13 of 19 bills it considered part of the urban program.

That total included four bills not specifically proposed by Carter in his urban message to Congress: legislation reauthorizing the Elementary and Secondary Education Act (ESEA), the Comprehensive Employment and Training Act (CETA), a measure providing loan guarantees for New York City, and legislation establishing the Consumer Cooperative Bank (which was initially opposed by the administration in 1977). *(Chart below gives brief description of each program)*

While some critics say including those bills distorts the administration's actual "won" and "lost" record, others point out that the legislation, especially CETA and ESEA, will pump millions of dollars into urban areas. Many urban advocates will argue that saving New York City alone was worth more than any of the small grant programs approved by Congress. Even excluding those bills, the administration still won approval of a majority of the bills proposed by the president in his urban message.

Spending Debate

If past response is any indication, the lack of substantial new spending by the administration in 1979 may bring renewed criticism, as was the case when Carter first unveiled his urban policy and legislative proposals in March 1978. Then, several urban advocates argued that the administration, while its intentions were good in developing

...How It Fared on Capitol Hill

● **Neighborhood Arts.** A "Livable Cities" program to stimulate cultural arts programs in urban communities and neighborhoods. Passed as part of the fiscal 1979 housing bill (S 3084) after authorization scaled down to $5 million for fiscal 1979 from initial proposal of $20 million.

● **Neighborhood Self Help.** A "Neighborhood Self-Help" program authorized at $15 million for fiscal 1979 to provide grants and other assistance to neighborhood organizations for various housing, economic development and other conservation and revitalization programs in low- and moderate-income neighborhoods. Also included in the fiscal 1979 housing bill.

● **Urban Affairs.** An urban parks and recreation program of matching grants to local governments for urban parks and recreation areas. Included in the omnibus parks bill (S 791). Final version authorized $150 million annually for fiscal 1979-82.

● **Mass Transit.** An urban mass transit program authorizing $200 million annually for fiscal 1979-83 in aid for urban areas to connect bus and transit lines and to fund economic development projects adjacent to mass transit operations. Included in HR 11733, the main highway bill passed by the 95th Congress.

● **Inner-City Health.** Inner-city health spending authorization of $50 million for fiscal 1979 for community health clinics and primary care centers in needy communities. Included in an omnibus health services and centers reauthorization (S 2474).

● **Education.** Increased federal aid under Title I of the Elementary and Secondary Education Act (ESEA) for cities and other areas with high concentrations of low-income families. Congress approved the administration proposal of a $600 million increase in the Title I authorization, $400 million of which is to be used for the aid to cities and other areas with high concentrations of poor

families. The administration submitted the ESEA proposal before the urban message, but it subsequently included the spending proposal in its catalog of urban legislation.

● **Consumer Bank.** A consumer cooperative bank to provide credit, equity and technical assistance to consumer cooperatives. The administration initially opposed formation of the bank when it was first proposed in 1977, but later switched and included it as part of its urban package.

● **Crime Prevention.** An increase of $10 million for fiscal 1979 for the Law Enforcement Assistance Administration (LEAA) to develop neighborhood crime prevention programs. Although included in the urban message, the administration later said the proposal would be considered next year as part of its reorganization plan for the LEAA.

● **State Incentive Grants.** A $400 million, two-year program of grants to states to encourage the development of urban revitalization programs at the state level. Hearings on the legislation (S 3209, HR 12893) were held in both the House and Senate, but no action was taken by either chamber.

● **CETA.** Reauthorization of the Comprehensive Employment and Training Act (CETA). Congress approved reauthorization legislation (S 2570) Oct. 15. Although not a part of the urban message, the administration included the CETA program in its catalog of urban bills. The measure does channel millions of dollars for public sector jobs into the nation's major urban areas.

● **New York City Loans.** Approval of New York City loan guarantees. The legislation (HR 12426) authorized the secretary of the Treasury to guarantee up to $1.7 billion in loans to New York City for up to 15 years. Although not a part of the urban message, the administration, which backed the measure, also included the New York City legislation in its urban package.

Executive Orders

Administration officials, members of Congress and others think four executive orders issued by President Carter could significantly help federal efforts to prevent further urban decay and promote urban revitalization.

The four orders, which were signed by Carter Aug. 16, are all designed to put existing federal resources — money, people and programs — to work where possible on behalf of urban areas.

The orders:

● Created an Interagency Coordinating Council to eliminate conflicts between federal agencies in operating urban programs. The council, headed by Jack H. Watson Jr., secretary to the Cabinet and assistant to the president for intergovernmental affairs, has actually been functioning since last March.

● Required the General Services Administration, the procuring agency for goods and services, to give priority to suppliers operating in areas of high unemployment.

● Required all federal agencies, including the GSA, to give priority consideration to central city areas in choosing sites for federal offices and facilities.

● Established a process whereby the Office of Management and Budget, in conjunction with various agencies, will analyze proposed new federal programs for their potential impact on urban areas. OMB officials said they have included the "urban and community impact" analysis in preparing the fiscal 1980 budget.

Some observers — and officials in charge of carrying out the various orders — believe it is much too early to assess their effect. The impact analysis, for example, does not have a requirement that programs with "anti-urban" potential be scrapped or altered. Rather, the potential impact will be presented to the White House as information to be considered in the final decision-making process.

Nevertheless, some persons have high hopes for the impact statements and other efforts to channel existing federal resources to urban areas and end, or at least curtail, federal programs and activities harmful to urban areas.

Praising the president's urban policy recently, Rep. Henry S. Reuss, D-Wis., chairman of the House Banking Committee, told a television interviewer, "I think what is needed is that the federal government stop doing so many of the wrong things that it's been doing for the last 20 years, breaking up the central city by unplanned expressways, by urban renewal bulldozers, by giving all sorts of unjustified tax incentives for jobs to leave town and go to the suburbs or to the countryside or to the Sun Belt."

the policy, had a long way to go to meet Carter's 1976 campaign commitment to revitalize the nation's cities.

That commitment included one statement, in an April 1, 1976, position paper, stating that, "Our cities needed financial assistance and the Republicans have given them crumbs."

Indeed, one major advocate for urban interests, the National Urban Coalition, bemoaned the administration's record on urban bills in the 95th Congress by pointing out

that only about $1 billion worth of programs was approved — as compared to a total of $8.3 billion in new spending authority called for in the package of legislation proposed by Carter in March. (The total spending included budget authority, revenue losses from tax breaks, and loan guarantees.)

Coalition Director M. Carl Holman, analyzing the record of the 95th Congress in a recent newsletter, termed the spending authorizations "extremely discouraging."

But that view is not shared by other urban analysts. David B. Walker, assistant director of the Advisory Commission on Intergovernmental Relations, argued in late 1978 that new spending at the federal level was not the answer to urban revitalization.

Recent figures compiled by the commission, Walker said, showed that in fiscal 1979 the federal government would distribute some $85 billion in funds to state and local governments (including income transfer payments such as Aid to Families with Dependent Children and Medicaid), with the bulk of it going to cities and counties. More aid than ever before is going to urban areas, he declared.

Walker said more results could be achieved at the state level, through changes in annexation and tax laws. The "business climate" set by leaders in the states was also important, he added.

Overall, Walker declared, economic stability at the national level would do more for urban areas than any specific urban grant programs.

Administration Goals

Administration officials, clearly reflecting the president's view that inflation is the primary domestic problem, seem to be making the same argument.

"Unless we do something now on inflation, the jobs that we have created will become meaningless and the gains which we have made will be threatened," Wexler said in her speech to the city planners and developers.

Marshall Kaplan, HUD's deputy assistant secretary for urban policy, described the 1979 agenda by saying HUD intended to "refine, extend, amend and toughen" the administration's urban policy.

HUD was preparing an interim report on urban policy, to be ready for public consumption in March 1979, on the first anniversary of Carter's message. That report was expected to include further recommendations.

Kaplan, in a 1978 interview, cited several agency actions that, he said, reflect the administration's "continuing commitment" to making the basic themes of the urban policy operating principles throughout the federal government. For example, he said, HUD and the Department of Transportation are scrutinizing the potential urban impact of planned highway improvement programs in four cities — Richmond, Va.; Rochester, N.Y.; Danbury, Conn.; and Dayton, Ohio. It was possible, he indicated, that DOT may seek to use the force of federal highway dollars to alter proposed improvements that could have a significant "anti-urban" impact.

Program Improvement

Wexler noted that, given the tight budget situation, the administration planned to concentrate on making sure that existing programs actually work, identifying and eliminating duplication in federal programs, and cutting out waste.

She and others indicated that special attention may be focused on such areas as urban economic development, where several agencies, including HUD and Commerce, through EDA, run very similar grant programs.

As part of the administration's overall reorganization program, a team in the Office of Management and Budget (OMB) has spent considerable time during 1977-78 studying various economic development activities sponsored by the federal government. Whether it would recommend broad reorganization was unclear; such a proposal undoubtedly would stir sharp bureaucratic infighting among the agencies involved.

But some idea of the scope of the problem was given by Lester A. Salamon, deputy associate OMB director for economic development, during a panel discussion at the same urban conference that heard Wexler and Schlosstein.

Salamon said his staff had identified 12 different programs — six grant and six loan efforts — that all were designed to accomplish basically the same goals. Agencies involved, Salamon said, included HUD, EDA, the Community Service Administration (CSA) and the Farmers Home Administration (FmHA). Terming it a "badly fragmented,...confusing...system," Salamon said there was "serious question" whether the existing organizational structure could carry out the urban development policies of the administration.

With HUD and EDA both seeking involvement in urban revitalization, Salamon said, HUD was busy recruiting economic development specialists from EDA, while EDA was busy recruiting urban specialists from HUD. The result, he said, was the creation of "duplicate staffs to do very similiar functions." Furthermore, he said, the "non-system," as he termed it, was wasting "scarce talent."

Executive Orders

Administration officials in the White House and various federal agencies also were attempting to carry out executive orders signed by Carter August 16 as part of the urban program. The orders were all designed to marshal existing resources — people, money and programs — on behalf of urban areas.

Administration advocates, defending the Carter program, point to the executive orders and some 100 administrative changes made in existing federal programs as potentially more important in the long run for developing a sustained national urban policy.

'Tote Board'

"A tote board that focuses only on new legislation doesn't tell the whole story," Kaplan said, arguing that the administrative changes and executive orders could produce significant results. But he indicated that many years would be required to determine whether the administrative and bureaucratic changes were actually producing results.

As part of the examination of current federal policies and programs, Kaplan said HUD intended to conduct a study during the next six months of federal tax law, and its impact on urban deterioration and revitalization. ∎

Carter's 19 Vetoes: Inflation Main Target

Five pocket vetoes by President Carter closed out Carter's action on legislation presented to him by the 95th Congress.

The disapprovals brought the total number of Carter vetoes to 19 during his first two years in office. His first veto of the 95th Congress, of a bill (S 1811) authorizing Energy Department appropriations, came on Nov. 5, 1977. His final 1978 veto, of HR 9937, dealing with textile import duties, occurred on Nov. 12.

Although substantial for a Democratic president with a Congress of his own party, Carter's veto mark was a significant drop from the record of his two immediate predecessors — both Republicans working with a Democratic Congress. Presidents Gerald R. Ford and Richard M. Nixon vetoed 66 and 43 bills, respectively. Unlike Ford or Nixon, Carter did not have any of his vetoes overridden at midterm.

Tops Kennedy, Johnson Figures

In two years in office, Carter already had vetoed more public bills than John F. Kennedy did in three years (nine) and Lyndon B. Johnson did in five years (13). Like Carter, Democrats Kennedy and Johnson had no vetoes overridden by the Democratic Congress.

Thirteen of Carter's 19 vetoes were pocket vetoes, accomplished by his refusal to sign certain bills after Congress adjourned.

Two vetoes occurred in the first session of the 95th Congress, and 17 in the second session.

Carter still trailed the all-time veto leaders by a large margin. Franklin D. Roosevelt vetoed 635 bills during his 12 years in office, and Grover Cleveland vetoed 584 during his two separate four-year terms.

Economic Reasons

The fight against inflation was a major theme of Carter's 1978 vetoes. For example, in rejecting HR 11545 he said that presidential flexibility in setting meat import levels "must be preserved as a weapon against inflation."

And Carter strongly pushed the anti-inflation theme in his Oct. 5 veto of HR 12928, the public works-water projects bill. He said that funding of the projects would be inflationary, and that Congress had resuscitated several water projects that could not be economically justified.

Carter's anti-inflation theme — along with a last minute advertising blitz against the bill by Proposition 13 leader Howard Jarvis — convinced the House to sustain his veto. In one of only two override attempts during his first two years in office, the House upheld Carter's stand on Oct. 5 by a 223-190 vote.

The other override attempt, also in the House, concerned HR 10929, the Defense Department fiscal 1979 weapons procurement bill. His main objection to the measure centered around funds for a fourth nuclear-powered aircraft carrier. The House upheld the veto Sept. 7, rejecting a motion to override it 191-206.

Vetoes November 8, 11

Carter vetoes included two on Nov. 8:

● S 1503, sponsored by five southern textile-state senators, would have compensated clothing manufacturers who used the chemical fire-retardant Tris. The government banned the product after discovering it contained cancer-causing chemicals. Carter objected to having the federal government indemnify the clothing manufacturers for their losses.

● HR 13719, a bill to give special payments to Guam and the Virgin Islands. Carter said the bill, which would have compensated the two territories for revenue losses resulting from changes in the U.S. tax code, was "a piecemeal approach to the growing revenue problems of the territories."

On Nov. 11, Carter vetoed three more bills:

● S 2416, to extend federal support for nurse training programs.

● HR 11545, the Meat Import Act of 1978. Carter objected to the level of the floor for meat imports and to restrictions on his authority to lift meat import quotas.

● HR 9937, which would have banned negotiated reductions in textile tariffs. Carter said the bill, pushed by Sen. Ernest F. Hollings, D-S.C., would "prompt our trading partners to retaliate" by withdrawing some of their tariffs from discussion during current trade talks. "The loss of these export areas is too high a price," he said, for "any transient benefits" in the bill.

Earlier Carter Vetoes

Following is a list of all of President Carter's vetoes up to Nov. 8, and the reasons he gave for the vetoes. None was overridden. An asterisk denotes those that were not pocket vetoes.

Date	Bill	Reason for Veto
1977		
Nov. 5	S 1811*	Objected to breeder reactor funds.
Nov. 9	HR 2521*	Unnecessary rabbit meat inspections.
1978		
June 19	HR 3161*	Firefighters' workweek cut did not equal pay cut, exceeded federal pay raise cap.
July 10	HR 10882*	Sikes Act amendments contained objectionable budget provisions and doubled the authorization unnecessarily. Congress later cleared a substitute bill (HR 13745).

Date	Bill	Reason for Veto
Aug. 17	HR 10929*	Weapons procurement bill contained funds for fourth nuclear-powered aircraft carrier, which Carter said would "weaken defense posture" by taking needed funds from other programs.
Oct. 5	HR 12928*	Public works water projects were inflationary.
Oct. 18	HR 9370	Aquaculture Act. Need for new subsidies not established.
Oct. 23	HR 11445	SBA amendments. Exceeds budget, duplicates programs.
Nov. 2	S 1104	Legionville historic site unnecessary.
Nov. 2	HR 11092	Navajo-Hopi lands bill unnecessary.
Nov. 2	HR 11861	Navy-Maritime Advisory Board Act requiring government-maritime industry meetings four times yearly duplicated present contacts.
Nov. 4	HR 11580	Lottery paraphernalia sales. (No veto message.)

Date	Bill	Reason for Veto
Nov. 4	HR 9518	Shipping act amendments. U.S. already seeking cooperative agreements with other countries.
Nov. 4	HR 6536	Cost of D.C. employees pension bill to federal government too high.

The following chart shows the number of public and private bills vetoed by all presidents since Harry S Truman:

President	All Bills Vetoed	Public Bills Vetoed			Vetoes Over-ridden
		Total Vetoed	Regular Vetoes	Pocket Vetoes	
Truman	250	83	54	29	11[1]
Eisenhower	181	81	36	45	2
Kennedy	21	9	4	5	0
Johnson	30	13	6	7	0
Nixon	43[2]	40	24	16[2]	5
Ford	66	61	45	16	12
Carter	19	19	6	13	0

1. Truman also had one private bill overridden, making a total of 12 Truman vetoes overridden.
2. Includes Nixon pocket veto of a bill during the 1970 congressional Christmas recess which was later ruled invalid by the District Court for the District of Columbia and the U.S. Court of Appeals for the District of Columbia. ∎

Energy and Environment

President Carter managed to get an energy bill through Congress in 1978, but the measure promised to have little effect on the way Americans produced and consumed increasing quantities of energy.

Its major purpose was to decrease oil imports by encouraging Americans to conserve oil and gas, to switch to other fuels such as coal when possible and to produce more oil and gas from domestic reservoirs.

On signing the bill, Carter remarked, "We have acquitted ourselves well as a nation while the world watched. We have shown the will and courage to face this complex problem."

But, while the legislation may have faced the energy problem, it stopped far short of solving it. Energy consumption in the United States continued to grow in 1978. It increased 2 percent over 1977 consumption and was expected to go up again in 1979.

About half of that energy was provided by oil and about 45 percent of that was imported. Only new supplies from Alaska's North Slope, in its first full year of production, kept imports below 1977 levels.

Concern increased in 1978 about the effect the high level of imports was having on the decline of the dollar on foreign money markets, the $34 billion trade deficit and continued inflation. The decision by the Organization of Petroleum Exporting Countries (OPEC) to increase prices by 14.49 percent in 1979 promised to exacerbate the situation.

Though perceived as a great political victory for the administration, the bill was drastically rewritten as it moved slowly through Congress.

Most painful to reach was the compromise on natural gas pricing policy, an incredibly complex scheme that by 1985 would end federal controls on the sale of newly discovered natural gas. The administration and its supporters struggled for months to overcome opposition from what one congressman called a "weird" coalition of legislators favoring continued controls and those preferring to lift controls.

But the administration failed to jar out of the Senate Finance Committee what was clearly the most important part of the original bill — a new policy to bring domestic oil prices up to world levels. Carter wanted to rebate the additional cost to consumers through a crude oil equalization tax, but Finance Chairman Russell B. Long, D-La., wanted the oil industry to get the extra revenues. His opposition, which stalled the bill in his committee, was enough to kill the measure even though the House passed it.

Other Energy Legislation

The attention paid the energy bill left Congress little time for other energy-related measures. For example, the fiscal 1979 authorization for the Department of Energy was not passed because of the threat of lengthy haggling over amendments, which congressional leaders feared would distract from work on the energy bill.

Other energy highlights of 1978 were:

● The first overhaul of offshore oil and gas leasing laws in 25 years. The new act, four years in the making, was expected to end uncertainty that had slowed development of frontier areas on the federally owned Outer Continental Shelf off the Atlantic coast.

● Defeat of efforts to spur construction of special pipelines to carry coal slurry — pulverized coal mixed with water. The railroad industry, joined by westerners concerned about depletion of scarce water supplies, got the credit for defeating the administration-backed bill.

● The first full year of operation of the Department of Energy, during which it spent more than $10 billion.

● Continued difficulties for the nuclear industry. Public concern about safe disposal of radioactive nuclear waste was one of the central problems plaguing the industry, but government in 1978 provided only studies of the waste, not solutions. Congress did not complete action on a bill supported by the industry that would have shortened the time it takes to get a nuclear plant licensed by the government.

● Writing of regulations to implement the strip mining law of 1977, which required coal miners to restore stripmined land. But the regulations were criticized by industry and even by some within the Carter administration, who considered them inflationary.

● No resolution of the long-running dispute between Carter and Congress over the plutonium-powered nuclear breeder reactor at Clinch River, Tenn. Carter continued his attempts to terminate the project, which he said was obsolete and over-priced.

Environmental Issues

Carter drew high praise from environmentalists for his record in 1978 on conservation and pollution control. Though noting some shortcomings, such as inadeqate funding of toxic substances control and "a contradictory and confusing nuclear policy," the leaders of major U.S. conservation organizations, in a year's end news conference, endorsed Carter's actions.

Among the highlights they cited were the president's veto of several water projects, protection of Alaska's wilderness and a "policy of unprecedented openness" that included meeting with environmentalists on numerous occasions.

Alaska Lands

The dominant event in 1978 that dealt with the environment was President Carter's sweeping move to restrict use of 56 million acres of federally owned wilderness in Alaska.

The action, based on authority from a 1906 law, earned Carter the highest praise from conservationists, who called

Carter Statements on Gas Deregulation

President Carter startled many observers at a March 9, 1978, press conference by endorsing a phased-in end to government regulation of natural gas prices.

The surprise came because for almost a year Carter had fought hard to continue government price controls over natural gas. In that time, some of the harshest rhetoric he has employed as president was issued to denounce the oil and gas companies for trying to end such federal gas price regulation.

From the record, it is clearly true that Carter as a candidate for president called for phased-in deregulation. It is also true that in his April 20, 1977, speech on energy to a joint session of Congress that he pledged to "work carefully toward deregulation."

Controlled Prices

But his National Energy Plan clearly called for continuing federal price controls on natural gas. The controlled prices would be higher and the control system would be different under Carter's plan. But the point was that gas would not be deregulated.

Most important, when it appeared that either house of Congress was about to vote to deregulate new natural gas, Carter strongly and publicly denounced the moves. At those times he seemed to argue that the oil and gas lobby was pushing for total deregulation of all natural gas, both newly discovered and that already flowing from old wells.

But that was not the case.

The gas deregulation legislation which threatened Carter's program in the House in July 1977 and which triumphed in the Senate in October aimed only at deregulating new natural gas — although "new" gas was liberally defined. In arguing against those deregulation measures, Carter incorrectly implied they would end regulation over all gas.

A representative compilation of Carter's statements on natural gas deregulation follows:

June 16, 1976

Presentation to the Democratic Platform Committee: "For natural gas, we should deregulate the price of only that natural gas not currently under existing contract (less than 5 percent) for a period of five years. At the end of this period of time, we should evaluate this program to see if it increases production and keeps gas-related products at prices the American people can afford."

Oct. 19, 1976

Letter to Texas Gov. Dolph Briscoe, D: "First, I will work with the Congress, as the Ford administration has been unable to do, to deregulate new natural gas."

April 20, 1977

Energy speech to joint session of Congress: "I want to work with the Congress to give gas producers an adequate incentive for exploration, working carefully toward deregulation of newly discovered natural gas as market conditions permit. I propose now that the price limit for all new gas sold anywhere in the country be set at the price of the equivalent energy value of domestic crude oil, beginning in 1978. This proposal will apply both to new gas and to expiring intrastate contracts. It would not affect existing contracts."

April 22, 1977

News conference: **Q:** "Mr. President, do you foresee a recommendation to eventually take the cap off of gas; that is, as long as there is a cap on it, it would seem to be regulated? . . .

A: "I think that would still have to remain for future analysis. I believe that . . . setting the natural gas price at its equivalent in oil is an adequate level of deregulation. Others, of course, want complete deregulation of oil and gas.

"I don't think it's possible for us to do that in the immediate future. I think the adverse impact on consumers and on our economy would just be too severe. . . ."

Sept. 24, 1977

Campaign speech at Norfolk, Va.: "I put forward to the Congress a comprehensive energy package. Part of it calls for deregulation, over a period of time, of natural gas. . . . But the gas companies — very powerful in Washington as you well know — want to deregulate immediately and add tremendous costs to the American public, not only for new gas to be discovered in the future but for gas that already has been discovered and that will be coming to you in any case. . . .

"I hate to veto a bill that a Democratic Congress passes, but you can depend upon it: I'll protect your interests when the bill crosses my desk."

Sept. 26, 1977

White House remarks: "The Congress has been lobbied continuously by the oil and gas industry to deregulate the price of new natural gas. . . . There comes a time when we must ask how much is enough. . . . It's time for the public interest to prevail over special interest lobbyists."

Sept. 29, 1977

Press conference: "I do not support complete deregulation of natural gas prices which would provide windfall profits without increasing supply. Deregulation would cost consumers an extra $70 billion by 1985 but would increase supplies very little, if any."

Oct. 13, 1977

News conference: Carter denounced "potential war profiteering in the impending energy crisis. This could develop with the passing months as the biggest ripoff in history." . . .[T]he oil companies apparently want it all. . . . If we deregulate natural gas prices, then the price will go to 15 times more than natural gas prices were before the oil embargo."

Oct. 28, 1977

Question and answer session with visiting newspaper executives: "As I said in my campaign and also as I said to the Congress when I made my energy speech last April, we are working toward deregulation of natural gas."

Nov. 4, 1977

Question and answer session: "I don't believe that I've changed my position. I don't interpret it that way. My position was that I would work with Congress, as had President Ford, for deregulation of natural gas. . . . The difference is in the rapidity with which natural gas is deregulated. . . .

March 9, 1978

News conference: **Q:** "Mr. President, are you willing to accept energy legislation that in a few years would lead to the deregulation of natural gas?"

A: "Yes, I am. This was a campaign statement and commitment of mine — that I thought natural gas should be deregulated. In my speech to the Congress last April, I repeated this hope and I think a long phased-in deregulation process without any shock to our national economy would be acceptable."

him the "greatest conservation president of all time." The president created 17 new national monuments.

Congress earlier had a chance to win similar praise by passing legislation to protect some of the federal land in Alaska in parks, wildlife refuges and other conservation units. But, despite an overwhelming vote by the House, months of work by committees and last minute negotiations, no legislation was given final approval.

The protections from mining, oil and gas drilling, logging and other harmful uses that were provided by Carter were permanent. However, Carter and Interior Secretary Cecil D. Andrus said the administration wanted the next Congress to pass legislation similar to what Carter supported in 1978.

Though it failed to act on Alaska lands, Congress did pass other sweeping legislation, which was considered to be the largest parks bill in history.

The measure authorized expenditure of $1.2 billion for more than 100 parks and projects in 44 states. Because it brought new federal money for parks to so many districts, the bill earned the label of "park barrel," in recognition of its similarity to "pork barrel" funding of hospitals, dams and other federal projects in a member's district.

Pollution Control

The dramatic move to protect Alaska's wilderness was in sharp contrast to the continuing, tedious implementation by federal agencies of laws designed to clean up the nation's water and air.

Clean air laws, for example, were amended in 1977, and regulations to carry out those revisions were written in 1978. States, cities and industry were starting to respond as the year ended. Clean water laws were also updated in 1977, and the court challenges to the regulations began in 1978.

Pollution control was increasingly focused on toxic substances and how they affected health. The danger of poisonous chemicals was vividly illustrated by the evacuation during the summer of 239 homes at Love Canal in Niagara Falls, N.Y., because they had been contaminated by chemical dumps.

But federal agencies writing regulations continued to face sharp disagreements about whether small amounts of toxic chemicals caused health risks, particularly risk of cancer. Often cleaning up the last bit of a poison was the most expensive part of pollution control.

Administration officials concerned about inflation had urged those writing regulations to pay more attention to the costs of health and environmental controls. Carter officials warned of the inflationary impact of regulations and adopted some of the same arguments used in the past by industries and by cities faced with cleaning up municipal water supplies.

To monitor inter-agency squabbles about balancing inflation and government regulations, Carter set up a Regulatory Analysis Review Group, headed by Environmental Protection Agency Administrator Douglas Costle.

Water Policy

When Carter and Congress fought in 1977 over several water projects he wanted to kill, the president promised to send Congress in 1978 a proposal for a new national water policy. The promised proposals went to Congress in June, but not in time to affect committee decisions about funding of dams and other projects for fiscal 1979.

Because of the timing and Carter's failure to propose legislation to carry out the policy, there was no debate in 1978 on general, overall questions of water policy. That was expected in 1979 when the legislation was to go to Capitol Hill.

Instead, Carter and Congress repeated the 1977 scenario and tangled over funding of several specific projects that Carter considered economically and environmentally unsound.

But rather than giving in to the powerful supporters of the projects, Carter carried out his threat to veto the public works appropriations bill that contained funding for six projects he thought were killed in a 1977 compromise.

Even though Democratic leaders of the House wanted to override the veto, they fell 53 votes short of the two-thirds needed. ∎

Carter Sets Aside 56 Million Acres in Alaska

The Carter administration Dec. 1, 1978, made sweeping use of a 1906 law to prevent mining, logging and other commercial development of an area in Alaska the size of Minnesota.

The creation of 17 new national monuments by presidential proclamation gives permanent protection to 56 million acres of federal wilderness in Alaska.

The move by President Carter more than doubles the size of the national park system. Not since President Theodore Roosevelt put 65 million acres in forest reserves has a president acted to protect so large a chunk of federal land.

A spokesman for conservationists in the Alaska Coalition said Carter had "exceeded the efforts" of Roosevelt and become "the greatest conservation president of all time."

But the move was made under a cloud of legal challenges. The state of Alaska had already filed suit Oct. 30 challenging the legality of such actions by the administration.

Congressional Action

Both Carter and Interior Secretary Cecil D. Andrus said the monuments were created to preserve the fragile scenery until Congress can try again in the next session to pass an Alaska lands bill. Previous restrictions on use of the land expired Dec. 17. Carter said the "risk of immediate damage to magnificent areas" made it "imperative to protect all the lands and preserve for Congress an unhampered opportunity to act next year."

Legislation (HR 39) setting aside more than 100 million acres of the state in parks, wildlife refuges and other conservation systems failed in the last days of the 95th Congress.

But the permanence of monuments, which only an act of Congress can change, prompted Alaska officials to accuse the administration of pre-empting the legislators.

Alaska Gov. Jay S. Hammond said Carter had "made unilaterally what should have been a congressional decision providing for public and state participation." Hammond said Carter's "extremely restrictive" actions had confirmed the state's "worst fears."

However, Andrus said the land would not have been adequately protected between Dec. 17 and the time Congress could act. "If we had adequate protection, I would not have put the president and myself through this exercise," Andrus told reporters. "We simply could not afford to gamble."

Layer of Protection

The president's decision adds another layer of protection to the 56 million acres. On Nov. 16, Andrus used authority in the Federal Land Policy and Management Act of 1976 (PL 94-579) to withdraw from development about 110 million acres of federal land in Alaska. But Interior Department lawyers were worried about legal challenges to the authority in the 1976 law. Of particular concern was whether the 1976 law could effectively bar the state from selecting the land after Dec. 17 as part of its statehood grant of 104 million acres.

The Antiquities Act of 1906, the law that authorizes monuments, was "by far the strongest authority we have available," said Andrus. The administration added that protection believing it was "in the best interests of the American people not to make light of these threats of litigation," Andrus added.

The bulk of the 56 million acres set aside as national monuments was included in the House and Senate bills as part of the national park system.

Carter could have made monuments of all of the 110 million acres being considered by legislators for parks, wildlife refuges and other conservation systems. But Andrus recommended designating only the 56 million acres because that action could be most readily defended under the 1906 law, he said. Monuments generally are operated with the same restrictions on use as parks. But wildlife refuges and forests are in some cases open to oil and gas drilling and logging — uses not permitted in monuments.

Wildlife Refuges

In addition to the creation of monuments, the administration is moving to use authority in the 1976 land management law to establish wildlife refuges in Alaska. That process could take several months, Andrus said. But the threat of additional executive action is expected to put pressure on Congress to act swiftly on Alaska lands legislation.

Andrus also predicted that sport hunters who found monuments closed to hunting will pressure Congress to change the boundaries of the areas. Many areas Congress opened to hunting as preserves were set aside as monuments.

Another spur to congressional action is the inclusion in the monuments of several million acres sought by the state of Alaska.

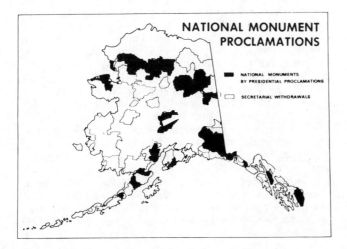

NATIONAL MONUMENT PROCLAMATIONS

■ NATIONAL MONUMENTS BY PRESIDENTIAL PROCLAMATIONS

☐ SECRETARIAL WITHDRAWALS

Thirteen of the monuments will be managed by the National Park Service:
- Aniakchak, 350,000 acres.
- Bering Land Bridge, 2.6 million acres.
- Cape Krusenstern, 560,000 acres.
- Denali, an enlargement of Mt. McKinley Park, 3.9 million acres.
- Gates of the Arctic, 8.2 million acres.
- Glacier Bay, an enlargement of 550,000 acres.
- Katmai, an enlargement of 1.4 million acres.

- Kenai Fjords, 570,000 acres.
- Kobuk Valley, 1.7 million acres.
- Lake Clark, 2.5 million acres.
- Noatak, 5.8 million acres.
- Wrangell-St. Elias, 11 million acres.
- Yukon-Charley, 1.7 million acres.

Two monuments will be managed by the Fish and Wildlife Service, which will allow sport hunting. The monuments are Yukon Flats, 10.6 million acres, and Becharof, 1.2 million acres.

Two monuments will be managed by the Forest Service: Admiralty Island, 1.1 million acres, and Misty Fjords, 2.2 million acres.

State Lawsuit

The state's lawsuit, filed Oct. 30, sought a permanent injunction against creation of monuments in Alaska. The state charged there was no basis for use of the Antiquities Act or the 1976 land management act. The state also claimed that the environmental impact statement on the administration's actions, issued in final form Nov. 28, was inadequate.

The state's appeal for additional time to comment on the impact statement was denied Nov. 24 by U.S. District Court Judge James von der Heydt in Anchorage. Comments on the impact statement, issued in draft form Oct. 25, were due Nov. 22.

The judge also refused to grant a temporary restraining order against any federal actions to restrict use of the federal Alaska lands. Pending was the request for a permanent injunction against such federal actions.

The Nov. 24 setback for the state followed a breakdown in efforts to reach a compromise with the federal government. Carter Nov. 17 rejected a proposed compromise, worked out between the state and federal officials, that would have held up the state's lawsuit for a year in return for a promise from Carter not to use establish monuments.

When Andrus restricted use of the 110 million acres he was criticized by Sen. Ted Stevens, R-Alaska. "I'm astounded," Stevens said, at the "arbitrary and capricious actions," which he asserted put an end to further "good faith" negotiations between federal and state officials on the state's lawsuit.

Andrus said his actions were "aimed at protecting the integrity of Alaska lands...because it assures that there will be no questionable mining claims or other complications regarding this land until final decisions are made."

Andrus was particularly concerned about mineral claims that could be made under an 1872 mining law. Such claims, officials said, could damage the fragile wilderness and complicate land ownership. The law, written when prospectors rode donkeys and carried pick axes, allowed a company that discovered minerals on public land open to mining to file a claim for ownership of the minerals and the site. Congress has been considering updating the law.

The section of the Land Policy and Management Act cited by Andrus, Section 204(e), allowed restrictions on development when the interior secretary, the Senate Energy Committee or the House Interior Committee determined existence of an "emergency situation" that threatened the natural state of the land.

The day before Andrus acted, he got a letter from House Interior Chairman Morris K. Udall, D-Ariz., in which Udall urged Andrus to take "extraordinary measures" to protect the land because of the current "emergency situation." ∎

Calling on a 1906 Law

The Statue of Liberty is one. So is Death Valley. And so are Indian burial grounds scattered across the southwestern United States.

These national monuments were first authorized by a 1906 law called the Antiquities Act that was President Carter's tool for protecting vast wilderness areas in Alaska from mining and other development.

All it takes to create a monument, usually treated as a park, is a presidential proclamation. When Carter established monuments in Alaska, he was following in the tradition of Theodore Roosevelt, who used the law to protect the Grand Canyon from homesteaders and commercial development. Congress acted later to create Grand Canyon National Park. In all, Roosevelt used the law to create nearly a dozen monuments.

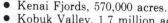

But Carter's opponents in Alaska have challenged that tradition of setting aside large areas as monuments. They argue that the law's original purpose was to protect small archaeological sites on federal land from people seeking old pottery and other artifacts.

The statute's legislative history is sketchy, but the law does say that monuments should be "historic landmarks, historic and prehistoric structures and other objects of historic or scientific interest." Monuments should be confined, the law says, to "the smallest area compatible with the proper care and management of the objects to be protected."

Using that limited authority to create millions of acres of monuments in Alaska is illegal, contend state officials and others.

But there is precedent for using the Antiquities Act to protect large chunks of Alaska. The largest existing monument is Glacier Bay, a wilderness sand beach along Alaska's Pacific Coast. The 2.8 million acre monument was established in 1925. Another Alaskan monument is Katmai, 2.7 million acres in the southern part of the state. It was established as a monument by President Woodrow Wilson in 1918.

There have been court challenges to use of the law, but as one congressional aide noted, "Nobody has ever succeeded in getting any of these things thrown out."

Foreign Policy

Negotiation was the key word in American foreign policy during 1978.

Peace talks sponsored by or directly involving the United States were under way in southern Africa, the Middle East, and Latin America. Even Congress and the Carter administration seemed to reach an understanding, through negotiation, on major foreign policy elements. The administration successfully concluded secret negotiations toward the establishment of diplomatic relations with the People's Republic of China, and neared agreement on a pact with the Soviet Union on strategic arms limitation.

But the chances for ultimate success in many crucial negotiations was uncertain as the year drew to a close.

Middle East

For President Carter, the Middle East meant euphoria and frustration in 1978. The euphoria came in September, when in 13 days at Camp David he coaxed and cajoled Egyptian President Anwar Sadat and Israeli Prime Minister Menachem Begin into accepting a "framework for peace" in the Middle East. But then followed three months of agonizing secret negotiations and public declarations by Egypt and Israel that threatened to undo the success of the Camp David accords.

A Dec. 17 deadline for agreement on an Egyptian-Israeli peace treaty passed as each side was accusing the other of reneging on Camp David promises. President Carter appeared to grow impatient as Sadat and Begin became less willing to compromise when the prospects for a peace treaty were so good. He rebuked both sides for squabbling about "little, tiny technicalities."

China

The Camp David meeting was equaled and perhaps surpassed only by the surprise announcement that the United States and the People's Republic of China would assume full diplomatic relations Jan. 1 and end U.S. ties to the nationalist regime on Taiwan.

Although it had long been assumed that the United States eventually would recognize Communist China and break relations with Taiwan, the suddenness of the Dec. 15 announcement startled the world. Particularly surprised were many members of Congress, especially conservatives, who thought Carter had promised to consult with them before severing ties with Taiwan. The president's decision not to involve members of Congress in the decision gave conservative opponents a ready-made issue to fight legislation implementing the new China policy.

Negotiations

United States-sponsored attempts to negotiate peaceful solutions to confrontations around the globe produced mixed results in 1978.

The SALT talks were moving relatively smoothly at the end of the year, in spite of various disagreements on provisions. But serious obstacles had developed in efforts to negotiate a peace in the Middle East and disputes in Nicaragua, Cyprus, Rhodesia and Namibia.

Generally, the American negotiating efforts proved moderately successful only in cases where all parties were predisposed to negotiate. In those cases where one or both parties saw a better chance of success through delay or military action, the negotiating efforts faced long odds.

● **SALT Talks**. The administration was close to completing a strategic arms limitation treaty (SALT) by the end of 1978. But opposition to the treaty was mounting in the United States. Conservative groups argued that the treaty would be a sell-out to the Russians, while a few liberal peace groups claimed the treaty wouldn't do much to end the arms race.

● **Rhodesia**. Along with Great Britain, the United States worked in 1978 to convene a peace conference involving all parties — government and guerrillas alike — in the war in Rhodesia. That attempt seemed close to success in the autumn, but it fell apart when guerrilla attacks escalated and the Rhodesian government expanded its attacks on guerrilla bases in Zambia and Mozambique. By the end of the year most of Rhodesia was under martial law.

Prime Minister Ian Smith established a coalition transition government with three black leaders in March, and said universal elections would be held by the end of the year. But Smith later postponed the elections to April 1979, and announced a new government plan to give whites effective control of the cabinet, further dimming the chances for a peace conference.

As the year ended the Carter administration debated whether to continue the negotiations or to simply withdraw and allow events to run their course, which might have meant an escalation of fighting.

Congress in 1978 again shifted its stand on economic sanctions against Rhodesia, primarily a ban on the importation of Rhodesian chrome. At the request of the Carter administration, Congress in 1977 reimposed a Rhodesian chrome ban that was first implemented in 1968 then lifted in 1971. But in 1978 conservatives moved to again lift the ban by ending all economic sanctions against the country. They didn't win, but Congress did approve language prohibiting the president from enforcing economic sanctions against Rhodesia after 1978 if Rhodesia had agreed to participate in an all-parties peace conference and if a government had been installed by universal, free elections. Because the elections were not held, the sanctions were still in effect at the beginning of 1979.

● **Cyprus**. In August, President Carter convinced Congress to end the arms embargo against Turkey. He argued that the embargo was a major obstacle to persuading Turkey to resume negotiations for a settlement in Cyprus, where traditional rivalries between Turkey and Greece were focused. Three months later the United States proposed a 12-point plan for a federal government in Cyprus with separate Turkish and Greek regions. But that plan met

Helping Hand: Republican Votes in Congress . . .

Congressional bipartisanship in foreign policy isn't quite dead yet.

Despite the ravages the concept suffered from the Vietnam War and more recently over dealing with the Soviet Union, President Carter won a string of key foreign policy votes in 1978 with the help of a small but consistent group of Republican members of Congress.

Without these votes, Carter's most important international initiatives probably would have gone down to defeat.

The GOP support has been primarily in the Senate. House Republicans delivered the necessary votes on one issue — arms for Turkey — to offset a majority of Democrats who voted against Carter.

The Carter proposals that Republican votes have helped the president win are:

● Ratification of the Panama Canal treaties.
● Sale of advanced fighter planes to Saudi Arabia.
● Lifting the arms sale embargo on Turkey.
● In the Senate, continuing a middle-of-the-road policy toward Rhodesia.

The first three were clear-cut Carter proposals and victories.

The Rhodesia issue has been murkier. The Senate — led by a Republican senator — helped out the administration by warding off a proposal to lift economic sanctions against that country — a policy change that opponents said would undercut Western efforts to bring about a peaceful change from minority white to majority black rule.

In the House, however, the administration didn't do as well on Rhodesia. That chamber lifted sanctions while giving Carter power to reimpose them. But the House

---

The Turkey arms embargo was "rammed through Congress by Democrats. . . . It seems a bit ludicrous that Democrats provided the votes to pass it, took the political credit and now are asking Republicans to furnish votes to help repeal it."

—House Minority Leader
John J. Rhodes, R-Ariz.

---

eliminated some of the key conditions that have been part of the efforts of the United States and Britain to accomplish a peaceful transition of power. Here, Republicans voted heavily against the administration view.

Senate Votes

In the Senate, CQ selected seven important foreign policy votes that occurred in 1978. Those votes, and the party divisions, are:

Canal. Panama Canal treaties — two identical votes on canal neutrality and transfer: 68-32: R 16-22; D 52-10 (ND 39-4; SD 13-6).

Planes. Sale of F-15 fighters to Saudi Arabia — the vote was on rejecting a resolution to block the sales: 44-54: R 11-26; D 33-28 (ND 26-17; SD 7-11).

Turkey. Lifting the arms embargo on Turkey: 57-42: R 27-10; D 30-32 (ND 17-26; SD 13-6).

The vote technically was on specifying future conditions for U.S. arms shipments; the vote on actually lifting the embargo, with the conditions attached, was by voice. But the 57-42 vote represented the Senate division on the basic embargo issue.

Rhodesia. There were three votes here. The first two involved a proposal by Sen. Clifford P. Case, R-N.J., to prohibit an end to U.S. economic sanctions against Rhodesia until the president decided that the Rhodesian government had "committed itself" to a conference of all groups contending for power in the nation and that free elections involving all population groups had been held under international supervision.

The third was an amendment by John C. Danforth, R-Mo., to lift the U.S. sanctions for three months at the end of 1978. According to Senate staffers closely involved in this fight, this vote was the highwater mark for advocates of lifting sanctions, led by Sen. Jesse Helms, R-N.C. Once the outcome on Danforth's amendment was clear, Helms decided not to push ahead with his own proposal to completely end sanctions.

Unlike the other issues, the Carter administration's position on the Rhodesia moves was never publicly made clear. But Senate sources say Carter lobbyists passed the word that the Case plan was acceptable when it became clear that nothing better could be obtained. Moreover, these sources say, it was clear to participants that had Case's plan not prevailed, Helms stood a good chance of winning — a prospect that was even more uninviting to the administration.

The three votes:

● Motion to table (kill) Case's proposal: rejected 39-57: R 27-11; D 12-46 (ND 2-38; SD 10-8).
● Adoption of the Case proposal: adopted 59-36: R 14-24; D 45-12 (ND 35-4; SD 10-8).
● Adoption of the Danforth proposal: rejected 42-54: R 28-10; D 14-44 (ND 3-37; SD 11-7).

Party Support. The party divisions on these votes reflected the crucial importance of Senate Republicans to sustaining Carter positions — either explicit as with Panama, the F-15 planes and Turkey arms, or acknowledged, as in the case of Rhodesia.

Although a majority of Senate Republicans backed the administration in only two cases — the plane sale and Turkey arms — in every case the GOP votes backing Carter were vital to his win. In the planes and arms sales votes, the Republican ballots helped offset the majority of Senate Democrats who went against the party's president on the issue.

Individual Support. Individually, the tabular list below shows the sources of Senate support for Carter proposals. The check marks indicate a vote that backed up the administration's position.

... Gave Carter Key Foreign Policy Victories

The list shows solid GOP support from just four senators: John H. Chafee, R.I.; Charles McC. Mathias, Jr., Md.; James B. Pearson, Kan.; and Robert T. Stafford, Vt.

But beyond 100 percent backing, the table reflects considerable support from another nine or 10 senators. This total of about 12 to 14 Republican senators seems to reflect the basic bipartisan support that the Senate GOP is able to deliver on foreign policy issues.

On the dozens of votes earlier in 1978 on the Panama Canal treaties, there was almost always a majority of Republicans voting against the administration position. But also on almost every vote there was a group of Republicans ranging from about 12 to 17 who consistently backed the administration. Those votes were important to prevent changes in the documents that probably would have sunk the treaties.

One Senate staffer who has followed foreign affairs for some years said that this group of Republicans reflects the party's basic internationalist wing that has traditionally supported bipartisanship in foreign policy "where the party line doesn't mean all that much." But he also noted that there has been increasing grumbling about why the GOP should have to continue "bailing out Jimmy" on these crucial issues.

On two issues, the plane sales and arms for Turkey, the Republican support for Carter's position was much higher than has been the pattern: 26 votes on the planes and 27 votes on Turkey.

The reasons for this are not completely clear. But in the case of Turkey, it appears the proposal to end the embargo drew support from both those Republican senators traditionally supportive of NATO and those senators who either don't have much of a Greek constituency or don't expect to get much support from that group anyway.

On the plane sales, there was evidence that when the issue was before the Senate last spring business interests with good access to Republicans, particularly conservatives, were urging support of the sales. One staffer speculated that these business groups were hoping to get some of the business from manufacturing the plane or, over a longer range, were looking at commercial dealings with all Middle East nations.

House Votes

There have been fewer House votes on crucial foreign policy issues.

One of the most important ones — on lifting the Turkey arms embargo — demonstrated the Republican Party's importance to Carter's foreign policy proposals.

The House went along with the Senate in backing Carter's request to end the embargo, but the vote was much closer: 208-205. Moreover, Carter's position prevailed only after two members — one a Republican, the other a Democrat — switched their votes at the end of the roll call.

On the vote, the party division was: R 78-64: D 130-141 (ND 64-123; SD 66-18). Thus on this vote a majority of the House Republicans voted with Carter to give the president an important victory. Carter was opposed by a majority of his own party, with most of those votes coming from northern members.

House Majority Leader John J. Rhodes, R-Ariz., couldn't resist the opportunity during the Turkey debate to turn the knife a bit on the issue.

Rhodes said he felt "very strongly about the political flim-flam that the Democratic Party has put over on the country."

He said the embargo had been "rammed through Congress by Democrats" over Ford administration protests. He added: "Personally, I am sorely tempted to tell the president, his secretary of state and the Speaker of the House that they should look for the votes necessary to repeal the Turkish embargo in the same place they got the votes to impose it. It seems a bit ludicrous that Democrats provided the votes to pass it, took the political credit and now are asking Republicans to furnish votes to help repeal it."

Senate GOP Support. In the table below, a check indicates a vote backing the administration position.

	Panama Canal	Panama Canal	F-15 Fighter Sales	Turkey Arms	Rhodesia Sanctions	Rhodesia Sanctions	Rhodesia Sanctions
Baker, Tenn.	✓	✓	✓	✓			
Bartlett, Okla.			✓	✓			
Bellmon, Okla.	✓	✓	✓	✓			
Brooke, Mass.	✓	✓			✓	✓	✓
Case, N.J.	✓	✓			✓	✓	✓
Chafee, R.I.	✓	✓	✓	✓	✓	✓	✓
Curtis, Neb.			✓	✓			
Danforth, Mo.	✓	✓	✓	✓		✓	
Dole, Kan.							
Domenici, N.M.					✓	✓	
Garn, Utah			✓	✓			
Goldwater, Ariz.			✓	✓			
Griffin, Mich.			✓	✓		✓	
Hansen, Wyo.			✓	✓			
Hatch, Utah			✓	✓			
Hatfield, Ore.	✓	✓	✓	✓	✓	✓	✓
Hayakawa, Calif.	✓	✓	✓	✓			
Heinz, Pa.	✓	✓					
Helms, N.C.			✓	✓			
Javits, N.Y.	✓	✓			✓	✓	✓
Laxalt, Nev.							
Lugar, Ind.			✓	✓			
Mathias, Md.	✓	✓	✓	✓	✓	✓	✓
McClure, Idaho			✓	✓			
Packwood, Ore.	✓	✓	✓	✓			
Pearson, Kan.	✓	✓	✓	✓	✓	✓	✓
Percy, Ill.	✓	✓	✓		✓	✓	✓
Roth, Del.					✓	✓	✓
Schmitt, N.M.			✓	✓			
Schweiker, Pa.				✓			
Scott, Va.			✓	✓			
Stafford, Vt.	✓	✓	✓	✓	✓	✓	✓
Stevens, Alaska			✓	✓		✓	
Thurmond, S.C.			✓	✓			
Tower, Texas			✓	✓			
Wallop, Wyo.			✓	✓			
Weicker, Conn.	✓	✓					
Young, N.D.			✓	✓			
	16	16	26	27	11	14	10

strong objections from both sides, clouding hopes that the ancient dispute could be resolved easily .

●**Nicaragua**. A violent insurrection in September, resulting in the deaths of some 1,500 persons, caused the United States to push for negotiations between President Anastasio Somoza Debayle and his opponents. Long an American-favored dictator, Somoza had lost popular support and the backing of the United States and was kept in power through the efforts of the military. Carter made it clear the United States wanted Somoza to resign.

After balking at U.S. mediation efforts, Somoza in December agreed to release hundreds of political prisoners and to accept a plebiscite on whether he would remain as president. But on Dec. 27 Somoza refused to agree to having the vote supervised by outsiders, which deadlocked negotiations at the end of the year.

●**Namibia**. Along with four other Western powers, the United States attempted in 1978 to persuade South Africa to accept United Nations-supervised elections in Namibia (South West Africa). The Western plan for elections was accepted by the United Nations and by the guerrilla force challenging South African rule of Namibia.

As part of the effort to persuade South Africa to accept U.N. involvement in Namibian elections, the United States softened its rhetoric against apartheid, and stalled U.N. action on economic sanctions against South Africa.

In December, however, South Africa conducted its own elections in Namibia, which it had controlled since 1920 under a League of Nations mandate. The election was won by a coalition friendly to South Africa.

Human Rights

The Carter administration continued its policy of publicly criticizing nations that violate the human rights of their citizens. But, as in 1977, the administration was itself taken to task for selective application of that policy. Conservatives argued that the United States wasn't paying enough attention to the human rights violations of Communist nations such as the Soviet Union, Vietnam and Cambodia, while liberals challenged the administration policy of near-silence on violations in Uganda, Iran, the Philippines, South Korea and other nations.

Carter himself said little about human rights problems during 1978 until December, when he declared that concern about human rights was the "soul" of U.S. foreign policy. "The effectiveness of our human rights policy is now an established fact," Carter said Dec. 6. "It has contributed to an atmosphere of change — sometimes disturbing — but which has encouraged progress in many ways and in many places."

In his December speech, celebrating the 30th anniversary of the United Nations Declaration of Human Rights, Carter singled out seven nations that "continue to practice repression": Cambodia, Chile, Uganda, South Africa, Nicaragua, Ethiopia and the Soviet Union.

Republican Support for Carter

Republicans supplied the crucial votes for several of President Carter's key foreign policy initiatives in 1978. The Republican aid was most evident — and most needed — in the Senate, where a handful of moderate and liberal Republicans consistently voted to support the Democratic president.

Major issues on which Republicans supplied the decisive votes were:

●Senate ratification of the Panama Canal treaties (16 Republicans supported the president);

●Senate approval of advanced fighter planes to Saudi Arabia (11 Republicans supported the president);

●Lifting the arms sale embargo against Turkey (27 Republican senators supported the president, and 78 Republican House members supported the president);

●Continuation of a moderate policy toward Rhodesia, especially in votes in the Senate (a minimum of 24 Republican senators supported the president on three separate votes).

In spite of their support for the president on specific votes, Republicans tended to paint a gloomy picture of American foreign policy failures resulting from unrestrained Russian blustering.

Senate Republicans in May issued a blistering attack on Carter's foreign policy: "In 15 short months of incoherence, inconsistence and ineptitude, our foreign policy and national security objectives are being challenged around the globe by Soviet arrogance."

American-Soviet Relations

While the United States was busy negotiating disputes around the globe in 1978, the Soviet Union was shoring up old alliances, creating new dependencies and exploiting some of the same conflicts the Americans were trying to resolve.

The result was that American-Soviet relations generally were cool, in spite of the importance each side attached to prospects for improved trade and for an arms control treaty.

Soviet involvement increased substantially in Vietnam, Ethiopia, Cuba and Afghanistan during 1978. Perhaps most significant, the Soviets were hoping to gain from the turmoil in oil-rich, strategically-important Iran, where American influence was closely tied to the waning power of Shah Mohammed Riza Pahlevi.

Administration officials claimed that the Soviet Union was actually losing ground, especially in Third World countries which needed more economic development support than the Russians could deliver.

For a few weeks in the late autumn a major confrontation appeared possible after the revelation that the Soviet Union had shipped an unstated number of advanced Mig 23 warplanes to Cuba. After a flurry of excitement that threatened a replay of the 1962 Cuban missile crisis, the Carter administration said the planes were not equipped to carry nuclear weapons and were not a direct threat to the United States.

Carter toughened his rhetoric toward the Soviet Union in mid-year, warning the Russians that he was willing to take a hard-line approach if their actions made it necessary.

"The Soviet Union can choose either confrontation or cooperation," the president said June 7. "The United States is adequately prepared to meet either choice." ∎

Jets for Saudis:

Middle East Plane Sales Backed by Senate Vote In Major Carter Victory

Given its first major role in shaping recent events in the Middle East, the Senate by a 10-vote margin went along with the Carter administration's controversial plan to sell $4.8 billion worth of jet fighters to Israel, Egypt and Saudi Arabia.

Under arms sales laws, House action was not required because the contracts automatically go through in 30 days unless rejected by both chambers.

A victory for the Carter administration but a bitter first defeat for Israel and U.S. Jewish organizations passionately opposed to the weapons package, the Senate's 44-54 decision May 15 to turn down a resolution (S Con Res 86) blocking the sales was preceded by 10 hours of emotional debate on the heavily-lobbied issue.

Sales critics objected to linking Israel's supplies to the Saudi contracts and asserted that the Carter policy would "sap the morale" of the Jewish state.

Contract supporters argued that the United States now must be "evenhanded" in relations with both Israel and Arab states because of the complex weave of U.S. economic and strategic interests in the Middle East.

Call for Courage

"We must have the courage, we must have the guts to face a changing world," said Abraham Ribicoff, D-Conn., referring to Saudi influence on international economic policies and Middle East peace efforts resulting from its oil riches. Ribicoff has been a longtime supporter of Israel.

Although Ribicoff and other administration supporters stressed that their position did not imply any lessening of support for Israel — that "commitment is unshakable," said Muriel Humphrey, D-Minn. — sales opponent Jacob K. Javits, R-N.Y., told the Senate the vote might not be read that way.

"The Israelis and Americans who feel as I do are likely to read the signal that is going to go out from this chamber quite differently. . . . The vote today may raise doubts now for the first time in 30 years respecting our commitment given the overtone and context of the debate," he said.

Earlier, Javits asserted that Carter's arms sales package — 60 F-15s for Saudi Arabia, 50 F-5Es for Egypt and 15 F-15s and 75 F-16s for Israel (half its original request) — was presented by President Carter "to teach the Israelis a lesson" to be more flexible in peace negotiations.

And other opponents said the sale was an expression of U.S. "nervelessness" in coming to grips with petroleum-based international economics.

Voting Pattern

It was clear throughout the debate that this was one vote many senators had hoped would not occur because of the difficult choice of siding either with Israel or the Arab states. But Senate Majority Leader Robert C. Byrd, D-W.Va., said he did not think a floor fight could have been avoided considering the way the sales were packaged.

In one of those odd voting patterns, where liberals oppose liberals, conservatives split with conservatives, it was Republican support that was the key to Carter's victory. Twenty-eight Democrats opposed the Biden resolution, but 33 backed the measure; 26 Republicans made the difference by supporting the sales, while only 11 Republicans voted against them.

On opposite sides were conservatives James B. Allen, D-Ala., and Harry F. Byrd Jr., Ind-Va.; liberals George McGovern, D-S.D., and Frank Church, D-Idaho; Majority Leader Byrd and Democratic Whip Alan Cranston, D-Calif., and Jewish members Javits and Ribicoff.

Lobby Impact

Pressure by the administration began to build May 12, the day after the deadlocked Foreign Relations Committee voted to send the resolution to the floor without a recommendation, when President Carter sent every member of the Senate a letter stating that a rejection of the aircraft for Egypt would be a "breach of trust" with Egyptian President Anwar Sadat who "has turned away from a relationship with the Soviet Union" to work with the United States in the search of peace.

The White House also disclosed that Carter was calling many in the Senate to argue his case. Members of the Cabinet and others in the administration also were reported to have contacted undecided senators before the vote.

On the opposite side, the American Jewish Committee and other pro-Israeli organizations were swamping Senate offices with telegrams, Mailgrams, letters and phone calls as the vote approached, according to aides. Outside the Senate chamber itself, the reception lobby was choked with lobbyists on both sides of the issue.

It was the pressure from Jewish organizations, however, that prompted Sen. Mike Gravel, D-Alaska, and others to state publicly that their votes had become a "litmus

Artist's Conception of F-15 in Flight

Senate Vote

The Senate's 44-54 vote against the resolution (S Con Res 86) to disapprove the $4.8 billion fighter sales to Israel, Egypt and Saudi Arabia was as follows:

Democrats Against Plane Sales (33)

Allen, Ala.	Matsunaga, Hawaii
Anderson, Minn.	McIntyre, N.H.
Bayh, Ind.	Melcher, Mont.
Biden, Del.	Metzenbaum, Ohio
Burdick, N.D.	Moynihan, N.Y.
Chiles, Fla.	Nelson, Wis.
Church, Idaho	Nunn, Ga.
Clark, Iowa	Pell, R.I.
Cranston, Calif.	Proxmire, Wis.
DeConcini, Ariz.	Riegle, Mich.
Durkin, N.H.	Sarbanes, Md.
Ford, Ky.	Sasser, Tenn.
Hart, Colo.	Stone, Fla.
Haskell, Colo.	Talmadge, Ga.
Hathaway, Maine	Williams, N.J.
Jackson, Wash.	Zorinsky, Neb.
Kennedy, Mass.	

Republicans Against Plane Sales (11)

Brooke, Mass.	Javits, N.Y.
Case, N.J.	Packwood, Ore.
Dole, Kan.	Roth, Del.
Domenici, N.M.	Schweiker, Pa.
Hatfield, Ore.	Weicker, Conn.
Heinz, Pa.	

Democrats For Plane Sales (28)

Abourezk, S.D.	Humphrey, Minn.
Bentsen, Texas	Inouye, Hawaii
Bumpers, Ark.	Johnston, La.
Byrd, Va.	Leahy, Vt.
Byrd, W.Va.	Long, La.
Cannon, Nev.	Magnuson, Wash.
Culver, Iowa	McGovern, S.D.
Eagleton, Mo.	Morgan, N.C.
Eastland, Miss.	Muskie, Maine
Glenn, Ohio	Randolph, W.Va.
Gravel, Alaska	Ribicoff, Conn.
Hatfield, Mont.	Sparkman, Ala.
Hodges, Ark.	Stennis, Miss.
Hollings, S.C.	Stevenson, Ill.

Republicans For Plane Sales (26)

Baker, Tenn.	Lugar, Ind.
Bartlett, Okla.	Mathias, Md.
Bellmon, Okla.	McClure, Idaho
Chafee, R.I.	Pearson, Kan.
Curtis, Neb.	Percy, Ill.
Danforth, Mo.	Schmitt, N.M.
Garn, Utah	Scott, Va.
Goldwater, Ariz.	Stafford, Vt.
Griffin, Mich.	Stevens, Alaska
Hansen, Wyo.	Thurmond, S.C.
Hatch, Utah	Tower, Texas
Hayakawa, Calif.	Wallop, Wyo.
Helms, N.C.	Young, N.D.

test" for future support from Jews, although they had supported Israel on every issue in the past.

"This vote, if it is not done properly, kisses away in the future all kinds of financial support that would inure to a candidate for office," said Gravel. More troublesome, he added, the vote "will cost me some very important personal friendships."

Earlier McGovern warned the U.S. Jewish community's members that if they "press the case for Israel to the point where America loses its capacity to influence the Arab leadership . . . that may set in motion a backlash both in the Middle East and in the United States that can only harm the Israeli cause."

Bob Packwood, R-Ore., defended the lobbying, insisting that Jews have an understandable interest in the homeland of their forefathers as do Poles, Greeks and blacks. "It is with sorrow and disgust, therefore, that I hear the State Department time and again refer to the Jewish lobby or the Israeli lobby in a tone suggestive of a group which puts the interests of another country ahead of the United States."

Administration Criticism

Although voting for the sales package, Senate Minority Leader Howard H. Baker Jr., R-Tenn., said that he was troubled by the way the contracts were linked. To maintain the balance of military forces in the Middle East and to assure Israel of its unique relationship to our interests in the region, Baker called upon Carter to double the number of F-16s to be sent Israel for a total of 150.

(The president May 11 offered to supply Israel 20 additional F-15s in the 1983-84 period to bring its total to 60, the number supplied the Saudis.)

Members of the president's own party as well questioned the way the sales contracts were presented to Congress. Paul S. Sarbanes, D-Md., for example, who had worked alongside Carter throughout the winter on the Panama Canal treaties, said that there "is a question of skill and competence in the art of government" missing on the handling of the aircraft sales.

Arguments for Sale

Administration lobbyists and senators supporting the sales on the floor stressed four major themes to support selling the F-15s to Saudi Arabia: the importance of the moderate Arab states to peace in the Middle East and the need for the United States to maintain balanced relationship in the region; the Soviet presence in the Horn of Africa, Syria and Iraq; the importance of Arab oil to the United States, 20 percent of which comes from the Middle East; and the possibility that Saudi Arabia would turn to France for fighters if the U.S. sale were rejected.

The question of the United States' need for Saudi-supplied petroleum was addressed directly by Ribicoff who said, "People try to avoid it, but let us talk about oil." Noting that the Saudis possess a quarter of the world's oil reserves and have the flexibility to contract or expand production for market stability, Ribicoff said "the fact is that without a stable, predictable supply of oil from Saudi Arabia . . . the West would face the worst depression in the industrial era."

"In essence," countered Daniel Patrick Moynihan, D-N.Y., the aircraft sale is a rationalization of "American nervelessness in the area of international economic policy as well as political and military policy." ∎

National Security

At first glance 1978 was a good year for President Carter in defense legislation.

Both the House and the Senate rejected decisively several moves to raise or lower the Defense Department's budget recommendations. And by unexpectedly large margins, Congress supported Carter's position on the year's two major battles over new weapons: the B-1 bomber and a fifth nuclear-powered aircraft carrier, both opposed by the president.

But some other important policy battles were not fought during the year, particularly those on a new strategic arms limitation treaty with the Soviet Union and on Carter's plan to withdraw all U.S. ground forces from South Korea. In each case the president stayed his hand, at least in part for fear of vehement congressional opposition.

Where Carter succeeded, he did so by committing his administration unconditionally to continued growth in Pentagon spending. He based his opposition to the bomber and the carrier on the argument that each would be less effective than other weapons programs: the cruise missile, which was still in the development stage, and smaller, but more numerous, warships.

Congress generally handled defense issues in 1978 the same way they had been handled in the previous four years — the period since the October 1973 Middle East War.

For all the rhetoric about a reassertion of the congressional role in foreign policy decisions, Congress continued to show a strong tendency to defer to the commander-in-chief on the details of military policy.

This presidential flexibility, however, appeared to be contingent on Carter's hewing to a fairly narrow path that depended on a real annual increase in the Defense Department's budget, modernization of Army and Air Force equipment in Western Europe and modernization of the U.S. strategic weapons arsenal.

Modernization Costs

Deferred at least until 1979 was a resolution of the dilemma that would confront both Carter and Congress as the modernization programs move into full swing and begin to cost substantial sums of money. A president who was committed to balancing the federal budget and a Congress elected in the year of a taxpayers' revolt would have to reconcile their fiscal conservatism with new programs that would be extremely costly, even by the Pentagon's standards.

And in the last weeks of 1978, Carter was severely criticized by liberal Democrats, many of whom long had been suspicious that he lacked sympathy with the party's traditional support of domestic welfare programs.

At issue was Carter's reported decision to allow the Pentagon's budget for fiscal 1980 to grow by 3 percent, after taking into account the cost of inflation. Major domestic programs, on the other hand, reportedly were to be severely constrained to keep the total federal budget deficit under $30 billion.

How Much Is Enough?

When the 95th Congress finally went home in mid-October, it became apparent that Congress, during fiscal 1979, would appropriate essentially the amount ($126 billion) the administration requested for national defense for the year.

The largest single money bill in the defense package, the Defense Department appropriations bill, actually was some $2 billion below the amount Carter requested. But this simply was the amount Congress had allocated for the aircraft carrier that Carter finally had killed through his veto of the annual arms procurement bill.

It was considered certain that the administration would submit — and Congress would pass — a supplemental appropriation early in 1979 to reallocate that money to other defense projects.

Through most of the year, Republicans and other conservative groups had bet heavily that Carter would be vulnerable to hard-line attacks on his defense policies. But during 1978 Moscow toned down some of the policies that had vividly conjured up the image of Soviet imperialism on the march, such as its harsh crackdown on Soviet dissidents and its military assistance to Ethiopia in that country's border war with Somalia.

3 Percent Growth Rate

Carter also scored important points in the skirmishing over the size of the defense budget by pledging his administration to a 3 percent annual growth rate. And he presented the budget as giving a strong boost to U.S. forces in NATO.

While hard-line critics charged that both claims were debatable, the administration stood by its position. Desperate to show their eagerness to hold down federal spending without jeopardizing important pork-barrel projects, most members found it comfortable to take Carter's claims at face value.

Carter's position also was buttressed by the fact that many of the weapons with which the hard-liners were most concerned could not have absorbed significant funding increases in any case during fiscal 1979:

● An effort by some members of the Senate Armed Services Committee to increase funds for development of a new intercontinental missile (called M-X) collapsed in May because the Air Force had not yet decided how the new missile would be protected against the large arsenal of increasingly accurate Soviet missiles.

● Several important Army programs — a new tank, two new anti-aircraft missiles, a new armored troop carrier, two new helicopters — all had been delayed at various points in their development cycle during the 1970s. As a result, these weapons had not yet entered production or were just beginning production at a relatively slow pace.

● Long drawn out disputes between the Navy and three of its largest shipbuilders over some $2 billion worth of contract claims left a general impression — even among some members who could be counted on to support a much larger shipbuilding program — that the Navy just could not absorb more money until it straightened out its management of ship construction programs.

The upshot was that both houses rejected by large margins floor amendments to the first budget resolution that would have increased or decreased the defense spending ceiling from the amounts recommended by the House and Senate Budget committees.

By the time each house acted on the defense appropriations bill, the anti-tax mood in the country, symbolized by California's "Proposition 13," was in full flight. But the few attempts to cut the bill did not present any serious threat. A Senate amendment that would have cut the budget request by a symbolic $1 billion received a mere 11 votes.

The Showdowns: B-1 and the Carrier

Carter beat the supporters of the B-1 and the nuclear carrier by unexpectedly large margins. And in each case the House, in backing the president, reversed at least one previous vote in favor of the new weapons.

But while the White House touted the two victories as clear evidence of Carter's prowess in dealing with Capitol Hill, the circumstances of the two battles suggested some narrow policy bounds within which Carter could exercise such clout.

Alternatives, Not Reductions

In each case, Carter insisted that he was opposing a weapon whose time had passed in order to invest in other projects that would do the same job more effectively. While the immediate effect was to kill a proposed defense expenditure, the promised alternatives would eventually cost about as much as the weapons they were to replace.

The long crusade against the B-1 had laid heavy emphasis on the plane's $100 million-a-copy price tag. But Carter and Defense Secretary Harold Brown based their decision to go with the cruise missile instead of the B-1 on the former's promise of greater effectiveness against Soviet air defenses.

Carter's strategy was even more clear in the White House's efforts to get Congress to sustain his veto of the $2 billion aircraft carrier.

At the insistence of the House Democratic leadership, he stressed that his purpose was not to cut the money from the budget, but rather to spend it on "higher priority" defense projects that would more directly beef up NATO's capability to defend Western Europe. And he unequivocally committed himself to requesting a slightly less expensive, non-nuclear carrier in 1979.

Symbols of Yesterday's War

Despite sophisticated arguments that tried to justify their role in future U.S. strategy, the bomber and the carrier were subjected to heavy criticism as symbols of military obsolescence.

With the end of the Vietnam War, the B-1 had become the surrogate target for critics of Pentagon spending. Capitalizing on the plane's price tag of $100 million-a-copy and its failure to meet some of more extravagant design goals planned for it, critics ridiculed the plane as a plaything for generals. An energetic anti-B-1 lobby bombarded the press and members of Congress with arguments against the plane.

Carrier Veto

Carrier opponents were not as organized as the anti-bomber lobby when Carter vetoed the big ship Aug. 17, but the same themes attracted liberals who were critical of the Pentagon's share of the federal budget and of its presumed influence on U.S. foreign policy: the ship was extremely expensive — $2 billion, without its deckload of planes — and opponents painted images of beribboned admirals swaggering around the quarterdeck to no real purpose.

Other expensive weapons had faced such attacks in the previous decade, but what sealed the doom of the B-1 and the carrier was the skepticism of many members who were not usually inclined to cut Pentagon programs.

House Appropriations Committee Chairman George Mahon, D-Texas, apparently spoke for many members when he said, in opposition to both the bomber and the carrier, that the weapon of the future clearly was the intercontinental missile. Neither the bomber nor the carrier would play more than a marginal role in any conflict with the Soviet Union, according to Mahon.

Skeptical of their value in wartime, horrified by their cost and presented with alternative weapons, which would not have to be paid for in 1978, enough moderates and hard-liners joined the traditional Pentagon critics to kill the two programs.

Brass Hat Support

In the case of the B-1, Carter had the additional advantage of strong support from ranking military leaders, including then-Air Force Chief of Staff Gen. David C. Jones. Jones had fought hard to save the plane, assisted by his colleagues on the Joint Chiefs of Staff. But when Carter decided to cancel the project, Jones decided that it was doomed.

Although the House on several occasions had voted in favor of the B-1, the Senate always had voted decisively against the project.

When House hard-liners tried to keep the program alive in 1978 by spending the money appropriated in 1976 for two of the planes, Jones supported Carter's effort to rescind the earlier appropriation.

The Air Force position was that it preferred to spend the $462 million on other programs that eventually would enter the Air Force arsenal.

The carrier case was different. Admirals campaigned vigorously in support of the nuclear carrier — until Carter vetoed the authorization bill that contained the ship. But many observers felt that the Navy's case was undermined by the long-festering problems with cost-overruns, schedule delays and contract

For 1980

The outrage expressed by liberal members over Carter's plan to increase the Pentagon budget while containing domestic programs was expected to help the president control the size of defense expenditures in fiscal 1980. He would be able to present whatever amount he requested as the middle-of-the-road position between demands for higher and lower Pentagon spending.

Also in 1979, Carter had to seek congressional action on a SALT treaty and, possibly, on his proposed withdrawal of ground troops from Korea.

In 1978 he was not really tested on his ability to sell Congress on other than hard-line positions on national security issues. ∎

White House Lobbying Helps Kill B-1

White House lobbying of rare intensity finally has killed the B-1 bomber program. The House Feb. 22, 1978, by a surprisingly large margin, 234-182, voted to rescind $462 million appropriated in fiscal 1977 to build two B-1s, thus reversing the position it took December 1977 when it rejected (166-191) the rescission.

Senior Air Force officers and some congressional defense experts had decided that as a matter of practical politics it would have been impossible to reverse President Carter's June 30, 1977, decision to cancel the B-1 in favor of the new cruise missile. Against that background, the White House and the House Democratic leadership were able to convince many members that voting against the rescission would not save the project, but only further delay the $7.8 billion supplemental appropriation bill (HR 9375) to which the rescission was attached.

Politically significant projects funded by the bill included sewage treatment plant construction grants ($4.5 billion), SBA disaster loans ($1.4 billion) and heating bill assistance for low-income households ($200 million).

Also provided by the bill was $346.5 million to accelerate development of the cruise missile and to modify existing B-52 bombers to carry them.

House acceptance of the Senate-sponsored rescission completed action on HR 9375. The Senate Feb. 1 had reaffirmed its position favoring the plane's cancellation. The conference report on the bill had been cleared Dec. 7.

An important factor in bringing several members around to Carter's position on the B-1 was the future of the demonstration fast breeder reactor at Clinch River, Tenn.

In November 1977 Carter vetoed the regular fiscal 1978 Energy Research and Development Administration (ERDA) authorization bill in hopes of killing the project. But Clinch River supporters then added to the supplemental $80 million for the project as well as language requiring Carter to use the money to advance the project. There was no resolution of the dispute in 1978.

Lobby Blitz

Problems in the B-1's early development and its cost — estimated in late 1977 at $101 million a copy — made it an easy target for critics of Pentagon spending.

But the project was supported by Presidents Nixon and Ford, and B-1 opponents were stymied by Congress' traditional reluctance to challenge the White House on major weapons decisions. Eventually, B-1 opponents hit on a tactical ploy that capitalized on this tendency. In 1976 a rider was attached to the annual defense funding bill stipulating that full-scale production of the B-1 would be subject to approval by the winner of the 1976 presidential election.

Carter's opposition to the B-1 appeared to waver once in office. But by June 30 the former engineer had become convinced the strategic wave of the future was the cruise missile.

Although deeply disappointed, the Air Force quickly accepted his decision. To override Carter would have required the approval of both houses.

Gradually, leading congressional defense experts joined the Air Force. By the fall of 1977, Appropriations Committee Chairman George Mahon, D-Texas, was leading the administration's fight in the House. Eventually, he was joined by Jack Edwards, D-Ala., the senior Republican on the Defense Appropriations Subcommittee. And on the Feb. 22 vote, Carter was supported by several usually hawkish members of the Armed Services Committee including Chairman Melvin Price, D-Ill., Mendel J. Davis, D-S.C., and Harold Runnels, D-N.M.

Carter secured congressional cancellation of fiscal 1978 B-1 money by Sept. 8. But B-1 supporters were able to keep the fiscal 1977 program alive because of members' concern over the possibility that a new strategic arms limitation treaty with Moscow (SALT II) might impose severe limitations on the cruise missile.

The SALT argument and high absenteeism among Democrats beat the rescission move in the House Dec. 6. But Carter was determined to kill the project, and he worked closely with the House Democratic leadership in preparing for a rematch.

At a White House meeting Feb. 17, congressional relations officials from several Cabinet departments were given four or five names from a list of 55 House members thought to be doubtful on the B-1 issue. They were instructed to call the members and press the case for rescinding the B-1 funds in order to free the money in the supplemental. "This is one we really want," a high White House aide told a reporter. "We're willing to spend capital to get it."

The Pentagon's case was pressed by Defense Secretary Harold Brown in phone calls to some members and in a briefing arranged by Mahon for several members the day before the vote. Mahon also circulated a letter from Air Force Chief of Staff Gen. David C. Jones urging the rescission, and he personally lobbied several members vigorously on behalf of Carter.

Carter phoned several members personally — including Price. And in meetings with some members about other subjects, he brought up the B-1, stressing his determination not to spend the fiscal 1977 money. He also sent a letter to each Democratic member of the Appropriations Committee soliciting support.

Vote Changes

Changing from opposition to Carter in the Dec. 6 vote to support on Feb. 22 were 31 members, of whom 22 were Democrats: Allen, Tenn.; Andrews, N.C.; Annunzio, Ill.; Bevill, Ala.; Burke, Mass.; Davis, S.C.; Dicks, Wash.; Flood, Pa.; Gammage, Texas; Holland, S.C.; Jenrette, S.C.; Levitas, Ga.; Lloyd, Tenn.; Mann, S.C.; Milford, Texas; Natcher, Tenn.; Patten, N.J.; Pepper, Fla.; Price, Ill.; Roybal, Calif.; Runnels, N.M. and Wright, Texas.

Also switching to support of the rescission were nine Republicans: Conable, N.Y.; Duncan, Tenn.; Quayle, Ind.; Quie, Minn.; Quillen, Tenn.; Ruppe, Mich.; Sawyer, Mich.; Sebelius, Kan. and Skubitz, Kan.

Switching from support of the rescission to opposition were Democrats Murphy, Pa., and Staggers, W.Va.

Floor Debate

B-1 proponents tried to bolster members against White House and congressional pressure to accept the Senate language in order to quickly clear the $7.9 billion bill. "The agencies could have had this money long weeks ago if the administration had been less engrossed in killing the B-1," said Robert L. F. Sikes, D-Fla. "If we win this fight today for the B-1, we will still get the supplemental."

John Buchanan, R-Ala., an apparent target of the White House lobbying campaign, denounced a phone call to his office by the Environmental Protection Agency's second-ranking congressional liaison official, Larry Snowhite. Snowhite had urged Buchanan to vote for the rescission with the argument that $57 million in sewage treatment money for Alabama was tied up in the supplemental. "Can anyone explain to me the connection between this and the B-1 bomber?" he demanded.

But Carter's supporters, led by Mahon and Joseph P. Addabbo, D-N.Y., noted that the Senate had shown no tendency to give in on its rescission language. And several members rose to recite the litany of pork-barrel projects that would be stalled until the supplemental was cleared.

The substantive discussion of the merits of the rescission retraced the arguments made during the four House B-1 debates in 1977.

Opponents of the rescission insisted the manned bomber could not be supplanted by the cruise missile. The new robot would be helpless against the Soviet Union's dense anti-aircraft defenses, they said, including a new ultra-high-speed missile now under development called the SA-10.

Moreover, the Carter administration already had agreed to limitations on the range of the cruise missile in the arms limitation talks with Moscow, opponents said. These would render the new weapon useless against vital targets deep inside the Soviet Union. Construction of the two planes would keep the contractors in business for 18 additional months. During that time the Pentagon would retain a realistic option to go ahead with B-1 production if U.S.-Soviet relations took a turn for the worse.

Carter's supporters maintained that in any future attack on the Soviet Union, swarms of the tiny cruise missiles would have a far better chance of slipping through the defenses than would a few hundred B-1s. Noting that no B-1 production money was included in the fiscal 1978 Pentagon budget nor in the fiscal 1979 request, they said that rescission of the fiscal 1977 money was just the logical extension of decisions Congress already had made last year.

Some members charged that the fight over the bomber had become an institutional test of strength. Robert K. Dornan, R-Calif., in whose district the planes would have been manufactured, argued that completion of the two B-1s would have been no more costly than the cost of their cancellation plus the welfare payments that would be needed for the 7,000 aerospace workers put out of work by terminating the plane. "What the president is saying here is that he does not want aircraft numbers five and six even if they are free. That is arrogant and absurd."

Armed Services Committee member Davis agreed with the diagnosis, but had a different prescription. "Let us cut out the argument between downtown and the House. Let us let the Air Force get on with the program that they need and let us try to improve them...and not sit here and waste time and money over two planes that will produce nothing."

Maneuvers

In a last ditch effort to save the planes, Jim Lloyd, D-Calif., then moved to table Mahon's motion that the House concur in the Senate's position. But Lloyd was defeated, 172-244.

Then Dornan demanded that the Mahon motion be split in two. After the House agreed to recede from its own position—the first part of the motion—by a standing vote of 126-110, Dornan moved to amend the second part accepting the Senate position. The Dornan version would have delayed implementation of the rescission until either house of Congress passed a resolution implementing it and, in any case, until 90 days after the Senate had ratified a new strategic arms limitation treaty (SALT II) with the Soviets.

O'Neill upheld Mahon's point of order that the Dornan motion was out of order since the SALT negotiations were not germane to the supplemental appropriations bill. The House then adopted the Senate position, 234-182. ∎

Members of Congress Fault Carter for Failure to Decide Future of 'Neutron Bomb'

The congressional furor over reports that President Carter had canceled the so-called neutron bomb abated only slightly after his announcement April 7, 1978, that he was only postponing a production decision.

The earlier report had drawn heavy criticism from defense hard-liners already upset by the slow pace of some new weapons programs under the Carter administration.

Members of Congress who tried in 1977 to kill the radiation weapon had applauded the cancellation report and urged Carter to stand up to the heavy political pressure in favor of going ahead with production. But opponents apparently lacked strong allies in the administration while supporters of the new weapon included most of Carter's senior defense and foreign policy advisers.

Carter followed up his April 7 announcement on Oct. 18 by ordering the Energy Department to begin production of components needed to convert tactical nuclear weapons into neutron bombs. However, the components would be stockpiled rather than inserted into warheads. The administration adopted the stockpile approach, recommended by the Senate Armed Services Committee, in hopes the Soviet Union would show corresponding restraint in its military buildup in Eastern Europe.

Background

The proposed enhanced radiation warheads for the Army's 60-mile-range Lance missile and its 8 inch and 155 mm howitzers were designed to produce an explosion with the force of only a few thousand tons of TNT. But they would produce the same surge of lethal radiation as an older nuclear weapon with 10 times the explosive power. While the heavy blast and fire damage from a neutron weapon would reach out only a few hundred yards, the radiation would be lethal over a radius of more than half a mile.

Tank Crews Vulnerable

The new warheads would be especially effective against the concentrated masses of tanks on which Soviet war planning is based. Armored vehicles, although resistant to the heat and blast of "regular" nuclear explosions, would give their crews little protection against neutron radiation.

According to defense planners, the limited nature of the blast and fire damage from neutron warheads made it a better weapon to counter a Soviet armored thrust into West Germany, the likely target of any Soviet attack on NATO.

The present U.S. tactical nuclear weapons in Europe would be destructive over a much larger radius and could not be used, in many situations, without causing massive damage and high civilian fatalities.

'Killer Bombs'

The Army had begun developing a new type of nuclear artillery shell in the early 1970s. But in 1973 Congress canceled the project, in part because of the high projected cost — $904 million for 2,000 8-inch artillery shells.

The Pentagon went back to the drawing board and, in 1974, returned with a new idea for modernizing the arsenal — enhanced radiation warheads, later to become known as neutron bombs. By 1977 the Energy Research and Development Administration (ERDA) — which by law had charge of all nuclear weapons research and production — was ready to begin manufacture of the warheads for the Lance missile and the 8-inch gun. But on June 6, 1977, the project received its first large-scale public notice in a *Washington Post* story headlined, "Killer Bombs Buried in ERDA Budget."

1977 Congressional Debate

In the ensuing congressional debate, opponents of the radiation weapon warned that because such warheads could be used to defend West Germany without destroying the country, they would make nuclear war more "thinkable" to NATO leaders. Accordingly, there would be pressure to use the weapon in certain circumstances. And once any type of nuclear weapon were used, according to this argument, the conflict would escalate to a global nuclear holocaust.

But proponents of the radiation weapon insisted that precisely because the Russians could more easily envision NATO using the new weapon to repel an attack, they would be deterred from launching the attack.

Attempts by opponents in Congress to halt production were turned back by large margins in both houses. But Congress did add to the fiscal 1978 ERDA authorization bill a proviso that it would have 45 days in which to veto any production decision.

President Carter had conceded during the 1977 congressional debate that he previously had been unaware of the enhanced radiation weapon program, which was initiated by the Ford administration. But he fought the attempts to kill the program, saying he wanted to retain the option of producing the new weapon. After Congress had acted, however, he said that a decision to produce the weapon would be contingent on a commitment by the NATO allies to allow its deployment on their territory.

Diplomatic Turmoil

Carter's hope that the other NATO members would share responsibility for producing the new weapon ran afoul of domestic politics in several European countries. Several political parties of the non-communist left attacked the new weapon as a peculiarly inhumane device that would accelerate the arms race. Egon Bahr, the general secretary of West German Chancellor Helmut Schmidt's Social Democratic Party, denounced the new weapons as "a symbol of mental perversion."

Schmidt reportedly feared that a public endorsement would jeopardize his governing coalition's 10-vote parliamentary majority. His government insisted that only the

United States could decide whether to proceed with production of the radiation warheads.

Exacerbating the situation was an intense Soviet campaign against the weapon. One strategy was to launch a propaganda blitz against it. At the Geneva disarmament conference, Moscow proposed a treaty banning radiation weapons; and 31 Soviet scientists wrote Carter that his decision on their production would test the sincerity of his campaign promises to slow the arms race.

In addition, Soviet leader Leonid Brezhnev reportedly warned the European NATO governments in strong terms against adding the new weapon to the NATO arsenal.

By March 1978 the Western alliance had moved toward a rough consensus on the issue. Washington would have to make the decision whether to produce the radiation warheads. If Carter decided to go ahead with it, then it would be up to Washington to try to negotiate a cancellation of the decision in return for some commensurate Soviet arms restraint, such as their cancellation of the 2,000-mile-range SS-20 missile or a reduction in Moscow's three-to-one advantage in the number of tanks stationed in central Europe.

Failing any agreement, West Germany then would accept deployment of the warheads on its territory if either Belgium or the Netherlands also endorsed the move. Administration officials pointed out that because of European sensitivity about German military activity, the Bonn government was unwilling to stand alone in calling for a controversial new weapon.

Final approval of the NATO strategy was scheduled for the week of March 20, but was canceled after President Carter became directly involved in the formulation of the U.S. position. Carter apparently wanted a firmer commitment from the NATO allies that the weapons would in fact be deployed if he approved their production. Deputy Secretary of State Warren M. Christopher carried this message to Bonn on March 27; and on April 4 West German Foreign Affairs Minister Hans-Dietrich Genscher came to Washington reportedly to urge Carter to go ahead.

Congressional Blowup

On April 4 *The New York Times* reported that Carter had decided to cancel the radiation weapon because its deployment would run counter to his goal of nuclear disarmament. According to the story, the decision overrode the advice of Carter's top foreign and defense policy advisers, but was backed by White House political operatives and U.S. Ambassador Andrew Young.

Defense hard-liners reacted swiftly. Many of them linked it to other allegedly unilateral arms decisions by Carter: cancellation of the B-1 bomber, slowing the development of a new intercontinental missile (called M-X) and blocking Navy plans for a new aircraft carrier.

Senate Armed Services Committee member Sam Nunn, D-Ga., who has acquired considerable influence as a NATO expert, warned that cancellation would "place in the minds of the Soviets the image of a timid and hesitant America which lacks the courage to confront the difficult defense choices ahead."

The chairman and several senior members of the House Armed Services Committee wrote Carter a letter protesting the reported decision and urging reconsideration. Bob Carr, D—Mich.,who had fought House moves to kill the radiation weapon in 1977, wrote separately to Carter urging him to proceed with the weapon.

Republican Attack

Republicans mounted a concerted attack, beginning with Senate Minority Leader Howard H. Baker Jr., R-Tenn. He told reporters April 4 that a cancellation would be "another in a long line of national defense mistakes," by Carter. "First we gave away the B-1 bomber and now we're going to give away the neutron bomb."

Despite White House insistence that no decision in fact had yet been made, the GOP continued its criticism. Former President Ford, former Secretary of State Henry A. Kissinger, and two of the party's 1980 presidential hopefuls, Sens. Baker and Robert Dole, R-Kan., denounced the reported cancellation at a series of fund-raising dinners April 6.

Also on April 6, Senate Majority Leader Robert C. Byrd, D-W.Va., wrote Carter urging that production proceed in the absence of any Soviet arms restraint in Europe. And he warned the president: "If the United States decides not to proceed with the neutron weapons, and does so without any parallel reduction in Soviet strength, the chances of any SALT agreement being ratified by the Senate are seriously jeopardized."

Rep. Ted Weiss, D-N.Y., and 60 other House members who voted in 1977 to kill the radiation weapon, wrote Carter April 4 to express their support for the cancellation. But more than a quarter of the House had joined Weiss in that 1977 effort.

And in the impending congressional battles over defense-related issues — the defense budget, the second Panama Canal treaty and a new SALT agreement — Carter's problem is to win over support of Republicans and conservatives in his own party.

Carter Decision

Throughout the controversy, the White House insisted that the Times story had been wrong — that no final decision had yet been made. On April 7 Carter announced the decision to delay production, but with an implicit threat to go ahead with it if Moscow showed no matching restraint.

Majority Leader Byrd's immediate reaction was cautious support of the president: "I feel the president is on solid ground if he hopes to use this as an option in disarmament talks and if he can secure similar concessions from the Soviet Union that are verifiable."

On April 8 at his weekly news conference, Byrd blamed the flap on the "faintheartedness" of NATO's European members. "We need a show of interest on their part to back up the president," he said.

But the hard-liners apparently were not mollified by Carter's announcement. "I believe it's a bad mistake that will hurt the NATO alliance, that will interrupt modernization of our tactical nuclear weapons in Europe and, overall, will be harmful to our national security," said Nunn.

Nunn added that Carter's threat to produce the weapon eventually would have no effect on the Russians: "I cannot envision the Soviets being willing to bargain a weapon that they either have on the line or in production for a weapon that the NATO alliance has been too timid and indecisive to produce."

From the other side of the issue, Rep. John Conyers, Jr., D-Mich., a signer of the Weiss letter, also professed disappointment at Carter's move, which he called a "mid-type compromise." He said he would be satisfied only if the weapon was killed outright. "When is enough going to be enough?" he asked. ∎

Health/Education/Welfare

A mood of budgetary austerity dominated consideration of health, education and welfare programs in 1978, both inside and outside of Congress.

The tax-cutting, anti-spending desires of the voters, symbolized by California's Proposition 13, had a great effect on social programs, which are often associated in the public mind with the worst of government waste and inefficiency.

The November election defeats of several liberal Democratic senators and the election of a Congress seen as somewhat to the right of the 95th foretold an even more conservative outlook on social spending in the future.

Rapid inflation added to the problems of the social service system, putting new strains on the local and private financing of health, education and welfare efforts, while discouraging increased federal assistance.

Carter administration hopes for major changes in health insurance and welfare systems were frustrated by the new conservative spirit. Congress was clearly reluctant to approve new programs with the potential to add billions of dollars to federal spending.

Social programs were also being curtailed on the local level. School operations in California and Ohio were cut back following voter rejection of taxes. And some states appeared to be moving toward "deliberalization" of welfare eligibility and benefits.

Health

The cost question clearly dominated debate on health programs. U.S. medical costs were growing about twice as fast as the overall rate of inflation, and spending for health services in 1978 averaged out to more than $800 per man, woman and child. In six years the nation's aggregate medical bill had nearly doubled, in 15 years it had quadrupled, and since 1950 it had increased more than eleven-fold, according to the Congressional Research Service.

The economics of national health insurance, pledged by President Carter in his 1976 campaign, caused a deep rift between Carter and Sen. Edward M. Kennedy, D-Mass. Carter favored a step-by-step approach, with benefits or coverage of groups phased in only if the economy permitted. Kennedy blasted this scheme, and launched extensive hearings on a labor-drafted health plan. He argued that the only way to eliminate the costly inequities and duplications of the existing "non-system" was to create at one time — and soon — an all-inclusive federal health system.

Congress' Mixed Record. Congress had a mixed record on saving health dollars in 1978. On the one hand, the Proposition 13 vote and general uneasiness about inflation prompted some cost-cutting votes on popular health programs. But when the proposed savings appeared to be at the expense of the powerful health care industry, thrift went out the window.

About 85 percent of federal health programs were up for renewal in 1978, and long-time observers were surprised at Congress' repeated pruning of authorizations well below levels recommended by health subcommittees. Often the cuts were recommended by the subcommittee chairmen after unusual floor defeats on health bills, to forestall further challenges.

While economizing on existing health programs, however, Congress balked at regulating hospital income, the one step the Carter administration said would significantly slow the ominous acceleration of health care spending.

One of the most significant factors in 1978 health policy debates appeared to be members' heightened sensitivity to the highly emotional issue of access to health care — much of it due to a 1977 fracas over proposed federal health planning guidelines intended to eliminate underused hospital beds and facilities. The guidelines had set off an avalanche of protests, mostly from rural and small-town constituents who feared they would force shutdowns of health resources in areas that already suffered from medical service shortages. Congress called on the Department of Health, Education and Welfare (HEW) to accommodate rural needs, and the 1978 final version included exemptions for small hospitals and clarified that the guidelines were advisory, not mandatory.

The 1977 experience brought the access issue strongly, and unpleasantly, to the attention of members, including many who usually paid little attention to health matters. The reported similarity of many of the protest letters suggested to some that the hospital industry had orchestrated the outcry. If so, it got good mileage out of its effort, for not only were the guidelines softened but the "rationing of health care" argument shaped many members' objections to the cost containment bill as well as a reauthorization of the planning system itself.

Other Cost-Control Developments. As Congress struggled with health legislation, the Carter administration moved ahead on several other fronts to deal with health cost problems. Anti-trust lawyers at the Federal Trade Commission (FTC) were scrutinizing the health care industry for evidence of anti-competitive patterns, such as restrictions on advertising by physicians, fee-setting and accreditation, and constraints on consumer information and state health regulation. In November, an FTC administrative law judge found that American Medical Association bans on physician advertising restricted competitive pricing for services, causing "substantial injury to the public." Opponents of the FTC anti-trust activities warned against such blunt interventions in medical economics.

On the theory that preventing illness was less expensive than treating it, a special HEW task force began surveying existing programs to prevent disease and promote health, and developing new initiatives. Only about 4 percent of federal health dollars were being spent on such activities. Creation of the task force came just as Congress was writing into several health bills modest new disease-prevention and health promotion programs. A third development was creation of a new disease-prevention and environmental health coalition that hoped to marshal efforts and resources of more than 100 lobby groups against business opposition to environmental and occupational health regulation.

Abortion Issue. The growing militance of the anti-abortion movement was apparent across the country. Members of Congress who opposed the use of any federal funds for abortion succeeded in attaching anti-abortion amendments to more bills than ever before. Anti-abortion forces played key roles in some 1978 congressional races, and vowed to continue their fight against those on their "hit list" for 1980. And at the urging of "pro-life" lobbyists, the legislatures of 13 states had petitioned Congress to call a constitutional convention to ban abortion in the United States; 34 were needed to require the convention call.

Education

Education was also a target of the taxpayers' revolt. At a time when total education spending represented almost 8 percent of the gross national product, a larger share than that consumed by defense, voters were becoming increasingly reluctant to approve new local taxes to pay for schools. In Ohio, for example, almost 60 percent of school bond issues were rejected by voters in June elections. In California, school officials announced service cutbacks and looked to more state aid to make up for shortages caused by Proposition 13's limit on local property taxes.

The schools' financial problems were compounded by militant demands by teachers for higher pay. The National Education Association counted more than 75 teachers' strikes in September, double the number in 1977.

Public concern over education continued to focus on the issue of discipline in the schools. According to the National Center for Education Statistics, more than twice as many persons polled cited discipline problems as the major problem facing education, as pointed to the next most frequently mentioned subject, school integration.

Another problem that attracted new efforts by state governments was the growing evidence that many students were graduating from the public education system without having acquired the basic skills needed to function adequately in society. The National Assessment of Education Progress estimated that 13 percent of 17-year-old high school students were functionally illiterate.

In response to this, 36 states had instituted some sort of minimal competency testing since 1975. But educators strongly resisted suggestions from some members of Congress that national competency standards be instituted.

In his Feb. 28 education message to Congress, President Carter called for a large increase in education funding to cope with these and other problems. Overall, he called for $12.9 billion for the education division of HEW, a 24 percent increase over fiscal 1978 and a total increase of 46 percent and $4 billion in the last two fiscal years. For elementary and secondary education, he proposed a 15 percent jump, for a total of $6.9 billion — the largest increase since enactment of the Elementary and Secondary Education Act (ESEA) of 1965. He also proposed new programs to improve basic skills and educational quality.

Desegregation. Another key educational issue, the use of affirmative action programs to correct past discrimination against minorities, was the topic of a historic Supreme Court decision in 1978 *(Regents of the University of California v. Bakke).*

Supporters of affirmative action reacted with cautious optimism to the court's finding that such programs were constitutional, arguing that the decision vindicated the consideration of race in university admissions. But opponents of the use of quotas in admissions also found much to be pleased by in the decision.

The use of busing to eliminate racial segregation in public schools continued in 1978 without much of the intense strife that surrounded it in the early 1970s. But polls showed that a large majority of Americans opposed the tactic. In Los Angeles, a busing plan went into effect without violence but with a boycott by thousands of white students, fueling charges by busing opponents that such plans added to "white flight" from big city schools.

Private Schools. The 1978 congressional debate over tuition tax credits for private elementary and secondary schools followed a decade-long decline in enrollments among the largest private education sector, parochial schools run by the Roman Catholic church. But there were some indications that the trend was slowing or reversing. Catholic educators said the increase in big-city parochial school enrollments was due to the desire of many parents to take their children out of the chaotic conditions prevailing in some public schools.

At the end of 1978, private school forces were mobilizing to fight a tentative decision by the Internal Revenue Service to review the tax-exempt status of private schools with low minority enrollments that had been formed at the time local public schools were being desegregated. The regulation was intended to enforce prohibitions against tax exemptions for segregated schools, but was strongly opposed by conservatives who claimed the ruling would declare schools guilty of segregation unless they could prove themselves innocent.

Welfare

The Carter administration began 1978 with high hopes of succeeding with a presidential campaign promise to overhaul the nation's welfare system. But within months it reluctantly had placed its comprehensive welfare reform measure on the back burner, where it remained for the rest of the year.

After the administration gave up its effort, several members of Congress offered less sweeping "reform" plans. Although the proposals generated some committee hearings, none made it to the floor of either the House or Senate. At the end of the year, officials in the White House and HEW and social welfare activists were debating whether to offer another, scaled-down welfare reform plan in 1979.

While voices from all sides of the political spectrum agreed that there were serious problems with the existing system, there was little consensus on the details of welfare reform, and this stymied efforts by both Democrats and Republicans to achieve legislative action. Some observers also suggested that the liberal coalition that had regularly lined up broad support for social welfare programs in the mid-1960s had lost considerable clout on Capitol Hill and was unable to muster the political leverage necessary to generate majority votes on behalf of key issues. ∎

Transportation/Commerce/Consumers

The Carter administration made some progress in 1978 toward its goal of developing a unified national transportation policy.

However, it found greater success in pushing legislation to let the transportation industries themselves work out their own policies.

But the administration's programs suffered at times from lackadaisical support from its own Transportation Department. Despite Transportation Secretary Brock Adams' congressional background and experience, he was unable to muster sufficient support for a number of administration initiatives and unwilling to go all out for others. And resistance from Congress and transportation interest groups blocked some major Carter goals.

Amidst persistent rumors that he was out of step with the president's program and out of touch with the president himself, Adams was forced to deny in July that he intended to resign from the Cabinet. By the end of the session, however, Adams enjoyed greater success in pushing the Carter proposals.

Deregulation Progress

The administration's most significant achievement was to convince Congress to begin to take the federal government out of the transportation regulation business.

It did this by seeking legislation phasing out federal controls on the commercial passenger airline industry. The airline deregulation legislation, a top Carter priority, was not cleared until the last day of the session.

However, the lengthy and thorough consideration it received in Congress served to allay the fears of its opponents and provided a forum for deregulation advocates to espouse their views. Its approval — and the resultant drop in air fares — was expected to pave the way for other transportation deregulation measures in the next Congress.

Another important legislative accomplishment was enactment of a waterway users fee bill. The payment of fees by users of the nation's inland waterways had been sought unsuccessfully by every administration since Franklin Delano Roosevelt's.

The other major transportation initiative mounted by the administration met with less success. A proposal to restructure the nation's highway and mass transit aid programs fizzled when Congress decided to focus on funding levels rather than on substantive changes.

The Carter administration played mostly a passive role in other transportation areas, seeking either to maintain the status quo or to let Congress set policy with little help from the Executive Branch.

In railroads and trucking, both Congress and the administration put off major policy decisions until 1979 or later. In shipping, Carter opposed most legislative initiatives originating in Congress while waiting for an administration task force to complete a study of the issues and to make recommendations. The task force failed to issue its recommendations before Congress adjourned.

Consumer groups found that heavy Democratic majorities in both houses did little to help along legislation that had enjoyed strong Democratic support in previous Congresses. Instead, moderate Democrats joined with conservative Democrats and Republicans to defeat or delay practically all newly proposed federal consumer programs. One of the few exceptions was passage of legislation creating a federally backed consumer cooperative bank.

After the defeat of a bill to create an agency for consumer affairs — Carter's top consumer priority — the president expanded the powers of his own White House consumer office. But that office was unable to accomplish what advocates of an independent agency had hoped for: a strong, politically unfettered voice for the consumer within the federal government.

Airline Deregulation

Carter's aides had predicted in 1977 that the new president could score an early and easy victory in Congress by supporting airline deregulation legislation because it already had been the subject of extensive congressional hearings during the previous Congress.

Though the victory was to elude him until the last day of the 95th Congress, Carter eventually scored political points through his decision to actively support the legislation.

Even before the deregulation bill was signed, a pioneering Civil Aeronautics Board had demonstrated the legislation's potential by introducing, on a limited basis, a new competitive environment in the commercial airline passenger industry. The board's experiment paved the way for enactment of the legislation by bringing about dramatic reductions in some air fares and increases in service on many routes. Airline company profits soared as ridership skyrocketed.

The success airline deregulation enjoyed was expected to facilitate similar Carter administration efforts involving the trucking and railroad industries.

Despite the airline deregulation measure's success, however, transportation industry deregulation remained a controversial issue in some quarters. Though the airline bill passed both houses by wide margins, for example, it encountered strong resistance in the Senate Commerce and House Public Works Committees. Those same committees were expected to play key roles in the development of trucking and railroad deregulation legislation, as well.

By year's end, a jurisdictional dispute already was brewing between the Senate Antitrust Subcommittee, chaired by Edward M. Kennedy, D-Mass. — a strong supporter of trucking deregulation — and the Senate Commerce Committee, chaired by Howard W. Cannon, D-Nev.

Waterway User Fees

With an assist from a bill dealing with bingo games, and under pressure from the Carter administration, Congress for the first time imposed user fees on the inland waterway barge industry. Legislation imposing the fees had been sought by federal transportation planners for 38 years, but the Carter administration's success in 1978 was due as much to the individual efforts of two key senators as to its own actions.

The Carter administration had asked Congress to require the barge industry to pay a portion of the government's cost of constructing and operating the nation's inland waterway system. But it was the strategy of Sen. Pete V. Domenici, R-N.M., that succeeded in making the fee legislation palatable to the barge industry.

By combining the unpopular fee requirement with approval of a new lock and dam on the Mississippi River at Alton, Ill. — a public works project popular with the barge industry — Domenici managed to steer the fees requirement through both the House and Senate.

That bill stalled, however, when Domenici's colleagues combined it with authorizations for additional water projects totaling several billion dollars, making the combined bill a prime veto candidate.

In a last-ditch effort to get a compromise through Congress, Sen. Russell B. Long, D-La., tacked a new version of the fee and lock and dam combination onto a bill clarifying the tax status of winnings from bingo games sponsored by tax-exempt and political organizations. Using his considerable powers of persuasion, Long pushed the compromise through both houses and on to the White House in only four days.

Highways and Mass Transit

President Carter proposed in January 1978 a modest revamping of the federal government's massive surface transportation aid programs. He also proposed funding levels only slightly above those approved for earlier years.

State and local governments, along with many members of Congress and representatives of transportation interest groups, objected to Carter's funding recommendations. Arguing that more money was needed to meet the nation's highway and mass transit needs, they convinced members of the House Public Works Committee to recommend greatly increased transportation spending.

The ensuing battle between the House and the administration over spending served to obscure the debate over the structural changes the administration had proposed. Though by the session's end Carter had managed to keep transportation spending close to what he considered an acceptable range, many of the structural changes he advocated ended up being lost in the debate over funding.

Though the legislation failed to integrate the highway and mass transit programs, as the administration had proposed, the Transportation Department at year's end proposed combining the Federal Highway and Urban Mass Transportation Administrations into a single Surface Transportation Administration. The merger was expected to substitute a mass transit-highway "partnership" for the competition that prevailed between the two modes of transportation under the existing structure.

Railroads

The nation's railroads remained in poor financial straits in 1978 — a condition that had persisted for over a decade — but the federal government did little to resolve the ailing industry's problems. Instead, both Congress and the administration continued existing programs and put off consideration of railroad policy changes until the next Congress.

Legislation was passed establishing a mechanism for the federal government to weed out unprofitable Amtrak railroad passenger routes in 1979, but leaving the actual choices of what routes to cut to the Transportation Department. The mechanism permitted Congress to veto the department's actions if it disagreed, however.

Congress voted to give the Consolidated Rail Corp. (ConRail) an additional infusion of federal funds to keep it afloat until 1979, when a comprehensive review of the federally subsidized railroad freight company was planned. At year's end, ConRail told Congress it would take substantial deregulation in addition to subsidies to keep it alive.

Commerce and Consumers

Congress' actions in the consumer area in 1978 were mostly negative, from the consumer movement's viewpoint. But Congress did approve legislation creating a national consumer cooperative bank that was expected to provide a boost for the nation's consumer cooperatives. The bank was to be backed by the federal government and was intended to provide loans and technical assistance to consumer cooperatives that had experienced difficulties in obtaining financing.

The Consumer Product Safety Commission, threatened early in the year with extinction by a White House task force, was instead renewed for a three-year period.

For most other consumer bills, however, there were only obituaries. The consumer protection agency, federal no-fault automobile insurance standards, subsidies for public interest group participation in federal agency proceedings, procedural changes for the Federal Trade Commission and legislation to reorganize the U.S. Postal Service all fell victim to a growing conservative trend in Congress during 1978.

In communications, Congress cleared legislation reorganizing the nation's public broadcasting system, accepting many recommendations advanced by the Carter administration. Carter paid little attention to other communications matters, however. Despite the policy vacuum, a House Commerce subcommittee began laying groundwork for a substantial revision of the nation's communications laws in 1979.

At year's end, key Senate Commerce Committee members indicated they agreed a revision was in order. ∎

Carter Plans Deregulation Drive in 1979

Having accomplished many of its goals in relaxing federal regulation of the airlines, the Carter administration hoped in 1979 to offer Congress similar plans to deregulate the railroad and trucking industries.

Of the two, the outlook was much more favorable for a railroad plan than for a trucking deregulation proposal, which faced resistance from employers and from the powerful Teamsters Union. The plans were being prepared in late 1978 by the Transportation Department, with help from the White House and other executive branch agencies.

The railroad industry wants to be deregulated. It claims that its worsening financial condition over the past decade stems from excessive government restrictions on the way it must operate. Unless the federal government eases its regulatory grip, the railroads argue, the amount of money the government will have to pay out in subsidies can be expected to continue to grow in coming years.

The trucking industry, on the other hand, is fighting deregulation. Because federal regulation of trucking limits new entry and keeps rates high, the existing firms are content with the status quo.

The truckers argue that efforts to make their industry more competitive will result in poorer service and harm the industry's economic stability. Further, the truckers claim, the railroads could be harmed by trucking deregulation, as

---

"There is lots of talk and worry and concern. If the administration decides to hold off on a bill until after the Teamsters' wage settlement, they'll have trouble getting it through. If we don't start pushing for this thing in the State of the Union message, it will probably be put over for whoever is president in 1981."

—White House aide

---

well. Railroads and trucks compete for the same freight in many instances. Lower prices for the transportation of goods by truck could force the railroads to cut into their already low earnings in order to remain competitive.

Airline Deregulation Success

The Carter administration is keen on deregulation at this time because of its recent success with airline deregulation legislation. After enactment of that bill, ticket prices fell as the airline companies began competing with each other for new business.

And, instead of disaster — as some airlines had predicted — the industry prospered as both ridership and profits increased.

Buoyed by the results of the airline bill, the administration decided to look at other parts of the economy where a lessening of federal regulation might promote better service to consumers at lower cost.

"Of all our weapons against inflation," Carter said Oct. 24, "competition is the most powerful. Without real competition, prices and wages go up, even when demand is going down."

Despite the airline bill's success, however, Carter's deregulatory drive remains controversial. Letting railroads set prices on their own, for example, while favored by the industry and by Carter policy-makers, could result in short-term increases in the cost of shipping some goods by rail, according to administration policy-makers.

And making it easier for the railroads to drop money-losing routes is likely to prove unpopular with members of Congress from areas that might lose rail service.

Trucking Controversies

In the same way, trucking deregulation also could prove a thorn in Carter's side. Because transportation costs represent only a small part of a piece of merchandise's final selling price, even a major decrease in transportation costs might result in only a small drop in the cost of goods to consumers.

Without the promise of big benefits to consumers, and, at the same time, under pressure by trucking interests not to deregulate, Congress may not see the urgency of adopting Carter's deregulation program.

Another potential stumbling block for trucking legislation is the powerful International Brotherhood of Teamsters, the nation's largest labor union. The Teamsters strongly oppose deregulation because they fear it may result in job losses for their members.

In a key test of his anti-inflation program, President Carter has asked the Teamsters to observe the administration's voluntary guidelines on wage increases.

Carter's inflation fighters fear that if they push a trucking deregulation bill too forcefully, an angered Teamsters Union — which began contract talks in mid-December — will retaliate by ignoring the administration's wage guidelines.

Carter's inflation chief, Alfred E. Kahn, has warned the Teamsters that for them to ignore the guidelines could strengthen Carter's hand in his deregulation drive.

On the other hand, there have been persistent rumors that the administration has not ruled out dropping the deregulation effort in return for a promise from the Teamsters that they will obey the guidelines. The rumors have come from the trucking industry as well as from administration sources.

Eizenstat's Decision

Before the latest options paper reaches the president, it will have to be cleared by White House domestic policy chief Stuart E. Eizenstat. Some administration officials note that Eizenstat still could choose to delay submission of a trucking bill to Congress, or to not submit legislation at all, in order to curry favor with the Teamsters.

"There is lots of talk and worry and concern," commented one Carter aide, who asked not to be named. "If the administration decides to hold off on a bill until after the Teamsters' wage settlement, they'll have trouble getting it through. If we don't start pushing for this thing in the State of the Union message next January, it will probably be put over for whoever is president in 1981."

Eizenstat was not available for comment on the rumors, but other White House aides flatly denied them.

"We intend to pursue trucking reform aggressively," White House policy aide Bill Johnston told *Congressional Quarterly*. "We will be sending up a bill and it will be a strong bill."

The latest trucking effort marks the third time the administration has set about preparing a "decision memo" for the president on trucking.

White House aides first studied trucking deregulation in March 1977. An options paper was drafted for Carter's consideration in January 1978. But the administration decided to put all of its deregulation muscle behind the airline bill.

In July 1978, a second memo was prepared for Carter, but that one also was never given to the president. The aides said at the time they still feared that another deregulation bill would jeopardize passage of the first. The airline deregulation bill finally was approved by Congress on Oct. 15.

ICC Initiatives

Since President Carter first announced in March 1977 that his administration would seek legislation to deregulate the trucking industry, the Interstate Commerce Commission (ICC) has acted in a number of ways to head off the need for new legislation by deregulating the industry administratively.

The ICC's actions, however, apparently have not altered the administration's conviction that legislation was needed to achieve deregulation of the trucking industry.

At a Nov. 9 press conference, Transportation Secretary Brock Adams characterized the ICC's deregulatory efforts as "good but not enough." Deregulation brought about administratively, Adams said in a brief interview, was fraught with delay, legal challenges and uncertainty. "The legislative route is preferable," he commented.

Conflicting Criticisms

At the same time as the administration was criticizing the commission for moving too slowly on trucking deregulation, the industry was criticizing the commission for moving too fast. One newly formed anti-deregulation group (called ACT — for "Assure Competitive Transportation") went so far as to circulate a petition calling for ICC Chairman A. Daniel O'Neal's resignation.

Particularly galling to the truckers was a Nov. 27 decision rejecting an application for a general rate increase proposed by the Southern Motor Carriers Rate Conference.

The conference had argued that the rate increase was necessary to offset higher labor costs based on its latest

---

Deregulation Dropouts

While many prominent business groups continue to press for an end to excessive government regulation of business, there continue to be exceptions.

Many airline companies strongly opposed airline deregulation legislation in the 95th Congress. Many trucking companies were lining up to oppose trucking deregulation legislation in 1979.

While the major airlines in 1978 fought among themselves, seeking — in vain — a unified industry position, Congress went ahead and approved legislation ending practically all federal regulation of their industry by 1982. While many airline companies welcomed the new competitive industry environment, others said they dreaded it.

One of the latter was Delta Air Lines, the fifth largest airline in the nation in terms of annual passenger revenues. With an eye to warning another industry to avoid a similar fate, a top Delta official showed up at the annual meeting of the American Trucking Associations (ATA).

"We now face very questionable and certainly distasteful legislation because we failed to join hands and present a solid front," Delta Air Lines Vice Chairman Richard S. Maurer warned the truckers at an ATA meeting in New York Nov. 1. "I would urge you as strongly as I can, at least within the confines of ATA, to agree on common principles with respect to the regulatory reform issue within your own industry."

"We were splintered," Maurer said. "Our trade association was absolutely unable to be effective on Capitol Hill. . . . And as a result, we went down to a resounding legislative defeat."

---

contract with the Teamsters. The ICC countered that industry profits already were too high. "We believe that the total effect of current regulation on motor common carriers of general freight has been to insulate them from price competition to a degree not found in industry generally," the ICC ruled.

Following the action, trucking company stocks tumbled as industry representatives warned that the ICC had endangered the industry's financial stability. American Trucking Associations President Bennett C. Whitlock Jr. said the commission had "performed open-heart surgery — blindfolded" and that its ruling "severely threatens the financial stability of numerous carriers and the very survival of others." Representatives of a number of companies urged members of Congress to push in the next session for curbs on the ICC's authority to move administratively to deregulate the industry.

Railroads: 'ICC Too Slow'

While the trucking industry criticized the ICC for moving too fast toward deregulation, the railroad industry was concerned that the ICC was moving too slowly.

In 1976 Congress had sought to ease the railroads' ability to raise and lower their fares and to drop service on unprofitable routes by passing the Railroad Revitalization and Regulatory Act (PL 94-210).

The measure had been proposed by the Ford administration a year earlier.

Trying to Deregulate the Regulated — Ford to Carter

In the summer of 1975 President Gerald R. Ford unveiled a plan to wage a major war against excessive government regulation.

"In many industries — transportation, energy, communications — federal regulatory commissions have actually thwarted competition," he said at the time. "The record is clear. They have burdened the consumer with the cost of misdirected regulation.... Government regulation is not an effective substitute for vigorous American competition."

Within months, however, Ford was forced to confront an uncomfortable truth: Those groups most opposed to his regulatory reform plan turned out to be the regulated industries themselves.

Though business groups publicly praised the president for his initiative, they privately geared up to fight the deregulation moves. The nation's banks fought proposed legislation to enable Savings and Loan Associations to compete with them. Broadcasters told top Ford advisers they would work to oppose his re-election, and proposed broadcast reform legislation was relegated to the status of a study.

Legislation to reform the trucking industry is stalled in the Office of Management and Budget (OMB), bitterly opposed by the American Trucking Associations and the Teamsters Union. But airline deregulation legislation — first proposed by Ford in October 1975 — finally won congressional approval in 1978.

Of the other Ford regulatory reform efforts, including those taken over by Congress and the Carter administration, the sole major successes so far have been the Railroad Revitalization and Regulatory Reform Act of 1976 (PL 94-210) — which permitted railroads and the Interstate Commerce Commission a measure of regulatory flexibility — and repeal of state Fair Trade laws (PL 94-145) in 1975 — which barred manufacturers and distributors from fixing retail prices for their goods.

The basis for business' opposition to reform is straightforward. Government regulators and the industries they regulate over the years have woven close relationships by which the industry agrees to follow certain rules and regulations in return for a reprieve from the rigors of the free marketplace.

In many cases, federal regulation has relieved private firms of worry over new market entry, price competition, safety standards, technological obsolescence and inefficient management.

Airline Industry

The airline industry is a pertinent example. When the House Aviation Subcommittee voted March 22 to reject a strong airline deregulation bill, it did so in accordance with the wishes of most of the major airlines, which had opposed the legislation since its inception.

Even though an airline deregulation bill finally was passed, same airlines continued to predict dire results.

"I think what has happened," commented James P. Carty, director of regulatory reform and consumer affairs for the National Association of Manufacturers — which supported airline deregulation — "is that people have paid lip service to reform, but when it comes down to moving on a proposal, economic self-interest comes to the fore."

Saving the Status Quo

"There's a vested interest in keeping things the way they are," remarked a former congressional aide active in regulatory reform who has since gone on to work at the White House. "In 1975 everyone blamed consumers for business regulation, but in fact business has been instrumental in creating and preserving regulation."

"Actually, we're a lot farther along than we might have been had Jerry Ford stayed in office," stated James C. Miller, a former member of Ford's Domestic Council and currently director of the American Enterprise Institute's Center for the Study of Government Regulation. "I think it would have been a lot slower and harder battle with a Republican President and a Democratic Congress...."

"The main problem with regulatory reform," Miller went on, "is that the ultimate beneficiaries of reform are large in number, they each have a relatively small stake in it, and they aren't organized very well. By contrast, those that benefit from regulation know their stake in it ... and they're well organized and very efficient in presenting their views."

Carter Initiatives

Carter appointed a number of strong advocates of reform to many of the regulatory agencies themselves: Alfred Kahn as chairman of the Civil Aeronautics Board, Michael Pertschuk as chairman of the Federal Trade Commission and Charles Ferris as chairman of the Federal Communications Commission. After his success with airline deregulation, Carter tapped Kahn to be his chief inflation fighter.

Trucking deregulation legislation still is a possibility, according to Stanley E. Morris, OMB deputy associate director for regulatory policy. "We are in the process of getting a memo to the president." And the White House was watching communications legislation being developed by the House Commerce Subcommittee on Communications.

Legislation to strengthen federal conflict of interest rules, require more detailed financial disclosure of federal officials and prevent former government officials from working to affect matters in which they were involved while in government service was signed into law by Carter in 1978.

And Carter early in the year released an executive order requiring all Executive Branch federal agencies to improve the quality of their regulation. The order would require, for example, that regulations be written in "plain English" and that officials responsible for the development of regulations personally approve them.

However, the actual implementation of the so-called "Four-R Act" was left to the ICC. Instead of acting quickly to ease its grip on the railroads, the commission interpreted the legislation conservatively and moved slowly.

According to an October 1978 Transportation Department report, "A Prospectus for Change in the Freight Railroad Industry," the effect of the new law "was minimized by the ICC." While the Four-R Act encouraged a reduction in government control, the Transportation Department concluded, "the ICC still constrains the railroads' freedom of action."

The railroad industry was even more critical of the ICC than the government. In July 1978 congressional testimony, Association of American Railroads (AAR) President William H. Dempsey accused the ICC of "a march toward more regulation" rather than deregulation. Unless the ICC eased its regulatory grip on the railroads, Dempsey said, the industry would end up "dead in the water."

"Every time Dan O'Neal opens his mouth," commented AAR Senior Vice President Carl V. Lyon in an interview, "I think it makes both the truckers and the railroads realize he doesn't have the best interests of the transportation industry in mind. He's much more interested in keeping the shippers happy. I don't think he cares whether there's a healthy railroad industry. The ICC is supposed to serve the public. The shipper is not the public."

The attacks on the ICC from both government and industry have stung O'Neal. Though O'Neal declined to be interviewed by Congressional Quarterly, he said in a statement: "The ICC is an independent regulatory agency. We will continue with what we feel is a proper course of deregulation and adjustment of the current machinery. As you know, we have a number of programs underway affecting entry and revenues. We expect to proceed with the orderly development of these and other initiatives."

Railroads' Poor Health

The Carter administration's advocacy of railroad deregulation legislation stems from the poor health of the industry, according to Ronald H. Reimann, deputy associate administrator of the Federal Railroad Administration (FRA).

Industry earnings have been on a decline for the past decade. In 1978 the industry was further troubled by freight car shortages during the grain harvest, a series of major railroad bankruptcies and a warning of impending financial disaster from the mammoth government-subsidized Consolidated Rail Corp. (ConRail).

As of the end of November 1978, the federal government had doled out $169.5 million in subsidies to the railroads since the subsidy programs began in April 1976, according to FRA figures. And all signs pointed to the need for greater and greater government subsidies in the future unless federal policies were changed, Reimann said.

According to the Transportation Department's October 1978 report on the rail industry's future, the railroads were expected to require from $13 billion to $16 billion in subsidies in order to maintain their existing level of service over the next 10 years, unless the industry's problems were solved.

As an alternative to subsidies, administration policy-makers proposed letting the railroads operate just like other businesses. If marketplace competition were substituted for federal regulation, the policy-makers reasoned, the railroads would drop unprofitable routes and raise some prices. But the remaining system would be healthier and more efficient.

"We're not saying that the railroads' problem is just regulatory," Reimann said, "but changing the regulation will make a significant difference."

Railroad Bill Provisions

Though the Transportation Department had not yet completed drafting its railroad deregulation bill, Reimann said that "we are looking, essentially, at a major restructuring of the regulatory environment of the railroad industry, one that would recognize the pervasiveness of competition in the transportation industry, and one which recognizes the need of the railroads to compete as real free enterprise companies."

Though no final decisions had been made, the legislation was expected to have two main components. To avoid disruptions, the legislation probably would be phased in over a number of years.

One component would give railroads considerable freedom to set their own rates, according to the individual market and commodity to be transported. "We want to give the railroads the opportunity to set prices at what the service is costing them," Reimann explained.

Even though prices might initially increase in some markets for some goods, "our hope is that, as the railroads become accustomed to the pricing and service competition, they're going to introduce efficiencies that would have the effect of reducing costs."

The other major deregulation component would broaden a railroad's ability to abandon unprofitable services or routes. Abandonments are permitted under existing law, but only after being approved by the ICC. Proposed abandonments that are opposed by a shipper or a state or local government currently require an ICC proceeding averaging 16 to 18 months, a commission spokesman said.

The legislation also was expected to deal with the financial problems of ConRail and may provide federal aid for retraining railroad employees facing job losses as a result of deregulation. The airline deregulation legislation was forcefully opposed by airline labor during the last Congress until an employee protection plan was included in the bill. ∎

Law Enforcement/Judiciary

For the first time since it was created in 1870, Justice Department officials went before congressional authorizing committees in 1978 to justify the agency's programs and expenditures.

The hearing record, including testimony of Attorney General Griffin B. Bell, detailed an ambitious set of legislative goals for the second session of the 95th Congress in the areas of law enforcement and the administration of justice.

A comparison of the department's goals and achievements in 1973 suggests that it was better at identifying problems than either it or Congress was in getting bills approved to solve them. Of 16 top legislative priorities outlined by the department in testimony given in March 1978 before the House Judiciary Committee, only five were enacted by Congress.

Nevertheless, several major pieces of legislation likely to have a long-lasting impact were approved. These included legislation increasing the size of the federal judiciary by more than 30 percent with the addition of 152 new district and circuit court judgeships, and a bill to control the use of wiretaps in the United States for foreign intelligence gathering purposes.

The new judges, to be appointed by President Carter, were likely to shape the character of the federal courts for several decades. The wiretap bill, on the other hand, established an important constitutional precedent in placing limits on executive branch "inherent power" in an attempt to protect the privacy of individual citizens. It was likely to have a considerable impact on legislation that was to be debated in the 96th Congress to further control intelligence agencies.

During 1978, the Congress also cleared a proposed constitutional amendment to give full voting representation in the House and Senate to residents of the District of Columbia, and extended by 39 months the deadline for ratification of the Equal Rights Amendment to the Constitution.

Left unfinished were the attorney general's top priority, recodification of the entire body of United States criminal law, as well as such other high priorities as legislation to require new registration and reporting requirements for lobbyists, a bill to provide attorneys fees to citizens who prevail in government suits brought against them, and bills dealing with class action lawsuits, antitrust improvements, and illegal aliens.

Many of the bills that failed to become law were approved by either the House or the Senate and were likely to be brought up early in the next Congress. Several of the Justice Department's top priorities — such as a bill to overturn a Supreme Court decision preventing indirect purchasers from suing price-fixers, and a bill to protect the constitutional rights of persons confined in state nursing homes and mental institutions — were killed as a result of filibuster threats in the Senate. Rules changes at the beginning of the 96th Congress were expected to diminish the possibility of the same thing happening to these bills again.

Criminal Code

The bill described by Attorney General Bell as his number one legislative priority in 1978, recodification of the entire body of U.S. criminal law, was the first major piece of legislation to clear the Senate in 1978.

The product of years of negotiations among Senate liberals and conservatives, representatives of conflicting civil liberties and national security interests, the massive bill passed the Senate by a surprisingly wide 72-15 margin. It was the first time in a decade of debate that a recodification bill had reached the floor of either house.

But the underlying assumptions of the Senate-passed bill, that liberals and conservatives had to compromise some of their most strongly held beliefs and that the measure had to be approved or rejected as a package, were resoundingly rejected when the bill was brought up in a House Judiciary subcommittee.

Subcommittee Chairman James R. Mann, D-S.C., summarized the thinking of subcommittee members when he said the criminal law "should not be subject to trade-offs and compromise in the name of reform." Many House committee members also argued that the Senate bill failed to account for the views of certain interested parties, notably defendants.

Wiretapping

Whether it would serve to protect innocent Americans from invasions of privacy by government intelligence agencies was yet to be seen. But the Foreign Intelligence Surveillance Act was clearly one of the most significant accomplishments of the 95th Congress.

A direct outgrowth of congressional hearings documenting widespread abuses by government intelligence agencies, the bill marked the first significant legislative effort to clamp down on invasions of citizens' privacy rights and violations of free speech that reached epidemic proportion in the 1960s.

Requiring a judicial warrant for most foreign intelligence agency electronic surveillance conducted in the United States, the bill was viewed as a major precedent in what promised to be a continuing debate over charters for the FBI, CIA, National Security Agency and other intelligence gathering networks. The Foreign Intelligence Surveillance Act was supported by all the federal intelligence agencies as well as the American Civil Liberties Union.

Administration of Justice

Shortly after taking office in 1977, Bell established a new Office for Improvements in the Administration of Justice which became the fount of numerous legislative proposals in the 95th Congress designed to make the federal court system operate more efficiently.

The most far-reaching achievement in the area was the judgeship bill, creating 117 new district court positions and 35 new spots on the appeals courts.

New judgeships to relieve overloaded court dockets had been called for in many judicial districts for years. But a

Major Justice Department Initiatives in the 95th Congress

Bill	Final Action
Foreign intelligence electronic surveillance controls	enacted
Creation of 152 new federal court judgeships	enacted
Special prosecutor to investigate wrongdoing in the executive branch	enacted
Pregnancy disability rights	enacted
District of Columbia voting representation (constitutional amendment)	cleared for state legislatures
Extension of ratification deadline for Equal Rights Amendment	cleared
Recodification of U.S. criminal laws	passed Senate
Expand jurisdiction of U.S. magistrates	died in House-Senate conference
Mandatory pretrial arbitration	died in committee
Diversity jurisdiction amendments	passed House*
Civil rights of institutionalized persons	passed House*
Lobbying reform	passed House
Federal tort claims amendments	died in committee
Illegal aliens	died in committee
Attorneys fees	died in committee
Class actions	died in committee
Indirect purchaser antitrust suits	died in committee

* Died as result of filibuster threat

Democratic Congress was never willing to give such an enormous patronage bonanza to a Republican president. So no bill was seriously considered until Democrats had one of their own in the White House.

An amendment to the bill, written in the House, required the president to issue standards and guidelines for merit selection of federal district judges. Carter had been sharply criticized in early 1978 when David W. Marston, a Republican U.S. attorney in Philadelphia, was replaced by a Democrat. Carter had pledged in his campaign to make all appointments of U.S. attorneys and judges on the basis of merit.

Shortly thereafter, Carter issued an executive order establishing merit selection commissions for the appeals courts. But the order did not cover district courts and House liberals and Republicans sought to force Carter into a strong position on merit selection. An executive order issued by the president in November sought to pressure senators to use merit commissions but left to senators the decision on whether the patronage system would be put to rest.

Access to Justice

Other successes in the area of court improvements were less significant than the judgeship bill. Congress gave approval to higher fees for witnesses and jurors to compensate for inflation and provided travel and living expenses that were frequently denied in the past. Congress also provided government paid interpreters to witnesses and parties to lawsuits who did not speak English or had hearing impairments.

But several major court improvement bills did not make it through in 1978. A bill to expand the jurisdiction of magistrates in civil and criminal trials died after the House attached it to a bill opposed by the American Bar Association and Association of Trial Lawyers of America. The more controversial diversity jurisdiction bills would have suspended or severely limited the right of litigants from different states to use federal rather than state courts to decide their disputes.

A bill to encourage use of district court arbitration in civil cases passed the Senate but no hearings were held in the House. The measure, which would have required use of pretrial arbitration on an experimental basis in five to eight districts was viewed as a quicker and less expensive means of resolving court disputes.

Other bills designed to increase access to federal courts, including one to overrule restrictive Supreme Court decisions on standing and another to provide attorneys fees to parties that would otherwise be unrepresented in agency rulemaking, failed to get out of committee. The attorneys fee legislation was subjected to heavy opposition from organized business lobbies.

Finally, a bill that would have given the federal government authority to sue state-run mental hospitals, prisons, and nursing homes where a "pattern or practice" of constitutional rights violations was found was killed by a Senate filibuster threat after winning House approval. ∎

Carter Gets Patronage Plum of 152 Judges

Legislation establishing 152 new federal court judgeships, the largest number ever created by a single act of Congress, cleared its final congressional hurdle Oct. 7, 1978, when the Senate approved it on a 67-15 vote.

The House had approved the compromise on the bill (HR 7843) Oct. 4 by a 292-112 vote.

The bill added 117 new district court judgeship positions and 35 new positions on the circuit courts of appeals to the existing 398 district court judgeships and 97 circuit court judgeships.

Proponents said the measure would improve access to the federal judiciary and relieve the backlog of court cases.

The bill provided President Carter with the largest block of judicial patronage in the nation's history. Some Republicans complained that passage of the measure without a merit selection process in place could lead to a wave of partisan political appointments. Although the bill required the president to establish standards and guidelines for the selection of judges on the basis of merit, the president was not required to follow these selection procedures.

The compromise was agreed on by Senate and House conferees Sept. 20, after a Senate proposal to split the southern Fifth Circuit Court of Appeals in two to create a new Eleventh Circuit was rejected. Conferees had been deadlocked over the Fifth Circuit issue for four months.

The conference report on HR 7843 was filed Sept. 28 (H Rept 95-1643).

Fifth Circuit

While conferees were deadlocked over splitting the Fifth Circuit Court of Appeals, the final compromise affected that circuit, which will have 26 judges under the bill, as well as the Ninth Circuit, which will have 23 judges.

Conferees agreed on deliberately ambiguous language designed to let Senate and House conferees interpret it as consistent with their own intentions for the Fifth Circuit.

The compromise provision allowed circuit courts having more than 15 judges to reorganize into "administrative units" for the performance of functions the bill left undefined.

The compromise allowed a large circuit court to perform its *en banc* functions with less than a full complement of judges. *En banc* hearings normally require the attendance of all judges in a circuit, as they are only held to resolve conflicting opinions within a circuit over issues of major importance.

While the bill left undefined the restraints on the administrative units, the two large circuits could create, the conference report noted that, "the Congress always has the power to make necessary changes by appropriate legislation," if those units reorganized in a manner not to the liking of the Congress.

The report also stated that with respect to the Fifth and Ninth circuits, "it would be appropriate" that the Judicial Conference submit a status report to Congress on

rules implemented in the circuit. The report would be required within one year after the last of the new judges was appointed.

While the compromise avoided directly addressing the Senate proposal for splitting the Fifth, most observers agreed that the Fifth Circuit judges could not reorganize to anywhere near the extent proposed by the Senate bill. Sen-

> *Although the bill required the president to establish standards and guidelines for the selection of judges on the basis of merit, the president was not required to follow these selection procedures.*

ate supporters of splitting the Fifth had argued that an *en banc* hearing with 26 judges would be unwieldy and that the large geographical area covered by the circuit already made it difficult for judges to hold *en banc* hearings. The House bill did not address splitting the Fifth Circuit.

New Judgeships

The conference report on HR 7843 increased the size of the federal judiciary by more than 30 percent. It provided 117 new judgeship positions on the district courts and 35 new positions on the circuit courts.

Both the House and Senate bills proposed increasing the size of the circuit courts by 35 judges, so there was no appeals court issue to be resolved in conference. They differed, however, over the number of district judgeships to be created — the Senate version containing nine positions not included in the House bill and the House six not included in the Senate.

Additional Circuit Court Judgeships

Circuit	Existing Judgeships	Added Under Conference Agreement	Total
District of Columbia	9	2	11
First	3	1	4
Second	9	2	11
Third	9	1	10
Fourth	7	3	10
Fifth	15	11	26
Sixth	9	2	11
Seventh	8	1	9
Eighth	8	1	9
Ninth	13	10	23
Tenth	7	1	8
Total	**97**	**35**	**132**

Additional District Judgeships

State or Territory	Current Number	Added by Senate Bill	Added by House Bill	Added Under Conference Agreement	State or Territory	Current Number	Added by Senate Bill	Added by House Bill	Added Under Conference Agreement
Ala.	8	3	4	4	Neb.	3	0	0	0
Alaska	2	0	0	0	Nev.	2	1	1	1
Ariz.	5	3	2	3	N.H.	1	1	1	1
Ark.	4	2	2	2	N.J.	9	1	2	2
Calif.	35	7	7	7	N.M.	3	1	1	1
Canal Zone	1	0	0	0	N.Y.	41	2	2	2
Colo.	4	2	2	2	N.C.	6	3	3	3
Conn.	4	1	1	1	N.D.	2	0	0	0
Del.	3	0	0	0	Ohio	13	2	3*	3*
D.C.	15	0	0	0	Okla.	6	2	2	2
Fla.	15	10*	8	9	Ore.	3	2	2	2
Ga.	10	6	5	6	Pa.	32	2	2	2
Guam	1	0	0	0	P.R.	3	4	3	4
Hawaii	2	0	0	0	R.I.	2	0	0	0
Idaho	2	0	0	0	S.C.	5	3	3	3
Ill.	17	3	4	4	S.D.	2	1	1	1
Ind.	7	2	1	2	Tenn.	8	1	1	1
Iowa	3	1	1	1	Texas	22	10	9	10
Kan.	4	1	1	1	Utah	2	1	1	1
Ky.	6	3*	3*	3*	Vt.	2	0	0	0
La.	14	6	5	6	Va.	8	4	4	4
Maine	1	1	1	1	V.I.	2	0	0	0
Md.	7	2	2	2	Wash.	5	2	2	2
Mass.	6	4	3	4	W.Va.	4	2*	2*	2*
Mich.	12	5	5	5	Wis.	4	1	2	2
Minn.	4	2*	2*	2*	Wyo.	1	0	1	0
Miss.	5	0	0	0					
Mo.	8	3	3	3	Total	398	113	110	117
Mont.	2	0	0	0					

Includes one temporary judgeship. The conference report provided that the first vacancy that occurred in each of these judicial districts five years or more after enactment of the bill shall not be filled.

Conferees eventually decided to pretty much follow the suggestion of Rep. Jack Brooks, D-Texas: "To save a lot of talk and discussion of who shot John it might be wise to accept all the House judges and all the Senate judges and everybody love everybody and just create judges abracadabra. . . ." The conference rejected only two of the proposed judgeships, one for Wyoming and one temporary judgeship for southern Florida.

Merit Selection

Conferees adopted a watered-down merit selection provision applicable to the new district judgeships. The conference report provided that the president promulgate and publish "standards and guidelines for the selection, on the basis of merit" of nominees for judgeships created by the bill.

But the merit selection provision was purely voluntary: "The president may waive such standards and guidelines with respect to any nomination by notifying the Sen-

ate of the reasons for such waiver." And the conference report stated that no nomination may be invalidated because the president failed to comply with the section.

The conference language differed from that proposed in the House bill — language the House had instructed its conferees to stick to on a 321-19 vote. House language, sponsored by John F. Seiberling, D-Ohio, would have required the president to set forth non-binding "procedures and guidelines" for choosing district court judges, but would have allowed the president to waive the criteria if he first notified the Senate.

Senate conferees resisted the "procedures" language in an effort to preserve so far as possible, the control they traditionally have wielded over nomination of judges. What remained to be seen was whether President Carter, in promulgating standards and guidelines, would also establish procedures that precisely defined the role of the Senate. Most observers were betting against such a course of action. ∎

Carter Order Raises Doubts Whether Judges Will Be Selected on Merit Basis

President Carter revived the debate over merit selection Nov. 8 when he issued an executive order urging senators to voluntarily forego their patronage prerogatives and establish commissions for the selection of U.S. district court judges on the basis of merit.

At a press conference called to explain the new order and recommended procedures and guidelines for their operation, Attorney General Griffin B. Bell made it clear the White House believed it could do no more than use "friendly persuasion" to get senators to establish merit selection commissions.

In an executive order released earlier in the year the president had established circuit court nominating commissions that were required to nominate appeals court judges on the basis of merit, leaving the final selection to the president rather than to senators, who have traditionally made the determinations.

But that order was based on a deal Carter made with James O. Eastland, D-Miss., chairman of the Senate Judiciary Committee. And Bell indicated no such agreement could have been reached on the district judgeships, which are considered more important to senators from a patronage point of view.

Nevertheless, Bell was confident that the new executive order would contribute to more highly qualified judges being placed on the bench. He said he expected more merit selection commissions to be created by senators than the 20 currently existing or proposed. And the Justice Department estimated that at least 62 of the 117 district judge positions created by the recently enacted Omnibus Judgeship Act (HR 7843 — PL 95-486) would be filled using names recommended by nominating commissions.

But while the administration exuded optimism over its district court selection proposal, the plan has come in for some harsh criticism and it is sure to be subjected to more as nominees begin appearing before the Senate Judiciary Committee for confirmation hearings.

In cases where senators chose not to establish commissions, Common Cause President David Cohen said, "the White House and the Justice Department have surrendered" to the patronage system. "There's an attitude in the Justice Department to do as little as possible, to change as little as possible and that has been sanctioned by the White House."

Other limitations of the purely voluntary Carter proposals were readily apparent. For example:

● While the White House proposed that commissions be composed of a balance of lawyers and non-lawyers, men and women, members of minority groups and persons of differing political affiliations, Bell said Carter would not reject recommendations from commissions that failed to conform to these and other proposed operating standards.

● Bell said the Justice Department planned to put together inventories of qualified women and minorities to be considered for judgeship vacancies. But the attorney general said the names would not be made available to commissions unless requested and that commission recommendations would not be rejected if they failed to include the names of qualified women or minorities identified by the Justice Department. When the judgeship bill passed, only 1 percent of federal judges were women and 4 percent black.

● Bell said the Justice Department would scrutinize the voluntary commissions to see if they conformed to the department's proposed operating standards. But he said the department's analyses of commission operations would not be made public, suggesting that while the White House is concerned that they operate effectively it is not so concerned it will criticize them.

● The proposed operating guidelines for merit selection commissions were not contained in the executive order. Such significant proposals as public notice of vacancies and the solicitation of names from non-lawyers as well as lawyers were not required by the executive order. Thus Carter left not only the establishment of commissions voluntary, but the way in which they operate once created. While the operation of many commissions may bear little resemblance to the White House recommendations, Bell said he expected recommendations of the nominating commissions would be accepted by the president in most cases. He said, however, that commissions would be asked to reconsider nominations if the process by which candidates were selected was not "fair."

● It was unclear if the White House would make public all of the names of nominees recommended by commissions or senators — publicity some observers say is essential to making the selection process more open and which would make it more difficult for the president to appoint someone other than the best qualified nominee.

Just what impact the president's order will have on the quality of future appointees to the federal courts remains to be seen. But the issues raised by the order are sure to come in for close scrutiny as the Senate Judiciary Committee begins confirmation hearings on 117 new federal district and 35 new circuit court judges.

Political Hot Potato

Merit selection has been a political hot potato ever since Carter pledged in his presidential campaign that all federal court judges would be appointed "strictly on the basis of merit without any consideration of political aspect or influence."

The issue was the subject of lengthy debate during House consideration of the Omnibus Judgeship Act, which gave Carter authority to appoint more federal judges than any other president in history. (The judgeship bill expanded the size of the federal judiciary by more than 30 percent from 495 judges to 647.)

While most parties to the debate agree that the most "meritorious" candidate should be appointed to fill any vacancy, they disagree over: 1) who should decide who is best qualified and, 2) the process and standards by which that final judgment is to be made.

The two sides in the congressional debate over merit selection started from differing assumptions. On the one hand there were those who argued that the politics of patronage could not or should not be taken out of the judicial appointment process, that senatorial appointments have generally been quite good, and that commissions would simply shift the appointments to someone other than senators.

On the other hand, there were those who insisted Carter could establish district nominating commissions such as he had created for federal appeals court vacancies, that commissions could be set up so as to be free of senatorial influence, and that they could be made to work so as to give consideration to a broader range of candidates than might be reviewed by a single senator.

The fight over merit selection found senators defending their traditional patronage domain, House lawmakers attempting to restore greater authority to the president at the expense of senators, and the president attempting to establish a middle ground that resisted the House solution while attempting to satisfy his campaign promise and not offend too many senators.

Can Carter's Plan Work?

Rather than usurping senatorial patronage, Carter chose a course that should make it more difficult for senators to use their patronage or, if they do make nominations on the basis of patronage, to be more circumspect about how they use it.

The president's decision merely to encourage use of commissions rather than to establish them was probably due to two key factors. First, the fact that he had no reason to want to alienate a large number of senators. And second, he recognized that a mandatory merit selection process would ultimately be at the mercy of an often arbitrary senatorial confirmation process.

While the Constitution gives the president appointment authority, suggesting that his judgment is the key factor in a judicial nomination, in actuality the president's involvement has been only incidental. "Senatorial courtesy" allows a senator from a judicial nominee's homestate to kill a nomination by withholding the "blue slip" giving the Senate Judiciary Committee approval to begin confirmation hearings. Recognizing that they stand to gain more going along with the Senate's patronage process than by attempting to fight it, presidents normally follow the recommendations of homestate senators.

Despite its purely hortatory nature, Carter's campaign of gentle persuasion may in the end contribute to selection of more qualified judges. Viewed in its best light the plan does put the White House on record in favor of merit commissions. It commits the attorney general to an active role in determining whether the selection process was fair before making recommendations to the president. Bell said he would personally call senators to encourage creation of merit panels where they don't already exist.

The plan adds further credence to the increasingly widespread view that there is a need for a new judicial selection process to replace the patronage system.

In addition to encouraging commissions, the White House plans to send questionnaires to senators and screen-ing commissions to determine what process they've used and what factors they've considered in selecting their nominees. (It does not, however, plan to make the responses to these questionnaires public.) Taken together, these factors may put pressure on senators to establish commissions or give more thoughtful consideration to their nominees.

Since most of the merit selection commissions in existence were created since Carter took office and at the urging of the president, there is reason to believe that Carter's gentle approach may work. Of the 52 district judges appointed by the president in 1977-78, 31 have been nominees of merit selection commissions.

Carter's executive order specifically required the attorney general, before making recommendations to the president, to "consider": 1) whether an effort was made to identify qualified candidates "including women and members of minority groups," 2) whether the process was "fair and reasonable" and 3) whether the candidates meet specified qualification standards including a "demonstrated commitment to equal justice under law," membership in good standing of the bar, a reputation for being "fair, experienced, even-tempered and free of biases against any class of citizens or any religious or racial group," and "outstanding legal ability and competence."

"There's an attitude in the Justice Department to do as little as possible, to change as little as possible and that has been sanctioned by the White House."

—Common Cause President David Cohen

Outlook

The composition of the federal judiciary for many years to come will be decided as the patronage system and a wide variety of selection processes begin nominating 152 life-tenured appointees.

That process is likely to find Republicans, who are fully aware of the enormity of Carter's patronage bonanza, charging that he has failed to live up to his campaign promise. And it may see an effort to get the Senate Judiciary Committee to modify the blue slip process.

What the best way of selecting candidates will be, probably won't be known for a long time. The 1978 confirmation of Iowa Judge Donald O'Brien raises serious doubts that there is any single best way of picking judges. In that case a highly regarded merit commission approved the nominee, only to find him rejected as unqualified by the American Bar Association, which has traditionally set the basic standards for appointments. The White House decided to accept the commission recommendation.

Curiously, despite all the discussion of the process, there have been relatively few attacks on the quality of sitting judges. That may, of course, be attributable as much to a failure of Congress and the news media to investigate candidates as it is to the success of the patronage system. As a result of the interest in merit selection, however, candidates are likely to be more closely scrutinized in the future. ∎

Agriculture

Two new elements in farm politics — a militant farmers' organization and farm legislation passed in 1977 — had more success in 1978 than their opponents predicted. As a result, farmers both made more money than the year before and convinced more people that they had some serious financial problems.

Between January and April, the months-old American Agriculture Movement (AAM) came close to forcing a major rewrite of the 1977 farm bill, and it won some unexpected concessions from the Carter administration and Congress. It also was covered extensively in the national media and "was successful in creating a national awareness" of farmers' problems, according to a Library of Congress study.

Meanwhile, the new farm programs that were the target of AAM protests worked well enough in 1978 to raise farm income 29 percent over 1977 levels, according to the Agriculture Department. At year's end, net farm income was expected to total $26 billion, compared with $20 billion in 1977.

Record commodity exports, up 50 percent compared to the 1973-75 period, were a major booster of farm income. Department officials said farmer participation in new set-aside and grain reserve programs, combined with the export sales, had kept farm prices strong enough for efficient producers. However, farmers with unusually high production costs still faced serious financial problems, department officials conceded.

AAM organizers, many from high-risk or low-productivity regions, promised renewed pressures on Washington in 1979 for more aid. But chances for further AAM success seemed dimmed by the improvements in farm income and by the increasingly dominant issue of inflation.

Food prices, a major component in the overall cost-of-living index, rose 10 percent in 1978, compared with a 6.5 percent rate of increase in 1977. Congressional and administration concern with high food costs was a major element in slowing AAM's impressive momentum in the spring. Much of the growth in food spending was caused by spiraling beef prices. Although more than half the retail price of food represents labor, transportation, advertising and other non-commodity costs, soaring cattle prices — up 50 percent from September 1977 — pushed retail prices up rapidly.

Over bitter protests from cattlemen, the president sought to deflate beef prices, first by admitting more cheap, foreign-produced meat into the country and later by vetoing a meat import bill. Even before the meat bill veto, administration lobbyists had wrung from congressional committees less favorable provisions than the cattlemen had wanted. They were similarly successful in winning cuts in sugar legislation, which ultimately failed. These developments suggested that members would be reluctant to risk further food price inflation to meet producer demands.

Farmer Protest. AAM began as a strike organization, but its promised withholding action on commodities never materialized and the movement had its strongest impact as an unorthodox pressure group in Washington, Clinging resolutely to its identity as a "movement," AAM never designated spokesmen, developed detailed positions on agriculture bills, allied itself with established farm lobbies or registered as a lobby.

And AAM as a group did not have any notable impact on the 1978 congressional elections, although members had vowed revenge at the polls on farm-district members who did not support them.

Sugar Legislation Dies

Sugar legislation unexpectedly died in the waning hours of the 95th Congress when the House balked at a conference agreement that had been drafted to Carter administration specifications.

The failure left a pending international sugar agreement without ratification, and left domestic producers with an expiring support program.

By a 177-194 vote the House Oct. 15 refused to accept a compromise five-year domestic sugar support program that the Senate had endorsed hours earlier. Before passing the compromise the Senate by a 36-20 vote had decided not to recommit — and thus kill — the bill.

In a weary session that began about 5 a.m. Oct. 15 conferees had bowed to presidential demands that they drop an automatic inflation adjustment to a base per-pound support price for sugar, and that they adopt a relatively low base or "price objective." Both houses had passed legislation establishing a domestic sugar price and authorizing import quotas and fees to keep sugar at that set price. But the president had threatened to veto the legislation as too inflationary.

Conferees finally agreed to the following: a base 15 cents per pound price — the figure adopted by the House — for fiscal year 1979 with a .75 cents supplementary payment for that year only. Thereafter, the price objective would rise 1 percent a year. The Senate bill had set the initial price at 16 cents.

Some sugar producers viewed the conference agreement as just barely adequate — to keep them going until 1979, when they planned to try again for more generous support. Their congressional advocates, led by Sen. Russell B. Long, D-La., pleaded for "aye" votes and the Senate went along.

But many producers, who claim production costs of 16 or 17 cents a pound, were angered by the conference agreement which they said guaranteed their bankruptcy.

What AAM did do was to dump delegations of angry farmers on congressional and administration offices for about three months. They failed to achieve their major goal of guaranteed 100 percent of parity prices. But before they went home to plant their spring crops, the farmer-lobbyists had:

● Won a moratorium from the administration on Farmers' Home Administration (FmHA) loan foreclosures.

● Won paid land diversion programs for cotton and feed grains and more favorable terms for the new grain reserve program from the administration.

● Prompted creation of a new "economic emergency" loan program under which farmers could refinance debts.

● Won a modest legislative adjustment of the 1977 act.

Farm Income. Near-perfect weather produced record yields in wheat and feed grains during 1978. But where bumper crops a year earlier had produced price-depressing surpluses, many farmers cut overall production in 1978 by idling part of their cropland in the new set-aside program.

Strong participation in a new farmer-held reserve program further controlled the flow of commodities to market.

Since September 1977, when Carter signed the farm bill, wheat prices had risen 32 percent and corn prices were up 18 percent. Estimated farm income for 1978 was still well below the 1973 high of $33.3 billion, and farmers' production costs also climbed about 11 percent in 1978. But federal payments to farmers were also up, with an estimated $1.3 billion in deficiency payments due farmers for their 1978 crops. The 1977 figure was $1.2 billion. (Deficiency payments, the difference between market prices and federal "target prices," were available for farmers participating in announced set-aside or land diversion programs.) The combined total of federal payouts to farmers for producer loans, deficiency and land diversion payments and disaster aid came to about $6.2 billion for the year.

Farmers had threatened to stay out of set-aside and reserve programs, and participation in the land program was running behind department expectations. But officials said the rate was "good" for a new program.

Farmer use of the reserve program exceeded department projections. ∎

Higher Prices Seen:

Carter Approval of New Sugar Bill Could End Impasse with Congress

Congress and the White House were stalemated over sugar price support legislation throughout 1978, in part because the Carter administration tried to hold the line on prices for the commodity.

Hoping to end the impasse, President Carter early in 1979 reportedly rejected the advice of his inflation fighters and agreed to a hefty price increase.

The move was triggered by a variety of factors, including a desire to get a sugar bill moving quickly in the Senate Finance and House Ways and Means committees before those committees were overwhelmed by trade legislation.

The administration decision represented a major narrowing of the gap between the White House and Congress over the issue of sugar prices. Administration officials in 1978 said any legislation that raised sugar prices to more than 15 cents a pound faced a veto. The new administration proposal would set a price objective of 15.8 cents a pound, with the possible addition of a half-cent-a-pound direct payment to producers.

Prospects for speedy passage of a sugar bill were tempered, however, by administration insistence that the 15.8 cent figure is non-negotiable.

"We really don't have any maneuvering room," said White House agriculture adviser Lynn Daft.

The proposal also could run into stiff opposition from sugar producers who say the 15.8-cent figure is still below their cost of production, and from consumer groups who object to a sharply higher market price for sugar.

Daft said the administration is considering attempting to graft its proposals onto an already introduced bill, such as the one (HR 2172) submitted jointly by House Agriculture Committee Chairman Thomas S. Foley, D-Wash., and Ways and Means Chairman Al Ullman, D-Ore., rather than drafting its own legislation.

"We're close enough that we could get an agreement," Daft said. "The mood in the White House and on the Hill is to get the differences out of the way and get some legislation on the books."

Background

The battle over sugar legislation in 1978 went down to the final hours of the session Oct. 15. The legislation finally died when the House rejected the conference report on a compromise bill (HR 13750) that acceded to administration demands to set a relatively low minimum price and eliminate any automatic increases to account for inflation.

The defeat left two issues dangling: ratification of the international sugar agreement (ISA), which would set up a system of quotas and stockpiling designed to stabilize the world market price of sugar, and a domestic price support

program for sugar, which was due to expire at the end of the 1978 crop year, in September 1979.

The core of the 1978 fight concerned conflicting claims about the costs of producing sugar. Domestic producers pushed hard to set a minimum price for sugar close to their production costs, which they said averaged 17 to 18 cents a pound. Administration spokesmen claimed average production costs were about 15 cents a pound.

A second issue was how to support the price. The administration first proposed setting a target price of about 14 cents a pound (when the market price fell below the target price, producers would be paid the difference), and adjusting it annually to reflect average production costs.

Congress favored using a system of import fees and quotas on foreign sugar to raise the price to 16 or 17 cents, with additional adjustments to reflect inflation. Administration officials later agreed to go along with the fee and tariff approach, but wanted direct federal payments to sugar producers rather than automatic inflation adjusters.

All the proposals included ratification of the ISA, an international agreement that would use export quotas and stockpiling to stabilize the world market price of sugar at between 11 and 21 cents a pound. Under the agreement, sugar would be stored and exports limited when the world market price fell below 15 cents a pound. The market system would operate normally when the price was between 15 and 19 cents; above 19 cents stocks would be released.

1978 House Action. The House Agriculture Committee reported a bill (HR 13750) in August that used fees and quotas to set a minimum price of 16 cents a pound. The bill included an automatic "escalator" that would adjust the price every three months to reflect inflation. It also included a minimum wage provision that guaranteed sugar workers $3 an hour immediately plus 20-cents-an-hour raises each crop year through 1983.

The Ways and Means Committee, which shared jurisdiction over the legislation, endorsed a less expensive version of HR 13750 that dropped the minimum price to 15 cents a pound and eliminated the automatic escalator. The committee said the president already had authority to make supplementary direct payments to producers if production costs rose above 15 cents a pound.

The compromise version passed by the House Oct. 6 set the price at 15 cents a pound, with semiannual adjustments to reflect changes in production costs.

Senate Action. The Senate passed its version of HR 13750 Oct. 13. The Senate bill set a minimum price of 16 cents a pound and included a semiannual inflation escalator. With the president threatening to veto any bill containing an escalator clause and a price objective over 15 cents, the Senate added two amendments designed to make the bill veto-proof: an extension of the president's authority to waive countervailing duties on some subsidized foreign imports — an item considered crucial to the success of the Multilateral Trade Negotiations — and an amendment authorizing the president to increase U.S. contributions to an international tin stockpile.

Final Action. Meeting on the final day of the session, conferees, under pressure from the administration, agreed to drop the automatic inflation adjustment feature and adopt a minimum price objective of 15 cents a pound plus a .75 cent a pound direct payment in fiscal 1979. The price objective would be increased to 15.8 cents a pound in fiscal 1980. The agreement also included minimum wage provisions, extension of the countervailing duty waiver authority and the international tin agreement provisions.

The Senate accepted the conference report by voice vote, but a few hours later the House rejected it by a 177-194 vote. A variety of objections combined to defeat the bill: some members from sugar states felt the price objective was too low, while many from corn states felt direct payments to sugar producers were unfair to corn sweetener producers. Other members said the bill was too costly.

A few days after the House rejected HR 13750, Agriculture Secretary Bob Bergland announced that the government would revise import fees to support the sugar price for the 1978 crop year (October 1978-September 1979) at 15 cents a pound.

Outlook

The 1979 sugar legislation was expected to attract the same diverse and powerful lineup of support and opposition that had characterized action on sugar bills in previous years. The one key change was the White House itself, which in 1978 was generally opposed to congressional proposals on sugar prices.

The inflationary impact of sugar legislation — each penny increase in the price objective costs consumers an estimated $200 million or more — has made sugar legislation a high priority for many consumer groups.

Kathleen Sheekey of the Consumer Federation of America said she was "very disappointed the president didn't hold the line" on sugar prices.

"We're going to continue to fight it," Sheekey said. "This is one of the areas where something can be done about rising food prices."

Industrial users and cane sugar refiners also are expected to fight any big jump in sugar prices that would raise their raw material costs.

Gregg R. Potvin of the U.S. Cane Sugar Refiners Association said it was "highly unfortunate the president felt impelled to give in to the intense pressure" for higher sugar prices.

Growers generally are expected to support the bill. David Carter, president of the U.S. Sugar Beet Growers Association, called the administration proposal a "long step in the right direction."

"We're substantially ahead of last year," he added.

Carter said he was "philosophically opposed" to the direct payments approach. "It's our preference to raise prices," he said. "We'd rather get it from the marketplace instead of from the taxpayer."

Congress and Government

Concerned about the federal government's tarnished public image, Congress took actions in 1978 aimed at boosting public opinion about ethics and efficiency in all three branches of government.

The two biggest steps taken toward that goal were enactment of laws reforming the federal civil service system and requiring detailed public disclosure of financial holdings by members of Congress and top officials in the executive and judicial branches.

But in trying to deal with ethics problems involving some individual members, Congress may have done its image more harm than good.

A series of embarrassing accusations of criminal or unethical behavior involving members plagued both the House and Senate in 1978. Three House members were indicted on felony charges during the year, and one of them later was convicted. Four members were charged with ethical violations by the House Committee on Standards of Official Conduct, and the Senate Ethics Committee investigated two of its members for alleged unethical behavior.

The full Senate was not called upon in 1978 to act in either ethics case investigated by its committee or in a separate probe of South Korean influence-peddling. But the House conducted a bitter, divisive debate after its ethics panel recommended punishment for three members charged with wrongdoing in the South Korean scandal.

The committee recommended that the House reprimand California Democrats Charles H. Wilson and John J. McFall and censure Edward R. Roybal, D-Calif. However, after a debate featuring criticism of the committee's procedures and its differing recommendations for punishment, the House rejected a resolution to censure Roybal and instead voted reprimands — the lightest possible punishment — for all three Californians.

Looking beyond its internal problems, Congress heeded election-year constituent complaints about the federal bureaucracy by passing two bills aimed at making the federal government more efficient and reducing waste in federal programs. One was the civil service reform bill, which was heavily promoted by the administration. The other was a measure setting up inspector general offices in 12 federal agencies. The new inspectors general, appointed by the president, were given subpoena and investigatory powers to fight waste and fraud in government programs.

A Senate subcommittee also held hearings on a scandal involving massive fraud and abuse in the General Services Administration, but no other congressional action was taken on the issue.

The subcommittee, investigating newspaper reports that had exposed the scandal, found abuses involving false claims for benefits and services, collusion among contractors and bribery of officials. Investigators said the abuses could be traced to lack of competitive bidding and irregular auditing procedures within GSA, as well as the traditional practice of filling GSA jobs by political patronage.

Constitutional Amendments

Two constitutional amendments were debated at great length during 1978.

One of them, giving full representation in Congress to the District of Columbia, was approved after opponents in the Senate abandoned their effort to kill it by filibuster. The amendment still had to be ratified by 38 state legislatures before it could take effect.

Also debated was a resolution giving the states 39 more months to ratify the Equal Rights Amendment (ERA). Congress approved ERA in 1972 and gave the states seven years to ratify it. However, only 35 of the 38 states needed for ratification had passed the amendment by the end of 1978. The new deadline set by the resolution was June 30, 1982.

Government Operations

Several legislative proposals that would have made fundamental changes in federal government operations were not acted on in 1978 but were expected to be revived in the 96th Congress. They included:

● **Sunset.** Sunset legislation, which would require automatic termination of funds for most federal spending programs if they were not specifically reauthorized after a comprehensive congressional review every 10 years. A sunset bill passed the Senate shortly before Congress adjourned for the year, but the House did not act on it.

● **Lobby Disclosure.** A lobby reform bill, calling for more detailed disclosure of lobbying activities by interest groups. The House passed a lobby disclosure bill but the Senate Governmental Affairs Committee never resolved a philosophical split among its members to produce a bill.

● **Campaign Financing.** Legislation to provide public financing for congressional races. House Republicans and southern Democrats twice blocked floor consideration of a public financing bill during 1978.

● **Congressional Veto.** Bills to give Congress a veto over regulations written by executive branch agencies. Broad legislative veto proposals, which traditionally have been rejected by the Senate, made no headway in the House during 1978. However, the House did include a legislative veto provision in a bill authorizing funds for the Federal Trade Commission. The bill eventually died because of House insistence that the legislative veto remain in it.

● **Appropriation Bill Riders.** Limitations on legislative riders offered as amendments to appropriations bills. Although many members of the House and Senate agreed that there should be restrictions on adding legislative amendments to appropriations bills, there was no consensus on what the restrictions should be. Neither body acted on proposals to limit legislative riders.

● **Senate Job Bias.** A resolution to give Senate employees protection from job discrimination. A filibuster threat prompted sponsors to withdraw the bill, which would have set up a mechanism for enforcing a new Senate anti-discrimination rule. The rule, scheduled to take effect in 1979, marked the first official protection for Senate employees from discrimination in hiring and firing.

The death of the resolution meant the Senate Ethics Committee had sole authority to enforce the rule when it took effect. But supporters of the resolution said its enforcement mechanism would have given Senate workers more protection than they were likely to get from the committee.

The House did not have any formal anti-discrimination rule.

● **Congressional Terms.** Resolutions limiting the number of terms members of Congress can serve. Although the Senate held hearings on several proposals, neither body showed much interest in term limitation bills. Similar proposals have been introduced — with no success — since the first Congress convened in 1789.

Televised Debate

Plans to begin televising House floor debates in 1978 were set back when the House Rules Committee decided it needed to come up with a more sophisticated broadcast system than the House originally had planned. The committee said a test system operated in 1977 produced poor pictures and sound, and House broadcasts were put off until the 96th Congress.

During 1978, television networks continued their battle to bring their own cameras into the House chamber. But the House leadership resisted network arguments and assured members that the cameras recording debate would be operated by House employees. The networks would be allowed to pick up a "feed" from the House-run broadcasts, the leadership said.

In the Senate, National Public Radio was permitted to broadcast floor debate of the Panama Canal treaties — the first time such broadcasts had been allowed. But there were no plans to broadcast other debates or to begin television broadcasts from the Senate.

Civil Service Reform

President Carter in March made civil service reform his top domestic legislative priority when he unveiled proposals to change the system. He said his plan would help fulfill his campaign promise to reorganize the federal bureaucracy and make it more responsive to the public.

Carter's plan — the most comprehensive reform of the system since the civil service was set up in 1883 — called for reorganizing the Civil Service Commission into two new agencies.

In addition, Carter proposed legislation that he said would put true merit in the civil service system by basing pay and job security on performance. Those and numerous other changes in the civil service were approved after months of intense administration lobbying, giving Carter one of the biggest legislative victories in his first two years as president.

Financial Disclosure

Although the ethics bill covered all three branches of the federal government, nearly all of the debate focused on how it would affect Congress.

The disclosure bill was the final piece of ethics legislation in a series of reform measures considered by the House and Senate in 1977 and 1978. A small but highly vocal group of House members managed to tie up the bill for months by threatening to use it as a vehicle for undoing a major reform in one of the earlier bills — the limit imposed on members' outside earned income.

House Democratic leaders considered passage of the financial disclosure bill essential as a *quid pro quo* for a House vote in 1977 raising congressional salaries. But they also wanted to keep intact the outside earned income limit.

The leaders put off House action until fall, when election-conscious members were unlikely to vote against the new ethics bill or for repeal of the previous ethics reform.

The ploy worked well: An effort to repeal the limit was soundly defeated and the bill passed with no trouble. ▌

The New Congress: A Small Step to the Right

The voters nudged Congress a step to the right in the 1978 elections, adding three Republicans in the Senate and 11 in the House, and allowing the GOP at least to entertain the notion that it is on the way back in national politics.

The numbers themselves are not exactly the stuff of which a renaissance is normally made. Free to campaign in opposition to the White House as well as Congress for the first time in 10 years, Republicans ought to have gained a few House seats, as they did. But for a party that suffered so badly in congressional voting four years ago, and failed to gain any of its strength back in 1976, 11 new House seats mark a beginning.

And the three new Senate seats may represent something more than a beginning. As important as the numerical change is the fact that Republicans managed to gain Senate strength in a year when they were defending half the seats at stake — a far higher proportion than they hold in the chamber as a whole.

Taking incumbents and newcomers together, the GOP elected 20 people to the Senate in 1978 — more than in any year since 1952.

So the congressional returns, combined with the news that six more Republican governors will supplement the current hardcore group of 12, allowed GOP leaders to claim an overall success in the 1978 election, even as the White House was pointing out — correctly — that the combined Democratic losses were relatively small compared with what has frequently happened to the party in power in midterm elections.

The Carter administration, which did not exactly exercise dictatorial control over the 95th Congress, can live with the still heavily Democratic lineup in both the House and Senate. But it may have some reason to be disturbed about Republican gains at the statehouse level.

Gubernatorial Results

The Republican Party appears, for the time being at least, to have checked the startling erosion in its gubernatorial strength that began in 1970, when the GOP controlled 32 statehouses, and still raged in 1976, when it had sunk to a compact but embarrassing 12.

Six new Republican governorships will not cause an earthquake in the presidential politics of 1980, but they will change the outlines somewhat. This is mainly because of the election of two men — William Clements in Texas and Richard L. Thornburgh in Pennsylvania. Republicans entered the 1978 campaign holding statehouses in only three of the 10 largest states. When the 1980 campaign begins, if it hasn't already, there will be GOP governors in half the "megastates," with the advantages in national media attention, fund raising and organization that they can provide.

And while statehouse control may be an overrated factor in presidential elections, there is an undeniable psychological advantage to being in charge in the states that draw most of the attention.

Possible Schism

Curiously, though, the separate gains for Republicans at the Senate and statehouse levels raised the possibility of a new split within the party between its congressional and gubernatorial factions.

On the gubernatorial side, it was the moderate Republicans who were the clear winners. Of the new "big five" Republican governors, Thornburgh and re-elected Govs. James R. Thompson in Illinois and William G. Milliken in Michigan are clearly identified with the party's left. James A. Rhodes, the veteran Republican narrowly returned in Ohio, is generally concerned with state issues, but has always sided with the moderates in national politics. Only Clements, still a political novice as he takes office in Texas, will add conservative influence at the big-state level.

The Republican left also re-elected Robert Ray of Iowa, the highly respected dean of American governors, to his fifth term. The right lost Meldrim Thomson Jr. of New Hampshire, who became nationally known for his outspoken extreme conservatism. It failed to elect Ted Strickland of Colorado, who would have been one of its leading spokesmen among the governors if he had won.

Congressional Results

The congressional picture is different. Moderate and liberal Republicans probably held even in Senate elections, gaining William S. Cohen in Maine, David Durenberger and Rudy Boschwitz in Minnesota, and Larry Pressler in South Dakota, all of whom replaced Democrats. But they lost national figures in Clifford P. Case in the New Jersey primary, Edward W. Brooke in the Massachusetts general election, and James B. Pearson of Kansas, who retired.

Pearson's replacement, Republican Nancy Landon Kassebaum, may also join the moderates. But Case and Brooke will be replaced by Democrats.

Conservative Republicans, on the other hand, lost virtually nothing. They won unexpected victories by ousting liberal Democrats Dick Clark of Iowa and Thomas J. McIntyre of New Hampshire, and gained a potential national leader in William L. Armstrong of Colorado. Thad Cochran of Mississippi, that state's first GOP senator ever chosen by popular vote, is certain to join the right on fiscal and defense issues, although he is likely to be a moderate on many social and some race-related questions.

New Right Gains

In general, the Senate returns represented a modest victory for the complex of conservative organizations loosely labeled the New Right. Groups like the Committee for the Survival of a Free Congress and the National Conservative Political Action Committee were major backers of Roger Jepsen against Clark and Gordon Humphrey against McIntyre, and were able to claim considerable credit for these two upsets that seemed to symbolize for many disappointed Democrats the small but significant rightward trend of the 1978 election.

The Humphrey and Jepsen triumphs were not won primarily on the Kemp-Roth tax cutting issue or other economic proposals most Republican candidates chose to emphasize, but on more emotional topics that national Republican strategists generally tried to avoid. Jepsen reduced Clark's vote in normally Democratic Catholic areas because Clark declined to endorse anti-abortion measures or support tuition tax credits for parochial schools. Humphrey made McIntyre's vote in favor of the Panama Canal treaties a centerpiece of his campaign.

In fact, it is difficult to find any Republican Senate candidate in the country who appears to owe his victory largely to his endorsement of a massive tax cut. New Jersey's Jeffrey Bell, who campaigned as hard and as effectively on this issue as anyone — "California had Proposition 13; New Jersey has Jeff Bell" — turned in a respectable showing but still found himself unable to overcome the personal popularity of his celebrity opponent, Democrat Bill Bradley, a former New York Knicks basketball player.

These results, scattered as they are, may strengthen the position of those conservatives centered around fundraiser Richard Viguerie, who believes social issues can be the basic vehicle for conservative success. The failure of the Kemp-Roth tax cut approach as a national campaign tool is likely to work against Rep. Jack Kemp, R-N.Y., and others who insist that a national majority can only be built on economic issues.

The Midwest

Perhaps as encouraging as anything else for Republicans in the election was the hint of recovery in the Midwest, the region which Republicans once monopolized but which has been systmatically torn from them by Democrats in the past decade.

A party without a regional base is a minority party, and since 1970 Republicans have had no stronghold they could use to counter Democrtic successes in other parts of the country.

They probably still do not have one, but Republicans did show surprising appeal in the farm states, where they

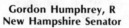

Gordon Humphrey, R
New Hampshire Senator

Bill Bradley, D
New Jersey Senator

have lost so badly in recent years. The GOP took eight of nine governorships contested in the Midwest, won two Democratic Senate seats in Minnesota and one each in South Dakota and Iowa, and gained House seats in Iowa, Kansas, Illinois, Indiana and Wisconsin.

Whether this phenomenon stems from problems with President Carter's farm policy, or whether it simply shows that the Democratic resurgence in the early 1970s in these states is petering out, the results will encourage midwestern Republicans at a point when some of them had begun to lose hope.

The South

For Republicans in the South, nothing can erase the legacy of 1974 and 1976, when first Watergate and then the Carter presidential candidacy wiped out the modest gains they had been making in the region since the early 1960s. Voting in 1978 still left the GOP far weaker than it was in 1972, the last time it made any overall progress in southern congressional representation. But there were a few signs that the Republican Party might still be able to grow in the South if it tries again.

Republicans took Democratic House seats in Arkansas, Georgia and South Carolina, the first such gains in six years. Cochran's election in a three-way contest as Mississippi's first popularly chosen Republican senator may have been a fluke, as Cochran himself has described it, but it is also a potent party-building tool for the GOP in that state.

Clements' election as governor of Texas gives Republicans an even more important boost there. And they needed it. Despite the victory of Clements and the re-election of incumbent Republican Sen. John G. Tower, GOP House candidates failed to take advantage of opportunities in several Texas House districts, capturing the seat of only one of eight departing Democrats after hoping earlier in this year to replace as many as six.

In Florida it was even worse. Presented with excellent opportunities to elect Republicans in two conservative districts Democrats vacated, Republicans not only lost both of those seats by embarrassing margins but failed to re-elect one of their own incumbents.

So the South offers conflicting evidence — glimmers of hope for a Republican future and obvious indications that the party is not even competitive yet in areas where it will have to be in order to win nationally. And in that respect, the results from the South simply offer in sharper focus a picture that applies to the rest of the country as well. ∎

Confirmation Process: Weaknesses Abound

One of the most damaging episodes of 1977 for the Carter administration, the "Lance affair," also was unpleasant for the Senate. And Carter's second year in office brought the "Marston affair," which similarly proved to be one of the banes of the year for the president and the Senate.

These and other cases demonstrate that there are pitfalls for both the executive and legislative branches in the way appointments to high government office are made. As the Senate undertakes its responsibility of examining and confirming major nominations, there is a continuing discussion of the problems in the process, and of potential remedies.

The Senate in 1978 handled such crucial nominations as that of G. William Miller to be chairman of the Federal Reserve Board, which determines monetary policy, and that of William H. Webster to head the FBI, the nation's top law enforcement agency. It also considered the nomination of James T. McIntyre Jr. to succeed his former boss, Bert Lance, as head of the Office of Management and Budget. All won approval.

Moreover, the controversial dismissal of David W. Marston, a Philadelphia U.S. attorney who was investigating state and federal officials, focused more than usual attention on the confirmation of his successor.

The Senate also had to pass judgment on a host of lesser presidential nominations. Carter in all submitted 3,054 civilian nominations to the Senate during 1978. All but 44 were confirmed. *(Nominations and confirmations, p. 75)*

'Rubber Stamp'

Even stalwart defenders of the Senate such as Majority Leader Robert C. Byrd (D W.Va.) have conceded that the confirmation process has not always worked as it should.

Common Cause, the citizens' lobbying group, in November 1977 published a report that skewered the Senate process as a "rubber-stamp machine."

And Sens. Abraham Ribicoff (D Conn.) and Charles H. Percy (R Ill.),

both among those most stung by the handling of the Lance confirmation, proposed legislation (S Res 258) in 1978 to standardize and centralize Senate confirmation.

Although the legislation went nowhere during a busy year for Ribicoff's Governmental Affairs Committee, Common Cause planned to renew its campaign for tighter procedures in the 96th Congress. The organization's president, David Cohen, wrote to all Senate members on Jan. 23, 1979, urging them to work for adoption of procedures "that establish the necessary institutional arrangements to ensure full and deliberative confirmation proceedings. . . ."

The gist of most of the dissatisfaction with the Senate's performance in confirming nominees to high office is typified by the case of Bert Lance: A brief, inadequately documented committee examination in January 1977 of his banking background failed to turn up the questionable aspects of his past career that led to his resignation under fire the following September. The failure in that case has led to criticism of Senate examinations in some cases.

Leading the charge for that viewpoint has been Common Cause, whose

1977 study was based on consideration of 50 Carter nominations. It concluded that the Senate inadequately examined the background and qualifications of most nominees, failed to build an adequate public record for the confirmation decision and rushed to confirmation without any affirmative finding that the calibre of the nominees met the requirements of their offices. *(Box, p. 72)*

Sen. Byrd already had told reporters that he felt the Senate had not performed as it should in confirmations. Calling the Lance case an "indictment" of the process, Byrd said that "confirmations often have been rubber-stamped. There has been a feeling that this is a nominee the president wants, and he should have who he wants. I believe our responsibility should go deeper than that."

But those criticisms signal the complexity of the confirmation task, which presents several distinct difficulties:

● Confirmation to high office increasingly must focus on potential conflicts of interest that turn on complex evaluations of financial information about both individuals and corporations for which they work.

G. William Miller, left, chairman of the Federal Reserve Board, chats with Sen. William Proxmire prior to hearing on Miller's nomination.

• Even traditional FBI inquiries into arrest records, youthful associations and other personal background data must be carefully weighed to avoid unfairly penalizing an individual for conduct that may be constitutionally protected even though not approved by many in society.

• Appointment to high office is patronage by any other name, and removing politics from patronage is no easier today than it has been since the days of Andrew Jackson.

• Besides being affected by partisan politics, the appointment process is constantly enmeshed with the conflict between the legislative and executive branches over both patronage and substantive policy.

Conflict of Interest

As the Lance case demonstrated, an adequate examination of a presidential nominee may require evaluation of bank records, a knowledge of banking practices and the ability to sift through complex financial statements.

In the more recent case of Fed nominee Miller, who headed the giant Textron conglomerate, evaluation of the nominee's qualifications required an understanding of the activities of a multibillion-dollar corporation. As one congressional observer put the problem of modern nominations, "It ain't as easy as looking for the old boy's arrest record."

It is primarily this problem that the Ribicoff-Percy bill addressed. A Governmental Affairs Committee aide said that the plan would provide the Senate with the staff expertise and the time needed to discharge this complicated part of the confirmation duty.

The proposal, introduced in 1977, called for creation of a Senate Office on Nominations, which would assume primary responsibility for conducting background inquiries into a nominee's integrity and fitness for office. The office would be headed by a director selected on a bipartisan basis and would have adequate staff to do the kind of investigative work implied by its mandate.

Moreover, the office would be empowered to demand detailed biographical and financial disclosure statements, which would be made available for public inspection. Finally, the Office on Nominations would have mandatory access to "any investigative reports prepared on the nominee by any federal agency and submitted to the President as part of his consideration of the nomination," including FBI summary reports.

This central office would compile a record on each major nominee and identify any questions about his or her integrity. It would then report to the committee having jurisdiction over the nomination, which would act according to a timetable that precluded a rush to confirmation.

Criticism

Critics of the proposal respond that a nominations office is not needed. They suggest there is little Senate committees cannot do now to scrutinize nominees if they take the trouble to do so.

"Just because one committee got into a lot of trouble by not doing a good job doesn't mean there's a problem with all the rest of us," said one aide, referring to Governmental Affairs' role in the Lance case.

Grenville Garside, chief of staff of the Energy and Natural Resources Committee, argues that "just because of the Lance case, it would be disastrous to rush in with an office, rules and regulations." Garside said that many tools already are at the disposal of examining committees, such as the use of the General Accounting Office (GAO) to aid in complex inquiries.

Above all, "we can put the burden on the executive," Garside said. "They are the advocates. If there's something we don't like, we don't have to confirm."

Those responsible for screening nominations in the White House are well aware of the ultimate weapon of Senate committees—rejection of nominees.

The office of White House counsel Robert J. Lipshutz has that job for the Carter administration. Associate counsel Michael H. Cardozo V, who handles the examination of a potential nominee's financial background and possible conflicts of interest, said he agrees that the Senate committees are in a position of strength in the confirmation process. "They can elicit anything they want to from a nominee, or just not confirm him," Cardozo said.

Tough Procedures

Even the critical Common Cause study corroborates the contention that an aggressive Senate committee can do a thorough confirmation investigation if it wishes.

That study reserves praise for a few committees, notably the Commerce Committee. In part due to its heavy responsibility for examining nominees to the numerous independent regulatory agencies, Commerce has developed tough procedures, including a comprehensive questionnaire to which all nominees before it must respond. A nominee's responses to the Commerce questionnaire may run as long as 400 pages, according to staff director Edward A. Merlis.

Several other committees also have developed extensive questionnaires that require a nominee to disclose wide-ranging information on his background, current finances and future employment plans.

To date, however, no uniform set of questions or standards has emerged, a fact which signals the second major criticism of the Ribicoff proposal. Senate committee aides state that "turf protection" by committee

---

The Constitutional Mandate

"The President...shall nominate, and by and with the Advice and Consent of the Senate shall appoint Ambassadors, other public Ministers and Consuls, Judges of the Supreme Court, and all other Officers of the United States, whose appointments are not herein otherwise provided for, and which shall be established by Law; but the Congress may by law vest the appointment of such inferior officers, as they think proper, in the President alone, in the courts of law, or in the heads of departments.

"The President shall have power to fill up all vacancies that may happen during the recess of the Senate, by granting commissions which shall expire at the end of their next session." *(Constitution of the United States, Article II, Section 2)*

The House has only one limited role in confirming officers of the executive branch. Under the Twenty-fifth Amendment to the Constitution, ratified in 1967, both the House and Senate must confirm, by majority vote, a new Vice President to succeed to any vacancy in that office.

chairmen is certain to stand in the way of creation of any central confirmation office. Powerful committee chairmen are considered unlikely to yield their confirmation prerogatives even partially to a staff that is not directly accountable to them.

Further, a number of aides argue that standardizing the inquiry into nominees would be a mistake, since the requirements for offices vary, and what constitutes a troublesome problem in a nominee's background may also vary. They add that individual committees can best muster the staff expertise relevant to their jurisdictions.

FBI Reports

Inquiries into the personal history and integrity of nominees continue to be a crucial element in confirmations.

Conflict Over Access

The principal tool in this part of the examination is the FBI "full field" investigation. The resulting report has long been a mainstay in the administration's way of assuring itself that a nominee's background is adequately pristine. But there has been conflict between the White House and the Senate over Senate access to those reports, and that historic conflict has come into the open because of the Lance case.

Senate committees have had differing experiences with previous administrations in gaining access to the FBI reports. With a few exceptions it appears, however, that past administrations did not allow members of confirming committees to look at the reports. At the very least, they discouraged committees from seeking access to them.

As a result, few committees regularly sought the reports. In fact, only one committee is known to have had regular access prior to the Carter administration: the Judiciary Committee. A special relationship has existed between that committee and the FBI, which the Judiciary Committee oversees. Also, the FBI in its manual of procedures has attached particular importance to the investigation of persons for life-tenure federal judgeship appointments, which are a major component of Judiciary's confirmation duties.

The Senate Judiciary Committee chairman thus has had longstanding personal access to the FBI reports on

---

Confirmation: A Major Task

One of the biggest chores any president faces is simply staffing his government. Review of those presidential personnel choices is likewise one of the Senate's major duties. Despite the number of government jobs controlled by the merit-based civil service system, the magnitude of the appointment and confirmation power, taken literally, remains enormous.

According to the Secretary of the Senate, the Carter administration had 62,850 appointments confirmed in 1978. Five nominations were withdrawn; none was rejected. That number is not exceptional. In the two years of the 93rd Congress (1973-74), for example, there were 131,254 confirmations.

Those figures are misleading, however, since the vast majority of those confirmations are of military promotions that traditionally have received no real scrutiny from the Senate. Nevertheless, John C. Stennis, D-Miss., chairman of the Armed Services Committee, announced in 1977 that that committee was instituting a new confirmation practice. The committee, he said, intends to "get a better picture as to

the type of men and women that are being nominated and proposed for promotion within the services," through a "system of random selection of officer nominees by the committee for confirmation hearings...."

Only 3,054 civilian nominations were included in the 62,850 total, and most of those were "routine" appointments to the Coast Guard, the National Oceanographic and Atmospheric Administration and the Public Health Service. Those appointments also have not received full-dress Senate attention in the past.

Still, Senate committees and the White House Counsel's office dealt in 1978 with some 200 nominations to policy-level positions deserving careful scrutiny.

The confirmation burden is unevenly distributed among Senate committees. Judiciary (judges, U.S. attorneys and U.S. marshals), Commerce (regulatory agencies), Foreign Relations (ambassadors) and Armed Services (primarily military) are among those committees with major confirmation duties. At least 14 committees have some confirmation responsibility.

---

nominees before his committee, with a deputy attorney general regularly bringing the reports to the chairman for his scrutiny.

Carter Policy

Cardozo, of Lipshutz' office, said that current Carter administration policy is to grant access to the FBI file only to the committee chairman and the ranking minority member, and only if they request to see it. If there is little or no derogatory information in the file, then the administration also will allow one staffer designated by the chairman to see the file.

Examination of the file is tightly guarded, however, even with committee chairmen. If a chairman asks to see a file, Cardozo, along with another counsel in Lipshutz' office, Patrick Apodaca, personally carry the file to the senator's office.

Cardozo remains with the senator while he reads the file. No reproductions are allowed, although notes can be taken. Afterward, Cardozo takes the file back to the White House.

That practice was formalized in the wake of the Lance affair, largely because more senators expressed an interest in seeing the FBI reports after observing how the Governmental Affairs Committee was burned by not seeing them.

Ribicoff complained after Lance's problems came to light that "the Senate is expected to act without having access to relevant investigative reports prepared on nominees by executive branch agencies. In the case of Mr. Lance, the [Governmental Affairs] committee was not given access to the FBI report on his nomination, nor did it have the opportunity to review reports prepared by the Comptroller of the Currency."

Cardozo responds it was Carter administration policy from the beginning to make the FBI reports available under those careful precautions. Garside, for one, corroborates that. He said that even before the Lance blowup in 1977, the Energy Committee requested and obtained FBI reports when they were considered necessary.

But the Carter administration has resisted granting the Senate access to the FBI reports on a routine basis. A 1977 letter from Lipshutz to Commerce Committee Chairman Warren G. Magnuson, D-Wash., and James B. Pearson, R-Kan., then ranking minority member, stated that "we are extremely reluctant to allow FBI reports to be read by others; they represent a significant intrusion into any nominee's privacy. To date, the policy of this administration, like others, has been not to submit FBI reports to the Senate, except on special occasions."

Lipshutz wrote in response to an earlier request to the president from Magnuson and Pearson asking regular access to FBI reports. Lipshutz outlined in his reply the procedure described by Cardozo.

"Making the FBI files available is a significant step, and can lead to invasions of privacy," Cardozo stated. "We want to be careful with it.... There have been problems with Senate staff. We have found that some staff members are not as discreet as they should be."

Damaging Allegations

The reason for this concern is rooted in the nature of the FBI reports themselves.

What the White House sees, and what it is now willing to show to committee chairmen, are "summary" reports that digest the results of interviews of various people who have had contact with the nominee in the past: neighbors, co-workers and friends.

The FBI does not make judgments, but passes along the statements of others. Many uncorroborated allegations about individuals may be included in the FBI reports, allegations that could be damaging to a person if leaked out, whether true or not.

A number of Senate aides privately argue that the real problem with the FBI reports is that they dwell on "gossip" about a person's social and sex life, without plumbing more complex questions of the individual's honesty or corruption. A major study by the then-Government Operations Committee in January 1977 quoted a number of past White House aides of both parties criticizing the reports as

an "irrelevant collection of gossip" and as "nonsense."

The FBI doesn't normally examine financial documents relevant to the individual's integrity. While the FBI report on Lance reportedly did not describe his controversial banking practices, it would have alerted the Ribicoff committee to existence of a criminal investigation of those activities in Atlanta. That investigation had been shut down at the time of Lance's nomination to the Carter Cabinet.

Loyalty Check

In addition, as the Government Operations study pointed out, the FBI inquiry has "McCarthy era" origins. The executive order mandating FBI investigations of top government appointees was signed by President Eisenhower in 1953. Under that order, one of the principal objectives is to check on a person's loyalty to the United States—and the methods used to measure loyalty are politically offensive to many observers today.

Notwithstanding those inadequacies, it seems clear that the Lance case has resulted in a heightened Senate determination to have regular access to the FBI product.

S Res 258 called for mandatory access to the reports, and the current administration policy guarantees carefully proscribed access. Cardozo said he believes that the senators appreciate the administration policy. "They feel we are strengthening the process," he said. "Senators want to make the confirmation process as comprehensive as possible and looking at the FBI files is one way of doing it."

Partisan Politics

The partisan nature of the confirmation process is most evident in the realm of judgeships and U.S. attorney appointments.

President Carter as a candidate pledged to remove politics from the consideration of appointments to these judicial offices. But the case of David Marston, who was fired by Attorney General Griffin B. Bell, has demonstrated the continuing political nature of those selections.

Under the system of senatorial courtesy that had its beginnings under President Washington, senators from each state who are of the same party as the president are given virtually a veto power over those appointments. As a

---

Study Calls Senate 'Rubber Stamp'

Procedures used by the Senate in confirmation cases were described as deficient in a November 1977 Common Cause report, "The Senate Rubber-Stamp Machine."

Common Cause examined procedures used in 50 Carter administration nominations. It was not a study of the nominees' actual qualifications.

Only two of the nominees were not confirmed:

• Donald L. Tucker was withdrawn from consideration to be a member of the Civil Aeronautics Board after opposition emerged in the Commerce Committee.

• Kent F. Hansen was rejected by the Environment and Public Works Committee as a nominee to the Nuclear Regulatory Commission.

The other 48 nominees were confirmed to Cabinet, sub-Cabinet, ambassadorial and regulatory agency posts.

Fourteen committees handled the nominations. Hearings were held on 49 of them, but only 10 of the hearings lasted longer than one day.

Only 14 nominees testified under oath.

Printed hearing records were made available to senators before their confirmation votes in only six of the 50 cases. Recorded votes in committee occurred in only half the cases, and recorded Senate floor votes came on only six.

More than half the nominees were fully confirmed within four weeks of their nomination. In 18 cases, committee approval came on the day the hearing was held. In the case of Energy Secretary James R. Schlesinger, a familiar figure to the members, full Senate confirmation was obtained the same day the Senate received his anticipated nomination.

In 14 cases committees opened to the public the financial disclosure statements tendered by the nominees. In 17 cases nominees were required to make public a statement of recent political activities and campaign contributions. In 39 cases potential conflicts of interest and their intended resolution were placed in the public record.

Judiciary Committee aide suggests, one reason for the practice is that these are offices held within the states themselves, not in Washington.

Thus the level of concern of a senator is apt to be somewhat higher for an appointment to a federal court than for an appointment, say, to a federal regulatory agency. As a corollary to the courtesy system, where the senators from a given state are not from the president's party, the president has been influenced in his choice by his party cohorts in the state's House delegation.

Marston Case

The Marston case stands as a clear example of the partisan approach of both parties to court-related appointments.

Marston had no prosecutorial experience and was recommended for appointment as U.S. attorney by President Ford because he had been an aide to Pennsylvania Republican Sen. Richard S. Schweiker.

The choice of Marston was harshly criticized at the time in many legal circles. Once in office, his anti-corruption record was good enough to turn some of his critics around. His removal by a Democratic administration responsive to the entreaties of Democratic congressmen, including one who had been touched by a Marston investigation, allowed Schweiker to shift the partisan label to the Democrats.

Partisan considerations historically have colored the discussion of the "merits" of an administration's nominees. President Carter has steadfastly clung to his pledge to move generally to merit consideration of nominees, but his record on overall appointments has been severely criticized by many observers. *(Merit selection of judges, pp. 57, 59)*

In particular, Carter has been charged with an excessive reliance on his fellow Georgians. In spite of that charge, Carter has continued that pattern. His selection of McIntyre, his Georgia budget director, to succeed Lance as OMB director is an important example of his belief that his Georgia associates are the best candidates for his national administration.

Tucker Case

In addition, some of his appointments have been criticized as political payoffs for early support in his presidential drive. A case often cited to back up that allegation was that of Donald Tucker, the speaker of the Florida House, who was nominated by Carter to be chairman of the Civil Aeronautics Board (CAB).

The CAB post is considered vital to air-travel-dependent Florida, and Tucker was an early Carter backer in the crucial 1976 Florida primary. Yet serious allegations about financial improprieties by Tucker had surfaced even before the nomination was announced. In the end, resistance to the nomination in the Commerce Committee forced Tucker's withdrawal, at some expense to the administration's claims to high ethical standards.

Despite the Tucker example, critics of the Carter performance on nominations also are critical of the Senate role in readily confirming most of those named. But Cardozo states that it is erroneous to suggest that presidential friends and political associates have been protected in the confirmation process.

"Our vulnerability is greater when the nominee is a friend of the president's, because it's bigger game for the press," he said. "The chase is harder. We all know that."

For that reason, Carodozo says that Carter personally scribbles notes instructing them to be particularly tough in examining the finances and potential conflicts of nominees close to the president, including his fellow Georgians.

Institutional Tensions

Overlaid on the personal and political partisanship of the appointment and confirmation process is the inherent institutional struggle between the two branches for patronage and policy control. *(Carter and Congress, p. 5)*

The point of the senatorial courtesy system is not only that members of a president's party have influence over appointments, but also that the Senate itself has wrested effective control over lower court and prosecutorial appointments from the president.

Historically, the Senate has not asserted such control over other nominations by the president, particularly those to his Cabinet. There, the sentiment expressed by Sen. Byrd that the president is entitled to "his own man" has been predominant.

Only eight men nominated to become Cabinet members have been rejected by Senate votes, although some others have not been nominated due to anticipated opposition. The last Cabinet-level rejection was the 1959 Eisenhower nomination of Lewis L. Strauss to be his Secretary of Commerce. *(Historical background, CQ Guide to Congress 2nd ed. p. 175)*

A slightly more aggressive Senate attitude has been taken to nominations more distant from a president's official working family. Nominations to the Supreme Court and to independent regulatory agencies have been considerably more likely to meet Senate opposition or even rejection. But the Senate's power over those nominations never has approached the control of the senatorial courtesy system over lower-level court appointments.

Policy Questions

There has even been a continuing debate over whether the "advice and consent" role of the Senate was intended to allow the Senate to affect policy, or whether it was intended only as a screen to weed out unqualified or corrupt appointments.

Particularly with regard to Cabinet nominees, many senators have felt that if an individual is shown to be honest and competent, then the president is entitled to name him without regard to policy beliefs.

A differing view holds that senators can and should inquire into the policy intentions and commitments of a nominee before confirming him to office. This view at present is maintained by a number of Senate committees, as reflected in their insistence that each major nominee testify under oath about his beliefs and plans, and in some cases, that he submit written statements on policy.

The most prominent example of such an approach to a Carter Cabinet member was the grilling received by Attorney General Bell in his confirmation hearings before Judiciary. Suspicions about Bell's civil rights record in particular, including his personal membership in some exclusionary clubs, led to days of questioning.

The result was that Bell was forced to pledge his resignation from such clubs, to commit himself to minority appointments to major Justice Department posts, and to take a number of actions once in office in the civil rights and civil liberties arena.

Common Cause and other critics of the Senate confirmation process contend that the eliciting of binding policy commitments from nominees ought to be the norm during confirmation.

Outlook

The lessons learned by many senators from the Lance case already are resulting in a perceptible shift toward a more stringent examination of presidential nominees.

Whether the trend becomes institutionalized in the form of a central and standardized confirmation process remains doubtful. What could emerge instead is a more limited set of improvements, such as a standard set of basic questions to be answered by a presidential nominee concerning his or her background and finances.

Cardozo says that the White House would be happy to cooperate in any such effort. Bob Thomson, who provides White House liaison with the Senate, adds that the White House "welcomes any Senate effort" to tighten the process.

Whatever the legislative outcome, both the White House and the Senate will continue to share the massive task of staffing the federal government. ∎

Senate Rejects Few Carter Appointments

Except for his efforts to fill vacancies on the Federal Election Commission (FEC), President Carter had little trouble getting his major nominees for federal office confirmed by the Senate in 1978.

Of 3,054 civilian nominations Carter sent to the Senate, 3,010 were confirmed. Four nominations were withdrawn and 40, mostly to relatively minor positions, failed to win confirmation. *(List of major 1978 confirmations, p. 79)*

FEC Fight

Two of the failed nominees, and one of the withdrawals, concerned the FEC — continuing Carter's problems with FEC nominees that began during his first year in office.

In 1977, Carter had named former congressional aides Samuel D. Zagoria and John W. McGarry to the bipartisan election agency, but political problems prevented the Senate from confirming either man. The controversies continued into 1978.

Zagoria, Friedersdorf. Carter resubmitted the Zagoria and McGarry nominations in early 1978, but the uproar continued. Concerning the Zagoria nomination, Republican congressional leaders Rep. John J. Rhodes of Arizona and Sen. Howard H. Baker Jr. of Tennessee reiterated that Carter broke his pledge that he would follow their recommendations in filling an open GOP seat on the FEC. Zagoria, a former aide to Sen. Clifford P. Case, R-N.J., had not been recommended by Baker or Rhodes. Carter eventually withdrew Zagoria's name on Aug. 15. (Zagoria won confirmation later for a slot on the Consumer Product Safety Commission.)

To fill the GOP slot, Carter on Oct. 10 nominated former White House legislative liaison Max L. Friedersdorf, who had been recommended by GOP congressional leaders. The Senate Rules Committee did not act on Friedersdorf's nomination before the 95th Congress adjourned.

McGarry. The Rules Committee approved McGarry's nomination by a 7-2 vote on Aug. 25, even though committee hearings had exposed discrepancies between the financial disclosure statements McGarry filed with the clerk of the House and his income tax returns.

McGarry, then special counsel for the House Administration Committee, also drew GOP fire for his close ties to House Speaker Thomas P. O'Neill Jr., D-Mass. A filibuster threat by the GOP leadership prevented the Senate from considering the McGarry nomination in the final days of the session.

Carter renewed the controversy by naming McGarry to a recess appointment to the FEC Oct. 25. Neil O. Staebler, a Democrat McGarry was supposed to replace, angrily said he would challenge the recess appontment in court. Staebler, whose term expired April 30, 1977, said he was entitled to serve until his successor was sworn in.

Staebler said that the Federal Election Campaign Act did not provide for a recess appointment to the commission.

The Constitution, however, empowered the president to make recess appointments.

Staebler also said such an appointment could be damaging to the commission. "It affects the conditions under which the president and Congress are elected," he told an Oct. 26 news conference. "If you get a person on the commission who is beholden, it could influence decisions one way or another."

White House press secretary Jody Powell said the Justice Department had cleared the recess appointment of McGarry as valid.

Besides a renewed fight over McGarry's nomination in 1979, Carter faced other FEC problems: The terms of two commissioners, Chairman Vernon W. Thomson, R, and Thomas E. Harris, D, were to expire April 30, 1979.

Civiletti: Justice Department

By a 72-22 vote, the Senate confirmed the nomination of Assistant Attorney General Benjamin A. Civiletti to be deputy attorney general. The vote came May 9 after the Senate Judiciary Committee reported the nomination on April 19.

Civiletti replaced former Pittsburgh Mayor Peter Flaherty in the Justice Department's second highest post. Flaherty resigned to make an unsuccessful race for the Pennsylvania governorship.

Judiciary Committee hearings on Civiletti quickly turned into a discussion of the so-called "Marston affair." Committtee Republicans demanded to know the role of Civiletti and of Attorney General Griffin B. Bell in the firing of David Marston, U.S. attorney for the eastern district of Pennsylvania (Philadelphia).

Marston, a Republican, had been told to leave by Carter, upon Bell's recommendation. Carter acted following a Nov. 4, 1977, telephone call from Rep. Joshua M. Eilberg, D-Pa. Marston charged that Carter and Bell had succumbed to political pressure in an effort to stop an investigation into criminal charges against Eilberg and Rep. Daniel J. Flood, D-Pa.

Judiciary Republicans quizzed Civiletti about the sequence of events.

Though the controversy continued on the Senate floor, Civiletti eventually won Senate confirmation over GOP protests. Marston tried to capitalize on the publicity he received by running for the Republican gubernatorial nomination in Pennsylvania, but finished third in a field of six.

To replace Marston, Carter nominated Peter F. Vaira, a Democrat. He was confirmed easily and continued the Marston investigations on Eilberg and Flood — producing indictments in the fall of 1978 against both men.

Morris: LEAA

Opposition led by the National Rifle Association (NRA) helped block action by the Senate Judiciary Committee on the nomination of law professor Norval Morris to head the Justice Department's Law Enforcement Assistance Administration (LEAA).

Judgeships

The prestige of a federal judgeship is high, and appointment to the judiciary is considered by most attorneys and politicians to be the apex of a legal and public career.

Federal judgeships are lifetime appointments and pay $57,500 in the circuit court and $54,500 in the district court annually. There is no mandatory retirement age, but judges may retire at full salary at age 65 after 15 years or at 70 after 10 years on the bench.

The following list gives the number of confirmed federal circuit and district court judges appointed by President Carter in 1977-78 and by his seven immediate predecessors.

	Democrats	Republicans
Roosevelt	188	6
Truman	116	9
Eisenhower	9	165
Kennedy[1]	111	11
Johnson	159	9
Nixon[2]	15	198
Ford	12	52
Carter (1977)	26	0
Carter (1978)[3]	26	2

1 One New York liberal also was appointed.

2 No party affiliation was available for one judge from Puerto Rico, and one independent was chosen.

3 No party affiliation was available for six judges, and one independent was chosen. The 1978 figures do not include a Democrat who failed to win Senate confirmation to a district court judgeship.

Morris, 54, dean of the University of Chicago law school since 1975, had criticized the LEAA for its overemphasis on "hardware." But the NRA objected to his stands favoring gun control.

The argument over Morris also delayed committee consideration of two proposed deputy LEAA administrators. None of the three men was given a recess appointment.

Gartner: Commodities Commission

One Carter nominee ran into trouble after his Senate confirmation. David G. Gartner, a former aide to Minnesota Democratic Sens. Hubert and Muriel Humphrey, was confirmed to a seat on the Commodity Futures Trading Commission (CFTC) on May 17.

Gartner had been recommended for the post by a fellow Minnesotan, Vice President Walter F. Mondale. During his confirmation hearings, however, some other Minnesota ties got him in trouble. Gartner voluntarily told the Senate Agriculture Committee that over a period of four years, Minneapolis grain magnate Dwayne Andreas had given $72,000 worth of stock to Gartner's four children. The stock was in Archer Davis Midland Inc., a major grain dealer regulated by the CFTC and chaired by Andreas, a longtime Humphrey financial supporter.

During questioning by the panel, Gartner agreed to sell the stock and to disqualify himself from any CFTC decisions involving Andreas' firm. The committee unanimously reported his nomination May 17 and the Senate confirmed it by voice vote the same day.

Criticism of the stockholdings and questions of conflict-of-interest rose when Gartner took his CFTC seat. The Agriculture Committee called him back for more hearings, and Carter reversed course and decided Gartner had to go. On June 26, he and Mondale took the unusual step of publicly asking Gartner to resign his CFTC seat. Gartner, pointing out that he had sold the stock and put the proceeds in trust for the children, refused to leave. He remained a CFTC member.

Judgeships

Nominations for judgeships caused three controversies in the Senate in 1977-78.

McKay. The first occurred in November 1977, after the judicial nominating commission for the 10th Circuit Court of Appeals presented five names to President Carter. Among them was that of Monroe G. McKay of Provo, Utah, a law professor at Brigham Young University, and brother of Rep. Gunn McKay, D-Utah.

Carter's nomination of McKay angered Sen. Orrin G. Hatch, R-Utah, who got the Senate Judiciary Committee to approve the nomination but not report it, pending further hearings. After the hearings were held, the panel reported McKay's name and the Senate confirmed it Nov. 29, 1977.

O'Brien. Longtime Iowa Democratic official Donald E. O'Brien was confirmed to an Iowa district judgeship on Oct. 4, but not before drawing fire from the American Bar Association (ABA).

The ABA opposed O'Brien's nomination on both political and judicial grounds. Its statement referred to incidents in his service as Woodbury County (Iowa) attorney from 1955-58. Politically, the ABA felt he was too partisan: O'Brien, once a member of the Democratic National Committee, was a twice-beaten Democratic congressional nominee, U.S. attorney for the northern district of Iowa from 1961-67, and a special counsel to the House Small Business Committee at the request of Chairman Neal Smith, D-Iowa, in 1978.

However, the Iowa Bar Association, represented by former Rep. Wiley T. Mayne, R-Iowa (1967-75), backed O'Brien, according to an aide to Sen. John C. Culver, D-Iowa. The aide added that the Iowa Judicial Selection Commission — a panel established by the two Iowa senators at President Carter's request to provide for merit selection of judges — had recommended O'Brien as well.

Following a six-hour hearing in which the Senate Judiciary Committee grilled the ABA on its opposition, the panel voted to report O'Brien's name. After putting a temporary "hold" on the nomination pending further evidence, Sen. Dennis DeConcini, D-Ariz., withdrew his objections. The Senate then approved O'Brien by voice vote Oct. 4.

Clauss. However, Carin Ann Clauss, nominated for a vacant district judgeship in the District of Columbia, was not so lucky. Numerous objections caused the Judiciary Committee to refuse to report her name before Congress adjourned.

Prior to the Sept. 20 nomination, the ABA attempted to block the consideration of Clauss, who was solicitor of the Labor Department. The ABA charged that Clauss' admitted lack of trial experience disqualified her for the job. The ABA screening panel for judicial nominees unanimously rejected her name when it was first offered in the spring of 1978.

(Continued on p. 78)

Membership of Federal Regulatory Agencies, 1978

Civil Aeronautics Board

(Five members appointed for six-year terms; not more than three members from one political party; agency due to expire Jan. 1, 1985)

Member	Party	Term Expires	Nominated	Confirmed by Senate
Vacancy				
Gloria Schaffer*	D	12/31/84	7/13/78	9/13/78
Marvin S. Cohen (C)	D	12/31/79	9/12/78	10/10/78
Richard J. O'Melia	R	12/31/80	5/16/74	9/19/74
Elizabeth E. Bailey*	R	12/31/83	7/8/77	7/28/77

Commodity Futures Trading Commission

(Five members appointed for five-year terms; not more than three members from one political party.)

Vacancy (C)				
Gary L. Seevers (VC)	I	4/15/79	3/19/75	4/10/75
Read P. Dunn Jr.‡	D	4/15/78	3/18/75	4/10/75
Robert L. Martin	R	6/19/81	6/3/76	6/17/76
David G. Gartner*	D	5/19/83	5/10/78	5/17/78

Consumer Product Safety Commission

(Five members appointed for seven-year terms; not more than three members from one political party.)

Susan B. King (C)*	D	10/26/84	1/20/78	2/28/78
Barbara H. Franklin	R	10/26/79	4/9/73	5/10/73
R. David Pittle**	D	10/26/82	1/20/78	2/1/78
Edith B. Sloan*	D	10/26/83	1/20/78	2/28/78
Samuel D. Zagoria*	R	10/26/85	9/29/78	10/10/78

Federal Communications Commission

(Seven members appointed for seven-year terms; not more than four members from one political party.)

Charles D. Ferris (C)*	D	6/30/84	9/12/77	10/10/77
Tyrone Brown*	D	6/30/79	10/17/77	11/9/77
James H. Quello	D	6/30/80	1/22/74	4/22/74
Robert E. Lee	R	6/30/81	5/17/74	6/27/74
Abbott Washburn	R	6/30/82	6/18/75	9/26/75
Joseph R. Fogarty	D	6/30/83	6/21/76	9/8/76
Vacancy				

Federal Election Commission

(Six members appointed for six-year terms; not more than three members from one political party)

William L. Springer†	R	4/30/77	5/17/76	5/21/76
Neil Staebler†	D	4/30/77	5/17/76	5/18/76
Thomas E. Harris	D	4/30/79	5/17/76	5/18/76
Vernon W. Thomson (C)	R	4/30/79	5/17/76	5/18/76
Joan D. Aikens	R	4/30/81	5/17/76	5/18/76
Robert O. Tiernan	D	4/30/81	5/17/76	5/18/76

† Members sitting on commission pending Senate confirmation of their replacements. John W. McGarry, D, was given a recess appointment by President Carter for the Staebler seat, but Staebler questioned the legality of the move.

Federal Energy Regulatory Commission

(Five members appointed to staggered four-year terms; not more than three members from one party.)

	Party	Term Expires	Nominated	Confirmed by Senate
Charles B. Curtis (C)*	I	6/22/80	9/30/77	10/20/77
Don S. Smith**	D	6/22/79	9/30/77	10/20/77
George R. Hall*	D	6/22/80	9/13/77	10/20/77
Georgiana R. Sheldon*	R	6/22/80	9/13/77	10/20/77
Matthew Holden Jr.*	D	6/22/81	9/26/77	10/20/77

Federal Reserve System Governors

(Seven members appointed for 14-year terms; no statutory limitation on political party membership.)

G. William Miller (C)*	D	1/31/92	1/25/78	3/3/78
Philip E. Caldwell	D	1/31/80	9/26/74	10/9/74
Nancy H. Teeters*	D	1/31/84	8/28/78	9/15/78
J. Charles Partee	I	1/31/86	12/8/75	12/19/75
Henry C. Wallich	R	1/31/88	1/11/74	2/8/74
Two vacancies				

Federal Trade Commission

(Five members appointed for seven-year terms; not more than three members from one party.)

Michael J. Pertschuk (C)*	D	9/25/84	3/25/77	4/6/77
Mary E. Hanford-Dole	I	9/25/80	9/5/73	11/20/73
Paul Rand Dixon	D	9/25/81	9/5/74	9/26/74
Robert Pitofsky*	D	9/25/82	5/25/78	6/28/78
David A. Clanton	R	9/25/83	7/20/76	7/29/76

Interstate Commerce Commission

(Eleven members appointed for seven-year terms; not more than six members from one political party; President Carter and Chairman O'Neal decided to cut the commission's size by not filling vacancies.)

Virginia Mae Brown	D	12/31/77	4/14/71	6/30/71
Betty Jo Christian	D	12/31/79	12/8/75	3/18/76
A. Daniel O'Neal Jr. (C)	D	12/31/79	3/6/73	4/6/73
George M. Stafford	R	12/31/80	1/15/74	2/27/74
Charles L. Clapp	R	12/31/80	1/22/74	2/27/74
Robert C. Gresham	R	12/31/81	6/3/74	9/19/74
Five vacancies				

Nuclear Regulatory Commission

(Five members appointed for five-year terms; not more than three members from one political party.)

Joseph M. Hendrie (C)*	R	6/30/81	6/29/77	8/3/77
Victor Gilinsky	D	6/30/79	12/12/74	12/19/74
Richard T. Kennedy	R	6/30/80	12/12/74	12/19/74
Peter A. Bradford*	D	6/30/82	6/12/77	8/3/77
James F. Ahearne*	—	6/30/83	5/18/78	7/21/78

Securities and Exchange Commission

(Five members appointed for five-year terms; not more than three members from one political party.)

Harold M. Williams (C)*	D	6/5/82	3/30/77	4/7/77
John R. Evans‡	R	6/5/78	5/29/73	6/1/73
Philip A. Loomis Jr.	R	6/5/79	7/15/74	8/8/74
Irving M. Pollack	D	6/5/80	7/1/75	8/1/75
Roberta S. Karmel*	D	6/5/81	8/1/77	9/22/77

* Carter appointment.
** Reappointed by Carter; first appointed by a previous administration.
‡ Continuing to serve pending filling of vacancy.

The ABA decision threw the nomination into limbo as Clauss attempted to gain further trial experience. The administration pledged to stand by her nomination, citing President Carter's desire to name more women and minority representatives to federal judgeships.

The administration, according to one official, also was determined to stand by its nominees and not let the ABA have a veto over them. Citing a judicial screening commission finding that "she is abundantly qualified despite the lack of trial experience," the official added that Carter would stand by the Clauss nomination "unless the ABA panel comes up with convincing evidence otherwise."

Clauss' trial experience during the summer of 1978 later caused the ABA panel to reverse its rejection of her, according to news reports — but that same trial experience cast another cloud over her nomination.

In a September 1978 opinion, the U.S. Court of Appeals for the Third Circuit criticized Clauss' office for its handling of an occupational safety case. The three-judge panel first criticized Labor Department lawyers — lawyers under Clauss' supervision — for filing a brief in August that was due in late April. The judges then added, "we register our most vigorous disapproval of the contumacious conduct of counsel in this case." They questioned the "competence of [government] counsel appearing in federal courts." The strong opinion damaged one of Clauss' main arguments for the nomination, namely that she ran an efficient and effective staff in the solicitor's office.

Energy Department Nominations

Two nomination fights from 1977 over Energy Department posts carried over into 1978. Both ended in confirmation of the controversial officials.

Coleman. Following the defeat of a motion to recommit his name to the Energy Committee, the Senate by voice vote May 9 approved the nomination of Lynn R. Coleman to be general counsel of the department.

Coleman had been under fire for his close ties to the energy industry. He had been a lawyer in the Washington office of Vinson and Elkins, a Texas law firm that included former Treasury Secretary and Texas Gov. John B. Connally among its partners and that represented many of the largest energy companies. Citing possible conflicts of interest, Sen. Howard M. Metzenbaum, D-Ohio, moved to kill Coleman's nomination by sending it back to committee. His motion was defeated 20-75.

Thorne. The controversy surrounding the nomination of Robert D. Thorne to be assistant secretary for energy technology ended much more quietly.

The Senate confirmed his nomination by voice vote on May 4.

Thorne's nomination had run into trouble in 1977 over his role in an anti-nuclear power referendum in California in 1976. Environmentalists charged that he was too pro-nuclear power to be put into the technology post.

They claimed that he used his position as head of the Energy Research and Development Administration's San Francisco office to put out pro-nuclear and anti-referendum material.

Mendelsohn Withdrawn

Following allegations of fiscal irregularities in an unsuccessful political campaign, President Carter on Nov. 14, 1977, withdrew the nomination of San Francisco supervisor Robert Mendelsohn as assistant interior secretary for management, program and budget.

After Mendelsohn was cleared of charges brought against him by the California Fair Political Practices Commission, Carter appointed him on June 5 to a post as assistant to Interior Secretary Cecil D. Andrus. Mendelsohn's new post did not require Senate confirmation.

Stewart: SBA

By an 88-11 vote, the Senate July 18 confirmed the nomination of Milton D. Stewart as chief counsel for advocacy in the Small Business Administration.

Proponents of the nomination pointed to Stewart's long record of concern for small businesses, especially minority small businesses. They also stressed the wide range of his support and his familiarity with the needs of the SBA's constituents.

Opponents, led by Sen. Lowell P. Weicker Jr., R-Conn., conceded these points about Stewart, but they questioned his role in the 1974 collapse of one small company, which was then taken over by another firm in which Stewart, Weicker said, had an interest.

Cottine: OSHA

By a 56-33 vote, the Senate on April 27 confirmed Carter's nomination of Bertram R. Cottine to be a member of the Occupational Safety and Health Review Commission.

Opposition to Cottine was led by Senate conservatives who had declared war on the Occupational Safety and Health Administration (OSHA). Pointing to Cottine's position as policy assistant in the office of Eula T. Bingham, assistant labor secretary for occupational safety, they claimed Cottine would not be objective in his decisions as a commission member.

Turner: Public Broadcasting

On Oct. 19, 1977, Carter nominated Irby Turner Jr. of Belzoni, Miss., to a seat on the board of directors of the Corporation for Public Broadcasting (CBP). But the Senate refused to act on his nomination before the end of the 1977 session and, unlike other such nominees, his name was not resubmitted in 1978.

Turner's nomination drew fire from national civil rights groups. They charged that during his service on the Mississippi Authority for Educational Television he had been insensitive to the need for minority-oriented programming on the state's public television stations.

Four 1978 Carter nominees for the CPB board were not acted upon by the Commerce Committee before adjournment: Geoffrey Cowan, Paul S. Friedlander, Kathleen Nolan and Howard A. White.

Sayre: Brazil

By a vote of 62-27, the Senate on April 27 tabled a motion to recommit the nomination of career diplomat Robert M. Sayre as ambassador to Brazil. The nomination was then confirmed by voice vote. The Sayre nomination was the only ambassadorial nomination to draw Senate fire in 1978.

The controversy around Sayre centered on his role in a 1972 incident in Panama. Sayre, who was U.S. ambassador at the time, received information that American drug enforcement agents were preparing to arrest Panamanian official Moises Torrijos on drug-smuggling charges when his plane landed in the Canal Zone. An arrest warrant had been issued in New York for Torrijos in connection with a smuggling ring.

Torrijos, the brother of Gen. Omar Torrijos, ruler of Panama, was then Panama's ambassador to Spain. Moises Torrijos' activities were questioned by senators opposed to the Panama Canal treaties earlier in 1978. They asked how a treaty could be concluded with a ruler whose brother was engaged in smuggling drugs.

Many of the senators who opposed the treaties opposed the Sayre nomination. They claimed that Sayre obstructed execution of the warrant by informing Gen. Torrijos of the fact that the United States knew his brother's destination. Torrijos informed his brother, the opponents added, who changed his landing place to one outside American jurisdiction, thus avoiding arrest.

Sayre told the Foreign Relations Committee that he had been informed of the plans regarding Moises Torrijos by the CIA Panama station chief. When he sought advice from his State Department superiors, they told him to communicate with Gen. Torrijos, as part of the U.S. campaign to soothe then-ruffled Panamanian feelings over the slow pace of negotiations on the treaties.

1978 Confirmations

Listed below are 163 persons named to major federal posts and confirmed by the Senate in 1978. Several major confirmations that occurred after the 1977 CQ Almanac went to press also are included. Information is given in the following order: name of office, salary, appointee, voting residence, last occupation before appointment, previous political or policy posts if any, date and place of birth, party affiliation (where available), confirmation date.

Also included are names of one person whose nomination was withdrawn (and later submitted for another agency), six who were not confirmed, one who was not confirmed but given a recess appointment by Carter, one who had been given a recess appointment prior to submission of his name for confirmation, and one whose post did not need confirmation.

Ambassadorial confirmations are listed only if the appointment was of more than routine interest.

EXECUTIVE OFFICE OF THE PRESIDENT

Central Intelligence Agency

Deputy director, $52,500 —**Frank Charles Carlucci III**; Bear Creek, Pa.; ambassador to Portugal (1974-78); under secretary of HEW (1972-74), associate and then deputy director, Office of Management and Budget (1971-72); director, Office of Economic Opportunity (1969-71); Oct. 18, 1930, in Scranton, Pa.; Feb. 9.

Council on Environmental Quality

Member, $50,000 — **Jane Hurt Yarn**; Atlanta, Ga.; chair, Charles A. Lindbergh Fund (1977-78); chair, Georgia Coastal Islands Committee (1969-70); Oct. 15, 1924, in Greenville, S.C.; Dem.; Aug. 18.

Office of Management and Budget

Director, $57,500 — **James T. McIntyre Jr.**; Alpharetta, Ga.; deputy director, OMB (1977-78); deputy Georgia revenue commissioner (1970-72); Dec. 17, 1940, in Vidalia, Ga.; Dem.; March 21.

Deputy director, $52,500 — **John Patrick White**; McLean, Va.; assistant secretary of defense for manpower and reserve affairs (1977-78); Feb. 27, 1938, in Syracuse, N.Y.; nominated Oct. 7; nomination not reported by Senate Governmental Affairs Committee before adjournment; recess appointment announced by Carter Nov. 1.

CABINET DEPARTMENTS

Agriculture Department

Assistant secretary for marketing and services and member of the board of directors of the Commodity Credit Corporation, $50,000 — **P. R. "Bobby" Smith**; Winder, Ga.; special assistant to the agriculture secretary (1977-78); national director, "Farmers for Carter" (1976); Feb. 25, 1925, in Winder; Dem.; Feb. 24 (assistant secretary) March 20 (CCC post).

Administrator, Rural Electrification Administration (terms expiring Oct. 30, 1988), $47,500 — **Robert W. Ferguson**; Reston, Va.; deputy REA administrator (1978); Jan. 28, 1925, in Minot, N.D.; Dem.; Oct. 15.

Commerce Department

Assistant secretary for congressional liaison, $50,000 — **Andrew E. Manatos**; Bethesda, Md.; counselor to the secretary of commerce for congressional liaison (1977); associate staff director, Senate District of Columbia Committee and legislative assistant to Sen. Thomas F. Eagleton, D-Mo. (1973-76); Dec. 7, 1944, in Washington, D.C.; Dem.; Dec. 15, 1977.

Assistant secretary for communications and information, $50,000 — **Henry Geller**; Alexandria, Va.; consultant to the Commerce Department (1977-78); special assistant to the chairman, Federal Communications Commission (FCC) (1970-73); FCC general counsel (1964-70); FCC deputy general counsel (1962-64); FCC associate general counsel (1961); March 14, 1924, in Springfield, Mass.; Dem.; June 28.

National Oceanographic and Atmospheric Administration

Deputy administrator, $50,000 — **James P. Walsh**; Washington, D.C.; general counsel, Senate Commerce Committee (1977-78); staff counsel, Commerce Committee (1972-77); assistant attorney general, Washington state (1971-72); Dec. 28, 1944, in North Bend, Ore.; Dem.; March 7.

Associate administrator, $47,500 — **George S. Benton**; Baltimore, Md.; assistant administrator for oceanic and atmospheric services, NOAA (1977-78); Sept. 24, 1917, in Oak Park, Ill.; June 28.

National Bureau of Standards

Director, $47,500 — **Ernest Ambler**; Bethesda, Md.; acting director, NBS (1975-78) and deputy director (1973-78); Nov. 20, 1923, in Yorkshire, England; Dem.; Feb. 1.

Patent and Trademark Office

Commissioner, $47,500 — **Donald Witte Banner**; Aurora, Ill.; General patent counsel, Borg-Warner Corp. (1964-78); Feb. 23, 1924, in Chicago, Ill.; Independent; May 24.

Defense Department

Under secretary for policy, $52,500 — **Stanley R. Resor**; New Canaan, Conn.; United States representative to the Mutual and Balanced Force Reduction negotiations (1973-78), secretary of the Army (1965-71), under secretary of the Army (1965); Dec. 5, 1917, in New York City; Rep.; Aug. 7.

Chairman, Defense Military Liaison Committee to the Department of Energy, $47,500 — **James P. Wade Jr.**; Reston, Va.; assistant to the defense secretary for atomic energy (1978 — concurrent post); Dec. 26, 1930, in Richmond Heights, Mo.; Aug. 7.

Air Force

Assistant secretary for financial management, $50,000 — **John Arnot Hewitt Jr.**; Princeton, N.J.; vice president for trust and fiduciary investment, Chase Manhattan Bank (1974-78); July 20, 1943, in Van Nuys, Calif.; Dem.; Feb. 24.

Joint Chiefs of Staff

Chairman (term expiring June 30, 1980), $47,500 — Gen. **David C. Jones**; Minot, N.D.; chief of staff, Air Force (1974-78); July 9, 1921, in Aberdeen, S.D.; May 24.

Air Force chief of staff (four-year term), $47,500 — Gen. **Lew Allen Jr.**; Gainesville, Texas; vice chief of staff, Air Force (1978); director, National Security Agency (1973-77); Sept. 30, 1925, in Miami, Fla.; May 24.

Chief of naval operations (four-year term), $47,500 — Adm. **Thomas B. Hayward**; Glendale, Calif.; commander-in-chief, U.S. Pacific Fleet (1976-78); May 3, 1924, in Glendale; May 24.

Department of Energy

Assistant secretary for conservation and solar applications, $50,000 — **Omi G. Walden**; Atlanta, Ga.; director, Georgia Office of Energy Resources (1976-78); policy adviser and federal-state relations coordinator for energy and environmental issues, office of the governor of Georgia (1973-76); Dec. 25, 1945 in Alma, Ga.; Dem.; July 26.

Assistant secretary for defense programs, $50,000 — **Duane C. Sewell**; Livermore, Calif.; Lawrence Livermore Laboratory, University of California since 1956, deputy director (1973-78); Aug. 15, 1918, in Oakland, Calif.; Dem.; Aug. 7.

Director of energy research (assistant secretary level), $50,000 — **John M. Deutch**; Lexington, Mass.; chairman, department of chemistry, Massachusetts Institute of Technology (1976-77); July 27, 1938, in Brussels, Belgium; Dec. 6, 1977.

Assistant secretary for resource applications, $50,000 — **George S. McIsaac**; Washington, D.C.; principal and director, McKinsey and Co. (consulting firm) (1962-78); July 25, 1930 in Auburn, N.Y.; Dem.; Feb. 10.

Assistant secretary for energy technology, $50,000 — **Robert D. Thorne**; Walnut Creek, Calif.; manager, San Francisco operations office, Energy Research and Development Administration (ERDA) (1978); acting assistant administrator for nuclear programs, ERDA (1977); July 22, 1938, in Laramie, Wyo.; Independent; May 4.

Assistant secretary for environment, $50,000 — **Ruth C. Clusen**; Green Bay, Wis.; president, League of Women Voters of U.S. (1974-78); member, U.S. delegation to U.S.-U.S.S.R. joint committee on environmental protection (1974); June 11, 1922, in Bruce, Wis.; Dem.; Aug. 25.

General counsel, $50,000 — **Lynn R. Coleman**; Washington, D.C.; lawyer, Vinson and Elkins (Texas law firm) (1965-78); campaign director, Barefoot Sanders for Senate (Texas Democratic primary candidate) (1972); Aug. 17, 1939, in Vernon, Texas; Dem.; May 9.

Inspector general, $50,000 — **John K. Mansfield**; Farmington, Conn.; special assistant to the assistant secretary of state for oceans and international environmental and scientific affairs (1974-78); inspector general of foreign assistance, State Department (1962-69); Oct. 8, 1921, in Chicago, Ill.; Dem.; May 3.

Deputy inspector general, $47,500 — **Thomas S. Williamson Jr.**; Washington, D.C.; associate with law firm of Covington and Burling (1974-78); July 14, 1946, in Plainfield, N.J.; Oct. 10.

Administrator, Energy Information Administration (assistant secretary level), $50,000 — **Lincoln E. Moses**; Stanford, Calif.; professor of statistics, Stanford University (1959-77); Dec. 21, 1921, in Kansas City, Mo.; Dem.; Dec. 15, 1977.

Department of Health, Education and Welfare

Administration on Aging

Commissioner, $47,500 — **Robert C. Benedict**; Mechanicsburg, Pa.; commissioner, Office of the Aging, Pennsylvania Department of Public Welfare (1972-78); Nov. 29, 1940, in Randolph, Vt.; Dem.; Feb. 10.

Alcohol, Drug Abuse and Mental Health Administration

Administrator, $50,000 — **Gerald L. Klerman**; Chestnut Hill, Mass.; professor of psychiatry, Harvard Medical School and director, Stanley Cobb Laboratories, Massachusetts General Hospital (1976-77); Dec. 29, 1928, in New York City; Dem.; Oct. 29, 1977.

Social Security Administration

Commissioner, $50,000 — **Stanford G. Ross**; Washington, D.C.; partner in D.C. law firm of Caplin and Drysdale (1969-78); Transportation Department general counsel (1968-69), White House staff assistant (1967-68), Treasury Department assistant counsel (1963-67); Oct. 9, 1931, in St. Louis, Mo.; Dem.; Sept. 27.

Institute of Museum Services

Director, $47,500 — **Leila I. Kimche**; Bethesda, Md.; executive director, Association of Science Technology Centers (1974-77); June 21, 1934, in New York City; Dec. 15, 1977.

Department of Housing and Urban Development

Federal Insurance Administration

Administrator, $50,000 — **Gloria Cusumano Jimenez**; Durham, N.C.; deputy commissioner and general counsel, North Carolina Department of Insurance (1975-78), director of housing and urban programs, N.C. Department of Local Affairs (1968-70); district aide to Rep. Richard L. Ottinger, D-N.Y. (1965-66); July 1, 1932, in New York City; Dem.; March 9.

Department of Interior

Director, Office of Surface Mining, $50,000 — **Walter N. Heine**; Newville, Pa.; associate deputy secretary for mines and land protection, Pennsylvania Department of Environmental Resources (1971-77); Feb. 21, 1934, in New York City; Rep.; Dec. 6, 1977.

Director, Bureau of Mines, $47,500 — **Roger A. Markle**; Salt Lake City, Utah; president, western division, Valley Camp Coal Co. (1974-78); Dec. 12, 1933, in Sidney, Mont.; Aug. 25.

Director, Bureau of Land Management, $47,500 — **Frank Gregg**; Hingham, Mass.; chairman, New England River Basins Commission (1967-78); staff assistant to the Interior secretary (1961-63); Dec. 12, 1925, in Denver, Colo.; Aug. 25.

United States Geological Survey

Director, $47,500 — **Harry William Menard**; La Jolla, Calif.; professor of geology, Scripps Institution of Oceanography (1955-78); Dec. 10, 1920, in Fresno, Calif.; March 23.

Department of Justice

Deputy attorney general, $57,500 — **Benjamin Civiletti**; Baltimore, Md.; assistant attorney general, Criminal Division (1977-78); assistant U.S. attorney for Maryland (1962-64); July 17, 1935, in Peekskill, N.Y.; Dem.; May 9.

Director, Federal Bureau of Investigation (10-year term) $57,500 — **William H. Webster;** Ladue, Mo.; judge, eighth U.S. Circuit Court of Appeals (1973-78); U.S. district judge, eastern Missouri (1971-73), U.S. attorney, eastern Missouri (1960-61); March 6, 1924, in Webster Groves, Mo.; Rep.; Feb. 9.

Assistant attorney general, Criminal Division, $50,000 — **Philip Benjamin Heymann;** Belmont, Mass.; professor of law, Harvard University (1969-78); associate Watergate special prosecutor (1973-75); Oct. 30, 1932, in Pittsburgh, Pa.; June 23.

Director, Community Relations Service, $50,000 — **Gilbert G. Pompa;** San Antonio, Texas; acting director, CRS (1977-78) and deputy director (1976-78); assistant district attorney, Bexar County (San Antonio) (1963-67) and assistant city attorney, San Antonio (1960-63); Oct. 1, 1931, in Devine, Texas; Dem.; May 26.

Law Enforcement Assistance Administration

Administrator, $52,500 — **Norval Morris;** Chicago, Ill.; dean of the University of Chicago law school (1975-); director of the UN Institute for Prevention of Crime and the Treatment of Offenders (1962-64); Oct. 1, 1923, in Auckland, New Zealand; nomination submitted to Judiciary Committee Sept. 19, but not reported before adjournment of Congress.

(Two assistant administrators also were nominated by Carter, but the names were not formally sent to the Judiciary Committee due to the delay in the Morris nomination.)

U.S. Parole Commission

Commissioner for term expiring Nov. 21, 1983, $47,500 — **Audrey A. Kaslow;** Pacoima, Calif.; probation director (not department chief), Los Angeles County probation department (1950-77); Sept. 9, 1921, in Miami, Ariz.; Nov. 15, 1977.

Commissioner for term expiring Oct. 17, 1984, $47,500 — **Richard T. Mulcrone;** Shakopee, Minn.; chairman of Minnesota Corrections Board (1973-78); May 23, 1934, in St. Paul, Minn.; Sept. 30.

Commissioner for term expiring Aug. 31, 1984, $47,500 — **Oliver James Keller Jr.;** Gainesville, Fla.; visiting professor of criminal justice studies at the University of Florida (1975-78); secretary of the Florida Department of Health and Rehabilitative Services (1973-75); April 21, 1923, in Lancaster, Pa.; July 14.

Department of Labor

Assistant secretary for mine safety and health, $50,000 — **Robert B. Lagather;** Arlington, Va.; deputy solicitor for regional operations, Labor Department (1975-78); deputy assistant secretary for labor-management relations administration, Labor Department (1973-75); Dec. 8, 1925, in Chisholm, Minn.; Dem.; Feb. 10.

Department of State

Under secretary for political affairs, $52,500 — **David D. Newsom;** Berkeley, Calif.; ambassador to the Philippines (1977-78); ambassador to Indonesia (1974-77); assistant secretary of state for African affairs (1969-74); ambassador to Libya (1965-69); Jan. 6, 1918, in Richmond, Calif.; April 12.

Assistant secretary for Near Eastern and South Asian Affairs, $50,000 — **Harold H. Saunders;** Falls Church, Va.; director, Bureau of Intelligence and Research, State Department (1975-78); deputy assistant secretary for Near Eastern and South Asian affairs (1974-75); Dec. 27, 1930, in Philadelphia, Pa.; April 6.

Assistant secretary for Inter-American Affairs, $50,000 — **Viron P. Vaky;** Corpus Christi, Texas; ambassador to Venezuela (1976-78); ambassador to Colombia (1974-76); ambassador to Costa Rica (1972-74); acting assistant secretary for Inter-American Affairs (1968-69); Sept. 13, 1926, in Corpus Christi; July 12.

Assistant secretary for oceans and international environmental and scientific affairs, $50,000 — **Thomas R. Pickering;** Ruther-

ford, N.J.; ambassador to Jordan (1974-78); special assistant to the secretary of state and executive secretary, State Department (1974); Nov. 5, 1931, in Orange, N.J.; Sept. 22.

Assistant secretary for educational and cultural affairs, $50,000 — **Alice Stone Ilchman;** Wellesley, Mass.; dean of the college and professor of economics and education, Wellesley College (1973-78); April 18, 1935, in Cincinnati, Ohio; Dem.; March 17. *(Post abolished April 1; see "International Communication Agency.")*

Agency for International Development

Assistant administrator for private and development cooperation, $50,000 — ***Calvin H. Raullerson;*** Lubbock, Texas; executive director, International Center for Arid and Semi-arid Land Studies, Texas Tech University (1973-78); Feb. 18, 1920, in Utica, N.Y.; Aug. 11.

Assistant administrator for intragovernmental and international affairs, $50,000 — **Donald Bromheim;** Washington, D.C.; vice-president, The Futures Group (part of Dreyfus Corp.) (1978); deputy coordinator, Alliance for Progress (1960-67); April 28, 1932, in New York; Dem.; May 2.

Ambassadors

(Salaries listed are those attached to the posts involved, according to the State Department.)

Chief of protocol (ambassadorial rank), $50,000 — **Edith Huntington Jones "Kit" Dobelle;** Pittsfield, Mass.; educational consultant, Massachusetts Education Department, Bureau of Equal Education Opportunity (1972-73); (1977-78: wife of Evan S. Dobelle, whom she succeeded as chief of protocol, and with whom she shared the office's duties); Sept. 2, 1944, in Hamden, Conn.; Dem.; Sept. 13.

Ambassador-at-large for Middle East peace negotiations, $57,500 — **Alfred L. "Roy" Atherton Jr.;** Palm Beach Gardens, Fla.; assistant secretary for Near Eastern and South Asian affairs (1974-78); deputy assistant secretary for Near Eastern and South Asian affairs (1973-74); Nov. 22, 1921, in Pittsburgh, Pa.; April 6.

Brazil, $57,500 — **Robert M. Sayre;** Falls Church, Va.; inspector general of the Foreign Service (1975-78); ambassador to Panama (1969-74) and Uruguay (1968-69); Aug. 18, 1924, in Hillsboro, Ore.; April 27.

Denmark, $47,500 — **Warren Demian Manshel;** New York City; editor and publisher, *Foreign Policy* magazine (1970-78) and *The Public Interest* magazine (1965-78); Jan. 26, 1924, in Berlin, Germany; June 22.

Ethiopia, $50,000 — **Frederic L. Chapin;** North Brunswick Township, N.J.; U.S. consul general, Sao Paulo, Brazil (1972-78); deputy executive secretary, AID (1965-68); July 13, 1929, in New York City; June 23.

Greece, $52,500 — **Robert J. McCloskey;** Chevy Chase, Md.; ambassador to Holland (1976-78); assistant secretary of state for congressional relations (1975-76); Nov. 25, 1922, in Philadelphia, Pa.; unaffiliated; March 1.

Jordan, $50,000 — **Nicholas A. Veliotes;** McLean, Va.; deputy assistant secretary, Bureau of Near Eastern and South Asian Affairs (1977-78); Oct. 28, 1928 in Oakland, Calif.; Aug. 18.

Korea, $57,500 — **William H. Gleysteen Jr.;** Jenkintown, Pa.; deputy assistant secretary for East Asian and Pacific affairs (1977-78 and 1974-76); May 8, 1926, in Peking, China; June 23.

Lebanon, $52,500 — **John Gunther Dean;** New York state; ambassador to Denmark (1975-78) and to Cambodia (1974-75); Feb. 26, 1926, in Germany; Sept. 30.

Netherlands, $50,000 — **Geri M. Joseph;** Minneapolis, Minn.; contributing editor and columnist, *Minneapolis Tribune* (1972-78); June 19, 1923, in St. Paul, Minn.; July 14.

Panama, $50,000 — **Ambler Holmes Moss Jr.,** Alexandria, Va.; attorney, Coudert Brothers, Washington, D.C. (1978); deputy assistant secretary for congressional relations (1977-78), member, Panama Canal treaty negotiating team (1977); Sept. 1, 1937, in Baltimore, Md.; Sept. 22.

Poland, $52,500 — **William E. Schaufele;** Avon Lake, Ohio; ambassador to Greece (1977-78); assistant secretary for African affairs (1975-77); deputy U.S. representative to the U.N. Security Council (1973-75); Dec. 7, 1923, in Lakewood, Ohio; Feb. 1.

Singapore, $47,500 — **Richard F. Kneip;** Pierre, S.D.; governor of South Dakota (D 1971-78); S.D. state senator (D 1965-71); Jan. 7, 1933, in Tyler, Minn.; Dem.; May 24.

South Africa, $52,500 — **William B. Edmondson;** Peru, Neb.; deputy assistant secretary for African affairs (1976-78); Feb. 26, 1927 in St. Joseph, Mo.; May 2.

Spain, $57,500 — **Terence A. Todman;** St. Thomas, Virgin Islands; assistant secretary for Inter-American Affairs (1977-78); March 13, 1926, in St. Thomas; Independent; May 24.

Vatican City (president's personal representative; does not need Senate confirmation), unpaid — **Robert F. Wagner;** New York City; senior partner, Finley, Kumble, Wagner, Heine and Underberg (New York law firm) (1975-78); ambassador to Spain (1968-69); mayor of New York City (D 1954-65); Manhattan borough president (D 1949-53); New York City planning commission chairman (1948), city housing commissioner (1947), city tax commissioner (1946), New York state assemblyman (D 1938-41); Dem.; does not require confirmation.

Transportation Department

Assistant secretary for budget and programs, $50,000 — **Mortimer L. Downey III;** Reston, Va.; deputy under secretary of transportation (1977); supervisor of rail public services for New York Port Authority (1973-75; worked for Port Authority since 1953); Aug. 9, 1936, in Springfield, Mass.; Dem.; Nov. 22, 1977.

Administrator, Federal Highway Administration, $57,500 — **Karl Smith Bowers;** Estill, S.C.; deputy FHA administrator (1977-78); Member and chairman (1976-77), South Carolina Highway Commission (1974-77); Oct. 13, 1941, in Estill; Dem.; Aug. 18.

Treasury Department

Assistant secretary for tax policy, $50,000 — **Donald C. Lubick;** Chevy Chase, Md.; deputy assistant secretary and acting (since December 1977) assistant secretary for tax policy (1977-78); April 29, 1926, in Buffalo, N.Y.; June 23.

INDEPENDENT AGENCIES

Civil Aeronautics Board

Member for term expiring Dec. 31, 1979, $50,000 — **Marvin S. Cohen;** Tucson, Ariz.; partner in law firm of Bilby, Shoenhair, Warnock and Dolph (1963-78); special assistant to the solicitor, Interior Department (1961-63); Oct. 16, 1931, in Akron, Ohio; Dem.; Oct. 10.

Member for term expiring Dec. 31, 1984, and term expiring Dec. 31, 1978, $50,000 — **Gloria Schaffer;** Woodbridge, Conn.; Connecticut secretary of state (D 1971-78); unsuccessful Democratic nominee for U.S. Senate (1976); Connecticut state senator (D 1959-71); Oct. 3, 1930 in New London, Conn.; Dem.; Sept. 13.

Commodity Futures Trading Commission

Commissioner for term expiring May 21, 1983, $50,000 — **David Gay Gartner;** Arlington, Va.; administrative assistant to Sens. Hubert H. and Muriel B. Humphrey (1971-78 and 1961-69); Sept. 27, 1935, in Des Moines, Iowa; Dem.; May 17.

Consumer Product Safety Commission

Chairman and commissioner for term expiring Oct. 26, 1984, $52,500 — **Susan B. King;** Washington, D.C.; special assistant to the chairman, Federal Election Commission (1975-77); April 29, 1940, in Sioux City, Iowa; Dem.; Feb. 28.

Commissioner for terms expiring Oct. 26, 1978, and Oct. 26, 1985, $50,000 — **Samuel D. Zagoria;** College Park, Md.; director, labor-management relations service, U.S. Conference of Mayors (1970-78); Member, National Labor Relations Board (1965-69); administrative assistant to Sen. Clifford L. Case, R-N.J. (1955-65); April 9, 1919, in Somerville, N.J.; Rep.; Oct. 10.

Commissioner for term expiring Oct. 26, 1982, $50,000 — **R. David Pittle;** Rockville, Md.; CPSC commissioner since Oct. 10, 1973; Oct. 7, 1938, in Washington, D.C.; Dem.; Feb. 1.

Commissioner for term expiring Oct. 26, 1983, $50,000 — **Edith B. Sloan;** Washington, D.C.; director, Washington, D.C., office of consumer protection (1976-78); New York City; Dem.; Feb. 28.

Equal Employment Opportunity Commission

Commissioner for term expiring July 1, 1982, $50,000 — **J. Clay Smith Jr.;** Washington, D.C.; associate general counsel, Federal Communications Commission (1976-78); April 15, 1942, in Omaha, Neb.; Rep.; Oct. 10.

Commissioner for term expiring July 1, 1983, $50,000 — **Armando M. Rodriguez,** Whittier, Calif.; president, East Los Angeles College (1973-78); assistant commissioner for regional office coordination, Office of Education (HEW) (1971-73); Sept. 30, 1921, in Mexico; Dem.; Oct. 10.

Environmental Protection Agency

Assistant administrator for research and development, $50,000 — **Stephen John Gage;** Bethesda, Md.; deputy assistant EPA administrator for minerals and industry, Office of Research and Development (1975-78); Sept. 27, 1940, in Palisade, Neb.; Independent; March 14.

Export-Import Bank

First vice-president and vice-chairman, $50,000 — **H. K. Allen;** Temple, Texas; chairman, Temple National Bank (1953-78); July 24, 1926, in Dallas, Texas; Dem.; March 23.

Federal Communications Commission

Commissioner, $50,000 — **Anne P. Jones;** Arlington, Mass.; general counsel for the Federal Home Loan Bank Board (1977-78); Feb. 9, 1935, in Somerville, Mass.; Rep.; not confirmed before Congress adjourned; no recess appointment.

Federal Deposit Insurance Corporation

Member of the board of directors for term expiring March 15, 1984, $50,000 — **William M. Isaac;** Louisville, Ky.; vice-president and general counsel, Kentucky National Corp. (bank holding company) (1974-78); Dec. 21, 1943 in Bryan, Ohio; Rep.; March 14.

Federal Election Commission

Commissioner, $50,000 — **John W. McGarry;** Boston, Mass.; partner, McGarry and Rovner (Boston law firm) (1977-78); special counsel on elections to the House Administration Committee (1973-77); June 11, 1922, in Boston; Dem.; nomination blocked in Senate; given recess (interim) appointment to FEC by President Carter on Oct. 25, 1978.

Commissioner, $50,000 — **Max L. Friedersdorf;** Alexandria, Va.; staff director, Senate Republican Policy Committee (1977-); assistant to the president for legislative affairs (1975-77); deputy assistant to the president (1973-75) and special assistant to the president (1971-73); July 7, 1929, in Grammer, Ind.; Rep.; not confirmed before Congress adjourned.

Commissioner, $50,000 — **Samuel D. Zagoria;** College Park, Md.; director of labor-management relations service, U.S. Conference of Mayors (1970-78); Member, National Labor Relations Board (1965-69); administrative assistant to Sen. Clifford L. Case, R-N.J. (1955-65); April 9, 1919, in Somerville, N.J.; Rep.; Nomination submitted April 7 and withdrawn Aug. 12.

Federal Home Loan Bank Board

Member for term expiring June 30, 1978, and term expiring June 30, 1982, $50,000 — **Anita Miller**; Ridgewood, N.J.; senior program officer, Ford Foundation (1972-78); April 20, 1931, in New York City; Dem.; April 25.

Federal Maritime Commission

Commissioner for term expiring June 30, 1983, $50,000 — **Thomas F. Moakley**; Whitman, Mass.; FMC commissioner since 1977 (reappointment); director of the Port of Boston for the Massachusetts Port Authority (1975-77); Nov. 3, 1921, in Boston; Dem. (cousin of Rep. Joe Moakley, D-Mass.); Aug. 11.

Commissioner for term expiring June 30, 1981, $50,000 — **Leslie Lazar Kanuk**; Englewood Cliffs, N.J.; professor and chairman, department of marketing, Baruch College, City University of New York (1967-78); Aug. 9, 1929, in New York City; Dem.; April 19.

Federal Reserve System

Chairman of the board of governors for term expiring Feb. 1, 1992, $57,500 — **G. William Miller**; Providence, R.I.; chief executive officer (1968-78) and chairman of the board (1974-78), Textron Inc.; Democratic National Convention delegate (1968); March 9, 1925, in Sapulpa, Okla.; Dem.; March 3.

Member of the board of governors for term expiring Feb. 1, 1984 — **Nancy Hays Teeters**; Washington, D.C.; assistant staff director and chief economist, House Budget Committee (1975-78); July 29, 1930, in Marion, Ind.; Dem.; Sept. 15.

Federal Trade Commission

Commissioner for term expiring Sept. 26, 1982, $50,000 — **Robert Pitofsky**; Chevy Chase, Md.; professor of law, Georgetown University and counsel, Arnold and Porter (both 1973-78); director, Bureau of Consumer Protection, FTC (1970-73); Dec. 27, 1929, in Patterson, N.J.; Dem.; June 28.

International Communication Agency

(New agency, combining old United States Information Agency and the State Department's Bureau of Educational and Cultural Affairs)

Director, $57,500 — **John E. Reinhardt**; Bethesda, Md.; director, USIA (1977-78); assistant secretary of state for public affairs (1975-77); March 8, 1920, in Glade Spring, Va.; March 17.

Deputy director, $52,500 — **Charles W. Bray III**; Bethesda, Md.; deputy director, USIA (1977-78); deputy assistant secretary of state for inter-American affairs (1976-77), for public affairs (1974-76) and for press relations (1973-74); Oct. 24, 1933, in New York City; March 17.

Associate director for educational and cultural affairs, $50,000 — **Alice Stone Ilchman**; Wellesley, Mass.; assistant secretary of state for educational and cultural affairs (1978); April 18, 1935, in Cincinnati, Ohio; Dem.; March 17.

Associate director for management, $50,000 — **James David Isbister**; Potomac, Md.; vice-president, Orkand Corp. (1977-78); administrator, Alcohol, Drug Abuse and Mental Health Administration, HEW (1974-77); March 31, 1937, in Mt. Clemens, Mich.; non-partisan; Aug. 18.

Associate director for programs, $50,000 — **Harold Frederick Schneidman**; Hazelton, Pa.; director, USIA Information Center Service (1971-78); June 23, 1922 in Hazelton; Aug. 18.

Associate director for the Voice of America, $50,000 — **R. Peter Straus**; New York City; assistant director, USIA and director of the Voice of America (1977-78); chairman, New York State Democratic Campaign Committee (1964); Feb. 15, 1923, in New York City; Dem.; July 14.

Interstate Commerce Commission

Director, Office of Rail Public Counsel, $47,500 — **Howard A. Heffron**; Bethesda, Md.; self-employed attorney, Washington, D.C. (1969-77); chief counsel, Federal Highway Administration (1967-69); Oct. 3, 1927, in New York City; Dec. 15, 1977.

National Labor Relations Board

Member for term expiring Aug. 27, 1983, $50,000 — **Howard Jenkins Jr.**; Kensington, Md.; member, NLRB since 1963 (reappointment); June 16, 1915, in Denver, Colo.; Rep.; Sept. 15.

National Mediation Board

Member for term expiring July 1, 1981, $50,000 — **George S. Ives**; Bethesda, Md.; member of board since 1969; administrative assistant to his father, Sen. Irving Ives, R-N.Y. (1953-58); Jan. 10, 1922 in Brooklyn, N.Y.; Rep.; Oct. 10.

National Science Foundation

Assistant director, $47,500 — **James A. Krumhansl**; Trumansburg, N.Y.; professor of physics, Cornell University; Aug. 2, 1919, in Cleveland, Ohio; Dec. 6, 1977.

National Transportation Safety Board

Chairman, $52,500 — **James B. King**; Boston, Mass.; member of the board (since 1977, chairmanship required separate confirmation); White House personnel assistant (1977); vice-president in charge of marketing for the Massachusetts Bay Transportation Authority (1975-76), administrative assistant to Sen. Edward M. Kennedy, D-Mass. (1967-75); March 27, 1935, in Ludlow, Mass.; Dem.; March 20.

Vice-chairman and member for term expiring Dec. 31, 1980, $50,000 — **Elwood T. Driver**; Reston, Va.; acting associate administrator, National Highway Traffic Safety Administration; Aug. 20, 1921, in Trenton, N.J.; Dem.; March 20.

Member for term expiring Dec. 31, 1982, $50,000 — **Francis H. McAdams**; Washington, D.C.; NTSB member since 1967 (reappointment); Dec. 27, 1915, in Brooklyn, N.Y.; Dem.; Aug. 11.

Nuclear Regulatory Commission

Commissioner for terms expiring June 30, 1978, and June 30, 1983, $52,500 — **John Francis Ahearne**; McLean, Va.; deputy assistant energy secretary for power applications (1977-78); staffer, White House Energy Policy and Planning Office (1977); June 14, 1934, in New Britain, Conn.; July 21.

Occupational Safety and Health Review Commission

Commissioner for term expiring April 27, 1983, $50,000 — **Bertram Robert Cottine**; Alexandria, Va.; special assistant for policy in office of the assistant secretary of labor for occupational safety and health (1977-78); April 2, 1947, in Kingston, N.Y.; unaffiliated; April 27.

Overseas Private Investment Corporation

President, $52,500 — **James Bruce Llewellyn**; The Bronx, N.Y.; president, Fedco Foods Corp. (1969-78); Small Business Administration regional director in New York (1965-66); July 16, 1927, in New York City; Dem.; Oct. 11.

United States Postal Service
Postal Rate Commission

Commissioner for the term expiring Oct. 14, 1982, $52,500 — **Alvin Harry Gandal;** Chevy Chase, Md.; director of the office of contract analysis of the Postal Service since 1976; Feb. 8, 1932, in Cleveland, Ohio; nomination submitted to Senate Governmental Affairs Committee Jan. 26, but not reported; not given a recess appointment.

Railroad Retirement Board

Chairman and member for the term expiring Aug. 29, 1982, $52,500 — **William P. Adams;** Naperville, Ill.; vice-president of the Motion Picture Association of America (1977-78); counsel, House Commerce Committee (1974-76) and in the Office of the Legislative Counsel of the House of Representatives (1955-74); Aug. 2, 1926, in Danville, Ill.; Independent; Feb. 10.

Member for the term expiring Aug. 28, 1983, $50,000 — **Earl Oliver;** Chicago, Ill.; member of the board since 1977 (reappointment); Feb. 25, 1917, in Monticello, Ky.; Dem.; Oct. 15.

Securities and Exchange Commission

Commissioner for term expiring June 5, 1981, $50,000 — **Roberta S. Karmel;** Potomac, Md.; partner in the New York City law firm of Rogers and Wells (1972-77); May 4, 1937 in Chicago, Ill.; Dem.; Sept. 22, 1977.

Small Business Administration

Chief counsel for advocacy, $47,500 — **Milton David Stewart;** Staten Island, New York; chairman of the Research Council for Small Business and the Professions (1975-78); research director, President's Committee on Civil Rights (1946), staff economist for the Senate Small Business Committee (1946-50); executive assistant administrator of the Small Defense Plants Administration (1950-52) and special counsel to Gov. Averell Harriman, D-N.Y. (1955-58); March 5, 1922, in Brooklyn, N.Y.; Dem.; July 18.

Tennessee Valley Authority

Member of the board for term expiring May 18, 1987, $50,000 — **Richard Merrell Freeman;** Glencoe, Ill.; vice-president, law, Chicago and Northwestern Transportation Co. (1967-78); July 2, 1941, in Crawfordsville, Ind.; Oct. 13.

United States Arms Control and Disarmament Agency

Director, $57,000 — Gen. (Ret.) **George M. Seignious II;** Charleston, S.C.; president of The Citadel (university) (1974-79); deputy assistant defense secretary for security assistance and director of the Defense Security Assistance Agency (1971-72); director of the Joint Staff of the Joint Chiefs of Staff (1972-74); June 21, 1921 in Orangeburg, S.C.; President Carter announced his "intention to nominate" Seignious to the post on Oct. 20 and gave him a recess appointment, beginning Dec. 1.

United States International Trade Commission

Commissioner for term expiring June 16, 1987, $50,000 — **Paula Stern;** Washington, D.C.; executive with Carnegie Endowment for International Peace (1977-78); legislative assistant to Sen. Gaylord Nelson, D-Wis. (1972-74, 1976); March 31, 1945, in Chicago, Ill.; Dem.; Sept. 27.

LEGISLATIVE BRANCH
Government Printing Office

Public Printer, $50,000 — **John P. Boyle;** Silver Spring, Md.; deputy public printer, GPO (1973-77); Jan. 25, 1919, in Honesdale, Pa.; Dem.; Oct. 27, 1977.

JUDICIARY
U.S. Circuit Courts of Appeals

Judge for the fourth circuit, $57,500 — **James Dickson Phillips Jr.;** Chapel Hill, N.C.; professor and dean of the law school (1964-74) at the University of North Carolina (1960-78); Sept. 23, 1922, in Scotland County, N.C.; Dem.; Aug. 11.

Judge for the fifth circuit, $57,500 — **Robert S. Vance;** Birmingham, Ala.; partner in the Birmingham law firm of Vance, Thompson and Brown (1964-77) and chairman of the Alabama Democratic Party (1966-77); chairman of the Alabama 1968 Democratic National Convention delegation, and delegate to the 1972 Democratic National Convention; May 10, 1931, in Talladega, Ala.; Dem.; Nov. 15, 1977.

Judge for the eighth circuit, $57,500 — **Theodore McMillian;** St. Louis, Mo.; judge on the Missouri Court of Appeals (1972-78); St. Louis circuit court judge (1956-72) and assistant circuit attorney (1952-56); Jan. 28, 1919, in St. Louis; Dem.; Sept. 22.

Judge for the tenth circuit, $57,500 — **James K. Logan;** Olathe, Kan.; senior partner in the Olathe law firm of Payne and Jones (1968-77); special assistant Kansas attorney general for antitrust programs (1971); Aug. 21, 1929, in Quenemo, Kan.; Dem.; Nov. 15, 1977.

Judge for the tenth circuit, $57,500 — **Monroe G. McKay;** Provo, Utah; professor at the Brigham Young University Law School (1974-77); May 30, 1928, in Huntsville, Utah; Dem.; Nov. 29, 1977.

U.S. Court of Claims

Chief judge, $57,500 — **Daniel M. Friedman;** Washington, D.C.; first deputy solicitor general, Justice Department (1968-78); Feb. 8, 1916, in New York City; Independent; May 17.

Associate judge, $57,500 — **Edward S. Smith;** Baltimore, Md.; member of the Baltimore law firm of Piper and Marbury (1963-78); supervisor of civil tax litigation, Justice Department (1961-63); March 27, 1919, in Birmingham, Ala.; Dem.; July 26.

U.S. Tax Court

Judge (15-year term), $54,500 — **Herbert L. Chabot;** Rockville, Md.; deputy chief of staff of the Joint Committee on Taxation (1977-78; with the committee since 1965); July 17, 1931, in New York City; Dem.; March 20.

U.S. District Courts

Judge for the eastern and western districts of Arkansas, $54,000 — **Richard S. Arnold;** Texarkana, Ark.; legislative assistant to Sen. Dale Bumpers, D-Ark. (1975-78); delegate to the Arkansas constitutional convention (1969-70), delegate to the Democratic National Convention from Arkansas (1968), candidate for Democratic nomination in the Fourth Congressional District of Arkansas (1966, 1972), member of the Arkansas Democratic state executive committee (1972-74), legislative secretary to then-Gov. Dale Bumpers, D-Ark. (1973-74); March 26, 1936, in Texarkana, Texas; Dem.; Sept. 20.

Judge for the central district of California, $54,500 — **Mariana R. Pfaelzer;** Los Angeles, Calif.; senior partner in the Los Angeles firm of Wyman, Bautzer, Rothman and Kuchel (1957-78); member, Los Angeles Board of Police Commissioners (1974-78); Feb. 4, 1926, in Wilmar, Calif.; Dem.; Sept. 22.

Judge for the district of Colorado, $54,500 — **John L. Kane Jr.;** Denver, Colo.; partner in Denver law firm of Holme, Robert and Owen (1972-77); Feb. 14, 1937, in Tucumcari, N.M.; Dem.; Nov. 15, 1977.

Judge for the district of Connecticut, $54,500 — **Ellen Bree Burns;** Hamden, Conn.; judge of the Connecticut Superior Court (1976-78); judge of the Connecticut Court of Common Pleas (1974-76), Connecticut circuit court judge (1973-74); Dec. 13, 1923, in New Haven, Conn.; Independent; May 17.

Judge for the district of the District of Columbia, $54,500 — **Harold H. Greene;** Washington, D.C.; chief judge, D.C. Court of General Sessions (1965-71) and its successor, D.C. Superior Court (1971-78); associate judge, Court of General Sessions (1965-66); Feb. 6, 1923, in Frankfort, Germany; May 17.

Judge for the district court of the District of Columbia, $54,500 — **Carin Ann Clauss;** Alexandria, Va.; solicitor of the Labor Department (1977-); associate solicitor, fair labor standards division, Labor Department (1972-77); Jan. 24, 1939, in Knoxville, Tenn.; Dem.; Not confirmed by the Senate before end of 95th Congress.

Judge for the southern district of Florida, $54,500 — **Jose A. Gonzalez Jr.;** Fort Lauderdale, Fla.; judge of the 17th Florida judicial circuit (1964-78); assistant state's attorney for the 15th Florida circuit (1961-64); Nov. 26, 1931, in Tampa, Fla.; July 26.

Judge for the middle district of Florida, $54,500 — **George C. Carr;** Lakeland, Fla.; partner in the Lakeland law firm of Peterson, Carr and Harris (1957-77); part-time county attorney, Polk County, Fla. (1973-77); Lakeland municipal judge (1965-66); July 26, 1929, in Lakeland; Dem.; Dec. 15, 1977.

Judge for the southern district of Georgia, $54,500 — **B. Avant Edenfield;** Statesboro, Ga.; partner in Statesboro law firm of Allen, Edenfield, Brown and Wright (1958-78); deputy assistant state attorney general (1970-78), Georgia state senator (D 1965-67); Aug. 2, 1934, in Bullock County, Ga.; Dem.; Oct. 10.

Judge for the eastern district of Illinois, $54,500 — **Harold A. Baker;** Champaign, Ill.; partner in Champaign law firm of Hatch and Baker (1956-78); senior counsel to the President's Commission on CIA Activities in the United States (Rockefeller Commission) (1975); Oct. 4, 1929, in Mount Kisco, N.Y.; Dem.; Sept. 22.

Judge for the northern and southern districts of Iowa, $54,500 — **Donald E. O'Brien;** Sioux City, Iowa; special counsel to the House Small Business Committee (1978); member of the Democratic National Committee (1977-78); director, Carter for President Michigan campaign (1976); director of McGovern for President Texas campaign (1972), U.S. attorney for the northern district of Iowa (1961-67), Sioux City municipal judge (1959-60) and Woodbury County attorney (1955-58), unsuccessful candidate for Congress (D 1958, 1960); Sept. 30, 1923, in Marcus, Iowa; Dem.; Oct. 4.

Judge for the eastern district of Louisiana, $54,500 — **Adrian G. Duplantier;** New Orleans, La.; judge in Division B of the Orleans Parish civil district court (1974-78); first assistant district attorney for Orleans Parish (1954-56); March 5, 1929, in New Orleans; Dem.; May 26.

Judge for the eastern district of Louisiana, $54,500 — **Robert F. Collins;** New Orleans, La.; magistrate-judge of the Louisiana criminal district court in New Orleans (1972-78); judge-ad-hoc of New Orleans traffic court (1969-72); Jan. 27, 1931, in New Orleans; Dem.; May 17.

Judge for the district of Massachusetts, $54,500 — **Armando David Mazzone;** Wakefield, Mass.; Massachusetts superior court judge (1975-78); assistant U.S. attorney for Massachusetts (1961-65); June 3, 1928, in Everett, Mass.; Dem.; Feb. 7.

Judge for the eastern district of Michigan, $54,500 — **Patricia Jean Ehrhardt Boyle;** Detroit, Mich.; Detroit Recorder's Court judge (1976-78); assistant Wayne County prosecutor (1968-76) and assistant U.S. attorney for the eastern district (1964-68); March 31, 1937, in Detroit; Sept. 22.

Judge for the eastern district of Michigan, $54,500 — **Julian A. Cook Jr.;** Oak Park, Mich.; partner in the Pontiac, Mich., law firm of Cook and Curry (1974-78); chairman of the Michigan Civil Rights Commission (1968-71); June 22, 1930, in Washington, D.C.; Dem.; Sept. 22.

Judge for the district of Nevada, $54,500 — **Harry E. Claiborne;** Las Vegas, Nev.; self-employed attorney in Las Vegas (1946-78); special counsel to the Senate Rules Committee for Rockefeller confirmation hearings (1974); Nevada state assemblyman and assistant majority leader (D 1948-50); July 2, 1917, in McRae, Ark.; Dem.; Aug. 11.

Judge for the district of New Hampshire, $54,500 — **Shane Devine;** Manchester, N.H.; partner in Manchester law firm of Devine, Millimet, Stahl and Branch (1955-78); Feb. 1, 1926, in Manchester; Dem.; June 23.

Judge for the district of New Mexico, $54,500 — **Santiago Eloy Campos;** Santa Fe, N.M.; self-employed attorney in Santa Fe (1975-78) and judge of the New Mexico district court (1972-78); assistant to the state attorney general (1955-57); Dec. 25, 1926, in Santa Rosa, N.M.; Dem.; July 10.

Judge for the southern district of New York, $54,500 — **Robert W. Sweet;** New York City; partner in New York City firm of Skadden, Arps, Slate, Meagher and Flom (1970-78); deputy mayor of New York under John V. Lindsay (1966-69), executive assistant to Lindsay (1965-66); assistant U.S. attorney for the southern district (1955-57); Oct. 15, 1922, in Yonkers, N.Y.; Rep.; April 25.

Judge for the southern district of New York, $54,500 — **Mary Johnson Lowe;** The Bronx, N.Y.; justice in Bronx County state supreme court (1975-78); acting justice, Bronx County state supreme court (1973-75); New York City criminal court judge (1971-73); June 10, 1924, in New York City; Dem.; June 23.

Judge for the southern district of New York, $54,500 — **Leonard Burke Sand;** New York City; partner in the New York City law firm of Robinson, Silverman, Pearce, Aronsohn, Sand and Berman (1959-78); state constitutional convention delegate (1967); assistant to the solicitor general of the United States (1956-59); assistant U.S. attorney for the southern district (1953-55); May 24, 1928, in New York City; May 17.

Judge for the eastern district of Pennsylvania, $54,500 — **Norma Levy Shapiro;** Narberth, Pa.; partner in the Philadelphia law firm of Deckert, Price and Rhoads (1973-78); July 28, 1928, in Philadelphia, Pa.; Rep.; Aug. 11.

Judge for the eastern district of Pennsylvania, $54,500 — **Louis H. Pollak;** Philadelphia, Pa.; dean of the University of Pennsylvania law school (1975-78); special assistant to the ambassador-at-large, State Department (1951-53); Dec. 7, 1922, in New York City; Dem.; July 10.

Judge for the western district of Pennsylvania, $54,500 — **Paul A. Simmons;** Monongahela, Pa.; state judge, Washington County Court of Common Pleas (1973-78; appointed 1973, then elected to full term with nominations from both parties 1975); member, Washington County Redevelopment Authority (1968-73), and commissioner, Pennsylvania Human Relations Commission (1963-68); Aug. 21, 1931, in Monongahela; Dem.; April 6.

Judge for the western district of Pennsylvania, $54,500 — **Gustave Diamond;** McMurray, Pa.; self-employed attorney in Washington, Pa. (1976-78); assistant U.S. attorney (1961-63) and U.S. attorney (1963-69) for the western district; Jan. 29, 1928, in Burgettstown, Pa.; Dem.; May 1.

Judge for the western district of Pennsylvania, $54,500 — **Donald E. Ziegler;** Pittsburgh, Pa.; judge of the criminal division of the Allegheny County Court of Common Pleas (1974-78); member of the Pennsylvania Unemployment Compensation Board of Review (1962); Oct. 1, 1936, in Pittsburgh; Dem.; May 1.

Judge for the middle district of Tennessee, $54,500 — **Thomas A. Wiseman Jr.;** Nashville, Tenn.; partner in the Nashville firm of Chambers and Wiseman (1974-78); unsuccessful candidate for the Democratic gubernatorial nomination (1974); Tennessee state treasurer (D 1971-73); Nov. 3, 1930, in Tullahoma, Tenn.; Dem.; Aug. 11.

Judge for the district of Utah, $54,500 — **Bruce Sterling Jenkins;** Salt Lake City, Utah; U.S. bankruptcy referee (1965-78); state senator (D 1958-65), minority leader (1963-65) and senate president (1965); May 27, 1927, in Salt Lake City; Dem.; Sept. 20.

Judge for the western district of Washington $54,500 — **Jack E. Tanner;** Tacoma, Wash.; self-employed attorney in Tacoma (1955-78); Jan. 28, 1919, in Tacoma; Dem.; May 17.

Judge for the district of the Canal Zone (eight-year term), $54,500 — **Robert H. McFarland;** Bay Springs, Miss.; partner in the Bay Springs firm of Roberts and McFarland; chairman of the Mississippi Oil and Gas Board (1962-70); Feb. 25, 1919, in Bay Springs, July 10.

Judge for the district of Guam (eight-year term), $54,500 — **Cristobal Camacho Duenas;** Agana, Guam; judge for the district of Guam since 1969 (reappointment to seat); judge of the Guam Island Court (1960-69); Sept. 12, 1920, in Agana, Guam; May 17.

Judge for the district of the Northern Mariana Islands (eight-year term), $54,500 — **Alfred Laureta;** Kapaa, Hawaii; Fifth Hawaii circuit court judge (1969-78); First Hawaii circuit judge (1967-69); Hawaii state director of labor and industrial relations (1963-67); administrative assistant to then-Rep. Daniel K. Inouye, D-Hawaii; May 21, 1924, in Ewa, Hawaii; Dem.; May 17.

Judge for the district of the Virgin Islands (eight-year term), $54,500 — **Almeric L. Christian;** St. Thomas, V.I.; U.S. district judge for the Virgin Islands since 1969, and chief judge since 1970 (reappointment); U.S. attorney for the Virgin Islands (1962-69); Nov. 23, 1919, in Christiansted, St. Thomas, V.I.; Dem.; April 6.

District of Columbia Superior Courts

Associate judge, $49,050 — **Carlisle Edward Pratt;** Washington, D.C.; member of law firm of Pratt and Queen (1975-77); Jan. 26, 1923, in Washington; Dem.; Dec. 15, 1977.

Associate judge, $49,050 — **Frederick Howard Weisberg;** Washington, D.C.; chief of the appellate division of the D.C. public defender service (1974-77); March 22, 1944, in Buffalo, N.Y.; Independent; Dec. 15, 1977.

Associate judge, $49,050 — **Peter Henry Wolf;** Washington, D.C.; partner in Washington law firm of Wolf and Kovner (1974); May 5, 1935, in New Jersey; Dem.; nomination sent to Senate Governmental Affairs Committee Sept. 18, 1978, but not reported by panel before adjournment of Congress.

Presidential Messages, Major Statements

CQ

Jimmy Carter's State of the Union Message

Following is the White House transcript of President Carter's State of the Union address, as delivered to a joint session of Congress Jan. 19, 1978:

Thank you very much.

Mr. President, Mr. Speaker, Members of the 95th Congress, ladies and gentlemen:

Two years ago today we had the first Caucus in Iowa and one year ago tomorrow, I walked from here to the White House to take up the duties of President of the United States. I didn't know it then when I walked, but I have been trying to save energy ever since. I return tonight to fulfill one of those duties of the Constitution: To "give to the Congress"—and to the Nation—"information on the state of the Union."

Militarily, politically, economically and in spirit, the state of our Union is sound.

We are a great country, a strong country, a vital and a dynamic country—and so we will remain.

We are a confident people and a hard-working people, a decent and a compassionate people—and so we will remain.

I want to speak to you tonight about where we are and where we must go, about what we have done and what we must do. And I want to pledge to you my best efforts and ask you to pledge yours.

Each generation of Americans has to face circumstances not of its own choosing, but by which its character is measured and its spirit is tested.

There are times of emergency, when a nation and its leaders must bring their energies to bear on a single urgent task. That was a duty Abraham Lincoln faced when our land was torn apart by conflict in the War Between the States. That was the duty faced by Franklin Roosevelt when he led America out of an economic depression and again when he led America to victory in war.

There are other times when there is no single overwhelming crisis—yet profound national interests are at stake.

At such times the risk of inaction can be equally great. It becomes the task of leaders to call forth the vast and restless energies of our people to build for the future.

That is what Harry Truman did in the years after the Second World War, when we helped Europe and Japan rebuild themselves and secured an international order that has protected freedom from aggression.

We live in such time now—and we face such duties.

We have come through a long period of turmoil and doubt, but we have once again found our moral course and with a new spirit, we are striving to express our best instincts to the rest of the world.

There is all across our land, a growing sense of peace and a sense of common purpose. This sense of unity cannot be expressed in programs or in legislation, or in dollars.

It is an achievement that belongs to every individual American. This unity ties together and it towers over all our efforts here in Washington, and it serves as an inspiring beacon for all of us who are elected to serve. This new atmosphere demands a new spirit, a partnership between those of us who lead and those who elect. The foundations of this partnership are truth, the courage to face hard decisions; concern for one another and the common good over special interests; and a basic faith and trust in the wisdom and strength and judgment of the American people.

For the first time in a generation, we are not haunted by a major international crisis or by domestic turmoil, and we now have a rare and a priceless opportunity to address persistent problems and burdens which come to us as a Nation—quietly and steadily getting worse over the years.

As President, I have had to ask you—the Members of Congress, and you, the American people—to come to grips with some of the most difficult and hard questions facing our society.

We must make a maximum effort—because if we do not aim for the best, we are very likely to achieve little.

I see no benefit to the country if we delay because the problems will only get worse.

We need patience and good will, but we really need to realize that there is a limit to the role and the function of government.

Government cannot solve all our problems, it can't set our goals, it cannot define our vision. Government cannot eliminate poverty, or provide a bountiful economy or reduce inflation or save our cities or cure illiteracy or provide energy, and government cannot mandate goodness. Only a true partnership between government and the people can ever hope to reach these goals.

Those of us who govern can sometimes inspire, and we can identify needs and marshal resources, but we simply cannot be the managers of everything and everybody.

We here in Washington must move away from crisis management, and we must establish clear goals for the immediate future and the distant future which will let us work together and not in conflict.

Never again should we neglect a growing crisis like the shortage of energy, where further delay will only lead to more harsh and painful solutions.

Every day we spend more than $120 million for foreign oil. This slows our economic growth. It lowers the value of the dollar overseas, and it aggravates unemployment and inflation here at home.

Now we know what we must do, increase production—

We must cut down on waste. And we must use more of those fuels which are plentiful and more permanent.

We must be fair to people and we must not disrupt our Nation's economy and our budget.

Now that sounds simple. But I recognize the difficulties involved. I know that it is not easy for the Congress to act. But the fact remains that on the energy legislation, we have failed the American people. Almost five years after the oil embargo dramatized the problem for us all, we still do not have a national energy program.

Not much longer can we tolerate this stalemate. It undermines our national interest both at home and abroad. We must succeed, and I believe we will.

Our main task at home this year, with energy a central element, is the Nation's economy. We must continue the recovery and further cut unemployment and inflation.

Last year was a good one for the United States. We reached all of our major economic goals for 1977. Four million new jobs were created—an all-time record—and the number of unemployed dropped by more than a million. Unemployment right now is the lowest it has been since 1974, and not since World War II has such a high percentage of American people been employed.

The rate of inflation went down. There was a good growth in business profits and investments, the source of more jobs for our workers, and a higher standard of living for all our people. After taxes and inflation, there was a healthy increase in workers' wages.

This year, our country will have the first two trillion dollar economy in the history of the world.

Now we are proud of this progress the first year, but we must do even better in the future.

We still have serious problems on which all of us must work together. Our trade deficit is too large. Inflation is still too high, and too many Americans still do not have a job. Now, I didn't have any simple answers for all these problems. But we have developed an economic policy that is working, because it is simple, balanced and fair. It is based on four principles:

First, the economy must keep on expanding to produce new jobs and better income which our people need. The fruits of growth must be widely shared. More jobs must be made available to those who have been by-passed until now, and the tax system must be made fairer and simpler.

Secondly, private business and not the government must lead the expansion in the future.

Third, we must lower the rate of inflation and keep it down. Inflation slows down economic growth, and it is the most cruel to the poor and also to the elderly and others who live on fixed incomes.

And fourth, we must contribute to the strength of the world economy.

I will announce detailed proposals for improving our tax system later this week. We can make our tax laws fairer, we can make them simpler and easier to understand; and at the same time, we can—and we will—reduce the tax burden on American citizens by $25 billion.

The tax reforms and the tax reductions go together. Only with the long overdue reforms will the full tax cut be advisable.

Almost $17 billion in income tax cuts will go to individuals. Ninety-six per cent of all American taxpayers will see their taxes go down. For a typical family of four, this means an annual saving of more than $250 a year, or a tax reduction of about 20 per cent.

A further $2 billion cut in excise taxes will give more relief and also contribute directly to lowering the rate of inflation.

We will also provide strong additional incentives for business investment and growth through substantial cuts in the corporate tax rates and improvement in the investment tax credit.

These tax proposals will increase opportunity everywhere in the Nation. But additional jobs for the disadvantaged deserve special attention.

We have already passed laws to assure equal access to the voting booth, and to restaurants, and to schools, and to housing; and laws to permit access to jobs. But job opportunity—the chance to earn a decent living—is also a basic human right which we cannot and will not ignore.

A major priority for our Nation is the final elimination of the barriers that restrict the opportunities available to women, and also to black people, Hispanics and other minorities. We have come a long way toward that goal. But there is still more to do.

What we inherited from the past must not be permitted to shackle us in the future.

I will be asking you for a substantial increase in funds for public jobs for our young people, and I also am recommending that the Congress continue the Public Service Employment Programs at more than twice the level of a year ago.

When welfare reform is completed, we will have more than a million additional jobs so that those on welfare who are able to work can work.

However, again, we know that in our free society, private business is still the best source of new jobs.

Therefore, I will propose a new program to encourage businesses to hire young and disadvantaged Americans. Those people only need skills and a chance, in order to take their place in our economic system. Let's give them the chance they need.

A major step in the right direction would be the early passage of a greatly improved Humphrey-Hawkins Bill.

My budget for 1979 addresses these national needs, but it is lean and tight. I have cut waste wherever possible.

I am proposing an increase of less than 2 per cent after adjusting for inflation—the smallest increase in the Federal budget in four years.

Lately, Federal spending has taken a steadily increasing portion of what Americans produce. Our new budget reverses that trend, and later I hope to bring the Government's toll down even further. And with your help, we will do that.

In time of high employment and a strong economy, deficit spending should not be a feature of our budget.

As the economy continues to gain strength and as our unemployment rates continue to fall, revenues will grow. With careful planning, efficient management and proper restraint on spending, we can move rapidly toward a balanced budget—and we will.

Next year the budget deficit will be only slightly less than this year. But one-third of the deficit is due to the necessary tax cuts that I have proposed. This year the right choice is to reduce the burden on tax-payers and provide more jobs for our people.

The third element in our program is a renewed attack on inflation. We have learned the hard way that high unemployment will not prevent or cure inflation. Government can help us by stimulating private investment and by maintaining a responsible economic policy. Through a new top level review process, we will do a better job of reducing government regulation that drives up costs and drives up prices.

But again, government alone cannot bring down the rate of inflation. When a level of high inflation is expected to continue, then companies raise prices to protect their profit margins against the prospective increases in wages and other costs; while workers demand higher wages as protection against the expected price increases. It's like an escalation in the arms race, and understandably, no one wants to disarm alone.

Voluntary Anti-inflation Program

No one firm or a group of workers can halt this process. It is an effort that we must all make together. I am therefore asking government, business, labor, and other groups to join in a voluntary program to moderate inflation by holding wage and price increases in each sector of the

economy during 1978 below the average increases of the last two years.

I do not believe in wage and price controls. A sincere commitment to voluntary constraints provides a way, perhaps the only way to fight inflation without government interference.

As I came into the Capitol tonight, I saw the farmers, my fellow farmers, standing out in the snow. I am familiar with their problem and I know from Congress' action that you are, too. When I was running Carter's Warehouse, we had spread on our own farms five, ten, fifteen fertilizers for about $40 a ton. The last time I was home, the price was about $100 a ton. The cost of nitrogen has gone up 150 per cent, and the price of products that farmers sell has either stayed the same or gone down a little. Now this past year in 1977, you the Congress and I together passed a new Agricultural Act. It went into effect October 1. It will have its first impact on the 1978 crops. It will help a great deal. It will add $8.5 billion or more to help the farmers with their price supports and target prices.

Last year we had the highest level of exports of farm products in the history of our country, $24 billion. We expect to have more this year. We will be working together. But I think it is incumbent on us to monitor very carefully the farm situation and continue to work harmoniously with the farmers of our country. What is best for the farmer, the farm families, in the long run is best for the consumers of our country.

Economic success at home is also the key to success in our international economic policy. An effective energy program, strong investment and productivity and controlled inflation will improve our trade balance and balance it, and it will help to protect the integrity of the dollar overseas.

By working closely with our friends abroad, we can promote the economic health of the whole world. With fair and balanced agreements lowering the barriers to trade.

Despite the inevitable pressures that build up when the world economy suffers from high unemployment, we must firmly resist the demands for self-defeating protectionism. But free trade must also be fair trade. And I am determined to protect the American industry and American workers against the foreign trade practices which are unfair or illegal.

In a separate written message to Congress, I have outlined other domestic initiatives, such as welfare reform, consumer protection, basic education skills, urban policy, reform of our labor laws and national health care later on this year. I will not repeat those tonight. But there are several other points that I would like to make directly to you.

During these past years, Americans have seen our government grow far from us.

Government Reorganization

For some citizens the government has almost become like a foreign country, so strange and distant that we have often had to deal with it through trained ambassadors who have sometimes become too powerful and too influential—lawyers, accountants and lobbyists. This cannot go on.

We must have what Abraham Lincoln wanted, a government for the people.

We have made progress toward that kind of government. You have given me the authority requested to reorganize the Federal bureaucracy. And I am using that authority.

We have already begun a series of reorganization plans which will be completed over a period of three years. We have also proposed abolishing almost 500 Federal advisory and other commissions and boards. But I know that the American people are still sick and tired of Federal paperwork and red tape. Bit by bit we are chopping down the thicket of unnecessary Federal regulations by which government too often interferes in our personal lives and our personal business. We have cut the public's Federal paperwork load by more than 12 percent in less than a year. And we are not through cutting.

We have made a good start on turning the gobbledygook of Federal regulations into plain English that people can understand. But we know that we still have a long way to go. We have brought together parts of eleven government agencies to create a new Department of Energy. And now it is time to take another major step by creating a separate Department of Education.

But even the best-organized government will only be as effective as the people who carry out its policies. For this reason, I consider Civil Service reform to be absolutely vital. Worked out with the civil servants themselves, this reorganization plan will restore the merit principle to a system which has grown into a bureaucratic maze. It will provide greater management flexibility and better rewards for better performance without compromising job security.

Then and only then can we have a government that is efficient, open, and truly worthy of our people's understanding and respect. I have promised that we will have such a government and I intend to keep that promise.

In our foreign policy, the separation of people from government has been in the past a source of weakness and error. In a democratic system like ours, foreign policy decisions must be able to stand the test of public examination and public debate. If we make a mistake in this Administration, it will be on the side of frankness and openness with the American people.

In our modern world when the deaths of literally millions of people can result from a few terrifying seconds of destruction, the path of national strength and security is identical to the path of peace. Tonight, I am happy to report that because we are strong, our Nation is at peace with the world.

Human Rights and Defense

We are a confident Nation. We have restored a moral basis for our foreign policy. The very heart of our identity as a Nation is our firm commitment to human rights.

We stand for human rights because we believe that government has as a purpose, to promote the well-being of its citizens. This is true in our domestic policy, it is also true in our foreign policy. The world must know that in support of human rights, the United States will stand firm.

We expect no quick or easy results, but there has been significant movement toward greater freedom and humanity in several parts of the world.

Thousands of political prisoners have been freed. The leaders of the world—even our ideological adversaries—now see that their attitude toward fundamental human rights affects their standing in the international community and it affects their relations with the United States.

To serve the interests of every American, our foreign policy has three major goals. The first and prime concern is and will remain the security of our country.

Security is based on our national will and security is based on the strength of our armed forces. We have the will, and militarily, we are very strong. Security also comes through the strength of our alliances. We have reconfirmed our commitment to the defense of Europe, and this year, we will demonstrate that commitment by further modernizing and strengthening our military capabilities there.

Security can also be enhanced by agreements with potential adversaries which reduce the threat of nuclear disaster while maintaining our own relative strategic capability.

In areas of peaceful competition with the Soviet Union, we will continue to more than hold our own.

At the same time, we are negotiating with quiet confidence, without haste, with careful determination, to ease the tension between us and to ensure greater stability and security.

The Strategic Arms Limitation Talks have been long and difficult. We want a mutual limit on both the quality and quantity of the giant nuclear arsenals of both nations—and then we want actual reductions in strategic arms as a major step toward the ultimate elimination of nuclear weapons from the face of the earth.

If those talks result in an agreement this year—and I trust they will—I pledge to you that the agreement will maintain and enhance the stability of the world's strategic balance and the security of the United States.

For 30 years, concerted but unsuccessful efforts have been made to ban the testing of atomic explosives—both military weapons and peaceful nuclear devices.

We are hard at work with Great Britain and the Soviet Union on an agreement which will stop testing and will protect our national security and provide for adequate verification of compliance.

We are now making progress, I believe good progress, toward this comprehensive ban on nuclear explosions.

We are also working vigorously to halt the proliferation of nuclear weapons among the nations of the world which do not now have them and to reduce the deadly global traffic in conventional arms sales. Our stand for peace is suspect if we are also the principal arms merchant of the world. So we have decided to cut down our arms transfers abroad on a year-by-year basis, and to work with other major arms exporters to encourage their similar restraint.

Every American has a stake in our second major goal—a world at peace. In a nuclear age, each of us is threatened when peace is not secured everywhere. We are trying to promote harmony in those parts of the world where major differences exist among other nations and threaten international peace.

In the Middle East, we are contributing our good offices to maintain the momentum of the current negotiations—and to keep open the lines of communication among the Middle Eastern leaders. The whole world has a great stake in the success of these efforts. This is a precious opportunity for a historic settlement of a longstanding conflict—an opportunity which may never come again in our lifetime.

Our role has been difficult and sometimes thankless and controversial. But it has been constructive and it has been necessary, and it will continue.

Our third major foreign policy goal is one that touches the life of every American citizen everyday: world economic growth and stability.

This requires strong economic performance by the industrialized democracies like ourselves and progress in resolving the global energy crisis. Last fall, with the help of others, we succeeded in our vigorous efforts to maintain the stability of the price of oil. But as many foreign leaders have emphasized to me personally, and I am sure to you, the greatest future contribution that America can make to the world economy would be an effective energy conservation program here at home.

We will not hesitate to take the actions needed to protect the integrity of the American dollar.

We are trying to develop a more just international system. And in this spirit, we are supporting the struggle for human development: in Africa, in Asia, and in Latin America.

Panama Canal Treaties

Finally, the world is watching to see how we act on one of our most important and controversial items of business: approval of the Panama Canal Treaties.

The treaties now before the Senate are the result of the work of four Administrations—two Democratic, two Republican.

They guarantee that the Canal will be open always for unrestricted use by the ships of the world. Our ships have the right to go to the head of the line for priority of passage in times of emergency or need.

We retain the permanent right to defend the Canal with our own military forces, if necessary, to guarantee its openness and its neutrality.

The treaties are to the clear advantage of ourselves, the Panamanians, and the other users of the Canal. Ratifying the Panama Canal Treaties will demonstrate our good faith to the world, discourage the spread of hostile ideologies in this hemisphere and directly contribute to the economic well-being and the security of the United States.

I have to say that that is very welcome applause.

There were two moments on my recent journey which, for me, confirmed the final aims of our foreign policy and what it always must be.

One was a little village in India, where I met a people as passionately attached to their rights and liberties as we are—but whose children have a far smaller chance for good health or food or education or human fulfillment than a child born in this country.

The other moment was in Warsaw, capital of a nation twice devastated by war in this century. Their people have rebuilt the city which war's destruction took from them; but what was new only emphasized clearly what was lost.

What I saw in those two places crystalized for me the purposes of our own Nation's policy: to ensure economic justice, to advance human rights, to resolve conflicts without violence, and to proclaim in our great democracy our constant faith in the liberty and dignity of human beings everywhere.

We Americans have a great deal of work to do together. In the end, how well we do that work will depend on the spirit in which we approach it.

We must seek fresh answers, unhindered by the stale prescriptions of the past.

It has been said that our best years are behind us. But I say again that America's best is still ahead. We have emerged from bitter experiences chastened but proud, confident once again, ready to face challenges once again, and united once again.

A Solemn Time

We come together tonight at a solemn time. Last week the Senate lost a good and honest man, Lee Metcalf of Montana.

And today, the flag of the United States flew at half-mast from this Capitol and from American installations and ships all over the world, in mourning for Senator Hubert Humphrey.

Because he exemplified so well the joy and the zest of living, his death reminds us not so much of our own mortality but of the possibilities offered to us by life. He always looked to the future with a special American kind of confidence, of hope and enthusiasm.

The best way that we can honor him is by following his example. Our task—to use the words of Senator Humphrey—is "reconciliation, rebuilding, and rebirth."

Reconciliation of private needs and interests into a higher purpose.

Rebuilding the old dreams of justice and liberty, and country and community.

Rebirth of our faith in the common good.

Each of us here tonight—and all who are listening in your homes—must rededicate ourselves to serving the common good.

We are a community, a beloved community, all of us; our individual fates are linked; our futures intertwined; and if we act in that knowledge and in that spirit, together, as the Bible says, we can move mountains.

Thank you very much. ∎

Accompanying Message

Following is the text of President Carter's message to Congress that accompanied his State of the Union address Jan. 19, 1978. The accompanying message was sent to Congress with the State of the Union address but was not delivered by Carter.

TO THE CONGRESS
OF THE UNITED STATES:

Tonight's State of the Union Address concentrates on this year's highest priorities—a strong energy bill; a coordinated economic program of job creation, tax reduction, tax reform and anti-inflation measures; making the government more effective and efficient; maintaining the peace through a strong national defense; and ratifying both the Panama Canal Treaties and, if completed, the SALT II treaty.

It is important that the Congress and the Nation also understand what our other important initiatives and goals will be for 1978. I am therefore sending to Congress this separate, more detailed State of the Union Message, which describes Administration priorities in the areas not fully covered in the Address.

DOMESTIC AFFAIRS

A number of serious domestic problems faced the Nation when I took office one year ago. The economy had not yet fully recovered from the recession; our country had no sound energy policy; the Federal government was operating inefficiently and ineffectively in many areas; concerns about the openness and integrity of our govern-

ment remained in the aftermath of Watergate; and many of our most pressing social problems had not been addressed.

In 1977, my Administration did not solve all of those problems. But Congress joined us in tackling many of these issues, and together we made progress. Now that a year has passed, I believe we are a more confident people, with more trust in our institutions. We are a country on the move again, prepared to address our problems with boldness and confidence, at home and abroad. We have reasserted our concern for the problems of people here at home and reaffirmed our position of moral leadership in the world.

This year, my domestic goals will continue to reflect those concerns that guided my actions in 1977: restoring economic prosperity; meeting our Nation's human needs; making the government more efficient and more responsive; and developing and protecting our natural resources.

RESTORING ECONOMIC PROSPERITY

I am devoting a substantial part of my State of the Union Address to the need for a comprehensive economic program, and I will devote the bulk of my Economic Report to Congress, to be delivered tomorrow, to a complete description of my Administration's economic goals and objectives. In this Message, therefore, I will not repeat those statements but I want to set forth briefly the key elements of those proposals:

—a $23 billion income tax cut in 1979, with $17 billion going to individuals and their families and $6 billion going to businesses;

—a tax reform program designed to make our tax laws fairer and simpler;

—an anti-inflation program, designed to reduce annual increases in wages and prices, with the cooperation of labor and business and with the Federal government setting an example; reductions of $2 billion in excise and payroll taxes will also make a contribution to reducing inflation;

—an extension of the funding for 725,000 public service (CETA) jobs, and a $700 million increase in spending for our youth employment efforts;

—a major new $400 million private sector jobs initiative, designed primarily to encourage businesses to hire unemployed minorities and youth.

I plan to work very closely with Congress to secure prompt action on these economic proposals. Their adoption will help achieve the kind of economic prosperity for our Nation that all of us want. Along with a sound energy bill, enactment of these economic proposals will be my highest domestic priority for 1978.

Energy

There can be no higher priority than prompt enactment of comprehensive energy legislation along the lines submitted to the Congress last spring.

Huge oil price increases in 1973-74 contributed to the double-digit inflation of 1974, and to the worst recession in 40 years. These price hikes were also the principal cause of our foreign trade deficit, which has contributed to the weakness of the dollar abroad.

Unless we act now, our energy problems will rapidly get worse. Failure to act will fuel inflation, erode the value of the dollar, render us vulnerable to disruptions in our oil supply, and limit our economic progress in the years to come.

I am confident that the Congress will respond to the Nation's clear need, by enacting responsible and balanced energy legislation early this year.

Employment

Last year we made considerable progress in our efforts to reduce unemployment. The unemployment rate decreased from 7.8% to 6.4%. During the year, 4.1 million new jobs were created. Unemployment fell by 1.1 million workers. The actions we took as part of our $21 billion economic stimulus package substantially helped us achieve these favorable results.

In 1978, the Administration will continue its efforts to reduce unemployment still further and to increase employment opportunities for all Americans. As part of the budget I will propose:

—additional funds to increase youth programs 260 per cent above the 1976 level, providing $2.3 billion in outlays and 450,000 man-years of employment and training for young workers;

—a $400 million private sector employment program focused on youth and other disadvantaged workers and aimed at mobilizing private industry to work with government in finding jobs. It will be implemented through business councils established throughout the country;

—maintenance of the 725,000 CETA jobs through 1979, while tying them in future years to national unemployment rates;

—beginning of a demonstration program for the jobs component of the Better Jobs and Income Program.

Humphrey-Hawkins Legislation

The Administration will seek passage of the Humphrey-Hawkins Full Employment and Balanced Growth Act.

This Act will help the Administration and the Congress in planning our efforts to reduce unemployment and to create jobs, while maintaining reasonable price stability. Its enactment would serve as a living memorial to the late Senator Hubert Humphrey.

Private Sector Jobs

The Administration plans a major $400 million effort to involve business and labor in the training and hiring of the hard-core unemployed.

The program will closely tie the Federal employment system with the private sector, through the use of business councils. I am confident that the private sector will respond positively to the call to help the Nation solve one of its most serious problems—the employment of our youth and minorities.

Inflation

Although inflation is lower now than in the recent past, we still must do more to keep it down. The steps my Administration will take include:

—incentives for business investment, contained in our tax proposals, which will increase production investment, and thereby help us hold down prices and costs;

—reduction in excise and unemployment taxes, proposed in the new budget;

—continuing reductions in needlessly complex Federal regulations. We have established a high-level inter-agency committee to review the effects of regulation in our economy, and we will continue our efforts for regulatory reform in the airline industry and elsewhere;

—a special effort to hold down the soaring costs of health care, through enactment of the Hospital Cost Containment Act.

But the government cannot solve this problem alone—especially once business, labor, and consumers have accepted inflation as a fact of life, and adjusted their behavior accordingly. I have therefore asked business and labor to undertake, voluntarily, a new program to reduce inflation. I will ask each industry to aim for smaller price and wage increases in 1978 than it averaged over the last two years. As a major employer the Federal government should take the lead in this effort. Voluntary cooperation is one way—perhaps the only way—to reduce inflation without unacceptable government interference and coercion.

Urban Assistance and Community Development

The Administration and Congress took major steps last year to meet the needs of our cities. We increased funding for Community Development Block Grants by $2.7 billion over three years, and provided an alternative formula for allocating funds that was more responsive to the needs of distressed urban areas. Next year we will recommend an increase of $150 million over the 1978 level for the Community Development Block Grant program. We enacted a new program of Urban Development Action Grants at an annual level of $400 million, and extended and expanded Anti-Recession Fiscal Assistance (ARFA).

I am proposing that the ARFA program, which expires September 30, 1978, be extended. We are evaluating possible revisions in programs and funding, and will make our recommendations to the Congress within two months.

The Administration is also studying closely the possible need for extended Federal lending to New York City. The current legislation expires on June 30, 1978. We are committed, along with the State and City, to preserving the City's solvency. If such extended lending is necessary for that purpose, we will propose it. However, all the interested parties must contribute to a permanent solution.

This spring I will submit to Congress a message outlining this Administration's urban policy, based on the work of the Urban and Regional Policy Group, chaired by the Secretary of Housing and Urban Development. It will be designed to make existing Federal programs more effective, and will involve new initiatives and resources to address our urban needs. The long-standing problems of our cities are structural in nature and cannot be corrected by short-term or one-time efforts. This Administration is committed to a long-term and continuing effort to meet stubborn problems and changing needs. Our urban policy proposals will:

—build a more effective partnership between the Federal government, State and local governments, the private sector, neighborhood groups and concerned citizens;

—be sufficiently flexible to meet the diverse needs of our urban areas and to respond to particular problems of distressed areas;

—address the fiscal needs of hard-pressed urban governments, as well as the economic and social needs of city residents;

—improve the urban physical environment and strengthen urban communities;

—use Federal assistance to stimulate job-creating investments by the private sector and to encourage innovative actions by the State and local governments.

Agriculture and Rural Development

Decent farm income and a strong family farm system are vital to our national economic stability and strength. For too long farm prices for many commodities have been severely depressed. Working with the Congress in the past year, we have adopted new programs and policies designed to strengthen farm income and to ensure abundant, reasonably priced food for consumers. Partially as a result of these policies and programs, farm prices are now improving. Nevertheless, we cannot be satisfied with the economic condition of many American farmers today. We will continue to monitor our agricultural economy and to work with Congressional and farm leaders to make certain that Federal programs and policies are carried out effectively.

Food and Agriculture Act

In the past year we have worked with the Congress to enact a new comprehensive Food and Agriculture Act, which will protect producers and consumers. We have also exercised set-aside authority for wheat and feed grains, which will protect farm income. This year we expect to pay farmers $7.3 billion for all price support programs. The new farm bill which became effective October 1, 1977, achieves long-needed changes in our agricultural policies, including:

—minimal governmental intervention in markets and in the decisions farmers make;

—price support loans for major commodities that permit us to remain competitive in world markets;

—a grain reserve designed to remove excess products from the market and hold them until supplies are short;

—income support levels based on cost-of-production.

Grain Reserve

Last year we initiated a plan to place 30-35 million metric tons of food and feed grains in reserve. Establishing this reserve will add further strength and stability to the market and provide a hedge against export control on grain. Most of this grain will be owned and controlled by farmers. To strengthen farmer control of the grain and to help keep the grain out of government ownership, terms of the farmer storage facility loan program were liberalized. In 1978, the Administration will propose an international emergency grain reserve of up to 6 million metric tons to help us meet our food aid commitments abroad.

Agricultural Disaster and Drought Aid

Because of the record droughts in 1977, I worked with Congress to pass an $844 million Emergency Drought Assistance Program. This year we will ask Congress to eliminate the many inconsistencies and inequities in existing disaster aid programs, and we will continue to give high priority to addressing the effects of the drought, which has begun to abate.

We are taking other steps to improve life in rural America. I recently signed a law to encourage better delivery of health services in rural communities. We will continue to expand the assignment of the National Health Service Corps' doctors, dentists and other health professionals to underserved rural areas. We will shortly be announcing methods to improve the effectiveness of rural housing programs with greater emphasis on home ownership for rural Americans.

Agricultural Exports

I want to increase our agricultural exports. To do so we need competitive prices, high quality products, and reserve supplies to meet all contingencies. We must remove unnecessary barriers to exports. And we must have an affirmative export policy. In 1977, the Administration more than doubled (to $1.7 billion) the short-term export credit program, increased Soviet grain purchase authorization to 15 million tons,

developed a risk assurance program, and expanded efforts to develop export markets around the world.

This year we will continue these efforts, especially to reduce barriers to agricultural trade.

Sugar

To stabilize world sugar prices and to protect domestic sugar-producers, we negotiated an international sugar agreement this year with the major sugar-producing countries. We will seek Congressional ratification of the agreement early in 1978. The sugar program required by the 1977 Food and Agricultural Act will protect the domestic sugar industry in the meantime.

Rural Development and Credit Policy

In fiscal year 1977, the Farmers Home Administration provided nearly $7 billion in loans in four areas: farming, housing, community facilities and business and industrial development. We expect to provide at least $1 billion more in the current fiscal year.

Small Business

This Administration took several steps in 1977 to strengthen small business. The Small Business Administration expanded its financial and management assistance to these firms and developed an advocacy program to represent small business interests before all Federal departments and agencies. In 1978, we will continue efforts to support small business through tax cuts and special tax incentives, reduced regulations and other programmatic reforms, and expanded SBA loan authority.

MEETING OUR NATION'S HUMAN NEEDS

The Administration's constant concern has been with meeting the human needs of all Americans. Over the past year, we have moved on a number of fronts to make certain our citizens will be well housed, better educated, and properly cared for when they are in need. This year we will pursue our current initiatives in these areas and launch new ones.

Health

This past year we were very active in the effort to improve the health of our citizens and to restrain skyrocketing health care costs, through:

—Establishment of a Mental Health Commission to help develop a national mental health program. The Commission will issue its final report later this year, and I expect to carefully consider the Commission's findings.

—A campaign to immunize the more than 20 million children not yet protected against communicable childhood diseases.

—Reorganization of part of HEW to allow more efficient delivery of Medicare/Medicaid services. The cost savings from the reorganizations will be realized more fully this year.

—Signing legislation to attack fraud and abuse in Medicare/Medicaid programs.

—Signing legislation to make Medicare/Medicaid reimbursement available to physician extenders in rural clinics. The beneficial effects of that bill will be felt in our Nation's rural areas for the first time this year.

In 1978, the Administration will continue these and other efforts to bring us better and less costly health care.

Hospital Cost Containment

One of my main legislative goals for this year is the Hospital Cost Containment Bill. That bill, which would save hospital users more than $7 billion in the first two years after enactment, is our principal weapon in the effort to decrease health care costs, which now double every five years.

National Health Insurance

I will submit to Congress later this year a National Health Insurance proposal. While Congress will not have the time to complete action on this proposal in 1978, it is important to begin the national debate on the many complex issues involved in National Health Insurance.

National Health Insurance will not solve all our health problems. A sensible national health policy also requires more effective delivery of preventive services, better nutrition, vigorous abatement of environmental and occupational threats to health, and efforts to change individual lifestyles that endanger health.

But National Health Insurance is a crucial step. It will protect our people from ruinous medical bills and provide each citizen with better access to sound and balanced health insurance coverage.

Medicaid Improvements for Children

Last year I proposed the Child Health Assessment Program to improve the early and preventive screening, diagnosis and treatment program for lower-income children under Medicaid. The Administration will press for enactment of this measure, and will urge its expansion to make an additional 1.7 million lower-income children eligible.

Teenage Pregnancy Proposal

I will propose legislation to establish networks of community based services to prevent unwanted adolescent pregnancies. We need and will urge expansion of existing family planning services to reach an additional 280,000 teenagers.

Drug Abuse

Drug Abuse threatens the health and safety of our children, here and abroad. We will continue the efforts begun last year to make our drug abuse prevention and control programs more effective and efficient.

World Health

This year I will present a strategy for working directly with other nations and through international organizations to raise the standards of health and nutrition around the world.

Education

Last year the Congress adopted with our cooperation a 15 per cent increase in education funding—the largest increase since enactment of the Elementary and Secondary Education Act.

This year we will continue to demonstrate our commitment to improving the Nation's education programs. HEW's education budget expenditures will be increased by 14 per cent, with the most significant increases coming in education of the disadvantaged, assistance to State programs for education of the handicapped, and college student financial aid.

The Administration will also work with the Congress for the creation of a separate Cabinet-level Department of Education, and for legislation to replace and reform expiring Federal education acts.

These legislative proposals will concentrate on:

—increasing basic literacy;

—ensuring that students are prepared for jobs;

—supporting post-secondary education and lifelong learning; and,

—strengthening the partnership between Federal, State, and local governments.

To augment existing programs, I will propose legislation to help low and middle-income families meet rising college tuition costs, and will also support a significant expansion of student aid programs.

Income Assistance

Over the past year we have made many far-reaching improvements in the programs that provide income assistance to the needy. My Administration will continue to assign great importance to this area in 1978.

Welfare Reform

I proposed last year a reform of the Nation's welfare system, through the Better Jobs and Income Act. This Act would fundamentally reform current programs to assist the poor by:

—consolidating the Aid to Families with Dependent Children, Supplemental Security Income and Food Stamps programs into a single consolidated cash assistance program that provides a basic nationally uniform Federal benefit;

—improving efforts to find jobs for the poor in the private sector, and creating up to 1.4 million public service jobs for heads of families who cannot be placed in unsubsidized employment; and

—improving work incentives by expanding the Earned Income Tax Credit.

We will work actively with the Congress in the coming year to pass the Better Jobs and Income Act, and we will provide in this year's budget for pilot employment programs so we will be ready to implement the welfare reform program.

Family and Children

My Administration will continue its strong commitment to strengthening the American family and to expanding programs for children.

The Administration will propose this year that the school breakfast program be made mandatory in schools with high concentrations of needy children. Further, we will propose a major expansion in special supplemental food programs for women, infants, and children.

Among other major actions in 1978 will be:

—convening a White House Conference on Families;

—pressing for enactment of our proposed reforms in foster care programs including new financial assistance to aid in the adoption of hard-to-place children;

—more than doubling the budget outlays for child welfare services, with an emphasis on services that help keep families together;

—continuing $200 million in special funding for day care under Title XX of the Social Security Act.

We will also depend upon the revitalized Community Services Administration to develop new approaches to assist the poor.

The Elderly

Last year saw the enactment of Social Security financing legislation that will assure the system's financial integrity into the next century. This year the Administration will continue to work for strengthened legislation against unwarranted age discrimination in the Federal and private sector. We will propose legislation to extend and strengthen the Older Americans Act and we will seek a 13 per cent increase in funding for programs providing daily meals to the elderly, raising the total of daily meals served to 385,000. In addition, the Administration will work to assure that the contributions of older Americans are sought in our efforts to meet national needs.

Housing

Last year we made progress toward our national goal of a decent home in a suitable environment for every American family. 1977 was a good year for housing, generally, with total new starts exceeding two million. And we have renewed the Federal government's commitment to housing for the needy.

Early last year, the Administration proposed major new intiatives to meet the housing needs of low- and moderate-income

Americans—initiatives which are central to our urban development strategy. We had about 118,000 starts under section 8 and public housing subsidized programs in 1977. We look forward to another 30 per cent increase in subsidized housing starts in these programs for 1978, and 92,000 starts in the Assisted Housing Rehabilitation Loan Programs. We will reassess our national housing needs and goals and our current housing and credit policies designed to meet those needs.

In 1978, the Administration will strengthen its commitment to meet the housing needs of all communities with a variety of expanded programs and new initiatives:

—Rental housing assistance to an additional 400,000 low-income families, and help to enable an additional 50,000 moderate-income families to own their own homes. The total number of families receiving housing assistance will increase from 2.6 million in 1977 to 3.1 million in 1979.

—More funds for the rehabilitation loan program under section 312, with an expansion of existing programs for substantial renovations and the creation of a new moderate rehabilitation program under section 8.

—A major new operating subsidy program for 1979. This new program, coupled with improved management controls and the monitoring of troubled projects, is intended to reduce the inventory of defaulted projects and aid in restoring distressed urban areas. The Department of Housing and Urban Development has made substantial progress in 1977 in reducing the stock of defaulted projects. This new program will give the Department additional tools. Outlays for this program are estimated to total $52 million in 1979.

—A Federal financing mechanism for assisted housing projects through use of the GNMA Tandem program.

—A targeted GNMA Tandem program which will provide subsidies designed to bring middle-income families back to the cities.

—Targeting of rural housing programs to lower-income residents, including a special program to help very poor families own their own homes.

—Continuing high levels of production of housing for the elderly and handicapped.

Transportation

This year we will build on the efforts we made last year to strengthen the Nation's transportation system by decreasing consumer costs, pursuing increased energy efficiency, and improving safety:

—negotiation of a new US-UK bilateral air services agreement;

—approval of new international air routes from a number of American cities;

—requiring passive restraint systems on all new automobiles by 1984;

—setting new fuel efficiency standards for 1981-1984 model automobiles;

—beginning work on the Northeast Corridor Railroad Improvement Program;

—passing an all-cargo airline deregulation bill.

We will also continue our policy of increasing competition and reducing airfares in international flights, and pursue additional bilateral agreements. Consumers have already benefited from reduced international fares and improved service.

Highway and Transit Programs

We will soon propose a comprehensive highway and transit program, which will provide more than $45 billion in total authorizations in the 1979-1982 period. The program will give states and localities more flexibility in planning and programming their highway and transit funding, by reducing the number of narrow, categorical accounts and by using consolidated accounts for a wider range of potential transportation projects.

In addition, we will make funding of transportation programs more uniform and give localities more control over highway and mass transit funds in large urban areas.

Highway Safety

The Administration will propose legislation to strengthen our efforts for highway safety and to reduce restrictions on the states' use of Federal highway safety grant funds. That legislation will earmark funds for the Department of Transportation to support important highway safety projects, such as the 55 mile per hour speed limit program.

Inland Waterway User Fees

Users of Federal inland waterways should pay fees which will pay a substantial part of the cost of constructing, operating and maintaining those waterways. My Administration will continue to work closely with Congress toward passage of a bill that will, for the first time, establish inland waterway user fees.

Aircraft Noise Abatement

My Administration will again seek passage of legislation to control aircraft noise.

No-Fault Automobile Insurance

We continue to support legislation to establish Federal minimum standards for no-fault automobile insurance.

Veterans

In 1977, we took a number of steps to make certain that the country continues to meet the special needs of our millions of veterans. Legislation was passed to increase compensation benefits for service-connected disabilities, benefits under the G.I. Bill, and veterans pension benefits. Millions of veterans will feel the effects of these increases this year.

In 1978, we will further improve our veterans programs by:

—initiating a government-wide review of the problems of Vietnam veterans and the means by which current programs can be made more effective in meeting their needs;

—beginning new programs to deal with problems of alcohol, drug abuse and psychological readjustment;

—proposing increased benefits for service-connected disabilities, and improvements in the veterans pension program;

—continuing special employment programs for Vietnam-era veterans.

Arts and Humanities

Americans are increasingly aware that the arts and humanities preserve and transmit our heritage, enrich our lives, and contribute significantly to the social and economic well-being of our Nation. This Administration is committed to fostering the highest standards of creativity and scholarship in an open partnership between public and private sectors—and we believe that the products of this commitment must be available to the many Americans who wish to share in them. This year's substantial increases in the budgets for the Arts and Humanities Endowments demonstrate my strong belief in the value of these programs.

MAKING THE GOVERNMENT MORE EFFICIENT AND MORE RESPONSIVE
Government Employees

Civil Service Reform

The Civil Service System is too often a bureaucratic maze which stifles the initiative of our dedicated Government employees while inadequately protecting their rights. Our 2.8 million civil servants are governed by outdated rules and institutions that keep them from being as efficient as they would like to be. No one is more frustrated by this system than hardworking public servants. Therefore, one of my major priorities in 1978 will be to ensure passage of the first comprehensive reform of the system since its creation nearly a century ago—reforms developed with the direct involvement of civil servants. Early this year, Congress will receive legislation and a reorganization plan to:

—restructure the institutions that run the Civil Service;

—increase safeguards against abuses of official power;

—provide greater incentives for managers to improve the Government's efficiency and responsiveness;

—reduce the system's red tape and delays;

—speed the procedures for dealing with employee grievances and disciplinary actions;

—make equal employment opportunities more effective.

Last year the Administration acted to protect Federal employees from the loss of a job due to reorganization. Such protection will be maintained.

Hatch Act Reform

I will continue to support reform of the Hatch Act, which would restore the right of most Civil Service employees to participate in the political process.

Part-time and Flexi-time Employment

To help obtain Federal jobs for the elderly, the handicapped, women, and others with family responsibilities, all Federal agencies will carry forward renewed efforts to increase part-time and flexi-time employment opportunities.

Reorganization, Management and Regulatory Reform

The Government Reorganization Project will keep working to make the Government more responsive and efficient. Last year we combined parts of 11 agencies into one Department of Energy, streamlined the Executive Office of the President and reduced the White House Staff, and proposed the abolition of nearly 500 advisory committees and small agencies.

In addition to the upcoming Civil Service and education reform efforts, we will soon submit proposals:

—to restructure our equal employment programs to provide better protection for the rights of minorities and women, and to ease the burden of compliance on State and local government as well as business;

—to improve the administration of justice; and

—to reorganize our disaster assistance programs.

Additional studies are under way in many other areas, and several of these will result in reorganization proposals later this year. Efforts to improve Federal cash management continue.

We are also vigorously pursuing the effort begun last year to reduce the burden of outdated, ineffective, and nit-picking regulations. For example, the Department of Health, Education and Welfare eliminated 5 per cent of their regulations, the Federal Trade Commission rescinded 111 outdated sets of rules on trade practices and both the Civil Aeronautics Board and the Interstate Commerce Commission have moved to allow more competition, which has led to lower prices. In 1978, we will continue these efforts.

Worker Health and Safety

The Occupational Health and Safety Administration has already slashed its paperwork requirements by 50 per cent and eliminated 1,100 unnecessary regulations, while improving its capacity to protect workers. This spring the Task Force on Worker Safety will make further recommendations to increase protection for workers and minimize employer cost.

Airline Regulatory Reform

Last year, I signed legislation deregulating all cargo air transportation. This year, I will continue to work for passage of the airline regulatory reform bill for passengers. That bill will allow air carriers to compete through lower fares, new services, and new markets, without excessive government interference or disruption of service to small communities.

Trucking Regulatory Reform

Forty years of tight government controls have not done enough to bring us competitive prices, good services, and efficient use of fuel. We will consider measures to bring more competition into the motor carrier area.

Drugs

We will propose legislation to reform regulation of the drug industry, which will protect the consumer and make regulations fairer and less burdensome.

Regulatory Process

Early in 1978, I will issue an Executive Order to improve the regulatory process. This Order will require officials responsible for regulations to sign them; assure that policy-level officials are fully involved in the process; require that regulations be written in plain English; make it easier for the public to participate in the process; increase coordination between agencies with overlapping responsibilities; require a closer look at the cost of regulations before they are issued; and require "sunset" reviews of existing regulations.

I have also set up an interagency committee to help regulatory agencies review the economic effects of major regulations, so that we can be sure that the costs of each proposed regulation have been fully considered. In this way we will be able to identify the least costly means of achieving our regulatory goals.

Paperwork Reduction

In 1977, my Administration decreased by 12 per cent the paperwork burden that the Government imposes on the people. This was done by eliminating, consolidating, simplifying, and decreasing the frequency of reports. That savings is the equivalent of 50,000 full-time workers filling out Federal forms for a full year. All departments and agencies are currently setting goals for further substantial reductions in 1978. All reporting requirements associated with grant-in-aid programs will be subject to "sunset" reviews, and ended unless they are found necessary. In addition, we are reviewing the recommendations of the Commission on Federal Paperwork.

Labor Law Reform

Last year we proposed legislation to reform our Nation's labor laws, in order to streamline the conduct of elections for employee representation and strengthen the enforcement powers of the National Labor Relations Board. We will work closely with Congress to ensure early passage of this bill, which is one of my highest legislative goals this year.

Election Reform

Last year, I supported proposals to make our elections fairer and more honest. These included public financing of Congressional campaigns, amendments to the Federal Election Campaign Act and other election reforms. The Administration will continue to support Congressional action on these measures.

Consumer Reform

We have taken many actions to benefit consumers by reducing the costs and improving the quality and safety of products. But one consumer initiative merits separate emphasis—the creation of the Office of Consumer Representation. We supported legislation last year to create such an Office, so that the interests of consumers could be represented in one government agency. The Office would not require additional government employees or expenditures since it would merely consolidate the consumer offices that already exist throughout the government. I am strongly committed to this legislation, and regard its enactment as one of the year's primary legislative priorities.

Public Broadcasting Reform

I proposed legislation last year to strengthen the public broadcasting service by providing increased long-term Federal support, insulation from political pressure, better coordination among the national organizations that run public broadcasting, and more opportunity for citizens to participate at the local level. My Administration will work with Congress this year to pass these reforms.

Openness and Integrity

One of our primary goals is to make certain that the government's ethical standards are high, and they they are fully observed. And we must ensure that our government is open and responsive to the American people.

Last year, I took steps in that direction by requiring that the senior officials of my Administration publicly disclose their income and assets and pledge not to do business with their agencies for two years after leaving government service. To increase the government's openness, we took steps to make certain that the spirit as well as the letter of the Freedom of Information Act was observed. And we tried to bring the Presidency to the people with citizen forums and discussion panels throughout the country.

This year, we will continue these efforts, concentrating our primary attention on these areas:

Lobby Reform

The Administration will press for legislation requiring registration of lobbyists and thorough public disclosure of their lobbying activities. This long-overdue legislation will help reestablish confidence and trust in government.

Ethics

I applaud the strong ethical codes adopted last year by the House and Senate. I believe those codes and the standards established for my Administration's officials should be made law, so that they will clearly apply to public officials in the future. I urge Congress to pass the Public Officials Integrity Act this year.

Classification

We are completing a study of classification systems for government documents and I will shortly issue an Executive Order designed to eliminate improper and unnecessary classification and to ensure that documents are declassified more rapidly.

Justice
Civil Rights and Equal Opportunity

All Americans have fundamental civil rights requiring government protection, and all must be afforded equal opportunities to participate as full members in our society. In 1977, this principle guided my Administration in numerous areas, and I plan to make certain that this year our efforts on behalf of civil rights and equal opportunities continue unabated. Our Nation's concern for human rights must be heard as clearly at home as abroad.

Educational Opportunities

In 1977, my Administration vigorously attacked educational discrimination on the elementary, secondary and higher education levels. A major suit was pursued to ensure non-discrimination at the university level. At the same time, we recognized and reaffirmed the importance of affirmative action programs to ensure equal opportunities at educational institutions through our brief in the *Bakke* case. Our efforts to eliminate discrimination and promote affirmative action programs, relying on flexible goals rather than on quotas, will continue in full force.

Handicapped

HEW issued regulations and guidelines to implement legislation guaranteeing equal access to programs receiving financial assistance from HEW. This year the other Cabinet Departments will issue similar regulations, so that the rights of handicapped Americans will begin to be fully observed. We are providing a $50 million loan fund to States and institutions to enable them to comply with these regulations and to eliminate barriers which prevent access by our handicapped citizens to federally assisted programs and activities. We are proposing a major increase in funding under the Education of all Handicapped Children Act.

Equal Opportunity

This past year the Administration reaffirmed Executive Order 11375, which prohibits discrimination on the basis of sex in Federal employment. In addition, I voluntarily placed the Executive Office of the President under Title VII of the Civil Rights Act. This year, as part of our effort to eliminate sex discrimination in unemployment *[sic]* and education, I will continue to urge the ratification of the Equal Rights Amendment to the Constitution.

This past year the Equal Employment Opportunity Commission was reorganized to increase its efficiency. As a result, the Commission made substantial progress on reducing its backlog of complaints. With the more than 40 per cent increase in funding that will be proposed in the 1979 budget, the EEOC will be able to further reduce its backlog. Early this year I will propose to Congress a reorganization plan concerning equal opportunity enforcement which will strengthen the EEOC.

Anti-Foreign Boycott

I strongly supported, and signed, legislation to prohibit American participation in secondary economic boycotts by foreign countries. That law will be strictly enforced by my Administration this year through the regulations just issued by the Department of Commerce.

Minority Business

Last year, we started a number of programs to make more opportunities available for minority-owned businesses. That effort will be continued and strengthened this year:

—We are half way toward our two-year goal of $2 billion in Federal purchases of services and goods from minority-owned firms. We will reach that goal by the end of the year.

—We will raise the goal for Federal deposits in minority-owned banks above the 1977 level of $100 billion.

—We will continue to enforce the $400 million minority business set-aside provision in the local public works act, and may exceed that target.

—We will continue to implement the minority business set-aside policy established for contracts let in the Northeast Corridor Railroad Improvement Program.

Undocumented Aliens

Last year, I proposed legislation to impose sanctions on employers who hire undocumented aliens and to change the legal status of the many undocumented aliens now residing in this country. That legislation would afford undocumented aliens residing here continuously since before 1970 the opportunity to apply for permanent resident status. It would create a new five-year temporary resident status for those undocumented aliens who resided here continuously from 1970 to January 1, 1977. I want to work with Congress this year toward passage of an undocumented aliens bill, for this social and economic problem can no longer be ignored.

Native Americans

The Administration has acted consistently to uphold its trusteeship responsibility to Native Americans. We also have elevated the post of Commissioner of Indian Affairs to the level of Assistant Secretary of Interior. In 1978, the Administration will review Federal Native American policy and will step up efforts to help Indian tribes assess and manage their natural resources.

Legal and Judicial Reform

Last year, my Administration began a number of major efforts to improve our Nation's legal and judicial system, and we intend to pursue those and related efforts fully this year.

Criminal Code Reform

We have worked closely with members of Congress to develop a proposed revision of the Nation's Criminal Code. That revision will codify in one part of the U.S. Code all Federal crime laws and will reform many outdated and inconsistent criminal laws. My Administration will work closely with Congress this year to seek passage of the first complete codification of the Nation's criminal laws.

Judicial Reform

The Federal judicial system has suffered for many years from an inadequate number of judges, and we will continue to work with Congress on an Omnibus Judgeship Bill to correct this problem. We will also continue our efforts to use our judges more effectively, through legislation which we have proposed to expand significantly the authority of magistrates, to increase the use of arbitration, and to tighten Federal jurisdiction. We will work this year to complete Congressional action on these bills.

Wiretap Reform

Last year we proposed legislation reforming our approach to electronic surveillance for foreign intelligence purposes, and affording greater protection to our citizens. Essentially, that legislation would require the government to obtain a court order before beginning any foreign intelligence wiretaps in this country. My Administration supports early passage of this much needed legislation.

Anti-trust Enforcement and Competition

Our Nation's anti-trust laws must be vigorously enforced. Therefore, I recently established a Presidential Commission to review Federal anti-trust enforcement, and to make its recommendations this year.

Last year, we initiated a new program, administered by the Department of Justice, to provide grant funds to State Attorneys General in order to strengthen anti-trust enforcement at the State level. We expect to see the results of this program this year.

By reducing government regulation, we can increase competition and thereby lower consumer costs. This year we will continue our deregulatory efforts in the legislative and administrative areas in order to reduce anti-competitive practices and abuses.

Crime Reduction and Criminal Justice

This past year the Reorganization Project and the Justice Department have been developing proposals to reorganize and to improve our Nation's criminal justice system, in order to strengthen enforcement and ensure equal justice. This year I will be sending a Message to Congress on criminal justice and crime reduction. My Message will include proposals to:

—reorganize the Federal Law Enforcement Assistance Administration;

—improve our criminal research efforts;

—develop better law enforcement methods against organized crime, white collar crime, drug abuse, and public corruption; and

—develop minimum standards for Federal correctional institutions.

FBI and Intelligence Agencies' Charters

I plan to issue a comprehensive Executive Order to govern the intelligence activities of the FBI, CIA, NSA and the Defense Department. That Executive Order will be the basis for the Administration's recommendations on legislative charters governing the activities of the FBI and various intelligence agencies.

Privacy

The Privacy Protection Study Committee recently proposed an extensive list of new legislative and regulatory safeguards. My Administration is analyzing these recent proposals and will develop this year a program to ensure that personal privacy is adequately protected.

District of Columbia

We proposed last year a series of reforms, including full voting representation in Congress, designed to give the residents of the District significantly greater control over their local affairs. My Administration will continue to work for the passage of those reforms this year.

DEVELOPING AND PROTECTING OUR NATURAL RESOURCES

National Energy Policy

In April 1977, I proposed to the Nation a comprehensive national energy policy. That policy is based on three principles, which will continue to guide our progress in 1978:

—we must learn to use energy more efficiently and more carefully, through conservation measures, including retrofitting our buildings, factories and homes;

—we must shift from oil and natural gas, which are becoming more scarce, to coal and renewable sources of energy which we have in abundance;

—we must provide fair prices to producers of energy, so as to encourage development of new supplies without permitting windfall profits.

The debate on this comprehensive policy has been long and arduous. A number of difficult, contentious issues remain to be settled. I am confident, however, that the Congress recognizes the seriousness of our energy problem and will act expeditiously on this program early this year. Securing passage of an acceptable energy bill—one which is fair to consumers, provides needed energy savings, and is prudent from a fiscal and budgetary standpoint—will continue as our highest and most urgent national priority in 1978.

Energy Statutes and Actions

We have already begun to lay a strong foundation for implementation of a national energy policy. In 1977 we took steps to put in place important policies and structural reforms needed to meet our energy goals:

—Creation of a new Department of Energy which combines, for the first time, major governmental functions of energy research, regulation, pricing policy, information collection and dissemination, and overall policy development. Without a strong organization, we would not hope to implement a comprehensive national policy.

—Congress has approved our proposed route for a pipeline to bring natural gas from the North Slope of Alaska to the lower 48 states.

—Passage of the Emergency Natural Gas Act to cope with the hardships of last winter's freeze and assure that high priority gas users were not cut off during supply emergencies.

—Funding of more than $4 billion to store the first 500 million barrels of oil in a strategic petroleum reserve. We have already begun to fill that reserve, and we remain committed to a 1 billion barrel strategic reserve by 1985.

Outer Continental Shelf Legislation

Legislation to improve the management of the Outer Continental Shelf for oil and gas development is a major item of un-finished business pending before Congress. Prompt passage is necessary so that we can have the benefit of the new law as we move to open more offshore areas to development and production. This bill mandates long-needed reforms in the leasing program to provide for the necessary development of offshore oil and gas while enhancing competition among oil companies, assuring that the public receives a fair return for the sale of the public's oil and gas resources, and protecting our marine and coastal resources.

Nuclear Energy

The United States has also advanced a policy to prevent the proliferation of nuclear weapons around the world. An International Nuclear Fuel Cycle Evaluation has been established with wide international participation to examine alternatives to existing proliferation-prone technologies. In addition, legislation was proposed last year to establish better controls on export of nuclear fuels and technologies. We will work with Congress to secure passage of that legislation early in 1978.

Our commitment to preventing the spread of nuclear weapons has led us to reorient our own domestic nuclear policies. I have deferred indefinitely the commercial reprocessing of spent nuclear fuel and plutonium recycling.

The Clinch River Plant itself would waste more than $2 billion while teaching us little that we do not already know, or cannot learn from our existing nuclear research and development program. I have recommended that the Clinch River Breeder Project be stopped, because it represents a premature and unwise commitment to commercialization of technology that we do not now need.

However, we intend to continue to develop the nuclear energy the Nation needs.

We will continue to move forward with a major research program on breeder technology.

We will begin to implement our program for government management of spent fuel from nuclear reactors.

In 1978, my Administration will work towards a policy for safe, permanent disposal of nuclear wastes.

In 1978 and beyond, we will carry on a vigorous nuclear research and development program designed to give us safe technologies that will reduce the danger of nuclear proliferation and will be environmentally responsible. We will also seek to improve the current system of licensing nuclear power reactors in order to cut bureaucratic delays, while firmly maintaining and strengthening health, safety and environmental requirements. I will propose nuclear licensing legislation to the Congress this year.

Environment

One of my deepest personal commitments is to a clean, healthy environ-ment for all of our citizens. Last May, I outlined this Administration's environmental priorities and policies in a comprehensive Environmental Message. Working closely with the Congress, we have made good progress on many of the measures contained in that Message; it will continue to guide our administrative and legislative actions in 1978. Overall, we will:

—increase our environmental outlays by more than 10 per cent, and provide the new staff resources necessary to ensure that the Nation's environmental laws are obeyed;

—determine the best way of enforcing the landmark environmental statutes enacted in 1977, taking considerations of science and public policy into account;

—pursue several important initiatives, including a National Heritage program and designation of national interest lands in Alaska, to manage our precious natural resources better and to preserve our heritage.

Environmental Statutes

In 1977, we worked closely with Congress to enact three of the most significant environmental statutes in recent years:

—The Surface Mining Control and Reclamation Act establishes a joint Federal-State program to make sure we use economically and environmentally sound strip-mining practices. It also sets up a fund to reclaim lands which have been ravaged by uncontrolled, careless mining, and provides clear, stable policy direction for operators.

—The Clean Air Act Amendments establish strict but achievable standards for auto emissions and ensure continued progress in reducing pollution from stationary air pollution sources.

—The Clean Water Act authorizes many of our most important water clean-up programs and will protect our Nation's wetlands without unnecessary Federal requirements. The Act also reforms the sewage treatment construction grant program and gives strong emphasis to the control of toxic chemicals in our environment.

We will provide the leadership and the funding necessary to carry out these new laws.

Water Policy

In 1977, an effort was begun to ensure that Federal programs and policies provide sound and fair management of our limited and valuable water resources. We began a complete review of Federal water policy, which will be completed this year. After close consultation with the Congress, the States, and the public, we will propose measures needed to carry out the recommendations of that study.

We will also continue with the strong dam safety inspection program which was initiated late last year to make sure our dams, public or private, are safe.

Alaska Lands

Last year, I sent Congress a proposal for use of Federal lands in Alaska. This proposal will protect 92 million acres for the public, will create or expand 13 national parks and reserves, 13 national wildlife refuges, and will confer wild and scenic river status on 33 waterways. I hope Congress will adopt these measures, which are needed this year to preserve the unique natural treasures of Alaska and, at the same time, permit the orderly development of Alaskan resources.

Redwood National Park

Redwood National Park contains some of the Nation's largest and oldest trees. Last year, to protect these trees from destruction by commercial logging at the edges of the Park, legislation was proposed to expand its boundaries. We will press for Congressional action on this bill in 1978.

National Heritage Program

We will shortly be proposing a Federal-State program to preserve unique elements of our natural and cultural heritage. This program, modeled after successful ones in several states, will be administered by the Department of the Interior. Although many of the necessary steps can be taken administratively, we will seek some new legislative authority in 1978.

Federal Compliance with Environmental Laws

My Administration is committed to the principle that the Federal government must set a good example of compliance with those environmental laws and regulations which have been established for the private sector. So far, unfortunately, the Federal record has been found wanting. My 1979 budget includes money to bring Federal facilities into compliance with existing environmental laws and regulations.

Federal Reclamation

In 1977, we began a thorough review of the 1902 Reclamation Act. After the study has been completed and reviewed this year, I will propose to Congress any changes needed to modernize the law.

Mining Law Reform

Last year the Administration proposed legislation to replace the archaic 1872 Mining Law with a modern leasing system for publicly-owned mineral resources. The 1872 system has resulted in withdrawal of large areas of land from mineral exploration as the only tool for environmental protection. The Administration's proposal would establish a balanced system where the public interests in mineral development, environmental protection and revenue to the U.S. Treasury will all be accomplished. Special provisions would minimize burdens on small operators and provide incentives for exploration.

Oil Spills

Last year I proposed to Congress legislation which would establish strict liability standards for oil tanker spills and would improve regulations aimed at preventing future oil spills. That legislation is still needed.

Science and Technology

The health of American science and technology and the creation of new knowledge is important to our economic well-being, to our national security, to our ability to help solve pressing national problems in such areas as energy, environment, health, natural resources. I am recommending a program of real growth of scientific research and other steps that will strengthen the Nation's research centers and encourage a new surge of technological innovation by American industry. The budget increase of 11 per cent for basic research will lead to improved opportunities for young scientists and engineers, and upgraded scientific equipment in the Nation's research centers. I am determined to maintain our Nation's leadership role in science and technology.

We will continue America's progress in the field of space exploration with continued development of the space shuttle system and procurement of four shuttle orbiters for operations from both East and West coasts, development of a spacecraft to study for the first time the polar regions of the Sun, and increased outlays for demonstrations of the practical applications of space-based systems and development of space technology.

FOREIGN AFFAIRS

A year ago I set five goals for United States foreign policy in the late 1970s and early 1980s: to reassert America's moral leadership; to strengthen our traditional ties with friends and allies; to work toward a more just international system; to promote regional reconciliation; and to preserve peace through preparedness and arms control. These goals continue to underlie my agenda for 1978.

MORAL LEADERSHIP

During the past year, we have placed American foreign policy on a new course consistent with the values and highest ideals of the American people. We are trying to limit the worldwide sale of arms; we are trying to prevent nuclear explosives—and the ability to make them—from spreading to more countries; we are building a new relationship with the developing countries, and we are promoting human rights throughout the world.

Human Rights

Virtually everywhere, human rights have become an important issue—especially in countries where they are systematical-

ly violated. There has been real progress, and for that the United States can take some credit.

We have taken the lead among Western nations at the Belgrade Review Conference on Security and Cooperation in Europe. Working closely with our Allies, and with neutral and non-aligned nations, our delegation—led by Ambassador Arthur Goldberg—has conducted a thorough review of implementation of the Helsinki Final Act, in all its aspects. We have made clear the United States is committed to the full implementation of the Final Act in this and other areas. We will seek a further Review Conference in two years; meanwhile, we will press for better implementation of the Helsinki Final Act.

Non-Proliferation

We must not ignore the enormous dangers posed by the unrestrained spread of nuclear weapons technology. We recognize the benefits of commercial nuclear power, but we also must acknowledge the risks. We believe that all countries can enjoy the benefits, while the risks are minimized, by developing safer technologies and creating new institutions to manage and safeguard all phases of the nuclear fuel cycle. Meanwhile, we have decided to postpone a premature commitment to technologies we cannot yet safely manage on a commercial scale; and we are seeking to persuade others that there are sound economic and energy reasons for them to do likewise.

Arms Sales

The world is threatened by the spiraling increase in trade of conventional arms. Not only do these arms increase the likelihood of conflict, they also divert resources from other human needs. It will not be easy to slow this spiral. We will begin to cut back on our own sales in recognition of the fact that, as the world's principal seller, we have a duty to take the first step. But we know that our efforts can only succeed if other major arms suppliers and recipients cooperate.

TIES WITH FRIENDS AND ALLIES

The energy crisis has underscored the reality of interdependence among nations and the need for a stable international financial and trading system. Our own actions reflect the belief that consultations with traditional friends and dialogue with developing nations are the only way that the United States can provide the economic and political leadership which the world expects of us.

Working with the Allies

During the past year, the United States restored our traditional friends and allies to the center of our foreign policy. Within days after his inauguration, the Vice President visited Brussels, Rome, Bonn, Paris, Reykjavik, and Tokyo. I met frequently in Washington with European and Japanese leaders. I participated in the Economic Summit in London, the 1977 NATO Summit, and a Four-Power Summit with leaders of Britain, Germany, and France. At the beginning of 1978, I visited France and Belgium—and while in Brussels, made the first visit by an American President to the headquarters of the European Community. We have also consulted with our European Allies on such diverse subjects as SALT, MBFR, the Middle East, Africa, human rights, the Belgrade Conference, energy, non-proliferation, the global economy, and North-South relations. We will intensify these efforts this year, expanding the list to include close consultations with the Allies on major arms control issues.

On May 30-31, we will host a NATO Summit in Washington, and we are also planning another Economic Summit this year.

We have shown in our dealings with Japan that close allies can find solutions to shared problems. Early in the year, we were concerned about nuclear reprocessing in Japan, but through flexibility and goodwill on both sides a suitable accommodation was reached on the building of a nuclear reprocessing plant there. Most recently, we reached agreement with the Japanese on ways to deal with their large current account surplus. Our trade and economic talks are another example of constructive action.

International Economic Cooperation

We are working to improve and extend the international economic system, to strengthen international economic institutions, and to ensure that international economic competition takes place in an orderly fashion. We will seek to improve cooperation among nations in the IMF, the GATT, the World Bank, the OECD, and other international organizations which have enabled us to maintain an open, liberal, trade and payments system.

The American economy remains strong. Our competitive position in international trade is excellent. In 1977 our merchandise exports exceeded imports (except for oil) by a large amount. Our inflation rate is among the lowest in the industrial world.

But our balance of trade and payments incurred a large and worrisome deficit. There were two main causes:

—In 1977, $45 billion flowed out to pay for imported oil. This wiped out what would otherwise have been a trade surplus.

—The demand here for foreign goods was much greater than the demand for American goods abroad. In 1977, American GNP increased roughly twice as fast in real terms as the GNP of our main trading partners.

Against this background, the exchange rate of the dollar declined relative to the currencies of Japan, Germany, Switzerland, and other European countries. These developments led to disorderly conditions in the exchange markets. In December I made clear that the United States would intervene to counter these disorders, and we have done so.

To assure the integrity of the dollar we must act now:

—We need a healthy and growing United States economy, with adequate investment, a prudent budget, and declining inflation. This will make us more competitive and more attractive to foreign investors.

—We need to conserve energy and develop alternative sources of supply. This will reduce our dependence on imported oil, and cut the outflow of dollars.

—We need to see a more vigorous world economy. Stronger growth, particularly in countries like Germany, Japan, Switzerland, and the Netherlands, can help reduce our own deficits and bring stability to international payments.

Factors already at work will reduce our trade deficit. Economic activity in Europe and elsewhere should rise. Our oil imports should level off this year. The effect of new exchange rates that have already occurred will, when their full effect is realized, improve our trade balance by several billions of dollars. While our trade and payments deficit in 1978 will be large, our external position should show some improvement.

We must also augment our capacity to deal with possible strains and pressures by strengthening our international trade and monetary system. I urge the Congress to act promptly to approve United States participation in the IMF's Supplementary Financing Facility.

The trading nations of the world are engaged in negotiations to reduce barriers and improve the international trading system by a reciprocal and balanced opening of markets. Freer trade will enable us all to use the world's resources more efficiently and will contribute to economic growth.

We will also attempt to strengthen the rules that have regulated international trade during the last 30 years. International competition must take place within a framework of agreed rules that are recognized as appropriate and fair.

THE DEVELOPING COUNTRIES

One of the most critical issues facing the United States is our economic and political relationship with developing countries. Our economy has become visibly dependent on the developing world for supplies and markets.

North-South Dialogue

Throughout 1975 and 1976 the United States and other developed countries worked with a group of developing nations in the Conference of International Economic Cooperations (CIEC). That "North-South Dialogue" reached agreement on some issues in June 1977, but there remain a number of unresolved questions. The United States will continue to consult and negotiate with developing countries on questions like commodity price stabilization, technology, and a common fund for international buffer stocks. We will pursue the North-South dialogue in the months ahead, confident that the developed nations and the developing nations can agree upon measures that will let all nations participate more fully in the management of the world economy.

Africa

Our relations with Africa involve energy, human rights, economic development, and the North-South dialogue. The Maputo and Lagos Conferences demonstrated that African countries can discuss difficult problems with us, to mutual advantage. Our relations with Nigeria have improved dramatically.

The Administration's FY 79 budget substantially increases development assistance to Africa, including continued support for the African Development Fund, and other programs to help African governments meet their people's basic human needs. The growth of African regional institutions like the Sahel Development Fund is important to African development.

Latin-America/Caribbean

The Administration's approach to Latin America and the Caribbean recognizes this region's diversity. We have placed great importance on the protection and defense of human rights, on halting the proliferation of nuclear weapons capabilities, on restraining conventional arms sales, on contributing to the settlement of disputes, and on engaging Latin governments in global economic negotiations.

We are now seeking Senate ratification of Protocol I of the Treaty of Tlatelolco, and the American Convention on Human Rights. Through the Caribbean Group, we are trying to promote regional development. And we intend to help several nations develop alternative energy sources.

Panama

General Torrijos and I signed the two Panama Canal Treaties on September 9, 1977. These treaties meet the legitimate interests of Panama and the United States and guarantee our permanent right to protect and defend the Canal. They will contribute importantly to regional stability.

Asia

The United States has sought to underline our desire for a close relationship with the developing countries of Asia through my visit to that continent and through regular contacts with the member countries of the Association of Southeast Asian Nations. We welcome the cooperation with ASEAN of the developed countries of the region, such as Japan and Australia.

PROMOTING REGIONAL RECONCILIATION

The greatest danger to world peace and stability is not war among the great powers, but war among small nations. During the past year, the United States has helped to promote productive negotiations in two troubled regions: the Middle East and Southern Africa. We have also tried to settle conflicts in the Horn of Africa and on Cyprus. And we have negotiated two Panama Canal Treaties that will enhance our country's relations with all the nations of Latin America.

The Middle East

In an effort to break with the rigid approaches of the past and bring about an overall peace settlement, I have looked to three basic principles: normalization of political, economic and cultural relations through peace treaties; withdrawal of armed forces from occupied territory to recognized and secure borders and the establishment of effective security measures; and a resolution of the Palestinian question.

Significant progress toward peace in the Middle East was made last year; we particularly applaud President Sadat's courageous initiative, reciprocated by Prime Minister Begin, in launching direct negotiations. The United States will continue this year to encourage all parties to resolve this deep-seated conflict.

Southern Africa

The entering Administration inherited problems in Rhodesia, Namibia, and South Africa.

—With the British, the United States launched new Rhodesian discussions last year. The Anglo-American Plan of September 1 sets forth fair and workable principles for majority rule: a transition period leading to free elections, a UN presence, a constitution with a judicially protected bill of rights, and a Zimbabwe Development Fund.

—The five-power Contact Group, in which the United States participates, has held discussions with South Africa and with the Southwest Africa Peoples Organization and other interested parties on an internationally acceptable settlement for an independent Namibia under majority rule. This effort has produced wide agreement, including provisions for a substantial UN presence.

—The United States has told the South African Prime Minister that unless his nation begins a progressive transformation toward full political participation for all its people, our relations will suffer. We supported a United Nations arms embargo on South Africa, prohibited "gray area" sales, and began a review of US/South African economic relations.

The Horn of Africa

Arms supplied by the Soviet Union now fuel both sides of a conflict in the Horn of Africa between Somalia and Ethiopia. There is a danger that the Soviet Union and Cuba will commit their own soldiers in this conflict, transforming it from a local war to a confrontation with broader strategic implications.

We deplore the fact that disagreements in this region have grown—with the assistance of outside powers—into bloody conflict. We have made clear to both sides that we will supply no arms for aggressive purposes. We will not recognize forcible changes in boundaries. We want to see the fighting end and the parties move from the battlefield to the negotiating table.

Cyprus

We hope that the groundwork was laid in 1977 for a permanent settlement in Cyprus and we are encouraging movement in that direction.

PRESERVING PEACE

During the past year, the Administration has assessed the threats to our own and our Allies' security, as well as our collective strength to combat these threats. We have sought to promote responsible arms control efforts and to reduce competition in arms. Recognizing that a strong defense is the foundation of our security, we have made certain that our defense spending will be sufficient and used to maximum effect.

Arms Control

The fundamental purposes of our arms limitations efforts are to promote our own national security and to strengthen international stability, thereby enhancing the prospects for peace everywhere.

—We are trying to move the Strategic Arms Limitation Talks toward more ambitious objectives. We want to reduce, not just contain, the competition in the number of strategic weapons possessed by the United States and the Soviet Union, and to limit qualitative improvements in weapons which merely raise the risks to all of us. Precisely because of our determination to obtain both of these objectives negotiations have been difficult and prolonged. However, I am confident that the agreement that we will present to the Congress will meet them.

—We have also made solid progress toward an objective that the United States has pursued for many years: a comprehensive treaty banning all nuclear explosions. This treaty will be open to all nations of the world. It will be a major step toward reduced reliance on these weapons and toward halting their further spread in the world.

—At the same time we are seeking arms limitations agreements with the Soviet Union that will contribute to security and stability in various regions of the world. In Europe we and our NATO Allies are seeking a mutual and balanced force reductions agreement that will achieve greater stability and balance at lower levels of forces. In the Indian Ocean, where neither we nor the Soviet Union has yet deployed military power on a large scale, we are working for an agreement to prevent a major military competition.

—For the first time, we have begun to negotiate with the Soviet Union the outlines of a treaty banning chemical warfare.

—An essential element of American security is the maintenance of stability in the Western Pacific, where the United States plays a major role in maintaining a balance of power. We are seeking to readjust our military presence in Korea by reducing our ground forces on the Peninsula and undertaking compensatory measures to ensure that an adequate balance of forces remain. We are talking with the Filipino government about the future of our military bases there.

—We are continuing the process of normalization of our relations with the People's Republic of China within the framework of the Shanghai Communique.

—In the last year, we have sought to halt the worldwide spread of nuclear weapons capacity. Nearly 40 nations have joined with us in an effort to find nuclear power sources that cannot be readily used for building nuclear weapons.

Defense Posture/Budget

The defense budget that I am recommending to Congress will fulfill our most pressing defense needs. I am requesting increases in defense spending that more than compensate for inflation. They are needed to maintain an adequate military balance in the face of continued Soviet military efforts.

—As we negotiate with the Soviets over strategic arms, we are continuing to preserve essential equivalence in strategic nuclear strength. Here our technological advantage over the Soviet Union is most apparent. We are building cruise missiles, which together with upgraded B-52s will assure the capability of this element of our Triad. We are continuing to develop the M-X missile system in case we need to deploy them. In this budget, I am requesting funds for continued increase in our Trident submarine force, which is our most important strategic program because submarines are so hard for any enemy to destroy.

—With our NATO Allies we are trying to improve the initial combat capability of NATO forces. We will improve the readiness of critical combat units, enhance American capability to send ground and tactical air forces reinforcements, and increase our permanent forces there. To lay the foundation for future improvements, the budget I propose requests 18 per cent increases in the procurement of equipment for the Army. The United States is not taking these steps alone; we are participating in a mutual effort.

—The importance of sea forces to United States national security is undisputed. The Navy receives the largest share of the defense budget, and I am requesting funds to continue its modernization. But, we need to examine the appropriate size and mix of United States naval forces in the future. Therefore, I have deferred spending for new aircraft carriers until a current Defense Department study is completed early this year. While we maintain our naval strength, we should have the capability to deploy rapidly a light but effective combat force worldwide, if necessary, without overseas base support. To this end, I am requesting funds for a vigorous airlift enhancement program.

In these and other ways, we are seeking to develop a foreign policy which is wider in scope; a foreign policy which recognizes global diversity; and a foreign policy which builds a more just and stable international system.

JIMMY CARTER

The White House,
January 19, 1978

Economic Message

Following is the text of President Carter's economic message to Congress Jan. 20, 1978:

TO THE CONGRESS
OF THE UNITED STATES:

I will be working closely with the Congress in 1978 to enact a program addressed to the immediate and the long-term needs of our economy. I am proposing tax reductions and reforms to continue our strong economic recovery, to encourage increased investment by American businesses, and to create a simpler and fairer tax system. I am seeking legislation to address the special problems of the disadvantaged and the unemployed. And I am taking new steps to combat inflation.

This report to the Congress on the condition of the economy sets forth the overall framework within which my economic proposals were formulated. It outlines, for you and for the Nation, my economic priorities for the years ahead and my strategies for achieving them.

I have begun from the premise that our economy is basically healthy, but that well-chosen Government policies will assure continued progress toward our economic goals.

Last year more than four million new jobs were created in our country—an all-time record—and unemployment was reduced by more than one million persons. Output rose by almost 6 per cent, and the benefits of this large increase were widely shared. The after-tax income of consumers, adjusted for inflation, rose substantially during 1977. Wages of the typical American worker increased by more than the rise of prices, and business profits also advanced.

The American economy is completing three years of recovery from the severe recession of 1974-75. Recovery in most other nations has lagged far behind our own. In the economies of our six major trading partners, seven million persons were unemployed at year's end—more than at the

depths of the 1974-75 recession. Our inflation rate is also lower than in most other nations around the world. We have a great many accomplishments. But much progress remains to be made, and there are problems to be dealt with along the way.

The recession of 1974-75 was the worst in 40 years, and the substantial increase in output over the past three years still leaves the economy operating below its productive potential. We cannot be content when almost 6½ million people actively seeking jobs cannot find work, when 3¼ million workers take part-time jobs because they cannot find fulltime employment, and when one million people have stopped looking for a job because they have lost hope of finding one. We cannot be content when a substantial portion of our industrial plant stands idle, as it does today.

We cannot be satisfied with an economic recovery that bypasses significant segments of the American people. Unemployment among minorities is more than twice as high as that among whites—and unemployment among minority teenagers is tragically high. Women have fewer satisfying job opportunities than men, and older Americans often find their access to the job market blocked. Farm incomes have dropped precipitously.

We must also address other problems if we are to assure full restoration of prosperity. Inflation is a serious economic concern for all Americans. The inflation rate is too high and must be brought down. Moreover, a residue of unease and caution about the future still pervades the thinking of some of our people. Businesses are still hesitant in their long-term investment planning, and the stock market remains depressed despite the substantial increase in business profits.

The economic difficulties that we face in the United States also confront most nations around the world. Our mutual problems are the legacy of the trauma suffered by the world economy during the early 1970s. The massive escalation of oil prices since 1973 continues to impose great burdens on the world economy. Oil imports drain away the purchasing power of oil-importing nations and upset the international balance of payments.

Many foreign governments have been reluctant to adopt policies needed to stimulate economic growth because they are concerned that inflationary pressures might be renewed or that their balance of international payments might be worsened. Abroad, as well as at home, concerns about the future have deterred business investment in new plants and equipment. As a consequence, economic growth has stagnated in many countries, and the rise in the capital stock needed to increase productivity, raise standards of living, and avoid future inflationary bottlenecks is not occurring.

The problems we face today are more complex and difficult than those of an earlier era. We cannot concentrate just on inflation, or just on unemployment, or just

on deficits in the Federal budget or our international payments. Nor can we act in isolation from other countries. We must deal with all of these problems simultaneously and on a worldwide basis.

Our problems cannot be solved overnight. But we can resolve them if we fix our sights on long-term objectives, adopt programs that will help us to realize our goals, and remain prepared to make adjustments as basic circumstances change.

In making my decisions on tax and budget policies for fiscal 1979, and in planning more generally for our Nation's future, I have been guided by four objectives for our economy that I believe our Nation should pursue.

We must continue to move steadily toward a high-employment economy in which the benefits of prosperity are widely shared. Progress in reducing unemployment of our labor and capital resources must be sure and sustainable. Over the next several years I believe we can increase our real output by 4½ to 5 per cent per year, and reduce unemployment by about one-half of a percentage point each year. An especially high priority is to increase job opportunities for the disadvantaged, particularly for black and Spanish-speaking Americans, and to deal more effectively with local pockets of unemployment, such as those in urban areas. We should eliminate unfair advantages through reform of the tax system, and restructure our welfare system to assure that the fruits of economic growth are enjoyed by all Americans.

We should rely principally on the private sector to lead the economic expansion and to create new jobs for a growing labor force. Five out of every six new jobs in the economy are created in the private sector. There are good reasons for continuing to rely mainly on the private sector in the years ahead. By emphasizing the creation of private jobs, our resources will be used more efficiently, our future capacity to produce will expand more rapidly, and the standard of living for our people will rise faster. Reliance upon the private sector does not mean neglecting the tasks that government can and must perform. The Federal Government can be an active partner to help achieve progress toward meeting national needs and, through competent management, still absorb a declining portion of the Nation's output.

We must contain and reduce the rate of inflation as we move toward a more fully employed economy. Inflation extracts a heavy toll from all Americans, and particularly from the poor and those on fixed incomes. Reducing inflation would benefit us all. A more stable price environment would make it easier for business firms and consumers to plan for the future. Thus, reduced inflation would substantially enhance our chances to maintain a strong economic expansion and return to a high-employment economy. In the years ahead we must seek to unwind the inflation we have inherited from the past and take the steps necessary to prevent new inflationary pressures as we approach high employment.

We must act in ways that contribute to the health of the world economy. As the strongest economy in the world, the United States has unique responsibilities to improve the international economic climate. The well-being of the United States depends on the condition of other nations around the world. Their economic destiny is, in turn, shaped by ours. The United States can retain its stature in the world only by pursuing policies that measure up to its role as a leader in international economic affairs.

These four economic objectives are sufficiently ambitious to constitute a serious challenge, but sufficiently realistic to be within our reach. A well-designed program will permit us to achieve them. The principal elements of my economic strategy are:

- Adopting promptly an effective national energy program;
- Managing Federal budget expenditures carefully and prudently, so that we can meet national needs while gradually reducing the share of our national output devoted to Federal spending;
- Using tax reductions to ensure steady growth of the private economy and reforming the tax system to make it fairer, simpler, and more progressive;
- Working to reduce the Federal deficit and balance the budget as rapidly as the developing strength of the economy allows;
- Improving existing programs and developing new ones to attack the problem of structural unemployment among the disadvantaged;
- Promoting greater business capital formation in order to enhance productivity gains, increase standards of living, and reduce the chances that capacity shortages would inhibit expansion later on;
- Adopting more effective programs to reduce the current rate of inflation and prevent a reacceleration of inflation as we approach high employment; and
- Pursuing international economic policies that promote economic recovery throughout the world, encourage an expansion of world trade, and maintain a strong international monetary system.

National Energy Plan

It has now been over four years since our economy was buffeted by the oil embargo and its aftermath of sharply increased oil prices. The massive oil price increase in 1973-74 contributed to the double-digit inflation of 1974 and to the worst recession in 40 years. It is a primary factor today behind the large deficit in our international balance of payments. Yet the United States still has not enacted a comprehensive and effective energy policy.

Our dependence on imported oil is sapping the strength of the American economy. Last year our imports of oil reached a total of about $45 billion, compared with $8½ billion in 1973. The increased expenditures on those imports have been like a sudden and massive tax imposed on the American people. Only part of the revenues have been returned to the United States in the form of higher exports of American goods to oil-producing countries. As a consequence, that "tax" has become a major obstacle to economic growth.

The huge deficit in foreign trade arising from our oil imports has contributed to the fall in the value of the dollar abroad. The dollar's decline has raised the cost of the goods we import and contributed to inflation. Our deficit also has unsettled international monetary markets, with adverse consequences for our international trading partners. Our response to the energy crisis is therefore a central element in our international and domestic economic policy. The energy program will not solve our problems at once, but it will pave the way for a balanced foreign trade position and a strong and sound dollar.

Our energy problems will worsen in the years to come unless we curb our appetite for oil and gas. Without decisive action, we will put additional pressure on the world oil market, aggravate inflationary pressures at home, and increase our vulnerability to the threat of oil supply disruptions. Together, these forces could severely limit the potential for continued economic progress over the coming decade.

The United States has no choice but to adjust to the new era of expensive energy. We can only choose when and how. If we act today, we have time to make a gradual transition to more efficient energy use—by conserving energy, increasing domestic energy production, and developing alternative sources of energy. If we delay, adjustment later will be harsh and painful, requiring draconian measures to accomplish what can now be done gradually and with far less anguish.

The energy problem we face is enormously complex. Finding an acceptable and effective solution has not been easy for me or for the Congress. I look forward to working closely with the Congress early this year to assure a speedy resolution. An acceptable bill must satisfy the following principles:

- First, the program must effectively reduce our consumption of limited energy supplies—oil and gas—while encouraging energy production and promoting a transition to the use of resources that are more abundant.
- Second, the program must be fair. No segment of the population should bear a disproportionate share of the cost or burden of adjustment, and no industry should reap unnecessary and undeserved windfall gains.
- Third, the program must be consistent with our overall economic strategy. It must neither undermine our efforts to continue the recovery nor obstruct achievement of our long-term budgetary goals.

Dealing with the energy problem is a difficult test for our Nation. It is a test of our economic and political maturity. Our people would surely react if there were an immediate crisis. But I am asking them to undertake sacrifices to *prevent* a crisis. If we fail to act today, we will bring a crisis upon ourselves and our children in years to come.

Federal Budget Expenditures

My Administration has given high priority to making more effective use of limited Federal resources. In fiscal 1976, Federal outlays amounted to 22½ per cent of the Nation's gross national product. This is considerably higher than the share devoted to government spending that prevailed for many years. To some degree, the recent higher share reflects the fact that the economy is still performing below its capacity, and that Federal programs to support the unemployed and the needy are larger than they would be in a high-employment economy. But it also stems from very rapid growth in a number of Federal programs instituted over the past 10 to 15 years.

Most of our Federal expenditure programs are designed to achieve important national goals that the private sector of the economy cannot accomplish. Only the government can provide for the national defense, and government resources are essential to cushion the hardships created by economic recession, to preserve our national resources, to protect the environment, and to meet other critical needs.

The Federal Government has a particular obligation to provide assistance to those who remain in need even during good times. Last year I presented to the Congress a program to reform the welfare system—the Better Jobs and Income Act of 1977—that is a concrete example of our commitment to devote resources to the most pressing national needs. My program will cost money. But it also will establish a more easily understood welfare system that is less costly to administer, less subject to abuse, and more responsive to the true needs of those who receive a helping hand from government. This program will create up to 1.4 million jobs for those able to work, and it will replace the patchwork of Federal, State, and local programs with a consistent income-support system that will relieve much of the enormous burden now placed on State and local governments.

In the management of a business enterprise, efficiency is enforced by the discipline of the market place. The collective judgments of millions of consumers establish an environment in which waste and efficiency are eventually penalized. The government, however, is not subject to that discipline. We in government must therefore impose stringent controls on ourselves to ensure greater efficiency and to make better choices among the possible uses of the taxpayers' money.

To assist us in this endeavor, I have adopted methods of budgetary control that have been tested in the business community. Early last year I asked the Office of Management and Budget to inaugurate a system of zero-based budgeting throughout the Federal Government. Within this budgetary system, every Federal program is given careful scrutiny—no matter how large or how small it may be, no matter how long it has been in existence or how recently established. This new system of budgetary planning helped to hold down less essential outlays in the budget for fiscal 1979 and focus our resources on our important national needs. It will produce even greater savings in subsequent years. A process of multi-year budgeting also has been inaugurated within the Federal Government that will require tentative budget plans to be developed and reviewed for three years ahead. With this system we can more effectively control future expenditures—by avoiding commitments now to endeavors that would grow in the future beyond the proportions we desire.

In formulating my recommendations for the 1979 budget, I have exercised very strict controls over spending. Adjusted for inflation, the increase in outlays has been held to less than 2 percent. I intend to continue prudent expenditure controls in the future. With good management we can, I believe, achieve our Nation's important social goals and still reduce over time the share of gross national product committed to Federal expenditures to about 21 percent.

Tax Reductions

I propose to rely principally upon growth in the private sector of the economy to reduce unemployment and raise incomes. Special Federal efforts will, of course, be necessary to deal with such problems as structural unemployment, but tax reductions will be the primary means by which Federal budget policy will promote growth. Careful management of budget outlays and a growing economy should permit substantial reductions in the years ahead. Tax reductions will be needed to strengthen consumer purchasing power and expand consumer markets. Stable growth in markets, together with added tax incentives for business, will lead to rising business investment and growing productivity.

As inflation and real economic growth raise the incomes of most Americans, they are pushed into higher income tax brackets. The tax burden on individuals is raised just as if higher rates had been enacted. The payroll taxes levied on workers and business firms for social security and unemployment insurance will also increase substantially over the year ahead. These are very large increases, but they are needed to keep our social security and unemployment insurance systems soundly financed.

Between 1977 and 1979, taxes on businesses and individuals will rise very sharply as a result of these several factors. Even though our economy is basically

healthy, this increasingly heavy tax burden would exert a mounting drag on economic growth. It must, therefore, be counteracted by tax reductions. The magnitude and timing of the reductions should be designed to maintain economic growth at a steady pace, taking into account the effects both of the growing tax burden and of other factors at work in the economy.

Consistent with this strategy, I am proposing a $25 billion program of net tax reductions accompanied by substantial tax reforms.

Individual income taxes will be reduced primarily through across-the-board reductions in personal tax rates, with special emphasis on low- and middle-income taxpayers. Personal taxes also will be simplified by my proposal to replace the existing personal exemption and credit with a tax credit of $240 for each person in the taxpayer's family.

There also will be important reforms that will improve the individual income tax system and raise substantial revenues, enabling me to recommend larger personal tax reductions.

Overall, I am proposing personal tax reductions of $24 billion, offset by $7 billion in tax reforms. These tax cuts, which will take effect next October 1, will significantly improve the progressivity of the tax system. The typical four-person family with $15,000 in income will receive a tax cut of $258—or more than 19 percent. As a result of the changes I am recommending, filling out tax returns will be simpler for many people.

Individuals also will benefit from reductions I have proposed in the Federal excise tax on telephone bills, and in the Federal payroll tax for unemployment insurance. These two proposals will add about $2 billion to consumers' purchasing power that will be realized principally through lower prices.

Business taxes will be reduced by more than $8 billion in 1979 under my tax program, offset partially by more than $2 billion in business tax reforms for a net tax reduction of nearly $6 billion. I have recommended that the overall corporate tax rate be reduced on October 1 from the current 48 percent to 45 percent, and be cut further to 44 percent in 1980. I also recommend that the existing 10-percent investment tax credit be made permanent, and that the benefits of this credit be extended to investments in industrial and utility structures. My proposal will enable businesses to use the investment tax credit to offset up to 90 percent of their Federal tax liability, compared with the 50-percent limit now imposed.

Important new tax reforms also will affect businesses. I am, for example, proposing to reduce the deductibility of a large class of business entertainment expenses. I have also proposed changes in the tax status of international business transactions that are of significant cost to taxpayers but that benefit the public insufficiently.

Because tax reform measures will raise $9 billion in revenue, it has been possible for

me to recommend $34 billion in overall tax reductions while keeping the net loss in revenues to $25 billion, the level I believe is appropriate given the state of our economy and the size of the budget deficit.

These proposals do not include any adjustment to take account of congressional action on my energy proposals. I proposed last April that the Congress pass a wellhead tax and rebate the proceeds of that tax directly to the American people. This is the best course to follow because it protects the real incomes of consumers and avoids a new source of fiscal drag. If the final energy bill includes a full rebate of the net proceeds of the wellhead tax, no further action on my part will be necessary. However, if the final bill allows for a rebate only for 1978—as provided in the House version—I will send a supplemental message to the Congress recommending that the individual tax reduction I am now proposing be increased by the amount of the net proceeds of the wellhead tax.

These tax reductions are essential to healthy economic recovery during 1978 and 1979. Prospects for continuation of that recovery in the near term are favorable. Consumers have been spending freely, and many other economic indicators recently have been moving up strongly. Without the tax reductions I have proposed, however, the longer-term prospects for economic growth would become increasingly poor. Because of the fiscal drag imposed by rising payroll taxes and inflation, economic growth would slow substantially in late 1978, and fall to about 3½ percent in 1979. The unemployment rate would stop declining and might begin to rise again, and the growth of investment outlays for new plant and equipment would slow significantly.

With the reductions in taxes I have proposed, on the other hand, the economy should grow by 4½ to 5 percent in both 1978 and 1979. Nearly one million new jobs would be created. Unemployment would therefore continue to fall and by late 1979 should be down to around 5½ to 6 percent. Capacity utilization and after-tax business profits would both improve, and thus the rate of investment in new plants and equipment should increase significantly.

Success in keeping a firm rein on spending will permit further tax reductions in years to come. Our ability to foresee the future course of the economy is not good enough, however, to enable us to know when additional reductions will be needed or how large they should be. It would therefore be imprudent to plan specific policy measures now for more than the current and the next fiscal year. But I will make recommendations for budget and tax policies for 1980 and beyond that are in keeping with our objectives of steady growth in the economy, more stable prices, and principal reliance on the private sector to achieve economic expansion.

Federal Deficit

Federal budgetary policy can play a constructive role in maintaining the health of the economy. There are times when large deficits in the Federal budget must be tolerated because they are needed to bolster the purchasing power of consumers and businesses. A budget deficit that persisted during a period of high employment and strong further growth of private demand, however, would put upward pressures on prices and would aggravate our inflationary problem. Under those circumstances, a budget deficit would also absorb savings that would be better used by the private sector to build new factories and offices and to purchase new machines. In order to assure that our economic progress remains on a solid footing and is not undermined by inflation, we must reduce the Federal budget deficit and achieve a balanced budget as soon as the developing strength in the economy allows.

The first requisite is careful management and control of Federal spending. The second is a prudent weighing of the need for tax reductions against the goal of budget balance.

This year I have proposed budgets that call for a deficit of $62 billion in 1978, and one only slightly smaller in 1979. Had I decided not to recommend a tax cut to put additional purchasing power in the hands of consumers and businesses, the deficit in 1979 could have been $15 to $20 billion smaller. But I believe that tax reduction is essential to continued progress in an economy still characterized by substantial unemployment and idle plant capacity.

How rapidly we can restore budget balance depends on the strength of the private economy. Over the next few years, two factors will be of particular importance.

The first is the financial condition of State and local governments. In the past, the aggregate budget of these governments tended to be approximately in balance. Today the State and local sector as a whole is in surplus. In 1977, for example, aggregate State and local receipts from all sources exceeded expenditures by nearly $30 billion. This overall surplus does not mean that every State and local government is in good financial condition. Many are hard pressed. Moreover, a large part of the aggregate surplus represents accumulations of pension funds for the 13 million employees of State and local governments.

Substantial surpluses in the State and local sector are likely to continue in the future. They absorb the incomes of consumers and business, and so act as a drag on the economy.

The second factor affecting the pace at which we can expect to move toward budget balance is the large deficit in America's foreign trade in goods and services. Imports into the United States have been swollen by the enormous quantity of oil we buy abroad to drive our cars, heat our homes, and fuel our industry. Our exports have grown only slowly, in large measure because economic growth abroad has been much slower than in the United States. As a result, the United States last year recorded a deficit of close to $18 billion in our current international accounts. This deficit has the same general effect on economic activity as a multibillion dollar increase in taxes.

Enactment of an effective energy program ultimately will reverse our growing dependence on oil imports. Moreover, economic growth in other countries should be improving over the next few years. But we may expect a current account deficit of some size to continue in the near future.

If strong economic expansion is to be maintained in the face of these major drains on the economy, additional tax reductions may be necessary beyond those I have proposed for 1979. But we will be better able to judge this question in a year or two, and we should not prejudge it now.

In formulating my budgetary decisions thus far, I have been careful to avoid commitments that would make it impossible for us to balance the budget by 1981. With unusually strong growth in the private economy, we would need a balanced Federal budget. In an economy growing less strongly, however, balancing the budget by 1981 would be possible only by forgoing tax reductions needed to reach our goal of high employment. In those circumstances, the date for reaching the goal of budget balance would have to be deferred.

What is important is that the planning and execution of Federal fiscal policies proceed in a prudent manner. Every decision on spending and taxes during my Administration has been, and will continue to be, made in the context of long-run budgetary planning that avoids the creation of excess demand during periods of high employment. That is an essential ingredient of responsible budgetary policy.

Structural Unemployment

Meaningful job opportunities ought to be available for all Americans who wish to work. But overall fiscal and monetary policy alone will not provide employment to many in our Nation. If we are to reduce unemployment satisfactorily, we must do more.

Eleven percent of adult American workers from minority groups are now jobless—close to the rate a year ago, and over twice as high as the unemployment rate for white adults. About 17 percent of our teenagers are unemployed today; among black teenagers the unemployment rate is nearly 40 percent. These intolerably high rates of unemployment must be brought down. This is an important goal, but achieving it will be a difficult task.

A generally healthy and growing economy is a prerequisite for dealing effectively with structural unemployment, but it is not enough. Even in good times some groups suffer from very high unemployment, which adds to the difficulty of achieving low unemployment and low inflation simultaneously. As the economy moves toward high employment, employers try to fill job vacancies from those groups of workers with substantial training and experience. Wage rates are bid up and prices follow, while large numbers from other groups are still looking unsuccessfully for work. Efforts to reduce unemployment among the unskilled and otherwise disadvantaged can be frustrated by inflationary pressures set off in those sectors of the labor market already fully employed.

To reach high levels of employment while maintaining reasonable price stability, we must take effective and adequate measures now to increase the employment opportunities of the disadvantaged. This principle is a key element of the Humphrey-Hawkins Bill—The Full Employment and Balanced Growth Act. I support this legislation and hope the Congress will enact it.

We have already taken several significant steps in this direction. Last year I proposed and the Congress appropriated $8.4 billion to expand the Public Service Employment Program to 725,000 jobs. These jobs are more sharply targeted on the long-term unemployed and the poor than previous programs under the Comprehensive Employment and Training Act. Direct opportunities for youth also have been expanded. The Youth Employment and Demonstration Projects Act of 1977, which is providing job experience and training in skills to unemployed youths, also was proposed by my Administration and enacted in 1977, providing 166,000 work and training positions for unemployed youths.

Several further measures are proposed in my 1979 budget. I have recommended that Public Service Employment be continued at the 725,000 job level throughout 1979, and that the number of jobs be phased down gradually in subsequent years as progress is made in reducing the overall level of unemployment. I have also recommended an expansion to $1.2 billion of the Youth Employment and Demonstration Projects Act to provide work opportunities and skill training for the unemployed youth who most need help. The Better Jobs and Income Program that I sent to the Congress in mid-1977 will create up to 1.4 million jobs, supplemented by cash allowances, for poor people who are able to work. An initial demonstration project for this program that will create 50,000 jobs is proposed in my 1979 budget, and more jobs will be phased in gradually once the welfare reform program is enacted.

Government programs can provide valuable assistance to the unemployed. In the end, however, we must turn to the private sector for the bulk of permanent job opportunities for the disadvantaged. It is in private industry that most productive jobs with opportunity for advancement are found. For this reason, I am requesting $400 million in my 1979 budget to begin a major new initiative for private sector hiring of the disadvantaged. Details of this proposal will be submitted to the Congress shortly. I am requesting the fullest cooperation of the business community in this initiative and have been assured by business leaders that it will be forthcoming.

Capital Formation

Over a broad expanse of years, improvement of the standard of living in this Nation depends primarily on growth in the productivity of the American work force. During the first two decades of the postwar period, the productivity of American labor increased at an average annual rate of about 3 percent. Over the past ten years, however, productivity growth has slowed markedly—to about 2 percent or less a year.

The reasons for this break with past trends are complex, but one factor that clearly stands out is the relatively slow growth in the stock of business plant and equipment. Historically, improvements in productivity have been linked closely to investment in plant and equipment. Investment in new facilities has embodied new and more productive technology and has provided our work force with more and better tools.

Business investment has lagged during the recovery for several reasons. Some of the fears engendered by the steep recession and severe inflation of 1973-75 have remained and have reduced the incentive for business to invest. Uncertainties about energy supplies and energy prices have also been a deterrent to investment, and so have concerns about governmental regulations in a variety of areas. Finally, high costs of capital goods and a depressed stock market have diminished the incentives and raised the costs to businesses of investment in new plant and equipment.

Industrial capacity is ample now. But without a substantial increase in investment over the next few years, problems would build for the future. Rapid growth of capacity is needed to assure that shortages of particular products do not emerge before we regain high employment. If capacity is not sufficient, bottlenecks may develop in some sectors, forcing up prices of industrial commodities. Inadequate rates of capital formation will also hold back the gains in productivity needed to improve standards of living and to avoid further aggravation of our inflation problem.

My tax and other economic proposals will encourage a greater rate of business investment in several ways. By promoting a sustainable rate of economic recovery, they will assure businesses of an expanding market for the output from new factories and equipment. The specific tax reductions for business I have proposed will increase after-tax profits and so directly provide additional incentives for investment.

We must also have conditions in financial markets that permit businesses to raise the funds they need for investment. Prudent Federal budgetary policies will contribute significantly to that end, as will policies that deal effectively with inflation. Both will ease the Federal Reserve's task of pursuing monetary policies that support full recovery.

Rate of Inflation

We cannot achieve full prosperity unless we deal effectively with inflation. We must take steps to reduce the high rate of inflation inherited from the past and to guard against a renewed outbreak of inflation as we regain a high-employment economy.

Our economy is not suffering at present from excess demand. Monetary growth in recent years has not been excessive, and Federal budget deficits have occurred in an economy with high unemployment and excess capacity. Yet prices continue to rise as a result of an inflationary process that has been under way for a decade.

Our present inflation began back in the late 1960s and accelerated sharply in the early years of the 1970s. Since 1974 the rate of consumer price inflation has declined substantially—from 12 percent to between 6 and 6½ percent at present. But that improvement is due largely to the termination of special influences affecting prices during 1974—the sharp rise of food and fuel prices, and the bulge in prices following the removal of wage and price controls.

Recent experience has demonstrated that the inflation we have inherited from the past cannot be cured by policies that slow growth and keep unemployment high. Since 1975, inflation has persisted stubbornly at a 6 to 6½ percent rate—even though unemployment went as high as 9 percent and still stands above 6 percent, and even though a substantial proportion of our industrial capacity has been idle. The human tragedy and waste of resources associated with policies of slow growth are intolerable, and the impact of such policies on the current inflation is very small. Moreover, by discouraging investment in new capacity, slow growth sows the seeds of future inflationary problems when the economy does return to high employment. Economic stagnation is not the answer to inflation.

Our first task in combating inflation is to guard against a renewed outbreak of higher price increases in the future. Firm discipline over the Federal budget and a prudent monetary policy are the most important steps that can be taken. Programs to attack structural pockets of unemployment among our people will make it possible to achieve higher levels of employment without exerting pressures on prices. Greater investment also will make a major contribution toward assuring that the capacity of our industry will be adequate to meet the needs of a high-employment economy.

Enactment of an energy program will eventually reduce the demand for oil imports—contributing to market conditions that discourage substantial oil price increases, and combating the inflation that results from a decline in the exchange value of the dollar. The programs I have inaugurated to build a 30- to 35-million metric ton grain reserve will provide a buffer against sudden upward movements in food prices in the event of bad weather.

Our second task—reducing the current rate of inflation—will be harder. Yet we must tackle the problem. Unless the inflation rate is brought down, the rate of price increase may well rise as unemployment falls to lower levels in later years, with consequences that would thwart our efforts to bring about full recovery.

The government has an obligation to set an example for the private sector, and we can play an important role in moderating inflation by reducing the effects of our own actions on prices. By adopting tax incentives and other policies to improve the growth of investment and productivity, we will help reduce the rise in costs and hence in prices.

The excise tax reductions I have proposed in my 1979 budget also will contribute moderately to lower costs and prices.

Government regulations also add to costs and raise prices. To some extent, this is the inevitable cost of much needed improvements in the environment and in the health and safety of workers and consumers. But there is no question that the scope of regulation has become excessive and that too little attention is given to its economic costs. We should not, and will not, give up our efforts to achieve cleaner air and water and a safer workplace. But, wherever possible, the extent of regulation should be reduced. We have eliminated hundreds of unneeded regulations already and will continue to pare down the remainder.

I also intend to put a high priority on minimizing the adverse effects of governmental regulations on the economy. To this end, I have established a high-level interagency committee that—together with the relevant regulatory agency—will review the economic effects of major regulations. This committee will seek to assure that the costs of each regulation have been fully considered, and that all alternatives have been explored, so that we may find and apply the least costly means of achieving our regulatory objectives. I have also directed my advisers to explore ways in which we can undertake an assessment of the impact of regulation on the economy as a whole and within each major sector. We need to find a way to set priorities among regulatory objectives and understand more fully the combined effects of our regulatory actions on the private economy.

Where regulation of economic activity has become outmoded and substantial overhaul is called for, I will pursue effective legislation. For example, I have supported actively congressional efforts to reform regulation of the airline industry, and I am considering proposals to reform the regulation of other industries.

I have given special attention to reducing the runaway costs of health care. The cost of a day in the hospital has more than doubled since 1970. Continuing escalation in the charges for hospital care can no longer be tolerated. I have submitted legislation, the Hospital Cost Containment Act of 1977, that would limit sharply the rate of growth in hospital spending, and I urge the Congress to enact this legislation in 1978.

The States can also play a role in moderating the current inflation. In 1976, State governments collected $50 billion in sales taxes. For the most part, these taxes enter directly into the cost of goods we buy and thus increase the price level. Today, State governments with significant surpluses are considering tax reductions. I urge those in a position to do so to consider the advantages to the national economy of reducing sales taxes, thereby helping to slow inflation.

Government alone cannot unwind the current inflation, however. Today's inflationary process is largely the consequence of self-fulfilling expectations. Businessmen, expecting inflation to continue, are less resistant to cost increases than they might be, since they have come to believe that, with all prices rising, their own increased costs can be passed on to consumers through higher prices. Wage increases are based on the expectation that prices will continue to rise. Wage gains in one sector spur similar demands in others.

There are gainers and losers in this process, since some groups in the economy are more successful than others at defending themselves against inflation. On the whole, however, the main result is continued inflation. No one group—neither business, nor labor, nor government—can stop this spiral on its own. What is needed is a joint effort.

Since the current inflation has developed strong momentum, it cannot be brought to a sudden halt. But we can achieve a gradual but sustained deceleration—having each succeeding year's inflation lower than the previous one. The benefits of slower growth of prices and wages would be broadly shared. Everyone would be better off. A conscious effort should be made by those who make wage and price decisions to take the individual actions necessary to bring about an economy-wide deceleration of inflation.

I am therefore asking the business community and American workers to participate in a voluntary program to decelerate the rate of price and wage increase. This program is based on the initial presumption that prices and wages in each industry should rise significantly less in 1978 than they did on average during the past two years.

I recognize that not all wages and prices can be expected to decelerate at the same pace. For example, where profit margins have been particularly squeezed, or where wages are lagging seriously, deceleration in 1978 would be less than for other firms or groups of workers. In exceptional cases deceleration may not be possible at all. Conversely, firms or groups that have done exceptionally well in the recent past may be expected to do more.

To enhance the prospects for success of this deceleration program, I have asked that major firms and unions respond to requests from members of my Administration to discuss with them on an informal basis steps that can be taken during the coming year to achieve deceleration in their industries. In reviewing the economic situation prior to making my recommendations to the Congress on the size of the pay raise for

Federal workers, due to take effect next October, I will keep this objective of deceleration in mind.

This program does not establish a uniform set of numerical standards against which each price or wage action is to be measured. The past inflation has introduced too many distortions into the economy to make that possible or desirable. But it does establish a standard of behavior for each industry for the coming year: every effort should be made to reduce the rate of wage and price increase in 1978 to below the average rate of the past two years.

I have chosen this approach after reviewing extensively all of the available options. There is no guarantee that establishing a voluntary deceleration standard will unwind the current inflation. I believe, however, that with the cooperation of business and labor, this proposal will work. Deceleration is a feasible standard of behavior, for it seeks restraint in wage and price actions in exchange for a general reduction in inflation. It is also a fair standard. Industries and workers with far different histories and current situations will not be asked to fit within the constraint of a single numerical guideline.

The inflation problem will not be easy to overcome. It will take time and patience. But the importance of these efforts cannot be overestimated. Unless we gain better control over the inflation rate, the prospects for regaining a fully employed economy will be seriously reduced. My Administration cannot and will not pursue policies in the future that threaten to trigger a new and more virulent round of inflation in this country. To do so would be the surest way of destroying the hopes of our citizens for a long-lasting prosperity.

International Economic Policies

Outside the United States, the world economy has seen a hesitant recovery from the deep recession of 1974-75. The rapid pace of economic growth that was widespread over most of the postwar years has all but disappeared. Unemployment is high, and in most industrial countries except the United States it is rising. Inflation is at high levels and declining only very slowly.

The imbalances in the international economic system continue to strain the world economy. Because of the surpluses of oil-exporting countries, many countries have sizable deficits, including the United States. Some industrial nations are also running large and persistent surpluses—thus increasing the pressures on countries in deficit. These imbalances have been a major factor contributing to disorder in exchange markets in recent months.

The condition of the world economy requires above all that nations work together to develop mutually beneficial solutions to global problems. If we fail to work together, we will lose the gains in living standards arising from the expansion of world commerce over the past three decades. If the world economy becomes a collection of

isolated and weak nations, we will all lose.

The first priority in our international economic policy is continued economic recovery throughout the industrial world. Growth of the U.S. economy—the largest and strongest in the world—is of vital importance. The economic program that I have proposed will ensure that America remains a leader and a source of strength in the world economy. It is important that other strong nations join with us to take direct actions to spur demand within their own economies. World recovery cannot proceed if nations rely upon exports as the principal source of economic expansion.

At the same time all countries must continue the battle against inflation. This will require prudent fiscal and monetary policies. Such policies must be supplemented by steps to reduce structural unemployment, measures to avoid bottlenecks by encouraging investment, and cooperation in the accumulation of commodity reserves to insulate the world from unforeseen shocks.

Reducing the widespread imbalances in international payments will require several parallel steps. To begin with, each individual country must ensure that its own policies help relieve the strains. The United States will do its part. In 1977 we had a current account deficit of about $18 billion. While not a cause for alarm, this is a matter of concern. We can take a most constructive step toward correcting this deficit by moving quickly to enact the National Energy Plan.

Countries in surplus should also do their part. Balance of payments surpluses in some countries have contributed to the economic stagnation among their trading partners. Where their own economies have slack, it is appropriate for nations in surplus to stimulate the growth of domestic demand—thereby increasing their imports and improving the prospects for growth in deficit countries. In some countries, lifting restraints on imports from abroad and reducing excessive government efforts to promote exports would be useful. After consultations with the United States, the Japanese have indicated they will take a series of steps toward reducing their large surplus.

The system of flexible exchange rates for currencies also can be helpful in correcting unsustainable imbalances in payments among countries. Since its inception in 1973, this system has operated well under unprecedented strains.

During 1977 the U.S. dollar has fallen in value against several key currencies. The decline in the dollar's value has occurred primarily against the currencies of those nations that have large trade and payments surpluses, and was not surprising in view of our large payments deficit and their surpluses. Late in 1977, however, movements in our exchange rate became both disorderly and excessively rapid. The United States reaffirmed its intention to step in when conditions in exchange markets become disorderly and to work in close cooperation with our friends abroad in this effort.

Under the flexible exchange rate system basic economic forces must continue to be the fundamental determinant of the value of currencies. However, we will not permit speculative activities in currency markets to disrupt our economy or those of our trading partners. We recognize fully our obligation in this regard, and we have taken steps to fulfill it.

Although substantial progress can be made toward a balanced world economy, some imbalances will persist for a substantial period of time. Financing requirements will remain large while adjustments occur. The private markets can and will continue to channel the bulk of the financing from surplus to deficit countries. But it is essential that adequate official financing also be available, in case of need, to encourage countries with severe payments problems to adopt orderly and responsible corrective measures. To meet this critical need the United States has strongly supported a proposal to strengthen the International Monetary Fund by the establishment of a new Supplementary Financing Facility.

The United States also will continue to contribute resources to promote growth in the economies of the developing nations. International assistance efforts—through bilateral aid and multilateral institutions—must continue to expand. We must also keep our doors open to imports from developing countries, so that their economies can grow and prosper through expanded trade.

A keystone of our international economic policy is to work with our trading partners to protect a free and open trading system. The American economy benefits by exporting those products that we make efficiently, and by importing those that we produce least efficiently. An open trading system increases our real incomes, strengthens competition in our markets, and contributes to combating inflation.

The United States will firmly resist the demands for protection that inevitably develop when the world economy suffers from high unemployment. The ensuing decline in world trade would worsen our problem of inflation, create inefficiencies in American enterprise, and lead to fewer jobs for American workers. But international competition must be fair. We have already taken and we will, when necessary, continue to take steps to ensure that our businesses and workers do not suffer from unfair trade practices.

I place great importance on the Multilateral Trade Negotiations now under way in Geneva. I believe our negotiators will bring home agreements that are fair and balanced and that will benefit our economy immensely over the years to come. The importance of these discussions can hardly be overemphasized. The trading system that emerges from the negotiations will set the tone for international commerce well into the 1980s. Our commitment to a successful conclusion to these talks underscores our long-term emphasis on the retention and expansion of open and fair trade among nations.

The Challenge Before Us

In this message I have outlined my fundamental economic goals and the strategy for attaining them. It is an ambitious, but I believe a realistic, agenda for the future. It calls for a broad range of actions to improve the health and fairness of the American economy. And it calls upon the American people to participate actively in many of these efforts.

I ask the Congress and the American people to join with me in a sustained effort to achieve a lasting prosperity. We all share the same fundamental goals. We can work together to reach them.

Jimmy Carter

January 20, 1978 ■

Tax Reform Proposals

Following is the text of President Carter's Jan. 20 message to Congress proposing changes in the nation's tax system:

TO THE CONGRESS
OF THE UNITED STATES:

I recommend that Congress enact a series of proposals that will reform our tax system and provide $25 billion in net tax reductions for individuals and businesses.

Fundamental reform of our tax laws is essential and should begin now. Tax relief and the maintenance of a strong economy are essential as well. The enactment of these proposals will constitute a major step towards sustaining our economic recovery and making our tax system fairer and simpler.

The Need for Tax Reduction

I propose net tax reductions consisting of:

—$17 billion in net income tax cuts for individuals, through across-the-board rate reductions and a new personal credit, focused primarily on low- and middle-income taxpayers.

—$6 billion in net income tax cuts for small and large corporations, through reductions in the corporate tax rates and extensions of the investment tax credit.

—$2 billion for elimination of the excise tax on telephone calls and a reduction in the payroll tax for unemployment insurance.

These tax reductions are a central part of the administration's overall economic strategy, which will rely principally upon growth in the private sector to create the new jobs we need to achieve our high-employment objective. The tax reductions will more than offset the recent increase in social security taxes and will provide the consumer purchasing power and business investment strength we need to keep our economy growing strongly and unemployment moving down.

Together with the programs that I will outline in my Budget Message, these tax cuts should assure that our economy will grow at a 4½ to 5 per cent pace through 1979, with unemployment declining to between 5½ and 6 per cent by the end of 1979. Without the tax cuts, economic growth would slow markedly toward the end

---

Summary of Revenue Effects of Income Tax Reductions, Tax Reforms and Telephone Excise and Unemployment Insurance Tax Reductions

($ billions)

	Fiscal Years				
	1979	**1980**	**1981**	**1982**	**1983**
Individual Income Tax:					
Tax reductions	− 22.5	− 25.7	− 29.2	− 33.4	− 38.5
Tax reforms	4.2	7.4	8.9	10.6	12.3
Net change	− 18.3	− 18.2	− 20.3	− 22.8	− 26.2
Corporation Income Tax:					
Tax reductions	− 6.3	− 9.4	− 11.1	− 11.8	− 12.8
Tax reforms	1.1	3.0	4.3	5.0	5.2
Net change	− 5.1	− 6.5	− 6.8	− 6.8	− 7.6
Telephone excise and unemployment insurance tax reductions	− 1.6	− 2.0	− 1.6	− 1.2	− 1.1
Total	**−25.0**	**−26.6**	**−28.6**	**−30.8**	**−34.9**

SOURCE: Treasury Department

of 1978 and fall to about 3½ per cent in 1979. Unemployment would be unlikely to fall below 6 per cent and, by the end of 1979, might be moving upward.

This tax program will mean up to one million additional jobs for American workers. It should lead to a pattern of economic growth which is steady, sustainable, and noninflationary.

In addition, I believe that our tax-payers, particularly those in the low- and middle-income brackets, *deserve* significant tax relief—I am determined to reduce federal taxes and expenditures as a share of our Gross National Product.

The Need for Tax Reform

The $25 billion in tax reductions are net reductions, *after* taking account of $9 billion in revenue-raising reforms which I am also proposing. Indeed, the full cuts in personal and corporate tax rates which I recommend would not be desirable in the absence of significant reform.

But these reforms stand on their own merits and would be long overdue even if I were not proposing any net tax reductions to accompany them. They focus on simplification for the individual taxpayer and the elimination of some of the most glaring tax preferences and loopholes.

Guided by the need for tax simplifica-tion and tax equity, I propose that Congress adopt reforms that would:

—Sharply curtail tax shelters.

—Eliminate the deductions claimed by businesses for theater and sporting tickets, yachts, hunting lodges, club dues, and first-class airfare and limit the deduction for the cost of meals to 50 per cent.

—Provide a taxable bond option for local governments and modify the tax treat-ment of industrial development bonds.

—Strengthen the minimum tax on items of preference income for individuals.

—Repeal the special alternative tax on capital gains, which only benefits in-dividuals in the highest tax brackets.

—Replace the personal exemption and general tax credits with a $240 per person credit.

—Simplify return preparation and recordkeeping by:

 • eliminating the deductions for sales, personal property, gasoline, and mis-cellaneous taxes;

 • combining the separate medical and casualty deductions and allowing them only to the extent they exceed 10 per cent of adjusted gross income;

 • repealing the deduction for political contributions but retaining the credit; and

 • liberalizing and modifying the Subchapter S and depreciation rules applicable to small businesses.

—Include unemployment compensation benefits in the taxable income of tax-payers above certain income levels.

—Ensure that the tax preferences available for fringe benefits assist rank-and-file workers as well as ex-ecutive officers.

—Eliminate the special bad debt deduc-tion for commercial banks, reduce the bad debt deduction available to savings and loan associations, and remove the tax exemption for credit unions.

—**Phase out the tax subsidies for** Domestic International Sales Cor-porations (DISCs) and the deferral of tax on foreign profits.

These reforms will make our tax system both fairer and simpler. Many of them are targeted at tax preferences and subsidies for activities that do not deserve special treat-ment and that largely benefit those who have no need for financial assistance. The average working man and woman pay for the loopholes and the special provisions in

our tax laws—because when some do not pay their fair share, the majority must pay higher taxes to make up the difference.

Low- and middle-income workers, struggling to make ends meet, are dis-couraged by tax laws that permit a few in-dividuals to live extravagantly at the ex-pense of government tax revenues. The privileged few are being subsidized by the rest of the taxpaying public when they routinely deduct the cost of country club dues, hunting lodges, elegant meals, theater and sports tickets, and night club shows. But the average worker's rare "night on the town" is paid for out of his *own* pocket with *after-tax* dollars.

Likewise, individuals who pay taxes on nearly every penny of earnings are treated unfairly compared to the few who are able to "shelter" their high incomes from taxes. Some persons with incomes exceeding $200,000 have little or no tax liability, while other high-income individuals return to the federal government nearly 60 cents of every dollar received. There is no good reason for next-door neighbors, in the same economic circumstances, to have vastly different tax bills because one has found tax shelters and loopholes.

In addition to the preferences for ex-pense account items and tax shelter ac-tivities, there are a number of equally in-appropriate and inefficient corporate tax subsidies. For example, there is no justifica-tion for the DISC export subsidy under which we pay over $1 billion a year in foregone tax revenue (mostly to our largest corporations) to encourage our firms to do what they would do anyway—export to profitable foreign markets. Nor can we rationalize proposals to reduce business taxes to increase investment at home while the deferral subsidy encourages mul-tinational corporations to invest overseas by letting them pay lower taxes on their foreign profits than they pay on money earned in the United States.

I ask Congress to join with me to end these unwarranted subsidies and return the revenue to the vast majority of our tax-payers who want no more or less than to pay their fair share.

The tax reforms and tax reductions which I am proposing have been carefully balanced to coordinate with our overall economic and budgetary strategy. Large tax reductions are premised on substantial reforms.

I must, therefore, caution that fiscal prudence will require significantly reduced tax cuts for low- and middle-income tax-payers if we cannot help finance the reduc-tions I have proposed through enactment of these revenue-raising reforms. I am propos-ing a balanced tax program, and I urge Congress to consider these recommen-dations as an integrated package.

Tax Reduction and Simplification for Individuals

Under this tax program, virtually all Americans will receive substantial tax relief, principally through a simple, across-

Income Tax and FICA Tax Changes
Four-Person, One-Earner Families*

Wage Income	Income Tax[1]	FICA TAX[2]	Total Tax
$ 5,000	$ 0	$ 14	$ 14
10,000	− 312	28	− 284
15,000	− 258	42	− 216
20,000	− 270	261	− 9
25,000	− 320	439	119
30,000	− 322	439	117
40,000	− 218	439	221
50,000	− 80	439	359
100,000	590	439	1,029

1. *Assumes deductible expenses equal to 23 percent of income under present law and 20 percent under the proposal.*

2. *Change in FICA tax calculated assuming present law rate and base for 1979 (6.13 per cent and $22,900), employees' share only; and assuming prior law rate and base for 1977 (5.85 per cent and $16,500), employees' share only.*

* *The above table was modified from the way it originally appeared in the President's tax message to conform to revised estimates released by the Treasury Department.*

SOURCE: Treasury Department

Income Tax Liabilities: Present Law and Administration Proposal (Personal Income Only)

(1976 Levels of Income)

Expanded Income Class ($000)	Present Law Tax Liability ($ millions)	Present Law Percentage Distribution (per cent)	Administration Proposal Tax Liability ($ millions)	Administration Proposal Percentage Distribution (per cent)	Tax Change Tax Liability ($ millions)	Tax Change Change as Per Cent of Present Law Tax (per cent)
Less than 5	$ 141	0.1%	$ −251	−0.2%	$ −392	−278.0%
5 - 10	8,227	6.1	6,368	5.2	−1,859	−22.6
10 - 15	18,071	13.4	15,361	12.4	−2,710	−15.0
15 - 20	23,009	17.0	20,148	16.3	−2,861	−12.4
20 - 30	32,778	24.2	29,593	23.9	−3,185	−9.7
30 - 50	22,017	16.3	20,971	17.0	−1,046	−4.8
50 - 100	16,492	12.2	16,344	13.2	−148	−0.9
100 - 200	8,084	6.0	8,261	6.7	177	2.2
200 and over	6,476	4.8	6,838	5.5	362	5.6
Total	$135,293	100.0%	$123,633	100.0%	$−11,660	− 8.6%

Note: Details may not add to totals due to rounding.

SOURCE: Office of the Secretary of the Treasury, Office of Tax Analysis

the-board reduction in personal tax rates. Lower withholding rates will be put into effect October 1, 1978, and taxpayers will experience an increase in take-home pay and purchasing power as of that date.

The typical taxpayer in all income classes up to $100,000 will pay lower taxes. But the bulk of relief has been targeted to low and middle-income taxpayers.

The $240 credit will be especially beneficial for low- and middle-income families. It will remove millions of Americans at or near the poverty level from the income tax rolls. No longer will the tax savings for dependents be worth more to high income than low income families. Instead, the credit will be worth just as much to the moderate income blue-collar worker as to the wealthy executive.

Over 94 per cent of the net individual tax relief will be provided to individuals and families earning less than $30,000 per year, and every income class up to $30,000 will bear a smaller share of the overall tax burden than it does now. *(See table above)*

Under my proposals, the typical family of four that earns $15,000 a year will save almost $260, a 19 per cent tax reduction.

For most persons in the low- and middle-income brackets, there will be a sizeable net reduction in combined income and payroll taxes even after the scheduled social security tax increases are taken into account. *(See table, previous page)*

Without this cut in income taxes, the social security tax increases would cause a reduction in the take-home pay of American workers. With this tax program, we will have restored the integrity of the Social Security system—returning that

system to a sound financial basis and assuring the stability of future benefits for retired workers—without increasing total taxes for most working people or causing a slowdown in our economic recovery.

We must also act to ease the burdens of tax return preparation and recordkeeping. We have a tax system that requires millions of individuals to compute their own tax liability. The government relies upon the good faith and conscientiousness of our taxpayers to an extent unparalleled in the rest of the world. But in order for our system to remain successful, it must be comprehensible to the average taxpayer.

Judged by this standard, the current tax structure is seriously defective. Millions of honest and intelligent Americans find themselves confused and frustrated by its complexity. The cost of this complexity is enormous in terms of hours and dollars spent.

Accordingly, tax simplification has been a goal of this administration from the outset. The tax return individuals will file between now and April 15 has been simplified as a result of the Tax Reduction and Simplification Act which I proposed and Congress enacted last year. The short form 1040A has been reduced from 25 lines to 15 lines. Form 1040 has been restructured so that it can be completed more systematically. Tax tables have been revised to reduce arithmetic computations. The language of the tax forms and the instructions has been made more understandable.

The simplification efforts that were begun in 1977 will be continued and expanded in the tax program I am presenting

today. The replacement of the existing personal exemption and general tax credits by the $240 personal credit will simplify return preparation for taxpayers and enable millions of individuals at or below the poverty level to file no tax return. Changes in itemized deductions (which will be more than offset by the rate cuts) will increase the number of nonitemizers to 84 per cent of all taxpayers. Six million Americans will be able to switch to the standard deduction and avoid keeping detailed records for tax purposes. The preparation of returns by itemizers will be simplified, and the tax program will reduce recordkeeping burdens on small businesses.

Business and Anti-Inflation Tax Reductions

Our Nation's employment and anti-inflation goals cannot be met without a strengthening of private business investment. In recent years, capital spending in the United States has been inadequate. Capacity growth in manufacturing has declined from a growth rate of about 4.5 per cent during the period 1948-1969, to 3.5 per cent from 1969-1973, and to 3 per cent from 1973-1976. Real business fixed investment in the third quarter of 1977 was 5 per cent below its 1974 peak.

In order to encourage needed capital outlays in the period ahead, my tax program contains annual net business tax reductions of approximately $6 billion. The corporate tax rate will be reduced on October 1, 1978, from 20 per cent to 18 per cent on the first $25,000 of income and from 22 per cent to 20 per cent on the second $25,000—this will result in a 10 per cent reduction in tax liability for most small corporations. The tax rate for large corporations will be cut from 48 per cent to 45 per cent on October 1, 1978, and to 44 per cent on January 1, 1980.

I also recommend several important changes in the existing 10 per cent investment tax credit: the 10 per cent credit should be made permanent; liberalized to cover up to 90 per cent of tax liability; made fully applicable to qualified pollution control facilities; and extended to investments in industrial and utility structures (including rehabilitation of existing structures). These changes should be particularly beneficial to developing businesses that are seeking to expand their productive facilities and should help to increase expenditures for the construction of new factories.

The corporate rate reductions and extensions of the investment tax credit which I am proposing will encourage capital formation by providing an immediate increase in cash flow to business and by enhancing the after-tax rewards of investment.

All small businesses will receive significant cuts in their tax rates under my program: reducing the bottom as well as the top corporate rates will be of special benefit to small corporations; small business proprietorships and partnerships will benefit from the individual rate cuts. In addition to these tax reductions, my program will simplify the depreciation rules applicable to small business and liberalize the provisions governing the deductions of losses on stock held in small companies.

Vigorous business investment will help ease inflationary pressure by averting capacity shortages that might otherwise occur as our economy continues to grow. The $2 billion reduction in telephone excise taxes and employer payroll taxes should provide additional relief from inflation by reducing costs and prices. These tax measures, applied in conjunction with other anti-inflation policies announced in my Economic Report, will support the objective of reducing and containing the rate of inflation.

The combination of these tax cuts and needed business tax reforms will result in a tax system that meets the needs of the broad spectrum of U.S. businesses more efficiently and equitably.

A detailed description of my program follows.

RECOMMENDATIONS TO REDUCE TAXES AND SIMPLIFY RETURNS FOR THE AVERAGE TAXPAYER

Tax Reductions for Individuals

Individual taxes will be reduced through across-the-board rate cuts and substitution of a single $240 personal credit for the existing personal exemption and alternative general credits. This tax relief will be reflected in decreased withholding rates for employees as of October 1, 1978.

The tax reductions I am now recommending do not include adjustments for congressional action on the National Energy Plan. In April, I proposed that Congress pass the crude oil equalization tax and rebate the proceeds to the American people on a per capita basis. This course is essential if we are to protect the real incomes of consumers. If the final energy bill includes a full rebate of the net proceeds of the crude oil tax, no further action on my part will be required. However, if the final bill contains a rebate provision only for 1978—as provided in the House version—I intend to send a supplemental message to Congress recommending that the individual tax reductions proposed in this message be increased by the net proceeds of the crude oil tax.

(1) **Rate Cuts.** The proposed rate schedule will range from a lowest bracket of 12 per cent to a top bracket of 68 per cent, compared with the current 14 to 70 per cent range. As under current law, the top rate bracket will apply with respect to income in excess of $200,000 for joint returns and $100,000 for single returns. The entire schedules are set forth in Tables 11 and 12. *(Tables, pp. 29-A, 30-A)*

This new rate structure will, in and of itself, increase the overall progressivity of the individual income tax because the cuts are proportionately larger in the low- and middle-income brackets.

(2) **Per Capita Tax Credit.** The tax benefits for dependents currently favor the wealthy over persons with modest incomes. A taxpayer is now entitled to a $750 exemption for each family member in addition to a general tax credit, which is equal to the greater of $35 per family member or 2 per cent of the first $9,000 of taxable income. The net effect of the complicated series of exemptions and credits is this: a family of four in the 50 per cent tax bracket enjoys a tax savings of $1,680 for dependents while families earning $10,000 save about one-third of that amount.

I propose that the existing exemption and general credits be replaced with a single credit of $240 per family member. Unlike the current structure, the new credit will provide the same benefit at all income levels; for a family with four members, the per capita credit will be worth $960 whether that family is middle class or wealthy. The $240 credit will ensure that most families at or near the poverty level will pay no taxes. Also, a single tax credit will simplify tax return preparation by eliminating the confusion caused by the existing combination of exemptions and alternative credits.

Changes in Itemized Deductions

The primary source of complexity in the tax laws for many middle-income individuals is itemized deductions. Average taxpayers have to maintain burdensome records in order to substantiate the deductions and are required to decipher complex tax rules to complete their tax returns. Restructuring of itemized deductions is essential if the tax laws are to be simplified

for typical, middle-class individuals and families.

I am recommending changes in itemized deductions that will enable approximately 6 million taxpayers to switch to the simple standard deduction. The number of taxpayers who use the standard deduction will be increased from 77 per cent to 84 per cent. And the calculation of the deductions for itemizers will be simplified greatly.

The deductions that will be curtailed are ones that add complexity and inequity to the tax system without advancing significant objectives of public policy. We will have a simpler, more efficient tax system if we eliminate these deductions and return the revenue directly to taxpayers through the rate cuts I propose.

(1) **State and Local Taxes.** The special deduction will be eliminated for general sales taxes, taxes on personal property (but not on residences or buildings), gasoline taxes, and miscellaneous taxes. These itemized deductions are claimed at nearly uniform rates by all itemizers and result in a relatively small tax benefit. For those taxpayers who do not use the published deduction tables, the recordkeeping burden can be substantial.

Moreover, a deduction for these types of taxes cannot be defended on public policy grounds. A deduction for gasoline taxes runs counter to our national effort to conserve energy. And the present level of state sales taxes cannot be said to depend upon the fact that those state taxes are deductible for federal income tax purposes.

(2) **Political Contributions Deduction.** Political contributions are now deductible as an itemized deduction in an amount not exceeding $200 for a joint return. Alternatively, a taxpayer may claim a credit against his tax for one-half of his political contributions, with a maximum credit of $50 on a joint return.

The reform proposal will repeal the political contribution deduction but retain the credit. The deduction is undesirable because it provides a larger subsidy to high-bracket contributors. Due to the present deduction, the wealthiest individuals can contribute $200 at an after-tax cost to them of only $60; middle-income Americans incur a cost of $150 for the same contribution. Elimination of the deduction will enhance tax equity and diminish the confusing complexity of the current scheme of deductions and credits.

(3) **Medical and Casualty Deductions.** The medical expense deduction is one of the most complicated items on the tax forms. Currently, one-half of the first $300 of health insurance premiums is deductible outright for those who itemize. Other medical expenses (including additional health insurance premiums) are deductible to the extent they are in excess of 3 per cent of adjusted gross income. The latter category of deductibility also includes medicines and drugs to the extent they exceed 1 per cent of adjusted gross income. And there is a separate deduction for

damage to property from a casualty (such as theft or fire) if the loss exceeds $100 and is not reimbursed by insurance.

I recommend substantial simplification of these provisions. The deductions for medical and casualty expenses will be combined, and a new "extraordinary expense" deduction will be available for medical and casualty expenses in excess of 10 per cent of adjusted gross income. In the case of casualty losses, the excess over $100 will be included in this computation. Medical insurance premiums and medicines will be treated the same as other medical expenses.

Medical and casualty expenditures should properly be deductible only when they are unusually large and have a significant impact on the taxpayer's ability to pay. The medical expense deduction originally met that standard. But, as a result of the changing relationship between medical costs and income, that standard is no longer satisfied. Substantial recordkeeping burdens and administrative problems can be eliminated through the proposed simplification of the deduction and the redefinition of "extraordinary" in the light of current experience among taxpayers.

Proposals to Curtail Inappropriate Subsidies, Special Privileges, Inequities and Abuses of the Tax System

Entertainment and Other Expenditures for Personal Consumption

One feature of the current tax system that is most disheartening to average taxpayers is the favorable tax treatment accorded extravagant entertainment expenses that are claimed to be business-related. Some individuals are able to deduct expenditures that provide personal enjoyment with little or no business benefit. And, even where entertainment expenditures may have some relationship to the production of income, they provide untaxed personal benefits to the participants. More than $2 billion of tax revenue is lost every year through these tax preferences.

For example, one person claimed a deduction of $17,000 for the cost of entertaining other members of his profession at his home, at a country club, at sporting events, at restaurants, and at a rental cottage. Another individual wrote off the cost of business lunches 338 days of the year at an average cost far exceeding $20 for each lunch. But there is no deduction in the tax laws for the factory worker's ticket to a football game or the secretary's lunch with fellow workers.

These special tax advantages for the privileged few undermine confidence in our Nation's tax system. The disparity must be eliminated by denying a deduction for expenditures to the extent they provide the participants with such untaxed personal enjoyment and benefits.

(1) **Theater and Sporting Events.** No deduction will be permitted for purchases of tickets to theater and sporting events. Present law, by allowing a deduction for the purchase of such tickets, provides a "two for the price of one" bargain to some taxpayers. As long as an individual is in the 50 per cent tax bracket or above, he may be able to invite a business friend at no cost to himself by having the Federal government pay for at least one-half of the total ticket costs. The overwhelming majority of our citizens pay for their theater and sports tickets out of their own after-tax dollars. No taxpayer should be asked to help subsidize someone else's personal entertainment.

(2) **Other Entertainment Expenses.** The tax reform program will also deny deductibility of any expenses of maintaining facilities such as yachts, hunting lodges and swimming pools and for fees paid to social, athletic, or sporting clubs. During a recent tax year, one small corporation deducted $67,000 for yacht expenses incurred in entertaining customers and potential customers on cruises and fishing trips. Another small company deducts over $100,000 a year to maintain hunting and fishing lodges to entertain employees of customers. Asking taxpayers to subsidize these kinds of activities for a tiny minority of our citizens strikes at the fairness and integrity of the tax system.

(3) **Business Meals.** Fifty per cent of currently deductible business entertainment expenses for food and beverages will remain deductible, and 50 percent will be disallowed. A substantial portion of business meal expenses represents the cost of personal consumption that must be incurred regardless of the business connection. The millions of Americans who work on farms, in factories and in offices should not be required to provide their tax dollars to support the high-priced lunches and dinners of a relatively small number of taxpayers. The 50 percent disallowance represents a reasonable and fair approach to compensate for the untaxed personal benefit involved.

(4) **Foreign Conventions.** Many professional, business, and trade organizations can furnish their members with tax-deductible foreign vacations. The method of conferring such tax-subsidized luxury is to sponsor a foreign convention or seminar. A brochure for one professional organization provides the appropriate atmosphere in promoting its foreign seminars:

"Decide where you would like to go this year: Rome. The Alps. The Holy Land. Paris and London. The Orient. Cruise the Rhine River or the Mediterranean. Visit the islands in the Caribbean. Delight in the art treasures of Florence."

The Tax Reform Act of 1976 placed some limits on the deductibility of foreign convention expenses. But the rules still permit taxpayers to take two foreign vacations a year partially at public expense—an exception that did not escape the attention of the organization whose 1977 brochure I have quoted.

I am proposing that the deductibility rules for foreign conventions be modified in a manner that will curb abuses while relaxing the current restrictions on conventions held in foreign countries for legitimate business purposes. The two convention rule will be stricken. In its place will be a rule that denies deductibility for foreign convention expenses unless factors such as the purpose and membership of the sponsor make it as reasonable to hold the convention outside the United States and possessions as within.

(5) **First Class Air Fare.** Another example of public support for private extravagance is the deductibility of first class air fare. Business travel constitutes a legitimate cost of producing income. However, the business purpose is served by purchasing a ticket at coach fare. The undue generosity of a deduction for first class air fare was recognized by Congress in 1976 when a deduction was denied for first class flights to foreign conventions. I propose that the rule be extended to tickets for domestic business travel.

Tax Shelters

Through tax shelters, persons can use "paper" losses to reduce taxes on high incomes from other sources. These shelter devices can slash the effective tax rate for many affluent individuals far below that of average income Americans. Moreover, such shelters attract investment dollars away from profit-seeking businesses and into ventures designed only for tax write-offs; legitimate businesses suffer competitive disadvantages as a result.

In the Tax Reform Act of 1976, Congress enacted reforms intended to restrict tax shelter abuses. The principal methods used in that legislation were revisions of the minimum tax and the adoption of an "at risk" rule to limit the deductibility of certain tax shelter losses.

However, some promoters have now adapted their operations to provide shelters in forms that were not specifically covered by the 1976 Act. In fact, shelter activity in 1977 may have surpassed the level reached in 1976. Form letters, addressed to "All of Us Who Wish to Reduce Our Taxes," boldly promise tax write-offs several times larger than the amount invested, and persons are urged to pass the message along "to anyone you think may have interest in tax reduction." Tax shelter experts promote their services in large and expensive advertisements in the financial sections of our Sunday papers.

Such flagrant manipulation of the tax laws should not be tolerated. I recommend action that will build upon the 1976 reforms and further reduce tax shelter abuses.

(1) **Strengthening of the Minimum Tax.** The minimum tax has proved to be one of the most useful devices to limit the attractiveness of tax shelter schemes, and it should be made still more effective. In its current form, the minimum tax is imposed at a rate of 15 per cent on the amount of certain tax preference items enjoyed by a tax-

payer. But the total amount of tax preferences can be reduced by the greater of $10,000 or one-half of regular liability (in the case of individuals) before the minimum tax is applied.

I recommend that the minimum tax for individuals be strengthened by eliminating the offset of one-half of regular tax liability against preference income. This change will make the minimum tax more progressive and a more sharply focused deterrent to the use of tax shelters. Persons making excessive use of preferences will be taxed on their preference income without regard to regular tax liability. On the other hand, those individuals with modest preference income will still be totally exempted from the minimum tax by the $10,000 preference offset, and the minimum tax will not be applied to capital gain realized on the sale of a personal residence. Ninety-eight per cent of the $284 million in revenue raised by this proposal will come from taxpayers with incomes exceeding $100,000 and more than 77 per cent will come from the income class over $200,000.

(2) **Extension of "at risk" Rule.** One of the 1976 reforms that should be toughened is the "at risk" rule. That rule denies deductibility for a shelter investor's paper losses that exceed his cash investment and indebtedness for which he has personal liability. My tax reform plan will generally extend the "at risk" provisions to cover all activities (except real estate) carried on individually, through partnerships, or by corporations controlled by five or fewer persons.

(3) **Changes in Real Estate Depreciation.** Reform of real estate depreciation practices is needed to reduce much of the wasteful tax shelter investment that has led to overbuilding of commercial real estate in such forms as shopping centers and office buildings. Real estate shelters were left virtually untouched by the 1976 Act. Consequently, these shelters have continued to thrive.

It is time to move depreciation for tax purposes more closely into line with a measurement of actual economic decline. The reform program will generally require taxpayers to base their depreciation for buildings on the straight-line method, using the present average tax lives claimed by taxpayers for different classes of property. Exceptions from the general rule will be granted until 1983 for new multi-family housing, which will be permitted to use a 150 per cent declining balance method; new low-income housing will remain eligible for a 200 per cent declining balance method until 1983, and for 150 per cent thereafter. Needed investment in industrial plants will be encouraged by an extension of the investment credit, as explained below. The investment credit is a more efficient and straight-forward means to provide a tax subsidy for such construction.

(4) **Taxation of Deferred Annuities.** Another flourishing tax shelter gimmick is the deferred annuity contract. Currently, a person can generally invest in an annuity

contract and postpone taxation on the interest build-up until the annuity is actually received. Although originally designed primarily to provide a safe flow of retirement income, the deferred annuity contract is now used commonly as a convenient tax dodge for a wide range of investment opportunities. The shelter benefits are aptly described by the promotional literature:

"HOW TO POSTPONE TAXES LEGALLY AND EARN INTEREST ON UNCLE SAM'S MONEY.... With An Investment That Never Goes Down, Always Goes Up, And Is Guaranteed Against Loss."

I recommend that this tax abuse be eliminated. Under my proposal, the earnings of most deferred annuities will be taxed currently to the purchaser. However, in order that an individual may still use a deferred annuity with guaranteed interest as a means to provide retirement income, the proposal will allow each person to designate a single contract, contributions to which may not exceed $1,000 annually, as a contract that will remain eligible for tax deferral. Also unaffected will be the tax treatment of qualified employee annuities.

(5) **Classification of Nominal Partnerships as Corporations for Tax Purposes.** In many cases, tax shelter schemes can offer the desired tax benefits to investors only if the shelter vehicle is organized as a partnership rather than a corporation. At the same time, limited partnerships can now provide traditional non-tax attributes of a corporation, such as limited personal liability, centralized management, and transferability of interests without sacrificing partnership tax benefits.

Promoters should not obtain the non-tax attributes of a corporation for their shelters while using technicalities to avoid corporate tax treatment. I recommend that new limited partnerships with more than 15 limited partners be treated as corporations for tax purposes; however, partnerships engaged primarily in housing activities will be excepted from this classification rule.

(6) **Tax Audit of Partnerships.** Tax shelter partnerships are not themselves subject to the tax assessment mechanism of the Internal Revenue Service; therefore, each individual partner must be audited separately even though the same substantive determinations may be involved. I recommend that legislation be enacted to permit a partnership to be treated as an entity for the purpose of determining tax issues. Tax shelters based on illegitimate deductions should not be permitted to succeed merely because of the difficulties involved in conducting an IRS examination of their activities.

Termination of Alternative Tax For Capital Gains

The wages of most workers are fully subject to tax at the rates contained in the published tax tables. But persons whose income arises from the sale of assets such as stock or land generally receive preferred

treatment; a deduction for long-term capital gains has the effect of taxing these gains at a rate that is one-half of the rate for ordinary income. This preference results in an annual revenue loss to the Treasury of $8 billion.

Taxpayers in the highest income brackets are granted an additional tax preference over and above the special capital gains deduction. Individuals above the 50 per cent tax bracket can take advantage of a 25 per cent tax ceiling on the first $50,000 of capital gains, a provision known as the "alternative tax." The benefits of this provision go exclusively to persons with taxable incomes exceeding $52,000 (if filing a joint return) or $38,000 (if filing a single return)—less than one per cent of all taxpayers.

Through the alternative tax, a wealthy investor can shield nearly 65 per cent of his capital gains from taxation—a benefit that is grossly inequitable when middle-class investors are taxed on one-half of such gains, and most workers are taxed on every cent of their wages and salaries. The alternative tax costs the Treasury over $100 million every year, almost 90 per cent of which goes to taxpayers in income classes above $100,000. I propose the repeal of this unfair and complicated tax benefit.

Fringe Benefits Unavailable to Rank-and-File Workers

Our tax system generally operates under the principle that employees should be taxed on their compensation no matter what form that compensation assumes. A worker who receives cash wages that he uses to provide benefits for his family should not ordinarily be taxed more heavily than the employee who receives those benefits directly from his employer. There are now exceptions to this general rule for certain types of employee benefits. I urge Congress to act so that these tax preferences benefit rank-and-file workers as well as the executive officers.

(1) **Non-discrimination Requirement for Health and Group Life Plans.** An example of a tax-preferred employee benefit is a health or group life insurance plan. If an individual purchases medical insurance, the premiums are deductible only within the limits applicable to the medical expense deduction. However, if an employer establishes a medical insurance program for its employees, the premium payments by the employer are deductible while neither the premiums nor the benefits are taxable to the employee.

Although this tax preference was designed in theory to secure basic protections for a wide range of employees, it often serves instead to subsidize expenses of only the high-level corporate managers. It is now possible for a businessman, through his controlled corporation, to establish a health plan that covers only one employee—himself—and permits all of his medical and dental expenses to be deducted. Meanwhile, that corporation's other employees have to provide health care

Individual Tax Rate Schedules for Joint Returns

	Present Law		Tax Proposal	
Taxable Income Bracket[1]	Tax at Low End of Bracket	Tax Rate on Income In Bracket	Tax at Low End of Bracket	Tax Rate on Income In Bracket
$ 0 - $ 500	$ 0	14%	$ 0	12%
500 - 1,000	70	14	60	12
1,000 - 2,000	140	15	120	14
2,000 - 3,000	290	16	260	16
3,000 - 4,000	450	17	420	17
4,000 - 8,000	620	19	590	18
8,000 - 12,000	1,380	22	1,310	19
12,000 - 16,000	2,260	25	2,070	20
16,000 - 20,000	3,250	28	2,870	23
20,000 - 24,000	4,380	32	3,790	27
24,000 - 28,000	5,660	36	4,870	32
28,000 - 32,000	7,100	39	6,150	36
32,000 - 36,000	8,660	42	7,590	39
36,000 - 40,000	10,340	45	9,150	42
40,000 - 44,000	12,140	48	10,830	44
44,000 - 48,000	14,060	50	12,590	48
48,000 - 52,000	16,060	50	14,510	48
52,000 - 54,000	18,060	53	16,430	51
54,000 - 62,000	19,120	53	17,450	51
62,000 - 64,000	23,360	53	21,530	51
64,000 - 76,000	24,420	55	22,550	54
76,000 - 88,000	31,020	58	29,030	57
88,000 - 90,000	37,980	60	35,870	57
90,000 - 100,000	39,180	60	37,010	60
100,000 - 110,000	45,180	62	43,010	60
110,000 - 120,000	51,380	62	49,010	62
120,000 - 130,000	57,580	64	55,210	62
130,000 - 140,000	63,980	64	61,410	64
140,000 - 150,000	70,380	66	67,810	64
150,000 - 160,000	76,980	66	74,210	65
160,000 - 175,000	83,580	68	80,710	65
175,000 - 180,000	98,780	68	90,460	66
180,000 - 200,000	97,180	69	93,760	66
200,000 and over	110,980	70	106,960	68

1. *The zero bracket is not shown in this table. To include the zero bracket, increase all taxable incomes shown by $3,200.*

SOURCE: Office of the Secretary of the Treasury, Office of Tax Analysis

for their families with nondeductible expenditures.

To curb this abuse, I recommend denial of the tax exemption for employer-established medical, disability, and group life insurance plans if those plans discriminate in favor of officers, shareholders, and higher-paid employees. Preferential tax treatment is now available to pension plans only if non-discrimination standards are met. The tax law should require similar non-discriminatory treatment for workers in the case of medical, disability, and group life insurance plans.

(2) **Employee Death Benefits.** Current law provides an exclusion for the first $5,000 of payments made by an employer on account of the death of an employee. I recommend the repeal of this exclusion. Typically, these death benefits are in the nature of deferred wages that would have been paid to employees in high tax brackets. Adequate tax relief for an employee's heirs is provided through a complete tax exemption for insurance proceeds.

(3) **Integration of Qualified Retirement Plans and Social Security.** Certain employer-sponsored retirement plans have a preferred tax status. Employer contributions to a qualified plan are currently deductible while the employee can defer taxation until retirement benefits are received. Although qualification for this special treatment is generally dependent upon non-discriminatory coverage of employees, the tax laws now permit a qualified plan to cover only employees who earn amounts exceeding the social security wage base—a base that will rise to $25,900 by 1980 under the recently enacted social security financing legislation.

Individual Tax Rate Schedules for Single Returns

Taxable Income Bracket[1]	Present Law		Tax Proposal	
	Tax at Low End of Bracket	Tax Rate on Income In Bracket	Tax at Low End of Bracket	Tax Rate on Income In Bracket
$ 0 - $ 500	$ 0	14%	$ 0	12%
500 - 1,000	70	15	60	13
1,000 - 1,500	145	16	125	15
1,500 - 2,000	225	17	200	15
2,000 - 3,000	310	19	275	18
3,000 - 4,000	500	19	455	19
4,000 - 6,000	690	21	645	20
6,000 - 8,000	1,110	24	1,045	20
8,000 - 10,000	1,590	25	1,445	22
10,000 - 12,000	2,090	27	1,885	23
12,000 - 14,000	2,630	29	2,345	25
14,000 - 16,000	3,210	31	2,845	25
16,000 - 18,000	3,830	34	3,345	29
18,000 - 20,000	4,510	36	3,925	29
20,000 - 22,000	5,230	38	4,505	33
22,000 - 24,000	5,990	40	5,165	33
24,000 - 26,000	6,790	40	5,825	38
26,000 - 28,000	7,590	45	6,585	38
28,000 - 32,000	8,490	45	7,345	41
32,000 - 36,000	10,290	50	8,985	46
36,000 - 38,000	12,290	50	10,825	50
38,000 - 40,000	13,290	55	11,825	50
40,000 - 44,000	14,390	55	12,825	51
44,000 - 48,000	16,590	60	14,865	57
48,000 - 50,000	18,990	60	17,145	58
50,000 - 52,000	20,190	62	18,305	58
52,000 - 54,000	21,430	62	19,465	60
54,000 - 60,000	22,670	62	20,665	60
60,000 - 62,000	26,390	64	24,265	60
62,000 - 64,000	27,670	64	25,465	63
64,000 - 70,000	28,950	64	26,725	63
70,000 - 76,000	32,790	66	30,505	63
76,000 - 80,000	36,750	66	34,285	66
80,000 - 88,000	39,390	68	36,925	66
88,000 - 90,000	44,830	68	42,205	66
90,000 - 100,000	46,190	69	43,525	67
100,000 and over	53,090	70	50,225	68

1. The zero bracket is not shown in this table. To include the zero bracket, increase all taxable incomes shown by $2,200.

SOURCE: Office of the Secretary of the Treasury, Office of Tax Analysis

It is unfair to grant tax preferences for private pension plans that bar all low- and middle-income employees from participation. I propose that a new integration formula be enacted so that a qualified pension plan cannot provide benefits to supplement social security for highly compensated employees unless all employees receive some coverage under the plan.

Unemployment Compensation

Unemployment compensation is a substitute for wages that generally provides needed relief to persons in financial distress. But, in some cases, the unemployment compensation system discourages work for taxable income. Since unemployment benefits are tax-free, they are more valuable than an equivalent amount of wages. This means that if two individuals have the same total income, the one who remains idle several months and receives unemployment compensation will be better off financially than his colleague who works the whole year. There can be no justification for conferring this tax-free benefit upon middle- and upper-income workers.

I propose that the current tax exemption for unemployment compensation benefits be phased out as an individual's income rises above $20,000 for single persons or $25,000 for married couples.

Taxable Bond Option and Industrial Development Bonds

Present law exempts from federal taxation the interest on certain bonds issued by state and local governments. There are now two general categories of tax-exempt bonds: obligations issued for the benefit of the state and local government itself, and industrial development bonds issued by the government to provide facilities such as pollution control equipment, sports facilities, waste disposal facilities, industrial parks, and facilities (including hospitals) of private, non-profit organizations. Also, there is a "small issue" exemption for certain industrial development bonds with face amounts that do not exceed $1 million, or $5 million where the total cost of capital expenditures on the financed facility does not exceed the $5 million amount.

My tax program preserves the freedom of state and local governments to issue tax-exempt bonds. I am recommending reforms that will restrict the tax avoidance opportunities available to the wealthy in the tax-exempt market while, at the same time, increasing the ability of state and local governments to obtain low-cost financing. In particular, I propose the following:

(1) **Option for Bonds Benefiting Governmental Units.** State and local governments will be given the option of continuing to issue tax-exempt bonds or issuing fully taxable bonds, accompanied by a direct federal interest subsidy to the governmental units. For bonds issued in 1979 and 1980, the subsidy will be equal to 35 per cent of the interest cost; the subsidy will rise to 40 per cent for bonds issued after 1980. The federal government will exercise no control over the purposes for which state and local governments use subsidized financing. State and local governments will benefit under the taxable bond option regardless of whether they decide to issue taxable or tax-exempt bonds: those issuing taxable bonds will benefit directly from the interest subsidy, and those continuing to issue tax-exempt bonds will benefit because the reduced supply of such bonds will allow governments to sell them at lower interest rates.

(2) **Pollution Control Bonds, Bonds for the Development of Industrial Parks, and Private Hospital Bonds.** The tax exemption will be removed for interest on pollution control bonds and bonds for the development of industrial parks. Also, the exemption will be removed for bonds issued to finance construction of hospital facilities for private, non-profit institutions unless there is a certification by the state that a new hospital is needed. These activities are essentially for the benefit of private users, and the tax exemption for the bonds has the effect of undermining the financing of governmental functions. Moreover, the general exemption for hospital bonds encourages excessive expansion of unneeded hospital facilities and runs counter to the administration's Hospital Cost Containment proposal.

(3) **Small Issue Exemption.** The existing "small issue" exemptions will be retained only for economically distressed areas; and, with respect to those areas, the $5 million exemption will be raised to $10 million.

(4) **Option for Certain Industrial Development Bonds.** Industrial development bonds which continue to enjoy tax-exempt status (such as those to finance sports facilities, housing, airports and convention facilities and small issues for economically distressed areas) will be eligible for the taxable bond option on the same terms as obligations issued for the benefit of state and local governments.

Accrual Accounting for Large Corporate Farms

Most taxpayers that are in the business of selling products must use an accrual method of accounting so that income is reflected accurately for tax purposes. However, farmers have historically been permitted to use the simpler cash method on the grounds that they lack the accounting and bookkeeping expertise required by the accrual system.

Congress acted in 1976 to deny the cash accounting privilege to most large corporate farms (with annual gross receipts exceeding $1 million), but retained an exception for large corporations that are "family owned." This distinction between family and nonfamily corporations bears no relationship to the rationale of preserving simple bookkeeping methods for small farmers. It has resulted in severe competitive imbalances between large corporations now required to use accrual accounting and those that are equally large but happen to fall within the definition of a "family farm."

This inequitable exception should now be eliminated. Corporate farms with gross receipts exceeding $1 million cannot fairly claim that they lack the sophistication necessary to comply with accrual accounting standards. Nor can lack of financial sophistication be claimed by farm syndicates used as investment vehicles by nonfarmers. Therefore, I recommend that the accrual accounting requirement cover corporations with gross receipts greater than $1 million, regardless of their ownership, and all farm syndicates.

Tax Treatment of Financial Institutions

Financial institutions now have a favored tax status that is based largely on outmoded concepts regarding the nature of these businesses. Commercial banks, mutual savings banks and savings and loan associations were permitted to deduct artificially inflated reserves for bad debts in order to protect the banking system from catastrophic losses that were prevalent prior to the extensive banking legislation of the 1930s. Credit unions were exempted from taxation in the days when these institutions were small entities with close bonds among the members and few powers to provide extensive financial services. I am recommending changes that will recognize the contemporary practices of financial institutions and will bring the tax treatment of commercial banks, savings and loan associations and credit unions more in line with the taxation of other businesses. These reforms will raise $300 million per year in revenue.

(1) **Commercial Banks.** Commercial banks may now claim bad debt deductions that greatly exceed their actual losses. Under legislation enacted in 1969, this special bad debt deduction is scheduled for elimination after 1987. I propose that the effective date for repeal be accelerated so that beginning in 1979 banks, like other businesses, will base their bad debt reserves on their own experience in the current and 5 preceding years.

(2) **Mutual Savings Banks and Savings and Loan Associations.** Mutual savings banks and savings and loan associations are also permitted a special bad debt deduction that bears no relationship to actual experience. These thrift institutions are generally entitled to deduct 40 per cent of their net income (this percentage is scheduled to apply in 1979) as a bad debt reserve as long as a significant portion of their deposits is invested in real estate loans. My tax program will reduce the percentage to 30 per cent over a 5-year period.

(3) **Credit Unions.** Credit unions are tax-exempt. Yet, their powers and functions are defined so broadly that the term "credit union" can include financial institutions that are functionally identical to a savings and loan association. The tax exemption provides them with an unfair financial advantage over their competitors. I propose that the percentage of exempt income be phased out over a 4-year period, and that credit unions be taxed in the same manner as mutual savings banks and savings and loan associations after 1982.

Domestic International Sales Corporation (DISC)

Business incentives form an integral part of my tax program. I am recommending measures that will encourage American businesses to invest in productive facilities and to create jobs. However, adoption of those incentives must be accompanied by the elimination of tax preferences that have proved to be wasteful. The so-called "DISC" provision is a prime example.

In 1971, Congress enacted a special tax program for exports. This program permitted tax benefits for exports channeled through a company's specially created subsidiary, usually a paper organization, known as a domestic international sales corporation (DISC). Artificial pricing rules on transactions between the parent company and its DISC permit a favorable allocation of export profits to the DISC, and the taxation of one-half of eligible DISC income is deferred as long as these profits are invested in export related assets.

DISC has proved to be a very inefficient and wasteful export subsidy in the current international monetary system. A recent Treasury study indicates that DISC may have contributed only $1 to $3 billion to U.S. exports in 1974—an increase of less than 3 per cent in total exports—at a tax revenue cost of $1.2 billion. In the long run, even these increased exports are probably offset by rising imports that result from the operation of the flexible exchange rate system. DISC does nothing for, and may even disadvantage, our import sensitive industries and our exporters not using the DISC provision. Independent experts believe that DISC may have had *no* positive effect on our balance of payments.

Congress has recognized the wasteful nature of DISC and, in 1976, limited its applicability. However, DISC continues to cost U.S. taxpayers over $1 billion per year, with 65 per cent of DISC benefits going to corporations with more than $250 million in assets.

I propose the elimination of one-third of DISC benefits in 1979, two-thirds in 1980, and all DISC benefits in 1981 and thereafter.

Foreign Tax Deferral

Domestic corporations can now avoid paying a U.S. tax on the earnings of their foreign subsidiaries as long as those earnings remain overseas. A U.S. tax is generally deferred until dividends are paid by the subsidiary to its domestic parent, and then U.S. tax liability is offset by a tax credit for foreign income taxes paid on those remitted earnings. Fifty per cent of all the benefits of tax deferral is obtained by 30 large multinational corporations.

I recommend that this deferral privilege be phased out over a 3-year period. At least one-third of a foreign subsidiary's earnings will be taxed to the U.S. parent in 1979, at least two-thirds in 1980, and all the **subsidiary's earnings after 1980. The tax** reform program is designed to create incentives for investment in the United States and the creation of jobs for American workers. Tax deferral runs counter to these objectives. By providing a preference for foreign source income, the current deferral provision provides an incentive for investing abroad rather than in the United States, thereby having the effect of reducing job opportunities for Americans. Moreover, deferral can encourage multinational corporations to manipulate internal transfer prices in order to allocate income to low-tax countries.

There is no reason to defer the imposition of a U.S. tax just because business operations are conducted abroad rather than in the United States, regardless of the motivation for creating a foreign subsidiary. Congress eliminated in 1969 certain special tax preferences for businesses conducted in

the United States through multi-layered corporations. I propose that Congress act in a similar manner to end the present preference for business operations conducted internationally through such multinational corporate structures.

The foreign tax credit will be retained in its present form. Therefore, elimination of deferral will not result in a double taxation of overseas earnings. And, in the event it appears to be in the national interest to permit tax deferral with respect to specific countries, such treatment can be provided selectively under negotiated tax treaties involving mutual concessions.

SPECIAL TAX REDUCTIONS PROPOSED TO REDUCE COSTS FOR CONSUMERS AND BUSINESSES

I propose two tax reduction measures—outside the income tax system—that will assist our efforts to attain price stability.

Repeal of Excise Tax on Telephone Services

The present 4 per cent excise tax on amounts paid for telephone services is now being phased out at the rate of 1 percentage point a year, with full repeal scheduled as of January 1, 1982.

I recommend complete repeal of this tax as of October 1, 1978. This action will reduce the cost of living directly. It will also lower consumer prices indirectly through a reduction of the business cost associated with telephone services.

Federal Unemployment Insurance Tax

I recommend a reduction in the federal unemployment insurance tax to reduce the payroll costs of employers. On January 1, 1978, the unemployment insurance tax rate rose from 0.5 per cent to 0.7 per cent of an employer's taxable wage base. This tax increase was instituted in order to replenish general revenue funds that have been loaned to the unemployment insurance trust fund during recent periods of high unemployment. But the issue of unemployment compensation financing requires a thorough reexamination to determine the best means of providing future benefits. To this end, I will soon appoint the National Commission on Unemployment Insurance which the Congress established to make this study and to offer recommendations. In the meantime, I am guided by my concerns about inflation. I propose that the tax rate be reduced to the 0.5 per cent level as of January 1, 1979.

RECOMMENDED BUSINESS INCENTIVES TO FOSTER GROWTH OF THE ECONOMY

Corporate Rate Cut

I recommend a corporate rate cut that will reduce business taxes by $6 billion. Tax

relief in this form is sizable, easily understood by taxpayers, and applicable across the board.

The corporate tax rate is now 20 per cent on the first $25,000 of income, 22 per cent on the next $25,000, and 48 per cent on corporate income exceeding $50,000. Effective October 1, 1978, this program will reduce the first two rate brackets to 18 and 20 per cent, respectively, and the rate to 45 per cent on taxable income in excess of $50,000. The top rate will be reduced an additional point, to 44 per cent, on January 1, 1980. Small as well as large corporations will benefit from these rate cuts.

A corporate rate reduction of this magnitude will increase capital formation and help to assure a sustained economic recovery. In recent years, the level of business fixed investment has been unsatisfactory. One of the primary causes of this inadequate investment performance has been the low rate of return businesses receive on their investments—after tax liability is taken into consideration. The lower tax rates I recommend will enhance the anticipated after-tax profits on corporate investment projects and increase cash flow immediately. Businesses will thereby be encouraged to increase capital spending and to create jobs for American workers. Corporate rate cuts this large are made possible by, and depend upon, passage of the revenue-raising business tax reforms I have described earlier.

Liberalization of Investment Tax Credit

The investment tax credit has proven to be one of the most potent tax incentives for capital formation. It provides a direct reduction in tax liability generally equal to 10 per cent of a business' qualifying investments. But there are now several limitations that restrict its effectiveness.

I recommend changes that will make the investment credit a stronger, more efficient, and more equitable incentive. These changes will reduce business taxes by approximately $2.5 billion per year.

(1) **Permanent 10 Per Cent Credit.** The present 10 per cent investment credit is not a permanent feature of the Internal Revenue Code. On January 1, 1981, the credit level is scheduled to revert to 7 per cent. I propose that the credit be extended permanently at a 10 per cent rate so that businesses can plan ahead with greater certainty of the tax benefits that will be associated with projected capital expenditures.

(2) **Increased Tax Liability Ceiling.** The investment credit claimed during any taxable year cannot generally exceed $25,000 plus 50 per cent of tax liability in excess of that amount (with excess credits being eligible for a 3-year carryback and a 7-year carry-forward). My tax program will provide a ceiling of 90 per cent of tax liability (including the first $25,000) and will thereby increase the incentive for those businesses with relatively high investment needs and low taxable incomes. Developing

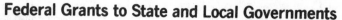

Federal Grants to State and Local Governments

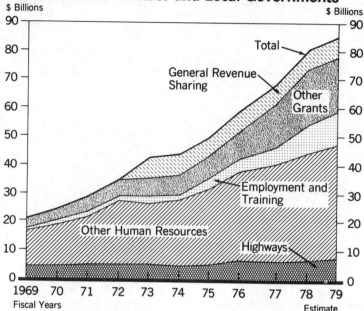

$ Billions ... $ Billions

90 ... 90
80 ... 80
70 ... 70
60 ... 60
50 ... 50
40 ... 40
30 ... 30
20 ... 20
10 ... 10
0 ... 0

Total
General Revenue Sharing
Other Grants
Employment and Training
Other Human Resources
Highways

1969 70 71 72 73 74 75 76 77 78 79
Fiscal Years   Estimate

businesses and firms suffering from temporary business reversals will be helped to compete more effectively with their larger or more stable competitors.

(3) **Eligibility of Structures.** The investment credit now applies only to machinery and equipment. My tax program will extend eligibility for the credit to utility and industrial structures, where investments have been especially sluggish. Investment in these structures reached its peak over 4 years ago and is now 16 per cent below that level. It is important that we act to remedy the existing tax bias against structures and encourage balanced industrial expansion. In order to ensure that this provision has no anti-urban bias, I propose that the investment credit be available for both new structures and the rehabilitation of existing structures.

I recommend that this provision apply to construction costs incurred after December 31, 1977. In the case of new structures, there will be an additional requirement that the facility be placed in service after that date.

(4) **Liberalized Credit for Pollution Control Facilities.** I propose that pollution abatement facilities placed in service after December 31, 1977, be allowed to qualify for a full 10 per cent credit even if special 5-year amortization is claimed under the provisions of existing law. Currently, only a 5 per cent credit may be combined with rapid amortization. This proposal will provide significant tax relief for industries that are forced to make pollution control expenditures in order to comply with environmental regulations.

Revision and Simplification of Regulations Under the Asset Depreciation Range System

The asset depreciation range (ADR) system provides substantial tax benefits to businesses. Under ADR, generous class lives are prescribed for categories of assets, and a taxpayer can select useful lives for depreciation purposes within a range that extends from 20 per cent below to 20 per cent above the designated class life. However, certain complexities in the ADR regulations discourage most businesses, especially small ones, from electing this depreciation system and impose administrative burdens on those businesses that do use ADR.

I recommend legislation expressly permitting the Treasury Department to issue regulations that will simplify the ADR system. Included among the changes will be a termination of the annual reporting requirement.

Proposals Focused on Small Business

The tax reductions I recommend will provide significant benefits for small businesses. For example, a small corporation with annual income of $50,000 will save $1,000 in taxes due to corporate rate reductions. For that corporation, tax liability will be reduced by nearly 10 per cent. Moreover, those small businesses conducted in partnership or sole proprietorship form will benefit substantially from the rate cuts I have proposed for individuals.

But in addition to providing these general tax incentives, I recommend three proposals designed specifically to assist small businesses. First, my tax program will simplify and liberalize the rules (Subchapter S) that treat certain small corporations as partnerships; the number of permissible shareholders will generally be increased from 10 to 15, and the rules governing subchapter S elections will be made less stringent. Second, a simplified method of depreciation will be authorized for small businesses that will provide tax

benefits similar to the current ADR system without complex recordkeeping requirements. And third, risk-taking will be encouraged by doubling the amount of a small corporation's stock (from $500,000 to $1 million) that can qualify for special ordinary loss treatment and by eliminating several technical requirements that needlessly restrict the ability of small businesses to use this provision.

Conclusion

Enactment of these recommendations will effect major reform of our tax laws, provide significant tax relief, and sustain our economic recovery.

This program will eliminate a number of the inequities that undermine the integrity of the tax system. It will make preparation of returns simpler and more understandable for millions of taxpayers. Prompt passage will strengthen the confidence of consumers and businesses in our growing economy and lead to the creation of up to one million new jobs for workers who need them.

I look forward to working in partnership with Congress to enact this program of tax reform and tax reduction.

JIMMY CARTER

The White House.
January 20, 1978

Budget Message

Following is the text of President Carter's fiscal 1979 budget message to Congress on January 23, 1978.

BUDGET MESSAGE OF THE PRESIDENT

*To the Congress
of the United States:*

The first complete budget of any new administration is its most important. It is the administration's first full statement of its priorities, policies, and proposals for meeting our national needs. Last February, after just one month in office, I submitted a revised budget to the Congress. That revision changed the direction of the prior administration's budget, but was—of necessity—based upon a review of limited scope. I promised then that future budgets would reflect detailed, zero-based reviews of Federal spending programs, reform of the tax system, and reorganization of the government. This budget is my first major step in meeting that promise. It reflects, I believe, **a determination to face and** make difficult decisions in a manner that places the common good above that of any particular interest.

This budget represents a careful balancing of several considerations:

—The importance of a fiscal policy that provides for a continuing recovery of the nation's economy from the 1974-75 recession;

—The obligation of the government to meet the critical needs of the nation and its people;

—The fact that resources are limited and that government must discipline its choices and its scope; and

—The need for careful and prudent management of the taxpayers' resources.

My budget provides for total outlays of $500 billion, an increase of $38 billion, or 8 per cent, over the 1978 target, and receipts of $400 billion. This budget total is a restrained one that:

—Meets essential national needs;

—Imposes strict priorities upon federal **expenditures; and**

—Decreases the share of the nation's gross national product taken by the federal government from 22.6 per cent to 22.0 per cent.

This budget places us on a path that will permit a balanced budget in the future if the private economy continues its recovery over the coming years.

At the same time, my budget embodies a fiscal policy that will strengthen the economic recovery. I propose a progressive tax reduction of $25 billion to help assure continued economic recovery and reduction in unemployment. An integral part of this tax reduction proposal is a set of recommendations for tax reform that will make the tax system simpler and more equitable. Without the reduction, I would have been able to announce a decline in the deficit of $15 to $20 billion between 1978 and 1979. With the reduction, the budget deficit will still decline slightly, because of careful restraints on expenditures. But I judged that the most important priority this year was to reduce the burdens on taxpayers. Only in this way can we ensure a vigorous economy, a declining unemployment rate, a strong expansion of private investment, and a stable budget balance in future years.

While the expenditures I recommend in this budget are restrained, they are, nevertheless, directed toward overcoming our nation's crucial problems. I have looked carefully at existing approaches to these problems and improved those approaches where possible. The spending priorities of the past are now being shifted toward long-neglected areas. These new priorities are based on the following judgments:

Energy Plan

—*An effective national energy plan is essential to reduce our increasingly critical dependence upon diminishing supplies of oil and gas, to encourage conservation of scarce energy resources, to stimulate conversion to more abundant fuels, and to reduce our large trade deficit.*

The national energy plan I proposed last spring defined these goals. This budget includes the programs and initiatives designed to meet those objectives. Included are increased emphases on conservation and nonnuclear research and development, energy grants and technical assistance to states and localities, accelerated acquisition of the strategic petroleum reserve, and greater emphases on nuclear waste management. I continue in the unswerving belief that the nation's leaders have the obligation to plan for the future, and that the national energy plan is essential to the future health and vigor of the American economy. The United States also must take the lead in minimizing the risks of nuclear weapons proliferation as we advance nuclear power technology. Thus, this budget increases research and development funding for systems that present fewer risks than the plutonium-fueled liquid metal fast breeder reactor.

Human Needs

—*The essential human needs of our citizens must be given high priority.*

In the spring of 1977 I proposed a long-overdue reform of the nation's welfare system. This reform recognizes that this is a nation of men and women who do not wish to be wards of the government but who want to work and to be self-sufficient. It includes a combination of employment opportunities and incentives for those who should work, and a basic income for those who cannot. This budget anticipates that Congress will pass the program for better jobs and income, and begins the process of careful planning for the implementation of an efficient and equitable system.

The budget also recognizes that ensuring the opportunity to compete and excel remains very important to our people. To give all children the healthiest possible start in life, I propose major expansion of medical care and nutritional supplements for low-income expectant mothers and infants. In addition, I propose major increases in educational assistance at all levels. Because of the continued high level of unemployment, particularly among minorities, I believe public employment programs should be continued at high levels for another year. Major increases in programs stressing employment for unemployed youth are recommended. A new effort will be mounted to place more disadvantaged persons in private sector jobs by increasing the involvement of the business community in local employment and training programs.

I view a workable urban strategy as an important link in a well-articulated domestic program and essential to the continuing recovery of the national economy. This budget includes increases for many programs benefiting urban areas and supports several efforts to improve these programs. I anticipate sending to the Congress early in the spring a set of further proposals dealing with the nation's urban problems.

Defense

—*The nation's armed forces must always stand sufficiently strong to deter aggression and to assure our security.*

My request for defense provides for the steady modernization of our strategic forces, and for substantial improvements in the combat readiness of our tactical forces. To parallel commitments made by our European allies, I am proposing significant increases in our overall defense effort, with special emphasis on those forces and capabilities most directly related to our NATO commitments. The defense budget I recommend also emphasizes modernization and research and development to meet future challenges to our security. But at the same time, I am restraining defense expenditures by introducing important efficiencies and by placing careful priorities upon our defense needs. The 1979 defense budget is prudent and tight, but consists of a real growth in outlays of 3 per cent above the cur-

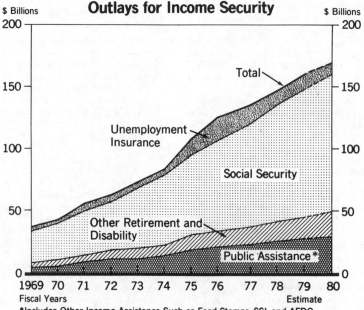

Outlays for Income Security

*Includes Other Income Assistance Such as Food Stamps, SSI, and AFDC

rent year's budget. Consistent with campaign pledges to the American people, it is $8 billion below the defense budget projected for 1979 by the previous administration.

Environment

—*The Federal Government has an obligation to nurture and protect our environment—the common resource, birthright and sustenance of the American people.*

This budget provides for substantially increased emphasis on protection of all our environmental resources, for new attention to our common heritage, and for substantial additions to our system of public lands. Planned use of our natural resources has been designed so that the most important of our unspoiled areas can remain forever in the hands of the people.

Technology

—*The Federal Government must lead the way in investing in the nation's technological future.*

Shortly after taking office, I determined that investment in basic research on the part of the federal government had fallen far too low over the past decade. Accordingly, I directed that a careful review be undertaken of appropriate basic research opportunities. As a result of that review, this budget proposes a real rate of growth of almost 5 per cent for basic research in 1979. I believe this emphasis is important to the continued vitality of our economy.

Government Operations

This budget also reflects this administration's commitment to two important approaches to making government work more efficiently and responsively: reorganization and zero-base budgeting.

The reorganization effort I have launched seeks more than just a streamlining of organization structure and the elimination of overlaps and duplication. It seeks to make our government more responsive, more efficient, and more clearly focused on the most pressing needs of our society. In 1977 I proposed—and the Congress accepted—a Cabinet-level Department of Energy, a streamlined Executive Office of the President, and a consolidation of our international information activities. In 1978 I will propose further reorganizations in such areas as the federal government's civil rights activities and the federal civil service system to make it more responsive and effective.

As I promised during my campaign, zero-base budgeting systems have been applied throughout the federal government. This budget is the product of a comprehensive zero-base review of all federal programs, both existing and new. In reviewing each agency's proposals, I have used zero-base budget alternatives and agency rankings to compare and evaluate the many requests competing for resources. As a result of the first year's effort, we have gained a better understanding of federal

Government Expenditures as a Percent of GNP*

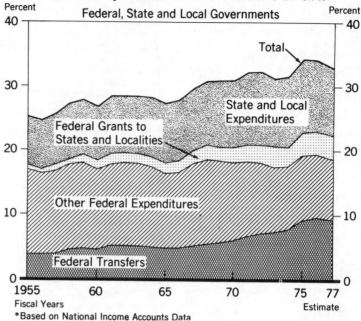

Percent — Federal, State and Local Governments — Percent

programs and have made better, more evenhanded judgments. Because of this system the budget includes dollar savings, and improvements in the way programs are operated. With experience, zero-based budgeting should be even more effective in future years.

Other significant changes in the budget process are reflected in this document. First: I have directed the Office of Management and Budget to establish a multi-year budget planning system using longer range budget projections. This will ensure that budget decisions are made with full awareness of their longer range implications. Second: we are using better techniques for estimating outlays so as to avoid the chronic "shortfalls" of recent years. Third: we have explicitly related the classification of the budget in terms of functions performed by government programs to the national needs and agency missions served, as called for in the Congressional Budget Act of 1974.

In formulating this budget I have been made acutely aware once more of the overwhelming number of demands upon the budget and of the finite nature of our resources. Public needs are critically important; but private needs are equally valid, and the only resources the government has are those it collects from the taxpayer. The competition for these resources and my belief and commitment that we must firmly limit what the government taxes and expends have led me to the premises on which my first budget is based.

—Critical national needs exist—particularly human and social ones—to which resources must be directed.

—Government resources are scarce; their use must be planned with the full awareness that they come from the

earnings of workers and profits of business firms.

—The span of government is not infinite. Priorities must be set and some old priorities changed. If we are to meet adequately the most critical needs, some demands must also be deferred. Government action must be limited to those areas where its intervention is more likely to solve problems than to compound them.

—We have an obligation to manage with excellence, and to maintain proper priorities within the $500 billion proposed in this budget. We all know that in a budget of this scale—larger than the gross national product of all but three nations in the world—there are dollars wasted and dollars misspent. These must be minimal.

These premises are unexceptionable in general, but difficult and controversial to apply. They have guided my actions in formulating this budget and they will continue to do so in the future. But to be successful I will need, and will work for, the help and cooperation of the Congress. Both the Congress and the Executive have a clear, joint interest in an approach that helps us to meet the demands of the future. In recent years the Congress has taken important steps—through the establishment of the congressional budget process—to improve its own means of establishing priorities. This administration has worked closely with the congressional appropriations and budget committees and has found them invaluable sources of advice. We will continue in this spirit of cooperation, and I look forward to working with the Congress and its leadership to obtain adoption of my budget for fiscal year 1979.

Jimmy Carter

January 20, 1978

Transportation Programs

Following is the text of President Carter's Jan. 26 message to Congress, transmitting his proposals to improve the federal highway and transit programs:

TO THE CONGRESS
OF THE UNITED STATES:

I am today transmitting to Congress proposed legislation that will significantly improve the organization and operation of the Federal Government's highway and transit programs.

One of the Administration's important goals is to develop a well balanced national transportation policy, one which takes account of our increased sensitivity to the effects of transportation on the social and economic life of our cities and rural communities. The reforms which are proposed in this legislation are designed to make certain that the nation has an effective transportation system, which uses energy more efficiently, enhances the quality of life in our urban and rural areas, and helps expand our economy.

The program I am proposing will intensify the Federal effort to complete the Interstate System and provide flexible assistance for highway construction and transit development. The legislation would authorize more than $50 billion over the next five years and proposes the following changes to meet national transportation needs:

—a comprehensive transportation planning program;
—measures to speed completion of the Interstate System and to improve maintenance;
—consolidation of more than 30 highway and public transportation grant programs into fewer and more flexible programs for both rural and urban areas;
—a uniform Federal share for all grant programs except Interstate construction and Interstate transfer projects;
—focusing the transit discretionary program on major investments;
—an expanded bridge replacement and rehabilitation program;
—a unified safety program; and
—greater flexibility for states and local governments to pursue their own priorities.

To achieve our objectives in this area, we propose a reorganization of a variety of highway and transit programs into a simpler and more manageable system of federal assistance. Certain aspects of our new approach to these programs should be emphasized.

Transportation Planning

To promote more efficient short-range and long-range planning by state and local officials, I propose to consolidate highway and transit planning funds and to distribute these funds as a single grant, under a formula to be determined by the Secretary of Transportation.

Planning grants will be made directly to designated metropolitan planning organizations in urbanized areas over one million in population. The Secretary will review transportation plans for such areas to ensure that they take reasonable account of such issues as air quality, energy conservation, environmental quality, accessibility to employment, effect on minorities, housing, land use and future development. The planning process for other areas will be strengthened as well.

Interstate System

Our first priority will be to complete the essential gaps in the Interstate System. Fifty per cent of the apportionment formula will be based on the cost to complete the essential gaps and 50 per cent on the cost to complete the total system. Highway projects substituted after an Interstate withdrawal will be funded from a state's Interstate apportionment, and substitute mass transit projects will be funded from the General Fund. Interstate substitute projects, both highway and transit, will be eligible for a ninety per cent federal share.

States will be required to have completed the Environmental Impact Statement process or to have submitted an application for an Interstate withdrawal on all uncompleted segments of the Interstate by September 30, 1982. Segments which have not met either requirement will be removed from the system. All incomplete Interstate segments must be under contract for construction and initial construction must have commenced by September 30, 1986.

Federal-Aid Primary System

To simplify an unduly restrictive funding structure, seven highway categories will be consolidated into a single Primary program. Funds will be apportioned by a formula specified in the legislation and the federal share will be eighty per cent. Up to 50 per cent of a state's primary system funds may be transferred to the urban highway or the small urban and rural transportation programs.

Urban Formula Grants

Two compatible programs will be established, one for highways and one for transit, for all urbanized areas with a population of 50,000 or more. The highway program will consolidate five categorical programs, and all urban roads not on the Interstate or primary systems will be eligible for assistance. The transit program will provide assistance for the acquisition, construction and improvement of facilities and equipment for use in public transportation services and the payment of operating expenses, including commuter rail operating expenses.

Funds will be apportioned by formula and the federal share for capital projects will be 80 per cent. The highway formula will be based on urbanized area population. Up to 50 per cent of the urban highway funds may be transferred to the Primary program or to the small urban and rural program. Up to 50 per cent of the transit funds may be transferred to the highway program. Highway funds will continue to be available for transit capital projects.

Governors and local officials will be required to designate a recipient or recipients for urban highway funds in urbanized areas with a population of one million or more. By this step we will significantly improve the opportunity for large cities to become more involved in the planning and programming of their highway systems. Urban highway funds for areas with small populations will go to the State.

Urban Discretionary Grant

This transit grant program will be focused on major expansion of bus fleets and new fixed guideway projects, including extensions of existing systems, and joint development projects.

Small Urban and Rural Formula Grant

To meet the unique needs of small cities and rural communities, we propose a consolidated grant program for highways and transit for all areas with a population below 50,000, with the state as the recipient.

Nine categorical highway programs will be consolidated into this new program, and all public roads not on the Interstate or primary systems will be eligible for assistance. The new program will provide assistance for both capital and operating expenses for public transportation in small urban and rural communities. Authorization for this program would come out of the Highway Trust Fund, but the Trust Fund would be reimbursed out of the General Fund for transit operating expenses.

Safety Program

To allow more flexible and rational use of funds, six highway safety programs will be consolidated into a single safety grant to states, with the federal share at 80 per cent.

Bridge Program

For the first time states will be able to use substantially increased funds for rehabilitation as well as replacements of deteriorating bridges. The federal share will be 80 per cent, and up to 30 per cent of the funds will be available for bridges not on the Federal-aid highway systems.

Authorizations

The proposed authorizations are designed to permit better long-term planning by those responsible for both highway and transit development. The Highway Trust Fund will be extended for an additional four years. The formula grant programs will be authorized for a four-year period, and the urban discretionary grant program will be authorized for a five-year period.

In proposing the reforms contained in this legislation I recognize the critical relationship between transportation, energy and development in urban and rural areas. I believe that these proposals will lead toward energy conservation and better land use. The enactment of this legislation will bring new opportunities and responsibilities to state and local officials, will respond to the problems of the present programs, and will help to place the surface transportation system on a sound financial basis.

I ask the Congress to move promptly to pass this highway and transit legislation.

JIMMY CARTER

The White House,
January 26, 1978

Arms Sales Cut

Following is the text of a statement by President Carter, issued Feb. 1, announcing reductions in the ceiling on arms sales abroad:

The United States Government, the Executive Branch and the Congress, are pledged to bring about a reduction in the trade in conventional arms. Last year, I promised to begin reducing U.S. arms sales as a necessary first step. I will continue that policy this year.

In the last fiscal year, the previous Administration and my Administration made sales commitments totaling many billions of dollars. While high, however, the total was considerably less than it would have been in the absence of new restraints we introduced, particularly in sales commitments to the developing countries of the world. Between January 20 and the close of the fiscal year, I approved and sent to Congress arms sales totaling $5.7 billion, which is less than half the total approved during the same period in 1976.

Today, I am announcing that arms transfer agreements covered by the ceiling which I have established will be reduced by $740 million in Fiscal Year 1978. This means that for the fiscal year which began on October 1, 1977, and which will end on September 30, 1978, new commitments under the Foreign Military Sales and Military Assistance programs for weapons and weapons-related items to all countries except NATO, Japan, Australia and New Zealand will not exceed $8.6 billion. The comparable figure for Fiscal Year 1977 was $9.3 billion. This is a reduction of 8 percent, figured on constant Fiscal Year 1976 dollars.

A larger cut in the ceiling would violate commitments already made, including our historic interest in the security of the Middle East, and would ignore the continuing realities of world politics and risk the confidence and security of those nations with whom the United States has vital and shared foreign policy and security interests. A smaller reduction would neglect our responsibility to set an example of restraint that others might follow.

I intend to make further reductions in the next fiscal year. The extent of next year's reduction will depend upon the world political situation and upon the degree of cooperation and understanding of other nations.

I want to emphasize that the restraint policy I announced on May 19, 1977, was not aimed exclusively at the volume of arms transfers. Equally important is restraint in the sophistication of arms being transferred and on the spreading capability to produce armaments. Therefore, in addition to the ceiling, I established five specific controls applicable to all transfers except those to our NATO allies, Japan, Australia, and New Zealand. These controls included: (1) a control on the first introduction of certain advanced systems into an area; (2) a prohibition on advanced systems for export only; (3) a prohibition on various types of coproduction arrangements; (4) tighter controls on retransfer; and (5) special controls on sales promotions.

These guidelines are at the heart of my decisions to approve or disapprove an arms transfer.

As I stated in my October 4 speech to the United Nations, genuine progress in this area will require multilateral efforts. But, we are committed to taking the first steps alone to stop the spiral of increasing arms transfers. I call upon suppliers and recipients alike to join us in a determined effort to make the world a safer place in which to live.

Nuclear Safeguards

Following is President Carter's Feb. 9 message to the Senate accompanying a proposed treaty with the International Atomic Energy Agency concerning safeguards for nuclear facilities:

TO THE SENATE
OF THE UNITED STATES:

I submit herewith, for Senate advice and consent to ratification, the Agreement between the United States of America and the International Atomic Energy Agency ("Agency") for the Application of Safeguards in the United States of America, with attached Protocol, approved by the Board of Governors of the Agency on September 17, 1976. This agreement provides for application of Agency safeguards to nuclear facilities in the United States, other than those having direct national security significance. The Agreement will enter into force when the United States notifies the Agency that its constitutional and statutory requirements for entry into force have been met.

The United States, as a nuclear weapons state party to the Treaty on the Non-Proliferation of Nuclear Weapons ("NPT"), is not obligated to accept Agency safeguards on its peaceful nuclear activities. On December 2, 1967, President Johnson offered to place United States nuclear facilities, except those with direct national security significance, under Agency safeguards in an effort to demonstrate that the application of those safeguards would not work to any nation's commercial disadvantage. Specifically, President Johnson stated:

"...I want to make it clear to the world that we in the United States are not asking any country to accept safeguards that we are unwilling to accept ourselves.

"So I am, today, announcing that when such safeguards are applied under the treaty, the United States will permit the International Atomic Energy Agency to apply its safeguards to all nuclear activities in the United States—excluding only those with direct national security significance.

"Under this offer the agency will be able to inspect a broad range of U.S. nuclear activities, both governmental and private, including the fuel in nuclear power reactors owned by utilities for generating electricity, and the fabrication, and chemical reprocessing of such fuel...."

Over the next ten years, both Presidents Nixon and Ford reaffirmed that offer.

I also transmit, for the information of the Senate, the report of the Department of State concerning the Agreement.

Universal participation in the NPT is a central goal of our non-proliferation policy. The entry into force of this Agreement would encourage that participation, and would fulfill our long-standing commitment to accept safeguards. I urge the Senate to act favorably on this Agreement at an early date and give its advice and consent to ratification.

JIMMY CARTER

The White House
Feb. 9, 1978

Jobs Program Renewal

Following is President Carter's Feb. 22 message to Congress requesting extension of the Comprehensive Employment and Training Act (CETA).

TO THE CONGRESS
OF THE UNITED STATES:

I am submitting today legislation to extend an improved Comprehensive Employment and Training Act through 1982.

This legislation is an essential complement to the balanced economic program I presented to the Congress last month. While our tax and budget proposals ensure that steady growth continues without inflation, the CETA legislation I am proposing today will make sure that more of our people share in the benefits of growth. With its training programs and direct job creation, this legislation is critical to reaching our employment goals.

In Fiscal Year 1979 we expect to spend $11.4 billion in this effort, providing jobs and training support for more than 4 million people under the CETA program.

This legislation will combine public and private efforts to attack the problem of *structural* unemployment, which affects groups, such as minorities and young people, who have difficulty finding work even when over-all economic prospects are good. Last year, for example, our employment situations improved markedly; 4.1 million more people held jobs at the end of 1977 than at the end of 1976, and the unemployment rate fell by 1.4 per cent. But even while unemployment was falling to 4 per cent among white males above the age of 20, it was rising—from 35 to 38 percent—among black teenagers.

Major Elements

The Comprehensive Employment and Training Act will enable us to concentrate on these groups that suffer structural problems, without putting inflationary pressures on the rest of the economy. Its major elements are:

—Public service jobs for the unemployed. In the last year, we have more than doubled the size of this program, increasing it from about 300,000 jobs to 725,000.

—The broad range of youth programs authorized by the Youth Employment and Demonstration Projects Act of 1977. Spending for youth programs has increased from about $660 million in Fiscal Year 1976 to about $2.3 billion in Fiscal Year 1979.

—The Administration's new Private Sector Initiative, which will provide opportunity for the private and public sectors to work together to provide jobs and training for the unemployed and disadvantaged.

—Other important related programs, such as the Job Corps, welfare reform demonstration projects, and the federal government's job training efforts.

These CETA programs have already played a role in reducing the unemployment rate from 7.8 per cent to 6.3 per cent in the last 13 months.

The bill I am submitting today, which will reauthorize the Comprehensive Employment and Training Act for an additional four years, from 1979 to 1982, will sustain the current programs, establish the foundation for future growth, and improve the operation of the CETA system.

A countercyclical program under Title VI, will maintain the 725,000 public service employment slots that were part of my stimulus program through Fiscal 1979. We are rapidly approaching the 700,000 mark in that effort, and I fully expect that the 725,-000 goal will be reached in the month of March.

Also, I am recommending to the Congress that we adopt a trigger formula, beginning in 1980, to insure that counter-cyclical public service employment is activated quickly when needed and is reduced as unemployment declines.

When the unemployment rate falls below four and three-quarters per cent, the triggering formula will reduce the number of slots to 100,000, targeted on areas that still have high unemployment. For each half percentage point that unemployment exceeds that 4.75 percent level, 100,000 public service employment positions will be added in Title VI.

Recent evidence indicates the effectiveness of countercyclical public service employment. Just last week, the National Commission on Manpower Policy released a study done by the Brookings Institution showing that the substitution problem, which limits the usefulness of public service employment when federal dollars are used to replace local funds, is not as serious as had previously been feared.

To reduce substitution, I am encouraging the use of a special project approach which, according to recent evidence, has been successful in meeting this problem.

I am also proposing strict limits on the use of these funds to support higher-wage public employment.

This new bill takes further steps to target jobs on those most in need and sharply limit substitution.

Only for Disadvantaged

In order to target more effectively, I am recommending that funds given out under the CETA system be used only for the economically disadvantaged—defined as those whose family income is no greater than 70 percent of the Bureau of Labor Statistics' lower-income family budget standard. I am also recommending that young people whose parents claimed them as income tax deductions in the previous year include their parents' income in establishing their eligibility for the current year.

This year, I propose that we demonstrate the jobs component of my welfare reform proposal by creating 50,000 positions in selected cities. Beginning in Fiscal 1980, with the passage of the welfare reform bill, we will increase the structural unemployment program until it can accommodate the 1.4 million people I anticipate will be served in the welfare reform plan. That should ensure that, for every family containing children and parents who want to work, there will be a job. Most families containing an employable person will see their income rise substantially above the poverty line.

The purpose of the Public Service Employment program will remain what it has been—to provide *useful* jobs. For example:

—Major parks in urban centers, such as Boston, that were once abandoned to overgrowth and vandalism have been reclaimed for the enjoyment of the public.

—In North Carolina, elderly people are being cared for, in their homes, by public service employment workers, rather than being forced to leave home and spend their last years in expensive, sometimes impersonal nursing homes.

—In Portland, Oregon, CETA workers install locks, window grates and other security devices in the homes of senior citizens and low-income families living in high-crime areas.

—In Memphis, workers are building ramps for the handicapped in five areas of the city used heavily by the handicapped and elderly.

—In Humboldt County, California, CETA workers help to staff day care centers serving low-income families.

—In Worthington, Minnesota, workers are providing home insulation and energy conservation assistance to low-income households in a four-county area.

As the economy improves, employment and training programs should shift their emphasis from creating jobs in the public sector to providing training and finding jobs in the private sector.

New Program

To help place CETA participants in private-sector jobs, to provide an opportunity for cooperation between the local CETA programs and the private sector, and to tap the goodwill and commitment of private-sector businessmen, large and small, as well as labor leaders, I am asking Congress for authority to establish a new Private Sector Employment Initiative, under a new Title VII. In the budget, I have set aside $400 million for this activity in 1979.

Private Industry Councils—made up of representatives of large and small businesses and union organizations—will be responsible for developing on-the-job training and other placement opportunities with private firms for young workers and other participants in the CETA system.

The CETA legislation that I am presenting today provides Congress with a plan for a rational, efficient and targeted structural and countercyclical employment program.

We need an employment and training system which is administratively clear, that helps those most in need, that creates needed jobs and provides maximum opportunity for cooperation between the public and private sectors. To reach the goal of full employment, and price stability which we have set in the Humphrey-Hawkins bill, we must make these programs work. The legislation I am sending to Congress today can provide a framework within which we can all work together to achieve that commitment.

JIMMY CARTER

The White House,
February 22, 1978   ∎

Equal Employment Plan

Following is President Carter's Feb. 23 message to Congress on

Reorganization Plan No. 1 of 1978, consolidating the federal government's equal employment opportunity activities.

TO THE CONGRESS
OF THE UNITED STATES:

I am submitting to you today Reorganization Plan No. 1 of 1978. This Plan makes the Equal Employment Opportunity Commission the principal Federal agency in fair employment enforcement. Together with actions I shall take by Executive Order, it consolidates Federal equal employment opportunity activities and lays, for the first time, the foundation of a unified, coherent Federal structure to combat job discrimination in all its forms.

In 1940 President Roosevelt issued the first Executive Order forbidding discrimination in employment by the Federal government. Since that time the Congress, the courts and the Executive Branch — spurred by the courage and sacrifice of many people and organizations — have taken historic steps to extend equal employment opportunity protection throughout the private as well as public sector. But each new prohibition against discrimination unfortunately has brought with it a further dispersal of Federal equal employment opportunity responsibility. This fragmentation of authority among a number of Federal agencies has meant confusion and ineffective enforcement for employees, regulatory duplication and needless expense for employers.

Fair employment is too vital for haphazard enforcement. My Administration will aggressively enforce our civil rights laws. Although discrimination in any area has severe consequences, limiting economic opportunity affects access to education, housing and health care. I, therefore, ask you to join with me to reorganize administration of the civil rights laws and to begin that effort by reorganizing the enforcement of those laws which ensure an equal opportunity to a job.

Streamlining Proposal

Eighteen government units now exercise important responsibilities under statutes, Executive Orders and regulations relating to equal employment opportunity:

• The Equal Employment Opportunity Commission (EEOC) enforces Title VII of the Civil Rights Act of 1964, which bans employment discrimination based on race, national origin, sex or religion. The EEOC acts on individual complaints and also initiates private sector cases involving a "pattern or practice" of discrimination.

• The Department of Labor and other agencies enforce Executive Order 11246. This prohibits discrimination in employment on the basis of race, national origin sex, or religion and requires affirmative action by government contractors. While the Department now coordinates enforcement of this "contract compliance" program, it is actually administered by eleven

other departments and agencies. The Department also administers those statutes requiring contractors to take affirmative action to employ handicapped people, disabled veterans and Vietnam veterans.

In addition, the Labor Department enforces the Equal Pay Act of 1963, which prohibits employers from paying unequal wages based on sex, and the Age Discrimination in Employment Act of 1967, which forbids age discrimination against persons between the ages of 40 and 65.

• The Department of Justice litigates Title VII cases involving public sector employers — State and local governments. The Department also represents the Federal government in lawsuits against Federal contractors and grant recipients who are in violation of Federal nondiscrimination prohibitions.

• The Civil Service Commission (CSC) enforces Title VII and all other nondiscrimination and affirmative action requirements for Federal employment. The CSC rules on complaints filed by individuals and monitors affirmative action plans submitted annually by other Federal agencies.

• The Equal Employment Opportunity Coordinating Council includes representatives from EEOC, Labor, Justice, CSC and the Civil Rights Commission. It is charged with coordinating the Federal equal employment opportunity enforcement effort and with eliminating overlap and inconsistent standards.

• In addition to these major government units, other agencies enforce various equal employment opportunity requirements which apply to specific grant programs. The Department of Treasury, for example, administers the anti-discrimination prohibitions applicable to recipients of revenue sharing funds.

These programs have had only limited success. Some of the past deficiencies include:

— inconsistent standards of compliance;

— duplicative, inconsistent paperwork requirements and investigative efforts;

— conflicts within agencies between their program responsibilities and their responsibility to enforce the civil rights laws;

— confusion on the part of workers about how and where to seek redress;

— lack of accountability.

I am proposing today a series of steps to bring coherence to the equal employment enforcement effort. These steps, to be accomplished by the Reorganization Plan and Executive Orders, constitute an important step toward consolidation of equal employment opportunity enforcement. They will be implemented over the next two years, so that the agencies involved may continue their internal reform.

EEOC Progress

Its experience and broad scope make the EEOC suitable for the role of principal Federal agency in fair employment enforcement. Located in the Executive Branch and responsible to the President, the

EEOC has developed considerable expertise in the field of employment discrimination since Congress created it by the Civil Rights Act of 1964. The Commission has played a pioneer role in defining both employment discrimination and its appropriate remedies.

While it has had management problems in past administrations, the EEOC's new leadership is making substantial progress in correcting them. In the last seven months the Commission has redesigned its internal structures and adopted proven management techniques. Early experience with these procedures indicates a high degree of success in reducing and expediting new cases. At my direction, the Office of Management and Budget is actively assisting the EEOC to ensure that these reforms continue.

The Reorganization Plan I am submitting will accomplish the following:

• On July 1, 1978, abolish the Equal Employment Opportunity Coordinating Council (42 U.S.C. 2000e-14) and transfer its duties to the EEOC (no positions or funds shifted).

• On October 1, 1978, shift enforcement of equal employment opportunity for Federal employees from the CSC to the EEOC (100 positions and $6.5 million shifted).

• On July 1, 1979, shift responsibility for enforcing both the Equal Pay Act and the Age Discrimination in Employment Act from the Labor Department to the EEOC (198 positions and $5.3 million shifted for Equal Pay; 119 positions and $3.5 million for Age Discrimination).

• Clarify the Attorney General's authority to initiate "pattern or practice" suits under Title VII in the public sector.

In addition, I will issue an Executive Order on October 1, 1978, to consolidate the contract compliance program — now the responsibility of Labor and eleven "compliance agencies" — into the Labor Department (1,517 positions and $33.1 million shifted).

These proposed transfers and consolidations reduce from fifteen to three the number of Federal agencies having important equal employment opportunity responsibilities under Title VII of the Civil Rights Act of 1964 and Federal contract compliance provisions.

Each element of my Plan is important to the success of the entire proposal.

By abolishing the Equal Employment Opportunity Coordinating Council and transferring its responsibilities to the EEOC, this plan places the Commission at the center of equal employment opportunity enforcement. With these new responsibilities, the EEOC can give coherence and direction to the government's efforts by developing strong uniform enforcement standards to apply throughout the government: standardized data collection procedures, joint training programs, programs to ensure the sharing of enforcement related data among agencies, and methods and priorities for complaint and compliance reviews. Such direction has been absent in the Equal Employment Opportunity Coordinating Council.

It should be stressed, however, that affected agencies will be consulted before EEOC takes any action. When the Plan has been approved, I intend to issue an Executive Order which will provide for consultation, as well as a procedure for reviewing major disputed issues within the Executive Office of the President. The Attorney General's responsibility to advise the Executive Branch on legal issues will also be preserved.

Federal Employees

Transfer of the Civil Service Commission's equal employment opportunity responsibilities to EEOC is needed to ensure that: (1) Federal employees have the same rights and remedies as those in the private sector and in State and local government; (2) Federal agencies meet the same standards as are required of other employers; and (3) potential conflicts between an agency's equal employment opportunity and personnel management functions are minimized. The Federal government must not fall below the standard of performance it expects of private employers.

The Civil Service Commission has in the past been lethargic in enforcing fair employment requirements within the Federal government. While the Chairman and other Commissioners I have appointed have already demonstrated their personal commitment to expanding equal employment opportunity, responsibility for ensuring fair employment for Federal employees should rest ultimately with the EEOC.

We must ensure that the transfer in no way undermines the important objectives of the comprehensive civil service reorganization which will be submitted to Congress in the near future. When the two plans take effect, I will direct the EEOC and the CSC to coordinate their procedures to prevent any duplication and overlap.

The Equal Pay Act, now administered by the Labor Department, prohibits employers from paying unequal wages based on sex. Title VII of the Civil Rights Act, which is enforced by EEOC, contains a broader ban on sex discrimination. The transfer of Equal Pay responsibility from the Labor Department to the EEOC will minimize overlap and centralize enforcement of statutory prohibitions against sex discrimination in employment.

The transfer will strengthen efforts to combat sex discrimination. Such efforts would be enhanced still further by passage of the legislation pending before you, which I support, that would prohibit employers from excluding women disabled by pregnancy from participating in disability programs.

There is now virtually complete overlap in the employers, labor organizations, and employment agencies covered by Title VII and by the Age Discrimination in Employment Act. This overlap is burdensome to employers and confusing to victims of discrimination. The proposed transfer of the age discrimination program from the Labor Department to the EEOC will eliminate the duplication.

The Plan I am proposing will not affect the Attorney General's responsibility to enforce Title VII against State or local governments or to represent the Federal government in suits against Federal contractors and grant recipients. In 1972, the Congress determined that the Attorney General should be involved in suits against State and local governments. This proposal reinforces that judgment and clarifies the Attorney General's authority to initiate litigation against State or local governments engaged in a "pattern or practice" of discrimination. This in no way diminishes the EEOC's existing authority to investigate complaints filed against State or local governments and, where appropriate, to refer them to the Attorney General. The Justice Department and the EEOC will cooperate so that the Department sues on valid referrals, as well as on its own "pattern or practice" cases.

Contractors' Compliance

A critical element of my proposals will be accomplished by Executive Order rather than by the Reorganization Plan. This involves consolidation in the Labor Department of the responsibility to ensure that Federal contractors comply with Executive Order 11246. Consolidation will achieve the following: promote consistent standards, procedures, and reporting requirements; remove contractors from the jurisdiction of multiple agencies; prevent an agency's equal employment objectives from being outweighed by its procurement and construction objectives; and produce more effective law enforcement through unification of planning, training and sanctions. By 1981, after I have had an opportunity to review the manner in which both the EEOC and the Labor Department are exercising their new responsibilities, I will determine whether further action is appropriate.

Finally, the responsibility for enforcing grant-related equal employment provisions will remain with the agencies administering the grant programs. With the EEOC acting as coordinator of Federal equal employment programs, we will be able to bring overlap and duplication to a minimum. We will be able, for example, to see that a university's employment practices are not subject to duplicative investigations under both Title IX of the Education Amendments of 1972 and the contract compliance program. Because of the similarities between the Executive Order program and those statutes requiring Federal contractors to take affirmative action to employ handicapped individuals and disabled and Vietnam veterans, I have determined that enforcement of these statutes should remain in the Labor Department.

Each of the changes set forth in the Reorganization Plan accompanying this message is necessary to accomplish one or more of the purposes set forth in Section 901(a) of Title 5 of the United States Code. I have taken care to determine that all functions abolished by the Plan are done only under the statutory authority provided by Section 903(b) of Title 5 of the United States Code.

I do not anticipate that the reorganizations contained in this Plan will result in any significant change in expenditures. They will result in a more efficient and manageable enforcement program.

The Plan I am submitting is moderate and measured. It gives the Equal Employment Opportunity Commission — an agency dedicated solely to this purpose — the primary Federal responsibility in the area of job discrimination, but it is designed to give this agency sufficient time to absorb its new responsibilities. This reorganization will produce consistent agency standards, as well as increased accountability. Combined with the intense commitment of those charged with these responsibilities, it will become possible for us to accelerate this nation's progress in ensuring equal job opportunities for all our people.

JIMMY CARTER

The White House,
February 23, 1978   ▮

Education Proposals

Following is President Carter's Feb. 28 message to Congress outlining his proposals for federal programs to aid elementary and secondary education.

TO THE CONGRESS
OF THE UNITED STATES:

I am submitting today my proposals to strengthen our major elementary and secondary education programs. These are one part of a concerted effort to re-establish education in the forefront of our domestic priorities. The other parts are major increases in the Federal education budget, establishment of a Cabinet-level Department of Education, and our proposal for a significant expansion of eligibility for college student assistance.

The proposals which I am now submitting for elementary and secondary education seek to enhance the primary role of the states and local communities in educating our Nation's children and reaffirm the need for a strong and supportive Federal commitment to education. They will:

— strengthen our commitment to basic skills education in Title I of the Elementary and Secondary Education program; and add a new provision to concentrate a major share of increased Title I funding on those school systems most in need;

— create a new program to encourage state implementation of their own compensatory education programs;

— provide additional flexibility in the Emergency School Aid Act, designed to assist in desegregation, so that funds can be retargeted from areas where they are no longer needed to areas of greater need;

— create a new research and demonstration effort in the area of basic skills, and enhance our efforts to link schools with employers and other community resources;

— implement a phased, gradual but substantial reform of the Impact Aid Program;

— strengthen the bilingual education program with emphasis on teaching English as a primary and overriding goal but permitting flexibility in use of first language and culturally sensitive approaches to help achieve this goal;

— strengthen participation of private schools in existing grant programs.

We can be justly proud of the accomplishments of our system of education. Education has promoted understanding among a diverse people; it has been the springboard to advancement for generations of our citizens; and it has produced the skills and knowledge required for this country to have the most advanced economy in the world.

Yet our schools face many important challenges. We must do a better job of teaching the basic skills of reading, writing and mathematics. We must remain committed to full and equal educational opportunity for all children. We must help students achieve educational excellence. We must responsibly reduce the financial barriers that limit access to higher education. And we must give education a more prominent and visible role in the Federal government.

We will face these challenges and overcome them. No asset is of greater value to our Nation and no commitment is so characteristic of the American people as our strong commitment to educate all our children.

Education Budget

The Administration's budget proposals for the coming year show the priority we give to education. Our FY 1979 budget contains $12.9 billion in appropriations for the Education Division of the Department of Health, Education and Welfare. That represents an increase of 24 percent above the FY 1978 level and a total increase of 46 percent and $4 billion in the last two fiscal years.

I have requested appropriations of $6.9 billion for elementary and secondary education, an increase of fifteen percent over FY 1978. This increase is the largest since the creation of the program and exceeds the FY 1977 budget by $1.7 billion. Along with these increases goes a forty percent increase in student assistance programs for higher education and a new effort to expand the reach of these programs to moderate income families hard-pressed by escalating tuition costs. Funding for these student assistance programs will rise from $3.8 billion in FY 1978 to $5.2 billion in FY 1979.

This budget reflects the judgment, widely shared by the Congress, that improving the education of our children is a wise investment in our future.

Department of Education

I have instructed the Office of Management and Budget and the Department of Health, Education and Welfare to work with Congress on legislation needed to establish a Department of Education which will:

— let us focus on Federal educational policy, at the highest levels of our government;

— permit closer coordination of Federal education programs and other related activities;

— reduce Federal regulations and reporting requirements and cut duplication;

— assist school districts, teachers, and parents to make better use of local resources and ingenuity.

A separate Cabinet-level department will enable the federal government to be a true partner with State, local and private education institutions in sustaining and improving the quality of our education system.

College Student Assistance

I recently proposed a major expansion of the programs providing financial assistance to students in higher education. Average college costs have increased by seventy-seven percent in the last ten years. At average costs of $4,500 per year in private higher education and $2,500 in public universities low and middle income families are finding it difficult to send their children to college. No able student should be denied a college education because his or her family cannot afford tuition, room and board.

My proposals will increase the number of students receiving assistance from three million to more than five million at a cost of $1.46 billion. The proposals would:

— expand the Basic Educational Opportunity Grants program to serve students from families with incomes up to $25,000 and increase the maximum grant to $1,800;

— make interest-subsidized Guaranteed Student Loans available to families with incomes up to $45,000;

— provide part-time jobs to college students through an expanded college Work-Study program.

This coordinated program is the best way to meet the needs of our students and their families. I strongly oppose the enactment of a tuition tax credit.

A college tuition tax credit would cost too much, would provide benefits to those without need, would provide less benefit to genuinely hard-pressed families than the proposals we have advanced, and would fragment educational policy within the executive and legislative branches of the Federal government.

A choice must be made. We cannot afford — and I will not accept — both a tuition tax credit and the increased student aid I have proposed. I strongly urge the Congress to act responsibly on the Administration's proposals.

Elementary and Secondary Education Amendments of 1978

The legislation I am submitting today involves the major elementary and secondary education programs. Since the Administration of Lyndon Johnson the primary role of these Federal programs has been to support improvements in educational quality for all children and improve the educational opportunities and achievements of the disadvantaged, the handicapped, those with limited English language skills, Native Americans and other minorities. I propose to continue and strengthen the use of Federal resources to meet special needs, and Federal leadership in research and innovation.

These programs must focus on the mastery of the basic skills necessary to function in our highly complex society. Every child should obtain the basic skills of reading, writing and mathematics early in his or her educational career. This should be the fundamental goal for our entire education system, and I hope that Federal leadership will help us meet that goal at every level of our school system.

Special Programs for Disadvantaged Children

I propose to improve Title I of the Elementary and Secondary Education Act which provides supplemental educational services to economically disadvantaged children.

1. Concentration of Resources

Recent evaluations show that Title I is beginning to raise the achievement levels of low-income students. I propose to build upon this success by incorporating in the reauthorization of the Act a separate authority to increase help for school districts with high concentrations of poor children. The amendments I propose will target additional Title I funds to school districts with large numbers of poor children (5,000 or more) or large proportions of poor children (20 percent or more), for use in programs with a strong emphasis on basic skills. I have requested $400 million in the 1979 budget for this proposal, which would aid 3,500 school districts and could increase the number of Title I eligible children served to 6.5 million.

This targeting of additional funds on areas of greatest need will be of special benefit to urban school systems with concentrations of low-income children. It is an important part of our efforts to help meet the needs of our cities. Yet the problems of educational disadvantage are not unique to cities; therefore, while 67 percent of the funds will flow to center-city school systems, 33 percent will flow to rural and suburban school systems which have similar needs.

2. State Programs for Disadvantaged Children

Strong State efforts are clearly necessary to fully meet the needs of disadvantaged children. Currently, however, fewer than twenty States have special programs to aid disadvantaged students. To encourage the creation of compensatory education programs at the State level, I recommend that a share of future increases in the Title I program be allocated, on the basis of one Federal dollar for every two State dollars, to States with qualified compensatory education programs of their own. In fiscal year 1980 twenty percent of any increases would be devoted to this matching program. In future years an increasing percentage would be made available. I hope this Federal incentive program will encourage a response at the State level which will give greater opportunities to millions of children.

Emergency School Aid Act

We must move aggressively to end the last vestiges of racial and ethnic mistrust and disharmony in our schools and in our society as a whole. Great progress toward that goal has been made, particularly in the South, but much remains to be done.

The Emergency School Aid Act has helped numerous local school districts respond to the problems of racial isolation and improve education for all their children. I recommend amendments to that legislation which would:

— encourage voluntary local initiatives to overcome the adverse effects of minority group isolation;

— offer flexibility to meet the needs of desegregating districts;

— and encourage multi-year planning and implementation of desegregation.

To give us more flexibility in meeting changing needs, I propose to increase the share of discretionary funds from 22 percent to 42 percent. This will permit allocation of resources to areas of greatest need. At the same time I am recommending a new system of multi-year grants which will sharply reduce paperwork and will help local school systems plan for the future.

Basic Skills

The Federal government can play an important role in funding research and demonstration projects which will show us how to improve the quality and effectiveness of our educational system. Student achievement can be improved through innovation, and a concentration on basic skills. I propose several improvements in this area:

— the creation of a new Basic Skills and Educational Quality title in the Elementary and Secondary Education Act which would encourage state and local demonstration efforts to improve basic skills in reading, writing and mathematics, including increased use of achievement testing and the participation by parents in teaching their children;

— the creation of a new Special Projects title in the Elementary and Secondary Education Act to consolidate educational quality developmental programs and provide greater flexibility; and strengthen our efforts, through the Community Schools program, to link the school with employers and other resources in the surrounding community;

— changes in the Adult Education Act to put more emphasis on competency in basic skills and on obtaining high school credentials, and to increase sponsorship of adult education programs by business, labor and other community organizations.

Impact Aid

Reform of Impact Aid is a challenge which must be faced. The purpose of the program is to compensate school districts for the cost of educating children when local revenues are reduced by tax-exempt federally-owned land and when local school enrollments are increased by children whose parents live and/or work on that land. Yet Impact Aid, as currently structured, has strayed far from that purpose.

The legislation I propose makes realistic and responsible reforms;

— elimination of payments for children whose parents work on Federal property outside the county in which the school district is located;

— two-year cap on payments which are based on public housing at the 1978 level followed by a phase out of the payments;

— an "absorption" provision which will reduce funding for lightly impacted districts by eliminating payments for children of Federal employees below three percent of non-federal enrollment.

To ease the adjustment to these changes I recommend a gradually declining "hold-harmless" provision under which no district will receive less than seventy-five percent of its previous year's payments over the next three years. I also propose that advance funding be made so that districts can be notified early of their allocations.

These proposals will save $76 million in FY 1979 and $336 million in FY 1982. I believe they are a realistic way to start bringing the Impact Aid program into line with the actual Federal burden on local school districts.

Bilingual Education

Three million children today lack equal access to education in our schools because of their limited English-speaking ability. The Bilingual Education Act is designed to help local school systems develop and implement programs to help these children. The proposals I am submitting today will improve the bilingual education program by:

— emphasizing the overriding goal of achieving proficiency in English;

— permitting the flexible use of instructional materials and teaching techniques appropriate and sensitive to the language, background and needs of the child;

— making parents more involved;

— requiring that individual programs be of sufficient scope and duration to have a substantial educational impact;

— allowing English speaking children to take part in bilingual education programs;

— providing more money for teacher training and emphasizing the use of bilingual teachers; and

— increasing research in new teaching techniques.

Because the Bilingual Education Program is a demonstration program, every effort must be made to ensure that funds are used to help local school districts to establish and maintain programs of their own. To ensure that Federal demonstration funds benefit as many children as possible, I am proposing that program grants ordinarily be limited to 5 years. Districts will be required to show how they will ensure that educational progress is maintained following the phase-out of grant monies.

In addition, I am proposing that the Office of Bilingual Education be made responsible for coordinating bilingual education aspects of other programs administered by the Office of Education.

Private Schools

Private schools — particularly parochial schools — are an important part of our diverse educational system. Federal education programs have long required benefits to go to eligible students in both public and private schools. But this requirement has not been effective in practice. I am committed to doing all that the Constitution allows to ensure students in private schools benefit from Federal programs.

I propose the following changes to improve services to private school students:

— States will be required to develop plans for ensuring the equitable participation of private school students in all Federal educational programs.

— The Title I program will be changed to require that economically disadvantaged children in private schools receive comparable funds to those received by public school students, with similar needs.

— Where a school district fails to provide appropriate Federal educational benefits under any program to eligible private school children, authority will be used to by-pass the district and use another agency to provide constitutionally permissible services.

Private school children must receive fair treatment under Federal education programs. However I cannot support a tax credit for private elementary and secondary school tuition. First, there is grave doubt that such a tax credit program can meet Constitutional requirements concerning separation of church and State. Second, the Federal government provides funding primarily to help meet the needs of public school children who are disadvantaged, or handicapped, or bilingual, or who have some other form of special need. We do not provide general support for public schools and it would be unfair to extend such support, through a general tax credit, to private schools.

I will continue to do all I can, within Constitutional limits, to provide for full and equitable participation of private schools and their students in Federal education efforts.

Women's Educational Equity Act

In order to assist in the elimination of sexual discrimination in education I propose to make the Women's Educational Equity Act an independent authority and expand its role in assisting local school districts.

Conclusion

The proposals I have outlined today — to strengthen our basic education laws, substantially increase the education budget and undertake major organizational reform aimed at creating a Cabinet-level Department of Education — set forth a far-reaching agenda for education. These proposals are important not only for what they offer to all of us in the future: a country that is stronger, more united and better equipped to meet the challenges that lie before us.

JIMMY CARTER

The White House,
February 28, 1978

Civil Service Reform

Following is President Carter's March 2 message to Congress outlining his proposals to revise the federal government's civil service system:

TO THE CONGRESS
OF THE UNITED STATES:

I am transmitting to the Congress today a comprehensive program to reform the Federal Civil Service system. My proposals are intended to increase the government's efficiency by placing new emphasis on the quality of performance of Federal workers. At the same time, my recommendations will ensure that employees and the public are protected against political abuse of the system.

Nearly a century has passed since enactment of the first Civil Service Act — the Pendleton Act of 1883. That Act established the United States Civil Service Commission and the merit system it administers. These institutions have served our Nation well in fostering development of a Federal workforce which is basically honest, competent, and dedicated to constitutional ideals and the public interest.

But the system has serious defects. It has become a bureaucratic maze which neglects merit, tolerates poor performance, permits abuse of legitimate employee rights, and mires every personnel action in red tape, delay and confusion.

Civil Service reform will be the centerpiece of government reorganization during my term in office.

I have seen at first hand the frustration among those who work within the bureaucracy. No one is more concerned at the inability of government to deliver on its promises than the worker who is trying to do a good job.

Most Civil Service employees perform with spirit and integrity. Nevertheless,

there is still widespread criticism of Federal government performance. The public suspects that there are too many government workers, that they are underworked, overpaid, and insulated from the consequences of incompetence.

Such sweeping criticisms are unfair to dedicated Federal workers who are conscientiously trying to do their best, but we have to recognize that the only way to restore public confidence in the vast majority who work well is to deal effectively and firmly with the few who do not.

For the past 7 months, a task force of more than 100 career civil servants has analyzed the Civil Service, explored its weaknesses and strengths and suggested how it can be improved.

The objectives of the Civil Service reform proposals I am transmitting today are:

—To strengthen the protection of legitimate employee rights;

—To provide incentives and opportunities for managers to improve the efficiency and responsiveness of the Federal Government;

—To reduce the red tape and costly delay in the present personnel system;

—To promote equal employment opportunity;

—To improve labor-management relations.

My specific proposals are these:

1. Replacing the Civil Service Commission with an Office of Personnel Management and a Merit Protection Board

Originally established to conduct Civil Service examinations, the Civil Service Commission has, over the years, assumed additional and inherently conflicting responsibilities. It serves simultaneously both as the protector of employee rights and as the promoter of efficient personnel management policy. It is a manager, rule-maker, prosecutor and judge. Consequently, none of these jobs are being done as effectively as they should be.

Acting under my existing reorganization authority, I propose to correct the inherent conflict of interest within the Civil Service Commission by abolishing the Commission and replacing it with a Merit Protection Board and Office of Personnel Management.

The Office of Personnel Management will be the center for personnel administration (including examination, training, and administration of pay and benefits); it will not have any prosecutorial or adjudicative powers against individuals. Its Director will be appointed by the President and confirmed by the Senate. The Director will be the government's management spokesman on Federal employee labor relations and will coordinate Federal personnel matters, except for Presidential appointments.

The Merit Protection Board will be the adjudicatory arm of the new personnel

system. It will be headed by a bipartisan board of three members, appointed for 7 years, serving non-renewable overlapping terms, and removable only for cause. This structure will guarantee independent and impartial protection to employees. I also propose to create a Special Counsel to the Board, appointed by the President and confirmed by the Senate, who will investigate and prosecute political abuses and merit system violations. This will help safeguard the rights of Federal employees who "blow the whistle" on violations of laws or regulations by other employees, including their supervisors.

In addition, these proposals will write into law for the first time the fundamental principles of the merit system and enumerate prohibited personnel practices.

2. A Senior Executive Service

A critical factor in determining whether Federal programs succeed or fail is the ability of the senior managers who run them. Throughout the Executive Branch, these 9,200 top administrators carry responsibilities that are often more challenging than comparable work in private industry. But under the Civil Service system, they lack the incentives for first-rate performance that managers in private industry have. The Civil Service system treats top managers just like the 2.1 million employees whose activities they direct. They are equally insulated from the risks of poor performance, and equally deprived of tangible rewards for excellence.

To help solve these problems I am proposing legislation to create a Senior Executive Service affecting managers in grades GS-16 through non-Presidentially appointed Executive Level IV or its equivalent. It would allow:

—Transfer of executives among senior positions on the basis of government need;

—Authority for agency heads to adjust salaries within a range set by law with the result that top managers would no longer receive automatic pay increases based on longevity;

—Annual performance reviews, with inadequate performance resulting in removal from the Senior Executive Service (back to GS-15) without any right of appeal to the Merit Protection Board.

Agency heads would be authorized to distribute bonuses for superior performance to not more than 50 percent of the senior executives each year. These would be allocated according to criteria prescribed by the Office of Personnel Management, and should average less than five percent of base salary per year. They would not constitute an increase in salary but rather a one-time payment. The Office of Personnel Management also would be empowered to award an additional stipend directly to a select group of senior executives, approximately five percent of the total of the Senior Executive Service, who have especially distinguished themselves in their work. The total of base salary, bonus, and honorary stipend should in no case exceed 95 percent of the salary level for an Executive Level II position.

No one now serving in the "supergrade" managerial positions would be required to join the Senior Executive Service. But all would have the opportunity to join. And the current percentage of noncareer supergrade managers — approximately 10 percent — would be written into law for the first time, so that the Office of Personnel Management would not retain the existing authority of the Civil Service Commission to expand the proportion of political appointees.

This new Senior Executive Service will provide a highly qualified corps of top managers with strong incentives and opportunities to improve the management of the Federal government.

3. Incentive Pay for Lower Level Federal Managers and Supervisors

The current Federal pay system provides virtually automatic "step" pay increases as well as further increases to keep Federal salaries comparable to those in private business. This may be appropriate for most Federal employees, but performance — not merely endurance — should determine the compensation of Federal managers and supervisors. I am proposing legislation to let the Office of Personnel Management establish an incentive pay system for government managers, starting with those in grades GS-13 through GS-15. Approximately 72,000 managers and supervisors would be affected by such a system which could later be extended by Congress to other managers and supervisors.

These managers and supervisors would no longer receive automatic "step" increases in pay and would receive only 50 percent of their annual comparability pay increase. They would, however, be eligible for "performance" pay increases of up to 12 percent of their existing salary. Such a change would not increase payroll costs, and it should be insulated against improprieties through the use of strong audit and performance reviews by the Office of Personnel Management.

4. A Fairer and Speedier Disciplinary System

The simple concept of a "merit system" has grown into a tangled web of complicated rules and regulations.

Managers are weakened in their ability to reward the best and most talented people — and to fire those few who are unwilling to work.

The sad fact is that it is easier to promote and transfer incompetent employees than to get rid of them.

It may take as long as 3 years merely to fire someone for just cause, and at the same time the protection of legitimate rights is a costly and time-consuming process for the employee.

A speedier and fairer disciplinary system will create a climate in which managers may discharge non-performing employees — using due process — with reasonable assurance that their judgment, if valid, will prevail.

At the same time, employees will receive a more rapid hearing for their grievances.

The procedures that exist to protect employee rights are absolutely essential.

But employee appeals must now go through the Civil Service Commission, which has a built-in conflict of interest by serving simultaneously as rule-maker, prosecutor, judge, and employee advocate.

The legislation I am proposing today would give all competitive employees a statutory right of appeal. It would spell out fair and sensible standards for the Merit Protection Board to apply in hearing appeals. Employees would be provided with attorneys' fees if they prevail and the agency's action were found to have been wholly without basis. Both employees and managers would have, for the first time, subpoena power to ensure witness participation and document submission. The subpoena power would expedite the appeals process, as would new provisions for prehearing discovery. One of the three existing appeal levels would be eliminated.

These changes would provide both employees and managers with speedier and fairer judgments on the appeal of disciplinary actions.

5. Improved Labor-Management Relations

In 1962, President John F. Kennedy issued Executive Order 10988, establishing a labor-management relations program in the Executive Branch. The Executive Order has demonstrated its value through five Administrations. However, I believe that the time has come to increase its effectiveness by abolishing the Federal Labor Relations Council created by Executive Order 10988 and transferring its functions, along with related functions of the Assistant Secretary of Labor for Labor Relations, to a newly established Federal Labor Relations Authority. The Authority will be composed of three full-time members appointed by the President with the advice and consent of the Senate.

I have also directed members of my Administration to develop, as part of Civil Service reform, a Labor-Management Relations legislative proposal by working with the appropriate Congressional Committees, Federal employees and their representatives. The goal of this legislation will be to make Executive Branch labor relations more comparable to those of private business, while recognizing the special requirements of the Federal Government and the paramount public interest in the effective conduct of the public's business. This will facilitate Civil Service reform of the managerial and supervisory elements of the Executive Branch, free of union involvement, and, at the same time, improve the collective bargaining process as an integral part of the personnel system for Federal workers.

It will permit the establishment through collective bargaining of grievance and arbitration systems, the cost of which will be borne largely by the parties to the dispute. Such procedures will largely displace the multiple appeals systems which now exist and which are unanimously perceived as too costly, too cumbersome and ineffective.

6. Decentralized Personnel Decisionmaking

Examining candidates for jobs in the career service is now done almost exclusively by the Civil Service Commission, which now may take as long as six or eight months to fill important agency positions.

In addition, many routine personnel management actions must be submitted to the Civil Service Commission for prior approval. Much red tape and delay are generated by these requirements; the public benefits little, if at all. My legislative proposals would authorize the Office of Personnel Management to delegate personnel authority to departments and agencies.

The risk of abuse would be minimized by performance agreements between agencies and the Office of Personnel Management, by requirements for reporting, and by follow-up evaluations.

7. Changes in the Veterans Preference Law

Granting preference in Federal employment to veterans of military service has long been an important and worthwhile national policy. It will remain our policy because of the debt we owe those who have served our nation. It is especially essential for disabled veterans, and there should be no change in current law which would adversely affect them. But the Veterans Preference Act of 1944 also conferred a *lifetime benefit* upon the nondisabled veteran, far beyond anything provided by other veterans readjustment laws like the GI Bill, the benefits of which are limited to 10 years following discharge from the service. Current law also severely limits agency ability to consider qualified applicants by forbidding consideration of all except the three highest-scoring applicants — the so-called rule of three. As a result of the 5-point lifetime preference and the "rule of three," women, minorities and other qualified non-veteran candidates often face insuperable obstacles in their quest for Federal jobs.

Similarly, where a manager believes a program would benefit from fewer employees, the veterans preference provides an absolute lifetime benefit to veterans. In any Reduction in Force, all veterans may "bump" all non-veterans, even those with far greater seniority. Thus women and minorities who have recently acquired middle management positions are more likely to lose their jobs in any cutback.

Therefore I propose:

—Limiting the 5-point veterans preference to the 10 year period following their discharge from the service, beginning 2 years after legislation is enacted;

—Expanding the number of applicants who may be considered by a hiring agency from three to seven, unless the Office of Personnel Management should determine that another number or category ranking is more appropriate;

—Eliminating the veterans preference for retired military officers of field grade rank or above and limiting its availability for other military personnel who have retired after at least 20 years in service to 3 years following their retirement;

—Restricting the absolute preference now accorded veterans in Reductions in Force to their first 3 years of Federal employment, after which time they would be granted 5 extra years of seniority for purposes of determining their rights when Reduction in Force occurs.

These changes would focus the veterans preference more sharply to help disabled veterans and veterans of the Viet Nam conflict. I have already proposed a 2-year extension of the Veterans Readjustment Appointment Authority to give these veterans easier entry into the Federal workforce; I support amendments to waive the educational limitation for disabled veterans and to expand Federal job openings for certain veterans in grades GS-5 to GS-7 under this authority. I propose that veterans with 50 percent or higher disability be eligible for non-competitive appointments.

These changes are intended to let the Federal Government meet the needs of the American people more effectively. At the same time, they would make the Federal work place a better environment for Federal employees. I ask the Congress to act promptly on Civil Service Reform and the Reorganization Plan which I will shortly submit.

JIMMY CARTER

The White House
March 2, 1978

Urban Policy

Following is President Carter's March 27 message to Congress, submitting his proposals for a comprehensive national urban policy:

TO THE CONGRESS
OF THE UNITED STATES:

I submit today my proposals for a comprehensive national urban policy. These proposals set a policy framework for actions my Administration has already taken, for proposed new initiatives, and for our efforts to assist America's communities and their residents in the years to come. The policy represents a comprehensive, long-term commitment to the Nation's urban areas.

The urban policy I am announcing today will build a *New Partnership* involving all levels of government, the private sector, and neighborhood and voluntary organizations in a major effort to make America's cities better places in which to live and work. It is a comprehensive policy aimed both at making cities more healthy and improving the lives of the people who live in them.

The major proposals will:

●Improve the effectiveness of existing Federal programs by coordinating these programs, simplifying planning requirements, reorienting resources, and reducing paperwork. And the proposals will make Federal actions more supportive of the urban policy effort and develop a process for analyzing the urban and community impact of all major Federal initiatives.

●Provide employment opportunities, primarily in the private sector, to the long-term unemployed and the disadvantaged in cities. This will be done through a labor-intensive public works program and tax and other incentives for business to hire the long-term unemployed.

●Provide fiscal relief to the most hard-pressed communities.

●Provide strong incentives to attract private investment to distressed communities, including the creation of a National Development Bank, expanded grant programs and targeted tax incentives.

●Encourage states to become partners in assisting urban areas through a new incentive grant program.

●Stimulate greater involvement by neighborhood organizations and voluntary associations through funding neighborhood development projects and by creating an Urban Volunteer Corps. These efforts will be undertaken with the approval of local elected officials.

●Increase access to opportunity for those disadvantaged by economic circumstance or a history of discrimination.

●Provide additional social and health services to disadvantaged people in cities and communities.

●Improve the urban physical environment and the cultural and aesthetic aspects of urban life by providing additional assistance for housing rehabilitation, mass transit, the arts, culture, parks and recreation facilities.

America's communities are an invaluable national asset. They are the center of our culture, the incubators of new ideas and inventions, the centers of commerce and finance, and the homes of our great museums, libraries and theatres. Cities contain trillions of dollars of public and private investments — investments which we must conserve, rehabilitate and fully use.

The New Partnership I am proposing today will focus the full energies of my Administration on a comprehensive, long-term effort. It will encourage States to redirect their own resources to support their urban areas more effectively. It will encourage local governments to streamline and coordinate their own activities. It will offer incentives to the private sector to make new investments in economically depressed communities. And it will involve citizens and neighborhood and voluntary organizations in meeting the economic and social needs of their communities.

The New Partnership will be guided by these principles:

●Simplifying and improving programs and policy at all levels of government.

●Combining the resources of federal, state and local government, and using them as a lever to involve the even greater strength of our private economy to conserve and strengthen our cities and communities.

●Being flexible enough to give help where it is most needed and to respond to the particular needs of each community.

●Increasing access to opportunity for those disadvantaged by economic circumstances or history of discrimination.

●And above all, drawing on the sense of community and voluntary effort that I believe is alive in America, and on the loyalty that Americans feel for their neighborhoods.

The need for a New Partnership is clear from the record of the last fifteen years. During the 1960s, the federal government took a strong leadership role in responding to the problems of the cities. The federal government attempted to identify the problems, develop the solutions and implement the programs. State and local governments and the private sector were not sufficiently involved. While many of these programs were successful, we learned an important lesson: that the federal government alone has neither the resources nor the knowledge to solve all urban problems.

An equally important lesson emerged from the experience of the early 1970s. During this period, the federal government retreated from its responsibilities, leaving states and localities with insufficient resources, interest or leadership to accomplish all that needed to be done. We learned that states and localities cannot solve the problems by themselves.

These experiences taught us that a successful urban policy must build a partnership that involves the leadership of the federal government and the participation of all levels of government, the private sector, neighborhood and voluntary organizations and individual citizens.

Prior Actions

The problems of our Nation's cities are complex and deep-seated. They have developed gradually over a generation as a result of private market and demographic forces and inadvertent government action; and the problems worsened markedly during the early 1970s.

These problems will not be solved immediately. They can be solved only by the long-term commitment which I offer today, and by the efforts of all levels of government, the private sector and neighborhood and voluntary organizations.

For my Administration, this commitment began on the day I took office and it will continue throughout my Presidency. With the cooperation of Congress, my Administration has already provided substantial increases in funding in many of the major urban assistance programs. Total assistance to state and local governments has increased by 25 percent, from $68 billion in FY 1977 to $85 billion in FY 1979. These increases are the direct result of actions we have taken during the past 14 months. They are as much a part of my Administration's urban policy as the initiatives which I am announcing today. Some of the most important programs have already been enacted into law or proposed to the Congress. These include:

● A $2.7 billion increase over three years in the Community Development Block Grant Program, accompanied by a change in the formula to provide more assistance to the older and declining cities.

● A $400 million a year Urban Development Action Grant Program providing assistance primarily to distressed cities.

● An expansion of youth and training programs and an increase in the number of public service employment jobs, from 325,000 to 725,000. Expenditures for employment and training doubled from FY '77 to FY '79 to over $12 billion.

● A $400 million private sector jobs proposal has been included in my proposal to reauthorize the CETA legislation. This initiative will encourage private businesses to hire the long-term unemployed and the disadvantaged.

● A sixty-five percent increase in grants provided by the Economic Development Administration to urban areas.

● A thirty percent increase in overall federal assistance to education, including a $400 million increase in the Elementary and Secondary Education Act, targeted in substantial part to large city school systems with a concentration of children from low-income families.

● An economic stimulus package enacted last year, (Anti-Recession Fiscal Assistance, Local Public Works and CETA) which provided almost $9 billion in additional aid to states and cities.

● A welfare reform proposal which, upon passage, will provide immediate fiscal relief to state and local governments.

● A doubling of outlays for the Section 312 housing rehabilitation loan program.

● Creation of a consumer cooperative bank which would provide financing assistance to consumer cooperatives which have difficulty obtaining conventional financing.

Improvements in Existing Programs

The Administration's Urban and Regional Policy Group (URPG) has examined all of the major urban assistance programs and proposed improvements. It also has worked with agencies traditionally not involved in urban policy, such as the Defense Department, the General Services Administration, and the Environmental

Protection Agency, and has developed proposals to make their actions more supportive of urban areas. As a result of this massive effort, the federal government has become more sensitive to urban problems and more committed to their solutions.

The review of existing federal programs has resulted in more than 150 improvements in existing programs. Most of these improvements can be undertaken immediately through administrative action. Some will require legislation. None will increase the federal budget.

A few examples of the improvements are:

● All agencies will develop goals and timetables for minority participation in their grants and contracts — five major agencies have already begun.

● The Defense Department will set up a new program to increase procurement in urban areas.

● EPA will modify its water and sewer program to discourage wasteful sprawl.

● HUD has retargeted the Tandem Mortgage Assistance Program to provide greater support for urban housing.

● The existing countercyclical fiscal assistance program will be retargeted to help governments with unemployment rates above the national average.

● HUD and EDA are developing common planning and application requirements.

● The General Services Administration will attempt to locate federal facilities in cities whenever such a location is not inconsistent with the agency's mission.

● The Department of Transportation has proposed legislation to consolidate many categories of urban highway and transit grants, and to standardize the local matching share. These steps will provide local governments with greater flexibility to develop transportation systems suited to their needs.

● The Environmental Protection Agency will amend its regulations to accommodate new economic development in high pollution areas. Localities will be permitted to "bank" reductions in pollution which result from firms going out of business. These reductions then can be transferred to new firms locating in the community.

The effect of all these changes may be greater than even the substantial new initiatives which I have proposed in this message.

New Initiatives

The new initiatives which I am announcing today address five major urban needs:

1) Improving the operation of federal, state and local governments

2) Employment and Economic Development

3) Fiscal Assistance

4) Community and Human Development

5) Neighborhoods and Voluntary Associations

These initiatives require $4.4 billion in

budget authority, $1.7 billion in new tax incentives, and $2.2 billion in guaranteed loan authority in FY 1979. For FY 1980 the budget authority will be $6.1 billion, the tax incentives $1.7 billion and the guaranteed loan authority $3.8 billion.

I. Improving the Operation of Federal, State and Local Governments

Federal Programs

Over the long run, reorganization of the economic and community development programs may be necessary. Last June, I directed my reorganization project staff in the Office of Management and Budget to begin exploring the reorganization options. They have completed the first stages of this work. During the next several months, they will consult with the Congress, state and local officials and the public to develop the best solution.

There are several actions I will take immediately.

● **Urban and Community Impact Analysis.** I am implementing a process through my Domestic Policy Staff (DPS) and Office of Management and Budget (OMB) to ensure that we do not inadvertently take actions which contradict the goals of the urban policy. Each agency submitting a major domestic initiative must include its own urban and community impact analysis. DPS and OMB will review these submissions and will ensure that any anti-urban impacts of proposed federal policies will be brought to my attention.

● **Interagency Coordinating Council.** To improve program coordination, I will form an Interagency Coordinating Council, composed of the Assistant Secretaries with major program responsibilities in the key urban departments. The Council will have two functions:

It will serve as a catalyst for operational improvements which cut across Departments (for example, instituting uniform grant applications); and it will encourage interagency cooperation on projects which are too large or too complex to be funded by one agency. This Council will, for the first time, provide a coordinated federal response to communities which develop comprehensive and multi-year projects. It will have direction from the Executive Office of the President.

● **Consolidating Planning Requirements and Other Management Improvements.** We soon will announce the consolidation of intra-agency planning requirements. I have asked the Director of the Office of Management and Budget to direct an interagency task force to improve the management of federal grant-in-aid programs and consolidate the numerous planning requirements in the community and economic development grant programs.

● **Improved Data and Information.** I have asked the Secretary of Commerce, in her capacity as Chair of the Statistical

Policy Coordination Committee, to design an improved urban data and information system. At the present time much of this data is inadequate or out of date.

- **The Role of State Governments.** State government policies, even more than federal policies, are important to the fiscal and economic health of cities. States affect their cities in a number of ways, including setting taxation and annexation powers, determining the placement of major development investments and apportioning the financial responsibility for welfare and education expenditures.

The federal government has little or no control over these developments, all of which clearly affect the economic and fiscal health of cities and communities.

These state responsibilities underscore the need for an urban policy which includes the states as full and equal partners. The effectiveness of our urban policy will be enhanced if the states can be encouraged to complement the federal effort.

To encourage states to support their urban areas, I will offer a new program of state incentive grants. These grants will be provided, on a discretionary basis, to states which adopt approved plans to help their cities and communities. The plans must be developed with the participation and approval of communities within the state. The grants will be provided to the states to finance a portion of the plan. The State Incentive Grant Program will be administered by HUD and will provide $400 million over two years.

- **Local Government Role.** Many communities and cities can improve management and planning improvements by reforming fiscal management practices, streamlining local regulatory procedures, and coordinating local community and economic development activities.

The federal government provides planning and technical assistance to communities through HUD and Commerce to help cities improve their management and planning practices. These funds will be used increasingly to build the local government's capacity to undertake the necessary fiscal and management reforms.

The federal government will offer special consideration in discretionary programs to cities which achieve coordinated action at the local level.

II. Employment and Economic Development

There is a serious shortage of jobs for many residents of our urban areas and a lack of investment to build the tax base of our cities.

The urban policy will address this issue in two ways.

In the short run, it will provide additional employment opportunities through a labor-intensive public works program, a targeted employment tax credit, and a private sector training and jobs initiative to encourage businesses to hire the hardcore unemployed, together with the extension I have already proposed in employment and training opportunities under the CETA Act.

In the long run, the policy attempts to rebuild the private sector economic base of these communities through a National Development Bank, a special tax incentive, an increase in economic development grants and other incentives.

Labor-intensive Public Works. I ask Congress for $1 billion a year for a program of labor-intensive public works, targeted on communities with high unemployment. Half of the estimated 60,000 full-time equivalent jobs created annually by this program will be reserved for the disadvantaged and the long-term unemployed. These workers will be paid at Davis-Bacon trainee wage levels.

This program will enable cities to make needed repairs on buildings, streets, parks, and other public facilities.

In contrast to the Local Public Works program — which involves projects requiring large equipment, material expenditures and a prolonged planning period — more of the funds under this labor-intensive program will go to job creation.

Targeted Employment Tax Credit. I also propose a Targeted Employment Tax Credit to encourage business to hire disadvantaged young workers between the ages of 18 and 24 who suffer the highest unemployment rates in the Nation.

Under my proposal, private employers of young and disadvantaged, or handicapped, workers would be entitled to claim a $2,000 tax credit for each eligible worker during the first year of employment and a $1,500 credit for each eligible worker during the second year.

I am proposing this Targeted Employment Tax Credit as a substitute for the expiring Employment Tax Credit. The current program costs $2.5 billion a year and has had little influence on hiring decisions. The Administration's targeted program will cost approximately $1.5 billion a year, with far greater impact.

Location of Federal Facilities. I will sign a new Executive Order directing the General Services Administration to give first priority to cities in locating new federal facilities or consolidating or relocating existing facilities. Under my Administration, federal facilities will be located in cities, unless such a location is inconsistent with the agency's mission.

Federal buildings and facilities can be an important source of jobs and of rental payments and, in many cities, a principal stabilizing force preventing decline.

The federal government should set an example for the private sector to invest in urban areas.

Federal Government Procurement. To assure that federal procurement is used to strengthen the economic base of our Nation's cities and communities, I will:

- strengthen the implementation of the existing procurement set-aside program for labor surplus areas, by directing the General Services Administration to work with each agency to develop specific procurement targets and to monitor their implementation. GSA will report to me every six months on the progress of each Agency;

- direct the Defense Department to implement an experimental program to target more of its procurement to high unemployment areas.

National Development Bank. I propose the creation of a National Development Bank, which would encourage businesses to locate or expand in economically distressed urban and rural areas. The Bank would be authorized to guarantee investments totaling $11 billion through 1981.

To lower operating costs in urban areas, the Bank would provide long-term, low-cost financing which, in conjunction with expanded grant programs administered by HUD and EDA, will reduce a firm's financing costs by up to 60 percent.

The Bank uses four major financing tools:

- Grants of up to 15 percent of a firm's total capital cost, to a maximum $3 million, for fixed assets of a project. The grants, which would be made under expanded EDA and HUD authorities, would cover expenditures for land assembly, site preparation, rehabilitation, and equipment.

- Loan guarantees, provided by the Bank to cover three-quarters of the remaining capital costs up to a maximum of $15 million per project. The Bank could, at its discretion, reduce the interest rate down to two and one-half percent for particularly desirable projects. Bank financing would be conditioned on obtaining 21 percent of the project's total costs from private lenders.

- The ceiling for industrial reserve bonds in economically distressed areas would be increased from $5 to $20 million with the approval of the Bank. A business which used this financing for a project could also receive a grant.

- The Bank also will provide a secondary loan market for private loans in eligible areas to finance capital expenditures. This will be particularly beneficial to small businesses.

Bank projects will require the approval of state or local government economic development entities, which would be responsible to the elected local leadership. Distressed urban and rural areas would be eligible. Additional employment would be a key test of project eligibility.

The Bank will be an interagency corporation, governed by a Board composed of the Secretaries of HUD, Commerce and the Treasury. This will ensure coordination between the major economic, community development and urban finance agencies of the government.

The Office of Management and Budget is currently assessing the organization of the federal economic and community development activities. The Bank will function on an interagency basis pending recommendations in this area.

Economic Development Grants. I propose substantial increases of $275 million each in the UDAG grant program and the EDA Title IX program. These increases will be used in conjunction with the financing incentives available from the National Development Bank.

Taken together these major increases will help leverage substantial new private sector investment in urban areas and address the long-term economic deterioration experienced by certain urban and rural areas.

Differential Investment Tax Credit. I propose that firms that locate or expand in economically distressed areas be eligible for a differential 5 percent investment tax credit, to a total of 15 percent for both structures and equipment. The credit would be available only to firms awarded "Certificates of Necessity" by the Commerce Department based on financing need and employment potential.

Commerce will be authorized to issue up to $200 million in certificates for each of the next two years.

Air Quality Planning Grants. I propose a $25 million planning grant program to help cities and communities comply with the Clean Air Act without limiting severely new, private sector investment within their areas.

I have also asked EPA, HUD and EDA to provide technical assistance to help local governments reconcile potential conflicts between air pollution and economic development goals.

Minority Business. Minority businesses are a critical part of the private sector economic base of many cities, communities and neighborhoods, and provide important employment opportunities to city residents.

I propose today two important initiatives which will increase the role of minority businesses in our economy. First, in comparison with FY 1977 levels, we will triple federal procurement from minority businesses by the end of FY 1979 — an increase over our earlier commitment to double minority procurement.

In addition, I intend to ask all federal agencies to include goals for minority business participation in their contract and grant-in-aid programs. Five agencies — HUD, Commerce, EPA, Interior and DOT — already have proposed improvements in minority business programs. These programs all build on our successful experience with the Local Public Works Program.

Finally, I intend to facilitate greater interaction between the minority business community and the leaders of our Nation's largest corporations.

Community Development Corporations. I propose that an additional $20 million be appropriated to the Community Services Administration as venture capital for the most effective Community Development Corporations. This assistance will

help them have a substantial impact on their designated areas.

The funding will be made available for projects that receive support from local elected officials, involve leveraging private sector funds and are coordinated with HUD, EDA or the Small Business Administration.

Role of Private Financial Institutions. An effective urban strategy must involve private financial institutions. I am asking the independent financial regulatory agencies to develop appropriate actions, consistent with safe, sound and prudent lending practices, to encourage financial institutions to play a greater role in meeting the credit needs of their communities.

First, I am requesting that financial regulatory agencies determine what further actions are necessary to halt the practice of redlining — the refusal to extend credit without a sound economic justification. I will encourage those agencies to develop strong, consistent and effective regulations to implement the Community Reinvestment Act.

Second, I propose the creation of an Institute for Community Investment, under the Federal Home Loan Bank Board. The Institute will bring together appraisers, realtors, lenders, building and insurance companies to develop a consistent approach toward urban lending and to train urban lending specialists.

Third, I propose a pilot program to create Neighborhood Commercial Reinvestment Centers under the Comptroller of the Currency. This proposal is an adaptation of the highly successful Urban Reinvestment Task Force housing credit concept to the commercial credit area. Neighborhood Commercial Reinvestment Centers will be local organizations, comprised of merchants and neighborhood residents, local government officials, and commercial banks which will provide business credit in urban neighborhoods. SBA, EDA, and HUD will work with the financial regulatory agencies to revitalize specific commercial areas.

Finally, I have asked the Secretary of Housing and Urban Development to chair an interagency task force to evaluate the availability of credit in urban areas and recommend appropriate further action. I have asked the task force to examine and make recommendations with respect to the following areas:

● The availability of mortgage and commercial credit in urban areas, and the impacts of the activities of federal agencies on such credit;

● Existing mortgage insurance, casualty insurance and business credit insurance programs;

● The full range of urban credit and insurance risk reduction techniques.

III. Fiscal Assistance

While the fiscal condition of many state and local governments has improved dramatically over the last three years,

many cities and communities still are experiencing severe problems. These cities and communities require fiscal assistance from the federal government, if they are to avoid severe service cutbacks or tax increases.

Supplemental Fiscal Assistance. Cities and communities currently receive fiscal assistance through the Anti-Recession Fiscal Assistance Act (ARFA), which expires on September 30, 1978. This program has been an effective tool for helping states and local governments withstand the fiscal impact of high unemployment.

Current unemployment projections, however, suggest that even if the ARFA program were extended in its current form, it would phase out by mid-FY 1979, when unemployment is expected to drop below six percent. If the program is permitted to phase out, many cities and communities will experience severe fiscal strain.

I propose today that ARFA be replaced with a Supplemental Fiscal Assistance Program, which will provide $1 billion of fiscal assistance annually for the next two fiscal years to local governments experiencing significant fiscal strain. Further extension of this program will be considered together with General Revenue Sharing.

Fiscal Relief in Welfare Proposal. In addition, I propose to phase in the fiscal relief component of the Better Jobs and Income Act as soon as Congress passes this legislation, rather than in 1981 as originally planned.

IV. Community and Human Development

A comprehensive program to revitalize America's cities must provide for community and human needs. This involves both physical facilities, such as parks, recreation facilities, housing and transportation systems, and the provision of health and social services.

Housing Rehabilitation. The conservation and upgrading of our housing stock is important to maintaining the strength of urban areas. Housing and rehabilitation improves the quality of community life and provides construction jobs in areas of high unemployment.

I propose an additional $150 million in FY 1979 for the Section 312 rehabilitation loan program, which will more than double the existing program. This expanded effort will permit the rehabilitation of small multi-family housing projects in distressed neighborhoods, for which financing presently is inadequate. In addition, expanded Section 312 funding will be used to strengthen the Urban Homesteading program.

Urban Transportation. In many cities, public transportation is inadequately financed. The federal government has begun to make substantial investments to rehabilitate, revitalize and construct urban transportation systems.

I have already submitted to Congress my proposals to extend and strengthen the highway and mass transit programs.

To supplement these efforts I today propose an additional $200 million for capital investments in intermodal urban transportation projects. These funds will be used to link existing transportation facilities in selected cities.

Resource Recovery Planning. Solid waste disposal is a growing problem in the many urban areas which face a shortage of landfill sites. At the same time, techniques to recover valuable resources and energy from solid waste have emerged.

I will request $15 million for the EPA to provide grants of $300,000 to $400,000 to cities for feasibility studies of solid waste recovery systems.

Arts and Culture. Cities are centers of culture and art, which thrive on the vitality of the urban environment.

To help renew and develop this artistic and cultural spirit, I propose a new Livable Cities program administered by the Department of Housing and Urban Development, with the participation of the National Endowment for the Arts. This program will provide up to $20 million in grants to states and communities for neighborhood- and community-based arts programs, urban design and planning, and the creation and display of art in public spaces. Historic preservation of buildings should also be encouraged.

Urban Parks and Recreation. The quality of life in urban areas is critically affected by the availability of open spaces and recreation facilities. Yet hard pressed communities often lack the resources to maintain and invest adequately in these amenities.

To address this problem, I propose a major new federal grant program. Urban communities will compete for funds to revive and rebuild parks and recreation facilities. Challenge grants totalling $150 million will be provided for construction and major rehabilitation of urban recreation systems, such as parks, tennis and basketball courts, swimming pools, bicycle paths, and other facilities. Cities will be awarded grants based on the quality of their planning, the degree of need and their ability to match the federal funds with private and local contributions.

Social Services. Urban revitalization efforts must be accompanied by efforts to help those in need to improve their own lives. A variety of income support and social service programs are designed to do this. Since 1974, however, the support given to state social service programs by the federal government has declined in real terms.

I propose an additional $150 million of new budget authority for the Title XX programs. These funds will be used to improve the delivery of social services in urban areas — ranging from Meals on Wheels for the elderly to day care for children of working mothers — and to develop greater coordination between local, public and private agencies.

Health Services. Nearly 50 million Americans live in areas without adequate health services. These areas, many of which are in inner cities, suffer from higher infant mortality rates, greater poverty and shortages of health care personnel.

In underserved areas, emergency room and outpatient departments of city hospitals are used as the routine source of medical care by the poor, primarily due to the lack of private physicians. As these departments were not designed to provide comprehensive medical care, the hospital resources are strained and the poor often go without adequate care.

To help meet the primary health care needs of the urban poor and reduce the strain on city hospitals, I propose to expand federally-supported Community Health Centers and to fund city-sponsored programs which provide comprehensive, but less costly, primary care services. The city-sponsored programs will enroll the medically indigent in existing health systems, such as HMOs. They also will help expand locally-supported centers, reform hospital outpatient departments and provide comprehensive health services.

Education. Schools are the focus of community activities in many places. Yet they are seldom fully used or linked to other community and social services.

I intend to provide $1.5 million to expand the experimental Cities in Schools program which seeks to bridge the gap by uniting a number of social services within schools to better serve both students and their families. We intend to expand this promising new program to 10 pilot schools.

In addition, I urge the Congress to enact the $600 million increase in the Title I program of the Elementary and Secondary Education Act, which I recently proposed, including my recommendation that $400 million of these funds be targeted to cities and other areas with high concentrations of low-income families.

V. Neighborhoods and Volunteer Organizations

No resource of our urban communities is more valuable than the commitment of our citizens.

Volunteer groups, which gain strength from the selfless efforts of many individuals, make an indispensable contribution to their cities.

Urban Volunteer Corps. I propose a $40 million program in ACTION to increase the effectiveness of voluntary activities at the local level. With the agreement of local government, the program will create a corps of volunteers at the local level and match their skills with the needs of local governments and community and neighborhood organizations.

It also will provide small grants averaging $5,000 for voluntary improvement and beautification projects.

ACTION would select, with the concurrence of local government, a lead agency in each city to administer the Urban Volunteer Corps.

Self-Help Development Program. Neighborhood associations are playing a key role in housing and neighborhood revitalization. We must strengthen that role.

I will request $15 million in FY 1979 for a self-help development program to be administered by the Office for Neighborhoods in HUD.

This new program will provide funds for specific housing and revitalization projects in poor and low-income areas. Each project would involve the participation of local residents, the private sector and local government and would require the concurrence of the mayor.

Crime Prevention. Street crime is a serious problem in America's cities and communities. Over the last few years a number of promising initiatives have been undertaken by community groups and local law enforcement agencies to combat street crime. Escort services for the elderly, centers to help the victims of crime, and neighborhood watchers are examples of promising developments.

I propose a program which will add $10 million in new resources to existing efforts in the Law Enforcement Assistance Administration for a program operated jointly by ACTION and LEAA. Under this program, mayors and local neighborhood groups will develop community crime prevention programs based on successful pilot models. My reorganization proposals for LEAA and the legislation I will submit to extend the Law Enforcement Assistance Act will strengthen our efforts at crime prevention.

Community Development Credit Unions. Some urban communities are not served by any financial institutions. Community Development Credit Unions address this problem by investing their assets in the communities in which they are established. This type of credit union was first established under the poverty programs in the 1960s. About 225 exist today, and many are the only financial institutions in their communities.

I am proposing a $12 million program to provide $200,000 seed capital for new Community Development Credit Unions, to provide them with an operating subsidy for staff, training and technical assistance.

* * *

The job of revitalizing the urban communities of our country will not be done overnight. Problems which have accumulated gradually over generations cannot be solved in a year or even in the term of a President.

But I believe that a New Partnership — bringing together in a common effort all who have a stake in the future of our communities — can bring us closer to our long-term goals. We can make America's cities more attractive places in which to live and work; we can help the people of urban America lead happier and more useful lives. But we can only do it together.

JIMMY CARTER

The White House,
March 27, 1978

Civil Service Commission Reorganization

Following is the text of President Carter's May 23 message to Congress accompanying his plan on reorganization of the Civil Service Commission.

TO THE CONGRESS
OF THE UNITED STATES:

On March 2 I sent to Congress a Civil Service reform proposal to enable the Federal Government to improve its service to the American people.

Today I am submitting another part of my comprehensive proposal to reform the Federal personnel management system through Reorganization Plan No. 2 of 1978. The plan will reorganize the Civil Service Commission and thereby create new institutions to increase the effectiveness of management and strengthen the protection of employee rights.

The Civil Service Commission has acquired inherently conflicting responsibilities: to help manage the Federal Government and to protect the rights of Federal employees. It has done neither job well. The plan would separate the two functions.

Office of Personnel Management

The positive personnel management tasks of the government — such as training, productivity programs, examinations, and pay and benefits administration — would be the responsibility of an Office of Personnel Management. Its director, appointed by the President and confirmed by the Senate, would be responsible for administering federal personnel matters except for presidential appointments. The director would be the government's principal representative in federal labor relations matters.

Merit Systems Protection Board

The adjudication and prosecution responsibilities of the Civil Service Commission will be performed by the Merit Systems Protection Board. The board will be headed by a bipartisan panel of three members appointed to 6-year, staggered terms. This board would be the first independent and institutionally impartial federal agency solely for the protection of federal employees.

The plan will create, within the board, a Special Counsel to investigate and prosecute political abuses and merit system violations. Under the civil service reform legislation now being considered by the Congress, the counsel would have power to investigate and prevent reprisals against employees who report illegal acts — the so-called "whistle-blowers." The counsel would be appointed by the President and confirmed by the Senate.

Federal Labor Relations Authority

An Executive Order now vests existing labor-management relations in a part-time Federal Labor Relations Council, comprised of three top government managers; other important functions are assigned to the Assistant Secretary of Labor for Labor-Management Relations. This arrangement is defective because the Council members are part-time, they come exclusively from the ranks of management and their jurisdiction is fragmented.

The plan I submit today would consolidate the central policymaking functions in labor-management relations now divided between the Council and the Assistant Secretary into one Federal Labor Relations Authority. The Authority would be composed of three full-time members appointed by the President with the advice and consent of the Senate. Its General Counsel, also appointed by the President and confirmed by the Senate, would present unfair labor practice complaints. The plan also provides for the continuance of the Federal Service Impasses Panel within the Authority to resolve negotiating impasses between federal employee unions and agencies.

The cost of replacing the Civil Service Commission can be paid by our present resources. The reorganization itself would neither increase nor decrease the costs of personnel management throughout the government. But taken together with the substantive reforms I have proposed, this plan will greatly improve the government's ability to manage programs, speed the delivery of federal services to the public, and aid in executing other reorganizations I will propose to the Congress, by improving federal personnel management.

Each of the provisions of this proposed reorganization would accomplish one or more of the purposes set forth in 5 U.S.C. 901 (a). No functions are abolished by the plan, but the offices referred to in 5 U.S.C. 5109 (b) and 5 U.S.C. 1103 (d) are abolished. The portions of the plan providing for the appointment and pay for the head and one or more officers of the Office of Personnel Management, the Merit Systems Protection Board, the Federal Labor Relations Authority and the Federal Service Impasses Panel, are necessary to carry out the reorganization. The rates of compensation are comparable to those for similar positions within the executive branch.

I am confident that this plan and the companion civil service reform legislation will both lead to more effective protection of federal employees' legitimate rights and a more rewarding workplace. At the same time the American people will benefit from a better managed, more productive and more efficient federal government.

JIMMY CARTER

The White House,
May 23, 1978

Water Policy

Following is the text of President Carter's June 6 message to Congress outlining his new water policy:

TO THE CONGRESS
OF THE UNITED STATES:

I am today sending to Congress water policy initiatives designed to:

— improve planning and efficient management of Federal water resource programs to prevent waste and to permit necessary water projects which are cost-effective, safe and environmentally sound to move forward expeditiously;

— provide a new, national emphasis on water conservation;

— enhance Federal-State cooperation and improved State water resources planning; and

— increase attention to environmental quality.

None of the initiatives would impose any new federal regulatory program for water management.

Last year, I directed the Water Resources Council, the Office of Management and Budget and the Council on Environmental Quality, under the chairmanship of Secretary [of the Interior] Cecil Andrus, to make a comprehensive review of Federal water policy and to recommend proposed reforms.

This new water policy results from their review, the study of water policy ordered by the Congress in Section 80 of the Water Resources Planning Act of 1974 and our extensive consultations with members of Congress, State, county, city and other local officials and the public.

Water is an essential resource, and over the years, the programs of the Bureau of Reclamation, the Corps of Engineers, the Soil Conservation Service and the Tennessee Valley Authority have helped permit a dramatic improvement in American agriculture, have provided irrigation water essential to the development of the West, and have developed community flood protection, electric power, navigation and recreation throughout the Nation.

I ordered this review of water policies and programs because of my concern that while Federal water resources programs have been of great benefit to our Nation, they are today plagued with problems and inefficiencies. In the course of this water policy review we found that:

— Twenty-five separate Federal agencies spend more than $10 billion per year on water resources projects and related programs.

— These projects often are planned without a uniform, standard basis for estimating benefits and costs.

— States are primarily responsible for water policy within their boundaries, yet are not integrally involved in setting priorities and sharing in Federal project planning and funding.

— There is a $34 billion backlog of authorized or uncompleted projects.

— Some water projects are unsafe or environmentally unwise and have caused losses of natural streams and rivers, fish and wildlife habitat and recreational opportunities.

The study also found that water conservation has not been addressed at a national level even though we have pressing water supply problems. Of 106 watershed subregions in the country, 21 already have severe water shortages. By the year 2000 this number could increase to 39 subregions. The Nation's cities are also beginning to experience water shortage problems which can only be solved at very high cost. In some areas, precious groundwater supplies are also being depleted at a faster rate than they are replenished. In many cases an effective water conservation program could play a key role in alleviating these problems.

These water policy initiatives will make the Federal government's water programs more efficient and responsive in meeting the Nation's water-related needs. They are designed to build on fundamentally sound statutes and on the Principles and Standards which govern the planning and development of Federal water projects, and also to enhance the role of the States, where the primary responsibilities for water policy must lie. For the first time, the Federal government will work with State and local governments and exert needed national leadership in the effort to conserve water. Above all, these policy reforms will encourage water projects which are economically and environmentally sound and will avoid projects which are wasteful or which benefit a few at the expense of many.

Across the Nation there is remarkable diversity in the role water plays. Over most of the West, water is scarce and must be managed carefully — and detailed traditions and laws have grown up to govern the use of water. In other parts of the country, flooding is more of a problem than drought, and in many areas, plentiful water resources have offered opportunities for hydroelectric power and navigation. In the urban areas of our Nation, water supply systems are the major concern — particularly where antiquated systems need rehabilitation in order to conserve water and assure continued economic growth.

Everywhere, water is fundamental to environmental quality. Clean drinking water, recreation, wildlife and beautiful natural areas depend on protection of our water resources.

Given this diversity, Federal water policy cannot attempt to prescribe water use patterns for the country. Nor should the Federal government preempt the primary responsibility of the States for water management and allocation. For those reasons, these water policy reforms will not preempt State or local water responsibilities. Yet water policy is an important national concern, and the Federal government has major responsibilities to exercise leadership, to protect the environment and to develop and maintain hydroelectric power, irrigated agriculture, flood control and navigation.

The primary focus of the proposals is on the water resources programs of the Corps of Engineers, the Bureau of Reclamation, the Soil Conservation Service and the Tennessee Valley Authority, where annual water program budgets total approximately $3.75 billion. These agencies perform the federal government's water resource development programs. In addition, a number of Federal agencies with water-related responsibilities will be affected by this water policy.

I am charging Secretary Andrus with the lead responsibility to see that these initiatives are carried out promptly and fully. With the assistance of the Office of Management and Budget and the Council on Environmental Quality, he will be responsible for working with the other Federal agencies, the Congress, State and local governments and the public to assure proper implementation of this policy and to make appropriate recommendations for reform in the future.

Specific Initiatives Improving Federal Water Resource Programs

The Federal government has played a vital role in developing the water resources of the United States. It is essential that Federal water programs be updated and better coordinated if they are to continue to serve the nation in the best way possible. The reforms I am proposing are designed to modernize and improve the coordination of federal water programs. In addition, in a few days, I will also be sending to the Congress a Budget amendment proposing funding for a number of new water project construction and planning starts. These projects meet the criteria I am announcing today. This is the first time the Executive Branch has proposed new water project starts since Fiscal Year 1975, four years ago.

The actions I am taking include:
● A directive to the Water Resources Council to improve the implementation of the Principles and Standards governing the planning of Federal water projects. The basic planning objectives of the Principles and Standards — national economic development and environmental quality — should be retained and given equal emphasis. In addition, the implementation of the Principles and Standards should be improved by:

— adding water conservation as a specific component of both the economic and environmental objectives;

— requiring the explicit formulation and consideration of a primarily non-structural plan as one alternative whenever structural water projects or programs are planned;

— instituting consistent, specific procedures for calculating benefits and costs in compliance with the Principles and Standards and other applicable planning and evaluation requirements. Benefit-cost analyses have not been uniformly applied by Federal agencies, and in some cases benefits have been improperly recognized,

"double-counted" or included when inconsistent with federal policy or sound economic rationale. I am directing the Water Resources Council to prepare within 12 months a manual which ensures that benefits and costs are calculated using the best techniques and provides for consistent application of the Principles and Standards and other requirements;

— ensuring that water projects have been planned in accordance with the Principles and Standards and other planning requirements by creating, by Executive Order, a project review function located in the Water Resources Council. A professional staff will ensure an impartial review of pre-construction project plans for their consistency with established planning and benefit-cost analysis procedures and applicable requirements. They will report on compliance with these requirements to agency heads, who will include their report, together with the agency recommendations, to the Office of Management and Budget. Project reviews will be completed within 60 days, before the Cabinet officer makes his or her Budget request for the coming fiscal year. Responsibility will rest with the Cabinet officer for Budget requests to the Office of Management and Budget, but timely independent review will be provided. This review must be completed within the same budget cycle in which the Cabinet officer intends to make Budget requests so that the process results in no delay.

— The manual, the Principles and Standards requirements and the independent review process will apply to all authorized projects (and separable project features) not yet under construction.

● Establishment of the following criteria for setting priorities each year among the water projects eligible for funding or authorization, which will form the basis of my decisions on specific water projects:

— Projects should have net national economic benefits unless there are environmental benefits which clearly more than compensate for any economic deficit. Net adverse environmental consequences should be significantly outweighed by economic benefits. Generally, projects with higher benefit/cost ratios and fewer adverse environmental consequences will be given priority within the limits of available funds.

— Projects should have widely distributed benefits.

— Projects should stress water conservation and appropriate non-structural measures.

— Projects should have no significant safety problems involving design, construction or operation.

— There should be evidence of active public support including support by State and local officials.

— Projects will be given expedited consideration where State governments assume a share of costs over and above existing cost-sharing.

— There should be no significant international or inter-governmental problems.

— Where vendible outputs are involved preference should be given to projects which provide for greater recovery of Federal and State costs, consistent with project purposes.

— The project's problem assessment, environmental impacts, costs and benefits should be based on up-to-date conditions (planning should not be obsolete).

— Projects should be in compliance with all relevant environmental statutes.

— Funding for mitigation of fish and wildlife damages should be provided concurrently and proportionately with construction funding.

● Preparation of a legislative proposal for improving cost-sharing for water projects. Improved cost-sharing will allow States to participate more actively in project decisions and will remove biases in the existing system against non-structural flood control measures. These changes will help assure project merit. This proposal, based on the study required by Section 80 of P.L. 93-251, has two parts:

— participation of States in the financing of federal water project construction. For project purposes with vendible outputs (such as water supply or hydroelectric power), States would contribute 10% of the costs, proportionate to and phased with federal appropriations. Revenues would be returned to the States proportionate to their contribution. For project purposes without vendible outputs (such as flood control), the State financing share would be 5%. There would be a cap on State participation per project per year of 1/4 of 1% of the State's general revenues so that a small State would not be precluded from having a very large project located in it. Where project benefits accrue to more than one State, State contributions would be calculated accordingly, but if a benefiting State did not choose to participate in cost-sharing, its share could be paid by other participating States. This State cost-sharing proposal would apply on a mandatory basis to projects not yet authorized. However, for projects in the authorized backlog, States which voluntarily enter into these cost-sharing arrangements will achieve expedited Executive Branch consideration and priority for project funding, as long as other project planning requirements are met. Soil Conservation Service projects will be completely exempt from this State cost-sharing proposal.

— equalizing cost-sharing for structural and non-structural flood control alternatives. There is existing authority for 80%-20%-Federal/non-Federal cost-sharing for non-structural flood control measures (including in-kind contributions such as land and easements). I will begin approving non-structural flood control projects with this funding arrangement and will propose that a parallel cost-sharing requirement (including in-kind contributions) be enacted for structural flood con-

trol measures, which currently have a multiplicity of cost-sharing rules.

Another policy issue raised in Section 80 of P.L. 93-251 is that of the appropriate discount rate for computing the present value of future estimated economic benefits of water projects. After careful consideration of a range of options I have decided that the currently legislated discount rate formula is reasonable, and I am therefore recommending that no change be made in the current formula. Nor will I recommend retroactive changes in the discount rate for currently authorized projects.

Water Conservation

Managing our vital water resources depends on a balance of supply, demand and wise use. Using water more efficiently is often cheaper and less damaging to the environment than developing additional supplies. While increases in supply will still be necessary, these reforms place emphasis on water conservation and make clear that this is now a national priority.

In addition to adding the consideration of water conservation to the Principles and Standards, the initiatives I am taking include:

● Directives to all Federal agencies with programs which affect water supply or consumption to encourage water conservation, including:

— making appropriate community water conservation measures a condition of the water supply and wastewater treatment grant and loan programs of the Environmental Protection Agency, the Department of Agriculture and the Department of Commerce;

— integrating water conservation requirements into the housing assistance programs of the Department of Housing and Urban Development, the Veterans Administration and the Department of Agriculture;

— providing technical assistance to farmers and urban dwellers on how to conserve water through existing programs of the Department of Agriculture, the Department of Interior and the Department of Housing and Urban Development;

— requiring development of water conservation programs as a condition of contracts for storage or delivery of municipal and industrial water supplies from federal projects;

— requiring the General Services Administration, in consultation with affected agencies, to establish water conservation goals and standards in Federal buildings and facilities;

— encouraging water conservation in the agricultural assistance programs of the Department of Agriculture and the Department of Interior which affect water consumption in water-short areas; and

— requesting all Federal agencies to examine their programs and policies so that they can implement appropriate measures to increase water conservation and re-use.

● A directive to the Secretary of the Interior to improve the implementation of irrigation repayment and water service contract procedures under existing authorities of the Bureau of Reclamation. The Secretary will:

— require that new and renegotiated contracts include provisions for recalculation and renegotiation of water rates every five years. This will replace the previous practice of 40-year contracts which often do not reflect inflation and thus do not meet the beneficiaries' repayment obligations;

— under existing authority add provisions to recover operation and maintenance costs when existing contracts are renegotiated, or earlier where existing contracts have adjustment clauses;

— more precisely calculate and implement the "ability to pay" provision in existing law which governs recovery of a portion of project capital costs.

● Preparation of legislation to allow States the option of requiring higher prices for municipal and industrial water supplies from Federal projects in order to promote conservation, provided that State revenues in excess of Federal costs would be returned to municipalities or other public water supply entities for use in water conservation or rehabilitation of water supply systems.

Federal-State Cooperation

States must be the focal point for water resource management. The water reforms are based on this guiding principle. Therefore, I am taking several initiatives to strengthen Federal-State relations in the water policy area and to develop a new, creative partnership. In addition to proposing that States increase their roles and responsibilities in water resources development through cost-sharing, the actions I am taking include:

● Proposing a substantial increase from $3 million to $25 million annually in the funding of State water planning under the existing 50%-50% matching program administered by the Water Resources Council. State water planning would integrate water management and implementation programs which emphasize water conservation and which are tailored to each State's needs including assessment of water delivery system rehabilitation needs and development of programs to protect and manage groundwater and instream flows.

● Preparation of legislation to provide $25 million annually in 50%-50% matching grant assistance to States to implement water conservation technical assistance programs. These funds could be passed through to counties and cities for use in urban or rural water conservation programs. This program will be administered by the Water Resources Council in conjunction with matching grants for water resources planning.

● Working with Governors to create a Task Force of Federal, State, county, city and other local officials to continue to address water-related problems. The administrative actions and legislative proposals in this Message are designed to initiate sound water management policy at the national level. However, the Federal government must work closely with the States, and with local governments as well, to continue identifying and examining water-related problems and to help implement the initiatives I am announcing today. This Task Force will be a continuing guide as we implement the water policy reforms and will ensure that the State and local role in our Nation's water policy is constant and meaningful.

● An instruction to Federal agencies to work promptly and expeditiously to inventory and quantify Federal reserved and Indian water rights. In several areas of the country, States have been unable to allocate water because these rights have not been determined. This quantification effort should focus first on high priority areas, should involve close consultation with the States and water users and should emphasize negotiations rather than litigation wherever possible.

Environmental Protection

Water is a basic requirement for human survival, is necessary for economic growth and prosperity, and is fundamental to protecting the natural environment. Existing environmental statutes relating to water and water projects generally are adequate, but these laws must be consistently applied and effectively enforced to achieve their purposes. Sensitivity to environmental protection must be an important aspect of all water-related planning and management decisions. I am particularly concerned about the need to improve the protection of instream flows and to evolve careful management of our nation's precious groundwater supplies, which are threatened by depletion and contamination.

My initiatives in this area include the following:

● A directive to the Secretary of the Interior and other Federal agency heads to implement vigorously the Fish and Wildlife Coordination Act, the Historic Preservation Act and other environmental statutes. Federal agencies will prepare formal implementing procedures for the Fish and Wildlife Coordination Act and other statutes where appropriate. Affected agencies will prepare reports on compliance with environmental statutes on a project-by-project basis for inclusion in annual submissions to the Office of Management and Budget.

● A directive to agency heads requiring them to include designated funds for environmental mitigation in water project appropriation requests to provide for concurrent and proportionate expenditure of mitigation funds.

● Accelerated implementation of Executive Order No. 11988 on floodplain management. This Order requires agencies to protect floodplains and to reduce risks of flood losses by not conducting, supporting or allowing actions in floodplains unless there are no practicable alternatives. Agency implementation is behind schedule and must be expedited.

● A directive to the Secretaries of Army, Commerce, Housing and Urban Development and Interior to help reduce flood damages through acquisition of flood-prone land and property, where consistent with primary program purposes.

● A directive to the Secretary of Agriculture to encourage more effective soil and water conservation through watershed programs of the Soil Conservation Service by:

— working with the Fish and Wildlife Service to apply fully the recently-adopted stream channel modification guidelines;

— encouraging accelerated land treatment measures prior to funding of structural measures on watershed projects, and making appropriate land treatment measures eligible for Federal cost-sharing;

— establishing periodic post-project monitoring to ensure implementation of land treatment and operation and maintenance activities specified in the work plan and to provide information helpful in improving the design of future projects.

● A directive to Federal agency heads to provide increased cooperation with States and leadership in maintaining instream flows and protecting groundwater through joint assessment of needs, increased assistance in the gathering and sharing of data, appropriate design and operation of Federal water facilities, and other means. I also call upon the Governors and the Congress to work with Federal agencies to protect the fish and wildlife and other values associated with adequate instream flows. New and existing projects should be planned and operated to protect instream flows, consistent with State law and in close consultation with States. Where prior commitments and economic feasibility permit, amendments to authorizing statutes should be sought in order to provide for streamflow maintenance.

Conclusion

These initiatives establish the goals and the framework for water policy reform. They do so without impinging on the rights of States and by calling for a closer partnership among the Federal, State, county, city and other local levels of government. I want to work with the Congress, State and local governments and the public to implement this policy. Together we can protect and manage our nation's water resources, putting water to use for society's benefit, preserving our rivers and streams for future generations of Americans, and averting critical water shortages in the future through adequate supply, conservation and wise planning.

JIMMY CARTER

The White House,
June 6, 1978 ∎

Disaster Aid Plan

Following is President Carter's June 19 message to Congress outlining his proposal to reorganize the federal disaster aid structure, along with a copy of the plan itself, Reorganization Plan No. 3 of 1978:

TO THE CONGRESS
OF THE UNITED STATES:

Today I am transmitting Reorganization Plan No. 3 of 1978. The Plan improves Federal emergency management and assistance. By consolidating emergency preparedness, mitigation and response activities, it cuts duplicative administrative costs and strengthens our ability to deal effectively with emergencies.

The Plan, together with changes I will make through executive action, would merge five agencies from the Departments of Defense, Commerce, HUD [Housing and Urban Development] and GSA [General Services Administration] into one new agency.

For the first time, key emergency management and assistance functions would be unified and made directly accountable to the President and Congress. This will reduce pressures for increased costs to serve similar goals.

The present situation has severely hampered Federal support of State and local emergency organizations and resources, which bear the primary responsibility for preserving life and property in times of calamity. This reorganization has been developed in close cooperation with State and local governments.

If approved by the Congress, the Plan will establish the Federal Emergency Management Agency, whose Director shall report directly to the President. The National Fire Prevention and Control Administration (in the Department of Commerce), the Federal Insurance Administration (in the Department of Housing and Urban Development) and oversight responsibility for the Federal emergency broadcast system (now assigned in the Executive Office of the President) would be transferred to the Agency. The Agency's Director, its Deputy Director, and its five principal program managers would be appointed by the President with the advice and consent of the Senate.

If the Plan takes effect, I will assign to the Federal Emergency Management Agency all authorities and functions vested by law in the President and presently delegated to the Defense Civil Preparedness Agency (in the Department of Defense). This will include certain engineering and communications support functions for civil defense now assigned to the U.S. Army.

I will also transfer to the new Agency all authorities and functions under the Disaster Relief Acts of 1970 and 1974 now delegated to the Federal Disaster Assistance Administration in the Department of Housing and Urban Development.

I will also transfer all Presidential authorities and functions now delegated to the Federal Preparedness Agency in the General Services Administration, including the establishment of policy for the National Stockpile. The stockpile disposal function, which is statutorily assigned to the General Services Administration, would remain there. Once these steps have been taken by Executive Order, these three agencies would be abolished.

Several additional transfers of emergency preparedness and mitigation functions would complete the consolidation. These include:

● Oversight of the Earthquake Hazards Reduction Program, under Public Law 95-124, now carried out by the Office of Science and Technology Policy in the Executive Office of the President.

● Coordination of Federal activities to promote dam safety, carried by the same Office.

● Responsibility for assistance to communities in the development of readiness plans for severe weather-related emergencies, including floods, hurricanes, and tornadoes.

● Coordination of natural and nuclear disaster warning systems.

● Coordination of preparedness and planning to reduce the consequences of major terrorist incidents. This would not alter the present responsibility of the Executive Branch for reacting to the incidents themselves.

This reorganization rests on several fundamental principles. First, Federal authorities to anticipate, prepare for, and respond to major civil emergencies should be supervised by one official responsible to the President and given attention by other officials at the highest levels.

The new Agency would be in this position. To increase White House oversight and involvement still further, I shall establish by Executive Order an Emergency Management Committee, to be chaired by the Federal Emergency Management Agency Director. Its membership shall be comprised of the Assistants to the President for National Security, Domestic Affairs and Policy and Intergovernmental Relations, and the Director, Office of Management and Budget. It will advise the President on ways to meet national civil emergencies. It will also oversee and provide guidance on the management of all Federal emergency authorities, advising the President on alternative approaches to improve performance and avoid excessive costs.

Second, an effective civil defense system requires the most efficient use of all available emergency resources. At the same time, civil defense systems, organization, and resources must be prepared to cope with any disasters which threaten our people. The Congress has clearly recognized this principle in recent changes in the civil defense legislation.

The communications, warning, evacuation, and public education processes involved in preparedness for a possible nu-

clear attack should be developed, tested, and used for major natural and accidental disaster as well. Consolidation of civil defense functions in the new Agency will assure that attack readiness programs are effectively integrated into the preparedness organizations and programs of State and local government, private industry, and volunteer organizations.

While serving an important "all-hazards" readiness and response role, civil defense must continue to be fully compatible with and be ready to play an important role in our Nation's overall strategic policy. Accordingly, to maintain a link between our strategic nuclear planning and our nuclear attack preparedness planning, I will make the Secretary of Defense and the National Security Council responsible for oversight of civil defense related programs and policies of the new Agency. This will also include appropriate Department of Defense support in areas like program development, technical support, research, communications, intelligence and emergency operations.

Third, whenever possible, emergency responsibilities should be extensions of the regular missions of Federal agencies. The primary task of the Federal Emergency Management Agency will be to coordinate and plan for the emergency deployment of resources that have other routine uses. There is no need to develop a separate set of Federal skills and capabilities for those rare occasions when catastrophe occurs.

Fourth, Federal hazard mitigation activities should be closely linked with emergency preparedness and response functions. This reorganization would permit more rational decisions on the relative costs and benefits of alternative approaches to disasters by making the Federal Emergency Management Agency the focal point of all Federal hazard mitigation activities and by combining these with the key Federal preparedness and response functions.

The affected hazard mitigation activities include the Federal Insurance Administration which seeks to reduce flood losses by assisting states and local governments in developing appropriate land uses and building standards and several agencies that presently seek to reduce fire and earthquake losses through research and education.

Most State and local governments have consolidated emergency planning, preparedness and response functions on an "all hazard" basis to take advantage of the similarities in preparing for and responding to the full range of potential emergencies. The Federal Government can and should follow this lead.

Each of the changes set forth in the plan is necessary to accomplish one or more of the purposes set forth in Section 901(a) of Title 5 of the United States Code. The Plan does not call for abolishing any functions now authorized by law. The provisions in the Plan for the appointment and pay of any head or officer of the new

agency have been found by me to be necessary.

I do not expect these actions to result in any significant changes in program expenditures for those authorities to be transferred. However, cost savings of between $10-$15 million annually can be achieved by consolidating headquarters and regional facilities and staffs. The elimination (through attrition) of about 300 jobs is also anticipated.

The emergency planning and response authorities involved in this Plan are vitally important to the security and well-being of our Nation. I urge the Congress to approve it.

JIMMY CARTER

The White House,
June 19, 1978   ∎

Reorganization Plan Number 3 of 1978

Prepared by the President and transmitted to the Senate and the House of Representatives in Congress assembled, June 19, 1978, pursuant to the provisions of Chapter 9 of Title 5 of the United States Code.

Part I. Federal Emergency Management Agency

Section 101. *Establishment of the Federal Emergency Management Agency.*

There is hereby established as an independent establishment in the Executive Branch, the Federal Emergency Management Agency (the "Agency").

Section 102. *The Director.*

The Agency shall be headed by a Director, who shall be appointed by the President, by and with the advice and consent of the Senate, and shall be compensated at the rate now or hereafter prescribed by law for level II of the Executive Schedule.

Section 103. *The Deputy Director.*

There shall be within the Agency a Deputy Director, who shall be appointed by the President, by and with the advice and consent of the Senate, and shall be compensated at the rate now or hereafter prescribed by law for level IV of the Executive Schedule. The Deputy Director shall perform such functions as the Director may from time to time prescribe and shall act as Director during the absence or disability of the Director or in the event of a vacancy in the Office of the Director.

Section 104. *Associate Directors.*

There shall be within the Agency not more than four Associate Directors, who shall be appointed by the President, by and with the advice and consent of the Senate, two of whom shall be compensated at the rate now or hereafter prescribed by law for level IV of the Executive Schedule, one of whom shall be compensated at the rate now or hereafter prescribed by law for level V of the Executive Schedule and one of whom shall be compensated at the rate now or hereafter prescribed by law for GS-18 of the General Schedule. The Associate Directors shall perform such functions as the Director may from time to time prescribe.

Section 105. *Regional Directors.*

There shall be within the Agency ten regional directors who shall be appointed by the Director in the excepted service and shall be compensated at the rate now or hereafter prescribed by law for GS-16 of the General Schedule.

Section 106. *Performance of Functions.*

The Director may establish bureaus, offices, divisions, and other units within the Agency. The Director may from time to time make provision for the performance of any function of the Director by any officer, employee, or unit of the Agency.

Part II. Transfer of Functions

Section 201. *Fire Prevention.*

There are hereby transferred to the Director all functions vested in the Secretary of Commerce, the Administrator and Deputy Administrator of the National Fire Prevention and Control Administration, and the Superintendent of the National Academy for Fire Prevention and Control pursuant to the Federal Fire Prevention and Control Act of 1974, as amended, (15 U.S.C. 2201 through 2219); exclusive of the functions set forth at Sections 18 and 23 of the Federal Fire Prevention and Control Act (15 U.S.C. 278 (f) and 1511).

Section 202. *Flood and Other Matters.*

There are hereby transferred to the Director all functions vested in the Secretary of Housing and Urban Development pursuant to the National Flood Insurance Act of 1968, as amended, and the Flood Disaster Protection Act of 1973, as amended, (42 U.S.C. 2414 and 42 U.S.C. 4001 through 4128), and Section 1 of the National Insurance Development Act of 1975, as amended, (89 Stat. 68).

Section 203. *Emergency Broadcast System.*

There are hereby transferred to the Director all functions concerning the Emergency Broadcast System, which were transferred to the President and all such functions transferred to the Secretary of Commerce, by Reorganization Plan Number 1.

Part III. General Provisions

Section 301. *Transfer and Abolishment of Agencies and Officers.*

The National Fire Prevention and Control Administration and the National Academy for Fire Prevention and Control and the positions of Administrator of said Administration and Superintendent of said Academy are hereby transferred to the Agency. The position of Deputy Administrator of said Administration (established by 15 U.S.C. 2204(c)) is hereby abolished.

Section 302. *Incidental Transfers.*

So much of the personnel, property, records, and unexpended balances of appropriations, allocations and other funds employed, used, held, available, or to be made available in connection with the functions transferred under this Plan, as the Director of the Office of Management and Budget shall determine, shall be transferred to the appropriate agency, or component at such time or times as the Director of the Office of Management and Budget shall provide, except that no such unexpended balances transferred shall be used for purposes other than those for which the appropriation was originally made. The Director of the Office of Management and Budget shall provide for terminating the affairs of any agencies abolished herein and for such further measures and dispositions as such Director deems necessary to effectuate the purposes of this Reorganization Plan.

Section 303. *Interim Officers.*

The President may authorize any persons who, immediately prior to the effective date of this Plan, held positions in the Executive Branch to which they were appointed by and with the advice and consent of the Senate, to act as Director, Deputy Director, and Associate Directors of the Agency, until those offices are for the first time filled pursuant to the provisions of this Reorganization Plan or by recess appointment, as the case may be. The President may authorize any such person to receive the compensation attached to the Office in respect of which that person so serves, in lieu of other compensation from the United States.

Section 304. *Effective Date.*

The provisions of this Reorganization Plan shall become effective at such time or times, on or before April 1, 1979, as the President shall specify, but not sooner than the earliest time allowable under Section 906 of title 5, United States Code.

Firefighters' Workweek Veto

Following is President Carter's June 19 message to Congress explaining his veto of HR 3161, a bill to shorten the workweek of federal firefighters. It was Carter's third veto.

TO THE HOUSE
OF REPRESENTATIVES:

I am returning, without my approval, H.R. 3161, a bill which would substantially reduce the work week for Federal firefighters, while maintaining their pay at nearly the present level. I have three principal objections to this bill.

First, this measure would reduce firefighters' work week without reducing the premium pay which was designed for a longer standby schedule. In effect, it would raise firefighters' total hourly pay by more than 15 percent. If only the basic hourly pay is considered, without overtime pay, the increase is almost 30 percent. I do not

believe this is justified, particularly in light of the 5.5 percent pay cap I have recommended for Federal employees as part of my efforts to hold down inflation. Moreover, the length of the work week for Federal firefighters must be considered in light of the nature of their duty. Fires tend to be less frequent at Federal installations than in urban areas. Comparatively, there is a very low incidence of fire and there are very few severe fires.

Second, H.R. 3161 would impair the ability of agency heads to manage the work force and regulate the work week.

Third, H.R. 3161 would require the Department of Defense alone to hire 4,600 additional employees, at an annual cost of $46.7 million, just to maintain existing fire protection. These additional personnel and payroll measures are unacceptable.

I am very proud of the superb record of Federal firefighters at our military installations. I know them to be hard-working and dedicated. The evidence is not compelling, however, that they are unfairly treated in matters of pay and length of work week. And in extending unwarranted advantages to them, H.R. 3161 offends the ideals of fairness that should guide this Administration. I am not prepared to accept its preferential approach.

JIMMY CARTER

The White House,
June 19, 1978

Legislative Veto Power

Following is President Carter's June 21 message to Congress opposing the legislative veto:

TO THE CONGRESS
OF THE UNITED STATES:

In recent years, the Congress has strengthened its oversight of Executive Branch decisions. I welcome that effort. Unfortunately, there has been increasing use of one oversight device that can do more harm than good — the "legislative veto."

In the past four years at least 48 of these provisions have been enacted — more than in the preceding twenty years. This proliferation threatens to upset the constitutional balance of responsibilities between the branches of government of the United States. It represents a fundamental departure from the way the government has been administered throughout American history. Unnecessary and unwarranted legislative veto procedures obstruct the efforts of my Administration and most members of Congress to make the administrative process quicker and simpler and divert attention from our common task of improving Federal programs and regulations.

Since taking office, I have several times expressed my deep reservations about legislative veto provisions in bills presented to me for signature. Herbert Hoover and every subsequent President have taken this position. The purpose of this message is to underscore and explain the concern and to propose alternatives.

The legislative veto was first used in the 1932 statute which authorized the President to reorganize the Executive Branch. The provision was repeated in subsequent reorganization acts, including the statute in effect today. This kind of legislative veto does not involve Congressional intrusion into the administration of on-going substantive programs, and it preserves the President's authority because he decides which proposals to submit to Congress. The Reorganization Act jeopardizes neither the President's responsibilities nor the prerogatives of Congress.

'Intrusive Device'

As employed in some recent legislation, however, the legislative veto injects the Congress into the details of administering substantive programs and laws. These new provisions require the President or an administrator of a Government agency to submit to Congress each decision or regulation adopted under a program. Instead of the decision going into effect, action is blocked for a set time — typically 60 congressional working days — while Congress studies it. A majority of both Houses, or either House, or even a single committee, is authorized to veto the action during that period.

Such intrusive devices infringe on the Executive's constitutional duty to faithfully execute the laws. They also authorize congressional action that has the effect of legislation while denying the President the opportunity to exercise his veto. Legislative vetoes thereby circumvent the President's role in the legislative process established by Article I, Section 7 of the Constitution.

These are fundamental constitutional issues. The Attorney General is seeking a definitive judgment on them from the courts, but no immediate resolution is in prospect. Pending a decision by the Supreme Court, it is my view, and that of the Attorney General, that these legislative veto provisions are unconstitutional.

Moreover, the legislative veto raises serious, practical policy problems.

Federal agencies issue thousands of complex regulations each year. Many are adopted after months or years of hearings and are based on many volumes of evidence. To act responsibly under a typical legislative veto provision, Congress would have to examine all of this evidence, hold its own hearings, and decide whether to overrule the agency — all in a few weeks. This task would add an additional burden to Congress' legislative agenda.

Causes Delay, Uncertainty

The regulatory process is rightly criticized for being slow and creating uncertainty which cripples planning by business, state, and local governments, and many others. The legislative veto greatly compounds both problems. At best, it prolongs the period of uncertainty for each

regulation by several months. At worst, it can mean years of delay. Under the legislative veto procedure, Congress can only block an agency's rules, not rewrite them. If the House and Senate agree that a regulation is needed but disagree with the agency or each other on the specifics, exercise of the veto can lead to indefinite deadlock.

This danger is illustrated by the regulations concerning President Nixon's papers. Three versions of these regulations were vetoed, and it took three years to reach agreement on them. Whatever the merits of the issues, this is clearly an unsatisfactory way to decide them. Such lengthy, expensive procedures could easily become commonplace under legislative veto statutes.

In addition to causing delay, legislative veto provisions can seriously harm the regulatory process. Regulators operating under such laws would seek to avoid vetoes. They would therefore tend to give more weight to the perceived political power of affected groups and less to their substantive arguments. Meetings of regulatory commissions could degenerate into speculation about how to write rules so they would escape future disapproval of future Congressional reviewers who are not present nor represented when the rules are being drafted. Many regulations would be evolved in negotiations between agency officials and Congressional staff members, subverting requirements in present law for public notice and comment and for decisions based on the record. Parties to regulatory proceedings, never knowing when a decision might be vetoed, would have to reargue each issue in Congress.

These problems would lead many regulators to reverse the constructive trend toward adopting uniform rules. They would revert to acting on a case-by-case basis, because the legislative veto cannot be applied to such decisions. This lack of uniformity would not reduce the scope of regulation, but it would reduce clarity and certainty. Those affected would have to determine how dozens of decisions on individual fact situations might apply to their own cases, instead of abiding by a single rule.

Treating Symptoms, Not Causes

The most troubling problem, however, is that the legislative veto treats symptoms, not causes. The vast effort required to second-guess individual regulatory decisions could impede the crucial task of revising the underlying statutes.

Agencies issue regulations because Congress passes laws authorizing them, or — frequently — mandating them. Many of these laws have not been seriously reexamined for years and need change. This year, Congress is working on key bills to reform airline regulation, encourage public participation in the regulatory process, require lobbyists to work more openly, and adopt "sunset" procedures. Next year's agenda may be even fuller. We need

legislation to speed up and simplify regulatory procedures, and we must reform a number of individual regulatory programs. We must deregulate where appropriate, make regulation easier to understand and to honor, and control the costs which regulations impose on our economy.

The President and the agency heads are responsible for improving the management of regulation, and we are doing so by administrative action encouraged by my Executive Order on improving the regulatory process. Only Congress through regulatory reform can deal with the underlying problems caused by a multitude of individual legislative mandates.

Regulation provides just one example of the problems caused by legislative vetoes; similarly severe problems arise in other areas of government. Thus, excessive use of legislative vetoes and other devices to restrict foreign policy actions can impede our ability to respond to rapidly changing world conditions. Reasonable flexibility is essential to effective government.

Overreaction to Abuses

In sum, for both constitutional and policy reasons I strongly oppose legislative vetoes over the execution of programs. The inclusion of such a provision in a bill will be an important factor in my decision to sign or to veto it.

I urge Congress to avoid including legislative veto provisions in legislation so that confrontations can be avoided. For areas where Congress feels special oversight of regulations or other actions is needed, I urge the adoption of "report-and-wait" provisions instead of legislative vetoes. Under such a provision, the Executive "reports" a proposed action to Congress and "waits" for a specified period before putting it into effect. This waiting period permits a dialogue with Congress to work out disagreements and gives Congress the opportunity to pass legislation, subject to my veto, to block or change the Executive action. Legislation establishing "report-and-wait" procedures has been introduced. Even these procedures consume resources and cause delays, however, so they should be used sparingly.

As for legislative vetoes over the execution of programs already described in legislation and in bills I must sign for other reasons, the Executive Branch will generally treat them as "report-and-wait" provisions. In such a case, if Congress subsequently adopts a resolution to veto an Executive action, we will give it serious consideration, but we will not, under our reading of the Constitution, consider it legally binding.

The desire for the legislative veto stems in part from Congress' mistrust of the Executive, due to the abuses of years past. Congress responded to those abuses by enacting constructive safeguards in such areas as war powers and the budget process. The legislative veto, however, is an overreaction which increases conflict between the branches of government. We need, instead, to focus on the future. By working together, we can restore trust and make the government more responsive and effective.

JIMMY CARTER

The White House
June 21, 1978

Earthquake Hazards Reduction

Following is the text of President Carter's message to Congress June 22, transmitting his plan to reduce the hazards of earthquakes:

TO THE CONGRESS
OF THE UNITED STATES:

Throughout its history, the human race has faced the threat of earthquakes, but in the last few years advances in science and technology have taught us more about earthquakes, and reduced the mystery of their origin and effects. These advances now permit us to anticipate earthquakes and to mitigate their potentially disastrous consequences. Today there is hope that we may eventually be able to predict earthquakes reliably.

Through the Earthquake Hazards Reduction Act of 1977 (Public Law 95-124), the Congress seeks to apply these advances by "the establishment and maintenance of an effective earthquake hazards reduction program." I am transmitting today a plan for a National Earthquake Hazards Reduction Program. This program is designed to meet the objectives of the important legislation you have passed. It deals with: predicting and preparing for earthquakes; ways in which government, industry, and the public can apply knowledge of seismic risk when making land-use decisions; and achieving earthquake-resistant design and construction.

As this program emphasizes, the Federal government must set a strong example in developing guidelines and standards for its own facilities. But Federal effort alone is not enough; to succeed in this effort, we must have the cooperative efforts of State and local governments, industry and business, professional and volunteer organizations, and the public.

JIMMY CARTER

The White House,
June 22, 1978

LEAA Overhaul

Following is President Carter's July 10 message to Congress, outlining his proposals to reorganize the programs being administered by the Law Enforcement Assistance Administration:

TO THE CONGRESS
OF THE UNITED STATES:

I am today sending to Congress the "Justice System Improvement Act of 1978," which will make significant changes in programs now being administered by the Law Enforcement Assistance Administration ("LEAA") and will revitalize our efforts to help State and local governments improve their justice systems.

For the past 10 years, Federal efforts to control crime through LEAA have been uncoordinated and ineffective. In providing financial assistance to State and local governments, the LEAA program has never been as efficient or effective as originally intended. A complex bureaucratic structure has enveloped the Federal effort, involving State and local law enforcement officials in excessive regulation, complexity, and mountains of redtape — rather than providing them with needed financial and technical assistance. Compliance with procedural guidelines has often overshadowed substantive accomplishments. Further, Federal research and statistics programs have not provided the types of information needed for sound management decisions by those involved in controlling crime and improving our justice system.

With the counsel and assistance of State and local officials and of Congressional leaders, particularly Senator Kennedy and Congressman Rodino, we have devoted more than a year to an intensive, thorough review of the LEAA program. Through that review, we sought to remedy the deficiencies in the LEAA program, while at the same time building upon the program's basic strengths. The Act which I am proposing today meets that goal: it effectively addresses LEAA's weaknesses and furthers our efforts, enhanced by our urban policy, to develop an effective partnership among the Federal government, State and local governments and community organizations.

Enactment of this bill will be a major step forward in our nation's efforts to control crime and improve the administration of justice. The bill contains the following major initiatives:

● It will streamline and redirect the LEAA program by simplifying the grant process and eliminating unnecessary paperwork; by targeting funds to areas of greatest need; by eliminating wasteful uses of LEAA funds; by strengthening the role of local governments; and by increasing community and neighborhood participation in program decisions.

● It will also consolidate within the Department of Justice civil and criminal research efforts in a new National Institute of Justice; and civil and criminal statistical programs in a new Bureau of Justice Statistics.

Law Enforcement Assistance Administration Eliminating Paperwork

The current statute authorizing LEAA imposes 25 broad planning requirements.

Implementation of these requirements has resulted in annual State plans of uncertain value and extraordinary length. Each year, State plans total about 55,000 pages often filled with needless and repetitive narrative. Over the program's history, about 500 plans filling some one-half million pages have been submitted to LEAA. Countless staff time has been devoted to plan development and review at the Federal, State and local level.

My proposal will reverse this trend. Statutorily mandated requirements regarding content of plans will be reduced from 25 to 8. Annual State plans — now averaging about 1,000 pages — will be replaced by simplified applications submitted once every three years. This change alone will decrease paperwork by as much as 75 percent.

In addition, under the Act, major local government units will be able to submit single applications for funding of all projects covering a three-year period. The impact of this change will be significant. Presently, cities like Atlanta, Denver, Detroit, Chicago, Los Angeles and Newark fill out on the average 40 project applications each year. Under the Act, they will be required to complete only one.

Targeting Funds

Under the existing statute, LEAA funds are distributed to States solely on the basis of population. There is no requirement that funds be distributed according to an area's need to fight crime.

Under the Act, a priority will be placed on focusing funds to the areas with the most severe crime problems, in line with the Administration's general policy of targeting funds from government programs to areas of greatest need.

At present 17 States have about 55 percent of the nation's serious crime and about 45 percent of the total population. Under our proposals, those 17 States would receive additional funds to distribute to their local areas with the greatest crime problems.

Wasteful Use of Funds

The existing LEAA statute does not place any meaningful limits on how funds are to be used, or incentives for efficient use. In recent years, it has become obvious that some LEAA funds have been wasted on useless equipment, hardware, projects and programs.

To avoid future wasteful use, and to insure that LEAA funds are spent in the most productive ways, my proposal contains reasonable limits on the use of LEAA funds.

Strict limitations will be placed on the use of funds for equipment, hardware, administrative expenses, and general salary expenses. These limitations should result in additional LEAA funds for programs which will directly impact on the fight against crime and which will improve our judicial system.

Local Governments

Under the current LEAA statute, local crime prevention and control efforts have frequently been undercut by uncertainty about funding levels, as well as by disagreements over State and local roles and responsibilities.

My proposal will eliminate the uncertainty concerning the funding level for local governments and will more clearly establish the relationship between State and local governments. Rather than having to file innumerable applications with their State governments, my proposal will enable municipalities of over 100,000 population and counties of over 250,000 population for the first time to receive a fixed allocation of LEAA funds each year.

In addition, decisions regarding funding are now made at the State level, often without adequate local consultation. Under my proposal, these cities and counties will be given greater discretion to select projects and programs particularly suited to their own crime reduction and criminal justice needs.

Community and Neighborhood Participation

All too often, a wide gulf separates law enforcement officials from the communities and people they protect. This has been particularly true of the LEAA program.

My proposal recognizes that crime prevention and justice system improvement are not solely the tasks of government or justice agencies. Private citizens and neighborhood and community organizations will have a vital role to play. The participation of neighborhood and community groups in the development and approval of State and local applications will be assured. Not only will public hearings be required before State and local LEAA funding decisions are made, but those groups will be fully represented on the State and local advisory boards that will be established to determine how LEAA funds are spent locally. These actions will reenforce the neighborhood anti-crime proposal announced recently in our urban policy.

National Institute of Justice

Although the Federal, State, and local governments spend billions of dollars each year in their effort to combat crime and improve their criminal justice systems, we do not have adequate tools to assess the impact of these dollars in reducing crime or improving our justice system.

To date, Federal leadership in developing the necessary tools has been uncoordinated, fragmented, and has generally lacked focus.

My proposal will remedy this problem by creating a National Institute of Justice within the Justice Department. The Institute will replace two existing units, the National Institute for Law Enforcement and

Criminal Justice and the National Institute of Corrections, and part of a third unit, the Institute of Juvenile Development and Research. The National Institute of Justice will be authorized to undertake basic and applied research and to conduct evaluations and sponsor demonstrations in the civil and criminal justice areas.

It will centralize the Federal effort to determine how the Federal, State and local governments can most effectively attack the crime problem and strengthen their justice system.

To ensure the independence and integrity of the Institute's efforts, its Director will have final authority for all grants and contracts made by the Institute.

An advisory board to the Institute will be composed of a broadly based group of academic experts, State and local officials, neighborhood and community leaders and citizens. The board will have authority to develop, in conjunction with the Director, policies and priorities for the National Institute of Justice.

Bureau of Justice Statistics

One of the most valuable services provided by the Federal government in the criminal justice area is the compilation of statistics. However, the Federal effort here has also lacked a central focus and direction.

Under my proposal, a Bureau of Justice Statistics will be created in the Department of Justice. The Bureau will be authorized to collect, analyze and disseminate statistics on criminal and civil justice matters. As a result, the Federal government will be able to provide crime statistics which are reliable and uniform.

An advisory board to the Bureau will consist of researchers, statisticians, State and local officials and citizens. The board would have authority to recommend to the Director policies and priorities for the Bureau of Justice Statistics.

To coordinate the operation of the streamlined LEAA, the National Institute of Justice and the Bureau of Justice Statistics, the Department of Justice will establish the Office of Justice Assistance, Research and Statistics. That Office will be responsible for ensuring that each of these three organizations attacks our criminal and civil justice problems in a focused and complementary way.

The "Justice System Improvement Act of 1978" lays the foundation for an effective Federal program of financial assistance, research and statistics and is vitally important to assist States, local governments and citizens groups in combating and improving the quality of the justice programs. I urge the Congress to give this proposal prompt and favorable consideration.

JIMMY CARTER

The White House
July 10, 1978

Sikes Act Veto

Following is President Carter's message to Congress giving his reasons for vetoing HR 10882. It was his fourth veto of a public bill.

TO THE HOUSE
OF REPRESENTATIVES:

I am returning without my approval H.R. 10882, the "Sikes Act Amendments of 1978."

The Sikes Act authorizes Federal-State cooperative programs for fish and wildlife conservation and public outdoor recreation on military reservations, National Forests, National Aeronautics and Space Administration sites, and certain Energy and Interior Department lands. It is intended to foster cooperation between the States and Federal land management agencies. H.R. 10882 would extend and increase appropriation authorizations under the act through 1981.

I am strongly committed to the wise management and conservation of fish and wildlife on public lands; I have recommended appropriations of approximately $35 million for fish and wildlife management on public lands subject to the Sikes Act. This total includes nearly $14.4 million for Federal/State cooperative programs of the type authorized by that Act, programs I believe are valuable and important.

However, these amendments are objectionable in two respects. First, the bill would more than double the current appropriation authorizations for Sikes Act programs — from $23.5 million in 1978 to $51 million in 1979, and $61 million in 1980 and 1981. These funds would be in addition to authorizations under other, more general, land management programs which are now used for carrying out most Sikes Act activities. I insist on adequate attention to the management of fish and wildlife resources on public lands, but the appropriations for these programs must be determined in the context of an effective and efficient management program encompassing all public land resources. These amendments provide unneeded authorization levels for Sikes Act programs.

Second, and more importantly, I object to the requirement in H.R. 10882 that directs the Secretaries of the Interior, Agriculture, and Defense to report to congressional authorizing committees whenever the President's budget request for Sikes Act activities is less than the amount authorized, and requires them to state specifically why the higher amount was not requested. This requirement is designed to bring pressure on the Administration to seek separate additional funds for Sikes Act programs and invites agencies to undercut the President's annual budget he has presented to the Congress. This is an unacceptable intrusion on the President's obligations and authority as Chief Executive. This approach would limit the President's ability to make his annual budget recommendations a positive, comprehensive, and balanced statement of the Administration's policies and budget priorities.

Disapproval of H.R. 10882 will not affect planned Federal expenditures for fish and wildlife management on public lands for 1979 which may be carried out under other more general land management authorities. This Administration will continue to move vigorously ahead in cooperation with the States to implement programs for the conservation and enhancement of fish and wildlife on public lands.

JIMMY CARTER

The White House,
July 10, 1978

Pension Regulation Plan

Following is President Carter's Aug. 10 message to Congress accompanying his Reorganization Plan No. 4 of 1978, which revises federal regulation of private pension and employee benefit plans:

TO THE CONGRESS
OF THE UNITED STATES:

Today I am submitting to the Congress my fourth Reorganization Plan for 1978. This proposal is designed to simplify and improve the unnecessarily complex administrative requirements of the Employee Retirement Income Security Act of 1974 (ERISA). The new plan will eliminate overlap and duplication in the administration of ERISA and help us achieve our goal of well regulated private pension plans.

ERISA was an essential step in the protection of worker pension rights. Its administrative provisions, however, have resulted in bureaucratic confusion and have been justifiably criticized by employers and unions alike. The biggest problem has been overlapping jurisdictional authority.

Under current ERISA provisions, the Departments of Treasury and Labor both have authority to issue regulations and decisions.

This dual jurisdiction has delayed a good many important rulings and, more importantly, produced bureaucratic runarounds and burdensome reporting requirements.

The new plan will significantly reduce these problems. In addition, both Departments are trying to cut red tape and paperwork, to eliminate unnecessary reporting requirements, and to streamline forms wherever possible.

Both Departments have already made considerable progress, and both will continue the effort to simplify their rules and their forms.

The Reorganization Plan is the most significant result of their joint effort to modify and simplify ERISA. It will eliminate most of the jurisdictional overlap between Treasury and Labor by making the following changes:

1) Treasury will have statutory authority for minimum standards. The new plan puts all responsibility for funding, participation, and vesting of benefit rights in the Department of Treasury. These standards are necessary to ensure that employee benefit plans are adequately funded and that all beneficiary rights are protected. Treasury is the most appropriate Department to administer these provisions; however, Labor will continue to have veto power over Treasury decisions that significantly affect collectively bargained plans.

2) Labor will have statutory authority for fiduciary obligations. ERISA prohibits transactions in which self-interest or conflict of interest could occur, but allows certain exemptions from these prohibitions. Labor will be responsible for overseeing fiduciary conduct under these provisions.

3) Both Departments will retain enforcement powers. The Reorganization Plan will continue Treasury's authority to audit plans and levy tax penalties for any deviation from standards. The plan will also continue Labor's authority to bring civil action against plans and fiduciaries. These provisions are retained in order to keep the special expertise of each Department available. New coordination between the Departments will eliminate duplicative investigations of alleged violations.

This reorganization will make an immediate improvement in ERISA's administration. It will eliminate almost all of the dual and overlapping authority in the two Departments and dramatically cut the time required to process applications for exemptions from prohibited transactions.

This plan is an interim arrangement. After the Departments have had a chance to administer ERISA under this new plan, the Office of Management and Budget and the Departments will jointly evaluate that experience. Based on that evaluation, early in 1980, the Administration will make appropriate legislative proposals to establish a long-term administrative structure for ERISA.

Each provision in this reorganization will accomplish one or more of the purposes in Title 5 of U.S.C. 901(a). There will be no change in expenditure or personnel levels, although a small number of people will be transferred from the Department of Treasury to the Department of Labor.

We all recognize that the administration of ERISA has been unduly burdensome. I am confident that this reorganization will significantly relieve much of that burden.

This plan is the culmination of our effort to streamline ERISA. It provides an administrative arrangement that will work. ERISA has been a symbol of unnecessarily complex government regulation. I hope this new step will become equally symbolic of my Administration's commitment to making government more effective and less intrusive in the lives of our people.

JIMMY CARTER

August 10, 1978

Weapons Procurement Veto

Following is President Carter's Aug. 17 message to Congress giving his reasons for vetoing HR 10929, the Defense Department weapons procurement bill. It was his fifth veto of a public bill.

TO THE HOUSE
OF REPRESENTATIVES:

I am returning without my approval HR 10929, the "Department of Defense Appropriation Authorization Act, 1979." I am doing so because I cannot, consistently with my constitutional responsibilities, sign into law a bill that in my view would weaken our national security in certain critical areas and wastes scarce defense dollars. The Congress' inclusion in this bill of a number of lower priority programs would force out of our defense budget certain central elements of our program, items needed now to modernize and bolster our military forces.

I believe that the defense of the United States needs to be strengthened. An adequate defense is the single most important concern I have as President. Accordingly, I submitted to the Congress in January of this year a budget request for the Department of Defense which would if enacted provide the defense we need. It requested $126.0 billion for the Department of Defense for Fiscal Year 1979. That amount was judged by me and by the Secretary of Defense to be adequate to provide for the military security of this country in Fiscal Year 1979, provided it was wisely spent.

The bill I am returning does not spend wisely. Instead, it actually would lead to less defense capability than I have requested. It does this by eliminating funds for high priority defense requirements and adding funds for purposes which do not meet our defense needs. Most notably, it would take nearly $2 billion from the total and set it aside for purchase of a nuclear-powered aircraft carrier — a ship which in the end would cost at least $2.4 billion, plus additional billions for its aircraft and the additional ships needed to defend and escort it.

We need more immediate improvements in our defense forces. A new nuclear-powered aircraft carrier would not be commissioned until 1987.

To spend $2 billion in defense dollars in that way would ignore much more serious and immediate defense needs. Other programs have been cut, during the appropriation process as well, to stay within Congressional budget limits. The effect would thus be to take away funds urgently needed by the Army, Navy, Air Force and Marine Corps for high priority programs — and to use those funds to build the most expensive ship in history. The result would be to weaken our military security in several critical areas, particularly during the next two years, at a time when we should be strengthening it. Within the $126.0 billion allocated for defense, we cannot have both an adequately balanced defense program and the luxury of an unneeded nuclear-powered aircraft carrier.

In pushing a nuclear-powered aircraft carrier into a $126.0 billion defense budget, HR 10929 would result in reduction or elimination of these essential programs, and a consequent weakening of our defense posture:

● **Weapons and equipment for the Army.** I requested a $1 billion increase to strengthen our ground forces, particularly our NATO-oriented forces, by providing more helicopters, combat vehicles and ammunition for our front-line forces. Adding the nuclear-powered aircraft carrier means eliminating $800 million of that increase.

● **Weapons and equipment for the Air Force.** I requested more funds for airlift, electronic warfare equipment and electronically guided ordnance. Adding the nuclear-powered aircraft carrier means eliminating $200 million of this increase.

● **Readiness funds.** It makes no sense to have military forces if their equipment is not in condition to fight. I requested an increase of $1 billion for items which are not glamorous, but which provide the immediate fighting capability of our forces — funds (requiring appropriation but not prior authorization) for repairs of weapons, spare parts for vehicles and aircraft, ship overhauls, training of personnel, communications, and logistical support to move equipment to where it is needed. Adding the nuclear-powered aircraft carrier means eliminating half of that increase in fighting capability — some $500 million.

● **Research and development.** To sustain our position of excellence in a world of weapons increasingly dependent on technology, I requested a 3% real growth in defense research and development. Adding the nuclear-powered aircraft carrier leads to an actual reduction in research and development. The bill also shifts some R&D funds from high priority programs to less important ones.

Our Navy has for a decade been moving in the direction of larger and larger, more-and-more-costly ships, and fewer of them. As a consequence our fleet today is smaller than at any time since 1940. We need a fleet that includes more vessels that can perform our Navy's mission but that are not, as this one would be, so designed as to be prohibitively expensive to build. The Navy does not need a fifth nuclear-powered aircraft carrier. It can maintain a twelve-carrier fleet and maintain the fighting capability it needs from a conventionally powered carrier, which I shall request in my budget for next year, at a saving of $1 billion for that single ship. Without this kind of discipline and control of the cost of ships, our Navy will not long be able to carry out its missions.

For these reasons, I must withhold my

approval from HR 10929. I adhere firmly to my request that the Congress provide $126.0 billion for defense in Fiscal Year 1979. But I ask that the Congress delete the authorization for the nuclear-powered aircraft carrier, and use that essential $2 billion of that $126.0 billion instead for as many of our programs as possible from the following critical areas:

● **$1 billion for Army and Air Force equipment** — For helicopters, transport aircraft, combat vehicles, electronic equipment, ammunition and ordnance and other weapons and equipment.

● **$500 million for improving readiness in all the armed services** — For a wide variety of items, ranging from repair of weapons to spare parts stockage to improved training and logistical support.

● **Up to $500 million for research and development** — For programs proposed in my FY 79 budget but deleted by one or another Congressional action.

● **Naval Ships** — It is crucial to maintain an appropriate overall annual level of ship construction. The Congress should return all of the general purpose ships requested in our budget.

These are the ways in which our defense dollars need to be spent. These are the ways in which they will add to our military security, by obtaining the greatest military capability for each dollar and by focusing the effort where more effort is needed.

In light of the continuing Soviet build-up, we must not reduce our own real defense capability, either by cutting the budget amount I have requested, or by substituting for high priority defense requirements programs which are less urgent or less effective.

If we do not spend our defense dollars wisely, we do not provide adequately for the security of our country. I know that the Congress and I share common goals. I ask the Congress to cooperate with me to help our armed forces use their funds in ways which produce the greatest fighting power, and to provide the men and women of our armed forces with the kinds of weapons, equipment and other items of support which they need to do their jobs.

JIMMY CARTER

The White House,
August 17, 1978   ∎

Public Works Bill Veto

Following is President Carter's Oct. 5 veto message on HR 12928, public works appropriations. It was his sixth veto of a public bill.

TO THE HOUSE
OF REPRESENTATIVES:

Today I am returning HR 12928, the Energy and Water Development Appropriations bill, to the Congress without my approval. This bill would hamper the nation's ability to control inflation, eliminate waste and make the government more efficient.

I respect the hard work and good intentions of the members of Congress who have prepared this legislation. I share with the Congress a commitment to a strong program of water resource development. Wise development and management of water resources are vital to American agriculture's continued prosperity, and to community and economic development in key areas of our nation. I have proposed $2.5 billion this year to support nearly 300 water projects — including twenty-six project starts, the first proposed by any president in four years. Much of the water development funding in this bill is sensible and necessary.

HR 12928 also contains energy research and development programs which are important to our nation's energy future. These appropriations are generally in accord with national needs, and I support them.

But this bill also contains provisions for excessive, wasteful water projects and ill-advised limitations on efficient program management; these require that I disapprove HR 12928 in its present form.

The bill would require expenditures on water projects which have already been evaluated objectively and found to be unsound or to fall short of planning, design and environmental assessment requirement. These requirements are essential to ensure that tax dollars are well spent and that future cost over-runs and litigation are avoided. The bill attempts to mandate an unnecessary major increase in the size of the federal bureaucracy. And it uses funding procedures which conceal from the taxpayers the true size of excessive federal spending commitments.

In its present form, this bill appears to appropriate less than my FY 1979 Budget. In fact, however, it commits the federal government to 27 additional new projects and reinstates six projects halted last year — three for construction and three for planning. These added water projects represent a total long-term commitment, including inflation, $1.8 billion in excess of those I proposed. Yet only a little more than $100 million is appropriated in this bill for these projects. *(Chart, next page)*

Purchasing water projects on the installment plan does not reduce their cost to American taxpayers. Nor does it justify funding projects which fail to meet reasonable standards. We can achieve an efficient budget only if we are prepared to admit the true costs of the actions we take.

No challenge the Congress and the Executive Branch must face together is more painful than the exercise of budgetary discipline in each individual case. But only consistent, determined discipline will enable us to achieve our shared objectives of controlling inflation, balancing the budget and making government more efficient. The action I am taking today is part of that effort.

This appropriations bill is a true and difficult test of our resolve to discipline the

Administration's 1979 Request for Water Resource Projects Compared with Amounts Contained in HR 12928
($ in millions)

	President's Request	Bill	Difference
Number of Projects			
New Construction Starts	$ 26	$ 53	$ + 27
Six projects halted [in 1977]*	—	6	+ 6
Total	26	59	+ 33
1979 Appropriation for Projects			
New Construction Starts	640	104	− 536
Six projects halted [in 1977]*	—	8	+ 8
Total	640	112	− 528
Actual Total Cost of Projects			
New Construction Starts	640	1,821	+1,181
Six projects halted [in 1977]*	—	586	+ 586
Total	$640	$2,407	$ 1,767

* Includes three projects funded for construction (total cost: $302 million) and three projects funded for further study (total cost: $284 million).

federal budget. Each bit of additional spending always looks small and unimportant against the total federal budget. The temptation to look the other way in each case is always great. But both Congress and the Executive Branch must recognize that there is no one single dramatic act which will control the budget. Budgetary control must be achieved by the cumulative impact of hard choices such as the one I am presenting to the Congress today.

Following are my specific objections to this bill:

— *Funding is reinstated in this bill for unsound water projects.* Six projects not funded last year by the Congress after thorough review determined them to be unwise investments would receive funding this year. The six projects would cost more than $580 million to complete. Three of these would be funded for construction and three for further study, even though no additional analysis is needed to augment the exhaustive information now available. One of the projects funded for further study would require an investment of over $1 million per farm family served. The majority of another "study" project's water supply "benefits" are to serve one catfish farm and several "potential" catfish farms. One project funded for construction, whose major benefit category is flatwater recreation, would be the sixth Corps of Engineers reservoir in a 50-mile radius. American taxpayers simply should not be forced to fund projects which provide such questionable public benefits.

— The bill commits the Federal government to excessive new water project construction starts. I requested funds for 26 new water project construction starts costing a total of $640 million, including an allowance for inflation. This is the first time a president has recommended new starts in four years. This request was well-considered and reflects my commitment to a strong continued program of water re-

source development. I believe these initiatives are of high priority in meeting agricultural, flood damage reduction, economic development, environmental and other needs. However, the bill goes far beyond this large request. It includes initial funding for an additional 27 projects which, allowing for inflation, would add $1.2 billion in total costs. In addition to unacceptable long-term budgetary impact, many of these projects lack required planning or engineering information, present unresolved economic or environmental problems, fail to meet legal requirements or meet low-priority needs.

There are competing uses for every federal dollar and difficult choices must be faced. Every program in government, no matter how vital, must focus first on matters of highest priority. The president and the Congress must join in this difficult effort. Particularly with taxes and inflation a major concern of every American, I cannot support undertaking expenditures such as a $412 million project where planning is incomplete, or a $117 million project which, without adequate consideration of the concerns of local farmers or of the availability of less damaging alternatives, would take large amounts of valuable farm, pasture and forest land out of production and displace 140 people. Other projects funded in excess of my recommendations pose similar serious problems.

— *I would be forced to enlarge the federal bureaucracy substantially and unnecessarily.* This bill would mandate the hiring of more than 2,300 additional federal employees in the Corps of Engineers and the Bureau of Reclamation — far exceeding actual need. This requirement is inconsistent with efficient program management and would cause growth in this segment of the federal workforce that would be difficult to reverse.

— *The true costs of the bill far exceed the amounts appropriated.* I believe that funds to meet the full cost of all new water

projects should be appropriated when the decision to go forward is made so that the true cost to the taxpayer is known and considered. Appropriating the full amount also helps ensure that, once a project is begun, funds are available to permit speedy, efficient completion. This bill continues the practice of committing the government to major financial investments for what appears on the surface to be very small appropriations. Thus, in making a relatively small appropriation of $103.6 million for new water project construction, HR 12928 is actually committing the government to total expenditures of $1.8 billion. At the same time, adding new starts each year without taking their full costs into account greatly increases the risk that budget pressures in the future will cause costly delays.

— *By eliminating funding for the Water Resources Council, the bill would seriously impair efforts to better coordinate water resources programs.* The Water Resources Council, composed of all the agencies with water programs, is our best assurance of consistent and efficient implementation of water programs throughout the government and close working relationships with other levels of government. The administration's new water policy stresses the need for systematic management of water resource programs and for increased coordination with state and local governments, and Congress recognized the importance of these objectives and of the Water Resources Council in reauthorizing the Council and its small staff this year.

I am pleased to note that the energy research and development portions of the bill are acceptable and meet important national needs. In a constructive step, this bill provides that decisions on the Clinch River Breeder Reactor project — or possible alternatives — will be determined in the Department of Energy authorization bill, the appropriate place to resolve this issue.

Vital energy programs and sound water development investments are important and shared goals of the Congress and my administration.

Yet the American people have the right to expect that their government will pursue these goals effectively, efficiently and with the budgetary discipline and careful planning essential to reduce inflation and continue economic growth. Citizens rightly demand sound programs to meet their needs. They rightly demand restraint and judgment in the allocation of public funds. And they expect those of us in public office to demonstrate the courage needed to face hard choices.

I call upon the Congress to join me in meeting our shared responsibility to the American people. I urge you to revise this bill expeditiously so that vital water and energy programs can continue unhampered by waste and inefficiency.

JIMMY CARTER

The White House,
October 5, 1978

Vietnam-Era Veterans

Following is President Carter's Oct. 10 message to Congress, outlining his proposals to assist veterans of the Vietnam War era:

TO THE CONGRESS
OF THE UNITED STATES:

I am submitting this message to report on the progress of Veterans of the Vietnam-era, and to describe the actions I will take to respond to the special problems a number of these Veterans still face.

Veterans of World War I, World War II and Korea have received the recognition and gratitude they deserve. They are honored and remembered as men and women who served their country. This has not always been the case for those who served during the War in Vietnam. In many ways, their service was more painful than in other eras: the selection process was often arbitrary; the war was long and brutal; the changes in warfare and innovations in medicine meant that fewer soldiers were killed than in other wars, but a far greater percentage survived with disabling injuries.

Because the war did not have the full backing of the American public, neither did those who fought in Vietnam. Many civilians came to confuse their view of the war with their view of those who were called upon to fight it. They confused the war with the warrior. Yet I know that all Americans join me in stating that the courage and patriotism of those who served in Vietnam have earned them full measure of honor and respect.

It is a tribute to the caliber of those who served that most Vietnam-era Veterans have already adjusted very successfully to civilian life. Still, in many ways, the effects of the war in Vietnam linger on. We have only begun to understand the full impact of the conflict. As part of healing its wounds, we have recognized our obligation to forget many harsh words and rash acts, and to forgive those who resisted the war. Of even greater importance is our determination to recognize those who did serve and to show our appreciation for the sacrifices they made.

I have directed the Secretary of Defense to honor the memory of all those who fought and died as well as those who are missing in action in Southeast Asia in ceremonies this fall at Arlington Cemetery.

As for those who did return, our review has found their personal and family median incomes are substantially higher than similar-aged non-Veterans, and their unemployment rates have been lowered. For the third quarter of 1978, Vietnam-era Veterans aged 20-34 had a 4.7 percent unemployment rate as compared to a 6.7 percent rate for the third quarter of 1977. Although rates vary from month to month, it is fair to say that most Vietnam-era Veterans have moved into the mainstream of economic life. Vietnam-era Veterans are making comparable or better use of their Veteran benefits than Veterans of previous wars. To date, nearly 65 percent have utilized their GI Bill benefits, which is far greater than under the World War II or Korean programs. We should not fail to recognize the hard work and determination that typify most Vietnam-era Veterans who have been successful in their military to civilian transition.

But for many Veterans — especially minority and disadvantaged Veterans — the transition to civilian life has led to unemployment, poverty and frustrations. The key to making our Veterans' programs successful — and efficient — is to target them carefully on those who continue to need help. By using our resources more skillfully and coordinating our efforts more closely, we can aid those ex-servicemen and women who are most in need of government assistance.

In my written State of the Union message to you last January, I indicated that my Administration would undertake a government-wide review of the status of the Vietnam-era Veteran and the programs designed to serve them. Since that time, the Veterans Administration, the Department of Labor, the Department of Defense, the Department of Justice, the Department of Health, Education and Welfare, the Community Services Administration, the Council of Economic Advisers, the Office of Management and Budget, and the Domestic Policy Staff have reviewed the status of these ex-servicemen and women and have prepared recommendations for improved government performance. On the basis of that policy review, I have ordered improvements in four areas of Veteran affairs:

- Employment Opportunities
- Educational Opportunities
- Other Veterans Services and Benefits
- Military Status

In order to implement my decisions in these areas and improve delivery of services to veterans, I have established an interagency Veterans Federal Coordinating Committee, composed of representatives of eight agencies, operating under the direction of the Executive Office of the President.

I am also conferring upon the Veterans Administration the status of a Cabinet Agency, for the purpose of attending Cabinet meetings. The Veterans Administration is a large and important part of our government. Its presence at Cabinet meetings will be useful for other departments with overlapping responsibilities, and for the Veterans Administration itself, which will have a stronger voice.

To better understand some of the issues that will continue to confront the Vietnam-era Veteran, I am instituting a survey of public attitudes toward those Veterans. This study will help us identify the real areas of concern, as well as accurately portray the public's overall support of Veterans' benefit programs generally.

I. Employment Opportunities

Most Vietnam-era Veterans are now doing better economically than non-veterans of the same age and background. In 1977, Vietnam-era Veterans aged 20-39 had median personal incomes of $12,680 compared to $9,820 for similar-aged non-veterans. When compared by family income, the figures are $15,040 and $12,850 respectively. For Vietnam-era Veterans aged 20-34, the unemployment rate of 7.4 percent for September one year ago declined to 4.9 percent in September 1978. As in all other sectors, unemployment rates for Veterans are substantially lower than they were when this Administration took office. We have hired nearly 98,000 Vietnam-era Veterans in public service jobs as part of the Administration's Economic Stimulus Package. Jobs and training assistance for Veterans became a top domestic priority when the Administration took office; the results are now clearly visible.

But if the overall employment picture for Vietnam-era Veterans is encouraging, the unemployment problems of minority, disabled, and disadvantaged Vietnam-era Veterans are cause for continued concern and attention. Black Vietnam-era Veterans, a significant percentage of whom saw active combat, face unemployment rates of 11.2 percent for the third quarter of 1978 compared to 15.9 percent for the third quarter of 1977. For the more seriously disabled Veterans, the unemployment rate is estimated to range as high as 50 percent. We have made great strides in every area of employment since the beginning of my Administration, but these jobless rates are still far too high. There is a clear need to better coordinate employment and employment assistance programs so that they are targeted on those Veterans most in need.

With that in mind, I have ordered a comprehensive review of the overall system for delivery of employment services to veterans. The review will yield further suggestions for improvement, but I have already initiated action to:

- improve the participation of Veterans in all Comprehensive Employment and Training Act (CETA) programs. We have designed a number of ways of making sure CETA prime sponsors take account of the special needs of Veterans. They include: inspecting grant plans and monitoring local prime sponsor systems to assure consideration of the Vietnam-era Veteran and seeking to have better Veterans representation on prime sponsor councils.

- continue operation of a national Help Through Industry Retraining and Employment (HIRE) program at a $40 million level, and supplement it with a $90 million HIRE II program, paid for with carry-over funds from the original HIRE effort. HIRE I is a national contract program operated through State Employment Services across the country, and through the National Alliance for Business. It hires and trains Veterans, members of Veterans' families eligible for Veterans' preference, and disadvantaged non-veteran youth for jobs in the private sector. HIRE II will decentralize sponsors to contract for and operate it in cooperation with State Employment Security agencies. HIRE II will be available exclusively for Veterans. Participants will also have access to all of the training, public employment and outreach services available through other CETA programs.

• secure from Congress authority to spend in Fiscal 1979 HIRE funds appropriated in 1977. Without this extension the unobligated funds would have reverted to the Treasury.

• continued support will be given for the special outreach programs for Veterans operated by the National Alliance for Business and selected community organizations. One of the most important contributions government can make to Vietnam-era Veterans is to support outreach programs. They extend Veterans services to those who are unaware of the availability of assistance or intimidated by the idea of seeking it. We have extended our outreach efforts through HIRE II program and Veterans organizations. The National Alliance for Business and 13 other private programs funded by the Department of Labor must have continued backing.

• maintain current funding levels for the Disabled Veterans Outreach Program (DVOP). DVOP was originally funded as part of the economic stimulus package, but the program deserves to continue at its current level of $30 million. DVOP employs 2,000 disabled Veterans to help find jobs for other disabled Veterans. So far, 26,000 disabled Veterans have found work through the program and it continues to be targeted at those Veterans with the severest employment problems.

• improve coordination between Department of Labor and Veterans Administration employment programs. These programs will become more efficient as departmental policy links are clarified by a new high-level joint committee appointed by the Secretary of Labor and the Veterans Administrator. Money-wasting duplication of effort will be ended.

• order all Federal agencies to make greater use of the Veterans Readjustment Appointment (VRA) authority to bring Vietnam-era Veterans, especially the disabled, into government service. I have already submitted legislation to liberalize and extend the authority to June 30, 1980. The bill has passed both Houses of Congress and is now in conference.

II. Educational Opportunities

Vietnam-era Veterans are in the process of becoming the best educated group of Veterans in our history. Already, 65 percent of Vietnam-era Veterans have taken advantage of the GI Bill. That compares to a final rate of some 51 percent for World War II Veterans and 43 percent for Veterans of the Korean War. The Nation has spent nearly $25 billion on the GI Bill for Vietnam-era Veterans compared with $14 billion for those who served in World War II and $4.5 billion for Veterans of the Korean conflict.

But these readjustment assistance benefits often have not been utilized by those Vietnam-era Veterans who need them the most. Many members of minority groups and those lacking a high school diploma have not taken full advantage of the GI Bill. For them, outreach efforts must be intensified and eligibility expanded. At present, eligibility for most benefits under the GI Bill generally ends ten years after discharge. Although these provisions are more liberal than for Veterans of previous wars, we will:

—submit legislation to the Congress that would extend eligibility beyond ten years for these Veterans the Veterans Administration defines as in need or educationally disadvantaged.

—continue a VA program called "Operation Boost" designed to seek out Veterans who are unaware of the time limit that is fast approaching for many of them.

III. Other Veterans Services and Benefits

In general, Veterans benefits have been generous for Vietnam-era Veterans, but these and other benefits to which they are entitled need to be targeted better on those who really need them. Among those benefits and services requiring improvement are ones relating to:

• Disabled Veterans
• Incarcerated Veterans
• Readjustment counseling and substance abuse treatment.

Disabled Veterans. Individuals with service-connected disabilities are especially in need of greater assistance from the government. This is particularly true for Vietnam-era Veterans, who suffered a 300 percent greater loss of lower extremities than Veterans of any other war. Altogether, 512,000 have sustained some kind of disability.

Our vocational rehabilitation programs must reflect our paramount concern for those Veterans who have service-connected disabilities. The current VA program is based on a 1943 model and requires major updating. I will submit legislation to the next Congress that will modernize and improve that program.

Readjustment Counseling and Substance Abuse Treatment. The frequent image of the Vietnam Veteran as unbalanced, unstable and drug-dependent is simply not borne out by available information. Most Veterans have adjusted well and the incidence of drug abuse, although greatly increased while in service, has for the most part declined to pre-Vietnam levels or lower. Nevertheless, there is evidence that suggests a significant minority of Vietnam Veterans have experienced problems of readjustment which continue even today.

Vietnam-era Veterans under age 34 have a suicide rate 23 percent higher than non-Veterans of the same age group. The number of hospitalized Vietnam-era Veterans identified as alcoholics or problem drinkers more than doubled from 13 percent in 1970 to 31 percent in 1977. And, although the drug abuse problems has declined, Vietnam-era Veterans account for 39 percent of all inpatients and 55 percent of all outpatients being treated by the VA for drug dependence problems.

The government is addressing these concerns, but more must be done:

—The Administration has already proposed legislation which would authorize psychological readjustment counseling to Vietnam-era Veterans and their families. The proposal is aimed at those Veterans who are not classified as mentally ill but nevertheless need some kind of counseling. I urge Congress to enact this proposal prior to adjournment.

The Administration also requested legislative authority to contract for halfway houses in the treatment of Vietnam-era Veterans with substance abuse problems. This authority, together with the activation of 20 new VA substance abuse treatment units in this coming fiscal year, should provide needed resources to treat those with continuing alcohol and drug abuse problems.

—Finally, more research needs to be done into the problems of Vietnam-era Veterans. I am directing both the Veterans Administration and the National Institute of Mental Health to initiate studies in this area. A major study contracted for by the Veterans Administration to be submitted next year should enable us to better identify the nature and extent of problems being experienced by Vietnam-era Veterans.

Incarcerated Veterans. Like Veterans of all wars, a certain percentage of Vietnam-era Veterans end up in prison after returning home. Available data suggest that there are about 29,000 Vietnam-era Veterans in State and Federal prisons. Many of these Veterans received discharges which entitle them to VA benefits. Unfortunately, we lack comprehensive information about imprisoned Veterans.

I have directed the Law Enforcement Assistance Administration (LEAA) to compile accurate data about incarcerated Veterans. I have also asked the LEAA and the Bureau of Prisons to develop an information dissemination program for criminal justice system officials aimed at informing Veterans of the benefits available to them.

IV. Military Status

Ninety-seven percent of all Vietnam-era Veterans received discharges under honorable conditions after completing service. It is only fair that those few individuals with discharges under other than honorable conditions be presented with the fullest possible justification for the action taken against them. Because of the serious harm such a discharge can do to a Veteran seeking a responsible place in society, the government must assure that discharge review is readily available to insure fair and humane treatment.

In this connection the Administration will:

—grant assistance to Veterans seeking discharge review. The Department of Defense has agreed to provide indices of discharge review/correction board cases to selective regional offices of the VA.

—submit legislation to modify the provisions of PL 95-196 which automatically barred VA benefits for combat Veterans discharged because of unauthorized absences of 180 days or more.

Conclusion

No steps we take can undo all the damage done by the war. There is no legislation that can bring those who died back to life, nor restore arms, legs, eyes to those who lost them in service. What we can do is to acknowledge our debt to those who sacrificed so much when their country asked service of them, and to repay that debt fully, gladly, and with a deep sense of respect.

JIMMY CARTER

The White House,
Oct. 10, 1978   ∎

Aquaculture Pocket Veto

Following is President Carter's Oct. 18 message to Congress explaining his decision to withhold approval of HR 9370, the aquaculture assistance bill. It was Carter's first use of the pocket veto and his seventh veto of a public bill:

I have withheld approval from HR 9370, "A bill to establish new Federal programs and assistance for the development of aquaculture in the United States."

While the underlying purpose of the bill, development of an active aquaculture industry, is sound, I am concerned that the numerous broad-reaching programs established under the bill are premature. HR 9370 would establish a National Aquaculture Council to assess the state of aquaculture in the U.S. and to prepare a National Aquaculture Development Plan — a detailed set of Federal activities to expand the commercial potential of certain aquatic species. It would establish substantial new programs of Federal assistance to carry out the plan and undertake demonstration projects in aquaculture. The bill also would create a Federal Aquaculture Assistance Fund to provide financial assistance and support to the aquaculture industry through a new Federal loan guarantee program and a new Federal insurance program.

The Administration recognizes the importance of aquaculture, the need for effec-

tive programs to support this, and the concept of an assessment of the aquaculture industry. In fact, many of the actions that the bill would require are already underway. Federal agencies are now involved in a wide variety of aquaculture activities, and they already have the legislative authorities they need to provide research and technical and financial assistance to the aquaculture industry. For example, the Small Business Administration can assist small business concerns which are engaged in aquaculture. The Department of Commerce, through its aquaculture research activities and the Sea Grant program, is supporting marine research, development, and advisory services. The Department of the Interior spends about $15 million yearly on freshwater aquaculture at its fish hatcheries, research and development laboratories, and cooperative fishery units. The Agriculture Department provides a complete range of information and technical assistance related to aquaculture. Additionally, the Farm Credit Administration is authorized to extend credit to harvesters of aquatic products.

We also have in place a way to coordinate the aquaculture programs of the Federal Government — namely, the Interagency Subcommittee on Aquaculture of the Federal Council on Science and Technology.

Given this array of Federal activities, I believe we should more carefully assess the need for additional programs in this area. In particular, I am concerned about offering major new government subsidies such as the loan guarantee and insurance programs unless and until a clear need for them has been established. Accordingly, I must withhold my approval of the bill.

My Administration will continue to assess the needs of aquaculture and the effectiveness and adequacy of the Federal programs in this area. We look forward to reviewing these programs next year with the sponsors of this measure in the hope we can agree on additional improvements in the government's aquaculture programs.

JIMMY CARTER

The White House,
October 18, 1978   ∎

SBA Amendments Veto

Following is President Carter's Oct. 23 statement giving his reasons for refusing to sign HR 11445, Small Business Act amendments. It was his second use of the pocket veto and his eighth veto of a public bill.

I am withholding my approval of HR 11445, omnibus amendments to the Small Business Act and the Small Business Investment Act. Because I recognize very personally the needs of the small business community and the dedication of

Congressman Neal Smith and Senator Gaylord Nelson, chairmen of the respective House and Senate small business committees, in developing this legislation, it is with great regret that I must take this action.

Having spent most of my adult life as a small businessman, I share with the Congress a strong commitment to the small business people of our country and I recognize the need for greater attention to small business needs by the federal government. Since I took office we have reduced the burden of federal regulations on small business, proposed significant tax reductions and increased lending under the guaranteed loan program by 40%. In May of this year I signed an Executive Order calling for a White House Conference on Small Business to be held in January 1980. This conference will involve over 25,000 small business people throughout the country helping us to develop a small business policy for this country. I intend to work with the Congress and particularly with Chairmen Smith and Nelson to develop and implement such a policy.

This legislation does have beneficial features. However, it is precisely because of my commitment to small business and an effective Small Business Administration, that I must withhold my approval from HR 11445. This bill, in its present form, is not the best we can do for small business in the United States and is inconsistent with the tight budget situation we will face in the next few years. Disapproval of the bill would not interrupt any existing SBA program since SBA programs are already authorized for fiscal year 1979, nor would it interfere with administration plans regarding the White House Conference on Small Business, since $4,000,000 has already been appropriated for the conference in fiscal year 1979. This conference is an important priority of mine and of my administration.

The bill authorizes over $2 billion in expenditures in excess of our budget projections through 1982. It continues a duplicative program of farm disaster lending by the SBA with excessively deep interest subsidies and terms which we believe to be wasteful. This has led to an unwarranted amount of farm disaster lending which should be done by the Farmers Home Administration. This administration has proposed that farm lending be consolidated in the Department of Agriculture which has the farm credit expertise and extensive field network necessary to operate the program effectively and efficiently. The Congress has failed to act on this recommendation.

Even more important is the effect this bill would have on the operations of the Small Business Administration. The bill virtually mandates significant staff increases. It would also interfere with the ability of the administrator of the SBA, my primary small business advisor and representative, to effectively run that agency. The legislation imposes specific titles and responsibilities upon agency officials and specifies funding and personnel levels for activities throughout SBA down to the smallest detail. These legislative strictures run counter to my efforts to better manage the federal government.

The bill also distorts the role of SBA's Chief Counsel for Advocacy. I supported the establishment of this office as a means to insure that the views of small business were adequately reflected in the policy-making processes of the government. But the legislation tends to move the Chief Counsel for Advocacy into policy and administrative areas more properly those of the administrator of the SBA. This bill also might begin to isolate the Chief Counsel for Advocacy from the executive policy-making process by calling for an annual report to Congress which could not be reviewed or coordinated with any other agency of the Executive Branch. Current statutes provide the Chief Counsel with sufficient authorities to evalute small business issues and serve as an ombudsman to small business interests.

I am also concerned by the loan pooling provision in this bill that would authorize private dealers to issue a new class of 100 percent federally guaranteed securities which would compete directly with the Treasury and other federally-backed securities in the bond markets.

I look forward to working with the Congress and the small business community who worked on this bill to develop a program to meet the needs of small business. It is my great hope that early in the next Congress an approach will be fashioned to meet the needs of the small business community, with the full involvement of my administration.

JIMMY CARTER

The White House,
October 25, 1978

Legionville Historic Site Veto

Following is President Carter's Nov. 2 statement giving his reasons for refusing to sign (pocket veto) S 1104:

I am withholding my approval from S 1104, a bill that would authorize the establishment of the Legionville National Historic Site in the State of Pennsylvania. I am withholding my signature because I do not believe the Legionville site is of sufficient national significance to merit the cost of establishing and maintaining it as a national historic site.

The site does not meet the national significance criteria for historical areas established by the Department of the Interior. The Pennsylvania State Historic Preservation Office judged the site of only local significance. A National Park Service report made in June 1977 agreed. Further, the site has been altered by such modern intrusions as a railroad and an interstate highway.

The career of General "Mad" Anthony Wayne has been amply commemorated at other designated sites and I do not believe the added expense of acquiring and developing this site is a worthwhile expenditure of Federal funds.

JIMMY CARTER

The White House,
November 2, 1978

Navajo-Hopi Relocation Veto

Following is President Carter's Nov. 2 statement giving his reasons for refusing to sign (a pocket veto) HR 11092.

I am withholding my approval of HR 11092, the "Navajo and Hopi Relocation Amendments of 1978." I have no objection to the authorization in this bill to fund the important and difficult work being performed by the Relocation Commission to administer the partitioning of land which has been jointly used by the Navajo and Hopi Tribes. My failure to approve this bill will not affect the ability of the Commission to continue its work, because appropriations for this fiscal year have already been approved.

My objections to the bill center on section 4, which would provide for a one-house veto of the relocation plan which is finally adopted by the Relocation Commission. I have previously informed the Congress of my view that such legislative veto devices are unconstitutional intrusions into the day-to-day administration of the law by the Executive Branch, including independent agencies such as the Relocation Commission. Congress is constitutionally empowered to overrule agency decisions executing the law only by enacting legislation subject to the veto power of the President under Article I, section 7 of the Constitution.

Where either Congress or the President is dissatisfied with the execution of the law by an independent agency of commission, legislation agreeable to both or enacted over the President's veto is an appropriate and constitutional means for overturning the result reached by that independent agency. If the Constitution required less, there would in fact be no true independence for agencies such as the Relocation Commission. This principle was adhered to by the Ninety-third Congress when it enacted the Navajo and Hopi Indian Relocation Commission Act in 1974 and is one from which we should not depart.

The bill also contains a provision which would oust incumbent members of the Navajo and Hopi Indian Relocation Commission if they happened to be Federal, State or local elected officials. This provision in section 2 has constitutional implications since it would allow for Congressional removal of officers in the Executive Branch. Further, as a matter of fairness and equity, interruption of the tenure of appointed officials by the imposition of new "qualifications" should not be lightly undertaken. Accordingly, I would suggest that the Ninety-sixth Congress, in any consideration of a similar bill, give due consideration to these problems.

The Administration will work with the Congress next year to develop any needed legislation to improve the operations of the Relocation Commission. The Commission needs to operate more effectively and I look forward to working with congressional leaders such as Senator DeConcini and Congressman Udall toward this end.

JIMMY CARTER

The White House,
November 4, 1978

Navy-Commerce Meetings Veto

Following is President Carter's Nov. 2 statement giving his reasons for refusing to sign (a pocket veto) HR 11861.

I am withholding my signature from HR 11861, which would require the Secretaries of Commerce and the Navy to meet at least four times a year with representatives of the maritime industry and to submit an annual report to the President and Congress on their activities and recommendations.

Both the Maritime Administration of the Commerce Department (MARAD) and the Navy already have numerous contacts with the maritime industry and with each other to study, develop, and implement the goals of the Merchant Marine Act. Navy and MARAD are currently working to improve their cooperation in this area by adding the Secretaries of Commerce and Navy to an existing inter-agency advisory board on maritime matters. They are also arranging to have the board meet at least four times a year, and at least one of these meetings will be open to maritime industry representatives.

In addition, in order to assure that the concerns that generated this bill are fully addressed, I am directing both Secretaries to consult regularly with maritime industry officials to discuss issues of mutual concern.

In light of these actions, I see no reason for this legislation. It is not necessary to achieve our goal of an adequate merchant marine. It would mandate a change in administrative functions which are currently satisfactory. It is an undue legislative intrusion into administrative activities which are the appropriate responsibility of the Executive Branch, and the required report would be an additional and unnecessary government expense. For these reasons, I am disapproving this bill.

The White House,   JIMMY CARTER
November 2, 1978   ▮

D.C. Employees' Pensions

Following is President Carter's Nov. 4 statement giving his reasons for refusing to sign (a pocket veto) the District of Columbia Employees' Pension bill.

I am withholding my approval from HR 6536 which would make certain changes in the retirement program for police, firefighters, teachers and judges of the District of Columbia.

This action today in no way alters my commitment to the basic principles of fairness and self-determination which must be the cornerstone of Federal-District relations. Included among our actions to fulfill this commitment have been (1) support of full voting representation, (2) support for expansion of "Home Rule" for the District and (3) support of efforts to provide greater equity and predictability to the financial relationship between the Federal government and the District.

I have also proposed removal of the Federal government from the District's Budgetary process by 1982, as well the development of an equitable Federal payment process on the District's revenues. This process must rest on an objective, equitable basis and not be used as a device to balance the District's budget. To achieve movement toward that goal, I recommended a Federal payment for Fiscal year 1979 totaling $317 million — the highest total ever recommended by a President.

It is against that background that my Administration last year expressed its willingness to work with the Congress and the District to develop a sound, reasonable solution to the District's current financial difficulties with its pension program for police, firemen, teachers and judges. Previous Administrations have declined to acknowledge any Federal responsibility for the District's current pension funding problems. In the bill that passed the House of Representatives, my Administration announced its willingness to assume sixty percent of the cost of making a transition to an actuarially sound system. This would have obligated the Federal government to make payments of $462 million over 25 years. Instead, the Congress ultimately adopted a different method of funding which identified the Federal responsibility as that portion of the unfunded liability attributable to employees who retired prior to Home Rule. This would require the Fed-

eral government to pay more than $1.6 billion over that same period.

This proposal fails to recognize that a large part of that liability derives from abuses of the disability retirement statutes which were permitted to flourish by those responsible for their effective administration. It undervalues or ignores the significance of Federal assistance through the Federal funding of benefits for thousands of District employees who participate in the Federal Civil Service Retirement System. I am therefore of the view that the enrolled bill overstates the degree of Federal responsibility.

Although the bill's benefit and disability retirement reforms are desirable, its failure to apply these reforms to current employees constitutes a serious and costly deficiency. While the bill contains a penalty clause, the purpose of which is to refuse the Federal payment if abuse persists, the application of basic statutory reforms to all employees would be a far more effective and efficient means of preventing a recurrence of the abuses which have prevailed in recent years.

Accordingly, I am compelled to withhold my approval from this bill.

I realize that many members of Congress have worked long and hard with the Administration on this question. I agree with them that there is indeed a Federal responsibility to see that this program is converted to one which is actuarially sound and which minimizes opportunity for abuse.

I look forward to working with the Congress and the elected representatives of session to develop acceptable retirement funding and reform legislation. We are prepared to consider a reasonable Federal financial contribution, providing that provisions are included that fully remedy the problem of retirement abuses. Working together, I am sure we can place the District retirement programs on a sound basis in a manner which both limits the extent of Federal financial responsibility, while also recognizing the Federal responsibility in this area.

JIMMY CARTER

The White House,
November 4, 1978   ▮

Shipping Rebates Veto

Following is President Carter's Nov. 4 statement giving his reasons for refusing to sign the Ocean Shipping Rebating bill.

I have decided not to sign into law HR 9518. This legislation, which would impose severe enforcement measures in the area of ocean shipping rebating, reflects concern with the possible disparity in enforcement of our anti-rebating laws against U.S.-flag carriers but not against foreign flag opera-

tors. I share that concern, and any disparity that exists must be eliminated.

The United States is currently engaged in important discussions with several European countries and Japan in an attempt to reach cooperative agreements involving a number of shipping problems, including rebating. Rather than taking immediate unilateral action undermining these efforts, I have directed the Secretary of State, in cooperation with the Federal Maritime Commission and other agencies to pursue these talks vigorously and to report to me on their progress. I am also directing the Administration's Maritime Policy Task Force to provide, by an early date, a set of recommendations that will address both the substance of our rebating laws as well procedures for enforcement, taking into account the inherently international character of ocean shipping.

In the interim, I am asking the Federal Maritime Commission to step up its enforcement efforts against illegal rebating under the authority now provided in the Shipping Act of 1916. The Administration is committed to assist the FMC in these efforts, and I urge the FMC to seek the assistance of the Department of State in obtaining any necessary cooperation from foreign governments.

Although I am withholding my signature on HR 9518 I believe the bill represents an important signal to foreign countries that we must work together to secure a cooperative shipping regime. I commit my Administration to work with the next Congress to develop a comprehensive maritime policy for the United States, in which the concerns reflected by this bill as well as broader policy issues can be fully addressed.

JIMMY CARTER

The White House,
November 4, 1978   ▮

Guam, Virgin Island Payments Veto

Following is President Carter's Nov. 8 statement giving his reasons for refusing to sign (a pocket veto) HR 13719:

I have withheld my approval of HR 13719, which would have authorized special Federal payments to Guam and the Virgin Islands to offset the local revenue losses during calendar years 1978 through 1982 caused by the Revenue Act of 1978.

Because income taxes paid by territorial residents to the governments of Guam and the Virgin Islands are based on the U.S. Internal Revenue Code, tax changes intended to reduce Federal income tax liabilities in the United States have a corresponding effect in reducing territorial tax liabilities. HR 13719 would have authorized direct grants to the territories to offset revenue losses associated with the 1978 tax Act.

While recognizing the defects in the current territorial tax structures which HR 13719 was designed to alleviate, particularly the effects of periodic Federal tax reductions on local revenues, I do not believe the bill provides an acceptable long-range solution. By replacing reasonable local tax efforts with direct Federal payments, the bill is simply another attempt to manage territorial deficits without addressing the underlying economic and financial problems which have led to those deficits. We can no longer afford a piecemeal approach to the growing revenue problems of the territories.

Accordingly, although I am disapproving HR 13719, I am directing the Secretaries of the Interior and the Treasury to study the financial situation of both the Virgin Islands and Guam to recommend a plan designed to help those governments achieve a higher degree of financial stability without perpetuating a piecemeal system which is costly to the Federal government and which does not sufficiently encourage responsible fianancial management in these territories.

JIMMY CARTER

The White House,
November 8, 1978

Tris Bill Veto

Following is President Carter's Nov. 8 statement giving reasons for refusing to sign S 1503.

I am withholding my approval of S 1503, a bill which would authorize Government indemnification, upon a judgment by the U.S. Court of Claims, of businesses which sustained losses as a result of the ban on the use of the chemical Tris in children's sleepwear.

In 1971 and 1974 the Government established strict fabric flammability standards on children's sleepwear to protect children against burns. To meet these flammability standards, the clothing industry treated fabric by using substantial quantities of the flame-retardant chemical Tris. In 1975, information became available that Tris was a carcinogenic risk to humans. Some firms stopped using Tris after this test information became available, but other firms did not.

On April 8, 1977, the Consumer Product Safety Commission ruled that children's sleepwear containing Tris was banned as a "hazardous substance" under the Federal Hazardous Substances Act. This led to the removal of Tris-treated children's sleepwear from the marketplace. Both the imposition of flammability standards and the subsequent ban on Tris-treated fabrics have caused expenditures and losses by industry.

The imposition of strict flammability standards to protect the Nation's children was fully justified. After it was discovered that Tris was hazardous to health, the removal of Tris-treated sleepwear from the marketplace, again to protect the Nation's children, was also fully justified.

S 1503 would establish an unprecedented and unwise use of taxpayer's funds to indemnify private companies for losses incurred as a result of compliance with a federal standard. The Government could be placed in the position in the future of having to pay industry each time new information arises which shows that a product used to meet regulatory standards is hazardous. This would be wrong. Producers and retailers have a basic responsibility for insuring the safety of the consumer goods they market.

If this bill became law the potential would exist for compensation of firms who marketed Tris-treated material after they knew, or should have known, that such products constituted a hazard to the health of children. Extensive, costly, and time-consuming litigation would be required to determine, in each instance, the liability involved and the loss attributable to the ban action in April 1977, without regard to profits the claimants may have earned on Tris-treated garments in earlier years.

While it is most regrettable that losses have resulted from the regulatory actions taken to protect the safety and health of the Nation's children, no basis exists to require a potential Federal expenditure of millions of dollars when the actions of the Government were fully justified. Accordingly, I am compelled to withhold my approval from this bill.

JIMMY CARTER

The White House,
November 8, 1978

Textile Tariff, Meat Import, Nurse Training Vetoes

Following are President Carter's Nov. 10 statements giving his reasons for refusing to sign (pocket veto) HR 9937, HR 11545 and S 2416.

I have decided not to sign into law HR 9937. This bill is an amendment to the Bank Holding Company Act which would authorize the General Services Administration to sell certain silver dollar coins at negotiated prices. I have determined that this legislation would not be in the national interest because of an unrelated amendment which exempts all textile and apparel items from any tariff reductions in the Multilateral Trade Negotiations (MTN) now underway in Geneva.

I am determined to assist the beleaguered textile industy. We are committed

to a healthy and growing textile and apparel industry. This legislation would not advance that cause, and could even harm the entire U.S. economy.

This bill would not address the real causes of the industry's difficulties. In return for any transient benefits, the bill would prompt our trading partners to retaliate by withdrawing offers in areas where our need for export markets is the greatest — products such as tobacco, grains, citrus, raw cotton, paper, machinery, poultry, and textile-related areas such as mill products and fashion clothing. The loss of these export areas is too high a price for our Nation to pay.

The cost of this bill might be even higher; at best, it would cost us many opportunities for export; at worst, it could cause the collapse of the trade talks and further restrict the growth of the world economy. If the two and a quarter million workers in the textile and apparel industry are to survive in their jobs, we must work to keep the world economy strong and international trade free.

Just within the last year we have taken a number of steps to improve the condition of the U.S. textile and apparel industry:

—We negotiated a renewal of the international Multifiber Arrangement through 1981, providing more responsive controls over disruptive imports.

—We have negotiatged 15 new bilateral export restraint agreements which are firmer and fairer than earlier versions, covering 80 percent of all imports from low-cost suppliers. And we are negotiating more.

—We have improved our monitoring of imports and implementation of restraints, through steps such as the new legislative initiatives I have approved.

—We have, despite the proposed small reduction in tariffs, the highest textile and apparel tariffs in the developed world.

—We have begun discussions with exporting countries not now under restraint to seek appropriate levels for their shipments.

—We have established a pilot program to improve productivity in the men's tailored clothing industry, and we have begun an export promotion program for the entire textile and apparel complex.

—And we have begun a review of existing and proposed Federal regulations affecting this industry to assess their impact.

This, however, is not enough. I pledge that we will do more:

—We will intensify our review of existing bilateral restraint agreements to be sure they really work, and if there are harmful surges we will work promptly to remedy them.

—We will not allow the effectiveness of our restraint agreements to be undermined by significant increases in shipments from uncontrolled suppliers, and we will maintain a world-wide evaluation of the imports of textile and apparel into the U.S. and seek appropriate action, country-by-country, where warranted.

—We will be prepared to expand the pilot project underway in the men's tailored clothing industry so that other sectors may benefit from that experience, and we will speed proposals for a similar program in the ladies apparel industry.

—We will negotiate strenuously for removal of non-tariff barriers to U.S. textile and apparel exports, including restrictive "rules of origin."

—The Office of the Special Representative for Trade Negotiations will begin a new policy review and report to me quarterly on developments in the domestic textile and apparel industry, with special emphasis on imports and exports, so that appropriate actions can be taken more promptly.

These steps, like those of the past year, will not be the limit of our assistance to this vital industry. But each step that we take must be directed toward the long-term health of this industry and the United States economy as a whole — unlike HR 9937 which on balance is detrimental to the textile industry, to its to million workers, and to the Nation as a whole.

JIMMY CARTER

The White House,
November 10, 1978

MEAT IMPORTS VETO

I have withheld my approval of HR 11545, the Meat Import Act of 1978.

I do so because the bill would severely restrict Presidential authority to increase meat imports and would place a floor or minimum access level for meat imports that I believe is too low. It deprives a President of the only anti-inflationary tool available in this area.

Current law allows the President substantial flexibility to increase meat imports when, in his judgment, domestic supplies are inadequate to meet demand at reasonable prices. I am convinced that this flexibility must be preserved, as a weapon against inflation.

Under this bill, however, authority to increase meat imports would be tied to declaration of a national emergency or natural disaster, or to a restrictive price formula. Under this formula, the farm price of cattle would have to increase faster than the retail meat price by more than ten percent during the first two calendar quarters of a year. Under this formula, quotas could have been relaxed only once in the last ten years.

I also believe that the United States must avoid imposing excessive restrictions on our trading partners who supply us with meat. HR 11545 would impose those restrictions by stipulating a minimum access level for meat imports of 1.2 billion pounds, instead of the 1.3 billion my Administration recommended. I am concerned that the bill's lower level could harm our trade relations with the meat exporting countries and thus impair their long-term reliability as souces of additional meat supplies when

our own production is low, particularly at a time when we are negotiating for greater access to foreign markets for both our industrial and agricultural products.

If the Congress had enacted HR 11545 without these objectionable provisions, I would have been pleased to sign it, as my advisers make clear repeatedly. The bill would have amended the Meat Import Act of 1964 to provide a new formula for determining meat import quotas. The new formula would have adjusted meat import quotas up when domestic production of meats subject to the quota went down. Under the 1964 meat import law, quotas are adjusted in the opposite way, so that as domestic production declines, the limits on meat imports are tightened, at exactly the wrong time. This defect has often compelled Presidents to increase or suspend the meat import quota, in order to ensure supplies of meat at reasonable prices. The new counter-cyclical formula would, in most years, automatically make the necessary adjustment in the meat import quota, without involving the President in the normal operation of the meat trade.

This Administration supports such counter-cyclical management of meat imports; in fact, the Department of Agriculture was instrumental in developing the formula which the Congress approved. But for all the advantages of the new formula, it is still an untested mechanical formula which may not respond ideally to all future situations. This is why I find the restrictions on the President's discretion to increase meat imports so objectionable and why my Administration's support for HR 11545 was so clearly conditioned upon removal of those restrictions and on increasing the minimum access level for meat imports to 1.3 billion pounds annually.

I am prepared to work with the Congress next year to pass a counter-cyclical meat import bill which will provide the stability and certainty the cattle industry requires, while preserving the President's existing discretionary authority and setting an acceptable minimum access level for imports.

JIMMY CARTER

The White House,
November 10, 1978

NURSE TRAINING ACT VETO

I am withholding my approval from S 2416, a bill that would extend a series of programs authorizing special Federal support for the training of nurses.

Although I support a number of its provisions, this bill would continue several Federal nurse training programs whose objectives have been accomplished and for which there is no longer a need. Moreover, the funding authorizations are excessive and unacceptable if we are to reduce the budget deficit to help fight inflation.

For the past 22 years, the Federal government has provided substantial financial support for nursing education. From 1956 through 1977, almost $1.4 billion was

awarded for student traineeships, loans, and scholarships; for construction and basic support for nursing education programs; and for projects to improve nursing education and recruitment.

With the help of this support, the number of active nurses has more than doubled since 1957 to over 1,000,000 in 1978. Ten years ago, in 1968, there were 300 active nurses per 100,000 population in the United States. By the beginning of 1977, this ratio had risen to 395 per 100,000 population.

The outlook is also good for adequate, sustained growth in the supply of nurses. There is, therefore, no reason for the government to provide special support to increase the total supply of professional nurses.

This year the Administration proposed to extend only the authorities for special projects in nursing education and for nurse practitioner training programs, in order to focus Federal nurse training support on areas of greatest national need. This proposal was based on the concept that future Federal assistance should be limited to geographic and specialty areas that need nurses most.

S 2416 would authorize more than $400 million for fiscal years 1979 and 1980, mostly for continued Federal funding of a number of unnecessary special nurse training programs, at a potential cost to the taxpayer far above my budget. At a time of urgent need for budget restraint, we cannot tolerate spending for any but truly essential purposes.

I must point out that nursing training is primarily undergraduate education, and nursing students are eligible for the assistance made available by the government to all students, based on need. I recently signed into law the Middle Income Student Assistance Act, which will significantly expand our basic grant and student loan guarantee programs. Nursing students are also eligible for National Health Service Corps scholarships.

Disapproval of this bill will not cause an abrupt termination of funding of the nurse training programs, since funds are available for fiscal year 1979 under the continuing resolution.

If the Nation is to meet its health care needs at reasonable cost, Federal nursing and other health professions programs must make the greatest contribution to adequate health care at the most reasonable cost. This bill does not meet that test.

The Administration is now conducting a major review of its support for all health professions training, including nursing. Legislative proposals in this area will be made to the 96th Congress. These proposals will recognize the key role of nurses in our society and the need for nurses to play an even greater role in the efficient delivery of health care services.

JIMMY CARTER

The White House,
November 10, 1978

News Conferences,
Major Statements

Texts of President Carter's 1978 News Conferences

January 12, 1978

Following is the White House transcript of President Carter's Jan. 12, 1978, news conference in Washington, D.C., his 23rd since taking office:

THE PRESIDENT: Good afternoon, everybody. Thank you very much.

It is nice to be back home. It is nice to start a new year. I have a brief statement to make before I answer questions.

Much has been said about the messages that I carried on behalf of the American people to leaders of the nations which I visited on the recent trip. But it is also important to focus on the message that I received from them and brought back home.

They are looking to our country to see whether we have the will, the resolve to deal squarely with our energy problems which are also becoming their problems. It is clear that our willingness to curb the enormous American national appetite for imported oil will be a consideration, for instance, in future OPEC oil prices.

As a nation, we are increasing our demand for foreign oil. We may have conservation forced on us by unexpected and rapid increases in oil prices in the future. Our consumers and our industries will pay more and more to foreign countries and with those dollars that go overseas we are in effect exporting American jobs.

In Paris and in Brussels, our own allies expressed concern about whether we can and will enact strong energy legislation. If our own economy is not strong, if our strength is being sapped by excessive imports, then we can't provide the kind of leadership and stability on which the economic well-being of the Western democracies rests so heavily.

The United States has had, and is still faced with, a very large trade deficit which has led recently to exchange market disorders and exchange rate speculation. It is clear that our heavy dependence on imported oil is the main part of our trade problem and that our failure to adopt a comprehensive energy program has badly weakened confidence in our ability to deal with that problem.

Almost every foreign leader stressed the importance of our energy program in terms of our responsibilities for international monetary order and the maintenance of the integrity of the dollar.

We all recognize that while the energy program will not reduce our oil imports overnight, that it will reduce our dependence on foreign oil over the long pull and also permanently. It would improve our trade position, our national economy, the strength of the dollar in a fundamental way.

I believe that we do have the resolve and the national will to deal with the energy problem. The debate in the Congress has been long and divisive and arduous. It has at times tried the patience of all of us. And delay has deferred action, unfortunately, on a number of other important national priorities.

But when we do succeed—and I believe we have an excellent chance to succeed early in this session—we will have accomplished something in which we can take pride; not just here at home, but before the other nations of the world as well.

Thank you. I would like to answer any questions you might have.

Energy Program - 1

Q: Mr. President, I have a question on energy. Has there been any kind of a compromise reached on natural gas pricing? Do you think you will get an energy program and, if you don't, what unilateral steps will you take? And I have a follow-up question.

A: A follow-up to all three of those questions?

There was a substantial amount of progress made by the conference committees just before Christmas. I think that many of the consumer-oriented House members were willing to accept a compromise that was acceptable to many of the senators. The problem has been and still is that there are nine senators for and nine senators against any sort of proposal that has been made up until this time.

Dr. James Schlesinger has been out on the West Coast to meet with the chairman of the committee, Senator Scoop Jackson, and I have talked to Senator Jackson on the phone and he has told me that he has a redetermination to exert his own leadership and profound influence in bringing about a resolution of the present deadlock.

My guess is that the Congress is beginning to realize, many of them have long realized, the importance of this legislation. It will be the first order of business. It is the first priority for this year's work and it is holding up other very important matters that the Congress is interested in.

So I think the answer to your second question is, yes, there will be a compromise reached. It will be acceptable to me and to the country. And I think it will come very early in this session.

The third thing, what will I do if the Congress does not act is something that I am not yet prepared to answer. There are authorities that I have and Dr. James Schlesinger has as head of the Energy Department that would be much more unsettling to our Nation's economy, the imposition of import charges on oil that we hope to avoid and I think the Members of the House and Senate want to avoid those kinds of disruptive actions just as much as we do.

The present laws are inadequate to deal with the increasing problems of the energy demands which are met so excessively by imports of oil. I think we do need to have passed adequate incentives. What we have proposed to the Congress would give oil producers for new oil the highest price in the world and it would mean that in natural gas, there would be a substantial increase in prices to the producers compared to what we have had in the past.

I think our proposal is fair and well balanced and I think there is a growing consensus within the Congress that this is a basis on which to reach an agreement and I hope to avoid having to take administrative action that would be damaging to the economy in order to protect us in the future.

NAACP Energy Statement

Q: My follow-up was simply were you surprised at the NAACP's opposition to your program and do you think it will have an impact?

A: I was surprised. I talked to the President of the NAACP this morning, Benjamin Hooks. He said the major thrust of their report was that they want to have a sustained growth in the economy and therefore provide additional jobs for people in our Nation. But I disagree strongly with the conclusion that the NAACP reached, that the way to do that was to channel enormous sums of money, 40, 50, 60, 70 billion dollars into the pockets of those who own the major oil companies, out of the pockets of consumers.

I want to have a strong economy, too. But I don't think that is the right way to do it.

Soviet Union, Cuba and Africa

Q: Mr. President, everywhere you traveled except Poland we were told that you and the leaders talked about Soviet and Cuban penetration in the Horn of Africa, but we only got very generalized and vague statements on this. Can you enunciate the depth of our concern and what can we do about it except jawbone?

A: We have taken a position concerning Africa that we would use our influence to bring about peace without shipping arms to the disputing parties and without our injecting ourselves into disputes that could best be resolved by Africans, both those parties that are in dispute and the Organization of African Unity. The Soviets have done just the opposite. They, in effect, contributed to the war that is presently taking place between Somalia and Ethiopia.

They sold excessive quantities of arms and weapons to both Somalia and to Ethiopia. The war began using Soviet weapons and now they are shipping large quantities of weapons, some men, and they are also dispatching Cubans into Ethiopia, perhaps to become combatants themselves. We have expressed our concern to the Soviets in very strong terms.

We have shared the concerns that we feel with the leaders that I have visited, both the cumulative group of countries that join with us in the NATO alliance, and specifically with France, the Middle Eastern countries and India. We have had unanimous response from them sharing our concern about the Soviet Union's unwarranted involvement in Africa. I am very concerned about the loss of life now.

Our hope is that the Somalians might call publicly for negotiations to begin immediately to resolve the Ogaden dispute. One possibility, of course, would be to go to the Security Council of the United Nations or to the permanent members of the Security Council. But the basic negotiation ought to take place between those two nations themselves.

So I think that there are things that we can do to express our concern publicly, to offer our good services in support of the African nations who are responsible, to support the Organization of African Unity and in the United Nations to let our voice be heard. But I hope that we can induce the Soviets and the Cubans not to send either soldiers or weapons into that area and call for and achieve a rapid initiation of negotiations.

Interest Rates

Q: Mr. President, on another subject, will Bill Miller, as head of the Fed, mean lower interest rates?

A: I want lower interest rates, and I know the Fed does also, I am sure, including Chairman Burns and certainly William Miller, who will be chairman in the future, I hope.

We have here a problem in stabilizing the value of the dollar, which is the basis for most international trade on the one hand, of preventing excessive inflation, which is compatible with that, and still having interest rates low enough to encourage businesses to invest in stocks, to encourage them to create jobs with expansion, and to make sure that we have an economy that is stable and predictable.

So I think that both Chairman Burns and Miller would like to have lower interest rates. I hate to repeat myself again, but I think that until the question of energy is resolved the uncertainty about this subject and the realization that our excessive imports of oil or adverse balance of trade is going to be permanent, those two things are going to contribute to the deleterious effects of increasing interest rates and also uncertainty in the stock market.

Mr. Bradley?

Marston Controversy - 1

Q: Mr. President, you promised during the campaign to appoint U.S. attorneys strictly—without any consideration of political aspects or influence—strictly on the basis of merit. May we first of all assume that is also your standard for removing political attorneys, U.S. attorneys, and, if so, why are you removing the U.S. attorney in Philadelphia, David Marston, who on the surface seems to have a credible record which includes the prosecution and conviction of a number of prominent Democrats?

A: The answer to the first part of your question is certainly yes. I intend to make sure that all the appointments that are made to federal judgeships and also to U.S. attorneys are made on the basis of merit, and I think until each appointment is observed very carefully—who was in office compared to who is the replacement for that person in office—that it would be hard to criticize a particular instance.

I have recently learned about the U.S. attorney named Marston. This is one of hundreds of U.S. attorneys in the country, and I was not familiar with the case until it became highly publicized. The Attorney General is handling the investigation of the replacement for Mr. Marston. I think the focusing of attention on this case will certainly doubly inspire him to make a selection that will be admirable and a credit to him and to me, and I have not interfered in it at all.

Before I first heard about Mr. Marston the Attorney General had already decided to replace him. We have encouraged the members of Congress, Democratic members of Congress, not to be involved in trying to influence the Attorney General about who should be the new U.S. attorney there.

I will be glad to answer a follow-up question.

Q: Is it the Attorney General's feeling, sir, that he has not done a good job?

A: I can't say that Mr. Marston has or has not done a good job. He was appointed at the last minute under the previous administration. He was not a practicing attorney, had never had any prosecuting experience. And the only criticism that I have heard about him was that he had a very heavy commitment to call in press conferences and so forth when he obtained evidence or when a grand jury took action in an indictment. I think this is not unique in the country.

I have not discussed the case with the Attorney General and asked him specifically what was wrong with Marston. I don't know who he will recommend to me for the replacement. But I can assure you that when the replacement is announced that there will be the emphasis on the quality of a replacement, his qualifications compared to the incumbent. And I have absolute confidence that the Attorney General will do a good job in that respect.

Energy Program - 2

Q: Could I have a follow-up on energy? You have said that you want a fair energy bill for Congress.

A: Yes, I do.

Q: And you have indicated repeatedly, today again, a warning about funneling undue amounts of money from the pockets of the consumers to the oil companies. Yet your Energy Department has told some northeastern congressmen that it will no longer continue weekly monitoring of home heating oil prices; that it will not monitor fuel prices at the refinery gates; and that if the prices to consumers do go up unduly this winter they will take action next winter. Now, how does that protect the consumers against a ripoff?

A: If what you say is true, then I don't see that it does protect the consumers adequately. I am not familiar with that statement, but I will find out an answer for you and let you know the answer.

Marston Controversy - 2

Q: Mr. President?

A: Yes.

Q: Mr. President, I would like to pursue the Marston question one step further. There have been reports that, first of all, Mr. Marston is in the midst of an investigation which involves two Democratic congressmen from Pennsylvania. There have been reports that at least one of them has sought to contact the White House or you yourself to in effect get Mr. Marston off their backs. I wonder if you are aware of any such contacts or intent, however informal, and what your reaction to such a contact would be?

A: The only contact I have had with any congressmen directly was I think Congressman Eilberg called me and asked that we look into it. At that time, the Attorney General had already decided to make the change. When I talked to the Attorney General about it, before Eilberg had let his views be known on the telephone call, he said that the replacement would be made and that he hoped that the Democratic Congress members who had shown an interest in it would not be involved in trying to decide who would be the replacement.

This has been an assurance given to us by Mr. Eilberg. As far as any investigation of members of Congress, however, I am not familiar with that at all and it was never mentioned to me.

Q: Could you tell me what reason Mr. Eilberg gave for asking you to look into it?

A: He wanted the replacement process to be expedited. The decision had already been made to replace Mr. Marston and I think the Attorney General can answer your question better specifically. And my importunity to Mr. Eilberg was that it would be better if the Congress members would let the Attorney General make the selection on the basis of merit alone and that was Mr. Eilberg's comment to me that he had no interest in who would be the replacement at all, but he thought that because of the confusion there, that the decision that the Attorney General had already made ought to be expedited and I feel the same way.

I have complete confidence that the replacement will be chosen on the basis of merit and not politics.

Tax Cuts

Q: Mr. President, it seems now that the economy is improving. Why should the tax cut that your administration is proposing be any larger than an amount necessary to compensate for the increased energy taxes and Social Security taxes?

A: The tax proposal that I intend to make to the Congress will have an effective date of October 1st. We anticipate if projections hold true, that the first two quarters of 1978 will show very good economic progress in the growth rate, in the controlling of unemployment and inflation. But we believe that by the end of the third quarter, October 1st, there will be a need to sustain the economic growth that we think we will experience.

We are not trying to deal with an economy that is tottering, or on the verge of collapse or in any danger. We have basically a very strong national economy.

The goal that we have set for ourselves for 1978 is a 5 per cent growth rate. We were very fortunate in 1977 in reaching the goals that we set for ourselves both in unemployment, as you know, and also in the growth rate. But we believe that a substantial tax reduction is needed for that purpose.

There are two other reasons. One is I want to reduce the portion of our gross national product that is collected and spent by the federal government. In my opinion, it is too high. It is approaching 23 per cent and by the time I go out of office, I would like to have that down to no more than 21 per cent. Also with the encroachment of inflation, it moves people into a higher tax bracket with paying a higher percentage of their income in taxes just because their dollars that they earn are cheaper and they get more of them.

So with inflation, you have in effect the imposition of higher and higher tax rates to the American people if the laws don't change. So for that reason also, I want to reduce the rate of taxes paid by the American people.

So I think that a substantial tax reduction is needed in 1978 and I believe the Congress will agree. So we intend to do all three things, to compensate for increases in Social Security tax, to keep the economy moving strongly, and also to compensate for the effects of inflation.

Oil Supplies

Q: Mr. President, when talking about the aggravation of oil imports to the U.S. government's strategic petroleum stockpile, I think your decision is to acquire one billion barrels of oil on the world market. The GAO and others have recommended that we use oil we already own, in the Elk Hills Naval Petroleum Reserve and that would save, I think, as you are doling out, about $20 billion you are going to spend in foreign oil. We could reduce this by half, $10 billion, saving if we used our existing naval supplies.

Why don't we do that?

A: We are in effect increasing the production of American oil to cut down on the amount that we have to purchase. At Elk Hills, at Teapot Dome, we are trying to increase the importing of oil to the continental United States from Alaska. We are trying to maintain the production of oil, sour oil to some degree, in California in addition to reducing overall consumption of oil and energy and shifting to coal.

At the same time, it is very important to us to have stability in the world oil market and protect us from some interruption in the future over which we have no control.

So we have set a goal for ourselves that by 1985, we will have a billion barrels of oil stored in a secure place in salt domes in the United States so that we can have an eight or 10-month supply in case overseas oil is interrupted in coming to us.

So the sum total of what we propose is to do exactly what you describe. Whether domestic oil actually goes into the supply system of our country and foreign oil goes into the underground storage really is of no consequence because the overall consumption of oil plus the import or use of oil to build up our reserves is the factor that it controls how much we import.

Q: My question is, it goes to the point there is a $10 billion savings. We already own the Elk Hills Naval oil reserve.

A: When we sell that oil, if it is on the commercial market the federal Treasury gets the money back for that oil. So it is really just swapping dollars. It may be very difficult to transport the oil from Elk Hills and identify a particular gallon or barrel of oil that has to go into a salt dome in Louisiana.

Q: They talk about swap arrangements particularly with Japan. Japan would be very happy to have that very sweet Elk Hills oil and they would give us their Mideast oil.

A: I understand. But we are trying to do what I have just said, build up the adequate supply of oil for reserve and cut down consumption and imports at the same time.

Yes:

Border Patrol

Q: Who did you say? (Laughter) I thought you were looking over there.

Sir, I have a question I want to take up with you. On Jan. 5, a helicopter, a border patrolman on board was shot at from the Mexican side of the border, and according to the Immigration Service, no plans are being made to make a formal, big, major protest on that through the White House or the State Department to the Mexican government. The families of the border patrolmen are very concerned. They think if you don't make a major protest, you will get this again.

A: Thank you very much. I will certainly look into it. We have only recently begun to use helicopters on the border patrol. We have in Mexico, however, in close cooperation with the Mexican government, used our helicopters for the detection of poppy fields that produce heroin and other hard drugs in Mexico.

My understanding was that the helicopter fired at was in the process of trying to destroy heroin poppy fields.

Q: No, sir, it was on this side of the border. The helicopter shot at was on this side of the border; was shot at from the Mexican side.

A: I understand.

Q: This has happened before with airplanes but not helicopters. It is very dangerous with helicopters.

A: Yes, until this past year we have never used helicopters for that purpose. But we are now.

Marston Controversy - 3

Q: Mr. President, to come back to the Marston matter for a minute, without again saying yourself and the Attorney General's intention to appoint someone at least as qualified as he is, it is still not clear to me why he is being removed in the first place. Could you expand on what you have said already a little bit?

A: I think I have covered it at least as far as I am able to. I have never looked into Mr. Marston's qualifications. I depend upon the Attorney General to assess the quality and the performance of duty of the U.S. attorneys around the country. And when he decides that a U.S. attorney needs to be replaced, then he makes the judgment about who ought to be the replacement.

He made, quite early in the past year, a decision that Mr. Marston should be replaced. I have never asked him to delineate all the reasons. My only involvement in it at all was to expedite the process.

As I have told you, I have complete confidence in the Attorney General's judgment. I think he will recommend to me someone who will make me and him proud and particularly since there has been such a large focusing of attention on the case the last few weeks. And by the publicity that has accrued to that case, I am not sure but I want to make sure now that when this selection is made it will be a superb person, and I hope and expect that it will be a man who is at least qualified, perhaps better qualified than Mr. Marston, or perhaps a woman.

Smoking and HEW

Q: Your Secretary of HEW wants to spend $23 million to persuade Americans to stop smoking, while there are people on your staff, Mr. President, who smoke in public like chimneys. Could you explain this apparent contradiction? (Laughter)

A: I don't see the contradiction there. I can't deny that the Secretary of HEW, who is responsible for the nation's health, points out as have his predecessors for 15 or 20 years, that smoking is a danger to health. The U.S. Surgeon General, as you know, years ago confirmed this in tests. I happen to think that that is his responsibility. It is not his responsibility to tell a particular American citizen whether they can or cannot smoke.

Q: I understand, sir. But would you ask your White House staff to set a national example? (Laughter)

A: No, sir.

Q: Okay.

Middle East

Q: When you were in Egypt meeting with President Sadat, President Sadat emerged from that meeting saying that your views and his on the Middle East were essentially identical. Does that mean that you think the Israelis should withdraw from all 20 settlements they have in the Sinai plus their West Bank settlements before there can be peace in the Middle East?

A: It is not for me to decide the specifics of an ultimate settlement; either between Israel and Egypt or Israel and Jordan or Israel and the other nations involved or the Palestinians.

I think that it is accurate that President Sadat and I see the Middle East question almost identically. I have not been involved and don't intend to get involved in the military settlement that is now being negotiated in Cairo. The position of our government is now and has been that Israeli settlements on occupied territory are illegal and that they contravene the Geneva Conference decisions that were made.

The UN Resolution 242 is the basis for the ultimate decision. All the nations involved have espoused 242, and 338 later on, which set up the Geneva Conference with ourselves and the Soviets as chairmen. We have in that language that says Israel will withdraw from occupied territory.

Combined with that requirement, though, is that Israel will have secure borders including a realization of security from the attitude of her neighbors. So this is an extremely complicated subject as you well know. I can't say that on every specific instance that President Sadat and I will agree on details. We didn't discuss those details.

I think that it is best for us just to add our good offices when we can, support both men as they go to the negotiating table. Secretary Vance will be in Jerusalem with the foreign ministers of the two countries involved and our position on the settlements has not changed.

FRANK CORMIER (AP): Thank you, Mr. President. ∎

January 30, 1978

Following is the White House transcript of President Carter's Jan. 30 news conference, his 24th since taking office:

THE PRESIDENT: Good afternoon. Please be seated.

I have two brief opening statements to make. The first one involves the major domestic programs that we will pursue in 1978. I would like to review briefly for you my proposals for reforming the tax system, for reducing taxes, for continuing to reduce the unemployment rate, and for preventing and controlling inflation.

These proposals are the centerpiece of the Administration's economic program for 1978. Economic policy depends, for its success, on a very careful balance between different interests, between sometimes conflicting national needs; between doing too much on the one hand, doing too little on the other. To modify one element of a balanced plan can often destroy this balance and can aggravate our economic problems.

I want to emphasize four elements of our proposals that carefully preserve this balance. First, there is tax reductions. We proposed a net tax reduction of $25 billion designed to create almost a million new jobs by the end of 1978. (The President meant to say 1979)

If they are enacted, the economy should continue to grow at a rate of about 4½ to 5 percent and unemployment should fall below 6 percent by the end of next year. For the vast majority of taxpayers, these reductions will offset the increase in rates that was necessary to prevent bankruptcy of our Social Security system. For 1978 there will be three times as much tax reduction as there is tax increase for the Social Security system. And the same ratio, three-to-one, will prevail in 1979.

Second, our tax reform proposal will allow us to have an immediate tax reduction while making substantial progress toward comprehensive reform, a simpler and a fairer tax system.

Without these needed reforms, we would not be able to afford so large a tax reduction. They comprise about $9 billion in savings, at the same time providing equality and fairness.

Third is jobs. I have asked for over $700 million more in new funds for youth jobs and, in addition, have asked the Congress to continue the high level of public service jobs for 1979, which is about twice as much as a year ago. In addition, I will shortly forward to the Congress a $400 million program to encourage private businesses to hire the hard core unemployed.

We are balancing the need for public service jobs with the need for private opportunities to reduce unemployment.

Fourth, inflation: Our program is voluntary, requiring the cooperation of government, business, labor and all our citizens. I have asked each group to hold its increases in wages and prices below the level that it averaged in increases for the last two years.

This fair and flexible program and voluntary program will not stop inflation overnight. But it is our best hope for bringing it under control. We simply cannot let inflation overtake us without taking action.

In sum, we proposed an economic program which is balanced. It will not please everyone. As I said in my State of the Union Address, we cannot do everything for everybody. We must be willing to face difficult decisions.

In developing our economic program, we have made difficult decisions and we propose an economic proposal or program that will sustain growth, that will increase employment, and reduce inflation.

The other thing I would like to do very briefly is to outline the history of the Soviet satellite, the Cosmos 954. This satellite, which had a nuclear power source on it, was launched on the 18th of September, last year. It was obvious to us later on that the Soviets were having trouble controlling the satellite. On the 19th of December, we set up a small task force in the White House. On the 6th of January, we felt that control had been lost, and I decided personally to notify the Soviets on the 12th of January that we were aware of their problems; to offer our help in monitoring the path of the satellite and to begin preparing jointly to predict where it would fall and also to prepare for handling it if it should contact the earth.

The Soviets replied that it was designed so that it would be destroyed as it came back into earth, and it was designed also so there was no possibility of an atomic explosion.

On the 17th and 18th of January, we notified the key Congressional leaders, some of our allies around the world who were capable of joining us in a tracking effort, and the Soviets a day later, on the 19th, repeated their comment it will not explode.

On the 22nd of January, we went back to the Soviets to ask them to give us an update to confirm the information we had from monitoring sources. And on the 23rd of January, the Soviets notified us that it would probably enter the atmosphere the following day, which was the 24th.

Early on the morning of the 24th, I was notified that the satellite would enter the atmosphere quite early. We did not know whether it would hit between Hawaii on a very high curve up to the northern part of Canada or the Western Coast of Africa, because sometimes the satellites can skip from one place to another as they enter the atmosphere. It, as you know, entered the atmosphere in Canada.

I immediately called Prime Minister Pierre Trudeau and informed him about the approximate location, which later turned out to be accurate, and on the 29th, as you know, just recently, the remains of the satellite have been recovered.

The last satellite we put into the earth's orbit with an atomic power source was in 1965. This satellite at the conclusion of its useful life was raised into a higher orbit that has a life span of at least 4,000 years.

I think we need to have more rigid safety precautions assured among all nations in earth-orbiting satellites. In fact, we would be glad to forego the deployment of any such satellite altogether and will pursue that option along with the Soviet Union.

The only time a satellite needs a long-lasting power source that is free of the use of solar energy which can be derived from the sun is when you go into deep outer space; for instance, if we send a probe to the outer planets there would not be an adequate source of energy from the sun to trigger our solar cells. We might need power from atomic sources then.

But I see no reason for us to continue with the option of nations to have earth-orbiting satellites unless much more advanced safety precautions can be initiated.

Middle East - 1

Q: Mr. President, since I assume the subject will come up when you meet with President Sadat, could you give us a general outline of your view toward our helping Egypt to acquire arms?

A: We have been, of course, facing the continuing prospect for a number of years of providing some weapons into the Mideast, heavily to Israel, also to Saudi Arabia, to Iran and to some degree the non-attack weapons to Egypt.

All these nations have requests to us for weapons. They have been committed to those nations to some degree by my two predecessors, and reconfirmed in some instances by me.

The National Security Council will make a report to me early this week recommending from the State Department, from the Defense Department, from the National Security Adviser, what weapons to recommend to the Congress.

After that point, the Congress will have a thirty-day plus a twenty-day period to respond affirmatively or not.

I will decide later on this week what to recommend to the Congress.

The Egyptians have, in the past, requested F-5-E fighter planes, one that is used extensively around the world for export purposes primarily and Israel and Saudi Arabia have requested other weapons. They have some F-5s.

Marston Firing - 1

Q: Mr. President, have you seen anything improper in the handling of the Marston affair? Have you learned any lessons from it, and all of its ramifications, and do you contemplate any changes in procedures for appointing and removing U.S. Attorneys?

A: In the first place, I see nothing improper in the handling of the case. I made a campaign commitment that any appointee to a position as U.S. Attorney or a judgeship would be appointed on the basis of merit and this campaign commitment will be carried out.

There has also been a statement made by me during the campaign that, all other factors equal, that I would choose someone for those positions, or even for the Supreme Court, whose basic political philosophy was compatible with mine. The fact is at this point we have about one-third of the U.S. Attorneys around the country who are Republicans. I think when I took office, only three Democrats were in office. And I don't think that Nixon or Ford appointed any Democrats during the eight-year period. So far as I know, they haven't.

I think that the Attorney General has handled the case as well as possible. I explained to you at the last press conference what I knew about the facts then and so far as I know, there is no impropriety at all. I understand from the Attorney General that he has now received recommendations for five highly-qualified nominees to take over that responsibility. He will begin interviewing them tomorrow. And the likelihood is that he would make a selection this week.

Q: Mr. President, but isn't it time to put aside the Justice Department and in that direction how about an end to the political firings of Federal judges and prosecutors wholly apart from seeing to it

that there are Democratic replacements highly qualified?

A: I think we have moved strongly in that direction. Obviously, a Federal Judge is not subject to being removed. The Constitution gives the President a responsibility to appoint those officials if confirmed by the Senate. And, of course, a U.S. Attorney can be fired or discharged from office only by the President himself. That does not apply to Federal judges. They, as you know, serve for life.

We have, I think, moved a great step in that direction. Over a period of many generations the Members of the Senate have become heavily involved in recommendations for judges. Since I have been in office we have set up selection boards for all Circuit judges. I think in fifteen states the Senators—which is a new development—have now set up selection boards to recommend highly-qualified District judges. But I agree with you that this is a move that we should make.

I think you will notice that when we have made selections for, say, Circuit judges or when we have made two selections now for Director of the FBI, there were Republicans involved in both cases, I think, for the FBI.

Q: How about setting up an independent blue ribbon committee that would monitor firings, as well as appointments, deciding each case on the merits, not on politics?

A: The Attorney General in the speech in May, and preceding that in March, advocated that this general procedure be followed. I don't remember the exact text of that speech. But I believe in every instance when the results have been made known that there has been no criticism of the person chosen. In some instances, U.S. Senators have specifically come forward and advocated that a Republican U.S. Attorney be kept in office.

I remember once in particular in New York that Pat Moynihan said to keep the Republicans in office and we have done so.

Q: Mr. President?

A: Yes?

Middle East - 2

Q: On the Middle East, do you have a clear idea now from Prime Minister Begin as to whether or not he will authorize new settlements in the West Bank and in the Sinai, and do you believe that Israel over a period of time ought to phase out those settlements in return for real peace?

A: I have covered this many times. Our position on settlements in occupied territory has been that they are illegal, that they are an obstacle to peace. When Prime Minister Begin was over here and when Foreign Minister Dayan was here, this question arose.

My understanding of their commitment was that no new settlements would be authorized by the Government, that any increase in settlers would be an expansion of existing settlements as much as possible within the aegis of the military.

The Geneva Conference agreement is that civilians should not go in to settle permanently in occupied territories. I think the Israeli Government has not authorized the Shilo settlement other than as an archaeological exploration project.

I have not yet heard from Prime Minister Begin directly but I have had information that this is a policy of the Israeli Government, that this is not an authorized settlement.

Marston Firing - 2

Q: Mr. President, let's sort of complete the record on that Marston Case. On the morning of January 12, according to your statement at the Justice Department, you learned that a Member of Congress was of investigative interest to either the Justice Department or the U.S. Attorney. Later that day at your news conference you said, "As far as any investigation of Members of Congress, however, I am not familiar with that at all and it was never mentioned to me." Do you see any conflict there?

A: No, I don't. I think if you read the question to which I referred, it is obviously related to whether or not I had known anything about any investigation in November. And the answer was no, no discussion ever had been made. The only inkling I had at all that Mr. Eilberg was involved with an investigation was that Frank Moore mentioned, just as I was leaving my office to come over to the press conference, that his name had been raised in conjunction with an investigation. I was not told at that time and had no idea that he was being investigated himself, Eilberg.

Q: Mr. President, could you tell us—this question goes more to philosophy, I guess, than anything—could you tell us why you felt compelled to respond to a phone call from a Congressman in Philadelphia to, as you put it, expedite the removal of a U.S. Attorney, one of more than 90 in the country? And secondly, do you really believe that these actions by your Administration over the last two or three weeks with regard to Mr. Marston square, really square, with the commitment you made in your campaign to remove the Justice Department from the spoils system traditional to American politics?

A: To answer your last question first, yes, I do think that our actions are compatible with my campaign statements which I have said earlier. On an average day, I get either personal letters from Congress Members or telephone calls about 10 or 12 inquiries or requests for the replacement of a public official or the appointment of someone to fill a vacancy. In most instances, as relates to the Federal Judiciary, the inquiries or recommendations come from U.S. Senators.

In historical terms, when both Senators are Republican Senators, then the Members of Congress and the Governors are consulted on who are qualified people and so forth. This was a routine matter for me and I did not consider my taking the

telephone call from Congressman Eilberg, nor relaying his request to the Attorney General, to be ill-advised at all. If it occurred now, I would do the same.

Middle East - 3

Q: Mr. President, do you have an overall view of the final borders you would like to see for Israel? Do you expect Israel to return to the 1967 borders in all aspects, especially East Jerusalem?

P: No. I don't have a map or a plan that ought to be the final border delineation between Israel and her neighbors. I have always operated and made my statements under the framework and within the constraints of United Nations Resolution 242, which calls for Israel to withdraw from occupied territories.

Israel interprets this language differently, of course, from the Arab neighbors. The Arab neighbors say that Israel ought to withdraw from all occupied territories. Israel says there is some flexibility there and that the thrust of UN Resolution 242 is an exchange, in effect, for portions of the occupied territory for guaranteed peace.

The three elements that I have pursued is, one, a delineation of final borders; secondly, a feeling or conviction on the part of the Israelis that their security was preserved, which would involve both their own military strength, the delineation of the borders and the attitude now and in the future of their neighbors.

The second question, of course, is the definition of real peace. What does peace mean? Does it simply mean a cessation of hostility or belligerency, or does it mean open borders, trade, tourism or diplomatic exchange, the location of ambassadors and so forth?

I have taken the more definitive definition as my own preference. And the other thing, of course, is to deal in all its aspects with the Palestinian question.

But I have never tried to put forward in my own mind or to any of the Mideastern leaders a map in saying this is where the lines should be drawn.

Coal Strike

Q: Mr. President, our Energy Secretary Schlesinger, has expressed some recent concern about the duration of the coal strike. I wonder to what extent you share that concern and whether you might see the necessity to use the Taft-Hartley Act?

A: We are very hopeful that the coal mine operators and the United Coal Workers will expedite a resolution of their differences. This past weekend the news was not good. I see no immediate prospect of having to exercise the Taft-Hartley provisions. It only provides for the President the authority to intercede if the national security is in danger. We certainly have not arrived at that point yet.

There are some things that we can do, and I have discussed them with the entire

Cabinet this morning and, of course, with Secretary Schlesinger in particular. The gaseous diffusion plants for the production of atomic fuels, for instance, are heavy users of energy. We are reducing the power consumed by them.

There is a need for citizens who live in the heavily hit regions, because of the snow storms, to cut down on consumption of energy because transportation won't let even the available supplies come into those regions. But I have no present intention at all of trying to intercede nor to exercise my authority under the Taft-Hartley Act.

Q: Mr. President?

A: Yes, sir?

Satellite Safety

Q: Mr. President, regarding your concern about satellites and the safety precautions, in taking this up with the Russians will you try to dissuade them from their practice of putting nuclear reactors into space in the future?

P: Yes; certainly in earth orbit. I think that this is something that we should explore. There are two factors, though. One is to try to evolve a surefire, safety requirement that would prevent a recurrence of any atomic active material reaching the earth or the atmosphere where human beings might breathe it. If we cannot evolve those fail-safe methods, then I think there ought to be a total prohibition against earth-orbiting satellites.

I would favor at this moment an agreement with the Soviets to prohibit earth-orbiting satellites with atomic radiation material in them.

Q: Mr. President, do you have any idea what the deal is on that satellite up there? We get all these reports. One day it is not radioactive; the next day it is. Do you have any late information about just what the status of that thing is? Or whether there is any danger?

A: No, I know nothing at this point that hasn't already been put into the press. One, I do know they have located a crater, about a nine-foot dimension, that it is radioactive and that a search group from one of our own helicopters working with the Canadians is at the site. But the configuration of the remains of the satellite or whether or not they are now retrieving it from the riverbed where it is located, I do not know.

Illegal Aliens

Q: Mr. President, last August in your Immigration Message, you said you were "not considering reintroduction of a bracero-type program for the temporary importation of farm workers."

Last week, Secretary Bergland down in Mexico City had an airport press conference at which he apparently gave some Mexican newspapers the idea that we were considering such a program and were considering importing three million braceros, and they have been writing a lot of stories about it.

He has tried to deny it. Could you state your position on it, sir?

A: We have no plans whatsoever to reinitiate a bracero program. Our own proposal to deal with the undocumented workers or illegal alien question has already been submitted to the public, and that encompasses what we proposed. It does not comprise a bracero-type program.

Soviet Killer Satellites

Q: There are reports that the Soviets have or will soon have the capability to disrupt sending of military orders by satellite. Could you tell us whether they are accurate or not?

P: My information is that that report is not accurate.

Nazi March

Q: Mr. President, there is a group of American Nazis in Skokie, a suburb of Chicago, which is contemplating a march that is in a predominantly Jewish neighborhood and there might be victims there of the Nazi concentration camps from World War II. Do you have any plan to use the moral weight of your office to try to discourage this kind of a march?

A: I deplore it. I wish that this demonstration of an abhorrent political and social philosophy would not be present at all. This is a matter that is in the American Federal courts, as you know, and under the framework of the Constitutional guarantee for free speech. I believe under carefully controlled conditions the courts have ruled that it is legal and that they have a right to act this way.

We have the same problem, as you know, in other parts of the Nation; in the South with the Ku Klux Klan, and others. I don't have any inclination to intercede further. I think it is best to leave it in the hands of the court.

Plan To Be Missionary

Q: Mr. President, is it true that you plan to become a missionary after leaving office and, if so, how soon after leaving, for how long and where—(Laughter)—and if I can pursue it, have you discussed this with Mrs. Carter? (Laughter)

A: I discussed it with my wife who was a member of the Sunday school class that I taught yesterday morning.

I have, as a Baptist layman, been part of the group that advocated an expanded church mission program, but I have not decided whether or not I would want to be a missionary after I complete my term as President.

Covert Surveillance

Q: Mr. President, on March 15th of 1976, you told the Chicago Council on Foreign Relations that the American people have had their fill of covert manipulation. The executive order you signed last week, January 24, provides a procedure for the NSC to approve covert manipulation.

I am wondering if the American people have had their fill of covert manipulation while you are continuing to provide this procedure for allowing it?

A: I don't believe that the executive order would permit, as you call it, covert manipulations. It does permit the surveillance of certain groups in the United States. The only way that an American citizen can be put under surveillence clandestine or secret surveillence is as a result of an order by a Federal judge with a warrant.

If someone is strongly suspected of being an agent of a foreign power, working against the security of our country, then with approval of the Attorney General to assure that it is a proper function and with my own approval, too, that is permitted.

But that is no departure from any past—

Q: I am talking about Section 1302. It says the SCC, Special Coordination Committee, shall consider and submit to the President a policy recommendation including all dissents on special activity and then Section 4.212 defines special activities as activities conducted abroad in support of national foreign policy objectives, which are planned and executed so that the role of the United States Government is not apparent or acknowledged publicly which seems to be a covert operation.

A: Covert, as you know, has a meaning of non-publicized or secret. Under any circumstance where we feel that it is necessary to have a so-called covert action of any kind overseas, then it has to be decided in the White House. The President is notified and approves it personally.

The Secretary of State and the Attorney General are involved and the Congressional Intelligence Committees are also informed. So this is a very careful prevention of any abuse if that should ever become necessary.

Farmers' Parity Demand

Q: Mr. President, could I ask you about the farmers' demands for 100 percent parity? They have been outside the White House gates several times recently.

Have you ever stated that you are flatly opposed to 100 percent parity, and if so—if not, what are your views on that specific demand; secondly, what would 100 percent parity cost in terms of increasing the Federal budget; and thirdly, what would it cost the American consumer?

A: I would guess to guarantee 100 percent parity for every farm product would cost 20 or 25 billion dollars in the Federal budget. It would also mean that the price of American farm products would be extraordinarily high and that they would be noncompetitive in international markets.

I think the request for or demand for 100 percent of parity is not well founded. There needs to be some flexibility obviously, and that is what is provided under the 1977 Agriculture Act.

This act, I believe, will go a long way toward meeting the legitimate needs of the American farmer. It only became effective the first day of October 1977. It has not been effective yet for a crop season and we, in implementing that bill, will have a greatly expanded financial benefit for the American farmer, increased support prices and target prices.

Also, we have had a very fine and successful effort for foreign sales and in establishing a reserve supply of feed grains and food grains primarily held and controlled by farmers, I think will bring some stability to the marketplace and prevent the wild fluctuations which hurt the farmer and the consumer. But 100 percent of parity in my opinion would be too costly.

Tax Cuts

Q: Mr. President, your Treasury Secretary this morning told the Ways and Means Committee that you would rather swallow a cut in your tax cuts rather than increase the $60 billion deficit. How are you going to deal with Chairman Ullman's intention to trim the reforms and probably trim the tax cuts, too?

A: You know Chairman Ullman is obviously entitled to his opinion, and I have never claimed that we had complete compatibility of opinion between myself and the chairmen of the committees either in the House or Senate.

As I pointed out in my opening statement, our entire economic package is a well-balanced one, and without the tax reforms which comprise about $9 billion it will not be possible to have even a $25 billion tax reduction without a very serious additional Federal deficit. I think the Federal deficit is enough. I wish it was much lower, and I intend to reduce it year-by-year until the end of my term.

We could have had about a $20 billion lower Federal deficit had we not advocated a tax cut. But there you have to balance off the advantages from a tax cut that is substantial and reducing the Federal deficit in a very rigid way. I think we made the right choice.

We also have to deal with the jobs programs, and we had an increase in Federal spending to put our people back to work, to cut down the unemployment rate. At the same time, we can't stimulate the economy too much or we would run into an increased rate of inflation.

So those four factors have to go together. I think we have put them together in a very careful way. If the Congress should change any of those factors—which I hope they will not—then we would have to use our own influence in the Congress and with the American people to try to induce them to accept some reasonable alternative which would still keep a balanced economic package.

FRANK CORMIER (AP): Thank you, Mr. President.

THE PRESIDENT: Thank you very much.

February 17, 1978

Following is the White House transcript of President Carter's news conference Feb. 17 in Cranston, R.I., his 25th news conference since taking office:

THE PRESIDENT: Thank you very much.

It is nice to be in New England, in Rhode Island, and I am very proud to have a press conference here for the Nation.

I have just talked to the Secretary of Labor about progress on the settlement of the coal strike. They are making good progress. No final agreement has been reached.

I have been in coal mines in Pennsylvania and other places to see the miners who work. I know that they are hard-working and patriotic Americans. They and the industry leaders both recognize there is a tremendous responsibility on their shoulders because the future of the Unions, the future of an effective collective bargaining process, the future of the coal industry, and the welfare of our Nation depends upon the success of these negotiations.

They have been bargaining now steadily since they began at the White House a day and a half ago. They continued in their discussions until 2:00 o'clock this morning and then after that management with the Secretary of Labor from 2:30 until 5:00 in the morning. And I have asked them to stay at the bargaining table until a final agreement is reached.

I have confidence that they will be successful because they and I want to avoid the necessity for me as President to take more serious action if the bargaining process is not effective. The whole Nation is looking to them with hope and confidence.

Before I answer your questions, I would like to cover one other point that is very crucial to New England, and that is the Nation's economy. In many ways our economy last year was good. The inflation rate went down; and wages, profits, production, housing starts, real income, investment, all went up.

Four million new jobs were created, an all-time record, and many of these jobs, I am glad to say were in New England. Employment here in New England last year went up 5½ percent. The unemployment rate dropped three full percentage points, from 8½ percent down to 5½ percent. But unemployment and inflation is still higher than I am willing to accept and so my top priority this year on the domestic scene is still the economy.

I have asked the Congress to help me put into effect a coherent program to make more jobs and to bring inflation closer under control. We need a cooperative anti-inflation effort, with voluntary action being taken by industry and by labor to keep wages and prices from pushing each other up.

We need an expanded jobs program to help those who are hit hardest by unemployment. Next week I will send to the Congress legislation that would reauthorize the $12 billion Comprehensive Employment and Training Act, provide for 725,000 public service jobs, and for a billion dollar youth employment and training program.

Also, we need tax reduction and tax reform. They go together. They add up to $25 billion in net cuts in the income taxes Americans have to pay, and they are also designed to create an additional one million new jobs. $17 billion of this tax cut will be for working families in our country, personal income tax reductions; and the rest in corporate tax reductions.

Corporations will also receive higher tax credits for investing in the sort of new plants, new equipment that will make New England and the rest of the Nation competitive with aggressive foreign exports.

But we can't have these cuts in taxes unless we help pay for them by eliminating some of our unnecessary and unwarranted income tax subsidies. Two of these are the deferral subsidy and the DISC subsidies. Both have a particularly bad effect in New England where competition from abroad has had such a terrible effect on businessmen and on workers alike.

The deferral subsidy sets a situation in effect where multinational corporations pay lower taxes on foreign profits than they pay on U.S. profits. This amounts to subsidizing corporations to export jobs overseas. The so-called DISC subsidies are just as bad. They let U.S. corporations set up "dummy" corporations to handle foreign exports so as to keep from paying U.S. taxes on half their profits. Both these give aways go overwhelmingly to a few of the largest multinational corporations. And both mean that the average taxpayer has to pay the bill, more taxes just to take up the slack caused by these subsidies.

Three-Martini Lunch

Both cost America and particularly New England, jobs. Both loopholes should be closed. As for the famous three-martini lunch, I don't care how many martinis anyone has with lunch, but I am concerned about who picks up the check.

I don't think a relatively small minority has some sort of divine right to have expensive meals, free theater tickets, country club dues, sporting events tickets, paid for by heavier taxes on everybody else.

If the Congress will help me by getting rid of these tax loopholes and by enacting the entire economic program, we could have a good start on correcting unemployment and inflation.

The economy won't turn around overnight, of course, any more than an ocean liner can turn around on a dime. The job will require slow, careful planning, not dramatic master strokes. It will require small corrections, of course, that we adhere to very patiently.

It will require careful planning, careful adjustment, careful tuning and cooperation.

The machinery of the American economy is sound. We have a lot to be thankful for. It has worked well despite severe shocks. But it can work better and that is our major goal in this country this year.

Now, I would be glad to answer your questions.

Mideast Airplane Sales - 1

Q: Do you think that Congress will go along with your decision to send sophisticated fighter jets to the Middle East? Can you give us the rationale for including for the first time in these sales Egypt and Saudi Arabia along with Israel?

P: Yes. I think Congress will go along with the proposal to sell a limited number of airplanes in the Middle East. F-15 planes are already being delivered to Israel. And in the new proposal Israel will receive additional F-15s and F-16s, very advanced fighter planes.

We have for a long time sold military equipment to Saudi Arabia, one of our closest allies, staunchest friends and economic partners. This is the first time we have sold F-15s to Saudi Arabia, but they have other advanced equipment.

The first planes will be delivered to Saudi Arabia not this year, or next year, but 1981 or 1982. The planes we have agreed to sell to Egypt are the F-5Es, not nearly so advanced a weapon as the F-15s or F-16s. But as you know, a few years ago, Egypt, which is now one of our staunchest friends and allies, severed their close relationship with the Soviet Union and in effect became an ally of ours. And I don't believe that there is any danger of this relatively short range not-advanced fighter causing a disruption in the peace between Egypt and Israel.

So for those reasons, I am advocating to the Congress that they approve these sales and I believe the Congress will do that.

Coal Strike - 1

Q: Without asking you for a deadline for a coal settlement, can you give us any clue as to the extent of your patience with the situation?

P: Well, the country is suffering already from the consequences of the coal strike. I have asked the Secretary of Labor and I have asked the negotiators from the workers and from the Coal Operators to stay at the bargaining table in constant sessions until they reach an agreement. There has been some progress made to date.

As you know, there is a division within the Labor Union itself but the Bargaining Council, which consists of 39 members, being kept as close as possible to the negotiating team that represents labor.

We hope that when an agreement is reached, that this will be in such a form and with close enough consultations ahead of time that it will be presented immediately to the membership of the United Mine Workers for approval.

So I think that all of us are determined. I have met personally at the White House with labor and management in the coal industry. And I can testify to you that they are sincere in wanting to reach an agreement.

Q: Do you see it going on for another week?

P: No. I don't think we can afford another week of negotiations. I would hope that they could conclude the negotiations within the next few hours or a day or so.

Aid to New England Workers

Q: Mr. President?

P: Yes.

Q: Dan Rea, WBZ-TV in Boston. Last week, as I am sure you very well know, Boston was in a very bad blizzard. Hundreds of thousands of hourly production workers in Massachusetts lost wages, wages that would be made up in some part by the Unemployment Compensation Fund. But the difference between the Unemployment Compensation Fund and the total salaries, for some families it is up to $100 or $125. Is the Federal Government prepared to do anything for the workers?

P: As you know, your own State and others in New England were so heavily damaged by the snowstorm and also by the actions of the seas and wind have been declared major disaster areas. This involves several elements of aid. One was an immediate dispatching here of Sea Bees and members of the other military forces to actually help in the clearing of the highways and the restoration of normal life in your economy.

I have also authorized personal loans for those who have damage to their homes, those who have serious economic problems and we worked very closely in harmony with the state and local officials on this element as well.

These loans are at very low interest. Sometimes the interest payments are almost non-existent. We hope that there can be some additional economic aid, if necessary, granted within the bounds of the law. But I do not know of any specific feature that would permit us to compensate workers for lost wages.

(The President's disaster declaration for Massachusetts, as well as for Rhode Island, does provide for the full legal amount of Federal unemployment compensation benefits to workers unemployed by the disaster.)

I think most of the industry here that employs people has now been restored to full employment; almost to full employment. But with that one exception, I think we are providing the maximum amount of aid that can be under the U.S. aid.

Q: Edward McHugh, Worcester Telegram, Worcester, Massachusetts.

Considering how deeply some of the New England states are already in hock to the Federal Government would you consider it proper for some of them to convert their unemployment insurance programs into disaster relief funds for people who lost wages during the storm?

P: I don't know enough about the answer to give you a response. I think in every instance of this kind the primary responsibility has got to be for the Governor or local officials in the state to make a judgment on what is best for that particular area. If a Governor or a legislator or a Mayor has made that decision, I would not want to contradict. When the unemployment compensation payment is more crucial at that one moment during or immediately following a disaster, or when it is more important to correct the consequences directly after the disaster in physical terms I would not want to judge. That is a decision the Governor would have to make.

Referendums on Nuclear Power

Q: Steve Bascade, WJAR-TV in Providence. The Federal Appeals Judge, Mr. President, has asked the Environmental Protection Agency to reconsider the approval of a cooling system for the nuclear plant in Seabrook, New Hampshire. Part of its reasoning is based on the fact that proponents of the plants didn't have access to all the relevant information.

My question is, how much say should people have over the construction of a plant and should they specifically have veto power in a referendum to oppose a nuclear plant if they so wish?

P: As you know, there are now no legal prohibitions at the Federal Government level from proceeding with the Seabrook plant. The Nuclear Regulatory Commission has not yet given a license. But the Environmental Protection Agency has ruled that the cooling system as proposed was adequate.

I do think that a State or the people within a State should have the right to determine the degree of shifting to nuclear power as a source for energy. As you know, some States have had referendums on this subject. This is a prerogative that the State Legislature and the Governor, and through some instances, through referenda, can be accomplished.

But the Federal Government does not have and would not want to have the right to prohibit the construction of a nuclear power plant in a State if the Federal laws were met. But I do think that in New Hampshire or Vermont or other States, that the legislature certainly should have the right to set the standards by which those plants should be built.

Q: What about the voters themselves in the referendum, not the legislature, the individual?

P: That depends upon whether or not there is a provision for a referendum to override a State law. As you know, in California, for instance, there is an initiative by which citizens can pass a law absent the legislature taking a stand.

But I think that—I know New Hampshire fairly well, having visited there several times during 1976, and I know how close your members of the legislature are to the people. I think there are just a very few people per Member of the House. I think that your legislators are adequately responsive.

U.S. Attorney in Rhode Island

Q: Mr. President, Jim Roberts, WEAN News in Providence. We have a U.S. Attorney here, Lincoln Almond, who is a Republican. You have not yet fired him, but Tom Murray of Newport has been recommended to take his place.

During your campaign, you promised to take the politics out of the selection process for U.S. Attorneys. Can you tell me first of all if you intend to replace Mr. Almond and if so, why?

P: I don't know. This matter has not come to my attention yet. Ordinarily I wait until the Attorney General gives me a recommendation about a replacement before I get involved in the process.

The number of Republican U.S. Attorneys in office now, I think, are about 25 out of 90-some. I think during the last eight years before I came in office, there was never a Democrat appointed to a U.S. Attorneyship. But we have tried to keep in office those who were doing a good job, and when we have made a replacement, I believe in every instance that the selection has been made on the basis of merit.

Whether or not that particular person is going to be replaced, I do not know.

Mideast Airplane Sales - 2

Q: Mr. President? Knowing tension already exists in the Israeli settlement policy, do you have any second thoughts about the timing of your announcements to sell war planes to Egypt or was the timing of that announcement and our public statements about the Israeli settlement policy a message to the Israelis to become more flexible in the current negotiations?

P: The two were not interrelated in my decision-making process. When I was in Saudi Arabia earlier in January, I told them that shortly after the Congress reconvened, I would send up a recommendation for military sales to the Middle East.

Every time I have ever met with Prime Minister Begin, both in the public sessions, that is with staff members, and also in private sessions with just him and me present, this has been the first item that he has brought up: "Please expedite the approval of the sales of military planes to Israel."

I think that the timing is proper. We are not trying to short circuit the allotted time for the Congress. As a matter of fact, we will not begin the process until after the Congress reconvenes, the Senate reconvenes. So there will be a full 50 days for the Congress to consider the matter. Twenty days after this coming Monday, I will send up official papers. I don't think it is a bad time to send it up.

I recognized ahead of time there would be some controversy about it. We did give it second and third thoughts before I made a decision about the composition of the package and the date for submitting it.

Q: Mr. President?

P: Mr. Bradley of CBS.

Coal Strike - 2

Q: Mr. President, back on the subject of the coal talks. Is that deadline Secretary Marshall talked about yesterday still in effect? If at the end of that period they have not reached an agreement, you can invoke the Taft-Hartley Act. The Miners have said they will not mine the coal and the army can't. If you do invoke those provisions and they refuse to mine coal, what can you do?

P: That is all spelled out in the law. The Miners, the Coal Operators, the Secretary of Labor, I, the Attorney General, the Governors, all would like, if possible, to avoid an invocation of the Taft-Hartley law and to let the coal dispute through collective bargaining lead to a new and acceptable contract. So there is no rigid time limit.

If it is obvious to me that progress is beind made, then my preference would be to keep the bargaining process going.

In the last 24 hours I have detected progress and we have not yet been able to get a final settlement. Even after our settlement is reached at the Labor Department, even after the Bargaining Council, who represents the Coal Miners approve the terms that have been derived with the negotiating team, it would still have to be submitted to the Union members back home for their approval. So that would take two, three weeks. And I think it would probably take an additional week or so before coal could start flowing to its destination after it has been mined.

So we still face a substantial delay. And I recognize that it is one of the most serious problems that I have faced as President. And I believe that the negotiators do, too. But I am not trying, and don't want to predict exactly what will happen in the future. And I don't want to set a rigid time limit on anyone. But I have had the urgency of this question imparted to me personally and constantly by the Secretary of Labor during this period of time.

Humphrey-Hawkins Bill

Q: Mr. President, Robert Goldman, University of Rhode Island.

You are an advocate of the Humphrey-Hawkins Bill. Will the bill help to provide job opportunities for college graduates?

P: Yes, I think the Humphrey-Hawkins Bill, if passed—and I think it has a good chance to be passed—would provide enhanced job opportunities for college graduates as well as others. It would set a goal of a 4 percent unemployment rate and

it would permit me to judge when this was in conflict with a control of inflation.

It would also bring into being a much closer coordination of effort between the President, the Federal Reserve Bank, Congress, and others in the government and in private industry to work together.

It would require me to submit to the Congress an economic plan over several years, four or five years, that would ultimately lead to the realization of those goals. So I think the planning concept, the involvement of all the elements who determine the outcome of our economic goals would be a step in the right direction itself, and it would put a heavy emphasis on the reduction of unemployment.

Maine Indian Claims

Q: Mr. President, John Day, Bangor News.

Mr. President, last October you were quoted as saying that Judge Gunter's recommendations for settling the Maine Indian suit were fair and equitable.

P: Yes.

Q: The new proposals which your task force has recently recommended have been severely criticized. What leads you to believe that the new recommendations are more fair and equitable than the old ones submitted by Judge Gunter, the difference being that the new recommendations call for substantial contributions from the private landowners of the State as opposed to no contributions under Judge Gunter's proposals?

P: As you know, Judge Gunter's proposal concerning the Maine land issue involving the Indians was not accepted by the Indians. And when it was rejected by the State, the landowners and the Indians, then I appointed a task force headed up by Bo Cutter, [Eliot Cutler] who happens coincidentally to be from Bangor, Maine, to try to work out an agreement.

We have now reached an agreement as far as the Federal Government is concerned represented by me and the Indian tribes. It would not require any further negotiation nor litigation by any landowner in Maine who owns less than 50,000 acress of land.

It does leave up to the State of Maine, and I think 14 landowners who have more than 50,000 acres, an option without any constraint on them—they can either accept the negotiated settlement, they can negotiate further for a better settlement for themselves, perhaps, or they can continue to litigate in court.

The reason that I got involved in it, reluctantly, I might say, was because almost every piece of property in Maine was potentially tied up in a lawsuit, could not be bought or sold, and I could foresee a very serious economic consequence to Maine unless I made some effort to address it.

This settlement would cost the Federal Government about $25 million. But I would like to point out, too, that we are bound by law that is, the Department of Interior—represented legally by the Attorney General, to represent the Indians.

This is a recent development, brought about, as you know, by the discovery of some old treaty papers, I think in 1971. And we tried to expedite the process. But there is no constraint on the large landowners nor the State to accept the settlement that we have evolved. That is up to them.

Coal Strike - 3

Q: Mr. President, as you know, the coal strike has passed all records in length.

P: Yes.

Q: Do you feel that the negotiators have really reached a point of being irresponsible in not reaching a settlement?

P: No, I don't ascribe irresponsibility to the negotiators.

When the negotiations broke down, when the bargaining council refused to accept for presentation to the miners the first agreement, that is the point at which I decided to intercede.

I invited both sides to come to the White House, which they did, and the union expanded their negotiating team from six members to nine members, to try to bring in some of those who did not agree with the first settlement to more closely assure when a new settlement was reached the miners would accept it. Now we are keeping the bargaining council in an adjacent room to the negotiators themselves, and there is a constant interrelationship of communications with them.

But I believe all the negotiators and the bargaining council on behalf of the union are negotiating in good faith.

Deficit Spending

Q: Mr. President, Joshua Resnek, Chelsea Record, Chelsea, Massachusetts.

Earlier you said the machinery of our economy is sound despite the shocks. However, shortly before the American Revolution the great economist Adam Smith wrote about governments like our own which consistently spend far more than they raise in taxes and which, as a result of such practices, are doomed to inevitable bankruptcy.

First I would like to ask you if you agree with economic reasoning like Mr. Smith's. Secondly, will your Administration continue to spend monies it is clearly incapable of raising?

P: Well, my goal, as you know, is to balance the budget. This year we are faced with a deficit that is about $15 billion or $20 billion higher than it would have been because we are trying to give a tax break, tax reduction, to the American people. In every instance you have to make a judgment on that.

One of the reasons that we are giving the tax reduction is because taxes are too high. Another one is that it would result in a stimulated economy, a million more people at work, and paying taxes rather than on the Federal dole. So you have to make a judgment.

We have expectations with some fairly accurate projections that the budget deficit next year, fiscal year 1980, will be considerably below 1979. If the economy continues to progress, then I have good hopes that in 1981 we would reach my goal. Obviously I don't have complete control over the economy. But I have not given up in trying to carry out the principles that Adam Smith espoused in your quote.

Mideast Airplane Sales - 3

Q: Mr. President, on the Middle East, arms to the Middle East, I want to ask a kind of philosophic question. How do you rationalize the idea of selling weapons, more sophisticated weapons of war, with the argument that they would help to bring about peace?

Does it bother you that these more and more sophisticated weapons are being sold to both sides and if a new war were to break out, it would be a more violent confrontation than any in the past?

P: As you know, we are not introducing new weapons into the Mdddle East. F-15s are already being delivered into the Middle East. Also, I have pledged myself to cut down on the volume of weapons each succeeding year as long as I am in office, barring some unpredictable worldwide military outbreak. This year there will be less weapons sales than last year. This will include, of course, the Middle East.

I think it is very good for nations to turn to us for their security needs instead of having to turn to the Soviet Union, as they have in the past. I am talking specifically about Egypt. You have to remember that Saudi Arabia has never had any active aggression against Israel. Saudi Arabia is our ally and friend. Egypt is our ally and friend. Israel is our ally and friend.

To maintain security in that region is important. Egypt has other threats against its security. The Soviets are shipping massive quantities of weapons into the Middle Eastern area now; into the Red Sea area, Ethiopia, Syria, Iraq, Libya, and we cannot abandon our own friends. So I don't think it is wrong at all to insure stability or the right to defend themselves in a region with arms sales.

We are continuing multinational negotiations with other sellers of weapons to get them to join with us in a constant step-by-step, year-by-year reduction in total arms sales. If they do, I think the world will be much more peaceful in the future.

FRANK CORMIER (AP): Thank you, Mr. President.

THE PRESIDENT: Thank you. ∎

March 2, 1978

Following is the White House text of President Carter's March 2 address to the National Press Club on civil service reorganization, followed by the White House transcript of the news conference, Carter's 26th since taking

office, that followed his press club speech:

PRESIDENT'S ADDRESS

I came to Washington with the promise—and the obligation—to help rebuild the faith of the American people in our government. We want a government that can be trusted, not feared; that will be efficient, not mired in its own red tape; a government that will respond to the needs of American citizens and not be preoccupied with needs of its own.

Taxpayers who work hard for their money want to see it wisely spent.

We all want a government worthy of confidence and respect.

That is what reorganization is all about.

We have no illusions that this task will be easy. Our government and its bureaucracy have evolved over many generations and the work of reform cannot be complete in a year or perhaps even during my service in the White House.

But we have begun. We have adopted zero-based budgeting. We have cut the burden of paperwork on the public, and excessive government regulation is being replaced with free market competition. At OSHA and in other federal agencies we are discarding obsolete regulations and rewriting rules in plain and comprehensible English. We have cut significantly the number of employees in the Executive Office of the President and abolished hundreds of unneeded advisory committees.

'Centerpiece of Government Reorganization'

But all that is not enough. The single most important step we can take is a thoroughgoing reform of the Civil Service system. Civil Service reform will be the centerpiece of government reorganization during my term in office.

I have seen at first hand the frustration among those who work within the bureaucracy. No one is more concerned at the inability of government to deliver on its promises than the worker who is trying to do a good job.

Most Civil Service employees perform with spirit and integrity. Nevertheless, there is still widespread criticism of federal government performance. The public suspects that there are too many government workers, that they are underworked, overpaid, and insulated from the consequences of incompetence.

Such sweeping criticisms are unfair to dedicated federal workers who are conscientiously trying to do their best, but we have to recognize that the only way to restore public confidence in the vast majority who work well is to deal effectively and firmly with the few who do not.

The two complaints most often heard against the present system are that Federal employees have too little protection against

political abuse—and too much protection against legitimate assessment of performance and skills. These charges sound contradictory, but both of them happen to be true. And the system that perpetuates them needs to be changed.

For the past seven months, a task force of more than 100 career civil servants has analyzed the Civil Service, explored its weaknesses and strengths and suggested how it can be improved. Their judgments are reflected in the Message I will send to the Congress today. I want to outline these proposals and explain the reasoning behind them. They represent the most sweeping reform of the Civil Service System since it was created nearly 100 years ago.

Merit System Bogged Down

The simple concept of a "merit system" has grown into a tangled web of complicated rules and regulations. Managers are weakened in their ability to reward the best and most talented people—and to fire those few who are unwilling to work.

The sad fact is that it is easier to promote and transfer incompetent employees than to get rid of them. It may take as long as three years merely to fire someone for just cause, and at the same time the protection of legitimate rights is a costly and time-consuming process for the employee.

You cannot run a farm that way, you cannot run a factory that way, and you certainly cannot run a government that way.

We have lost sight of the original purpose—which was to reward merit. More than 99 percent of all federal employees get a so-called "merit" rating and last year out of about 2 million employees only 226 people lost their jobs for inefficiency.

So my first proposition is this: There is not enough merit in the merit system. There is inadequate motivation because we have too few rewards for excellence and too few penalties for unsatisfactory work.

We must encourage better performance in ways that are used widely and effectively in private industry. Top federal workers are ready and willing to respond to the risks and rewards of competitive life, and public service will be healthier when they have that chance.

Management Incentives

We must strike a new balance that preserves the merit principle while giving managers the incentive and the authority to manage.

We propose to do this, first, by creating a Senior Executive Service, whose 9200 members will be available to serve wherever in the government they are most needed. They will be eligible for annual bonuses for superior performance, and can be moved from the Senior Executive Service back to their previous Civil Service status for poor performance.

I will also ask Congress to authorize the use of incentive pay for the 72,000 Federal managers and supervisors in grades GS-13 through GS-15, which is a far more attractive and sensible acknowledgment of merit than the silver water carafes and thicker carpets that pass for recognition today. They will no longer receive automatic "step" increases in pay without regard to performance.

Another proposal which will improve managerial excellence is a speedier and fairer disciplinary system, which will create a climate in which managers may discharge non-performing employees—using due process—with reasonable assurance that their judgment, if valid, will prevail. At the same time, employees will receive a more rapid hearing for their grievances.

The procedures that exist to protect employee rights are absolutely essential. But employee appeals must now go through the Civil Service Commission, which has a built-in conflict of interest by serving simultaneously as rulemaker, prosecutor, judge, and employee advocate.

More Protection

So, my second proposition is: Employees still have too little protection for their rights.

I propose to divide the present Civil Service Commission into two bodies—an Office of Personnel Management to improve the productivity and performance of Federal workers, and a Merit Protection Board to stand watch against merit abuses and resolve the appeals brought by employees.

I will also propose an Office of Special Counsel to investigate merit violations and protect "whistleblowers" who expose gross management errors and abuses.

Finally, I propose the creation of a federal labor relations authority to remedy unfair labor practices within the government much as the National Labor Relations Board does in the private sector. In addition, we will continue to work with Congress and federal employees to develop legislation which, while recognizing the special requirements of the Federal Government, will improve federal labor practices.

One other serious defect remains. That is the network of rules governing hiring, staffing, and tenure. We should let each agency do its own hiring, rather than the Civil Service Commission which now may take as long as six to eight months to fill important positions.

Veterans' Preference

Current rules often impede the hiring of qualified women, minorities, and the handicapped by giving veterans a lifetime advantage under Civil Service laws—far beyond the benefits provided under other veterans programs which are designed to ease the readjustment from military to civilian life. Therefore, we propose to reduce the preferential advantage given to non-disabled veterans to a 10-year period, and to end this preference altogether for

senior military officers who retire with pension benefits after a full military career. At the same time, we will strengthen provisions to ensure that disabled veterans and those who served during and since Vietnam are fully protected under our Civil Service laws.

These Civil Service reforms are the heart of our government reorganization effort.

Let me be straightforward about the implications of all this.

Our proposals will mean less job security for incompetent Federal employees, but conscientious civil servants will benefit from a change that recognizes and rewards good performance.

Our proposals deal with the major changes that must now be made. By enacting them we will make employment in the Civil Service more challenging, more productive, and a more prosperous and gratifying career.

But the greatest beneficiaries will be the American people, who can expect to see a more competent and efficient and responsive government—one that is worthy of the people it was created to serve.

NEWS CONFERENCE

Declining Dollar

Q: Oddly enough, we have questions which don't relate to what your speech was about, Mr. President.

The first question which has been in the news much lately is—this comes from James Cary of the Copley News Service: What are you going to do about the deteriorating dollar and the basic cause of its collapse, soaring foreign oil imports? And a related question by Joseph Slevin of the Slevin Economic report saying that European financial officials say the U.S. should defend the dollar more vigorously.

P: Thank you, Frank. I spent a lot of time studying about the American dollar, its value in international monetary markets, the causes for the recent deterioration as it relates to other major currencies. I can say with complete assurance that the basic principles of monetary values are not being adequately assessed on the current international monetary markets. There are three that I would like to mention specifically.

First of all, the attractiveness of investment in our own country compared to other nations is rapidly increasing. One of the reasons is a higher interest rate that can be paid on investments in our country.

Another one is the rapidly increasing consumption of oil that occurred during 1977. This caused us a great deal of concern. In 1978, we will not have that circumstance. The present trends and future projections show that at the worst we will have a leveling off of imports of foreign oil, one of the major causes of legitimate deterioration in the quality of the dollar.

And the other point is the degree with which American economic recovery or growth compares to potential purchases of

our own goods. In the last year, our own rate of growth was about 3 percent greater than the average of our major trading partners. That difference will be substantially less in 1978. We will still have adequate growth, but our major trading partners will have better growth than they had last year.

So these three basic causes in 1977 for some lowering in the dollar's value will be much better in 1978. We do move aggressively and adequately to prevent disorderly market circumstances when that need is obvious to us. We will continue to do that. But my own belief is that these basic principles that assess the legitimate value of the dollar have not been adequately observed recently. And my guess is that in the future over a longer period of time what I just told you will be observed and the dollar will remain in good shape.

Coal Strike

Q: We have a number of questions on coal. This one from Richard Stroud of the Christian Science Monitor. Do you feel that the Administration waited too long before intervening in the coal strike?

P: No. (Laughter)

Popularity Rating

Q: On another subject—(laughter)—recent public opinion polls—this from Judy Woodruff of NBC—show a continuing decline in the rating people give you for your job performance as President. How concerned are you that your Administration is perhaps developing a reputation for fumbling and ineptitude because of incidents like the Marston firing or for a failure to exert leadership because of the stalemate on the energy bill?

P: I might say that we have had to deal, and have decided to deal, with some longstanding, very difficult, controversial issues that in some instances had not been adequately addressed by my predecessors. I say that without criticism, but obviously we needed a comprehensive energy policy years ago.

No one has ever proposed it to the Congress from the White House until last April 20th. This needs to be acted upon immediately by the Congress. The House completed its action last August. We still have not been able to break a deadlock in the Senate Energy committees. Hard work is going on on that right now. It is one of the contributing causes to the lowered value of the dollar overseas. I think if we can get a resolution of the natural gas issue alone in the conference committees, immediately there would be a restoration of confidence in our Nation's will to act on a difficult question and our competence to deal with those complicated issues.

Obviously, we have addressed other measures that are difficult as well. We have had remarkable success, I think, in the last year, in holding down the increase in inflation, in reducing substantially the unemployment rate, in having a carefully predicted increase in our gross national product. We have got a good record on budget preparation, cooperation with the House and the Senate and we have learned in this last year there is some criticism that we acted too late in the coal strike and too early by others.

My own deep commitment is that whenever the collective bargaining system can function, Government ought to let it function. And I think had we precipitously imposed our will in the coal strike deliberations, that effort would have been counterproductive. I don't know what the miners will do this weekend. I hope they will vote affirmatively on the negotiated settlement. But I think it was not an exhibition of irresoluteness on our part. I was a carefully balanced judgment about what we should do.

We have addressed some questions on the Middle East that in the past had too long been ignored, trying to bring about a comprehensive settlement there. This is a very difficult, complicated issue over which we do not have control. We have encouraged direct negotiations with Israel and the major Arab countries. We have been successful in seeing that occur because of the action by foreign leaders between Begin and Sadat, something that was hoped for for generations, or for at least decades. We have seen a recognition of Israel's right to exist by Egypt and progress has been made; obviously, not yet have we been successful.

So I think that the polls show that my own personal popularity is very high. The assessment of how successful our Administration has been is disappointing, but it is a partnership between us and Congress, between us and the nations in the Middle East, between us and the coal miners and the coal operators. And Government doesn't have the unilateral, autocratic control over some of these very difficult issues.

So I am concerned that there has not been a resolution of all of these major confrontations and disputes. But we are making good progress and I am not disappointed at the progress that we have made. I am certainly not disappointed at our willingness to tackle issues that have historically been difficult to resolve.

New York Aid

Q: You mentioned your predecessors. This question relates to one of them. It is from Paul Healy of the New York News.

Mr. President, two years ago President Ford said from this podium that there would be no emergency Federal financial aid to New York City, prompting the famous Daily News headline, "Ford to City: 'Drop Dead.'" Yet President Ford later supported a money program to the City that seems more generous than the one outlined on Capitol Hill today by Secretary Blumenthal. What is your response to this?

P: In the first place, as you know, the Congress moved well to prevent bankruptcy of the New York City Government. We have very close personal consultations with the Mayor and other city officials, the banks, the unions, the Governor, and the Congressional Delegation here in Washington.

Yesterday afternoon I talked to the Mayor, Mayor Koch, to the Governor, Governor Carey, and to Senator Moynihan, yesterday and this morning to Secretary of Treasury Mike Blumenthal. I think the proposal that has been put forward is basically adequate. It is obviously not everything that the New York City officials would want.

We believe in sharing the responsibility between the Federal Government—with the guaranteed loans, and those other entities that I described, local lending institutions, the Union Trust Fund, City Government and the State Government.

This does provide a long-range guarantee of loans. It is not month by month or even year by year. Secretary Blumenthal recommended a 15-year period during which we would guarantee up to $2 billion in loans. I think it is a very reasonable and also very adequate proposal, and it is one we are not presenting to the Congress idly. We intend to fight for it. And I know that there is a great deal of concern in the Congress that this might be a proposal that is too generous. I think it is adequate, not overly generous and one that is worthy of our support, and it will get our support.

Middle East

Q: Later this month you will be meeting with Prime Minister Menachem Begin from Israel. Dick Ryan of the Detroit News asks: What do you hope to achieve during your meetings with the Prime Minister?

P: This will be my third meeting with Prime Minister Begin since he has been the leader of Israel. In addition, I communicate with him fairly frequently by personal letter, by diplomatic message, and on occasion by telephone. And both our own Secretary of State and other officials and his Secretary of State and other officials come here frequently. Defense Minister Weizman will be here shortly to consult with me and the Secretary of Defense, the Secretary of State and others.

We are looking for some common ground on which the Egyptians, Israelis, Jordanians, residents of the West Bank and other areas can agree.

This is a difficult and sensitive question. As you know, the Gaza Strip has had an affiliation in the past with Egypt, the West Bank with Jordan, both now occupied by Israel, and we hope to search out at the top level of government some resolution of the differences on specifics relating to the Sinai and also on a statement of principles relating to the occupied territories of the West Bank and the Gaza Strip, hoping at that time that Egypt and the Jordanians and the Palestinian Arabs who live in the West Bank Gaza Strip would be satisfied to conclude perhaps some agreements and proceed with further negotiations leading to an ultimate resolution of the issue, based on United Nations Resolution 242.

One of the crucial elements of any progress in the Middle East is a cleaving to the commitment that UN 242 is a basis for continued negotiations and a solution. The abandonment of that would put us back many months or years. So this is what I hope to accomplish with Prime Minister Begin, to frankly discuss with him my previous agreements and discussions with President Sadat; to encourage direct negotiations to be resumed; and to search out common ground based on advice given to me by Secretary of State Vance and also by Mr. Atherton on the latest possible language changes that might be necessary to let Egypt and Israel agree. So this is what I hope to accomplish and I believe the personal discussions will be good.

I would much prefer that the personal discussions be carried on between Sadat and Begin. But in the absence of that possibility at this moment we hope to restore it and act as an intermediary.

Civil Service Reorganization

Q: There are several questions here related to the Civil Service reorganization. This is a combined question from Mary McGrory of the Washington Star and Mark Goodin of the Houston Post.

The first part is, what sort of protection will the Office of Special Counsel provide for whistle-blowers? And the other part is that Frank Snepp, the ex-CIA agent, is the most famous whistle-blower of all, writing a book exposing incompetence and treachery. After a report to the Inspector General produced no results, you are prosecuting. How does this encourage whistle-blowing?

P: I would like to respond to those completely unbiased questions. (Laughter) I don't look on Frank Snepp as one of the greatest whistle-blowers of all times. He signed voluntarily a contract, later confirmed this agreement with the Director of the CIA that before his book was published, that it would be examined to assure there were no revelations of secret material. And I have not read the book; don't know the substance of it; don't believe that he has revealed anything that would lead to an improvement in our security apparatus or the protection of Americans' civil rights.

But the Attorney General has decided that when a contract is signed that it ought to be honored. If everyone who came into the CIA or other highly secret organizations in government felt free to resign because of a dispute or to retire at the end of satisfactory service and then write a book revealing our Nation's utmost secrets, it would be very devastating to our Nation's ability to protect ourselves in peace or war and to negotiate on a confidential and successful basis with other government leaders.

So I believe that this is important as a distinction to be drawn. The Special Counsel will be there independent from me to protect through the courts, if necessary, those who are legitimate whistle-blowers and who do point out violations of ethics, or those who through serious error hurt our country. And this is a function that is not presently extant. I think it will be a step in the right direction and there will be presentation after investigation to both the public and, if necessary, to the mechanism by which employees' rights are protected and, on an appeal basis, to the courts themselves.

SALT-Africa Linkage

Q: Mr. President, this is from Warren Rogers of The Tribune of New York. With the Soviets active now in the Horn of Africa and with other strains in U.S.-Soviet relations, what hope do you have for early resumption of SALT talks?

P: The SALT talks have never been discontinued or delayed. They are ongoing now and the Soviet involvement in the Horn has not interrupted that process. We do not initiate any government policy that is a linkage between the Soviet involvement in Ethiopia-Somalia dispute on the one hand and SALT or the comprehensive test bans negotiations on the other.

Obviously any negotiation, if concluded successfully at the Executive level, would have to be ratified by the Congress, who would be heavily influenced by the opinion of the American people. And the fact that the Soviets have over-armed to the teeth. The Somalians who then use Soviet weapons to invade Ethiopia and now are over-arming Ethiopia and directing their military effort has caused a threat to peace in the Horn area of Africa.

We have added our own importunities for a peaceful resolution and our own caution comments to the Soviets. They have assured me directly through Foreign Minister Gromyko that the Ethiopians would not cross the Somalia border.

We have sent a delegation to meet with President Mengistu who assured me personally that they would not cross the Somalia border. We have three hopes there that we trust and certainly hope that the Soviets will honor.

One is a Somalian withdrawal from the territories which they occupy in Eastern Ethiopia in the Ogaden area. Secondly, a removal from Ethiopia of Cuban and Soviet troops; third, a lessening of the tensions that exist between those countries and an honoring of the sometimes arbitrarily drawn international boundaries in Africa.

And we would hope that the OAU, the Organization of African Unity, would become more successful in their efforts to resolve this dispute in a peaceful way. But at this time, Somalia is the invading nation. We have refused to send any weapons into that area or permit third countries who bought weapons from us to transfer them into that area, and I think our policy is completely accurate.

The Soviets violating of these principles would be a cause of concern to me, would lessen the confidence of the American people in the word and peaceful intentions of the Soviet Union, would make it more difficult to ratify a SALT agreement or comprehensive test ban agreement

if concluded. And therefore, the two are linked because of actions by the Soviets. We don't initiate the linkage.

Dallas-London Air Service

Q: Mr. President, we have several questions related to the Braniff Airways low-cost service between Dallas and London, one from Ross Mark of the Daily Express of London, and another from Roy Bode of the Dallas Times-Herald.

First of all, have you received a recommendation from the CAB for retaliatory action, and do you plan to take such action against the British carrier? Secondly, do you believe that the British Government is abiding by its commitments in the Bermuda II airline agreements?

P: I have not received a recommendation from the CAB at this moment. When the recommendation gets to me, by law, I will have to act and will act immediately.

I don't know enough about the issue, the details of the British Government ruling, to know whether or not they have violated the agreement that was concluded this past year. My guess is, knowing the British, that they have not violated the agreements specifically. But, as you know, an agreement can't be that detailed to anticipate every individual ruling that will be concluded by the CAB on our side or its equivalent agency on the British side. I don't know much about the issue yet.

But if there is a violation, we would express our concern directly to Prime Minister Callaghan. And when the CAB gives me a report and a recommendation, the chances are that I would honor it.

We have had notable success in 1977 in increasing competition, particularly in international routes of air carriers. We have encouraged the additional competition of American airlines in this area, as well. We hope to get the Congress to act on substantial deregulation in the airline industry within our country. I believe that we have made notable success already and we have withstood a tremendous pressure from the British to have more Government protection, which would be contrary to competition in the agreement that we reached last year.

Social Security Taxes

Q: At the risk of showing favoritism, I will ask a question from Jack Cole of the Milwaukee Journal. Will you support legislation to reduce Social Security payroll taxes by transferring the hospital care and disability portions of the program to funding by general Treasury funds?

P: I don't think that 1978 is a time to further modify in any substantial way the Social Security law which was just passed this past year. Our own recommendation to Congress in 1977 did involve some transfer of funds and some use of general funds from the Treasury if the unemployment rate and/or the inflation rate caused excessive drains on the reserve funds. I think the Congress was very courageous and acted

properly in increasing Social Security payments into the funds to maintain the integrity of the system itself.

Had we not acted, we would be in a crisis stage right now. We are convinced that the recommendations that I have made to the Congress to lower income taxes will compensate in almost every instance for the increase in Social Security tax payments that were passed by a previous Administration, and also increased this past year.

So I don't think 1978 is the proper time to change it. I think that the principles of partial use of general funds under certain circumstances is a sound one that we did advocate, and transfer of moneys from one fund to another is a principle which we would also espouse when the time comes, if it does, for additional changes in the Social Security law. That is what we recommended last year.

Hamilton Jordan Incident

Q: Mr. President, we thank you very much for appearing here today and I have one final question for you for which I will take full responsibility.

In view of the 33-page so-called Jordan report, is there any truth to the rumor that you are planning a White House conference on etiquette in singles bars? (Laughter)

P: This is a matter that had not previously come to my attention until just before this press conference. (Laughter) I have known Hamilton Jordan a long time and I have discounted the story because they said he was drinking amaretto and cream. (Laughter) The White House conference is certainly worthy of consideration. My own personal advice would be that perhaps in the future Hamilton might substitute peaches for the amaretto. (Laughter)

(Applause)

March 9, 1978

Following is the White House transcript of President Carter's March 9 news conference, his 27th since taking office:

THE PRESIDENT: Good afternoon. Thank you.

I have two brief statements to make before I answer questions. Three days ago, I appointed a Board of Inquiry whose purpose under the Taft-Hartley Act was to investigate the negotiating stalemate and we know that this has closed our Nation's coal mines.

This morning, the board presented its report to me. Its finding was that an impasse does exist, and that the situation is serious. This morning, using the authority of the Taft-Hartley Act, I directed the Attorney General to seek this afternoon a court injunction which will order the miners to return to work and the operators to open the mines during the 80-day cooling off period during which time negotiations will proceed.

The welfare of our Nation requires this difficult step and I expect that all parties will obey the law. The Federal Government will use its resources to minimize the national economic and social dislocations caused by this labor dispute.

The Department of Energy and the State Governors will improve the distribution of energy resources by moving our supplies of coal to places where the need is most urgent. The relief agencies of the Federal Government are prepared, if necessary, to act in a coordinated fashion to assist local areas which are particularly hard hit.

This is a time for cooling off. We will do everything in our power to be sure that it does not become a time of confrontation. The law must be enforced.

I have met this afternoon with the Attorney General and I have asked him to assume personal direction of Federal law enforcement activities in this area.

The Secretary of Labor just informed me that he has asked the Board of Inquiry as an extension of their duties to go into the coal mining areas and consult with the miners, to encourage compliance with the law and return to the negotiating area.

There is no easy solution to this problem. What is required from all of us now is reason, patience, and a willingness to cooperate with one another and to obey the laws of the United States.

I am confident that with the support of the miners and the coal owners, the mine operators and the American people, and all public officials, that we can resolve this dispute without further damage to the well-being of our Nation.

Somalia Withdrawing Forces

I have another statement to make. Last night, I was informed by President Siad Barre of Somalia that he was agreeing to withdraw his forces from the Ogaden area, the occupied areas of Ethiopia, and just the last few minutes, he confirmed this commitment to me with a public statement.

I welcome President Siad Barre's announcement of this decision. The United States hopes that this decision will result in an immediate halt of the bloodshed in that area of the Horn of Africa. We hope that the Organization of African Unity can move quickly to assist all parties to terminate hostilities, to agree quickly on rules that can be observed so that Somalian forces can retire rapidly into their own territory and to ensure that peaceful conditions are restored among the civilian population.

As soon as Somalia forces have withdrawn completely, and as soon as Ethiopian forces have reestablished control over their own territory, withdrawal of the Soviet and Cuban combat presence should begin.

The United States looks forward to the complete withdrawal of all foreign forces from the two countries, Ethiopia and Somalia, at an early date. We stand ready to assist the Organization of African Unity in working out the basis for negotiations between Ethiopia and Somalia which would ensure the territorial integrity of all countries in the region and the honoring of international boundaries.

Somalia Arms Request

Q: Mr. President, does that Somalia announcement cause you to look any more favorably on Somali requests for American arms, assuming they go through with it?

P: We notified Somalia many months ago that as long as they were in occupied territory, that there would be no consideration on our part for defensive arms of any kind. I think it would require a tangible demonstration of the carrying out of this commitment on the part of the Somalians and also a renewed commitment not to dishonor the international boundaries of either Ethiopia or Kenya before we would be willing to discuss with them economic aid or defensive arms supplies.

In this case, working with the Organization of African Unity and the Congress, we would consider this in a routine manner, but not until.

Coal Strike - 1

P: Mr. President, there seem to be conflicting signals on what you would do if miners do not return to work. Would you consider seeking legislation to seize the mines, or do you have any other alternatives?

P: My firm belief and my firm commitment is that the Taft-Hartley Act will be enforced, that this will be adequate to assure supplies of coal to our country to avoid an additional crisis and that it will also be an adequate incentive to bring the bargaining parties back to the negotiating table for successful resolution.

I have absolutely no plans to seek Congressional action authorizing seizure of the coal mines.

Middle East - 1

Q: Mr. President, on the Middle East, the State Department today reaffirmed that UN Security Council Resolution 242 remains in our view the bedrock of our efforts to bring peace to that area and more or less served notice on the Israeli Government not to take any decision to renounce that. Could you state for us what your understanding or your interpretation of Security Council Resolution 242 is and what your understanding of the Israeli position on this is?

P: Well, United Nations Resolution 242 was passed about ten years ago. Since then it has been endorsed with practically no equivocation by our own country, by the entire international community, by the Israeli Government, and by the Arab countries who border on Israel. It calls for the withdrawal of Israel from territories occupied in the 1967 war. It calls for the restoration of security of Israel behind recognized and defensible borders. And this has been the basis on which all of our efforts since I have been in office, and also my predecessors' efforts have been based.

For any nation now to reject the application of 242 to the occupied territories, including the West Bank, the Sinai, the Golan Heights, would be a very serious blow to the prospects of peace in the Middle East. In addition to the principles that I have just described to you, we have also been working with complete commitment and with some substantial success, particularly in the case of Egypt, to ensure that Israel will not only be blessed with a cessation of hostilities, but also with a full restoration of peace, open borders, diplomatic relations, free trade, exchange of tourism and students and cultural exchanges. This is a prospect that we still have. But the abandonment of United Nations Resolution 242 as it applies to the West Bank and other occupied territories would be a very serious blow to the prospects of peace and a complete reversal of the policy of the Israeli Government and other governments in the area.

Siegel Resignation - 1

Q: Mr. President, have you given thought to abolishing the job of liaison with the Jewish community?

P: No. We have many members of our Administration who work directly with Jewish Americans who are interested particularly in the Middle East and other similar matters of interest to other groups in our country.

I meet frequently with groups of Jewish Americans who come to the White House, so does the Vice President, the Secretary of State does at the State Department, Dr. Brzezinski, Hamilton Jordan, Stu Eizenstat and so does Mark Siegel.

So we have a concerted effort to present our views and to receive the views of those interested parties and I think one of the most crucial elements of a successful achievement of peace in the Middle East is to continue those consultations and we will of course do that.

Q: Mr. President, isn't it discriminatory? I understand there are some two million Arabs in this country. Do you give this kind of consideration to them?

P: I have also met, I should have said, with Arab leaders from all over the country on the same subject.

Q: To follow that up—

Middle East - 2

Q: Thank you, Mr. President.

You have spoken many times of the commitment that the United States has for the security of Israel. In 1975, in September, the Sinai II agreement said specifically that the United States would promise to give advanced aircraft such as the F-16, an unspecified time and number, to Israel.

Why is that promise of the United States now made part of a package deal? In other words, why is it tied to approval for aircraft to other countries, Egypt and Saudi Arabia?

P: We are honoring completely the commitments made to Israel in the fall of 1975 concerning an adherence on our part to the adequate defense capabilities of Israel, including advanced aircraft like the F-15 and the F-16.

Some orders of this kind have already been placed, accepted and deliveries are in prospect. Some planes have already been delivered. And the proposal that I have made to Congress on the arms sales package is compatible with that commitment.

In the fall of 1975, commitments were also made to the Saudi Arabians, to provide them with advanced aircraft, to replace their present Lightning planes which are becoming obsolete.

Later in the Ford Administration in 1976, in the fall, a commitment was made to them to send Defense Department officials to Saudi Arabia, to give them some assessment of the characteristics of the F-15s and F-16s with a commitment then made that they would have their choice between the F-16s and the F-15s.

When Crown Prince Fahd came to our country last spring, I repeated this commitment that had been made by my own predecessors in the White House and so the sale of F-15s to Saudi Arabia is consistent with the commitment also made in the fall of 1975 and repeatedly reconfirmed.

The sale of the F-5Es—a much less capable airplane, by the way—to the Egyptians is, I think, a very legitimate proposal because Egyptians in effect have severed their supply of weapons that used to come from the Soviet Union and have cast their lot with us which is a very favorable development in the Middle East, one of the most profound developments of all.

I have no apology at all to make for this proposal. It maintains the military balance that exists in the Middle East. I can say without any doubt that the superior capabilities of the Israeli Air Force compared to their neighbors is maintained, and at the same time, it reconfirms our own relationship with the moderate Arab leaders and nations for the future to ensure that peace can be and will be maintained in the Middle East.

Middle East - 3

Q: Mr. Carter, on the same subject, we have seen reports in recent days from the Middle East from both Cairo and Jerusalem that in effect President Sadat's initiative has come to an end, that it has come aground. We also see reports from Jerusalem that Ministers in the Israeli Government have decided that there is no deal to be made at this time. Could you give us your assessment of where this stands and where you think it is going to go?

P: Well, as is the case in the White House and in the Congress, and in the United States, there is a difference in Israel, a very heated debate in prospect and already in progress about what should be done to bring about peace in the Middle East.

There are obviously differences also between nations, between Egypt and Israel, between Israel and their other neighbors. So I would say that in comparison to the situation a year ago, the prospects for comprehensive peace in the Middle East are quite good. We would hope that there could be an immediate resolution of all the differences. That is not immediately in prospect.

Prime Minister Begin will be coming to visit with me this coming week. I know him very well. I have met with him twice before. He is a very strong advocate, a very dedicated advocate of the position of the Israeli Government. He is a forceful and outspoken person. I am sure after our meeting, we will at least understand each other better.

I hope we can move another step toward peace. I had an equivalent opportunity this year to meet and to have long discussions with President Sadat.

I would say there has been a great deal of progress made. Just looking at the changes from the viewpoint of the Israelis, we have now the major Arab nation who has recognized Israel's right to exist, right to exist in peace, right to exist permanently, has offered the full definition of peace which I described earlier. They have been meeting directly and personally, Begin and Sadat and their representatives, which was not in prospect at all a year ago.

There are still differences between them—relatively minor differences in the Sinai, more major strategic kinds of differences involving the Palestinian question and the implementation of UN 242. So we have got a long way to go. It is a difficult question that has been one of the most challenging, I guess, in the last 30 years for the world, to bring about peace in the Middle East. But I am not discouraged about it. We are going to stick with it. And even if it takes a lot of time and much abuse and much debate and many differences expressed by all public officials, I intend to stay with it and I believe the American people are deeply committed to two things. One is the security of Israel under any circumstances, and secondly, the achievement of comprehensive peace.

Coal Strike - 2

Q: Mr. President, do you agree with the position of the Coal Operators as stated in the latest contract on both the issues of the right to strike and pension benefits? And can you explain why or why not?

P: Well, I would rather not single out any particular aspect of the contract for my approbation or rejection. There are issues of that kind that have been in deep contention. The Coal Operators want to eliminate the possibility of wildcat strikes and to increase production. The coal miners want the security of their retirement funds and they want to have continuation of the health benefits without contributing to the fund out of their salaries. Those have been the major items in contention. And I don't want to comment on the degree of my

approval of them. One thing on which there has been general and early agreement is the wage package and this I think, would be a basis for a resolution of the differences.

But I don't want to comment as a President on my approval or disapproval of individual items.

Q: Do you think the miners should have gone along with the contract as it was last submitted?

P: I was hoping that they would. As you know, there have been two contracts negotiated between the Mine Leaders and the Coal Operators. One was rejected by the Bargaining Council. The other contract was approved by the Bargaining Council, 39 members, ostensibly representing all the miners throughout the country and rejected by the membership.

But I was hoping that those contracts would be accepted. I have never gotten involved in saying that a particular provision should be in or out of the contract, but one that is freely negotiated. I was obviously hoping that it would be approved.

Middle East - 4

Q: Mr. President, Mark Siegel, one of your aides, quit today and you accepted his resignation with regret. He cited as his reason differences with your Middle East policy.

His resignation, to many, symbolized the split in the American and Jewish community over the internal debate that is going on over our Middle East policy. And with Begin coming, I wonder if you could tell us what differences there are between the two of us, what your position will be on these differences, and a comment on the report that you are going to pressure him to make significant concessions?

P: I don't have any intention to pressure Prime Minister Begin. I don't have any desire to do it and couldn't if I wanted to. He is a very strong and independent person representing a strong and independent nation. Our role has been that of an intermediary. And one of the most pleasant respites that I have had since I have been in office was the brief time when Prime Minister Begin and President Sadat were negotiating directly and I was out of the role of carrying messages back and forth.

That is, however, a situation that has now deteriorated to some degree since President Sadat went to Jerusalem. Both the military and the political talks are now interrupted—we hope temporarily.

One of the things I will be doing is to repeat to Prime Minister Begin personally the request and the negotiating positions of President Sadat and we have tried to do this through our Ambassadors and through out negotiator, Mr. Atherton, in the Mideast and I think perhaps I can do it perhaps a little more effectively.

But the differences that exist between them are well-known. In the Sinai, as I said, they are relatively easy to resolve. The Jewish settlements, the placement of Egyptian forces in the Sinai and some continuation of Israeli control over some airfields or aerodromes and the rapidity with which Israel would withdraw from the Sinai itself.

In the West Bank, Gaza Strip, this involves implementation of U.N. Resolution 242 and some resolution of the Palestinian question. We do not and never have favored an independent Palestinian nation. And within that bound of constraint, how to give the Palestinians who live in the West Bank Gaza Strip some voice in the determination of their own future, is an issue still unresolved.

That outlines very briefly the situation that we presently are in.

Upper-Bracket Taxes

Q: Mr. President, in the past, you have indicated an interest to make taxes in the upper brackets more equitable. Yet in your present tax message, there is nothing to have a limit of 50 percent on all taxable income, including dividends and interest as well as earned income at the present. Is there still hope that this is going to be done?

P: There will be an alleviation of the tax burden on almost every American under the tax proposal that we put forward to the Congress.

Within the constraints of a $25 billion net reduction, you can't make this an all-inclusive proposal. I would say that most of the reductions are not at the $200,000 or $250,000 or higher level. Most of the reductions are in the low and middle-income family tax payments.

I think, though, that in general, the proposal provides greater equity. It eliminates some of the unwarranted tax privileges that have existed too long. And of course, the net effect of it is the substantial reduction in both personal and corporate taxes.

But the higher income families that you have described above $100,000 income would not be benefited on a percentage basis nearly so much as the middle and lower-income families.

Rhodesia Settlement

Q: Mr. President, in view of the great amount of discussion that is going on now about internal Rhodesian settlement which excludes the Patriotic Front, is it possible in your view to have a settlement of the Rhodesian Conference without including Mr. Nkomo and Mr. Mugabe?

P: I would doubt we could have a permanent settlement without including a right for all the Nationalist leaders to participate. That would include Mugabe, Sithole, and would also, of course, include Nkomo as well. Muzorewa, the other leader, was here yesterday and met with Secretary Vance. We have had a meeting yesterday afternoon between myself, Secretary Vance, and the Foreign Minister of Great Britain, David Owen, and we reconfirmed our position, which has been consistent that the Anglo-American plan is the best basis for a permanent resolution of the Rhodesian or Zimbabwe question. It is

one that is substantially supported by the front line Presidents, Presidents of those nations surrounding Rhodesia, and it has not been accepted completely by Nkomo and Mugabe, the Freedom Force leaders outside of Rhodesia.

We hope now that we can have a conference of all the interested Nationalist leaders to try to work out the disparity between the internal settlement proposal, which is not adequate, and the so-called Anglo-American plan, which we believe to be adequate.

We have not rejected the individual component parts of the so-called internal settlement plan. To the extent that they are consistent with the overall Anglo-American plan provisions, they are a step in the right direction. But I think that it must be that any permanent settlement would include the right of all the interested Nationalist leaders to seek the leadership of Rhodesia.

Coal Strike - 3

Q: Mr. President, what are your plans if the coal miners refuse to obey Taft-Hartley and return to work? What do you do then?

P: The injunction, if it is granted—and the hearing for temporary restraining order is commencing now, about 3:30. It is a far-reaching injunction. It prevents the interference of any law violators with those who want to go back to work. It prevents a picketing against those who are complying with the law and mining coal. It requires the coal mine owners and the Mine Workers to recommence negotiation efforts. It prevents the interference with the transportation of coal in any form, and it provides a legal mechanism by which the Federal law enforcement officials and the State and local law enforcement officials can provide for the protection of lives and property.

I believe the coal miners to be law-abiding and patriotic citizens. And I believe that a substantial portion of them, an adequate proportion of them, will comply with the law. We also have modified the historic provisions of the Taft-Hartley Law by encouraging the operators and the Mine Workers to negotiate during this period regional settlements based on the wage package which was in general agreement from the very beginning weeks of the negotiations themselves.

I believe that the law will be obeyed. I might say one other thing. We have got about, I think, 82 percent of the Mine Workers who are not now working. We are still producing about 50 percent as much coal, and the reserve supplies of coal are down below, December 5th, only about 45 percent. So I believe that if we can get a moderate number—hopefully all, but a moderate number—of coal miners to go back to work, that we can prevent a crisis evolving in our country.

The distribution of existing energy supplies, electricity, oil, natural gas and coal, will also help to alleviate the problem. The injunction has broad coverage and I

think the sum total of all I have described will be adequate.

Siegel Resignation - 2

Q: Mr. President, to come back to the Dr. Siegel resignation, Dr. Siegel, as I understand it, resigned for two reasons; one, he was being asked to defend Administration policy in the Middle East; and two, he was unable to affect that decision-making process within the White House.

Does his resignation cause you to have any doubts about his not being able to have played a more prominent role in forming that policy? And two, does it cause you to wonder about the entire decision-making process in the Middle East within the White House and its future implications?

P: The answer to both your questions is no. Mark Siegel is a fine young man and an excellent employee and he has done his job well in the White House, dealing with one of the most difficult issues that I have had to face as President, an issue on which there is sharp disagreement in the White House, sometimes disagreements between myself and the Secretary of State or myself and the Secretary of Defense or myself and the National Security Advisor or myself and my own staff.

But we resolve those differences as best we can harmoniously. When there is continued disharmony, I make the final decision about the Administration policy. But this is an issue that is almost inherently a subject for dispute and disagreement.

As I pointed out earlier, there is a sharp public dispute in the Israeli Cabinet itself, not limited to a difference between parties in Israel. And obviously there are sharp disputes between Israel and her neighbors. But I think we are now addressing these difficult but crucial issues which are easier, politically speaking, to leave alone in a proper fashion.

We are not trying to impose our will on anyone. But I have to say that within the White House, when there is a continuing disagreement, that I make the final decision. That is what I was elected to do.

I think that Mark Siegel has had a strong input in his conversations and negotiating sessions with the Vice President, with Hamilton Jordan, with Dr. Brzezinski, and on occasion with me, not very often directly with me. But he has a perfect right to decide whether or not he prefers to continue performing that service. To explain the Administration positions to very interested American Jewish groups has been a difficult task for me as well as him.

And I honor his right to make that decision. I don't think that we have a breakdown in communications and consultations within the White House. And after constant reconsideration, I believe that our policy on the Middle East is the proper one.

Natural Gas Deregulation

Q: Mr. President, are you willing to accept energy legislation that in a few years would lead to the deregulation of natural gas?

P: Yes. I am. This was a campaign statement and commitment of mine that I thought natural gas should be deregulated. In my speech to the Congress last April the 20th, I repeated this hope and I think that a long phased-in deregulation process without any shocks to our national economy would be acceptable.

Marston Case

Q: Mr. President, it now appears that there were some significant deletions in the Justice Department affidavits on the Marston case bearing upon his competence and upon the nature of politics in Pennsylvania. And this has led to new charges of a cover-up by some people high up in the Justice Department, or at the very least, some incompetence on the part of Justice Department people.

What is your assessment of how your Justice Department has handled this, and if I may ask my follow-up before I sit down, are you irritated by the delay in naming Marston's successor?

P: The answer to your last question is no. Because of the high degree of attention focused on this particular appointment, the almost natural delay has been a matter of some interest. But it takes a long time to screen many applicants to make sure that we satisfy the desires of the judges in that area or of the responsible lawyers in that area and that we satisfy ourselves that there is an adequate FBI check of their background, that their financial status is good, that there is nothing that can be brought up later on that would be embarrassing to the appointee when a thorough discussion or investigation is made.

It is a time-consuming process. I am not dissatisfied. We are moving as rapidly as we can on that. I didn't know anything about the information presented to the Congressional committees. I think in retrospect it would have been better to go ahead and include the statement of the FBI agent.

Dollar Decline

Q: Mr. President, can you tell us why you think the dollar is declining abroad? What are you going to do about it and do you think it is time for more tougher measures to curb inflation here in the United States?

P: This is a matter with international implications. I had a long talk this morning on the phone with Chancellor Helmut Schmidt. This was one of the subjects that we did discuss. And German and American officials will be meeting this weekend to try to have a common approach to eliminating, or certainly reducing the disorderly marketing of the currencies of the world.

We have had a policy of intervening in the monetary markets only when disorder did occur, when there were fluctuations that were not warranted or that caused us some concern. I think recently the value of

the dollar has been fairly well stable with the deutsche mark, at about 2.02.

One of the things that has been pointed out to me is that the factors that caused a lowering of the dollar's value compared to some of the stronger currencies, Swiss francs, Japanese yen, German deutsche marks in this past year are being alleviated.

Higher interest rates in our country now, caused by various factors, now make investments in the United States more attractive than we were last year. We had a high increase in 1977 in the amount of oil imported.

My guess is that this year, we will not have that increase in imported oil.

Last year, we had a much higher increase in our gross national product, a much more vigorous economy, that made it possible for us to buy foreign goods better than foreigners could buy our goods.

I think the difference was about a three percent rate of growth. Because of the more vigorous economies in some of our foreign trading partners, countries, this year, that difference is certainly likely to narrow.

Chancellor Schmidt told me that the last quarter in 1977 in Germany the GNP growth was six percent. This was higher than he had anticipated and he didn't think it was going to be maintained constantly, but he was pleased with that.

So I think those factors all point to the very good strength of the dollar and on a long-term basis, it being fairly well priced compared to foreign currencies.

But any shocks to the market, any disorderly marketing will require us to intercede, and I will do so.

FRANK CORMIER (AP): Thank you, Mr. President. ∎

March 30, 1978

Following is the White House transcript of President Carter's news conference March 30 in Brasilia, Brazil. It was his 28th news conference since taking office:

THE PRESIDENT: Good morning, ladies and gentlemen. I am very delighted to be here in Brasilia to participate in a live press conference, and I will alternate questions from the Brazilian and the American press.

I will begin with Mr. Bonfim.

U.S.-Brazil Relations

Q: Mr. President, at the beginning of your Administration there was a clear tendency to isolate and treat Brazil coldly in favor of democratically-elected governments, elected by the people.

Yesterday at the airport you stressed the need for cooperation between Brazil and the United States as equal partners. Who has changed; Brazil or you?

P: I certainly have not changed. The experience that I have had in Brazil as Governor of Georgia before I became President made Brazil the most important

country to me. I and my wife visited it frequently. We had a partnership arrangement between my own State and the State of Pernambuco.

We studied the background, the history, the culture and the government of Brazil and there has not ever been any inclination on my part or the part of my Administration to underestimate the extreme importance of Brazil as a major world power, nor to underestimate the extreme importance of very close and harmonious relationships between the United States and Brazil.

There are some differences of opinion between ourselves and Brazil which have been very highly publicized.

But on the long scale of things, both in the past history and in the future, the major factors which bind us in harmony with Brazil far transcend — are much more important than the differences that have been published between our approach to human rights, for instance, and the subject of nonproliferation weapons. But our commitment to Brazil as a friend, our need for Brazil as a partner and a friend has always been the case and is presently very important to us and will always be that important in the future.

Helen?

Airplane Sales

Q: Regarding the use of American military supplies to invade a country and to cause untold suffering to hundreds of thousands, some say it is a violation of U.S. law. In view of the facts that you have before you, is it a violation; and two, what would cause you to reassess your war plane package to the Middle East?

P: Are you referring to the Lebanon question?

Q: Yes.

P: As you know, when the terrorist atack in Israel precipitated the countermove by Israel into Lebanon which has been a haven for the Palestinian terrorists the United States took the initiative in the United Nations, I might say, without the approval of Israel, to initiate United Nations action there to expedite the removal of Israeli forces from Lebanon.

We have obviously attempted to comply with the law and this is a matter that we are still addressing. The other part of your question?

Q: What would cause you to reassess your war plane package to the Middle East and how do you think you have attempted to comply with the law?

P: We are attempting to terminate as rapidly as possible the military presence of Israel in Southern Lebanon through United Nations action. I believe this is the proper way to do it rather than unilateral action on our part which would probably be unsuccessful in any case to get Israel to withdraw. The presence of United Nation forces, the French, Swedes, and others, I believe is the preferable way and it marshals the opinion of the entire world through the United Nations against the Israeli presence being retained in Lebanon.

This has not caused me to reassess the American position on the sale of war planes and other equipment to the Middle East. This is a very well balanced package. It emphasizes our interest in military security of the Middle East. It does not change at all the fact that Israel still retains a predominant air capability and military capability. There is no threat to their security. But it also lets the nations involved and the world know that our friendship, our partnership, our sharing of military equipment with the moderate Arab nations is an important permanent force of our foreign policy.

Loans and Human Rights

Q: The American commerical banks are the main Brazilian source of external credit. It seems to some people in Washington that sooner or later a Congressman may try to establish a link between commercial banking loans and the human rights policy. I would like to know your opinion about this subject.

P: Brazil is a major trading partner of the United States, in commercial goods and also in loans and I might say timely repayments. The debt of Brazil is very manageable. The loans of the American banks to Brazil are sound. Additional loans are being pursued by the American banks as an excellent advantage for their future investments in Brazil based on the strength of your country. It would be inconceivable to me that any act of Congress would try to restrict the lending of money by American private banks to Brazil under any circumstance.

This would violate the principles of our own free enterprise system and if such an act was passed by Congress, I would not approve it.

Q: What is in the first place for you: the private enterprise and the private system or the human rights policy?

P: They are both important to us. And I don't see any incompatability between a belief in a free enterprise system where government does not dominate the banks or the production of agricultural products or commercial products on the one hand and a deep and consistent and permanent and strong belief in enhancing human rights around the world.

I might say that the American business community, the Congress of the United States, the general populace of the United States supports completely a commitment of our Nation to human rights. It is a basic element of our national consciousness that is not a violation at all or no conflict between human rights on the one hand and the free enterprise system on the other.

Namibia Compromise

Q: Mr. President, tomorrow you fly to Africa. What can you tell us today about the revised five-power proposal?

P: As you know, under the auspices of the United Nations, our own country, Canada, Britain, France and the Federal Republic of Germany have been working jointly to present to South Africa and to the so-called SWAPO Organization, Southwest Africa Political Organization, a compromise solution to restoring majority rule in Namibia.

We have presented this proposal this week to the South African government, which now controls Namibia, and also to the SWAPO leaders. We are hopeful that if the proposal is not completely acceptable to both those parties, that it will at least be acceptable enough to prevent unilateral action on the part of South Africa to hold elections in complete violation of the United Nations resolutions and in complete violation of the principle of restoring majority rule to Namibia.

I cannot tell you what the outcome of those consultations will be. I will get a more complete report when I arrive in Lagos. Ambassador Young has been in Africa now for about a week. This is one of the reasons that he is there. And I will be glad to give you a more detailed report after I get additional information.

Brazil and Nuclear Weapons

Q: Mr. President, now that you have a broad nonproliferation act in your hands, do you expect you can persuade Brazil to give up reprocessing and enrichment technology being acquired from Germany? And in that case, what are the carrots you might specifically use to further the power of your arguments in your meeting with President Geisel?

P: We strongly favor the right of any country to have part of its energy supplies come from nuclear power. As you know, our country has been the leader in the evolution of atomic power for peaceful uses and we would do nothing to prevent this trend from continuing both in Brazil and in other countries around the world.

Our own nuclear nonproliferation policy, however, tries to draw a distinction between the right and the meeting of needs of countries to produce energy from atomic power on the one hand, and the right of the country to evolve weapons-grade nuclear materials through either enrichment processes or through reprocessing.

We have no authority over either West Germany or Brazil, nor do we want any. But as a friend of both countries, we reserve the right to express our opinion to them that it would be very good to have, and possible to have a complete nuclear fuel system throughout a country without having the ability to reprocess spent fuel from the power reactors. In the United States, for instance, in the last 25 years or so, on several occasions major investments, multi-billion-dollar investments in all, have been made in reprocessing plants. So far as I know, for the civilian nuclear technology, all those plants have now been **abandoned as being noneconomical.**

So this is a difference that does exist between Brazil and the United States. The right of Brazil and West Germany to continue with their agreement is one that we do not challenge, but we have reserved the right and have used the right to express our concern both to the Brazilian government and to the West German government.

I think it is accurate to say that the European nations have now announced that in the future, they will not make reprocessing plants part of their overseas sales inventory. And we are very deeply concerned about this. Of course, Brazil has announced that they have no intention of producing nuclear explosives. Brazil is the signatory to the Treaty of Tlatalolco. So far, however, Brazil has retained a caveat that it will not apply to them until all other nations sign it. And Argentina, Cuba, France, Russia have not yet signed the Tlatalolco Treaty.

We would hope that every effort would be made by Brazil and other countries as it is on the part of our own country to prevent the spread of nuclear explosive capability to any nation which does not presently have it.

Q: Mr. President, what are the carrots?

P: We have no specific carrots to offer except that we are making available to countries and now in a much more predictable way with the new Congressional law enriched uranium which is suitable for production of power but not suitable for explosives and technological advice and counsel, both in the use of uranium with which Brazil is not blessed as a natural resource, and also thorium which we have in our own country and which Brazil already has.

The new thorium technology is a much safer one to provide power without going to plutonium. Recently Brazil, I think very wisely, signed an additional agreement with West Germany which would open up advice and technological ability to use thorium. But the right of Brazil and the advisability of Brazil to have a very advanced nuclear power capability is one that we don't dispute, but on the other hand, approve.

I might add one other point, and that is that we see a clear need for all nations to sign the nonproliferation treaty. We are signatories of it. So are the Soviet Union, the Germans, most of the countries in the world, and this combined with international atomic agency safeguards is a good guarantee within a country and throughout the developed and developing world that there will not be a trend in the future toward other nations developing nuclear explosive capability.

Trying to Oust Begin?

Q: Mr. President, have you or any other top U.S.-officials — Dr. Brzezinski, for instance — suggested that Prime Minister Begin may not be the right man to head that government in the present circumstances? And apart from what may or may not have been said, do you now think that the Begin government can make the hard decisions necessary to move the peace process forward?

P: I can say unequivocally that no one in any position of responsibility in the United States Administration has ever insinuated that Prime Minister Begin is not qualified to be Prime Minister or that he should be replaced. This report, the origin of which I do not know, is completely false.

I think that Prime Minister Begin and his government are able to negotiate in an adequately flexible way to reach an agreement with Egypt, later Jordan and other of the neighboring countries. This is our hope and this is our belief.

We have not given up on the possibility of a negotiated peace settlement in the Middle East.

Under the Begin government with him as Prime Minister, recently arrangements have been made between Israel and Egypt for Ezer Weizman to go to Egypt again which will be a continuation of the probing for compatability. I think it is obvious now that with the issues so sharply drawn that key differences remain that must be addressed on the side of Israel. The things that are of deepest concern is Israel's refusal to acknowledge that United Nations Resolution 242 as applies clearly to the West Bank, their unwillingness to grant to the West Bank Palestinians, the Palestinian Arabs, a right to participate in the determination of their own future by voting at the end of a five-year period and so forth for the kind of affiliation they would have with Israel or Jordan or under a joint administration, and this is a problem for which I have no clear solution yet. But I believe that the Begin government is completely capable of negotiating an agreement with Egypt.

I promised this gentleman right here.

Future Visits

Q: I am from Channel 13, Argentina. Excuse me, my colleague.

In connection with your visit now in Latin America, do you expect in the future — do you consider the possibility of another visit to the other countries of Latin America — like in my case, Argentina, and do you have an eventual visit date for this?

P: We have not yet set any date, nor made any plans for future visits. As you may know, I have visited Argentina in the past. So has my wife. And this year, this past year, Secretary of State — our Secretary of State, Cyrus Vance, visited Argentina, too, and your own leader, Videla, came to visit us in Washington. I have no plans now for any additional trips anywhere after I return to Washington.

Yes, sir?

Meeting With Cardinal

Q: What is the purpose of this meeting that you are having in Rio with Cardinal Arns and five other people? I mean

what specifically are you intending to discuss with them, and —

P: I don't have any agenda prepared for my visit with Cardinal Arns and the others. In a diverse society like you have here in Brazil, it is important for me to visit with different persons who represent different views. I will have thorough discussions, as you know, with President Geisel and his Administration and I want to meet with as many other people as I can. I have, by the way, met and talked to Cardinal Arns previously in the United States. I think this is typical of leaders who visit other countries. I noticed, for instance, with some interest that when President Geisel visited the Federal Republic of Germany recently, he not only met with Chancellor Schmidt, but he met with the leaders of the opposition parties.

And as a leader of a nation, I reserve the right to meet with whom I please. And I think this is a constructive thing, which will give me a much better overall understanding of what exists in Brazil, and I think the right of people to speak to me as a foreign visitor is one that is important to Brazil to preserve and to cherish, and I am thankful that I have that right when I visit your country.

Inflation Program

Q: Mr. President, when you return from this Latin American and African trip, do you have any plans to combat the number one concern of the American people? I refer to inflation. Specifically, do you have any changes in mind in your up-to-now voluntary program of price and wage restraints?

P: Yes. My Administration, during the last couple of weeks, has been evolving a complete analysis of what we can do, both through administrative action, through public statements, through working with the business community and the labor community, and through Congressional action to control inflation, which is becoming an increasingly important problem for us.

I think the consumer price index figures that were released this week, the day we left Washington, were much better than we had anticipated, but still a cause for concern.

So when I get home, one of the first acts that I shall take is to make public the decisions that we are now putting together.

Q: Will they change the voluntary nature of the program, Mr. President?

P: I will address the details when I get back home.

Yes, I will get you next.

Brazil Government — 1

Q: I would like to know whether in your meeting with General Figueiredo yesterday you discussed the program of the general political opening up of the Brazilian Government and the implementation of that plan?

P: I did not have an opportunity to discuss any matters of importance with General Figueiredo. I only met him very briefly in a larger group of people, thirty or forty people, and in the receiving line when I came into the airport. So I have not had a chance to discuss this with him.

Ann?

Steel Price Hike

Q: Mr. President, despite some jawboning pressure from your Administration, U.S. Steel has raised its prices again. How does that fit in with your overall plans on inflation that is going to have some substantial impact nationwide?

P: It fits in very poorly. (Laughter) I think the prices announced by U.S. Steel, as their plans, are excessive, and although I have not been thoroughly briefed on what the Council on Wage and Price Stability has recommended, I will get that report today, but I think any such increase as I have heard, approximately $10 a ton, is excessive and does cause additional, very serious inflationary pressures in our country, and I think is much greater than would be warranted by the recent coal settlement.

Yes, ma'am?

Brazil Government — 2

Q: I am from the State of Sao Paulo. My basic question was the same as he asked, but I would like to know how you view the succession here in Brazil and how do you view the problem of political and civil rights in Brazil?

P: I think the type of succession and the process through which you choose your leaders, or your leaders are chosen, is one to be decided in Brazil. I am not here to tell you how to form your government. I have no inclination to do that. The Brazilian people are completely aware of the process and that is a judgment for you to make.

Brazil, like the United States, is struggling with the very difficult question of identifying human rights and civil rights violations, enhancing the democratic processes and also encouraging confidence among the people in my government in the United States and in the government here in Brazil and other countries.

The differences that have arisen on the human rights issue is not based upon the lack of commitment to enhance human rights. I think great progress has been made in your country and also in ours. We do have a sharp difference of opinion, however, on how the human rights issue should be addressed, how specific allegations should be investigated, and what action can be taken to correct any defects that exist in your country or mine or others.

We believe that this is an international problem, that the focusing of world attention and world pressure on us and other countries is a very beneficial factor, that high publicity should be given to any proven violation of human rights. It is a commitment that our nation has that I want not to abandon but to enhance and to strengthen.

Brazil, on the other hand, also struggling with the same problem trying to give greater human rights, does not believe that the international organizations and multinational opinions should be marshaled. However, I do note that recently Brazil did vote for an increase in the financing of the Inter-American Human Rights Commission.

We think that when an allegation is made in our own country, in Brazil, in the European countries, wherever, that some responsible delegation from the Inter-American Human Rights Commission or the United Nations should go in, get the facts, make the facts public. If there is an actual violation, there would be a great incentive to the government involved, ours or yours or others, to correct the defect.

If the allegation is false, then the exposition of the error, or the false allegation, would be good for the world to know.

So I think this is a very deep and important consideration. One of the best things about the development on human rights in the last year or so has been the worldwide attention to it. It was kind of a dormant issue for too long. Now I doubt that there is a world leader who exists that doesn't constantly feel the pressure of considering the human rights question — to analyze one's own Administration, one's own country, what the rest of the world thinks about us and how we can correct any defects and prevent allegations in the future either true or false.

Middle East Visit

Q: Mr, President, with the new movement which is now apparent in the Middle East question, is there any possibility of a Middle East stop on your way back home?

P: No. No. I have no intention to stop in the Middle East. I will go from here to Nigeria, from there to Liberia, and then back home.

Maybe one more question.

Human Rights in Brazil

Q: The restraint of your public words until now, your specific desire to meet with the new President, all these facts amount to a virtual blessing of the Brazilian mission. Is your interest in civil rights and political dissidents fading away, or are American economic interests in this country so strong that Brazil is already a special case?

P: I might say that the history, the culture, the common defense requirements, trade, common purpose bind, the people of Brazil, all bind the people of Brazil and the people of the United States together in an unbreakable commitment regardless of the identity of the leaders in our own country or yours. The people of Brazil and the United States are bound together. There is no lessening of our commitment to the principles that you described. The basic freedoms to democratic government, to the protection of human rights, to the preven-

tion of nuclear proliferation, these commitments are also very deep for us.

Obviously, the overwhelming responsibility when I come to a foreign country, no matter where it is, is to meet with the leaders who are in office. But I also will be visiting the Congress this morning. I am sure that I will be meeting with the Chairman of a Foreign Relations Committee who is also a candidate for President.

We have already pointed out I will be meeting with religious leaders and I hope that in this process that I will have a chance to get views from all elements, at least some of the major elements of the Brazilian society. But I am not endorsing any candidates, and I think that the overwhelming sense of my visit already has been that the strength of our friendship and the mutuality of our purposes now and in the future far override any sharply expressed differences of opinion on even the major and very important issues of human rights, nonproliferation, trade, and so forth.

MR. CORMIER (AP): Thank you, Mr. President. ∎

April 11, 1978

Following is the White House transcript of President Carter's April 11 news conference, following his speech to the American Society of Newspaper Editors. It was Carter's 29th news conference since taking office:

Administration Image

Q: Mr. President, whatever the reaction to your economic speech here today, it seems clear that this administration faces a continuing image problem. You, sir, came into office with an image of freshness, with promises of efficiency and reform, and above all, with promises to run an open administration, close to the public. But after 15 months, the polls seem to indicate declining public hope in your administration.

Some of our newspapers criticize you for being indecisive and above all have said that the presidency, far from being open, is increasingly dependent on a small group of intimate advisors.

Whether these charges are fair or unfair, sir, are you concerned by this dramatic shift in image, and, if so, how do you hope to redress the situation?

P: I don't agree that there is a dramatic shift in image. I think the poll results have been fairly stable for the last four or five months. And as has been the case with previous presidents, after the flush of victory is over and the very difficult responsibilities descend on the shoulders of a president, the high expectations of the people that the problems would be resolved overnight tend to cause a deterioration in public expectancy and sometimes a feeling of discouragement.

We have deliberately addressed some of the more difficult and intransigent, even historic, problems of our country. We are having, I think, good progress in resolving most of these problems. In domestic affairs, we have begun to reorganize the government. Every proposal that I have put to the Congress so far has been accepted. We have formed a new Department of Energy. The Congress has now been working for 12 months on a comprehensive energy policy.

These are the same matters that were addressed when Harry Truman was president back in 1948, deregulation of natural gas, dealing with excessive energy consumption. They are extremely controversial and very difficult.

We put forward our proposals on economic stimulus. I believe that last year we achieved a remarkable degree of success in meeting the goals that we set for our administration with unemployment dropping drastically, as I already pointed out, inflation holding steady, good economic growth.

We have, I think, helped to revitalize the interest not only of our own country, but our European allies in the strength of NATO, a recommitment to a long range military program that will resubmit that alliance. We are dealing with a very difficult Middle East problem. And I think if anyone would take an inventory of what did occur a year ago, what circumstance did prevail, the progress that has been made — although success is still doubtful — is notable.

We are making good steady progress on the SALT negotiations, a subject that has been a matter of public international debate for decades. I think that we have a good prospect this year of having success in that respect. For the first time, we are addressing actual reducing the number of atomic weapons held by ourselves and the Soviet Union.

We are making good progress along with the British and the Soviets with a comprehensive test ban, for the first time prohibiting, if we are successful, the testing of any atomic explosions, either military weapons or peaceful devices, an unprecedented attempt at a very difficult subject.

I think it is accurate to say that a year or so ago, almost everyone felt the nuclear genie was out of the bottle, that many of the nations that don't have atomic explosive capability were on the verge of achieving it through the free sale of reprocessing plans around the world.

I think that has now been stopped. I think our effort to put forward an image of our country that would give us a source of pride in human rights has been a profound impact around the world. I don't think there is a single leader of a nation anywhere that is not now constantly aware of the question of how my country, how my actions are measuring up against international standards in preserving basic human rights.

So we have got a lot of things we haven't yet solved. We are trying to deal with them; energy, inflation, continued government efficiency, welfare reform, tax reform. But I think the Congress has had a notable achievement. I feel at ease with the job, I have enjoyed it. I roll easily with the punches of criticism, whether I think it is deserved or not deserved. Our poll status is holding steady at this point. I think in general, I could characterize our administration as dealing with some of the most difficult questions that face our nation without restraint and without attention being given to the political consequences or possible failure, and I believe that the successes in the future will prove that we were right. I will keep the other answers briefer.

Tom, good to see you.

Election Plans

Q: I can't resist saying how satisfying it is to all of us to finally see you live, as it were. As you remember, I think we had a couple of encounters, rather shaky telephonic communications, once from opposite sides of a picket line in Washington and once in Honolulu. It is nice to see you here.

My question: You have been in office 15 months, roughly. How comfortable do you feel in the job, what is your biggest surprise that you have encountered in this job, and do you definitely plan to run for re-election?

P: The answer to the last question is no, I don't definitely plan to run for re-election. I haven't addressed that question at all.

Secondly, my biggest surprise — I guess you mean in the nature of a disappointment. I think I have found it is much easier for me in my own administration to evolve a very complex proposal for resolving a difficult issue than it is for Congress to pass legislation and to make that same decision.

The energy legislation is one example. I never dreamed a year ago in April when I proposed this matter to the Congress that a year later it still would not be resolved. I think I have got a growing understanding of the Congress, its limitations, and its capabilities and also its leadership, which was a new experience for me altogether, never having lived or served in the federal government in Washington.

As far as my attitude toward the job is concerned, I like it. I have got a good staff. We have now evolved, I think, a good means by which we address major issues and let everyone's views be known. We sometimes have, contrary to what Mr. Hughes said, too open an examination of our debate process and decision-making process, where the news media quite often takes a preliminary proposal by a secretary or a matter we are considering as a final judgment, and I only make one judgment, which is then released to the press. That has been a problem for us. I think I have got an outstanding Cabinet. After this first 15 months, there is none on the Cabinet

that I would have preferred to have changed. I am very satisfied with them. I hope they are also satisfied.

So I like the job. I feel at ease with it. I am doing the best I can with difficult problems. All presidents have shared them. And I think compared with my predecessors we have done okay.

Wage and Price Controls

Q: Mr. President, I am Abe Rosenthal, *New York Times.*

In your speech you have taken a position against imposed wage and price controls.

P: Yes.

Q: And yet in your speech you yourself impose wage controls on the federal part of the work force. That is not very voluntary. And you also talk about a federal pricing policy. Do you have any mental tripwire at which point you will say that this country must have an imposed wage and price control policy, that the inflation has gone too high, and that volunteerism simply has not worked?

P: No, I do not. I think even if inflation should continue to escalate and reach a very high level, that wage and price controls, mandatory wage and price controls would be ill-advised and also counterproductive. I don't think they would work. The only instance of which I can think where wage and price controls might be applied would be a case of national emergency, like an all-out war, some tragedy of that kind, where normal economic processes would not be at work.

I don't think that my dealing with the wages of people that I appoint or whose executive management is my responsibility is under the category of wage and price controls. I think that the normal processes of wages will be observed and I hope that the federal government can break the deadlock that now exists between the private and public sector by setting an example.

I think that what I have proposed in the top executives in my own staff members having no increases this year, and a 5½ percent increase for the white-collar workers of the federal government, is reasonable. But I cannot imagine any circumstance under which I would favor mandatory wage and price controls.

Q: Mr. President, Dick Harwood with *The Washington Post.* To further clarify your remarks on this question of wage and price restraint, are you proposing that the 5½ percent should be a standard for private wage settlements this year? And are you proposing any numerical ceiling or guideline on price increase?

P: No, the level that I have set as a target for the private sector — a voluntary compliance provision — is to take the increases for the last two years and have the 1978 increases be less than that two-year average. That would apply to both prices and wages. Once we turn the corner on inflation and start with a slight downward trend instead of a continued upward trend, I think we would have a very healthy result

throughout the country without anyone suffering.

As I pointed out, all of us anticipate continued inflation. We make our plans accordingly and therefore perpetuate the inflation rate. There is an underlying inflation rate that has existed in our country for a number of years of 6 to 6½ percent. I certainly don't want to see that underlying inflation rate increase. I would like to bring it downward, and we have set that as a goal for ourselves.

Last year we met this goal both in inflation and the unemployment rate and also in natural growth rate. But I think that if everyone would voluntarily comply with the standard that I have described to you, it would be an extremely beneficial thing for our country and no one would suffer in the process.

Tuition Tax Credits

Q: Mr. President, Christy Bulkeley, Danville, Illinois; *Commercial News.* You expressed concern about the tuition tax credits that are in Congress.

P: Yes.

Q: Do you intend to veto the bill if it reaches you as proposed, or do you see an acceptable level of tuition tax credits?

P: My present intention would be to veto any bill that was costly and which was unconstitutional. All of the proposals that I have seen in the Congress so far are both costly and unconstitutional, particularly as they apply to elementary and secondary schools. But until I see legislation actually on my desk, I couldn't give you a firm commitment that I would veto it. But unless those two provisions are corrected, that I have just described as potential defects, then I would veto it.

Q: The second question I have is, do you see a possible compromise on a level that you would consider acceptable?

P: No. I don't favor tuition tax credits under any circumstance, even if it was at a very slight level, because this would inevitably rapidly grow with each succeeding budget, and the first thing you know, tuition tax credits would be the major federal expenditure for all education in the United States. So I think that the tuition tax credits itself, as a subject, is very detrimental to the future of education in our country.

It gives credit to those who need them least, and it makes the average parent who is a working class person, particularly who has his children in the public schools, pay for high tax benefits for families in a higher tax group who have their children in private schools. So I think the whole concept is fallacious, and I don't like it. (Applause)

Social Security Tax Rollback

Q: Mr. President, Jim Squires with the *Orlando Sentinel Star.* You did not mention a possible veto of the rollback in Congress of Social Security taxes. There is a report that you might accept that rollback if it were tied to a proposal that would levy a crude oil tax and devote the revenue to financing the Social Security project.

Could you tell me if that report is true, and if you would veto the bill if it passes in its present form?

P: Well, I have made it clear to the congressional leadership in the House and the Senate that I do not favor any modification in the Social Security laws or financing structure this year.

The Congress, I think last year, very courageously passed Social Security legislation that would bring order out of chaos and put the Social Security reserve funds back on a sound basis for 25 or 30 years in the future. They were on the verge of bankruptcy. Also, those who are particularly affected with higher Social Security payments, beginning next year — not this year, by the way — are those in a higher income group who will have their retirement benefits increased.

The tax reform proposals and the tax reduction proposals submitted to Congress this year will in almost every instance more than compensate for any increase in Social Security payments.

So for all those reasons, I do not favor any Social Security legislation this year. I can't say unequivocally that I would veto any such measure that came to my desk. My guess is that the furor that was originally raised about Social Security benefits, after more careful examination by the American people and the news media has now ceased to be a burning issue. My prediction is that the Congress will not send to me any legislation on Social Security.

Q: Do you see any possibility of compromise with the energy bill, of a tie between those two?

P: Not at this moment, I don't.

Race Relations Leadership

Q: Mr. President, Bob Haiman from the *St. Petersburg Times,* St. Petersburg, Florida.

Mr. President, this is the Tenth Anniversary of the report of the Kerner Commission on race problems in America. Those who look at that report and its allegations and what has happened since '68 are inclined to believe there has been some progress for black Americans, but not much. The Carnegie Corporation, in trying to account for why we still seem to be moving toward two separate and unequal societies in this country, last night issued a report which says very briefly in one sentence, and I quote, "It is because there seems to be no leader who is capable of evoking a nation's latent sense of conscience and mobilizing it to action."

My question is, sir, could you be that leader, should you be that leader, are you that leader, and if you are, then how do you plan to lead?

P: I think it is incumbent on a president to speak for the nation and particular-

ly to speak for those citizens of our nation who are deprived, who are needy, who are poor, who are non-influential, who are inarticulate, and who suffer because of the past discriminations that have fallen upon black people and other minority groups and who still have their own families devastated by poverty and unemployment out of all proportion to their percentage of national population.

We have increased greatly the economic benefits, at least, the job opportunities of minority groups since I have been in office, not only in the appointments that I have made of major leaders for positions of executive authority but in other ways.

For instance, we set as the goal of the first year of our administration to have more than $100 million in federal deposits in black-owned banks, minority-owned banks. We have reached that goal. Congress passed legislation requiring that in the public works legislation, a $4 billion program, that 10 percent of this money be spent with businesses owned by minority stockholders as a dominant stockholding group. That goal has been exceeded.

We have now proposed to the Congress — and I predict immediate passage, no delay — a complete reorganization of the Equal Employment Opportunity functions within the federal government. We are struggling to bring up the unemployment rate among minority citizens. And I think that in the housing area, in our urban policy program that we have just put forward, all these things have been done.

So to measure my own effectiveness as a leader in this respect is something I am not able to do. I don't think we have achieved notable success as yet. But I think I, combining my voice with congressional leaders, those in private business, the minority organization leaders who are very evocative and very effective, the sum total of that plus obviously, editorial support from all of you, can make the difference.

My own belief is that minority groups have prospered in this country in the last ten years, compared to their previous circumstances. But they have a long way to go, and I feel responsible to make sure they go that long way toward equality of opportunity in this country. (Applause)

China Policy

Q: Bob Smyser, *Honolulu Star-Bulletin.* I would like to ask about your China policy and about Taiwan in particular.

The present Peking government says it will not use force in the near term to settle the Taiwan question, but it will not rule out the use of force for the indefinite future. Does this reservation by Peking pose an insurmountable obstacle to our full diplomatic recognition of Peking?

P: I would not acknowledge any insurmountable obstacle. In reaching the goals expressed in the Shanghai Communique, which is binding on us, and which I

fully support, and binding on the People's Republic of China leaders, we recognize the concept that is shared in Taiwan and on the Mainland there is only one China. We recognize it is for the best interests of our own nation to have full diplomatic relationships with China. And my hope is that over a period of months — we are not in any big hurry; neither are the People's Republic of China leaders — that we will completely realize the hopes expressed in the Shanghai Communique.

Rising Utility Bills

Q: Mr. President, Al Fitzpatrick from the *Beacon Journal* in Akron, Ohio.

You mentioned in your speech conserving energy and that we all ought to conserve energy. I think many people have done just that. But how does one justify saving energy when those monthly utility bills continue to rise?

P: Well, I think the rising monthly utility bills is an additional incentive to save energy, and not a contrary factor. Obviously, when we consume more energy than we produce in our country, it means that there is a pressure on limited supplies and competition for those available supplies, and the prices go up. As the price of coal and oil go up to the consuming homeowner, they also go up to the utility companies that produce electric power.

Many utility companies around this nation have an automatic escalator clause where without any approval by the regulatory agency in a state they can pass on those increased fuel costs to the consumer. Obviously, the more we can hold down our consumption of energy, the more we can save on our monthly fuel bills and the more we can hold down the increase in oil, natural gas and coal prices.

One of the additional problems with the lack of conservation is that we have now increased our oil [imports] to $45 billion a year and they comprise about 50 percent of all the oil we use. If we should have — and heaven knows, I hope we never have — another oil embargo where those supply interruptions would afflict our nation, it would be a much more serious problem to our national security, to our own economic prosperity and even national existence than it was back in 1973 when that temporary interruption took place.

So we have got to do at least two major things, among others: Each one of us conserve the energy we consume by every possible means; and second, to increase the production of available supplies in our country of energy — coal, which can last several hundred years; and particularly those replenishable supplies derived from wood, from solar sources, from geothermal supplies and so forth.

Bergland Quitting?

Q: Jean Alice Small, the *Daily Journal,* Kankakee, Illinois.

Mr. President, recently it was reported that Secretary of Agriculture Bergland is considering resignation from his Cabinet post because of your position on agriculture and the farm bill. May I ask if this is true? And in reference to your Cabinet, do you plan to make any Cabinet changes in the near future or after the election?

P: That report was absolutely erroneous. There was no basis for it at all. There has not been any difference of opinion between myself and Bob Bergland about agricultural policy. At the Cabinet meeting Monday morning, Bob Bergland said that, as was the case when Mark Twain said the report of his own death had been exaggerated, he had never contemplated resigning from the Cabinet. As a matter of fact, if Bob Bergland and I have ever disagreed on a basic agricultural policy, I am not aware of it. I contemplate no changes in my Cabinet. Nothing would please me better than to finish four years with the same Cabinet I presently have.

Q: Thank you for straightening it out.

P: Thank you.

FBI Disciplinary Action

Q: Mr. President, Bailey of *The Minneapolis Tribune*.

P: Yes.

Q: Sir, the Attorney General said yesterday that 68 FBI agents will be disciplined but not prosecuted in connection with the burglary indictments, conspiracy indictments that were handed down yesterday.

Two questions related to that: Will the names of those 68 agents and the discipline applied be a matter of public record; and second, the decision not to prosecute them was apparently based on the theory that they were following orders. I wonder if you regard that as an appropriate reason for deciding not to prosecute a law enforcement officer who violates the law?

P: I don't know whether or not they will be, whether their names will be made public. I will have to ask the Attorney General about this. I don't know the legalities of it. I think that Griffin Bell made the right decision. He made it on his own — without consultation with me, by the way — to prosecute the ones who issued the order.

Obviously there are some instances in the military and otherwise when a heinous crime, when committed by someone under orders, should be punished. But I think in this case the Attorney General made the right decision.

FRANK CORMIER (AP): Thank you Mr. President.

(Applause)   ∎

April 25, 1978

Following is the White House transcript of President Carter's April 25 news conference, his 30th since taking office:

THE PRESIDENT: Before I became President I realized and was warned that dealing with the federal bureaucracy would be one of the worst problems I would have to face. It has been even worse than I had anticipated. Of all the steps that we can take to make government more efficient and effective, reforming the civil service system is the most important of all.

The civil service reform proposals which I submitted last month will return the civil service to some system of reward and incentive for the tens of thousands of superb public servants who want to do a good job for the American people.

This will also give managers a chance to manage. It will reward excellence, good service, dedication, and will protect employees' vital and legitimate rights.

It will also expand the protection against political abuse that employees need in order to do their jobs well, and will make our civil service one of the most dependable and one of the most effective and honest in the whole world.

Nearly everyone in our country will benefit from the civil service reform proposals. For those in private business, it will mean faster government action, less intrusion in the private sector of our economy. For taxpayers, it will mean that we get more for the money that we pay. For those who depend on government for help, it will mean better services to them, quicker, more effective.

And most of all, for the civil service employees, for the government employees, it will mean that they can do their jobs better and more effectively. They only have one life to live, and sometimes in a sacrificial way they want to dedicate their lives to public service, and this will let them do a better job.

When criticism and debate in the Congress lead to a stronger plan, then I will support these changes. But I will object very strenuously to weakening our proposal, and I do object also very strenuously to false accusations, specifically one that has been raised recently that this will intrude into the privacy of public servants and inject politics and possible abuse into the system to damage those who serve the government. In fact, to the creation of a Merit Protection Board and an Office of Special Counsel, political abuse is specifically removed.

I know that everyone wants a better government, particularly those of us like myself who are responsible for leadership and management of the United States Government.

In a way, I believe that our nation is being tested these days. We have a period of relative calm, free from great crisis or threat to our national security. And we are being tested to see whether or not we can take advantage of this opportunity for improvement.

It will reveal, I think, whether we can deal with conflicting narrow special interests and act in the national interest of our country.

Civil service reform is now before the Congress. It will test me and the Congress as well, and I believe that the Congress will give the right answer to the question: Can we have a better government? I think we can.

Oil Import Fees

Q: Mr. President, where do you stand now on the possibility of imposing by Executive Order or administrative action, oil import fees, and how soon might you act?

I understand that a couple of your advisers are suggesting a May 1 deadline.

P: Well, no one has suggested a deadline that early. As a matter of fact, we have just finished the fourth major element of a five-part comprehensive fuel or energy program with natural gas deregulation. And now this is being recommended to the complete Conference Committee.

The next step is the crude oil equalization tax which will be addressed by the Finance Committee in the Senate and the Ways and Means Committee in the House, representatives of them in the Conference Committee.

I have talked to the chairmen of both those committees about the crude oil equalization tax, the fifth element of our major proposals.

It is too early, I think, to consider administrative action. I still hope and expect that the Congress will act and will complete the fifth element of our energy plan and present the entire package as it should be to the Congress in one body.

Neutron Bomb

Q: Mr. President, President Brezhnev has offered to not build the neutron bomb if you agree or the U.S. agrees to do likewise.

Is that the word you are looking for to halt the program?

P: No. The Soviets know and President Brezhnev knows that the neutron weapon is designed to be used against massive and perhaps overwhelming tank forces in the Western and Eastern European areas.

The Soviets, over a period of years, have greatly built up their tank forces and others stronger than have the NATO allies.

The neutron weapons are designed to equalize that inequality, along with many other steps that our country is now taking. The Soviets have no use for a neutron weapon, so the offer by Brezhnev to refrain from building the neutron weapons has no significance in the European theatre. And he knows this.

We are strengthening NATO in other ways. Ourselves, our NATO allies, will meet here in Washington the last of May with a recommitment, which is already well in progress, for a long-range strengthening of NATO and all its aspects.

But this statement by Brezhnev concerning the neutron weapon has no significance at all.

Fighter Plane Sales — 1

Q: Mr. President, are you going to heed the calls of the congressional leadership of your own party and delay formal submission of the package sale of warplanes to the Congress or break it up in any way?

P: Well, I have not been asked by the leadership in the Congress to delay. I have had one senator who came to see me about holding off on this proposal. Secretary Vance and I have been in close communication, both with one another and with leaders in the Congress, for a number of weeks concerning the arms sale package that will be presented to the Congress very shortly. This package will be presented in individual component parts to the Congress. It is the only legal way to do it.

The Congress will act on those major sales proposals individually to Israel, to Egypt, and to Saudi Arabia. Each one is important. Each one completes a commitment that has been made by either me, or, even in the case of the Saudis and Israel, our predecessors for these sales.

I look upon them as a package. And if the Congress should accept a portion and reject another, then my intent is to withdraw the sales proposal altogether. But the Congress will not receive nor act on these proposals as a package. They have to act, according to the law, on individual items.

These proposals are in the national interest. I think it is important to our country to meet our commitments. The one that is perhaps the most controversial is the sale of F-15s to the Saudi Arabians. This was a promise that was made to the Saudi Arabians in September of 1975 to let them have a choice of F-16s or F-15s. They want these weapons for defensive purposes.

I recommitted this nation to provide these planes both last year and again this year. And my deep belief is that since in the Middle East our preeminent consideration is the long-range and permanent security and peacefulness for the people of Israel, that to treat the moderate Arabs with fairness and friendship and strengthen their commitment to us in return is in the best interests of our own country and of Israel.

We are negotiating or discussing these matters with the Congress. But there will be no delay of the sales proposal beyond the point where it can be completed by the time the Congress goes into recess — maybe two or three days; no longer than that.

Q: Mr. President, do you think it proper or do you think it right for the Foreign Minister of another government to interfere in the legislative processes of this government? I am talking particularly about your Middle East arms package here, legislation which you said is in the best interest of the United States. Do you think it is right?

P: Well, I have made my decision about the arms sales package after very careful consideration, a close study of de-

cisions and opinions expressed by my predecessors in the White House, careful consultation with the State Department and our Defense Department, our military leaders, and I have made my recommendation to the Congress. I will make it shortly on what I consider to be in the best interests of our allies and friends in the Middle East.

In each one of these instances, the arms sales proposals were made as a result of requests by the governments involved. And I think that is the basis on which the decision should be made, by my making the request to the Congress, by Congress considering my request for approval of the sales in the best interests of our country as judged by me and the Congress.

Tax Cut

Q: Mr. President, many Democrats in the House Ways and Means Committee, including the Chairman, are urging you to scale back your net tax cut to something under $20 billion, and the Federal Reserve chairman today suggested that you delay the effect of whatever tax cut until next January first, all because apparently they feel it is inflationary now, looking down the road.

Will you consider either of those suggestions?

P: No. A $25 billion reduction in taxes on the American people would not be inflationary. It is, in my judgment and the best judgment of the economic advisers who work with me, about the right figure. We only have about an 82 percent utilization of our production capacity now. We do not have excessive demand as a cause for inflationary increases in prices of our products.

We have a cycle of wage increases, price increases, that kind of grow on one another and I don't believe it would be advisable, and I do not intend to change my recommendation that the net between the tax reforms and the tax reductions would be approximately equal to $25 billion.

I think that the best time to make it effective is the first of October. I hope that Congress can act rapidly enough to make the reduction effective then.

The last quarter's results of growth in our national products showed some leveling off. It needs to be kept strong and vigorous. If this tax proposal does not go through, by the end of 1979, it would cost every family in America on the average $600 in income, about $40 billion in reduced income, because of a constrained economy that did not continue to grow.

If the tax reduction of $25 billion was eliminated, it would mean that we would have a million more people out of work by the end of the first 12 months after the tax reduction than we would have otherwise.

So for all those reasons and others, I think the $25 billion in tax reduction on our people, which is needed and which would help them, is about the right figure.

Fighter Plane Sales — 2

Q: Mr. President, just to follow up on the Middle East thing, I would like to pursue it just a little bit more maybe from a slightly different angle. The Israeli Foreign Minister, Mr. Dayan, has suggested that Israel might be willing to give up its own fighter planes in your package, if the sales were stopped to Saudi Arabia and Egypt.

In the light of your own professed interest in cutting back on foreign arms sales, would you consider withdrawing the entire package to prevent a new escalation of the arms race in the Middle East?

P: No, I would not. As I said earlier, the process through which we sell arms — and this sales proposal, would be completed five years in the future, by — I think the last deliveries would be 1983 — is initiated by a request from governments, foreign governments, that we permit the sale of arms to them. As I said earlier, we committed ourselves to help Saudi Arabia with arms sales to protect themselves in September of 1975.

At the same time, approximately, in the fall of 1975, our government committed to help Israel with their proposal, by making arms sales available to them. Obviously, if any nation withdrew its request for arms sales, that would change the entire procedure.

I have never heard of Foreign Minister Dayan's statement that they did not need the weapons or would withdraw their request for weapons until today. Mr. Dayan is on the way to our country. He will be meeting shortly with the Secretary of State and others, and I think only after very close consultations with them can we determine whether or not Israel desires to go ahead with the arms sales commitment that I have made to them.

But I do not intend to withdraw the arms sales proposals after they are submitted to the Congress, and I do not intend to delay.

Q: If Mr. Dayan did in fact tell you that Israel would withdraw its request, would you then be willing to pull back the whole package?

P: I can't imagine that happening, and I would rather not answer a hypothetical question of that kind.

Middle East Negotiations

Q: You mentioned that Mr. Dayan is coming. I just wonder, sir, do you have any reason at all to feel optimistic that the negotiations between Israel and Egypt can somehow be brought off dead center?

I know Mr. Atherton has been in Cairo and you have had consultations. What is the outlook now?

P: I have reason to be optimistic but I can't predict success any time soon. This has been going on for 30 years.

I think compared to a year ago, for instance, remarkable progress has been made. After the visit of President Sadat to

Jerusalem, there was a remarkable sense of excessive hope or euphoria that swept the world that peace was imminent.

Since then I have met extensively with President Sadat and with Prime Minister Begin and also with the foreign ministers of the two countries involved. And there is still hope that we can move toward a peaceful settlement.

I think if there were not hope, that Foreign Minister Dayan would not be coming to Washington to meet with our own officials to explore further avenues for progress.

As you know, since Prime Minister Begin was here, Ezer Weizman, who is the Defense Minister of Israel, has been to Egypt (once) to meet with President Sadat. So discussions are going on and explorations are continuing.

And I am firmly convinced that both the Israelis and Egyptians want peace. They both are concerned about the terms of peace. After years of hatred and even active combat, there is still an element of distrust about the future intentions of each other.

But I am hopeful that we can continue to make progress. My commitment is deep and irreversible. As long as I am in the White House as President, I will continue to pursue without any slackening of my interests or commitment, the avenue toward peace.

And I anticipate that now and in the future there will be temporary periods of discouragement and withdrawal of the negotiating parties. So I think every evidence that I have both publicly and privately known is that both sides want peace and the progress toward peace is steady.

Criticizing Congress

Q: Mr. President, last week you used very strong language to criticize Congress for wasting a year on energy legislation, and you also urged Congress to be more responsive to the public desire for tax reform.

Since this allegedly laggardly, unresponsive Congress is controlled by the Democrats, and since congressional elections will be held this fall, doesn't that constitute an attack on members of your own party?

P: Well, I wouldn't characterize it as an attack. I think it was an accurate description of the fact that for 12 months Congress had had a very good energy proposal before it and had not acted conclusively on it.

The day after I made that statement, the negotiating team within the Conference Committee did resolve to their own satisfaction the question of the regulation and pricing of natural gas.

One of the most difficult political questions that ever addressed Congress. This has been kicking around now for at least 30 years. I think Truman vetoed the first natural gas deregulation bill. I think it is a step in the right direction.

Now, out of the five major categories of proposals I made to the Congress a year ago, four of them have been resolved at least at the conference level and now the remaining issue is the pricing of oil.

We, last year, imported $45 billion worth of oil, too much, and I believe the Congress is beginning to see the public supports action on the energy legislation and that when they do act it will help our whole economy.

I think one of the reasons that the stock market has gone up, I think almost 75 points in the last two weeks, unprecedented rise, is, among other things, a new commitment to fighting inflation and the apparent willingness of Congress now to act on the energy legislation; those two things.

So I am not attacking the Congress, but I reserve the right to point out the inactivity of Congress which I think on occasion does inspire them to act more rapidly.

Inflation and Unemployment

Q: Mr. President, a few days ago you met with some top executives of big corporations to discuss inflation. Did you discuss unemployment at the same time? If so, could you tell us about that as it relates to unemployment?

P: Yes, we did discuss unemployment. I pointed out to the executives who were here that in the last, I would say 12 months, because of the good action on the part of the Democratic Congress, in putting into law our stimulus package, that we had had a dramatic drop in the unemployment rate; and that a year ago, they around that table including myself and the members of my Cabinet who were there, had been almost completely committed or concerned about unemployment. That is now going in the right direction. I think, the last three or four months show that the unemployment rate is at 6 percent or a little above, almost two full percentage points less than it was 15 months ago when I became President. This has got to continue.

We also discussed the fact that the focusing of federal programs concerning reducing unemployment can now be placed upon those who are most difficult to employ — minority citizens, women and others who are the last ones hired and the first ones fired, and the young people who also have a very high unemployment rate.

So we are not slackening off at all on the employment question. The programs that we put into effect are still in effect. They are getting more and more specifically effective with different groups as time goes on. My belief is that the unemployment rate will continue to decrease, particularly among those groups that I have just described and, at the same time, we can tackle inflation with a much higher concentration of our own effort and commitment and public awareness.

The two are not in conflict. We have seen that when the last administration, which happens to have been Republican, concentrated on inflation by letting unemployment go up, it did not work. So I believe the best thing is to do what we have already done, and that is to try to hold down inflation and bring down unemployment at the same time. That is what we are trying to do.

Lobby Disclosure Bill

Q: Mr. President, in view of the increased lobbying on the Hill, witness the Panama Canal and your civil service reform and all of this, can you support Senator Kennedy's new expected legislation on lobbies?

P: I strongly support the lobby control legislation that is now before the Congress. I am not sure that I know exactly the terms of Senator Kennedy's own bill. The Congress will vote this week, the House of Representatives will vote this week, on a very effective lobby control bill, a lobby reform bill, and I support that strongly.

It was one of the themes that I pursued during my own campaign for President. We have been actively involved in drafting it in the strongest possible terms, and I do support it.

Interest Rates

Q: Mr. President, were you surprised last week when the Federal Reserve raised the short-term interest rate, and have you any reaction to it?

P: I didn't have any prior knowledge that the Federal Reserve was going to raise the interest rates. I do get a report frequently and regularly about the supply of money and how much it is increasing. I understand after the action was taken, because of an explanation by the Chairman to Charlie Schultze, that the reason they did raise the interest rates was because the money supply was increasing more rapidly than they desired or thought was advisable for our country. And obviously, as you know, the Federal Reserve Board is completely independent of me. They have no reason to consult with me before they make a decision, and don't do it as a matter of policy.

But I think that the interest rates ought to be kept as low as possible and, as you know, I can help to control that by the form of economic proposals I make to the Congress, the budget levels and so forth, and the Congress can help to determine that by the rate of taxation and the size of the deficit and the Federal Reserve primarily by controlling in indirect means the supply of money.

But that is an independent action. I did not know about it ahead of time. I understand the reason that they did it. I would like to do everything I can — I know that Bill Miller would, too — to hold down interest rate levels.

Fighter Plane Sales - 3

Q: Mr. President, you said there will be written assurances from Saudi Arabia and Egypt they will not use the war planes against Israel in any future conflict. Further, various Administration spokesmen have pointed out that the Saudi Arabian Government will be dependent on the U.S. for technical support for these planes and this support could always be cut off in the event that a future conflict would start, and that the Saudis desire to use the weapons against Israel.

Is it your understanding that both types of assurances will be in effect?

P: We would not sell the planes to the Saudi Arabians if we thought that the desire was to use them against Israel. I am completely convinced that the Saudis want their airplanes to be used to protect their own country.

The Saudis have informed officials in our government that they do not desire to deploy them at Tabuk, which is the airfield nearest to Israel, and I know for a fact that the configuration of the weapons on the F-15 that the Saudis have offered is primarily a defensive configuration. And for those reasons I feel sure that the problems that you described are adequately addressed in the proposals that I have made to the Congress and in the statements that the Saudis have already made.

New York City Aid

Q: Mr. President, the long-term loan package for New York City is in a great deal of trouble on Capitol Hill. I am curious, sir, just how much of a commitment are you prepared to make to push for that legislation in the coming weeks?

P: It is one of the major goals of our Administration to have economic aid for New York City. The Secretary of the Treasury, Mike Blumenthal, has discussed this since the first day, first few days that we were in office, with the Mayor of New York, Beame and now Koch, and also with Governor Carey and other officials in New York, the labor leaders, the bankers in New York City and others.

We have also had close consultations with the committees in Congress. We have proposed a package that I think would alleviate New York City's short-term and long-term financial problems, but a major part of the responsibility has got to fall upon the people in New York City itself. Unless New York is willing to commit themselves and to prove to us that they can and will balance the budget through careful consideration of how money is expended to the levels of taxation involved, unless the leaders in New York City, both in and out of government, prove to us and the Congress that they will operate or cooperate together to put New York City back on a sound basis, I don't think it is possible for the Congress to pass the New York City legislative proposal that we have already submitted to the Congress.

I think that so far indications are that all persons involved, ourselves, the Congressional leaders and the New York City officials in and out of government, are committed to this common goal. So I believe the Congress will pass the legislation. I think the proposal we made will help to solve New York City's problems without costing the American taxpayers anything. And I believe that it will bring all of us together in a much more cooperative way.

Middle Income Taxpayers

Q: Mr. President, if I could just follow up on an earlier tax question, how unfair do you think the tax burden is that this country now places on the middle class? And if you do think it is unfair, then why are you so insistent on pushing tax reform that most people believe are going to hit the middle class the worst and on resisting a rollback in the social security taxes that would also penalize the middle class?

P: Let me answer your last question first.

One of the things that we had to do last year was to bring the social security system out of near bankruptcy into a sound economic position. Two of the three major reserve funds for the social security system were on the verge of bankruptcy and the Congress had to increase the social security payments to keep the social security system sound. They acted courageously and properly in that respect.

In order to make sure that the taxpayers in all categories, with very few exceptions, have a net reduction in their taxes this year, even after paying increased social security benefits, that is where the tax reduction proposal comes in.

If the Congress should not act in accordance with my request and lower income taxes, then there would be a net increase in taxes paid by the middle income groups.

Another factor that has not been adequately publicized is those very people who pay high income taxes, those 20, 25, 30 thousand dollar citizens, having that much income per year, also get better benefits when they retire. So in a way it is kind of an investment for them.

We have a lot of abuses in the system that ought to be eliminated. Last year, for instance, one medical doctor, a surgeon, owns a yacht and he took a $14,000 tax credit, tax exemption, for entertaining other doctors on his yacht. This is legal under the present law. Most American citizens don't have a yacht and when they go for a small pleasure ride, if they do have a small boat, they can't deduct it as an income tax deduction. And when that doctor didn't pay his $14,000 in taxes, other average working American families had to pay his taxes for him.

We have another instance that I recall from the statistics I have read, that one businessman charged off 338 lunches last year, more than $10,000 in so-called business lunches, more than many American

families make in all, and the average working American had to pay that guy's taxes for him.

I think that is a gross abuse of the average American family. And that is the kind of corrections that we are trying to put in. On Capitol Hill now there is a concentrated and unbelievable number of highly qualified, very intelligent, very effective lobbyists trying to induce the Members of Congress to preserve those special privileges for people who have them because they are so powerful and so influential now and in the past that they could carve out for themselves some special deal in the income tax laws of our country at the expense of the average American family. That is where tax reform comes in.

So tax reduction is important to make sure we don't put an extra tax burden on our people; even counting Social Security. Tax reform is necessary to let our tax code be simple and fair for a change. Both those changes, both those recommendations are urgently needed.

FRANK CORMIER (AP): Thank you, Mr. President. ∎

May 4, 1978

Following is the White House transcript of President Carter's May 4 news conference in Portland, Ore. It was his 31st news conference as president.

THE PRESIDENT: Good evening, everybody.

First of all, let me say it is a great pleasure to be back here in Portland. I have come West on this trip to talk about the most pressing issues that we face, energy and environment, urban policy, agriculture, jobs, inflation, criminal justice, tax reform, and also to listen to what Westerners have to say. Our national agenda is a full one. We have a lot to discuss, a lot to do.

One of the things at the very top of that list is making our government work better. Reform of the civil service is the single most important step that we can take to insure that the government does what it is supposed to do — meet the needs of the American people with the minimum of waste and a maximum of efficiency.

We all want a government that is worthy of confidence and respect. That is what civil service reform is all about. Westerners have an extra stake in the efficiency of the civil service in the Federal Government because the Federal Government plays the larger role in the life of this region than perhaps any other. For example, the amount of public land in the West gives you a special stake in Federal decisions in the way they are implemented.

Since so many critical decisions are made in Washington and Washington is physically remote from the West, responsiveness of our government depends upon the ability to learn your needs and to give them a full and a fair consideration.

Civil Service Reform

Two months ago, I submitted to the Congress a comprehensive program of reform for the civil service. My aim has been to clear a path for honest, hard working and industrious civil servants and to give them the tools to get the job done.

I want to reward competence and dedication. I want to clear out the incompetence and the unresponsiveness that cheat the American taxpayer and give all governments a bad name.

And I want to make government more effective by establishing clear assignments of responsibility and authority.

We need to put the work ethic back in public service and we need to put merit back in the merit system.

We are trying to do that in a way that honors and protects every Federal employee's rights while giving managers in the Federal Government the authority that they need to do their job.

It is virtually impossible now to discipline those Federal employees who fail to perform. This is an issue of efficiency and good management, but it goes beyond that. It is also an issue of the performance and the vigor, the very life of our democratic system.

I think the American people in the West and all across the country are going to be watching how the Congress handles this very difficult but very important assignment to reform the bureaucracy of our government, the keystone of which is to make the civil service work better.

Mr. Cadera.

Timber Policy

Q: Mr. President, Jim Cadera, *Oregonian.* Soon you will receive recommendations from your staff implementation of your proposal to increase lumber supplies by cutting more public and private timber. Would you allow a variance from the policy of even flow in national forest timber harvesting if it is recommended? And I have a follow-up.

P: Well, what I am interested in, first of all, is to sustain the rate of harvest for our national forests on a constant basis in the years ahead. I would not want to have a crash program to harvest too much timber at this time. We now waste probably six billion board-feet of timber every year. So we want to improve the efficiency of harvesting the public lands' timber that we have now. We also want to make sure that after the logs are harvested, that the output of them is increased in efficiency and we want to assess whether or not we need to improve or increase the harvesting on private and state lands.

But no matter what the recommendations are to me, I would increase production only to the extent that we could do this and have a constant future of sustained production in our national forests.

Q: Will you order the Office of Management and Budget to increase forest ser-

vice job ceilings to allow intensive management and dramatically increase timber harvesting?

P: That is one of the things we will be addressing within the next few weeks. We have in the past been putting out for sale eleven, twelve billion board-feet of lumber per year. And if there is a decision made to increase this harvest rate and to sustain our permanent harvest capabilities, then it might call for additional forest personnel. But I think in any instance of what personnel we have working in our national forest need to do a better job to enhance production of the forests that we have. There are about, I think, 300,000 acres of national forests in Oregon, Governor Straub told me, which was over-harvested in the past which is now relatively nonproductive. This kind of over-harvesting in past years needs to be protected. So to improve the efficiency of acres we have is a very important element and may need more personnel.

If so, I would not hesitate to put them to work.

Carter Income Tax

Q: Mr. President, have you resolved the IRS audit of the 1975 income taxes and did you have to pay income taxes in 1977? And if so, how much?

P: Yes. I had to pay income taxes in 1977. I don't remember the exact figure. But it was a substantial amount. The 1975 audit, as far as I know, has not yet been completed. The last time I heard about it, the prospect was that it would be accurate within a couple hundred dollars.

Yes?

Nuclear Waste Disposal

Q: Mr. President, Federal officials tell us that there will be no permanent nuclear waste disposal program until the middle eighties. Nuclear plants across the nation will fill the temporary storage facilities by then. What do you propose to do in the interim and would you impose a storage site on the state that decided that it did not want to have a storage site?

P: We have had nuclear power for peaceful purposes now for more than 30 years. I think you know that in addition to that, we have had the production of atomic materials for weapons even earlier. There never has yet been a workable Federal policy for disposing of nuclear wastes on a permanent basis in Richland, Washington, for instance, where early supplies were produced.

I visited there often while I was in the Navy and the underground storage there has sprung some leaks in recent years that have been detected.

We are now looking into the prospect of storing nuclear wastes in underground caverns which perhaps are salt dome type enclosures, in some parts of the Central Southwest.

We have also many commercial producers of atomic power who store their own

spent nuclear fuel in various kinds of enclosures, both on the surface of the ground, in water tanks, and also buried underneath the surface of the ground.

By the end of this year. Dr. James Schlesinger will present to me a comprehensive proposal for a permanent waste disposal plan and to answer the last part of your question, I would not try to store nuclear wastes on any private lands in a state where opposition existed.

There may be some very large military areas owned by the Federal Government where storage would be proper, and where there may be some opposition from the State. But we are trying to work that out now. One of the places we are looking at, for instance, is in New Mexico and the process is including close consultations with local and state officials. It is a difficult problem that has not been resolved anywhere in the world yet.

Nuclear Power Policy

Q: Mr. President, I would also like to ask a question about nuclear power, but it goes beyond the storage of nuclear waste.

I am told by anti-nuclear groups here that their national goal is to shut down all nuclear plants. The tactic so far has been the same tactic that was used to shut down the Vietnam War, civil disobedience. So far as our Trojan plant is concerned, that has so far resulted in about 200 arrests and the consequent legal costs threaten to break the back of the tiny county trying the cases against them.

More than that, the issue of nuclear power seems to be enlarging into an issue that could be seriously divisive for the people of the country as a whole. What I would like to know is, is this in your thinking and do you have a plan for such a possibility?

P: Well, our national policy is to permit the planning, siting and construction of nuclear power plants. Obviously this is a decision to be made by local and state officials. I think when I ran for President in 1976 there were referendum ballots in 22 states of varying reforms to restrict the building of nuclear power plants in those states. In almost every instance the referenda were voted down by people who were residents in that area.

We have, I think, some very good existing regulations which protect the public from the siting of nuclear power plants in places that are dangerous. And I believe that the best solution to this problem is for people to abide by the law and for the local or state governments and people through referenda to decide whether they want nuclear power plants there.

Obviously, the State Legislature can pass laws prohibiting it. When I was Governor of Georgia, I did approve construction of a nuclear power plant in Georgia. It was located in a place that was acceptable to the environmentalists, which I considered myself to be one. So I think the best way for people to handle this is to abide by the law, state and local officials work out the locations of state power plants and if people object to their being constructed at all, through the legislative process or referendum prohibit their construction in a state.

Campaign Plans

Q: Mr. President, concerning your trip out here to the Western states and the upcoming Congressional campaign, some Democrats have been quoted as saying you may prove more a liability than an asset in the upcoming campaign. Assuming you disagree with that, sir, how do you respond and how active will you be in the Congressional campaign?

P: Well, if I had heard any Democrat, which I haven't, I would certainly not require them to attend the political rallies and the events in which I participate. I have no control over Members of the Congress. But I have never heard one say that. As a matter of fact, hardly a day goes by that some Member of the Congress, Governors don't request that I go with them to campaign in their States. I have been in two states so far already on the trip; one in Colorado, where there was a very strong and constructive relationship between me and the Congressional delegation, some of whom were running for re-election, the Governors involved, and I think there was a very warm reception for me there.

So I feel very good about the trip, don't think I am a political handicap for Democrats who are running for office. If any of them think so, then their proximity to me is a voluntary matter.

Water Policy

Q: Mr. President, with growing pressure on your Administration not to drastically reform the nation's water policy, and also in light of the critical energy picture, what, or how much of a reform do you plan to make in the nation's water policy? What would be the reason for any changes in your earlier plan for reform of that policy?

P: Long before I became President, there was a growing series of conflicts in this country concerning the use of water — conflicts between native Americans and white Americans, conflicts between environmentalists and those who desire increased power production from damming up free-flowing streams, conflicts between agricultural users, primarily through irrigation and the producers of minerals and particularly fuel like coal, and many of these long-standing disputes have begun to reach a crisis stage resulting in interminable lawsuits, divisiveness, arguments, debates, and also there had never been created in our country a comprehensive water policy that was evolved through close consultation among those conflicting groups.

We have never either had a way for Governors, Mayors, Members of the Congress, the President, the Cabinet, to consult with one another, to say, this is what we hope to do in the future with the water supplies that we have, and we have never had a way to set priorities on the expenditure of Federal and other funds.

Quite often we have approved, in the Congress, dams and other water projects that had a very low benefit-cost ratio. Sometimes they cost much more than the total benefits ever to be derived from the water project because a Member of Congress had enough seniority or influence or the patience to wait for his or her project to get to the top of the list and be financed by public funds. There is a limited amount of money that can be spent for these very expensive water projects. I want to be sure when we do approve a project — and there will be many approved in the future under my Administration and others — that the most needed projects are the ones to be funded first and we don't continue to waste money on projects that are not needed and are wasteful and sometimes even dangerous.

So I think the evolution of the water policy is a very constructive thing. It is long overdue. I will have the water policy options presented to me when I get back to Washington. This next week my own staff and Secretary Andrus will be meeting with the staff, Members of the Congress, and also the Governors and the following week I will meet with the Western Governors, and then I will make a decision on what the water policy of our country syould be. Many of those decisions will later have to be considered by Congress.

But I think the whole process is a very constructive one, long overdue, badly needed to be sure we do harness water and use water to the best advantage in the future, protecting the interests of the people who are involved.

Mideast Warplane Sales

Q: Are you willing to compromise on the number of warplanes you propose to sell to Egypt and Saudi Arabia and Israel in order to achieve Congressional approval of those sales and the second part of my question is do you see the same linkage between Saudi Arabian support of the American dollar in oil prices that Sheik Yamani did last week when he looked at the sale?

P: I think Sheik Yamani has recently denied saying what was reported about him about a close interconnection between continued involvement with the American dollar and friendship between Saudi Arabia and the United States and the sale of warplanes to Saudi Arabia. I think he has denied that.

I think the proposals that we have made to Congress, to Egypt, Saudi Arabia and Israel for warplanes ought not to be changed at all and I hope and expect that Congress will approve this proposal as we submitted it.

Obviously, there will be a lot of hard work to be done in the Congress. We will be presenting to the House committee on the 8th and 9th of May — and we have also testified yesterday for six or seven hours in the Senate committee. I think we will win this proposal because it is right. It is good for our country, and very badly needed.

One of the most crucial elements of a permanent maintenance of peace in the Middle East and the security of Israel is for us to have a relationship with the moderate Arab nations, like Egypt and Saudi Arabia, where they depend upon us to keep our word and where there is a clear recognition of the friendship and mutual trust between our countries.

We have provided these planes for Saudi Arabia, not to attack Israel; they are defensive-type of airplane. And the Saudis have ordered configuration — or appurtenances on the planes, fittings on the planes that are defensive in nature. So they are designed and needed to defend Saudi Arabia. I see no reason to change any of those proposals.

Action on Inflation

Q: Mr. President, Ted Natt, *Daily News*, Longview, Washington. Today there was more bad news about the economy and also the price index went up a larger than usual amount. Do you have a point in your mind beyond which you will take stronger action on inflation than you have taken thus far, and if so, what is it?

P: I don't intend to impose wage and price controls. We are consulting now with labor and business leaders to get them to reduce their rate of increase of both wages and prices below what they did the last two years. We call that deceleration of inflation. I am going to be very strict in vetoing any proposals that the Congress makes that would increase the deficit that we already face for next year's fiscal budget, 1979.

My own admonitions to the American people — I spoke to lawyers today and asked them to hold down their rate of fee increases. They have increased professional fees, maybe news people included, in the last five years even more than oil prices have gone up. So I think that this is going to be a matter for all Americans to address. Everyone wants other people to be the ones to take action to hold down inflation, to hold down wages, to hold down prices. But it is going to have to be a common effort and I will do everything I can within the power of the Presidency to hold down the inflation rate.

A year ago, my primary consideration was putting American people back to work and the Congress rallied with me, the American people, the private business sector rallied with me and we have had remarkable success in the last 15 months in bringing the unemployment rate down.

We added more than four million jobs last year. I think the unemployment rate in Oregon went down three full percentage points. Now we are going to address the same degree of determination to holding down the inflation rate without abandoning our effort to further reduce the unemployment rate.

Q: Mr. President, follow-up, if I may: General Motors' response to your deceleration program was to announce an average increase of about $100 on each, on most, new model lines. AT&T's response, with estimated profits this year of five to six billion dollars, was a statement by Chairman deButts that AT&T probably will have a rate increase this year and the response of several unions has been that they do indeed consider the coal settlement as a pattern for wage increases next year of ten, twelve or thirteen percent.

In the light of that, what possible assurance can you give the American people that there is going to be any progress in fighting inflation?

P: I can't guarantee success. The only thing I can do is the best effort in my power. I can't mandate action by those people involved. That is not compatible with what I have heard from Tom Murphy, who is head of General Motors or Mr. deButts who is head of AT&T. My hope is still that the automobile manufacturers, Ford, General Motors and others, that they will hold their price increases below the six percent increase for the last two years.

And we have two major labor settlements this year, as you know — railroads and Post Office employees.

We are going to do the best we can, I, Bob Strauss and others, to hold down those wage settlements below the average that they got for the last two years on a nationwide wage rate basis. And I believe we have a good chance to succeed, but it is going to take the concerted effort of all Americans to hold down the inflation rate. It is not something government can do by itself. It is not something one labor union can do by itself nor one major corporation.

There is a common goal that we share not only with Americans but also with other countries. But it is a top priority in my economic package this year to hold down the inflation rate, and I hope we will have equal success as we did with unemployment last year.

Indian Land Claims

Q: Mr. President, you mentioned Native Americans. That brings me to a question that is quite serious in the State of Washington, and that is growing resentment toward land claims that Native Americans are making, claiming treaty rights. There is also resentment that the Federal Government is taking an active role in supporting these land claims against the property rights of non-Indians.

Are you aware of this feeling and do you think there is a reassessment of this Federal role needed?

P: Yes, I am aware of the feeling, of course. As you know, the disputes between Native Indians and other Americans have been growing in recent years, primarily through the Federal courts. The ruling in this area concerning harvesting of fish between Indians and other Americans has been one of great importance to me, and I know it is important to all the people in this area.

We have had our Secretaries of Interior and Commerce working with the Department of Justice, trying to evolve a compromise between Indians and other Americans to try to take this case out of court.

We had a similar case that came to a head in Maine. I appointed Judge William Gunter to work out a compromise between the Indians and other residents in that area. And hopefully we can reach a solution there.

The Federal Government is charged with responsibility of representing the Indian claims. Secretary Cecil Andrus, Department of Interior, is in the audience here.

This creates an additional problem for us, but what we want is fairness and equity between Native Americans and others. The case is not one that I can resolve from the White House. We can use our good offices as an intermediary, sometimes our negotiating services, and the members of my Cabinet can work with all elements involved. But even then we have to get permission from the judges in the Federal courts to intercede even to that degree.

Congress has acted in several instances with legislation which I have signed into law. But it is a long-standing problem. It is one I hope we can resolve in the next few years. There are high disputes on both sides and great quantities of money involved. It is a serious problem, one we did not create. But it has been growing in importance for decades.

That is about the best answer I can give you. I don't know an easy answer to it.

Angola

Q: What is your view, Mr. President, of the South African military action against Angola taken today and what can the United States do in this case?

P: Well, our Congress and my predecessor in the White House finally reached an agreement that we would not intercede in Angola, a decision with which I agree.

We are not about to send American troops to Angola to participate in a war in that Western African country.

We want to see peace maintained. There have been so-called UNIDA forces under Savimbi, operating in the south part of Angola ever since the last war a couple of years ago. President Neto, who heads up the government in Angola, has been quite concerned about this. There are about 20,-000 Cubans, also, in Angola supporting the Neto government.

Savimbi has denied to some of the European leaders to whom I have talked any supply of weapons or supply or other armaments from South Africa. I think he does get supplies from some other sources, not from us.

But we have no intention to intercede in any war in Angola.

Popularity in Polls

Q: Mr. President, before you arrived, much was written and said and made of the fact you are perceived by critics to be unresponsive to problems of the West. Today there is a new national poll that shows only 29 percent of those questioned think you are doing a good or excellent job as President. Presumably you don't agree with these perceptions.

My question is, do you think these perceptions hamper you in what you are trying to accomplish? And, if so, do you have plans to try to counter them?

P: One of the ways to counter them is to come to places where my policies might be in dispute or misunderstood and try to clarify the issues that are very difficult to solve and which involve not only me, but involve the Congress, the Governors, Mayors, and private citizens of our nation. We have addressed some issues that are very difficult to resolve. The unemployment rate was very high, the inflation rate was very high, growth in our country was quite low and disturbing. We didn't have a strong enough relationship with the countries of Africa and Europe. The Middle East dispute has been going on for 30 years. We needed very badly, and still need, to have a SALT agreement with the Soviet Union. We had been negotiating the Panama Canal Treaties for 14 years before I became President.

We tried to address these issues as strongly, openly and as aggressively as is humanly capable to do. In addition to that, we have tried to bring some order out of chaos with some of the problems in the Federal Government, with welfare reform, with the creation of the Department of Energy, to have a comprehensive energy policy for the first time, to put the Civil Service back in the proper working order and all of these things cause some disturbance in the political structure of our country.

I feel very sure that almost all of the attempts that we have made are in the best interests of the American people. And I believe that as they are understood, that the present low rating in the polls will be improving. So I am hopeful that my popularity in the polls will go up. I think any politician would feel the same, but I am satisfied with the Administration's progress so far. I have also had a very good reception on this trip to the West, better, I might say, than the last time I was out here.

Progress On SALT

Q: Mr. President, this week you and some members of your Administration have indicated there was not a new SALT compromise reached when Secretary Vance was in Moscow. Could you tell us what the United States has on the negotiating table in terms of SALT negotiations and whether the chances are better than remote that you and President Brezhnev would meet this summer?

P: We have not discussed any time for President Brezhnev to come here to the United States to meet with me. We extended him an invitation in the early days of my Administration because the last visit had been by President Ford to Vladivostok in the Soviet Union. I think the essence of it is that he is likely to come over here when we see a SALT agreement imminent so that he and I perhaps can resolve the last very few remaining issues that the negotiators can't resolve themselves.

Our determination is that any SALT agreement would protect the ability of the United States to defend itself against any conceivable attack. We would also insist upon the maintenance of equivalent capability, destructive power, between the nuclear armaments of our country and the Soviet Union. And on top of that, any SALT agreement would have to provide for adequate proof, verifiability of the other nation carrying out the terms of the agreement.

This is a very complicated subject. We have made a lot of progress in the last year and my hope is that we can reach an agreement this year. But there are still several issues that have not been resolved.

Q: Have you put number figures, can you put number figures on what the United States is proposing at this point?

P: No. I think the American proposal has been revealed four or five months ago with the number of MIRVs that can be kept, the number of land-based missiles that can be kept by each side and the total number of missiles of all kinds that can be kept. That is our proposal, but we have not reached agreement on all of those matters because they are interrelated. Any yielding on our part involving one of those figures would have to result in an equivalent advantage to our country by the Soviets yielding on a comparable figure.

We have not reached any point yet for revealing the details of our recent discussions with the Soviet Union.

HELEN THOMAS (UPI): Thank you, Mr. President. ∎

May 25, 1978

Following is The New York Times *transcript of President Carter's May 25 news conference in Chicago. It was his 32nd news conference as president.*

P: Thank you very much. It's always good for me to visit Chicago, one of our most beautiful cities and perhaps the best managed large city in our country or perhaps the world. This afternoon I have a brief statement to make, and then I'll be glad to answer any questions that you might have.

Our action to help rescue those who have been threatened in Zaire has virtually come to an end. Our transport aircraft, having completed their mission, will be returning to their bases within the next few days.

I know that I speak for all Americans in expressing my abhorrence and distress over the violence and the killing that resulted from the Katangan invasion from Angola into Zaire.

As great as the human tragedy was, it could have been much worse for the European nationals and for the Zairians and the consequences much more severe for that country if we had not joined in with our allies in a common effort. Our action in Zaire was an appropriate and measured response to the situation. In this endeavor we demonstrated both our ability to cooperate with our allies and our willingness to consult fully with the Congress before taking any actions.

I imposed strict limits on the scope of our involvement, and they were rigorously observed. I'm gratified that we had the full support of Congressional leaders before and during the rescue effort in Zaire.

The Government of Angola must bear a heavy responsibility for the deadly attack, which was launched from its territory, and it's a burden and a responsibility shared by Cuba.

We believe that Cuba had known of the Katangan plan to invade and obviously did nothing to restrain them from crossing the border. We also know that the Cubans have played a key role in training and equipping the Katangans who attacked.

Our action to support the rescue efforts in Zaire was taken pursuant to present law and under my constitutional powers and duties as Commander-in-Chief. However, the tragedy in Zaire as well as other recent developments has caused me to reflect on the ability of our Government, without becoming involved in combat, to act promptly and decisively to help countries whose security is threatened by external forces.

Our military and economic assistance programs are one of the most important means of assisting our friends. Some of the legislation governing these foreign aid programs has the effect of placing very narrow limits on where and when they can be used. Some of these limitations, though they were enacted many years ago and under special circumstances, continue to be entirely appropriate and advisable today. Others may be outmoded.

For that reason I have concluded that we should review the full range of legislation which now governs the operation of these programs. I've asked the Secretary of State to conduct this review and to consult with Congress constantly in preparing this study for me.

We want to take a careful look at whether our legislation and procedures are fully responsive to the challenges that we face today. I will meet with the Congressional leadership myself in the year — in the near future, so that we can reach a joint decision on the appropriate steps to be taken.

As for the Clark Amendment, which prohibits action in regard to Angola, I have no present intention of seeking its modifi-

cation nor that of any other special piece of legislation. Any proposal for modifications will await our view of all restrictions and consultations with the appropriate committees of the Congress.

In the meantime, the existing provisions of law will, of course, be faithfully observed by me. But also, in the meantime, we must resist further restrictions being attached to legislation now before the Congress.

As we consider new legislation, it is vital that we recognize our need to be able to adapt to rapidly changing circumstances. The foreign assistance legislation now pending in Congress contains several proposed restrictions on Presidential authority in economic and military aid programs.

While I'm prepared to report to Congress and to remain fully accountable to the American people, I will oppose further restrictions. I do so not necessarily because I intend to exercise my authority in the areas in question but to preserve Presidential capacity to act in the national interest at a time of rapidly changing circumstances.

I believe that the Congressional leadership and the American people will support this position.

Thank you very much. I'd like to now call on Melody McDowell for a question.

Programs for Jobless

Q: What kind of programs have you or do you plan to institute which would allow those who are in progress being given not only a job but also to gain marketable career-oriented skills, particularly among black youth where the unemployment rate is disproportionately higher than in any other group?

P: The Humphrey-Hawkins bill does not include specific programs designed to reduce unemployment. The Humphrey-Hawkins bill devises a system by which the President, the Congress, state and local governments, the private sector can work together with a common goal of reduced unemployment over a period of years.

This legislation puts a constraint on me as President when I put forward a proposal to Congress, when I put forward a budget, for instance, to explain to the Congress how it will be impacted by and how it will help the unemployment rate in the country.

In the last 16 months since I've been in office, we've seen a dramatic reduction in the unemployment rate. We've added a net increase of five and a half million jobs. The unemployment rate has dropped from about 8 percent down to 6 percent on a nationwide basis.

We still have a very high unemployment rate, however, as Melody pointed out, among young people, minority groups and, in some areas, women. We have sharply focused Federal programs to put people back to work. And the National Alliance of Businessmen, the labor organizations and others are also helping us, for instance, with veterans, with minority groups and with young people.

Sixteen months ago one of the highest unemployed groups in the country were Vietnam veterans. They now have a lower unemployment rate because of these specially focused programs than the average Americans who are in their age group. And as we put the general populace back to work, we can focus much more narrowly now on those who are the so-called hard core unemployed; that is, the last ones hired and the first ones to be fired.

So the Humphrey-Hawkins bill has nothing in it that would put excessive constraints on the American public or Government; it gives us a framework by which we can plan together to continue to bring down an unemployment rate that has been improved but which is still too high.

Arms Talks and Africa Link

Q: Mr. President, Frank Cormier, Associated Press. Former President Ford suggested today there should be an interrelationship between progress on SALT and Soviet willingness to show restraint in Africa. Do you agree with his position on that?

P: Well, I read President Ford's statement that he made today, and I think that his analysis is that we ought not necessarily to let the Soviet action in other areas interfere with the progress of SALT. But he pointed out, and I agree, that unless the Soviets do honor the constraints on basic human rights, unless they also honor constraints on their involvement in places like Africa, that it will have a strong adverse affect on our country and make it much more difficult to sell to the American people and to have ratification in Congress of a SALT agreement if it should be negotiated between me and Brezhnev and those who work under us.

So I never have favored the establishment by me or Brezhnev of a linkage between the two, saying that if the Soviets and the Cubans stay in Ethiopia, for instance, we would cancel the SALT talks. I think that the SALT agreement is so important for our country, for the safety of the entire world, that we ought not to let any impediment come between us and the reaching of a successful agreement.

But there is no doubt that if the Soviets continue to abuse human rights, to punish people who are monitoring the Soviets' compliance with the Helsinki Agreement, which they signed of their own free will, and unless they show some constraints on their own involvement in Africa and on their sending Cuban troops to be involved in Africa, it will make it much more difficult to conclude a SALT agreement and to have it ratified once it is written.

Closing of Illinois Bases

Q: One of the Democratic candidates you are here in Chicago to campaign for, Alex Seith, said Illinois will be crucial to

you for re-election in 1980, that your popularity is on the wane here and that one thing hurting it is the possibility of closing at least three bases in Illinois — Fort Sheridan, Great Lakes Naval Station and Chanute Air Force Base. I wonder, sir, if you're going to have any private conversations with local Democratic officials to heat up the relationship, so to speak, and if you have any comment on the possibility of those bases staying open?

P: Well, I have to say that I flew from Washington to Chicago on Air Force One with several members of the Illinois delegation, I think almost all the Democrats. They very quickly brought up this subject and discussed it thoroughly with me, and I have already had a chance to discuss this with Mayor Bilandic on the way in from the airport and with Adlai Stevenson, the Senator. He was with us, also.

There's no doubt that if, say, these three major bases were closed under my Administration it would be a severe political blow to me. I think it's accurate to point out, though, that we'll make the decision in the final analysis not on the basis of political considerations but on the basis of what's best for the national defense of our country now and prospectively in the future.

The fact that these bases are on a potential list to be assessed has no significance at all. For instance, if we have three major Marine recruit training facilities in our nation and the Defense Department decides that we only need two of them and will close one, they put all three on the list to be assessed so that after their assessment is complete, they will present to me and to the Congress proposals for the closing down of a base or changing its character.

But before that is done, there will be nine or 10 months of very careful analysis plus a very careful study being done, which will continue for a long period of time, on the economic consequences to that area and to the country if it is closed down.

You've got the military assessment of need, a very long list, very few of the bases will actually be closed in the final analysis, not more than a third or so, and the economic consequences if a base is closed. So I recognize the political consequences, but even then I'll have to make a final judgment and so will the Congress on the basis of what's best for our country, not how much a local — or a community — might react adversely if a decision is made against them.

Q: Would you have any private discussion to warm up the political relationship with the Cook County organization?

P: Well, I've already begun those discussions. I was met by many of the candidates for office at the airport. All the members of the House of Representatives running for re-election, as you know — I met with them today. I've already met and ridden in and been up in the hotel room with Mayor Bilandic, who also happens to be here.

Obviously, one of the reasons that I came here to Chicago is not only to meet and address the Legislature tomorrow morning, which will be a bipartisan effort, but to help the Cook County Democrats and the Illinois Democrats win in the fall.

And my heart's in it. There is no difference of opinion between me and the Democratic candidates or leaders here about what should be done by the Illinois people in the elections this fall.

Restrictions on Africa Aid — 1

Q: Mr. President, a question about Africa again. Can you be more specific in the kinds of changes you would seek in this review? For instance, how do you feel that your hands are tied in sending aid to these nations in Africa? And further, under what conditions would you want to be able to extend aid, lethal or nonlethal, to such troops as the opposition forces in Angola?

P: Well, you know I have no intention of getting involved in any conflict in Angola. This is not my intention at all. But the Congress has had an increasing inclination recently, beginning long before I came in office, to impose one-house vetoes and to put very tight constraints on what countries we could give any aid to and prohibit even World Bank loans for countries, say that produced competitive crops in the United States. For instance, last year the Congress attempted to impose a prohibition against any loans by the World Bank against a country that produced sugar products, because it competed with sugar produced in our own country, or to prevent any aid being given to a country that produced tung oil because it competed with soybean oil grown in our own country.

That means that we are prohibited from giving much needed friendship, mutual support, building up a trade relationship, giving aid when it's necessary to countries that might desperately desire our help but be forced, because of an absence of it, to turn to the Soviet Union or to turn to Eastern bloc countries to help them sustain themselves.

There's a borderline region where I think the President ought to exert leadership and authority, keeping the Congress and the American people informed about countries that are not democraries, that might be socialistic in nature, but who don't want to be dominated by the Soviet Union or the Eastern bloc countries. Some of them are already very good friends of ours. For instance, we are prohibited, except under special circumstances, from giving any aid to Zambia.

Now President Kaunda was here this past week. He's a very fine African leader whose friendship we want. Tanzania is another one. President Nyerere is one of our good friends now. He wasn't three or four years ago. Another one that would be an even more borderline case would be Mozambique, Machel being the President.

I think that many of these African leaders are very strongly nationalistic in their attitude; they don't want to be dominated by us or anyone else. But if we're prevented from giving them any aid of a peaceful nature, even food, then they've got to turn somewhere else. And it ties my hands too much.

It might be that when the Congress passes an amendment like this on a foreign aid bill that the reasons are sound. But then times change. Maybe after a year or two years, when that provision is still on the law books, there might be different leaders or different political circumstances there. I can't act to deal with the changing circumstance.

I might say that this problem was raised not be me with the Congress, but by Congressional leaders with me. And I'm not going to advocate any changes in present law until we have thoroughly discussed it with the Congressional leaders in both houses — both Democrats and Republicans.

But I am opposed to any tightly restraining amendments that are now being proposed by the Congress on the foreign aid legislation that we are considering this year.

Water User Fees

Q: Mr. President, if Congress sent you a public works bill with the fees on one-way users at the level set by the Senate, will you veto that bill as Secretary Adams said you would? And if so, sir, what alternative solution would you propose for problems of Alton's Locks and Dams 26?

P: If the — I would veto the Senate passed bill, yes. We asked the Congress to impose water user fees so that we might get back a part of the cost of operating locks, dams — other very expensive waterway facilities — and also to get back part of the cost of the original capital investment.

In my opinion, at the present time the barge traffic has a major advantage over other forms of transportation. Also, these facilities, when they are modified or built anew, cost very great sums of money, and I believe that it's proper for the Congress to pass a law that would let very modest user fees be imposed so that those who do use those facilities that are built by the taxpayers all over the country at least partially share in the cost of them. This is the case with other forms of transportation; I think it ought to be the case with water user fees as well.

Restrictions on Africa Aid — 2

Q: Mr. President, I suppose most of these restrictions that were written into the law were written with the idea of keeping the United States from becoming bogged down in another Vietnam, but I just wonder, sir, do you see a comparison in the choices you now face and the choices that were faced by President Kennedy and President Johnson back in those early days when we began to put — get in — just a little ways and then more and more came

on. What differences are there in this situation and what they faced?

P: No, I don't think there's any comparison at all. In my opinion, if President Johnson, President Nixon, President Eisenhower, Kennedy were in office now, having experienced the Vietnam War, they would be very cautious and very careful not to become involved again militarily. And I have that deep feeling myself.

We are talking here about the kinds of amendments that I described to Wes Clifford a few minutes ago, an amendment that says we cannot either give any aid or even vote in the World Bank board of directors for a loan to a foreign country just because their form of government might be different from ours, or because they have had some past — or even present — human rights violations, or even because they produce competitive crops that might be competing with crops grown in the United States. And there's a trend in Congress that is building up that puts too much constraint on a President to deal with rapidly changing circumstances.

We do not want to send our military forces into Africa to meet the challenge of Soviet and Cuban intrusion. The Soviets and Cubans are eager to give either military aid, and even the Soviets send Cuban troops into a country to fight. We don't want to do that at all. But if we can't even give a shipment of wheat, or give a sound commercial loan or vote for a loan by the World Bank to that same people — or that same country — it means that I can't compete at all, even peacefully, with the Soviet or Cuban military action in those countries. That's what concerns me very deeply. And I might say that it's not just my concern. I had a long conversation yesterday with President Ford.

He's, I think, perhaps at least as deeply concerned as I am. And the Congressional leaders share this same concern.

Inflation Fight

Q: Mr. President, when you were in Illinois campaigning you said, in Springfield and other places, that if you were elected we could depend on your doing something about inflation, and now we hear we're going to get a 9.3 for April and maybe the same for May. I wonder, sir, if you cannot control it, what the political consequences will be to you. And secondly, would you consider taking a $20,000 a year pay cut, which was suggested as a symbol for the nation by Arthur Burns?

P: I don't remember Mr. Burns volunteering to take a pay cut while I was in Government, but —. We have imposed a zero increase on all executive pay in the Federal Government in the Executive Branch. The Congress is now considering imposing the same zero increase in high-level pay for members of Congress and members of the Judiciary as well. I think that's well advised.

It's obvious to me, looking back historically, that a year ago, or 16 months

ago, the primary concern in our country was unemployment. But my goal has been, as President, to bring down both unemployment and inflation. Last year we experienced about a 6 percent inflation rate — 6, 6-1/2 percent. Now our projections for this year are that it might be 6-1/2 or 7 percent.

I think the 9 percent that you referred to is a temporary aberration brought about primarily by the high food costs because of bad weather.

We're doing everything we can, now, to cut down the rate of inflation short of wage and price controls, which I do not ever intend to impose, barring a national calamity. And we've gotten good support so far from some of the major business leaders and the labor leaders as well. General Motors, for instance, AT&T have already publicly announced they're going to hold down the price of their products and also put tight constraints on executive salaries and other salaries over which they have control. The worst economic problem — the worst domestic problem — that we have now is inflation. And I had a meeting this morning with my Cabinet officers to tell them that the 1980 fiscal year budget, which I'm now considering in its early stage, will be very tight, with severe cutbacks in what we had anticipated recommending to the Congress next January.

I'm perfectly willing to meet any special interest group, no matter how benevolent, and hold my own in spite of the political consequences. And that includes business. It includes transportation. It includes farmers. It includes all those groups who are very sincere and very good Americans but who have to recognize that this year at least, and perhaps next year as well, we have got to constrain inflation. And I'm willing to take the political heat to do it, because it's very difficult for anyone of those groups to agree to join in a common effort. But I think if we can get a spirit of deep concern, which I feel and a common willingness to sacrifice, that I can meet my commitments to the American people and hold down inflation.

As you know, the Government does play a major role. It sets a tone, and it controls the depth of the deficit, and it orients where spending programs are implemented and how much taxes are collected. We've already cut back our tax proposal, which results in a decrease in the deficit for next year of about $10 billion below what we proposed in January.

So I'm determined to fight inflation. I can't do it by myself. It's going to take all Americans to help, but I recognize that I have the leadership role.

Restrictions on Africa Aid — 3

Q: Mr. President, Walt Rodgers with A.P. It was just about a year ago at Notre Dame University that you told Americans it was time to end their inordinate concern and alarm with communism. And yet you seem to have fallen into that same preoccupation in Africa. My question is: What is America's vested interest in Africa, and why is it so important that we oppose the Soviets and Cubans on that continent?

P: Well, I have no fear of communism and no inordinate concern about communism. I'm not preoccupied with the Soviet Union. I don't fear them. I see the inherent strength of the United States, economically and politically and militarily, and I'm determined as President to maintain that strength, which is in almost every respect superior to that of the Soviet Union.

We are concerned that the Soviets don't impose upon themselves the same constraint that we do. They have no reticence about becoming involved militarily in internal affairs in Africa. I think the Organization of African Unity, the United Nations, the O.A.S. in this hemisphere and other similar regional and worldwide organizations can handle those disputes either within a country or across an international boundary without military forces being sent there.

And that's the subject of my concern, and I feel that one of my responsibilities and one of the authorities that I have is to raise public awareness of it. I think that Cuba, for instance, claiming to be a non-aligned country, is probably one of the most intensely aligned countries in the world. It's a joke to call Cuba nonaligned. They have military alliances with the Soviet Union; they act at the Soviet Union's direction; they're economically dependent upon the Soviet Union; they act as a surrogate for the Soviet Union.

And so I think it's important for me as President, not being preoccupied or fearful, to let the world know what the circumstances are, because I think it's contrary to the hope that we all have for peace.

We have a major vested interest in Africa. Our trade relationships are there. There's a tremendous developing continent. It goes all the way from ancient and highly developed civilizations, as you well know, in Egypt, in the northern part of Africa, through a burgeoning black population in the southern part of Africa.

In the past we've not had an adequate interest there. And almost by default. Because we came in late, or because we were not involved in a friendly, normal trade relationships where mutual trust and mutual friendships existed, we saw those countries turning to Marxist countries or Eastern countries for their support and their friendship.

I think they would rather have a balanced relationship between us and the Soviets. I think in many instances they would rather have a democratic friend than to have a totalitarian friend. And I want to make sure they have that option.

Politics and Polls

Q: Basil Talbott of *The Chicago Sun Times.* Recent polls have showed your popularity dropping. I guess a Harris Poll released this week showed that either Senator Kennedy or former President Ford could beat you if the election were held today. And there are some reports that your aides have urged you to get out around the nation and try to bolster that image. I wonder if your trips to places like this — is that one of the purposes of this trip? And if it is, does that mean that you're a candidate for re-election? And whether you are or not, are you concerned about those polls?

P: Well, I'm not a candidate for re-election. That's a question that I'll decide much later.

I've never been particularly excited about very good polls, and I've never been particularly concerned about very poor polls. They go up and down, as you well know. And quite often polls vary among themselves at a particular time.

We've tried to address the crucial issues of our nation without being fearful about political consequences. In some cases, they are long overdue in being addressed — reorganization of government, welfare reform, energy policy, the Turkey arms embargo, which is now coming up, Mideast arms sales, the Panama Canal treaties. These things are not easy to do.

And I could very well make every decision that I have confronting me on the basis of how it would affect me in the polls. I don't think that's the best leadership attitude for me to have.

But I am concerned about it. I wish my popularity in the country was much higher. And obviously one of my duties as President is to get among the people throughout the country, because I learn in the process. And in having these regional press conferences like this, talking to your legislature tomorrow, meeting with Democratic people tonight and so forth — which I've done periodically ever since I've been in office, even when my opinion poll results were very high — I think it helps me to understand our country better.

So I'd say it's a combination of hoping the people will understand and therefore like what I do, or at least sympathize with me, and in the process let me learn more about this country.

Q: Thank you, Mr. President.

P: Thank you very much.   ∎

June 14, 1978

Following is the White House transcript of President Carter's June 14 news conference. It was his 33rd news conference since taking office:

THE PRESIDENT: Good afternoon, everybody.

I have two brief statements to make before I answer questions.

The most immediate and urgent foreign policy decision to be made by the current legislative session is in lifting the arms embargo against Turkey. The points that the Congress intended to underscore three years ago, when the embargo was imposed, have all been made, but now the embargo is not contributing to a settlement of the Cyprus dispute, nor is it helping to improve our relationship with our allies, Turkey and Greece. It has driven a wedge between those two countries and has weakened the cohesion and the readiness of NATO. It has thereby harmed our own national security interests in the eastern Mediterranean, an area which is crucial to the defense of the southern flank of Europe and also our own access, and that of others to the Middle East.

It is important to implement an effective policy in this area of the eastern Mediterranean, Greece, Turkey, Cyprus area. We have three purposes, all of which are equally important. First to serve U.S. and NATO security interests, as well as the security interests of Greece and Turkey as nations; second, to improve the relationship between Greece and Turkey; and third, to facilitate progress toward a Cyprus settlement.

I am asking the Congress to support me in enacting the full program, which, in addition to removing the embargo against arms sales to Turkey, provides for military sales credits to both Turkey and to Greece, provides for economic aid to Turkey, and provides further funds for relief and rehabilitation for refugees in Cyrpus.

Both Greece and Turkey are valuable friends and allies of our own. Lifting the embargo is essential to our hopes for peace and stability in the eastern region of the Mediterranean. I hope that the American people and the Congress will give me their support in the realization of U.S. interests in this critical area of the world.

The domestic issue that I would like to pursue is that of inflation. Last week I emphasized how important it is to hold the -line on Federal budget expenditures, as a series of appropriations bills are considered by the Congress during the next few weeks.

I cannot make this point too strongly, nor repeat it too often, because much of the fight against inflation from the perspective of the federal government, itself, depends on Congress' action in the days ahead. Unless the Congress is responsible, the federal deficit will rise at a time when it must and can be reduced. Unless the Congress shows restraint in spending, it will set the worst possible example for our workers and businessmen whom I have asked to restrain their own wage and price increases in order to hold down inflation.

Unless we recognize the limits on our ability to spend in the federal government, then both American citizens and those in foreign countries will see that we cannot make the difficult decisions that are necessary if inflation is to be controlled.

I am concerned in particular at this time about the Public Works Appropriations bill that the House will begin voting on tomorrow. That bill, as passed by the Appropriations Committee, would add not only $1.4 billion in spending over the life of

46 new water projects, but it also continues spending for the unsound water projects which the Congress agreed not to fund until last year.

It would waste far too much of our taxpayers' money and we just can't afford it. With the help of many of the House members who are also concerned about the inflationary impact of the Public Works bill, we will be working to eliminate the unnecessary spending proposals for water projects in that bill.

Unless they are all eliminated, I intend to veto it.

Cuba Role in Africa—1

Q: Mr. President, do you think that Fidel Castro is lying when he says that there has been no Cuban involvement in the recent invasion of Zaire, and since you made the charge contrary to Castro's word, do you have proof that he did not attempt to restrain the rebels?

P: I don't really desire to get into a public dispute with Mr. Castro through the news media. The facts are these: In Zaire, the Cubans now have more than 20,000 armed troops plus other support personnel; in Angola — excuse me. They also are deeply involved in the ministries of the Angolan government itself and they have substantial control over the transportation facilities in Angola — the seaports, the airports and so forth.

In the southeastern (northeastern) part of Angola from which the Katangan attack was launched, the Cubans have around 4,000 or more troops. They are a heavy influence both with all personnel in Angola, including the Katangans and also, of course, with the NATO government itself.

There is no doubt about the fact that Cuba has been involved in the training of Katangan people who did invade. We have firm proof of this fact. And the knowledge that Cuba had of the impending invasion has been admitted by Castro himself.

This was a story published, I think in *Time* magazine the last week in May and later Castro informed one of our own diplomats that he knew about the impending invasion ahead of time and that he attempted to notify President Neto in Angola and was unsuccessful. (Castro informed one of our own diplomats that he knew about the impending invasion ahead of time and that he attempted to notify President Neto in Angola and was unsuccessful, and later there was a story published in *Time* magazine.)

The fact is that Castro could have done much more had he genuinely wanted to stop the invasion. He could have interceded with the Katangans themselves. He could certainly have imposed Cuban troops near the border, because they are spread throughout Angola, to impede the invasion. He could have notified the Zambian government of this fact. He could have notified the Organization of African Unity. He could have notified the world at large that an invasion designed to cross

and to disturb an international border was in prospect. And he did not do any of these things.

At the present time, Mr. Castro has still not condemned the invasion of Zaire by the Katangan rebels. So there is no doubt in my mind that just on the basis of these facts alone my statement is true. Rather than look backward, I would like very much for Mr. Castro to pledge himself and for the Neto government in Angola to pledge themselves to prevent any further crossing of the Angolan border which would permit future invasions of Zaire.

Of course, we would also relish the withdrawal of Cuban troops in the future both there and Ethiopia, and support for the American, British and other efforts to bring about peace in the southern part of Africa.

Q: Would you be willing to see him on that subject?

P: No, I don't think it is appropriate for me to see Mr. Castro.

California Taxpayer Revolt—1

Q: Mr. President, Proposition 13 would have appeared to have sent some politicians into shock, including some in this town. You don't appear to be in shock. But I wonder if the California vote will have any influence on your possibly reassessing your own policies and approaches.

P: Obviously we will have to observe very carefully the developments in California in the future the full impact of Proposition 13 is felt. It will reduce property taxes perhaps as much as 60 percent in California.

One of the reasons for the decision made by the citizens of California is that property taxes there are very high compared to those in other parts of the nation, most other parts of the nation. The property valuations have increased rapidly and the taxes levied have increased rapidly. That, combined with the well-known fact that the State Government had accumulated four and a half or five billion dollars or so in surplus funds I think combined to increase the desire of the California people to impose this limit on property taxes. Those factors would be unlikely to prevail in other states of the nation at this time. But the two-to-one margin of approval by the California people to restrain public spending and taxation is obviously a message that has been well received and observed by all of us throughout the country. I think this is not incompatible with the fact that we want to hold down spending; we want to reduce taxes at the Federal Government level.

There will be some indirect impact on the Federal Government now and more direct influence in the future, because there is no doubt about the fact the unemployment will go up in California, as government workers are laid off because of stringent budget requirements, and, of course, our unemployment compensation payments will have to increase.

Also, I think we have about 50,000 CETA jobs, Comprehensive Education Training Administration jobs worked out jointly with local governments. Many of those may be in danger.

We have no way yet to anticipate what other consequences will accrue. But all of us are concerned about the budget levels, about unnecessary spending, about more efficient operation of government and about lower taxation. These were proposals that have already been made by us here in Washington. But I think they strengthen support now in the Congress for those considerations.

Zavala County Funds Cutoff

Q: Mr. President, the head of the Community Services Administration testified yesterday in Federal Court that some of your top aides, including Frank Moore, asked the CSA to cut off funds to the Zavala County Economic Development Corporation. Why does your administration want to cut off funds to this Texas Mexican-American group?

P: I think there has been — I don't know many details about the proposal, but I do know that the Governor of Texas had complained earlier about the way the funds were managed and this question was raised with the CSA. Later after the CSA, following an investigation, decided that some of the funding should be either cut back or terminated unless the management was improved, the people involved in the Zavala County effort tried to get the Federal Government to reverse its decision.

When that request was refused, the Zavala County officials went to court. A decision was made by Graciela Olivarez, Administrator of CSA, that the Federal Government position was the proper one. And we are prepared to go to court and to have the full information revealed to the court and let the court decide whether it should be administered or not.

Q: I would like to follow that up.

P: Please do.

Q: Why did you claim Executive privilege on the nine memos regarding that from various aides to you and so forth?

P: I think as a general rule when I have a wide range of advice coming to me following the complaint of a Mayor or a Governor or a State Legislator or some other responsible official, when some of the complaints are based on hearsay or allegations or personalities or specific criticisms of the qualifications of administering officials, it would not be appropriate to reveal all those memos to the public.

This is something that has been honored for generations in our government. And I think that if there was a possibility that those kind of confidential memoranda were later to be made public when they have to be very frank and open and free expressions of even contradictory views, there would be a tight reluctance on the part of my subordinates to give me free advice because they would have to assess every document presented to me or every expression of opinion to see whether or not it could stand up to scrutiny later on for public analysis, or maybe two years later.

So I think the confidential privilege of having my own subordinates give me free advice without their memoranda being revealed to the public is something that I would have to preserve.

Cuba Role in Africa—2

Q: Mr. President, other than being critical of the Cubans and the Russians for their involvement in Africa, what can this government do specifically to discourage any further involvement in the future and specifically, have you made a decision about any possible retaliatory action against the Cubans, in the way of trade or travel restrictions or against the Soviet Union because of their recent activities in Africa?

P: No, I don't contemplate any retaliatory action. As you know, we have a trade embargo against Cuba at this time and we do not have diplomatic relations with Cuba. We do have a representative in Washington and Havana that provides us communication service, if nothing else.

We are doing the best we can to acquaint the world with the hazards and the consequences of increasing involvement of the Soviets and the Cubans in Africa. I think it is accurate to say that they take advantage of local disturbances and move in with massive intrusions, both of military weapons, which contribute to further bloodshed among Africans themselves, and when they are permitted by the local government, they send in large quantities of troops. There are now more than 20,000 troops by Cuba in Angola. This number has increased within the last 12 months.

We believe that in Ethiopia there are more than 15,000 Cuban troops there now, even though the armed combat in the Ogaden area between Somalia and Ethiopia is over. I think drawing public opinion to this not only in this country but around the world has been relatively effective. We now have the prospect of a further armed outbreak between Eritrea and Ethiopia. I would hope that our expressions of concern would induce the Cubans not to become involved in that fighting itself.

I think it is time for the Cuban troops to withdraw from Ethiopia. Ethiopia has been heavily armed now by the rapid intrusion of Soviet weapons to them after Somalia did attack in the Ogaden area. I think Ethiopia is perfectly capable of defending themselves without Cuban troops, and it would certainly be contributory to world peace if Cuba would withdraw. But I think other than acting in a way to acquaint the world with their actions, the only other thing we can do is, through peaceful means, to provide some strength to nations that do want to be autonomous, that do want to see African problems settled by African people themselves.

We are providing a limited amount of economic aid, some limited military aid on occasion. The other thing that we are trying to do is involve multinational organizations to help in controlling outside intrusion into Africa.

The Organization of African Unity is a good organization, but it has been relatively reluctant in the past to deal with very controversial issues. Quite often the African nations themselves are divided on the controversial issues. The United Nations is one to whom we have turned and we are working under the auspices of the United Nations in trying to deal with the Namibian question. I think you know that in Namibia and Rhodesia we are working with other countries in trying to bring about majority rule, and a peaceful settlement. We have had no help at all from either the Cubans or the Soviets in trying to deal with these very sensitive questions. So I think these brief things that I have outlined are some of the things, short of armed involvement, which we do not intend to do, to bring about some lessening of the Cuban-Soviet intrusion into Africa.

Q: I have a follow-up.

P: Go ahead.

U.S. Role in Africa

Q: Nyerere has been critical, at the same time, of our involvement in Africa. There are people in your own administration who have been critical, who think we have made too much of the Cuban activities. Is there a possibility that all the recent criticism may in some way endanger potential resolution of other more serious problems in Africa, like Ethiopia?

P: I think any military disturbance in Africa when exacerbated by the intrusion of foreign troops and weapons tends to spill over across other borders. One of the things that made it so important to draw the line on Cuba and hopefully the Katangans in the future in the violation of Zairean borders was that principle of leaving those international borders undisturbed.

I think the reason that Nyerere expressed concern was that he thought that we were supporting a so-called pan-African force, that we were developing a strike force of some kind that could be used whenever called upon to go to anywhere in Africa to try to intercede militarily to bring about peace.

This is a proposition that we have never considered. Our only involvement has been for the Shaba province in the southern part of Zaire to try to stabilize the situation there. As you know, we only provided logistical support to other nations; we have not provided any troops and don't intend to. So that is the limit of our involvement and I don't think we will go any further than that.

Gartner Appointment

Q: Mr. President, in light of your Code of Ethics pledge never to appoint anyone with a conflict of interest or even the appearance of conflict, how do you justify appointing former Humphrey aide David Gartner to the Commission regulating commodities when he had accepted for his children $72,000 in stocks from a major commodities dealer, Dwayne Andreas? Did you know these facts before you made the appointment?

P: No. I didn't.

Q: How do you justify it?

P: I believe that the Senate committee and the full Senate did have this information before they decided that Mr. Gartner was qualified. Also he has pledged himself not to become involved at all in the consideration of any matter that related to that particular company. So although I didn't know about it before I submitted his name, we knew about this before the Senate committee and the Senate at large considered his appointment.

It was approved overwhelmingly, as you know....

Q: You believe it does not constitute a conflict of interest or the appearance of conflict?

P: That is correct. I think that the circumstances and the facts have been made known thoroughly so far as I am able to tell. In spite of this, accommodating this, the Senate did approve his appointment and he has pledged himself not to become involved in any matter that related to that particular company.

California Taxpayer Revolt—2

Q: Mr. President, to get back to Proposition 13, sir, today Budget Director McIntyre called it wishful thinking to suggest that communities in California could ask the federal government to bail them out of difficulties with their local payrolls and so forth. How do you — there was an indication he was speaking for you on this. Was he, and how do you feel about that? And if you were to get such requests from localities, what would you tell them?

P: Well, within the constraints of the presently existing programs for transportation, education, for air and water pollution control, crime control and the LEAA-CETA jobs for public service and training, of course we would be glad to help the communities of California on the same basis as we helped communities around the country. If there should evolve a crisis in a community, after careful assessment, within the bounds of the law and administrative procedures, we would obviously help them.

The federal impact of the California decision will be felt long in the future. I think with a $5 billion surplus that presently exists in the State government for several months in the future, this can be used as Governor Brown has very wisely proposed to deal with those special needs.

Following that time, of course, we will have to assess what role the Federal Government might play, but I don't think there would be any possibility of our passing a specific law just to deal with California. The reason for the interrelation on taxes, for instance, is to prevent double taxation and I think even with the reduced taxes on property in California, the taxes, for instance, in states like Georgia or Alabama, would still be quite a lot lower than those in California. So we still have no means, no inclination to single out California for special federal programs just because they have lowered property taxes.

Carter Taxes

Q: Mr. President, as a presidential candidate you often cited the need for timely financial disclosure as a means of avoiding conflicts of interest; or appearance of it. Yet, as President, you have not yet released your income tax filing from last year, nor your 1976, nor your 1977 net worth statements, as you pledged to do. My question is, what are your plans with regard to disclosure?

P: Jody Powell now has all those data and they are available for release. The reason we held this up is because we had an Internal Revenue Service audit of my 1975 and 1976 tax returns. I have forgotten the exact figures, but one of the years we had no change at all in the tax return. The other one, when I was Governor, I put in normal contributions as a state employee into the retirement system. When I got the money back at the end of my service as Governor, there was a $350 increase in value because of interest earned, and we did not pay income taxes on that. We owe $160 back taxes. In the analysis of that year, however, the Internal Revenue Service found that there was owed to me from a previous year either $5,000 or $6,000 — (laughter) — I have forgotten the exact figures — in back taxes. So I will have to pay $160, approximately, to the IRS, and I will get a $5,000 or $6,000 refund that I had not known about. But that confirmation from the IRS just came to us this morning and my wife came over at lunch and told me about it. That is what Jody has been waiting for. It is good news.

Yes, ma'am?

Turkish Arms Embargo

Q: Mr. President, Turkey has openly stated that she is in a very bad situation in a military incapability. What is the alternative of the U.S. Government if the embargo is still not lifted and if Soviet-Russia proposes a military aid to Turkey in this very desperate situation?

P: I would guess that Turkey would be reluctant to turn away from her historical alliance with the Western nations, those nations of NATO. Obviously we are not the only source of weapons or supplies for Turkey. And even under the present provisions of the arms embargo, the Congress last year did approve the sale, I think, of some F-4s, some fighter planes to Turkey, about $90 million worth.

Turkey has been very greatly disturbed because of the arms embargo, brought about, I think, three years ago by the fact that Turkey did violate the American law in using American-supplied weapons to go into Cyprus. I think that it is accurate to say that the Congress had good intentions three years ago when the embargo was enforced in hopes that it would have beneficial results.

The fact is, as I said earlier, it has not had beneficial results. It has driven a wedge between Greece and Turkey, between Greece and the United States, between Turkey and the United States, and has weakened the alliance of Turkey and Greece toward NATO, and has, I think, brought into a deadlock or perpetuated a deadlock on Cyprus.

So we have tried it. It didn't work. My guess is we will continue, we and other NATO allies, to include Turkey in all the plans — we will give them adequate supplies for their own defense within the capabilities of our nation's and in compliance with the law.

My hope and my expectations are that the Congress will remove the embargo this year.

Individual Rights

Q: Mr. President, on May 24, your Deputy Attorney General Mr. Civiletti urged Congress to pass a law that would require an American citizen to go to court to protect the privacy of his own personal records and be said that to expect the government to show reasonable cause to believe that a crime was involved was "just not realistic."

Now, as a leader in a world campaign to expand human rights throughout the world, how do you justify your administration's trying to punch holes into individual rights here at home?

P: My analysis of the attitude of the Attorney General is that he has been a foremost proponent of protecting individual rights. He has never deviated from this commitment so far as I know. I am not familiar with the particular case to which you refer and I am hesitant to comment on it without being more thoroughly familiar with it, but if you would provide it to the Press Secretary, I will be glad to try to answer it more definitively.

Q: Mr. President?

P: Yes, sir, on the aisle back there.

Wilmington 10

Q: Mr. President, Congressman Don Edwards had suggested that the administration file a friend of the court brief for the Wilmington 10 since no action has been taken on the part of the administration. Do you plan to follow the fate of the Wilmington 10, and if not, why?

P: I don't know. As you recognize, the case has been in the past in the Federal Court. My understanding is that this group through their attorneys have now filed in the Federal Court for some relief. I think the Attorney General in the past, the Justice Department has inquired into the proper treatment of these defendants. But I don't believe that the Attorney General has any intention that — certainly that he has relayed to me — of joining in as a party to the Wilmington 10's application in court.

Q: Mr. President?

P: Yes, sir.

Aid to New York City

Q: Mr. President, tomorrow the Senate Banking Committee will begin to consider the proposal you made to provide long-term federal loans for New York City. How do you feel about the statements by some senators that the banks and the unions in the city have not done enough and actually should be required to do more as a condition for further federal aid and about the apprehension by some senators that this would allow excess spending by other cities?

P: My own belief is that the requirements placed on New York City through their own volition and also because of the requests of the Secretary of the Treasury, Mr. Blumenthal, are adequate. And the House of Representatives considered this matter very carefully and voted with a margin, I think, of more than 90 votes to go along with both short-term financing and also long-term financing.

My own belief is that long-term financing is preferable. This would not endanger the Federal Government at all, we would not lose a penny on the guarantee of those loans, in fact, we would gain somewhat from interest paid by New York City on the guaranteed loans of the Federal Government. And I think it would remove the requirement that New York City act on an emergency basis in just two or three years at the most when if they were given seven or eight years to work out their problems with careful constraints and monitoring of their actions, this would be a much more businesslike approach.

It would also let the labor unions, with their retirement funds, private investors, the banks and others in New York, the sale of bonds themselves which would be guaranteed by the federal government and action by local and state officials to be much more carefully planned and much more harmonious.

So for all practical purposes that I have been able to consider, I think that the long-range guarantee of those borrowed funds, those debts of New York City, is the best approach. My hope is that even though the committee may be much more adverse to the proposal, that on the Senate floor itself, that the vote will be favorable and that the Senate will emulate what the House has done and approve those loan guarantees for New York City.

Human Rights in Russia

Q: In addition to the impending trial of Anatoly Scharansky, who you have very vigorously denied was a CIA agent or had any intelligence functions, the Soviets have now arrested and imprisoned Vladmire Slepak who you cabled in a telegram in November 1976 you would make a cardinal element of your policy when you were elected, his defense and the defense of other Soviets who have been accused.

Do you regard the arrest of Mr. Slepak and some of the other Soviet actions in this field as a personal response to your human rights campaign?

P: No. I don't believe it is a personal response to a campaign that I have launched on human rights. I think the fact of the matter is long before I came in office, the Soviet Union voluntarily signed the agreement at Helsinki, the last portion of which guaranteed certain basic civil rights within the boundaries of individual nations.

It is not as though other nations were intruding into the internal affairs of the Soviet Union. The Soviet Union voluntarily agreed to meet certain standards under the protection of the rights of its own citizens. There was set up a group within the Soviet Union and other countries to monitor compliance with the agreement which the Soviets themselves had signed and a substantial portion of that group in the Soviet Union have now been either harassed, or imprisoned or tried, and I think this is something that is continuing.

I don't believe it is an attack on me. I think it is a matter, as I said in my speech in Annapolis, of whether or not the Soviet Union can stand internal dissension and monitoring of the actions of the government by private citizens or private citizen groups.

I have expressed in the strongest possible terms both publicly and through diplomatic channels our concern about the actions of the Soviet Government. And I believe that even though they obviously have a right to make decisions within their own country, this works against the best interests of harmony and peace between the Soviet Union and other countries because they look with concern upon the attitude of the Soviet Union towards its own citizens and they see in these actions a violation of an agreement, a solemn agreement, which the Soviet Union voluntarily signed.

Q: May I follow that up, Mr. President? Some of the people who have been arrested have said you have ceased to talk about particular cases, and that you just speak now about human rights in general, and that that has left them victim to the Soviet crackdown.

Have you, in fact, ceased to come to the defense of people like Mr. Slepak and Mr. Scharansky?

P: You just mentioned three cases, and maybe you mentioned four. I have commented on all of those and I think that it is important for the world to monitor what goes on in the Soviet Union. I have not avoided a reference both publicly and privately to the Soviet Union on specific cases, and I intend to continue to do so.

FRANK CORMIER (AP): Thank you, Mr. President.

THE PRESIDENT: Thank you very much.   ∎

June 26, 1978

Following is the White House transcript of President Carter's June 26 news conference, his 34th since taking office:

THE PRESIDENT: At the beginning of this year, I proposed to Congress substantial tax relief for almost every taxpayer in our country. I also asked that some important and long-overdue reforms be made in our unfair and very complicated tax laws.

Last week it became clear that the Congress is seriously considering a tax bill that contains no major reforms at all. That is bad enough; but this new Congressional proposal is even worse. It actually attempts to take a step backward through some version of a so-called Steiger capital gains amendment. This proposal would add more than $2 billion to the Federal budget deficit. Eighty percent of its tax benefits would go to one-half of one percent of the American taxpayers who make more than $100,000 a year. Three thousand millionaires would get tax reductions averaging $214,000. The other 99.5 percent of our taxpayers would not do quite so well.

For instance, a middle-income family making between $20,000 and $30,000 a year would get a tax reduction from this proposal of less than $1.00. And the working man or woman who makes $20,000 or less a year would get no more than 25 cents.

The American people want some tax relief from the heavy burden of taxation on their shoulders, but neither they nor I will tolerate a plan that provides huge tax windfalls for millionaires and two bits for the average American. That underestimates the intelligence of the American people.

My proposal, to reduce the taxes paid by large and small businesses so that they can invest in new investments, new businesses, new equipment, new jobs, is a much more fair and effective approach than providing huge tax give-aways to millionaires.

Both businesses and also American working families deserve a real tax cut this year and our tax code barely needs to be made simpler, fairer and more effective.

I am working hard for tax reduction and tax reform, but only Congress can pass laws. I am still confident that in response to the obvious desires of the American people, the Congress will act responsibly on the tax package I have submitted. The American people expect and deserve no less.

Thank you very much.

Mr. Cormier?

Mideast Peace Prospects

Q: Mr. President, could you give us your current assessment of Middle East peace prospects at this time when Israel and Egypt are again apparently at an impasse?

P: My experience in dealing with the Mideast peace proposals leads me not to be surprised when we have temporary setbacks or rejections from one side or the other.

I thought the Israeli Cabinet response to our two basic questions was very disappointing. And I thought this weekend the Israeli Cabinet rejected an Egyptian proposal that has not yet even been made. It is not in final form, I understand. It certainly has not been presented to us to present to the Israelis. It has already been rejected.

Our commitment to pursuing a comprehensive and effective peace agreement in the Middle East is constant and very dedicated. We will not back off on this. After we receive the Egyptian proposal when it is put in final form, we will be sure to relay it to the Israelis as the Egyptians will request, and then both proposals, the Israeli proposal, the Egyptian proposal, will be on the table.

At that time it might be appropriate, if the Israelis and Egyptians agree, for a meeting between their foreign ministers, perhaps, and our own Secretary of State. I would hope that at that point we could make real progress toward searching out the common ground on which they might stand and alleviating the differences that still remain. But I can't predict the rate of progress. It obviously will require good faith and some flexibility on both sides.

U.S.-Soviet Relations—1

Q: Mr. President, in the current war of words you said you are not going to let the Russians push us around, and Mr. Brezhnev says that you are pursuing a dangerous policy by playing the Chinese card.

My question is: Are they pushing us around and are you playing the Chinese card?

P: Well, we are too strong and powerful and deeply committed a nation to be pushed around. Economic, military, political strength: the basic principles on which our Nation is founded, are too strongly held and preserved by the American people to permit us to be weak enough to be pushed around.

As I said in Annapolis, and as we have had as a constant policy, we want to be friends with the Soviet Union. We want to have rapid progress made on the SALT negotiations, the Comprehensive Test Ban, increased trade, better communications. Some of the things the Soviets do cause us deep concern. The human rights questions within the Soviet Union in violation of the Helsinki Agreement, their intrusion, along with the Cubans, into Africa, these things do cause us some concern and create in the American people some doubt about the

Soviets' good and peaceful intentions. But I have a deep belief that the underlying relationship between ourselves and the Soviets is stable and that Mr. Brezhnev, along with myself, wants peace, and wants to have better friendship.

We are not trying, nor will we ever try, to play the Soviets against the People's Republic of China, nor vice versa. We have some very important relationships with the Chinese that need to be pursued. They are worldwide common hopes that we share with the Chinese. We have bilateral relations that we want to expand — trade, exchange of science and technology, and so forth, and at the same time we want to have peace with the Chinese, almost a billion people. These are the goals that we have maintained during my own Administration, the same identical goals that were evoked clearly by President Nixon and President Ford.

So we won't let any temporary disharmonies or disputes about transient circumstances delay our pursuit of peace with the Soviet Union, nor our ability nor commitment toward better relationships with the People's Republic of China.

Q: Mr. President, to follow that up, you are consciously not linking the progress in the strategic arms negotiations to Soviet behavior either in Africa or the dissident problem. There is a suggestion made by a member of the National Security Council Staff that there should be linkage, however, between trade with the Soviet Union and the transfer of technology to the Soviet Union and their actions throughout the rest of the world.

Do you favor using trade and economic incentives as a means of moderating Soviet behavior?

P: I have not heard that proposal that you describe. As you know, the Soviets have arrested an American businessman. We have had a very hard time trying to determine if there is any grounds for his arrest, and the Soviet press, which is the spokesman for their Soviet government, has already condemned him without a trial or even without thorough investigation. This kind of an episode naturally causes concern among the American business community who does look upon the Soviet Union, as do I, as a good place for the sale of American-manufactured products, American farm and agricultural products and other things. But we have never tried to threaten the Soviet Union, we have never held out the prospect of increased or decreased trade if they did or did not do a certain thing that we thought was best.

We have tried to pursue peace as an overwhelmingly sense of our goals with the Soviet Union and I think that is shared in good faith by President Brezhnev.

So I think the word "linkage" is sometimes inappropriately used. It is obvious that there is a good factor in progress with the Soviet Union if the American people, the Congress, the business community, feel that they are acting in good faith toward us, they have a friendly attitude toward us, they treat our citizens over there trying to enhance trade with respect and with fairness.

All of these things are tightly interrelated, but I think the word "linkage" is one that is inappropriately used.

Capital Gains Tax—1

Q: Mr. President, in your opening remarks on the tax legislation and the Steiger Amendment, the implication is strong there, but you stop short of actually saying you would veto legislation with the Steiger Amendment. Will you veto such legislation if it comes to your desk?

P: I said neither the American people nor I will tolerate a plan that does what the Steiger Amendment does. I think that is clear enough. I don't see any way that I could accept a major tax proposal of this kind that did cost the Federal Treasury $2 billion, an increase of budget deficit that much, and channel almost all of the money to the very rich people. So I don't see any possibility of my approving such a plan.

Police Brutality Cases

Q: Mr. President, your Justice Department has set up a dual prosecution policy in cases of police brutality where the victims' civil rights may have been violated. But there seems to be some confusion over whether the dual prosecution policy should be used. I wonder if you could clarify.

P: I doubt it, but I will try.

When I came in office and when Griffin Bell became the Attorney General, there was a concern that we shared about the mistreatment of minority citizens in this country — blacks, those who speak Spanish, and others. I believe that at the present time, we are investigating about 192 cases of that sort. Each case has to be assessed on its own merits. There is a duality in culpability among those who commit some crime. I am speaking in generalities now. One is the actual criminal case where you punish someone for abusing another person.

Sometimes the abuse extends to the death of the victim. Another element of criminality is the violation of the American Civil Rights Act, where a person's rights are deprived, even the loss of life.

If in the judgment of the Attorney General — and he makes the judgment, I don't — the original case is not adequately pursued nor the punishment, if meted out, adequate for the crime, if that is a gross abuse of that, then the Attorney General reserves the right to enter the case and try the perpetrator of the crime on the basis of a civil rights violation.

This has been historically the case, but we have revived this issue. Without referring to a particular case, this is our policy. As I said, to repeat myself, each case has to be decided on its own merits, though, and the Attorney General makes the ultimate decision.

Q: If I could follow that up, in the Rodriguez case in Dallas it has been reported that Drew Days at the Justice Department decided not to prosecute that case, and that you talked to some Mexican-Americans while you were down in Texas and promised that Attorney General Bell would go ahead and look into it himself personally.

Why was that decision made? Why was it decided that Bell would go ahead and prosecute when Days had decided not to?

P: There was an erroneous press report, which sometimes occurs in our nation, which indicated that Drew Days had made a decision and that he had recommended to Mr. Civiletti, who pursues criminal cases, that this case not be pursued further.

We inquired of Mr. Days about the accuracy of that report. He has not yet made a decision about whether he would recommend any further Justice Department involvement, and I asked the Attorney General, which is appropriate, to look into the case himself. This is a case of high interest to the Spanish-speaking community in the Southwest, and again, his decision would be made on the basis of the merits of the case. But Mr. Days has not made any decision on his own. He has not made any recommendation to Mr. Civiletti, which was erroneously reported by the press.

Gartner Refusal to Resign

Q: Mr. President, it has been reported that you have asked David Gartner to resign from the Commodity Futures Trading Commission and it has been rumored that he has told you that he wouldn't. Are these things true? And if so, what are you going to do about them?

P: I might say I don't know Mr. Gartner. He is one of the roughly 700 people that we have recommended to the Congress be appointed to positions of importance. In assessing the factors in his case during the last week or so, both I and my staff members, after consultation with the Vice President, who does know Mr. Gartner well, we have decided Mr. Gartner ought to resign.

He has not committed a crime, he has not violated the law, but the image of impropriety, resulting from the acceptance by his children of a substantial gift, leads me to think it would be better if he did resign. I understand that Friday Mr. Gartner called my staff members and said that he did not intend to resign. So the description that you made is substantially correct. I do not have authority to remove Mr. Gartner from office once he has been confirmed by the Senate. But I think he should resign. The decision now is up to him.

Q: Mr. President, so there is no further step that you feel you can take at this point?

P: No, except to encourage him to reconsider and resign.

Q: Sir, it was my impression at your last news conference here that you had already assessed the case because you seemed at that time to indicate that you saw nothing wrong with the circumstances surrounding all of this. What has caused you to change your mind?

P: I have looked into it much more thoroughly than I had before I came to the last press conference. The report I made last time was basically accurate, that he had reported voluntarily the acceptance of the gift to his children, that the Senate Agriculture Committee had been thoroughly conversant with this fact, and that the Senate Committee and the Senate itself had confirmed him, that he had not committed any crime. I believe, though, in light of the fact that there is an allegation of impropriety on his part, with which I agree, that he should resign.

U.S.-Soviet Relations—2

Q: Mr. President, along with the recent tougher rhetoric from Moscow, there has also reportedly been an important concession by the Soviets that the talks over reducing the number of NATO and Warsaw Pact troops based in Europe, I wonder in light of that, what are the prospects now for an agreement at those talks?

P: The prospects are much better than they were a month ago. We, along with our NATO allies, have been pursuing what we call a mutual and balanced force reductions in the European Theatre for a number of years in the talks at Vienna. And the Soviets, this past two weeks, I think within the last two weeks, replied in a very affirmative way. Over the weekend President Brezhnev made a speech, I think at Minsk, where he said that this was a major reply on the part of the Soviet Union. He thought that we should assess it very carefully.

So I don't know what the future results should be. There is a difference in estimate of the number of Soviet forces in the Warsaw Pact Region, Eastern Europe, compared to what we think they have there. We think the Soviets have a superior force in the number of men, the number of tanks, to us. The Soviets' estimates are considerably lower.

We are negotiating now with the Soviets to see where the disparity lies. And what we want is to have a balanced reduction so that at the end of this reduction the two forces will be roughly equivalent to each other, and that they will be at a lower level than before. So I would say it is a step in the right direction, and we will pursue it.

Criticism of Brzezinski

Q: Mr. President, last week in Texas in the course of defending Mr. Brzezinski, you criticized the Soviet Union and Cuba for attacking and you also criticized special interest groups, which presumably are domestic organizations. Many people think that you had reference to the Jewish Community, which has been critical of Mr. Brzezinski.

Could you explain, sir — two parts to this question — who or what special interest groups do you mean, and what limits, if any, do you think there ought to be on the criticism of officials like Mr. Brzezinski involved in the making of foreign policy?

P: It is open season on me or officials in the Government, as you well know, and I think that is part of the American system, which I don't deplore. I didn't have any particular special interest group in mind. I said "special interest groups" and then following that specifically referred to the Cubans, the Soviets, and their apologists. And that is an adequate example, I think, of special interest groups to whom I refer. The point is that I make the ultimate decisions in foreign policy.

There is a minimum of disagreement between the National Security Council and the State Department. I do get advice from various sources, both in and out of Government. And obviously, in a complicated issue, I get recommendations that sometimes are at variance with one another, but when I make the final decision, then I want to be, and am the one responsible. I make the judgment and neither the Secretary of State nor Dr. Brzezinski makes those judgments. I think it is easy for someone who disagrees with a decision I make to single out Dr. Brzezinski as a target, insinuating I am either ineffective or incompetent or ignorant, that I don't actually make the decisions, but that my subordinates make them for me. And it gives an easy target for them without attacking the President of the United States.

But I have noticed that President Brezhnev, Mr. Castro and others always single out Dr. Brzezinski as their target. It is not fair to him. I think it overly exaggerates any possible disagreement that the State Department and the National Security Council have, even in the formative stages of a decision, and it takes away from the fact that in this country I am the President. I make the decisions, and I want to be responsible for those decisions once they are made.

U.S.-Soviet Relations—3

Q: Mr. President, what precisely is our position with relation to the Soviets? It isn't always easy for us to discern the precise position. Is it hard-nosed or is it conciliatory or somewhere in between? I wonder whether you could refine your answer on this a bit.

P: I don't know any clearer way to express it than I did in the speech I made in Annapolis a few weeks ago which I very carefully wrote myself, and a speech that I went over with my advisers, almost every word in it.

We want to be friends with the Soviets. We want to improve our relationship with the Soviets. We want to make progress, and I might say we are making progress on a SALT agreement, on a comprehensive test ban agreement, the prohibition against attacks on one another's sat-

ellites, the reduction of forces in Eastern and Western Europe, which I have already discussed, and so forth.

These discussions, these negotiations, are going along very well. We are making good progress. And as I said in my speech in Annapolis, I believe Mr. Brezhnev wants the same thing I do. He wants peace between our country and theirs.

We do, however, stay in a state of competition. This is inevitable. I think it is going to be that way 15, 20 years in the future. We want to have accommodation when we can mutually benefit from that accommodation. We are willing to meet the Soviets in competition of a peaceful nature.

When the Soviets commit some act with which we disagree, I have to make a judgment whether to be quiet about it or to speak out openly and acquaint the American people with the facts so that Americans can understand the interrelationship between us and the Soviet Union.

As I said, I think in an interview with a Dallas newspaper a couple of weeks ago, though, our relationship with the Soviet Union overall is stable. It is not in danger. There is no present threat to peace.

The negotiations are proceeding in good faith. There is no cause for alarm. And I think this is pretty much a normal circumstance. I would hope that when we conclude the SALT and the comprehensive test ban negotiations, hopefully without too much delay, that Mr. Brezhnev and I might meet personally and to ratify the agreement that has basically been hammered out.

We are much closer to an agreement than we were a few weeks ago. We have made good progress.

Q: What about a visit from Mr. Brezhnev? What are the chances of a meeting beforehand?

P: I have extended an almost standing invitiation to Mr. Brezhnev to come over and meet with me. My belief is, however, that he will not meet until the prospect for an agreement is quite imminent. But I welcome this. And I feel quite at ease about our relationship with the Soviet Union, although there are public debates, public disputes, sometimes public disagreements.

Weapons for Angola Rebels

Q: Secretary of State Vance has said that we want to cooperate with the Neto government in Angola and we just sent a diplomat over to Angola to do just that, talk to them. A few weeks earlier, the CIA Director had been up on the Hill to try to get approval from the Senate for a plan of back-door weapons to the rebels in Angola. What is the consistency in these two positions and would you have approved that plan?

P: There was never any plan put forward to send back-door weapons to the rebels because that would have been in violation of the American law. I don't believe any responsible person in my Administration would have violated the so-called Clark Amendment which prevents us from either direct or indirect involvement in the internal affairs in Angola. Our relationship with the Angolan officials has been a fairly consistent one. Ever since I have been in office, we have had negotiations or consultations directly with Angolan officials.

This is important, first of all, because we want to have peace in Southern Africa. And Mr. Neto, who is the leader of the Angolan Government, has some influence on other African leaders, particularly the leaders of SWAPO where we want an agreement in Namibia. Also, we have wanted to hold the Angolan leaders responsible for any future possible invasions into the Shaba Province in Zaire.

I also would like to see the Cubans begin to remove their troops from Angola. And a few weeks ago in New York, their Foreign Minister, Angolan Foreign Minister, met with our Secretary of State and suggested additional consultations, which is a continuation of what we have done all the time.

We have no desire at this point, no plans, to normalize our relationship with Angola. But we have never contemplated getting militarily involved in Angola, directly nor indirectly, and this present visit by Mr. McHenry to Angola is part of a series of consultations with them.

Q: Mr. President, let me follow that up. I am not quite sure what you are saying when you say there was no plan presented to the Senate. The CIA Director, Mr. Turner, did present a document, a written plan, to Senator Clark to try to see if Senator Clark thought that this would be acceptable, and would not violate the Clark Amendment. The plan called for sending arms through a third country to the rebel forces in Angola.

Did you know about that meeting? Did you know about that document? And since others around the Administration did, would you have approved it?

P: I didn't have any idea that the CIA Director had even talked to Senator Clark about it. My impression of it from the news reports and from subsequent information was that he went to consult with Senator Clark to see within the bounds of the law what involvement would be possible in Angola. But I had no knowledge of that, nor have I ever intended to send weapons to Angola, either directly nor indirectly.

(Continued on p. 134-A)

July 20, 1978

Following is President Carter's July 20 news conference, his 35th since taking office.

THE PRESIDENT: Good evening, everybody. Before I answer questions I would like to make one brief comment. Dr. Peter Bourne, out of consideration for my Administration, has submitted his resignation this afternoon which I have accepted with regret.

Dr. Bourne is a close friend of mine and my family. He is an able and dedicated public servant. Because of this unfortunate occurrence, he has left the government.

There are some allegations which will be the subject of investigation and because I would not want my comments inadvertently to affect or to influence those investigations, I will have no further comment on this subject this evening and will not answer questions on this subject. I will be glad to answer questions on other items.

Relations with Soviet Union

Q: Mr. President, you seem to be embarked on an eye-for-an-eye diplomacy with the Soviets, and they are accusing you of blackmail in terms of human rights.

My question is how far in the direction of reprisals do you plan to go and what do you intend to accomplish?

P: We have a deep commitment in our nation to the enhancement of human rights, not only here but around the world. The Soviets, when they signed the final act of the Helsinki Agreement voluntarily, along with 35 or so other nations, committed themselves to certain principles to be honored among their own citizens — the right of citizens to emigrate from the Soviet Union, the right of families to be united, and the right of government in a legitimate way even to be criticized by their citizens.

The recent trials in the Soviet Union have been aimed against Soviet citizens who were monitoring compliance with the Helsinki Act which the Soviets themselves signed. And we, along with voices throughout the world, have expressed our displeasure at these actions.

I have not embarked on a vendetta against the Soviet Union. I know that we cannot interfere in the internal affairs of the Soviet Union. I would like to have better relationships with the Soviets.

We have continued our discussions with the Soviet Union on SALT and other matters. We would like to even enhance trade with the Soviet Union. But we have to let our own foreign policy be carried out.

I might add that in addition to those highly publicized dissidents that have been tried recently, Mr. Shcharansky, Pektus and others, Orlov and others, that there is a Lithuanian named Petkus who has also been tried and sentenced, and when I was in East Germany recently — West Berlin — there have been two men tried in East Germany, a Mr. Huebner and also a Mr. Bahro.

I met with the six leaders of other Western democracies. All of us are concerned about this move in the Soviet Union to punish dissidents for monitoring compliance with the Helsinki Agreement. But I would like to have better relationships with the Soviet Union. We have expressed our displeasure, I think, in a very moderate way.

Capital Gains Tax Cut

Q: Mr. President, the House Ways and Means Committee seems intent on approving one of the capital gains tax-cut proposals that you said here on June 26th you saw no possibility you could accept. Would you veto the Jones or Steiger amendments or would you accept some sort of compromise such as cutting the capital gains tax only on the sale of homes?

P: We put forward to the Congress a tax reduction and tax reform proposal that I think is adequate and necessary. First of all, it would reduce the tax burden on the American people substantially. It would permit an efficient formation of increased capital to invest back in plant and equipment and to provide better jobs for the American people. It would protect the average homeowner, the average working family against shifting the tax burden on their shoulders and away from the shoulders of the very rich, the very powerful and the very influential.

It would also result in a simplification of the tax system. These are principles that I feel very deeply about. In my opinion, as I expressed at the last press conference, I believe, the Jones and Steiger amendment would violate some of those principles. I will have to wait until the final tax package is placed on my desk after it has been considered and complete action from both Houses of Congress is concluded.

At that time, I will decide whether or not that tax bill is in the best interests of our country. If it is not, I will veto it.

Civil Service Reform

Q: Mr. President, what are you going to do to save your civil service reform? Or is it snagged now hopelessly in Congress?

P: The reorganization plans in the House and Senate that relate to civil service has been approved overwhelmingly. The House recently took action, I think 36 to nothing, to approve it. This is a key element. The Senate passed the reorganization proposal relating to civil service very strongly in the committee. The only thing they changed was one element concerning veterans' preference. The House Post Office and Civil Service Committee has passed a bill last night after long debate and some delay with some very adverse attachments to the bill which we hope to get removed either in the Rules Committee or the House Floor or in conference.

This is a crucial element of my attempt to control the bureaucracy in the federal government, and it is such a burning issue in the minds of the American people to finally do something about waste and control to the federal bureaucracy that I am really convinced that the House members and Senate members of the Congress will not go home to face election not having acted upon it.

So because of that, I believe that the unsatisfactory amendments will be removed and I predict that the civil service reform bill will be passed because it is so badly needed and because the American people and I demand that something be done.

Raising Oil Policies

Q: You told the economic summit conference in Germany that the price of domestic oil in the United States is too low and the heart of your energy program is to raise it. But how would conservation justify the hardship that would have on American consumers and its own inflationary effect as well?

P: The long run impact of excessive oil consumption and waste is one of the major contributing factors to the underlying inflation rate we have now.

We simply waste too much oil, we use too much oil, we import too much oil. One reason is the price is extraordinarily low. I am committed to a comprehensive energy package that I put to the Congress 15 months ago in April of 1977. The Congress has still not acted finally on any one of the five crucial elements.

Conference committees have completed work now on four of the five, almost completed. And the Senate has acted on one of those elements. The one that the conference committees have not yet considered is the crude oil equalization tax. There are four basic ways, if I can remember them all, where we can increase the price of oil just to the world level price to discourage waste. One is to let the oil companies decide how much they should raise the price of oil, which I think would be very bad for the American consumers. Two other ways are for me to impose quotas or oil import fees which would result in administrative difficulties but which is presently permitted under the law.

The fourth way is much preferable to impose a crude oil equalization tax to raise the price of oil and within that act of the Congress to restore that money collected immediately back to the consumers of this country. There would be no net shift away from the consumers of money. But the price of oil would be raised to encourage conservation.

That is my preference, and I still hope and believe that the Congress will take action accordingly.

Andrew Young's Remark

Q: Mr. President, what effect has the statement made by Ambassador Andrew Young had on your human rights campaign and do you agree with him that there are political prisoners in the United States?

P: The statement by Andy Young was unfortunate and I do not agree with it. I don't think there are thousands of political prisoners in this country. He went on to explain what he meant — that 10, 15 years ago during the civil rights demonstrations and debates, that he and others were imprisoned because of their belief that the

laws of the United States should be changed. They were changed. We made great progress, which Andy Young pointed out.

This is a subject that I have discussed with Andy Young. He knows that I disapprove of his statement. I do not agree. We have, I think, persisted in our human rights commitment in spite of that statement and I have discussed this with Andy Young. And I don't believe that he will make a similar statement again.

The fact of the matter is that Andy Young has been and is very valuable to our country. He has opened up new areas of communications and mutual trust and cooperation, among the nations of Africa, in particular.

At almost the same time when Andy made that unfortunate statement, he had been remarkably successful in bringing about a conclusion of the Namibian question which could have exploded into a very unsatisfactory conflict in southern Africa.

So I know that Andy regrets having made that statement which was embarrassing to me. I don't believe he will do it again.

National Health Insurance

Q: Mr. President, you have been promising for the last six months to provide the American people with some sort of national health insurance. Are you going to provide that to the people this summer? Are you going to propose something and send it up to the Hill this summer?

P: By the end of this month, I will have a directive to the secretary of HEW to consult with governors, with mayors, with members of the Congress, with those who provide health care in our country. And expressed in that direction to him will be the principles on which a comprehensive health care system will be established in our country.

The Congress obviously will not have time to take action on this comprehensive proposal this year, but I want the American people and the members of Congress to know the principles under which it will be formed.

One of the very discouraging aspects of our present health care system is the enormous increase in costs that have burdened down the American people.

The average increase in cost of health care per year has been more than twice as much as the overall inflation rate. I can't think of anything the Congress could do that would benefit consumers more than to pass the hospital cost containment bill that we proposed and which the Commerce Committee in the House voted down or gutted with an unsatisfactory amendment this week.

This will cost the American consumers over the next five years $56 billion in unnecessary health-care costs and will cost the American taxpayer, through federal expenditures, $19 billion.

This is an extraordinary and unnecessary burden on the American people but the Congress, Commerce Committee was not able to deal with it.

So we have got to control costs even under the present system and this year the American people will know the principles and the framework for a comprehensive health care system that cannot be acted upon this year but I believe the Congress will consider next year.

Prescriptions by Bourne

Q: Mr. President, I hope that this doesn't fall within the area of legal issues that you prefer not to discuss tonight, but the health of the president himself has always been a matter of great concern to the country.

Can you say whether any of the prescriptions that were signed by Dr. Bourne for the substances went either to you or members of your family?

P: Dr. Bourne has never given me any treatment of any kind.

Q: None of those substances went to you?

P: No, sir.

Strikes

Q: The City of Washington has been devastated now by a subway strike. We are facing a possible mail strike. Philadelphia has had a sanitation strike, Louisville a police strike. There have been fires accompanying a fireman's strike in Memphis. How long do you think the people are going to stand for this and what are your thoughts about strikes by public employees?

P: I deplore the circumstances that finally result in a strike. We obviously prefer that through regular legal bargaining procedures that disputes can be settled without disruptive strikes. This evening, for instance, we are waiting with great interest the outcome of the Postal Workers' negotiations, and we hope that they will be resolved successfully before midnight, which is the deadline.

If they are not, then legal procedures provide a mechanism by which some extension can be granted. I deplore strikes but recognize the right of workers to conduct labor negotiations if they aren't successful, sometimes strikes are advisable. But I prefer of course to see disputes settled without strikes.

Turkey Embargo

Q: Mr. President, during your summit in Bonn, did the Western leaders bring up the subject of the Turkish embargo? And if so, what was your reaction? Could you tell us, please?

P: Yes. Every member of NATO, including five of the members who were there with me — the only exception is Japan, who is not a member of NATO — are deeply interested in removing the embargo against Turkey. This embargo was imposed, I think, properly three years ago.

The results that were expected have not been realized. It has not resulted in any progress being made in resolving the Cyprus dispute or restoring the human rights of the Greek Cypriots who have indeed suffered and who suffer today. It has driven a wedge between Turkey and the rest of the NATO countries, between Greece and NATO, between Turkey and Greece, between us and Turkey. And I hope that the Congress will act expeditiously to remove the Turkey arms embargo.

There is a unanimous belief that is the proper action within NATO with the exception of Greece. And I believe this action will in the long run benefit Greece as well. It is a very important subject, the most important foreign affairs subject that the Congress will consider the rest of this session.

Anti-Inflation Program

Q: Mr. President, Barry Bosworth, your counsel on Wage and Price Stability, said there will be a restructuring of the anti-inflation program in the administration. The feeling is the present program isn't doing the job. Is that at your instigation and are you happy with the anti-inflation program?

P: No, it is not at my instigation. We are doing what we can from the president's office, trying to control inflation. We are cutting down the federal budget deficit. In 1976, the budget deficit was in the 60 billions of dollars. In 1978, it was in the 50's of billions of dollars. In 1979, in the 40's of billions of dollars. I hope the next time we can bring that down to at least the 30 billions of dollars.

We are being very constrained on the Congress in not having excessive expenditures. We also have announced that the wages of federal employees, blue-collar and white-collar employees, will be limited to about five-and-a-half percent. I have put a complete freeze from my own sense of responsibility on executive salaries. There will be no increase this year.

We have tried to induce business and labor to have less of a price or wage increase this year and the next year than they did in the two preceding years. So we are trying to do everything without mandatory controls to limit inflation.

One of the most serious needs to control inflation is to cut down on the waste of energy. This puts an enormous burden on the American people. And I hope that the Congress will act here. As I said earlier, Congress has not acted yet on the civil service reform legislation or on hospital cost containment.

Airline deregulation is another bill that is being considered by Congress that will control inflation. So we have a comprehensive program that we want put forward. In some cases, the Congress has acted, in other cases they have not. I think the more American people's interest is built up and the more political influence they use themselves as individuals on Congress to act against inflation, the better chance we will have to succeed.

I think some business leaders have complied with our request, some labor leaders have acquired [sic] with our request, some have not. But we are building momentum, and I believe that we can at least let inflation top off this year. Someone has got to control it. It has got to be a partnership between the American people, the Congress and myself. I am doing all I can.

U.S. Olympic Boycott

Q: Mr. President, do you agree or disagree with those who urge that American athletes boycott the 1980 Olympic games in Moscow as a protest against Soviet treatment of dissidents?

P: This is a decision that will be made by the United States Olympic Committee. My own hope is that the American athletes will participate in the 1980 Olympics.

Texas Shooting Case

Q: Mr. President, Ben Reyes, a Mexican-American in the Texas Legislature, said today that you called him to express your embarrassment about Attorney General Bell's decision not to initiate federal prosecution of the Dallas policeman who shot a 12-year-old Mexican-American boy while handcuffed in the rear seat of a patrol car.

Are you embarrassed by this politically sensitive decision, and did you either ask the Justice Department to prosecute the case or express your disapproval when Mr. Bell declined prosecution?

P: When I was in Texas a few weeks ago, I studied the details of this case. It is one of about 150 cases that the Justice Department has been re-examining to make sure that there was no deprivation of the political rights or criminal justice rights or civil rights of people because — who are minorities or who speak Spanish.

I think the Justice Department has done a good job. This was a particularly disturbing case because the person killed was only 12 years old. He was handcuffed in the custody of police officers. At that time, I called Griffin Bell, the Attorney General, and told him I was deeply concerned about it and asked him to look into the case personally. He promised me that he would, and he did.

I did not ask Griffin Bell nor his subordinates to either prosecute or not prosecute. This is a legal decision over which the president has no control. It is one made by the Justice Department officials themselves.

They have decided not to prosecute this case further. It is a very complicated legal issue. The primary reason that they quote was that there was an enthusiastic prosecution of this case by the state officials.

The relatively low sentence, I think a five-year imprisonment for this death, was granted by the jury and because of that, the Justice Department decided not to prosecute under the present provisions of the law. But I have no authority, nor inclination, to direct the Justice Department to reverse their decision.

Shcharansky, Ginzburg Release

Q: Mr. President, are you aware of any negotiations underway for the release of Anatoly Shcharansky or Alexander Ginzburg?

P: No, not specifically. I think it would be inappropriate for me to talk about the negotiations that go on between ourselves and other governments about release of prisoners in general or specifically.

Q: In principle, is the United States willing to negotiate the release of these men?

P: We would like to see the prisoners released, but I can't go into that now.

Political Prisoners

Q: Mr. President, there has been a lot of talk about this term "political prisoners." I would like to follow up Ed's question. What is your definition of a political prisoner? Do you believe that Ben Chavis of the Wilmington 10 is a political prisoner or not?

P: It is hard for me to define in a brief period of time what is a political prisoner. I think that if there is a commission of crime involving violence, damage to another person's property or health or life, and if they are prosecuted for that under the rules of our government, that would certainly not come under the categorization of political prisoners. What we deplore in the Soviet Union is the prosecution of persons who speak out, even in accordance with international agreements that have been signed by the country involved.

I might add very quickly that the Soviet Union is not the only country guilty of that.

Bourne Resignation

Q: I, too, have a question about the Bourne case which does not touch on the allegations against him. It is simply this: Whether you agree with Dr. Bourne as he stated in his letter of resignation that the attacks on him were really designed to harm you through him.

P: I would prefer not to answer that question.

Business Losses

Q: There have been some published analyses that you have lost somewhere in the neighborhood of $300,000 in your interest in your warehouse firms. If those allegations or analyses are true, are you considering replacing your friend, Mr. Kirbo, as trustee?

P: I would rather have made a profit on the warehouse last year. When I was sworn in as president, I agreed with the public and Mr. Kirbo and others that I would not become even knowledgeable about the details of the operation of my former businesses. And I don't know what caused the loss. I am authorized to sign the tax return which showed the loss, but I am not contemplating changing the trustees.

Ending Paraquat Use

Q: Dr. Bourne, about six months ago, helped initiate a report of the National Institute on Drug Abuse that said paraquat, one of at least 13 herbicides being used on marijuana in Mexico, caused lung fibrosis when smoked by marijuana consumers here in the United States. The report went on to say that maybe we should halt this spraying program.

Right now in the Congress, Senator Percy has a bill which would outlaw the future expenditures of money, men or DEA material, to Mexico to spray marijuana which is later harvested, brought to the United States, and smoked. My question, sir, is are you willing to support Senator Percy in stopping the spraying of paraquat and other herbicides on marijuana in Mexico?

P: I am not familiar with the bill. My understanding is that American money is not used to purchase the paraquat. I think Mexico buys this material from other countries and they use their own personnel to spray it with. My preference is that marijuana not be grown nor smoked. It is illegal.

Q: What about $13 million a year that is being channeled into Mexico now that is being used with the helicopters to go out spraying the fields or DEA, drug enforcement administration intelligence that goes out to help eradicate these fields?

P: I favor this relationship with Mexico. When I came into office, about 75 percent, for instance, of all the heroin used in our country was coming from Mexico. Because of the work of Dr. Bourne and the officials at the DEA, the Drug Enforcement Agency, we and the new president and officials of Mexico, President Lopez Portillo, we have mounted a very successful campaign and now we have almost stopped the flow of heroin, for instance, from Mexico to our country.

Marijuana happens to be an illicit drug that is included under the overall Drug Control Program, and I favor this program very strongly.

Park Chung Hee Visit

Q: Mr. President? Thank you, Mr. President. There is the expressed speculation in Japan and South Korea that you would invite General Park Chung Hee of South Korea to Washington in next January for talks. Could you comment on this?

P: I don't know of any invitation that is planned for President Park.

I would certainly have no objection to meeting him, but we have not extended an invitation to him so far as I know.

Sales to Soviet Union

Q: Mr. President, could you tell us how you are leaning on the sale of the Dresser equipment to the Soviet Union and what are some of the factors involved in the decision?

P: We have taken all the action that I intend to take for the time being. We terminated the sale of a very advanced computer to the Soviet Union — roughly a six or seven million dollar sale — which would have provided a quantum jump in computer capability, multiplying the speed of the computer, I think, twenty-fold.

This was supposed to have been bought by Tass one of the Soviet news agencies, to, I think, handle the requirements for the 1980 Olympics.

This was far in excess of what they needed for that purpose and I have put under the control agreement in our country where different government agencies assess the need for sales equipment that would result in increased oil production in the Soviet Union.

On the particular case to which you refer, I have not cancelled that.

This sale of technology — Germans will install it — was approved, I think, the last day of May before we reassessed this proposal. There is still pending one element of this sale, some kind of arc welding, that I have not yet approved. I have not decided what to do about it.

Statements by Young

Q: Mr. President, news secretary Powell has indicated that in the future when Ambassador Young speaks out on issues such as human rights, that perhaps this will be a subject for discussion at the White House beforehand, perhaps indicating that he might require your prior approval on a number of topics. Will this be the case?

P: No. I don't think so. I trust Andy to realize that he will be more careful in the future. It would be almost a full-time job for me if I tried to assess — (Laughter) — if I tried to assess every statement that Andy Young and other ambassadors make, or other officials who have the same opportunity to consult directly with the press.

And I don't intend to get into the censoring business. I have to trust the sound judgment of those — I have made mistakes myself and I have tried to correct them in the future. I think in this particular case Andy made a mistake. And I think he will try to correct it on his own initiative.

Human Rights in U.S.

Q: Mr. President, members of your administration, including yourself, have often cited the findings of Amnesty International with regard to political prisoners in other countries.

Why is it, then, that you did not accept the group's findings with respect to Reverend Chambers and the Wilmington 10, and also, sir, are you not aware or concerned that what is called by some black

leaders a dichotomy in your human rights policy with respect to foreign dissidents and with respect to human rights in this country is threatening your black constituency?

P: I have been concerned about human rights violations in our own country as well as others. The Justice Department reassessed the case of the Wilmington 10 after the governor decided the action to be taken this past year. Now, so far as I know, there is no legal basis for further action on the case by the Justice Department. The attorneys for the Wilmington 10 have the right to appeal to the federal courts on their own initiative, and I presume they can under a *habeus corpus* request or some other. But so far as I have been able to determine from the position of the presidency itself, having no direct responsibility for it, the case is still being considered, appeals are still permissible under certain federal codes, and I believe that the justice system in our country has worked well.

MS. THOMAS (UPI): Thank you, Mr. President.

August 17, 1978

Following is President Carter's Aug. 17 news conference, his 36th as president:

THE PRESIDENT: I have one statement, and then I would like to answer your questions.

As President of the United States, my ultimate responsibility is to the protection of our Nation's security, and as Commander-in-Chief of our armed forces, it is my obligation to see that those forces are operationally ready, fully equipped, and prepared for any contingency. Because I take these responsibilities seriously, I submitted this spring a defense budget designed to improve our military preparedness and calling for increased spending in real terms above and beyond the cost of inflation, especially for enhanced readiness and for the urgent requirement of strengthening our NATO forces.

Because of these same obligations, and with the concurrence of the Secretary of Defense, I have decided to veto the defense authorization bill which the Congress passed last week.

This is not a question of money. The Congress has reduced only slightly the amount of money that I recommended for our Nation's defense. It is a question of how that money is going to be spent, whether it will be concentrated in the most vital areas of need, or diverted to less crucial projects.

We must have the strongest possible defense within the budget limits set by Congress. We cannot afford to waste our national defense dollars. We need better maintenance and logistical support, more research and development, a more flexible navy and we need these improvements now, not eight or ten years in the future.

The defense authorization bill does not meet any of these requirements.

'Cutting into the Muscle'

There are four particularly disturbing areas in which this bill, by cutting into the muscle of our military request, could weaken our defenses and erode our contributions to NATO.

This bill, for instance, cuts $800 million for weapons and equipment for our Army forces, undermining our commitment to NATO at the very time when our allies recognize the urgent need to improve the power and the readiness of our forces in Europe.

This bill would also cut $200 million for Air Force weapons and equipment, which would add flexibility and strength to our military forces, not only in NATO and this country but throughout the world.

This bill would also cause a cut of half a billion dollars, $500 million, from readiness funds. This is an unglamorous part, but it is necessary for expenditures for ship overhauls, weapon repairs, spare parts, personnel training, and the logistical support which guarantees that we can move our forces and have them act immediately when they are needed.

And this bill also cuts very heavily from military research and development funds. I had requested a substantial increase in these funds to sustain our position of technical excellence in a world where circumstances change rapidly and where weapons are increasingly dependent on advanced technology.

The bill that has passed the Congress could lead to an actual decrease in these funds for next year.

The ultimate effect of this bill would also weaken our Navy by aggravating the dangerous trend away from a larger number of different kinds of ships, which can maintain our military presence on the high seas, and toward a disturbingly small number of ships which are increasingly costly.

What the Congress has done with the money being cut from these vital areas is to authorize a fifth nuclear-powered aircraft carrier which we do not need.

This would be the most expensive ship ever built. The purchase price even estimated now would be at least $2 billion and the aircraft it would carry and the extra ships required to escort and defend it would cost billions more in years to come.

In order to use our dollars for their maximum effect, we must choose the armor, artillery, aircraft, and support that will immediately bolster our strength, especially in NATO. By diverting funds away from more important defense needs in order to build a very expensive nuclear aircraft carrier, this bill would reduce our commitment to NATO, waste the resources available for defense and weaken our nation's military capabilities in the future.

I will be glad to cooperate with Congress in passing a more responsible bill and I urge the Members of Congress to face

that duty as soon as they return from their recess. The nation's interest and my oath of office require me to veto this bill and to seek a stronger defense for our country.

Mr. Gerstenzang?

Camp David Meeting on Middle East

Q: Mr. President, your direct involvement in the Middle East summit conference next month is seeming to be a high-risk gamble. Can you say what made you take this step and what are the risks? What happens if this effort fails?

P: Let me say, first of all, that we don't act just as a noninterested mediator or message carrier in the Mideast negotiations. Our own national security is vitally involved, not only in maintaining peace around the world, but especially in the Middle East, and we have devoted our utmost effort to bringing about a peaceful resolution of the long-standing Middle Eastern dispute. I have met in small groups and privately with Prime Minister Begin and with President Sadat on many occasions.

I think I know them both quite well, and I am absolutely convinced that both men want peace, and the people in both nations genuinely want peace. All of us were pleased last November when the exchange of visits took place, Sadat going to Jerusalem, Begin going to Ismalia. It was one of the happiest few weeks of my career as President not to be involved in those negotiations and see them face to face trying to work out the differences between them.

Since then, the interrelationships which brought us such high hopes last winter have deteriorated rapidly. In spite of our best efforts, recently, those peace talks broke down completely, not only at the high level of Prime Minister and President, but even at a lower level involving Cabinet officers themselves.

Even when Secretary Vance had scheduled a trip to the Mideast, we could not get the leaders to agree to meet. It is a very high risk thing for me politically because now I think if we are unsuccessful at Camp David, I will certainly have to share a part of the blame for that failure. But I don't see that I could do anything differently because I am afraid if the leaders do not meet and do not permit their subordinates to meet in a continuing series of tough negotiations, that the situation in the Middle East might be much more serious in the future, even than it is now.

So I decided on my own, and later got the concurrence of my top advisers, including Secretary of State Vance and the Vice President and others, to invite both those men to meet with me at Camp David. We do not have any assurance of success. I do not anticipate being completely successful there and having a peace treaty signed in that brief period of time. But if we can get them to sit down and discuss honestly and sincerely their desires for peace, to explore the compatibilities among them, to identi-

fy very clearly the differences, try to resolve those differences, then I think we can set a framework for peace in the future.

It may result only in a redetermination or recommitment to continue subsequent negotiations. We might make more progress than that. But we will go there as a full partner in the discussions, depending primarily, however, on the two national leaders, themselves, to work out the differences between them.

I pray and I hope the whole Nation, the whole world will pray that we do not fail, because failure could result in a new conflict in the Middle East which could severely damage the security of our own country.

Dollar Crisis

Q: Mr. President, you are said to be very deeply concerned about the dollar. Is there a dollar crisis? What are you going to do about it? Why haven't you done something yet? And I have a follow-up. (Laughter)

P: I am deeply concerned about the dollar. And I have asked Secretary of Treasury Mike Blumenthal and the Chairman of the Federal Reserve, Bill Miller, and others to consult with one another and to give me advice on steps that can be taken by them and by me.

There are some factors that are encouraging in the long run. Recent monthly data have shown that our balance-of-trade deficit is going down. I believe that we've made good progress in seeing an increase in the economic growth of other nations overseas so that they are better able now and in the future to buy our goods than they have been in the past, when we were growing fast and we could afford to buy their goods.

The Congress can contribute. The single most important thing that Congress can do to control inflation and also to ease the pressures on the dollar and to reduce our severe adverse trade balance is to pass an energy bill. I have done everything in the world that I could do and so have my Cabinet members and all my staff members and many hundreds of people around the country to induce Congress to go ahead and act on a comprehensive energy bill.

They have not yet done so. They have been working on it since April of 1977. We still have hopes that the Congress will act successfully.

Another underlying problem, of course, is inflation, and we are dealing with that on many levels. One, of course, is to hold down the size of the Federal deficit. We have made good progress there. I know that when I ran for President in 1976, the Federal deficit was in the sixties of billions of dollars. By 1978, it was down to the fifties of billions of dollars; '79 the forties of billions of dollars, low forties; and by the 1980 fiscal year, I am determined to have it down in the thirties of billions of dollars.

We are eliminating excessive spending and demonstrating to our country and the rest of the world that we are determined to hold down inflation. But it is a tenacious thing. It would be erroneous for me to insinuate to the American people it is easy and we are going to solve it overnight. Everybody has got to help. But if we can top it out, inflationary curve this year, I think that will send a good signal to the world monetary markets.

We have a combination of problems, some of which we are addressing successfully, some of which are very difficult, but we are all working in concert.

I believe that the underlying economic strength of our Nation will prevent a further deterioration in the status of our Nation and a further deterioration in the dollar, particularly if the Congress will act and if we can act in the Administration to address those questions that I have described.

Camp David Summit - 2

Q. Mr. President, back to the summit, whatever preparations may have been made, just try to push one step further, if I may, is there an agreement or an arrangement or even a slight arrangement already in place before you go into this big meeting?

P: In my letter to both Prime Minister Begin and Sadat, I outlined some of the principles on which we should meet, not negotiating principles, but the need, for instance, to lessen the vituperation that had been sweeping back and forth between government leaders, to express in a positive fashion their determination to come to Camp David with flexibility and with an ability on the part of those government leaders to act.

The immediacy of their response — they did not delay at all when they read my letter to say "I will come to Camp David" — is indicative of good faith on their part. But I do not have any commitment from them to change their previously expressed positions as a prerequisite or prelude to coming to Camp David.

Relations With Congress

Q: Mr. President, your Agriculture Secretary was quoted as saying earlier this week that you intended to retaliate against the cheap-shot artists in Congress who oppose some of your programs. What is your attitude toward Congress as you come up to the Labor Day recess?

P: I would say that in general, the Congress has been very cooperative and very constructive. I think any analysis of the accomplishments of Congress last year in the domestic field would be favorable. We addressed the most difficult questions of all successfully. The energy question was put off until this year and still has not yet been addressed.

In foreign affairs this year, I think the Congress has acted with great judgment and also with great courage to deal with some longstanding questions involving sales of weapons to the moderate Arab nations, approval of the Panama Canal

treaties, removal of the embargo against Turkey, and so forth.

I have never discussed this subject with the Secretry of Agriculture, and he's never discussed it with me. But I certainly don't have any animosity against any Member of Congress. I do not have a list of Congress Members who are worthy of punishment. I have no inclination to do that; it's not part of my nature. And I think it would be counterproductive if I attempted it.

Oil Imports

Q: Mr. President, earlier this year, you suggested the time might come when you would have to move administratively to impose import fees or quotas on foreign oil. My question is are we near that time, and if Congress should adjourn this year, without passing what you consider to be a substantial energy bill, will you do it?

P: That is an option that I will maintain open for myself. Obviously there are several options that can be exercised, the most advantageous of which to consumers, to oil producers, to our own country and I think to the rest of the world is to pass the energy proposal as I presented it to the Congress, to impose a tax on oil, to reduce its waste and to encourage more use of American oil in the first place, and to distribute the revenues from that tax back immediately to the American people.

This would be a very constructive attitude. The second one would be in the absence of Congressional action for me to impose, through executive order under the present law, either import quotas, limiting the amount of oil that could come in, or import fees which would charge extra for oil coming into the Nation. And, of course, the other option, which is one that I think would be at the bottom of the list, would be to permit the oil companies to unilaterally increase the price of their oil very high and to let the consumers pay for it to the enrichment of the oil companies themselves.

That is a list of the options I can think of at this moment that exist for me. My preference, of course, is for the Congress to act. But I cannot foreclose the option that I have to act unilaterally through executive order if the Congress does not act.

Costanza Successor

Q: Why do you think Midge Costanza felt obliged to resign and do you have a new appointee to take her place?

P: Midge resigned without any encouragement from me. As a matter of fact, I asked Midge to stay on. She left in very good spirits. She has announced to the press and has told me privately she has several very good offers to utilize her superb services. And she has worked very closely with us, no later than yesterday as a matter of fact, in the White House West Wing, to help us choose a successor to take her place. I think that describes the situation quite accurately.

Q: Do you have any successor in mind?

P: We have several ones whom we are considering. We have not yet made a choice.

Trade With Soviet Union

Q: Do you plan to continue selective trade sanctions against the Soviet Union since some allied nations, such as France, are unwilling to cooperate in technological boycotts?

P: We obviously don't have any inclination to declare a trade embargo against the Soviet Union to stop all trade. It is to the advantage of our own country to have trade with the Soviet Union. I think embargoes that have been imposed in the past by previous Administrations, for instance, and unannounced and unilaterally opening of shipments of feed grains and food grains and soybeans overseas has been very detrimental to our country. I do not intend to do that. But we will assess each individual sale on the basis of several criteria, one of the most important criteria of which is does this sale contribute to the enhancement of the Soviet military capabilities and is this country the only reasonable source of a supply for that particular item. And we have a very well established procedure in the government for carrying out that analysis. And I believe that my own cancellation of the sale of a very large computer a month or so ago was well advised, but we will have to consider each one of those additional items as they are proposed on its own merits.

It takes a long time for a decision like that to get to my desk. Most of them are simply canceled before they even come to my attention. The Commerce Department and others assess it, State Department has to approve it before it comes to me. We will have to assess them on an individual basis.

Defense Authorization Veto

Q: Getting back to energy and the veto today, Senator Jackson was suggesting this is going to be a big problem for the energy bill now that you have vetoed the defense bill because he said the aircraft carrier was kind of the glue that held that thing together and it took them six months to get the bill. He said now it is going to be a problem. He said we have so many headaches and this is another one. It seems rather significant to me in that he is the man that is carrying that energy bill for you.

P: I met this morning with Senator Jackson and others to go over the reasons for my veto. He did not disagree with the reasons that I expressed. I have not had a single adviser who told me that we ought to go ahead with the nuclear aircraft carrier. The only concerns that anyone has expressed to me is that it might create additional work for Congress in correcting an error that they made, or that it might cause me political problems in having vetoed a bill and having a confrontation with Congress.

I don't desire to do anything with Congress but cooperate with them. We are working now in the House, which will first take up the veto since the bill originated in the House to make sure we can sustain my veto on the basis of its own merits. I don't see any reason to link the building of a nuclear aircraft carrier, which will be completed maybe in 1987, with the approval of a conference committee report on natural gas that has been negotiated now for almost 16 months.

Q: You notice someone up there can't see. Are you confident someone up there might not see it?

P: I can't guarantee nobody considers it, but I can tell you this — it wouldn't be the first problem we had with the natural gas bill. (Laughter)

Tuition Tax Relief

Q: Mr. President, Congress appears bent on passing some sort of tuition tax relief this year. I would like to know what your current position is now as regards to Congress passing tuition tax relief for parents with children in universities, and your position on parents with children in parochial schools?

Is it your intention to veto any tuition tax relief that comes down?

P: I do not favor the tuition tax credit approach to college students and I even more strongly oppose on constitutional grounds government financing of the elementary and secondary schools which are privately operated.

On the tax bill, I am not satisfied with the bill that the House passed. It does not meet the basic criteria that I set for fairness, for equity, for simplicity, for progressivity and the efficient enhancement of capital investment funds.

A veto is a prerogative that a President is given under the Constitution. It is not an abnormal authority. It is one that should be a routine part of the interrelationship between the White House and Capitol Hill. And it is not only a pleasure to have that authority to make my own leverage more effective, but it is a duty that falls on me and I want to keep that option open.

I reserve the right after a bill gets on my desk to either veto it or sign it. I have no reticence about vetoing a bill that I think is contrary to the best interests of our country. My hope is that Congress will pass a bill after close consultation with us that would be acceptable.

My position on the tax credits is clear. I have not changed my position at all. I don't think anybody's position on the tax bill, the tax reduction bill, is clear. It is very, very confused, and my hope is that the Senate will correct some of the basic errors that the House made; if not, that in the conference committee the bill can be made acceptable to me. If it is not acceptable to me, I would have no hesitancy about vetoing it.

Relations With China

Q: Mr. President, during a recent interview you made the point that both we and the Chinese are patient on the subject of establishing full diplomatic relations.

My question concerns the extent of that patience on your part, whether now it might be something indefinitely on the back burner or something you would like to see accomplished between now and, let's say, the end of 1980?

P: The normalization of relations with the People's Republic of China has always been a goal of my Administration. It was the goal of my predecessors under the general provisions of the Shanghai Communique that was signed by President Nixon on his historic visit to China.

The pace of negotiations must be one that is mutually set. We have a very good representative in China, Leonard Woodcock. They have a very fine representative here, a new representative not known as an Ambassador in Washington whom I have not yet met.

But we are constantly exploring ways to have better relationships with China. First of all, no matter what our relationship is with them on a bilateral basis, we want China to be a peaceful nation, to be secure and to have their beneficial effects felt around the world.

Secondly, we want our bilateral relationships with them to be better, to enhance trade, communications, student exchange and so forth, whether or not we have diplomatic relations as such. And then, of course, the final thing is to hope for diplomatic relations when we are both willing to proceed expeditiously and when we are both willing to accommodate one another's wishes.

I can't tell you what the pace of that might be. It is not something that I could unilaterally impose upon them and I have to judge by what their response might be.

I think there is a new impression — certainly that I have of the leadership in China — that they are more outreaching now, they are more outgoing.

The present visit of Chairman Hua, for instance, to Romania, is a good indication, an almost unprecedented thing for them to go out into the Eastern European world and perhaps other countries as well later on to make visits. So I think they are reaching out in a spirit of friendship. If they do, I will respond in good faith. I just cannot give you a time schedule.

Effort to Appear Tougher?

Q: Mr. President, aside from the merits of the defense bill, which you have covered, some of your advisers are saying that part of your reason for vetoing it is a desire to undo the impression you are a pushover, so to speak, when it comes to dealing with Congress. Do you think you have been too willing in the past to go along with what the Members of Congress wanted and how much does this veto have

to do with an effort to make you appear tougher?

P: That really is not a factor involved in it. There have been times in the past when I have had a major difference with Congress, at least with a number of Congress Members, and have ultimately prevailed.

Some of the foreign affairs debates which I just described a few minutes ago are examples of this. Early in the session last year, there was a great opposition in the Congress, particularly the Democratic leadership, against re-establishing a reorganization authority for me. And they did it reluctantly, but now it is assumed to be a routine thing. There have been cases when I have erred on the side of not vetoing a bill. I think that last year I should have vetoed the appropriation bill that authorized unnecessary water projects. If I had it to do over again, I would have vetoed it. But that is one of the rare occasions when I think I have been too lenient in accommodating the desires of Congress. But the Congress is now trying to reimpose those water projects on me as President and even additional ones, that are worse.

So I think that I have had a fairly well-balanced approach to Congress. We have close consultations with Congress on a continuing basis. I don't have any fear of the Congress. I am sure they don't have any fear of me.

Rickover View on Carrier

Q: Mr. President, in your book "Why Not the Best?", you describe Admiral Rickover as having had a great influence on your life.

I wonder if in light of the veto, Mr. President, that you did discuss your decision against a new nuclear carrier, the Nimitz class, with Admiral Rickover, and what that conversation consisted of?

P: I did not discuss it with him. When I had my first visit with Admiral Rickover after becoming President, it was obvious to me then and now that he is a very outspoken person. He presents his case to the Congress in an effective way and he has a great influence on them and on me.

He pointed out then his inclination was not to try to influence my decision on individual items in the Defense budget, that he knew I had special problems as President and a special perspective that he could not have himself. And because of our close relationship in the past, which still exists, by the way, he was going to refrain from that particular aspect of my responsibilities.

He does meet with me quite frequently, and we have very frank discussions, but I think more in general terms. And he has not had any inclination to try to influence me on this particular matter.

Gen. Walker Resignation

Q: Mr. President, sir, I want to point out to you to see if you think this is not an injustice. Robert Griffin of General Services Administration, number two man, was fired because of his conduct there. And then a job was created for him by you giving him $50,000 a year. Then we have a four-star general out in the Pentagon, Walton Walker, with an exemplary record, and he is having to get out of the service and take retirement, which will cost the taxpayers a lot of money simply because his position at NATO was abolished. They gave it to a Turkish general to ease the tension over the arms embargo, and there is no other four-star slot for Walton Walker, so a good man has to get out of the service. Don't you think that is an injustice?

P: I will try to respond as best I can. In the first place, I don't know of any item that has been reported by the press in a more distorted way than the one relating to Robert Griffin. Griffin was not fired because he was incompetent. He was not fired because there was any allegation about his honesty and integrity. He was moved from the General Services Administration because he was incompatible with the Director of the General Services Administration, Mr. Solomon. He was not promoted. He was transferred to another position with the same salary exactly and the same pay grade exactly.

He is not a member of the White House staff. He works for the Special Trade Representative, which is not in the White House at all.

There has been a general distortion of what happened in that respect. I have no apology to make for having moved him out of GSA. I have no apology to make for having put a good man with great integrity and great knowledge in a productive job.

The general to whom you refer was recently promoted to four-star status. He was assigned to Turkey to fill a position. NATO leaders, not completely controlled by us, decided that that position would be filled by a non-American. It was no reflection on General Walker at all. There is no other four-star position in the entire armed forces, and he was offered a three-star position.

He decided that in place of going back to a three-star position, which he had just recently occupied, that he would prefer to resign. And he is a good man also. There is no reflection on him. There has never been any reflection on him.

I have looked into both these cases myself. I am familiar with both of them and I can tell you there is no reflection on either man. They were given jobs, offered jobs compatible with their rank. General Walker performed superbly in Turkey and I regret he did not stay in the Army as a four-star general.

HELEN THOMAS (UPI): Thank you. ∎

September 28, 1978

Following is the White House transcript of President Carter's Sept. 28 news conference, his 37th since taking office:

THE PRESIDENT: Be seated, please.

I would like to comment first on two very courageous actions that have been taken recently. The first is by the Israeli Knesset, their parliament, late last night, when they voted overwhelmingly by more than a four to one margin for peace in the Middle East, including the removal of the Israeli settlers from the Sinai which is Egyptian territory.

This is a continuation of the courageous action that has already been demonstrated by Prime Minister Begin who led the parliament debate, gave his full weight to this peace move, and by President Sadat who cooperated at Camp David in making it possible.

Since the Knesset vote, I have talked to Prime Minister Begin, also just a few minutes ago since lunch to President Sadat. Both of them agree that there are no remaining obstacles to proceeding as rapidly as possible to conclude a peace treaty between Israel and Egypt.

I am very proud of this action on their part. We will cooperate again as full partners in the negotiations to conclude the final terms of the Israeli-Egyptian peace treaty.

The other courageous vote that was taken yesterday was by the United States Senate, under the great leadership of Majority Leader Robert Byrd and committee chairman, Senator Scoop Jackson, to approve the natural gas legislation. This is a bill that will provide the centerpiece for establishing a United States energy policy. It is very good for consumers, particularly in those states that are faced with very urgent shortage of natural gas in years to come.

It is also fair to producers. I think it would make us much less dependent upon imported foreign oil. And I congratulate the Senate on this action.

Now the House must act on the same legislation. I hope that they will do so expeditiously and expect that this will be the case.

One other report, briefly. We have not been successful after 28 hours or more of negotiation, to reach a settlement between the striking railway workers and the rail lines. We now have almost a complete shutdown of rail service in our country. I have just recently issued an order establishing an emergency board which will take over the responsibility for negotiating a settlement between the workers and the railroads themselves.

This is necessary action. I think it is accurate to say that both sides do want a settlement. The differences between them are relatively small compared to what they were originally. This will take the railway workers back on the job. If there is any opposition to this action, then I would not hesitate to go to Federal Court to enforce it. I believe this is the first step to getting our railway service back into operation in our country.

Middle East Treaty — I

Q: Mr. President, what will you do to make Prime Minister Begin comply with your understanding that Israel must eventually withdraw from the West Bank and further to build no settlements there during the five years of negotiation? And will you consider a Christmas trip to the Middle East for a signing of the peace treaty?

P: There is nothing I can make Prime Minister Begin do. He is an independent leader of an autonomous and independent nation. I can only use persuasion and depend upon the mutual trust that exists between me and him.

There were 20 or 30 very crucial issues that were obstacles at the beginning of the Camp David negotiations. This was one of them. I would guess that it was after midnight Saturday, less than 24 hours after the final agreement was signed, that we reached these agreements.

There are two elements of the dispute. One is at what time will the agreement not to build any more segments be concluded. Prime Minister Begin's interpretation is that this is to be maintained, the prohibition against new settlements, during the negotiations concerning the Sinai with Egypt.

My very clear understanding is that it related to the negotiation for conclusion in the West Bank-Gaza Strip of the establishment of a self-government. The other question concerns whether or not Israel would initiate new settlements after this negotiating period was concluded and the self-government was established.

I think the best answer to that is that this is an honest difference of opinion. The best answer I can give is to quote from a statement by Foreign Minister Dayan, who was with us at that midnight meeting, and this is a statement he made at the Ben Gurion Airport on the 19th of September, when he arrived in Israel. "Let us not delude ourselves" — I am quoting him — "I have no doubt that when we enter into deliberations with the other parties concerning what is to happen in the area in the five years of transition. That is the West Bank-Gaza Strip. This question will come up and will be discussed and agreement will have to be reached on this subject."

So the degree of participation of the residents of the West Bank has still got to be determined. It is an honest difference of opinion. It would certainly be no obstacle to the progress towards peace.

But I can't say we have resolved it yet. There is no personal animosity between myself and Prime Minister Begin.

I certainly do not allege any improper action on his part. It is just an honest difference of opinion, which I think will be resolved.

As far as my going to the Mideast is concerned, nothing would please me more than to participate in the signing of a peace treaty at an early date. But that is still to be negotiated. The only request that President Sadat made of me in the entire Camp

David proceedings was that I come to Egypt. I promised him that I would, sometime in the future.

Q: If Prime Minister Begin persists, would you consider cancelling the U.S. agreement to build air bases in the Negev for Israel?

P: No. The letter to Israel concerning the two airports to be put in the Negev, I have already directed that that letter be sent to Israel. It is not being sent from me to Prime Minister Begin. It is being sent from Defense Secretary Harold Brown to Defense Minister Weizman.

We have not agreed to build the air bases. We have agreed to consult with the Israelis and participate in the cost of those rebuilt air bases, to the degree that we negotiate in the future. We will certainly participate in the cost, the degree to be determined in the future.

Rating in Polls

Q: Mr. President, I am sure you have been enjoying your big resurgence in the polls lately, but I wonder if you are fairly confident you can keep them up there.

P: I am not sure about that. I hope so. My interpretation is the polls have been much more accurate the last week or two than they were before. (Laughter) But I will do the best I can. I think it is not an accurate conclusion that the culmination of our efforts on, say, natural gas, civil service reform and other major endeavors in the Congress, is the result of the Camp David accords.

Obviously, my own reputation as a capable leader was enhanced by that agreement, but we have been working very long months to bring about the conclusion of some highly controversial issues. I will continue to do the best I can. But my actions will never be predicated on what is the most popular. But I will do what I think is best for our country. I will take my chances on whether the people approve or not.

Full Employment Bill

Q: Mr. President, it was recently reported that you said in a meeting with the Congressional Black Caucus that a Camp David-type meeting on the Humphrey-Hawkins Full Employment Bill would be ill-advised —

P: Yes.

Q: — causing John Conyers to storm out as everyone knows. I was wondering first, why would such a meeting be ill-advised; and secondly, if Camp David meetings are to be focused on international affairs, might such a meeting take place involving the principal ones in South Africa and Rhodesia where these situations could be equally as violent and turmoil could equally exist?

P: I have been in office now for 20 months. I have faced many very difficult issues, in foreign affairs and domestic affairs. I have never called a caucus or a meeting at Camp David except once in my life. This was a unique set of circumstances where I felt that extended negotiations over several

days — as you know, it turned out to be two weeks — in almost complete seclusion was absolutely necessary to reach an agreement.

I would guess that this might never again occur. It may on very rare occasions. But I don't ever intend to use a Camp David meeting to settle matters that ought best to be resolved within the Congress where they can best handle them. I will use my utmost influence to determine the outcome of those deliberations in the Congress.

As far as the Humphrey-Hawkins Bill goes, I think it is very important that this bill be passed. It is a full employment commitment of our country, which I share. We have helped to get the bill passed through the House. It is now on the Senate calendar. I talked to Majority Leader Byrd since lunch about this. He is proceeding as rapidly as he can. He is trying to get a time certain, an agreement by some Republican Members of the Senate to vote on the Humphrey-Hawkins Bill. But it is just not appropriate and I think it would be ill-advised for me to take a group of Senators or Congressmen in the last two weeks of the session up to Camp David to spend a week or two in seclusion. It is just impractical.

SALT Talks — 1

Q: Mr. President, we hear reports that you feel pretty good about how the SALT negotiations are coming along these days. How close are we to a SALT agreement now?

P: The issues that divide us and the Soviet Union on SALT have been constantly narrowed over the last 18 months of negotiation. Now the issues are quite few.

I also talked to Secretary Vance since lunch. He has been meeting today and yesterday with Foreign Minister Gromyko of the Soviet Union. I think both men are negotiating aggressively and in good faith to reach a conclusion of the differences.

I don't know what the outcome will be. It takes two to reach agreement. We hope to conclude a SALT agreement this year.

I will be meeting with Foreign Minister Gromyko Saturday to capitalize upon the progress that I think Vance and Gromyko are making now. I don't see any insurmountable obstacles. But if the Soviets are forthcoming and cooperative and are willing to compromise some of their positions, we will have an agreement.

Welfare Fraud

Q: It has been reported this week that some Federal employees who are on the payroll and also drawing welfare benefits have been charged. It is also reported outside of Washington recently that the Federal Government has made what amounts to a conscious decision not to pursue fraud by individual welfare recipients and leave that instead to the local and state government.

Are you aware of this policy, and do you approve of it?

P: When I came into office, we were determined, I and my administration, I

think shared by the Congress, to proceed aggressively to eliminate fraud from government. We have a problem in GSA. We have had some good success in other areas, including rooting out of people who have tried to defraud the Government by drawing welfare payments when they were on a payroll and didn't deserve it, according to the law.

My own inclination would be let the Justice Department decide whether or not an indictment and prosecution should be pursued or whether repayment of the funds with some penalty would be adequate. I am not familiar with the individual cases. But the fact is we have initiated for the first time an attempt to root out these violators of the law and make them provide some recompense to the Government that is according to what is proper and right.

I wouldn't say that every case ought to be pursued as a criminal proceeding, to put them in jail. Sometimes they might be discharged from their job, sometimes to repay the money, sometimes to pay a penalty. If it is a gross case, I would favor them going to jail.

Inflation Program — 1

Q: The Fed's discount rate is now nearly 10 percent. You are about to announce some top anti-inflation measures. How can any anti-inflation program be credible when you have interest rates this high and do you think 10 percent interest rates is the proper way to fight inflation?

P: The discount rate is not that high but I think it is too high and I wish it was lower. There are three entities in the government that have a great individual independent impact on either controlling inflation or enhancing inflation.

One is the President and my Cabinet members, in the preparation of the budget, do we advocate reducing the deficits? Do we advocate spending too much? The other is the Congress who makes the final determination on the budget and also prescribes, to a major degree, tax policy.

The third, of course, is the independent Federal Reserve. My own hope is that our present efforts to control inflation will be so successful that those interest rates now as determined by the Federal Reserve can be brought down.

When I came into office, we had a budget deficit of almost $70 billion — I think $66 billion. By the end of this Congressional session, I hope we will almost have brought that down below $40 billion, maybe even lower. We are cutting down the Federal deficit. We have a very tight constraint on spending. This is important in controlling inflation.

I am going to be very persistent in my own role as President in holding down unwarranted spending in individual bills that come to me from the Congress. I think the time for wasteful spending is over. And I think if we can show that we can get inflation under control through those actions by me and the Congress, that would be an inducement for the Federal Reserve to start bringing the interest rate down. But each one of those elements of our Government, Federal Reserve, Congress, President, are independent. I cannot control the other two. I can set a good example. That is what I am trying to do.

SALT Talks — 2

Q: Going back to SALT, the military is pushing an idea of digging a lot of holes in the ground for our land-based intercontinental ballistic missiles. So you truck them around; the Russians never know which hole the missile is in. The theory is the Russians have to hit all the holes in order to get all the missiles. Do you think that is a good idea and how does that affect the SALT negotiations?

P: That is one among many ideas. I think over a period of time, it has become obvious that our fixed silo-type intercontinental ballistic missiles are becoming more and more vulnerable because of the accuracy of the Soviet missiles; ours are even more accurate and the MIRVing of the Soviet missiles where they have many warheads on each missile which we have had for a long time.

The so-called multiple aim points of many silos for each missile is one idea that has been put forward. It has some very serious defects. I can only mention two at this time. One is how do you verify that all the holes don't have missiles in them. It is obvious that we would be keeping the agreement, we would not violate it.

We don't know that that would be the case on the other side. I believe that we would find, as we proceed further with it, that it would not only be very difficult if the Soviets adopted this same policy, but very expensive as well. But that is one option that we are considering. I would guess that by the end of this year, we would have gone through all the options including that one, and at that time, certainly at the time that SALT II agreement is reached, I will explain to the American people in the most careful and complete terms what our future plans for adequate strategic strength will be, probably going for the next five years.

That is just one of the options now. It has some very serious defects. It is being considered.

Middle East Treaty — 2

Q: Mr. President, there is a report that you are working for a settlement in Lebanon and that Syria and Israel would be involved. Could you verify this, sir?

P: This is a subject that President Sadat raised with me several times at Camp David. It is one in which we have been involved, as you know, for many months. There is a tragedy in Lebanon that the rest of the world has not adequately addressed, including ourselves.

The suffering of the people of Lebanon, through no fault of their own in almost every case, has been extraordinary. Obviously the responsibility for resolving the

Lebanon question rests primarily on the shoulders of those who live there.

My commitment has been to strengthen the Sarkis Government, politically, economically and militarily. We gave them some aid so that the President of that country can control the affairs of the country itself. When we were flying back from Camp David on the helicopter, President Sadat and I were talking about this, Prime Minister Begin joined in the conversation. All three of us committed ourselves to renew our support for the Sarkis Government, the Lebanese Government. So they have the prime responsibility.

The next two nations I would say that are most intimately involved are Syria, which has large forces in Lebanon, invited in by the Lebanese Government because they cannot maintain order by themselves under existing circumstances and Israel, who obviously wants a stable government, stable people on their northern border.

Other countries more removed geographically also have an intense interest and influence in Lebanon. I would say two of them would be Saudi Arabia and Egypt.

More distantly, other countries that have a direct historical interest like the United States and France would be involved. All this could be done under the aegis of the United Nations. But I think it is time for us to take joint action to call a conference of those who are involved, primarily the people who live in Lebanon, the different factions there and try to reach some solution that may involve a new charter for Lebanon.

I am not in favor of a partitioned Lebanon. I would like to see a unified Lebanon at peace with a strong enough central government to control the situation there and protect its own people.

Veto Plans

Q: Mr. President, I understand that you are considering vetoing the public works water projects bill and in addition to that, that you are considering vetoing four other bills — tuition tax credit, surface transportation, tax cut bill, and Labor-HEW. Can you tell us is this part of your anti-inflation program? Will you veto the bills? Or is this a President Carter who has come down from Camp David and is trying to show he can handle his own Congress as well as the Israelis and the Egyptians?

P: I don't want to show that I can handle the Congress. What I want to do is work in harmony with the Congress. I think we have done that to a substantial degree, a provable degree. The legislation to which you refer causes me deep concern because some of it is wasteful, some of it has elements in it which I consider to be unconstitutional. And my own objection to certain features of that legislation has been well-known to the Congress and also to the public.

The public works bill has now passed the conference committee and both the House and Senate have adopted the con-

ference report. This bill in its present form is completely unacceptable to me. And I will decide whether or not to veto it when it gets to my desk. It is up to the leaders of the Congress to decide when to submit it to me. My objection to some of its features are well-known. I think that we have got to establish a policy in Washington, the Congress and I, particularly in these crucial days when inflation is our number one concern, at least on the domestic scene, that will be an example for the rest of the nation to follow.

If we continue the age-old policy of pork barrel allocations in the public works bill, this is a horrible example to set for the rest of the country. It would make it very difficult for me to control inflation if the Congress and I couldn't set a good example for the rest of the nation. So I am willing to meet the Congress on this issue — we have an honest difference of opinion with some of the Members of the Congress — and have it resolved in a constitutional and appropriate way.

If it involves a veto, the Congress has a right to express their displeasure by attempting to override my veto. I am going to do the best I can, if I do veto the bill, to get enough votes to sustain my veto. There have been some allegations made that the Congress might try to connect this bill with the energy bill. I don't believe they will do that. The proper way for the Congress to express its displeasure over the veto of the public works bill is to override the veto. I believe the energy legislation is too important for any responsible Member of the House of Representatives to connect it with the public works bill.

Inflation Program — 2

Q: Mr. President, President Ford said this week that you made a mistake last year in concentrating on unemployment rather than inflation. Do you agree with that, first of all? And secondly, do you wish you had moved sooner to do something about inflation?

P: No, I don't agree with that at all. When I was running for President, after I became President, I never singularly attacked the unemployment problem without also trying to deal with the inflationary problem. President Ford left me with a $66 billion deficit. We have tried to turn that around and cut down deficit spending. We have been remarkably successful.

At the same time, we have provided the American people with a much better life, better education programs, better housing programs, better transportation programs, substantial tax reductions — six or seven billion dollars last year, perhaps as much as $20 billion this year.

I believe that we have seen in 1977 a very substantial reduction in the inflation rate. The last 6 months of 1977, the inflation rate was quite low, 4-1/2 to 5 percent; an average for the entire year of about 6 or 6-1/2 percent. It grew this year more than we had anticipated for several reasons, the most important of which was the high food prices that occurred the first six months of the year.

We have always had a very strong anti-inflation program. Since we have had very good luck so far, success, in bringing down the unemployment rate, adding 6-1/2 million new jobs, bringing the unemployment rate down by about 25 percent already, we are able to focus our attention much more specifically on inflation.

It is much more of a threat now than it was a year ago. But I am determined to deal with inflation as effectively as we have already proven we could deal with unemployment.

Middle East Treaty — 3

Q: Mr. President, you said in your opening statement that both President Sadat and Prime Minister Begin said there are no remaining obstacles to concluding the Sinai treaty. Have they set a date yet for starting these talks? And how long would you estimate it would take to go through the formalities that still remain?

P: I would hope that we could commence the talks within two weeks, but no specific date has been set. Both Prime Minister Begin and President Sadat today, when I talked to them on the phone, on their own initiative, said they were expecting us to be full partners as I was at Camp David, and they could see no obstacles to the peace talks beginning without delay.

I think it will take two weeks to prepare for the talks. There are some official responsibilities that President Sadat has in his own country that will take place and be concluded within two weeks. But that would be the approximate time frame. I am not trying to be presumptuous because no date has been set.

Q: If I could follow that up, Prime Minister Begin is supposed to be sending a letter dealing with the Israeli position on the West Bank. Has that letter been received yet? And would any delay on that letter perhaps hold up these talks on the Sinai?

P: Prime Minister Begin has sent me a letter expressing his position and I have also sent him a letter expressing my position. Now I think the next step would be for me and him in good faith and in a friendly, cooperative attitude to try to work out the differences between us.

Q: Will you make those letters available?

P: I will think it over. I can't answer because I would really — it suits me okay for the letters to be made available but I can't unilaterally release the letter that I sent to him or received from him without his approval.

My own inclination is to let all the correspondence be made public that relates to the Mideast settlements. We have done that so far, even when where we had differences of opinion. But I would have to get his permission before we could release the letters.

Steel Imports

Q: Mr. President, your trigger price program for steel has managed to reduce the foreign imports. But foreign steel still takes a large part of the U.S. market and the floor under steel prices does drive up the inflationary forces.

What modifications, if any, do you plan in your trigger price program?

P: As you know, the steel trigger price program went into effect, I think, only in May. We have only had a few months of experience with it. So far it has been very successful. We have had a net increase this year of, I think, 24,000 jobs in the steel industry alone.

In spite of a fairly dormant construction industry, we have had 5 percent increase in the shipments of domestic steel. I understand that the Japanese steel exports have actually gone down this year. The most important measure, I think, of success so far is that a year or so ago, the steel industry plants were only being used at about 76 percent capacity. Now that use has increased to almost 90 percent capacity. So we have got a very vigorous steel industry now.

I think the price of steel has been held reasonably well under control. We are obviously fine-tuning the trigger price system as we get more experience with it.

There are special kinds of steel that might be involved. We have some problems still in Europe because the steel price, as you know, is based on Japanese cost. But I think we have stopped the unwarranted dumping of foreign steel on our American market.

I think we have protected the jobs of steel workers and we have added a new degree of prosperity to the steel industry.

I believe that the second quarter this year, compared to the second quarter of last year, steel industry profits were up 71 percent, which means that they have a lot more to invest back into more modern plants and more jobs for better steel production in our country.

Q: Mr. President, can you tell us a little more, sir, about the nature of your participation in this next round of talks? You mentioned full partnership. Will you be personally involved with that, or will Secretary Vance be?

P: I would guess that I would not be personally involved except in a case where the leaders of the other two nations were involved. If there was a dispute about a particular drawing of a line, or a phased withdrawal, or something of that kind, that could not be resolved at the Foreign Minister or delegate level, then I would get involved, if necessary.

I wouldn't want to see the talks break down because of any timidity on my part. I consider it to be one of the most important responsibilities that I have. I would guess, though, that the negotiations will be carried on at a fairly high level below the President and Prime Minister level.

I understand from Prime Minister Begin that the leader of his delegation will be Foreign Minister Dayan. I don't know yet who will head the Egyptian delegation. I have not yet decided on the American delegation leader. But it will be at a fairly high level and the principles for settling the Sinai disagreements have all been resolved.

Now the details which I don't think are going to be highly controversial are the only things remaining to be resolved. The exact decision of whether a particular road intersection or a hilltop would be at the first withdrawal line, those are the kinds of things that would be settled, and I believe we have a good relationship between the two leaders that wouldn't cause a deterioration in the negotiations.

FRANK CORMIER: Thank you, Mr. President.

THE PRESIDENT: Thank you very much. I enjoyed it.   ∎

October 10, 1978

Following is the White House transcript of President Carter's Oct. 10 news conference, his 38th since taking office:

THE PRESIDENT: I have a brief statement to make to begin with.

As all of you know, we are approaching the end of the 95th congressional session with a great deal of work still to be done. We are searching for a fair tax bill that would be simple, equitable, progressive in nature. The Senate, after it completes its deliberations on the tax bill, will take up the full employment and balanced growth legislation which expresses in clear legislative terms a commitment that has been longstanding in our nation that any American has a right to a job. This right must be balanced with stable pricing structures.

The passage of this legislation was very greatly needed and I hope the Senate will act expeditiously on it. The House has already passed it overwhelmingly.

The most important bill left in the House is on energy. We have been working on a comprehensive energy policy for our nation now for 18 or 20 months. The most important single element in the energy package is natural gas, a difficult, complicated, highly debated question.

In addition to that, we will have bills designed to conserve energy, to shift to coal, a more plentiful supply of energy, utility rate reform, and also energy taxes and credits to encourage people to take actions to make their houses more efficient and their businesses more efficient, and to save energy throughout the nation.

The most important single portion of this legislation is on natural gas. Because of our excessive dependence on foreign oil we have seen the value of the dollar decline, large sums of American money have gone to foreign nations unnecessarily, and the excessive imports have caused at least one percent to be added to our inflation rate.

The vote on these bills in the House will come at the end of this week.

The natural gas bill will result in a decrease by 1985 of 1.4 million barrels of imported oil per day.

I believe that this vote is the most important that will be cast by the members of the Congress during this year. And it will be a measure of the effectiveness of the Congress, of our government, and also a measure of achievement for the year. I sincerely hope that the House members will vote affirmatively on the natural gas legislation and other packages of the energy policy for our country at the end of this week.

Tax Bill Veto — 1

QUESTION: Mr. President, you mentioned taxes. Almost certain the tax bill you get from Congress will significantly exceed your own goals. Do you think that a tax veto is inevitable?

P: Well, the goals that the tax bill will exceed — I presume you mean the amount of money that it will cost the Treasury. Right?

The House bill is within the guidelines that I established for the cost to the Treasury. I think it would not be excessively inflationary. The Senate is still deliberating on the tax bill so far as I know, unless they just recently finished it, and what they are considering would not be satisfactory in its present form. If the House and Senate conferees the rest of this week can get together and take the best elements of both the House bill on the one hand and the Senate bill on the other, and combine them, we can have an acceptable tax bill to present to me and which I will sign.

The bill must be simple, fair, equitable, progressive in nature, that is putting the tax burden where people can most afford it, and a substantial tax reduction on our people. If it meets those requirements, then I will sign it. But at present, the issue is still in doubt.

Q: Would you hesitate to veto if it doesn't meet those criteria?

P: No, I would not hesitate to veto it if it does not meet those criteria.

Middle East Treaty — 1

Q: Mr. President, are the separate peace talks that open Thursday between Israel and Egypt linked in any way to negotiations on other Arab lands under Israeli occupation and have you ever answered King Hussein's questions concerning the clarification on the sovereignty issues?

P: The two discussions on the Sinai, which relates to Egypt and Israel only, on the one hand and the West Bank-Gaza Strip discussions on the other are not legally interconnected, but I think throughout the Camp David talks and in the minds of myself, Prime Minister Begin, and President Sadat, they are interrelated. We have been trying to induce the Jordanians, and to some lesser degree so far the Palestin-

ians who live on the West Bank-Gaza Strip area to participate in the talks.

We hope they will both participate along with the Egyptians and Israelis. There is no doubt in my mind that while the negotiating teams are in Washington, we will discuss both the Sinai questions leading to an Egyptian-Israeli peace treaty and also the questions concerning the West Bank and Gaza Strip.

I have not yet responded to the questions that King Hussein sent to me. I saw him on one of the television programs reading the questions. They are in the process of being assessed by the State Department and I presume when they get to me —

Q: They were given to you privately, were they not?

P: No, they were not. I have not yet received them personally. But I know basically what is in them. It is important this be done expeditiously and I will not delay it, but it will be several days.

Shevchenko Defection

Q: Mr. President, what is your view of the Shevchenko defection case in which a high level Russian defector had his whereabouts revealed by a paid woman companion who says that the funds for her companionship came from the CIA?

P: If the figures the woman quoted were accurate, which they aren't, it would be highly inflationary, — (Laughter) — contrary to my policy there. But Shevchenko, I understand, had large sums of money paid to him by the United Nations when he terminated his service there and I understand, had other bank accounts as well.

I have also heard that he is writing a book or more than one book and will receive in the future substantial advanced payments for that authorship. The payments that we have made to him, the CIA, I am not familiar with completely.

I am sure Admiral Turner would be glad to answer that question, but they don't equal what the woman said was paid for her services or favors.

SALT Talks — 1

Q: Mr. President, does Mr. Warnke's resignation have anything to do with the idea that perhaps he is not the right man to try to sell this treaty to the Senate; and, second, to the SALT Treaty, can you say today that you will submit a SALT agreement to the Senate for ratification or are you still holding out the possibility that you might just do it in an executive capacity?

P: Mr. Warnke came to help us with the SALT negotiations as Director of the ACDA organization with the understanding that he could only stay for a limited period of time.

At that time, last year, we thought we would have a SALT agreement in 1977. Several months ago he told me that for personal reasons he would still like to step down. Quite early this past summer I induced him to stay on. He will be the head

of the Arms Control and Disarmament Agency until after Secretary Vance's upcoming trip to Moscow, after which he will step down. I wish he would stay on. He is a very good man and he will be available to testify to the Congress even after he returns to private life.

I have not yet decided how to submit the agreement or the treaty to the Congress. I think it would depend upon when it was concluded, but my preference would be to submit it as a treaty.

Q: Mr. President, you don't rule out the other, sir?

P: My preference is to submit it as a treaty.

Rhodesia Policy — 1

Q: Mr. President, will you see Ian Smith now that he is in the United States? And there is a second part to that question. Are you aware of any agreement Henry Kissinger made with Smith such that the United States would give Rhodesia full diplomatic recognition and an end to sanctions in return for a trend toward majority rule?

P: I am not familiar with that executive agreement. I do not intend to see Mr. Smith. He has had a meeting with the members of the Congress who invited him over and also had, I think, a two-hour meeting with Secretary Vance. There is no reason for me to meet with him.

I think that the essence of it is what we are trying to do is to end the bloodshed in Rhodesia. We have not caused the bloodshed. We have not caused the war. We have put forward publicly, without any secrecy about it, along with the British, to the front line presidents, to the patriotic front, the Smith regime, our proposals, that there will be all-parties conferences where people that are in dispute can get together and talk and try to work out a means by which free and democratic elections can be held in Rhodesia, so that anyone who is can run for office, and let the people of Rhodesia decide what kind of government they want.

This is a proposal that Mr. Smith and his regime have not been willing to accept. But this is what we propose.

If the parties in dispute prefer a different proposal and agree upon it, we would have no objection to that.

SALT Talks — 2

Q: Mr. President, we are currently prosecuting a former CIA warrant officer for allegedly selling a manual on one of our spy satellites to the Soviets. Can you tell us whether or not the Soviets having that manual has in any way compromised U.S. security and whether or not it has affected our SALT negotiations because it might make it more difficult for us to verify their strategic weapons system?

P: I would not want to comment on that particular case. Whenever the Soviets discover any information about our classified material, it is obviously potentially damaging to our country. It has not affected our SALT negotiations. I stated publicly, I think for the first time a president has done so, down at Cape Kennedy, Cape Canaveral, two or three Sundays ago, that we did have aerial surveillance. And I think it is important for the American people to know that in the past and present and in the future, that our aerial surveillance capability would be adequate to affirm that the agreement on SALT, those in existence and those in the future, would be adequate.

So the revelation of any secret information or classified information is something to be avoided. It has not affected the SALT talks. Our ability to verify compliance will be adequate in the future.

Moscow Embassy as Asylum

Q: Mr. President, a family of Russian Pentecostals, the Shevchenkos, are seeking asylum and are lodged in the U.S. Embassy in Moscow. They said in letters that have been smuggled out that the embassy is bringing subtle, emotional pressure to dispel them into the hands of the Russians probably at great risk.

Did you direct the embassy to seek their ouster or are you willing to give them asylum and visas?

P: They are Russian citizens, as you know, and have been in the embassy in the Soviet Union in Moscow, the American Embassy, for months. We have provided them a place to stay, we provided them a room to live in, even though this is not a residence with normal quarters for them. I would presume they have no reason to smuggle out correspondence to this country since they have the embassy officials' ability to transmit messages.

I have not directed the embassy to discharge them from the embassy, no.

Inflation Program — 1

Q: Mr. President, the current underlying inflation rate is between seven and eight percent. Under your new anti-inflation program to be revealed soon, could we expect that rate to drop very much next year?

P: Well, I would hope so. I have been working on the anti-inflation package for a number of weeks, as you know, as you may know. I think that when the Congress completes its work, then I will be able to put the final touches on the anti-inflation program and reveal it to the public and pursue it aggressively.

My best effort at this moment in dealing with inflation is to be involved in the passage or modification of laws during these last few days of the congressional session. And this is what I have been trying to do, sometimes with private meetings with conference committees, sometimes with individual members of Congress, on a rare occasion with a veto of a bill which I found to be unacceptable.

But I would hope and I believe that the anti-inflation proposals I make, along with a tight constraint on budget spending by the Congress and myself, would be enough to bring down the inflation rate.

ERA Deadline Extension

Q: When do you think the ERA amendment will be fully ratified?

P: I don't know. We have been very pleased to have the Congress extend the time for three years. But that is a decision on ratification for the states to make. So far, 35 states have ratified it. Three more need to do so to make 38 or a three-fourths majority. But I am not qualified to predict when those three states might take that action. I hope without delay.

Education Department

Q: How high a priority do you still set on the creation of a Department of Education, first at this session of Congress, and if it doesn't happen at this session, then the next one?

P: I have advocated and have worked hard this year for the establishment of an independent Department of Education. I don't think that education in our country has gotten an adequate hearing in my own administration or previous ones because it has been a part of HEW, with health and welfare the dominant portions of that department.

I think at this point, it is unlikely that the bill will pass this year. The Senate did pass the bill. The House was not able or willing to take it up. But I still have it as an important goal of mine to establish this department.

I think it is important that a more efficient delivery of educational opportunity to children in our country be achieved. I think the primary control of the schools, obviously, ought to be at the local and state level, but I think it will make it more effective.

Q: In that connection, would it trouble you if the Congress appears to be wanting to drop Headstart from that department?

P: I think that issue has already been resolved. We don't want to do anything to weaken Headstart and I believe it has been a belief on the part of those who have managed Headstart in the past that it ought not to be part of the Education Department. And when I was a young man just home from the Navy, I headed up the Headstart Program in Georgia the first year, believe in it, and want to strengthen it, not weaken it. But I don't believe that it is likely that Headstart will be a part of the new Department of Education.

Middle East Treaty — 2

Q: Mr. President, to follow up Helen's opening question on the Middle East, you said there was no doubt that the subject of the West Bank would come up in the talks as well as that of Sinai. One of the Egyptian delegates has indicated that the Egyptians might be unwilling to sign a peace treaty without evidence of Israeli flexibility on the future question of settlements on the West Bank. Have the Israelis given any indication yet — for example, have they yet responded in this question of the exchange of letters and come around to the U.S. position on the future settlements in the West Bank?

P: I don't believe that your opinion accurately expresses what President Sadat has told me. I don't think he would let any single element of the West Bank-Gaza Strip settlement prevent a conclusion of a treaty between Egypt and Israel.

And I think the Israelis have been very forthcoming, in my experience with them at Camp David over long days of negotiations, concerning the West Bank and Gaza Strip. I think they are acting in good faith to set up an autonomous governing entity in the West Bank-Gaza Strip to withdraw their military government very expeditiously and I think the settlements issue still remains open. But it is subject to a negotiation.

The last time I had a press conference, I read the statement that Foreign Minister Dayan made in Israel, which I think is adequate, combined with a cessation of settlement activity altogether between now and the time the self-government is set up.

The role of our government, our position has always been that settlements in occupied territory are illegal and are an obstacle to peace. I have not changed my opinion, but to summarize, I don't believe this one issue, if unresolved expeditiously, would prevent the peace treaty between Israel and Egypt.

Policy Toward Iran

Q: Mr. President, I would like to ask you about Iran. How do we view the situation involving the Shah there now? Is he secure? How important is it to U.S. interests that the Shah remain in power and what if anything can the United States government do to keep him in power?

P: The strategic importance to our country, I think to the entire Western World, of a good relationship with a strong and independent Iran is crucial. We have historic friendships with Iran. I think they are a great stabilizing force in their part of the world. They are a very important trade partner. They have acted very responsibly. My own belief is that the Shah has moved aggressively to establish democratic principles in Iran and to have a progressive attitude towards social questions, social problems. This has been the source of much of the opposition to him in Iran.

We have no inclination to try to decide the internal affairs of Iran. My own hopes have been that there could be peace there, and an end to bloodshed in an orderly transformation into more progressive social arrangements and also increased democratization of the government itself which I believe the Shah also espouses. He may not be moving fast enough for some, he may be moving too fast for others. I don't want to get involved in that specific.

Popularity In West

Q: Mr. President, could I just ask you a political question? You have been making a rapid rise in the polls lately but some Democrats out in the West don't seem to believe that. Governor Lamm said something to the effect that you are about as popular in the West as Sherman in Georgia, said he was not even sure you would feel welcome there, was not sure it would be of benefit to Democrats out there even if you came out to campaign for them.

I was just wondering, sir, how do you think that situation has developed?

P: I don't think my popularity with Governor Lamm has fluctuated very much since I have been in office. It has always been about the same as you have just described, but I have been to Colorado to campaign in his presence and also for Senator Haskell and the congressional delegation, and was well received there.

I think it is accurate to say that most of the Western governors, and I think most of the members of the Congress from the West, have been strongly supportive of the basic positions that I have taken on issues that were highly controversial. And I feel at ease and I feel very welcomed when I go there.

Obviously, public opinion polls go up and down. They went up substantially at the end of the Camp David agreement. I think it is inevitable that they will go down somewhat, but I can't modify my own positions on issues or my basic commitments to the American people on the basis of public opinion polls.

If I happen to be unpopular with a particular governor or a group of people, I will just have to accept that and do the best I can.

Tax Bill Veto — 2

Q: Mr. President, I know you have answered one tax question, but what do you think of the $142 billion five-year tax cut bill passed by the Senate? Do you think there are enough safeguards in it against inflation. And what do you think of the concept of passing annual tax cuts so far for as long as five years ahead?

P: I am really not qualified to answer that question because I have not studied the actions that the Senate has taken in the last few hours. It would be very difficult to consummate as far-reaching and as controversial and as innovative a concept as that in the last few hours of a congressional session.

This is something in which the House has not been involved and for that to be analyzed completely as to its impact on the American taxpayers in such a short time would be very difficult.

In general, I believe that the Senate-passed bill has a much greater tax reduction than I can accept and has some features in it which I cannot accept.

My hope is, as I expressed originally, that the House and the Senate conferees over the next two or three days can reach an agreement, extracting the most acceptable elements from the House bill, combining them with the most acceptable elements of the Senate bill so that I can sign the final bill as passed.

If not, then there will be no tax bill this year because I will veto it. The only option would be for the Senate and the House to come back in a special session after the election, which I would not favor personally.

If this should occur, and I hope it won't occur, a veto, then, of course, early next year tax reduction would again be at the top of the agenda so that it could be passed as soon as possible, making some provisions of it as appropriate, even retroactive to the first of the year.

But my hope and expectation is still that the House and Senate conferees can meet and resolve the differences between them. I will be meeting tomorrow with the chairmen of the two committes from the House and Senate and, hopefully, the three of us can agree on an acceptable package.

Rhodesia Policy — 2

Q: Mr. President, a follow-up on the Rhodesia question. You indicated that if an all-parties conference would take place this would be an advantage to possibly settling the problems in Rhodesia?

Would you host such a conference in the United States?

P: I have no preference about where it should be held. My thinking is it would be better, perhaps, to hold it where the parties to the conference prefer.

Two or three weeks ago I instructed Secretary Vance to propose to the Front Line presidents and others that an all-parties conference be held in New York. This was not acceptable to some of them and the idea was not carried to completion.

But the important thing is to get the members who are in dispute who head armed forces that are killing each other in Rhodesia, Zimbabwe, the surrounding areas, and bring them to a table to talk about the differences and try to resolve them.

I believe that this is the best approach and, as I say, we are not wedded to a particular plan, although I think the Anglo-American plan, so-called, has been accepted in its basic elements by all the Front Line presidents and on occasion major parts of it by the Smith internal group and also the Patriotic Front. It is a good basis for negotiation.

So we are doing the best we can to end the bloodshed and to bring peace without any tendency to force people to come to a certain place or to force people even to accept the elements of the settlement that we think are best.

Balanced Budget

Q: Mr. President, there was a time when you spoke of a balanced federal budget by 1981 and now the Senate is talking of that as a factor in whether or not there would be a gigantic tax cut.

If and when do you ever see a balanced federal budget and how important is that anymore as a long-range consideration?

P: I still have a balanced budget as a goal, an important goal. You have to judge very carefully how much you can reduce taxes which takes money away from the federal government that it could use to balance a budget on the one hand and how much that tax reduction would stimulate the economy to bring in additional revenues at a lower tax rate.

I have been trying to bring the federal deficit down. As I have said many times, when I was running for President in 1976, the deficit was $66 billion. The Congress is very likely to pass a budget this year of about $38 billion deficit. So we have cut down the deficit $28 billion already in just two years. And I would hope that this trend would continue downward. The 1980 budget deficit, I hope, would be even less.

You can't predict what the economic forces will be and then the following year, I hope to get it down further. I would certainly like to have a balanced budget but it depends to a great degree on the strength of the economy and what tax reductions we give.

By the end of this year, if things go well on the tax bill, we will have reduced taxes on the American people $25 billion. Had we not given a tax reduction, of course that would be additional revenue to help balance the budget. So you have to balance the budget itself on one hand, how much deficit you have, against tax reductions to the people to keep jobs available and the economy growing.

That is a very difficult thing to do. We are just doing the best we can. It is unpredictable what will occur.

Inflation Program — 2

Q: Mr. President, I would like to ask you about the future of the dollar, sir. Do you feel that the inflationary, anti-inflationary steps that you plan to take after Congress leaves, combined with making good on the pledges of bond which would occur if the Congress acts on your energy plan, would that in some way turn the dollar around or do you feel you have to do more than that in order to stem the erosion of the value of the dollar against other currencies?

P: You have to do more than any particular two items. I think the most important thing the Congress can do is to pass an energy package to give us an identifiable American energy policy. I think this would restore confidence in our government, confidence in our people, more than anything I can think of, among foreign nations who trade with us and who trade in our currency and therefore cause it sometimes to go down in an unwarranted degree.

Obviously, controlling inflation is another very major step forward that we can take to strengthen the dollar.

We have done other things as well. We are trying to increase our exports to reduce our balance of trade deficit. We have sold additional amounts of gold which is predictable policy now, and I think this helps to strengthen the dollar.

One of the most important things that is occurring outside of our own control, but modified in a beneficial way at Bonn, was to strengthen the economies of our major trading partners, notably Japan and Germany. As their economies are stronger, they can buy goods more from other countries including ourselves.

So I think all these factors combined would lower our trade deficit and lead to a stronger dollar.

FRANK CORMIER (AP): Thank you, Mr. President.

November 9, 1978

Following is the White House transcript of President Carter's Nov. 9 news conference, held in Kansas City, Mo. It was his 39th news conference as president.

Farm Set-aside Programs

THE PRESIDENT: I'm glad to be in Kansas City, and I would like to call on Mr. Scott Feldman [KNBC-TV, Kansas City] for the first question.

QUESTION: Thank you, Mr. President. It's been suggested that American farmers would be immensely helped if the Government were to drop its set-aside programs and urge farmers to produce simply everything they could, while at the same time the government would push agricultural exports even harder.

My question to you, sir, is would you consider dropping the farm set-aside program, and how far will your administration go in demanding in world trade talks that the United States not open its market any wider to foreign goods unless those countries let in more American farm goods?

P: Thank you, Mr. Feldman.

I think it's highly likely that we will have set-asides. On a nationwide basis, we have had very good crop in corn, this year in particular, averaging for the first time over 100 bushels per acre.

The policy of our own Government, my administration, has been to try to increase farm income, and we've increased farm income about 25 percent.

We've also, every year, set records on farm exports. We have gotten recent information that the worldwide feed grain stocks are fairly high, but we anticipate very large exports of farm products this coming year.

I would say a moderate set-aside program, continued storage of farm products under the farmer's control, not so that the middle grain dealers can make the extraordinary profits as they have in the past, no embargoes on the shipment of farm products in the future, as they have been under

previous administrations — this combination, I think, is the best to pursue.

I don't believe that the erection of tariffs or trade barriers would help us at all in the agricultural economy, because we export so many more agricultural products than we import. But we have recently signed a bill — as a matter of fact, in Kansas — passed by the Congress, that would improve greatly our opportunity to export farm products in the future with additional loans for those that might purchase our farm products, with additional opening of farm export offices to represent our farmers in foreign countries where markets are possible.

Mr. Pippert [Wes Pippert, United Press International].

Results of the Election - 1

Q: Mr. President, I'm very interested in your assessment of the election, and a couple of specific questions: Why did Democrats do so poorly in this region of the Middle West; and secondly, with regard to Congress, how much does the more conservative nature of the Senate jeopardize approval of a SALT agreement, either as a treaty or as an executive agreement? And will the new makeup of the Senate make you hesitate to introduce such legislation as urban aid and welfare reform?

P: I hope I can remember those four questions. Well, in the first place, I think the Democrats did fairly well on a nationwide basis. We lost some very key races, some of them in the Midwest. I'd say one of the most serious was the loss of the Senate seat, Dick Clark in Iowa. But I just rode in from the airport with the new Governor-elect of Kansas, who happens to be a Democrat.

I think there was a general expression around the country of approval for the Democratic Party and its policies. I don't look on it as a referendum of whether I've done a good job or not. We retained well over 60 percent of the Members of the House of Representatives, Congress, about 60 percent in the Senate, and about 60 percent in the Governorships.

The election of Republican Senators and their effect on the SALT ratification — I think both liberals and conservatives, Democrats and Republicans favor an agreement with the Soviet Union which would limit the threat of nuclear arms in the future. We have been negotiating the SALT II agreement now for almost 2 years, even longer, including the time my own predecessors spent on this effort. And I believe that if the SALT treaty is well balanced — and it certainly will be — it will be infinitely superior to no treaty at all and much better than the SALT I agreement under which we presently live.

So, I believe that we will have a tough fight in the Senate, as we've always anticipated, but I don't anticipate that partisanship will play a role in the passage or ratification of the SALT agreement.

I would never be hesitant about presenting any sort of controversial legislation

to Congress because I feared failure. If I had had this inclination toward fear, I would not have been able to sign an energy bill this morning; we would not have had the Panama treaties ratified; we would not have had many achievements that we've already realized.

So, I wouldn't let the makeup of the Congress, which is still heavily Democratic by the way, preventing my introducing bills that I thought were good for the country.

Mr. Brooks Jackson [Associated Press].

Defense Spending

Q: Mr. President, as you draw up the budget for next year, which you will be doing the next few weeks, you're facing the choice between, to some extent, guns and butter. We've committed to our NATO Allies to let the military budget grow. At the same time, you want to hold down, decrease the Federal deficit to $30 billion or below.

Is it true, as reported, that you've decided to let the whole military budget grow by about 3 percent faster than the rate of inflation while ordering a $4 billion, $5 billion cut of the projected gross of social programs? And if so, where are those cuts going to come from — Amtrak subsidies or Federal pensions or farm programs or where?

P: Well, I've been working on the 1980 fiscal year budget for months. I had my first hearings, preliminary hearings with the agency heads last April or May, and now almost daily, I meet with the Office of Management and Budget on future decisions to be made in the budget itself. I won't make final decisions on the fiscal year '80 budget until sometime next month, after meeting with the heads of the different agencies and departments of the Federal Government to let them appeal, in effect, decisions that the OMB, Office of Management and Budget, and I have made together.

There's no way that I can cut down the ability of our Nation to defend itself. Our security obviously comes first. And we have encouraged our NATO Allies in particular to increase their expenditures for a joint defense of Europe and therefore us by 3 percent a year above the inflation rate. I intend to honor that commitment. The final figures, though, on individual departments, and clearly the Defense Department, have not yet been decided.

I might point out I will meet my goal, which I announced in the anti-inflation speech a couple of weeks ago, of having a budget deficit less than half what it was when I was running for President. The budget deficit will be below $30 billion. It's going to be a very tight, very stringent, very difficult budget to achieve, but I will achieve it. And I'm sure Congress will back me in this effort. I'm also continuing a freeze on hiring of Federal employees. I have limited this year, with the Congress' approval, the pay increases for Federal employees — there is no increase at all for executives in the Federal Government. And I'll do other things as well to control inflation.

I consider it to be my top domestic commitment, and I don't intend to fail.

Meat Imports

Q: Mr. President, Jim Fitzpatrick, *Kansas City Times.*

Do you intend to sign the meat import bill, and if not, why not?

P: The bill has not gotten to my desk yet. And I expect to receive it tomorrow or Saturday. I'll make a decision then.

I might point out that I'm strongly in favor of the countercyclical approach to beef imports, where on a predictable basis, when the supply of beef in this country is high, that imports would be lower, and vice versa. There are some factors that concern me about the beef import bill. One is the — I understand to be a severe limitation on the President's right to make decisions in case of emergency. But I'll have to assess the bill in its entirety. If I should make a decision against the legislation, however, because of the feature that I just described to you, then I would work with the Congress to include early next year a countercyclical approach. I think it's a very good approach. And I'll just have to make a decision before the end of this week.

Judy [Judy Woodruff, NBC News].

Revenue Act of 1978

Q: Mr. President, the tax bill that you have signed contains cuts in capital gains taxes, which is the opposite of what you would have liked. It also contains cuts for people in the middle-income level, who are making between $10,000 to $15,000 a year. That is not going to be enough to offset the increases in social security taxes.

Why did you sign the bill?

P: Well, there were many features about the tax bill which were not my original preference. The reforms included in the bill — and they're substantial — did not measure up to what I asked the Congress to do. The final reduction in capital gains taxes was substantially below that approved by either the House or Senate. It was as low as the conference committee could go.

I think that we do need tax reduction, and the bill involves about $21 billion in tax reductions — and a part of it, by the way, is the continuation of the present tax reductions, which would have increased $13 billion, roughly, had I not signed the bill at all.

We did the best we could in the last few days — as a matter of fact, the last few hours of the congressional session — to make the bill more acceptable to me. In balance, it was acceptable. It was necessary. And I think that we do benefit greatly from the fact that the people of our country will not be saddled with $20 to $30 billion in increased taxes at the first of the next year, had I not signed the bill.

I've not given up on my hope that we can have additional reforms in the future.

And I think the capital gains reductions were reasonable, compared to what the House and Senate had both considered.

Social Security Payments

Q: In line with that, Mr. President, last week in Kansas City, Senator Eagleton expressed concern over the social security tax increase, the bill that was passed. He termed it as a bad bill and one that needed to be reviewed. Do you agree with the review and possibly a reduction in the social security tax increase?

P: The original proposal that I made to the Congress last year, in 1977, was that the social security be handled slightly different from the way it was and that we have a reduction, as you know, in social security payments. The Congress — and I approved, finally — decided that the social security system was in such imminent danger of bankruptcy that it had to be saved; and it was saved by increase in rates.

I have no present plans to advocate a substantial change in the present legislation. If so, if I did have a reduction in social security payments, that redution would have to be made up by allocations of funds from the general Treasury. I know for a fact that Senator Long, head of the Finance Committee in the Senate, is strongly opposed to this procedure. And I think even if I desired it, it would be highly unlikely that we could achieve it. It's one of the options that we will consider, but I certainly have no present plans to do so.

Anti-inflation Program

Q: Mr. President, considering George Meany's reaction to your anti-inflation proposals, and in view of the fact that negotiations are coming up in a number of industries, major industries, during the next few months, what do you intend to do to keep the unions involved to adhere to your 7-percent wage cap?

P: Well, Mr. Meany did not reject the voluntary wage and price standards that I proposed. He expressed a preference that the Congress be called back into session to impose an extensive mandatory Government wage and price standard throughout the entire free enterprise system of our country. I do not have any intention of doing this. And if I attempted it, I have no feeling at all that the Congress would approve.

In the absence of that, Mr. Meany, I think, made clear in one of the Sunday afternoon talk shows that he did encourage individual labor unions to cooperate, within the bounds of their desire and what's best for their own members. So, I've got, I'd say, a minimal, at least, degree of support from the AFL-CIO President. Of course, he recognized, as do I, that we have international presidents, themselves, to make decisions. There are several thousand bargaining units in the country. We've gotten fairly substantial encouragement from the UAW, one of the major labor unions,

and also from the Teamsters, who will be negotiating a contract next year.

I'm determined, as is Alfred Kahn and other members of my administration, to make the anti-inflation package work. I don't intend to back down. I'll do everything I can that's legal within the bounds of my own authority and my influence with Congress to assure that the anti-inflation package is successful. And I think that most labor members, in organized unions or otherwise, feel that it's much better for them to control inflation than it is to let it run rampant, even if they were to get some small increases in — temporary increases in wages that are then overcome by increased inflation.

Everybody wants inflation to be controlled, including the members of labor unions.

Q: Mr. President, Stan Karmack, KCMO, Kansas City. We have confirmed with the Hershey Corporation this morning that the price of a Hershey bar is going up 9.3 percent. Since that is above your wage and price guidelines, will you try to put the bite on the Hershey bar? [*Laughter*]

P: If the report is true, then I would disapprove it strongly. We do have some persuasion that we can exercise. I would hope that the Hershey Company and all other companies would comply with our policy proposed, that any increase that they implement would be at least one-half percent below the average of their increase for 1976 and 1977. I'm not adequately familiar with the Hershey prices in the past to see if this is in compliance with it.

But through purchasing policies of the Federal Government, through competition, through the disapproval expressed by myself, other leaders of our Nation, and individual consumers, I would hope that any deviation from our policies could be controlled.

The Middle East

Q: Mr. President, question on the Middle East. Do you agree with President Sadat's view that the two agreements, the one on the West Bank and the agreement now being negotiated for peace between Israel and Egypt, have to be linked in some way?

P: Well, there's never been any doubt in my mind, nor President Sadat's, nor Prime Minister Begin's, that one of the premises for the Camp David negotiations was a comprehensive peace settlement that includes not just an isolated peace treaty between Israel and Egypt but includes a continuation of a solution for the West Bank, Gaza Strip, and ultimately for the Golan Heights as well. There is some difference of opinion between the two leaders about how specifically it should be expressed in the Sinai treaty.

I personally favor the presently negotiated language, which in the preamble does say that both nations commit themselves to carry out the comprehensive peace agreement as was agreed at Camp David. This is a matter for negotiation between the two leaders.

I have heard President (Prime Minister)[1] Begin say in my presence that he did not desire a separate peace treaty with Egypt. And, of course, this is also the opinion and strongly felt view of President Sadat.

We've been negotiating on the Mideast peace agreement for months. I have personally put hundreds of hours into it. We have reached, on more than one occasion so far, agreement on the text between the negotiators themselves. When they refer the text back to the leaders at home in Egypt and Israel, sometimes the work that has been done is partially undone. But I think that the present language as approved by the negotiators is adequate, and our presumption is to adhere to that language as our preference. But I would like to point out that we are not trying to impose our will on the leaders themselves or on those nations, and we hope that they will rapidly reach a conclusion.

There's no doubt in my mind that this kind of difference in language and how a linkage is actually expressed is a matter for negotiation. It does not violate the commitments made at Camp David, no matter what the decision might be as reached jointly by Egypt and Israel.

Farm Set-aside Programs

Q: Mr. President, may I retrack to the '79 — Sam Nelson, Commodity News Service — may I retrack to the '79 feed grain set-aside program?

P: Yes.

Q: You said you plan on a moderate program. Is a 20-percent acreage set-aside considered by you moderate, and do you plan to wait until the November 15 deadline to make your announcement?

P: I did not plan to wait until the November 15 deadline. I intend to move on it as quickly as I can. We did want to wait until after today, because as you know, this is the date on which we get November crop estimates. And we wanted to have that information available before we put the final touches on the decision.

I would not want to give you any figure yet, because I haven't decided. But I will try to decide that either this week or very early next week. I don't intend to wait until the 15th.

Results of the Election - 2

Q: Mr. President, looking at the won-and-lost column of the Democratic candidates for whom you campaigned in this election, how would you assess your impact in these races?

P: I would say when they lost, I had a substantial impact. When they won, they did it on their own merit. [*Laughter*]

Q: Mr. President, may I follow up? Seriously, do you believe that in modern times that a President coming into a city to campaign for a candidate really does sway the vote one way or the other?

P: It's hard to say. My time to campaign around the country is very limited. There are hundreds and hundreds of candidates, as you know. I think I tried to help roughly 50 candidates for the Congress, in the Senate and House, including Governors, I believe. And a few more than half those won. But I couldn't say that my presence either caused a victory or a defeat.

We did choose for my own presence those elections in almost every instance where there were marginal prospects for victory. When you go into a State, for instance, like California, it's obvious that Governor Brown was a heavy favorite. There were other Democrats running for the Congress, for instance, in the Sacramento area, whose elections were quite doubtful, and the same thing applied all over the country.

So, I don't think the President has too much of an impact on an individual race. The major purpose of my last swing was to encourage American people to get out to vote. The vote turnout was higher than we anticipated. It was not nearly high enough. I think three voters out of eight went to the polls. Five voters out of eight did not. But that was the primary purpose of my last swing, to help Democrats, yes, but to get out a large vote. I doubt that my presence had much of an impact on the outcome of those who won.

Agricultural Economy

Q: Mr. President, Steve Saunders from KBCM Radio. You've already mentioned the countercyclical measure and the set-aside program. But aren't you playing with the profits of agriculture, maybe one of the only facets of our economy by itself that can help with the inflation problem, the devaluation of the dollar problem, and the balance-of-trade deficit, all in one, not by signing the countercyclical bill, by waiting until this late for that set-aside program, when most farmers wanted it earlier, and by allowing about 50 percent of the world's reserves of grain stocks to build up in this country?

P: No. [*Laughter*] We inherited a situation in the agricultural communities that was very depressing and of great concern to me. The farmers were actually faced with another depression. The Congress passed, with bipartisan support last year, a comprehensive agriculture bill. It went into effect the first day of October 1977. Since then, farm income has increased $7 billion this year compared to last year, a 25-percent increase in farm income.

In spite of very depressed prices in 1977, the exports hit an alltime record. this year, we expect to export over $27 billion, which is substantially above the alltime record set last year. We'll continue this balanced approach.

The farmers will have to do some sacrificing along with all other Americans. We can't concentrate all of our government's effort and ignore inflationary pressures,

erect trade barriers just to protect farmers. I'm a farmer myself, and I never have met a farmer who, in a showdown, wanted to do something deleterious or harmful to his own country just for selfish advantage.

I think we've been very fair with farmers; I continue to be fair with the farmers; and of course my own stand is corroborated by the action taken by the Congress. And my decisions will be made very shortly, before the statutory limit, after the information on production that was received today, with which I'm not yet familiar. And I'm not waiting until the last minute.

The reporter with the large diamond ring on her finger.[2] [*Laughter*]

National Energy Bills

Q: Mr. President, you said when the energy bill finally passed that you were not pleased with all aspects of it and that you would work year after year to try to improve it. What specifically will you propose in January to change the energy bill that you signed today?

P: I don't know yet. As was pointed out this morning in the signing ceremony, this is one of the most difficult legislative tasks that the Congress has ever undertaken, possibly, in the history of our country. It's complicated; it's contentious; it's very difficult to understand. It has international implications, and politically I don't think anyone could win from it. It was not something that's politically attractive.

The proposal that I made originally with substantial taxes imposed on oil, the taxes to be refunded to the American people immediately, would have saved additional oil consumption. The bills that I signed this morning will result in savings of about 2-1/2 million barrels of oil per day by 1985. The original proposals would have saved an estimated 4-1/2 million barrels per day. So, we've got about 60 or 65 percent of what we asked for. But we do now have a comprehensive energy policy for the first time.

As we go into the implementation of this legislation, we'll obviously have some accomplishments, which means that regulation can be reduced. We'll obviously find some defects, I'm sure, in this complicated legislation, that I'll try to correct. But I've not given up on my original proposal that there should be a constraint on the excessive consumption of oil and therefore the excessive importation of oil. How we'll go about it, I don't yet know.

The President's Religion

Q: Mr. President, you're in the Bible Belt of the United States. And I was wondering if it's made a difference to you, that that you're a born-again Christian, in the last 2 years in office?

P: I think my religious beliefs are well known. And in my own opinion, a deep religious faith is a very sound basis on

---

[1] *Printed in the transcript.*

[2] *Ann Compton of ABC News had recently announced her engagement to be married.*

which to make difficult decisions and to have some assurance that you are doing the proper things. But I've been very careful not to interrelate my Christian beliefs with my responsibilities as President. But it is a great personal gratification for me to have that religious faith.

Nicaragua

Q: Mr. President, you're being confronted with a growing number of pleas to help bring about a mediated peace in the Latin American country of Nicaragua. Is the U.S. going to act to prevent further bloodshed and repression, or do you feel that your hands are tied because you don't want to interfere in the internal affairs of another country? What can you do?

P: We are participating actively and daily in the negotiations to bring about a settlement in Nicaragua. I get daily reports from Mr. Bowdler. He was one of the three major negotiators there. We're working in harmony with two other Latin American countries in this effort.

We are trying to bring about a resolution of the Nicaraguan question. And I think you know in the last few weeks since these negotiations began, the bloodshed has certainly been drastically reduced. It's one of the most difficult tasks that we've undertaken.

And we proposed others to be the negotiators at first. We were unable to find an acceptable group. With our absence, both sides — I guess all sides, there are many more than two — wanted the United States to be negotiators. So, we are negotiating actively now to reach an agreement in Nicaragua to control bloodshed, to minimize disputes, and to set up a government there that will have the full support of the Nicaraguan people.

Right-to-Work Laws

Q: Mr. President, Bill Stilley of Raytown and William Jewell College Radio Station, KWPB. Missouri voters defeated the right-to-work amendment Tuesday. And I was wanting to know what effect do you see will this have on the right-to-work movement in efforts to repeal section 14(b) of Taft-Hartley?

P: I think obviously the outcome of the vote in Missouri will have a great effect on attempts that might have been made in other States to repeal right to work or to establish right-to-work laws.

This is a matter that I doubt the Congress will address in any concerted fashion during the coming year. So, I don't think that the Missouri decision will have a great effect on the National Government. It's a very highly controversial issue. The Missouri people spoke, I think, clearly, by a 3-to-2 margin. And I think this would be certainly a discouragement for an attempt in other States to impose right to work.

MR. JACKSON. Thank you, Mr. President.

THE PRESIDENT. Thank you very much. I've enjoyed being here. And I'm

going now to speak to the 50th anniversary of the FFA organization of our country, of which I was a member early in my life. ∎

November 30, 1978

Following is the transcript of President Carter's Nov. 30 news conference, his 40th since taking office.

THE PRESIDENT: Good afternoon. Mr. Cormier?

Inflation Fight

Q: Mr. President, if worse came to worse, and I know that you don't anticipate this eventuality, but if the choice came down to continuing the fight against inflation and reconciling yourself to being a one-term President, which choice would you make? (Laughter)

P: I would maintain the fight against inflation, and at the same time I would like to add a comment that I believe this is exactly what the American people want. Instead of being an unpopular act, I think it would be a popular act to maintain it. I think we will be successful in leveling off the rate of inflation and then bringing it down, and I don't see any adverse political consequences from doing so.

I would like to add one other point, and that is that the decisions are not easy ones. As we go into a very tight 1980 fiscal year budget, I am beginning to see more and more clearly how difficult it will be, but I intend to do it.

Q: On that subject, Mr. President, do you plan to stay with your pledge to increase your defense budget by 3 percent despite your anti-inflation drive, and also, on defense there are published reports that you are going to change your nuclear strategy to focus more on massive retaliation.

Is that true?

P: Well, let me answer the last part first. Our nuclear policy basically is one of deterrence; to take actions that are well known by the American people and that are well known by the Soviets and other nations; that any attack on us would result in devastating destruction by the nation which launched an attack against us. So the basic policy is one of deterrence.

We obviously constantly assess the quality of our own nuclear weapon systems as times change, as technological advances are made, and as the change takes place in the Soviet Union's arsenal. We keep our weapons up to date; we improve our communications and command and information systems, but we will maintain basically a deterrent policy rather than to change the basic policy itself.

The other answer to your question is that our goal and that of other NATO nations is to increase the real level of defense expenditures. This is our goal. Each expenditure on defense, each system for which we spend the taxpayers' money, will be much more carefully assessed this year to make sure that we are efficient and

effective in the funds that we do expend.

Over the last number of years, including since I have been in office even, the percentage of our total budget and our gross national product that goes into defense has been decreasing and at the conclusion of the budget cycle when I make the budget public to the Congress and to the people in about six weeks, I know that I will be responsible to make sure that the social and other domestic needs of our Nation are met, our international obligations are fulfilled, and an adequate defense is assured and that there be a proper balance among these different, sometimes conflicting, demands.

So I will be responsible and I will assure you and other Americans that when the budget is assessed that I will carry out my responsibilities well.

Relations with China

Q: Mr. President, I would like to ask you about China. What is your timetable for reaching full normalization of relations with China, and have the recent events that are now going on in China — have those altered that policy and do you envision China as a potential military ally at any time against the Soviet Union?

P: We don't have any intention of selling any weapons to either China or the Soviet Union. We are improving our relationships with the People's Republic of China as time goes on, even short of complete diplomatic normalization.

Our goal, however, is to move toward normalization in accordance with the Shanghai Communique agreements. The attitude of China, the domestic attitude in China, has changed, and we watch it with great interest.

Tax Bill

Q: Mr. President, the austerity budget you are now working on is for spending that begins October 1 of next year, as I understand it. In view of that, and in view of the inflationary pressure we have today, would it have been more effective to veto the tax bill which would have had an immediate impact on the inflationary economy, rather than waiting until next October?

P: No, in balance, it would not have been good for our country. It might have had some tendency to control inflation, but at the same time, I think it would have added a tremendous additional tax burden on our people and restrained greatly the normal growth that we anticipate maintaining throughout next year.

Our growth rate will be reduced somewhat, to maybe below 3 percent. I don't think we will have a recession. But we took that into very careful account as we put together our overall anti-inflation program.

So, in balance, I decided to sign and put into effect the Tax Reduction Bill. I think that in spite of that, maybe compatibly with that, we will still be successful in adequately fighting inflation.

Missiles and SALT

Q: Mr. President, is it correct that you have decided to go ahead with the MX mobile missile and the Trident II in the next budget, and will you comment on the suggestion that that decision, if you take it, the decision on civil defense, is actually a part of a plan to sort of pull the fangs of the anti-SALT people, but it is part of a SALT dance, rather than an independent action?

P: I don't think it is part of a SALT dance. I have not decided yet on what types of new weapons systems, if any, we will advocate in the 1980 fiscal year budget for our strategic arms arsenal.

The press reports about a $2 billion civil defense program have been completely erroneous, and I have never been able to find where the origin of that story might have derived. No proposal has even been made to me for a civil defense program of that magnitude.

We are considering the advisability of pursuing some civil defense assessments, including the fairly long-term evacuation of some of our major cities if we should think that nuclear war would be likely, which is obviously not a very likely project in itself, proposal in itself. But I have not yet decided to move on the MX or, if to move on the MX, what to do about making sure that our present silo missiles are secure.

The Soviet missiles, as have ours in recent years, have been improved in their quality, particularly in their accuracy. And this makes the one leg of our so-called triad more vulnerable, that is, the fixed silo missiles.

We are addressing this question with a series of analyses, but I have not yet made a decision on how to do it.

Nixon Speaking Out

Q: Mr. President, what do you think about Richard Nixon beginning to speak out on the public issues? Could this become a problem for you?

P: I think Mr. Nixon has the same right to speak out as any other American, and it doesn't cause me any concern.

Inflation Fight - 2

Q: Mr. President, there have been a number of reports about the problems that the people who are running your anti-inflation program have been having, and we are now being told that the wage and price guidelines are going to be modified in some cases. How satisfied are you at this point with the way the program has gotten off the ground? And how concerned are you that some of this early confusion is going to make it more difficult to get people to comply with it?

P: I am satisfied with the way the anti-inflation program has commenced. Alfred Kahn, who is heading up the entire program, until a week or 10 days ago — I have forgotten the exact time — was completing his service as the Chairman of the Civil Aeronautics Board, and it has only been

that brief period where he has been full-time on the job.

In accordance with the law of our country, whenever new proposals are promulgated from an administrative point of view, as have been the anti-inflation proposals, they have to be published and after a certain period of time for requisite public comment among those who are most directly affected by a regulation, then the regulations are made final. The time for that public comment has not yet terminated. It won't be until the end of this week.

So as is always the case, as is required by law, we are now in the phase of letting the public and interested groups respond to the proposals that have been made. I might say that we are moving expeditiously on the anti-inflation effort. My guidelines expressed to the public in an evening television address have not been modified at all.

Obviously, with more than a thousand different kinds of decisions to be made, there will be some flexibility, and the reason for this public discussion, as I say again, required by law, is to let special groups that might be affected in an unanticipated way have an opportunity to present their case before the regulations are made final.

Human Rights

Q: Mr. President, I would like to follow up on Mr. Sperling's question and ask a more specific Nixon question, if I could.

He was at Oxford University today and he said of your human rights policy, quite critically, that it is designed to win a lot of publicity and votes but it won't achieve results. I was wondering if you would care to respond to that criticism; and secondly, do you see the events in China as an outcome of your human rights policy?

P: I can make a career out of responding to all of the criticisms that are made and comments made by other political figures, even including ex-Presidents. I don't intend to do so.

I personally think the human rights policy of our Government is well advised and has had broad-ranging, beneficial effect. I don't claim credit for the American human rights policy when political prisoners are released from certain countries or when those countries move toward more democratic means, or even when — as is in the case of China now — they are public and apparently permitting demands or requests for more democratic government policies and enhanced human rights.

But I think our policy is right. It is well founded. It is one that I will maintain tenaciously, and I think it is demonstrated around the world that it has already had good effect.

Guyana

Q: Mr. President, I want to ask about Guyana. Do you think that the nature of that cult says anything about America?

And secondly, what can the Government do to avoid future Jonestowns?

P: I obviously don't think that the Jonestown cult was typical in any way of America. I think these were people who became obsessed with a particular leader's philosophy. They were obviously misled; a tragedy resulted. It did not take place in our own country.

In retrospect, all of us can deplore what did occur. It is unconstitutional for the Government of our country to investigate or to issue laws against any group, no matter how much they might depart from normal custom, which is based on religious belief. The only exception is when there is some substantive allegation that the activities of those religious groups directly violate a Federal law.

I might point out that Congressman Ryan and other Congressmen did go to the Justice Department several weeks or months ago to go into the so-called brainwashing aspects of a few religious cults around the country. My understanding is that the so-called People's Temple was not one of those thought by them at that time to be indulging into brainwashing. It was a recent, late development that no one, so far as I know, was able to anticipate or assess adequately. So I don't think we ought to have an over-reaction because of the Jonestown tragedy by injecting Government into trying to control people's religious beliefs.

And I believe that we also don't need to deplore on a nationwide basis the fact that the Jonestown cult, so-called, was typical of America, because it is not.

Middle East

Q: Mr. President, where do we stand on a Middle East accord between Egypt and Israel, and what can you or are you doing to try to bring these two parties together?

P: Well, we are negotiating and communicating with both the leaders of Israel and Egypt on a constant and sustained basis. I have been dissatisfied and disappointed at the length of time required to bring about a peace treaty that was signed by both Israel and Egypt.

I have already outlined in the past my assessment of why this delay has taken place, as contrasted with Camp David. I am not dealing directly with the principals simultaneously, and a lot of the negotiation has, unfortunately, been conducted through the press because of political reasons, domestically speaking, or other reasons.

Although I am somewhat discouraged, we are certainly not going to give up on the effort. Tomorrow, I will be meeting with the Prime Minister of Egypt, Mr. Khalil, who is coming, I understand, with a personal message to me from President Sadat.

We have a need, obviously, to get a treaty text pinned down and approved by both governments, and to resolve the very difficult question of the so-called linkage, whether or not certain acts in the West Bank-Gaza Strip have to be taking place at the same time the Sinai agreement is consummated. But regardless of temporary disappointments and setbacks that we have experienced since Camp David, they are no more serious, nor of any greater concern, than some that I experienced at Camp David. And we will continue to pursue our efforts to bring about a peace treaty there.

My reason for what optimism I keep is that I know for certain that both President Sadat and Prime Minister Begin want a peace treaty. I know that their people want a peace treaty. And I think as long as this determination on their part is extant, that our own good offices are very likely to be fruitful. So I will continue the effort, no matter how difficult it might be in the future.

Inflation Fight - 3

Q: Mr. President, it seems that we are all being asked to settle basically for our present standard of living, something that we don't find easy to accept after all these years of expecting more, and it does seem, indeed, from your anti-inflation program that either one has to get a promotion or increase his or her productivity greatly; otherwise there could be no more money. And how important is an acceptance of that to the success of your wage-price standards?

P: We anticipate that America will continue to be strong, viable, prosperous, progressive, growing, and the quality of life of our own citizens measured in a multi-faceted way. We don't anticipate a recession or depression next year.

The free enterprise system of our country will still reward outstanding effort or outstanding ability, or perhaps good fortune on occasion, and I see no reason for despair at all.

Most people, many people, look upon an effort to control inflation as a negative or adverse factor in our country's life. I don't look on it that way. It takes a strong, viable, dynamic, competent nation to deal successfully with the question of inflation.

This is not something that has recently arisen as a problem. The last 10 years we have had an inflation rate of about 6 percent, and I just think now is the time for us to make every effort we can to correct it. But I don't think that the American people need to fear that if we are successful in controlling inflation that their lives are going to be constrained or less pleasant or prosperous in the future.

My belief is that to the extent we are successful in controlling inflation, the quality of life of Americans will be enhanced, not hurt.

MIGs in Cuba

Q: Mr. President, I would like to ask you about the MIGs in Cuba. Have you come to a decision yet on whether the MIG-23s in Cuba represent any increased threat to the United States? Have you asked the Russians to take them out? And do you believe the 1962 understandings with the Soviet Union have been violated?

P: There have been MIG-23s in Cuba for a long time. There is a model of the MIG-23 that has been introduced there late last spring which we have been observing since that time.

We would consider it to be a very serious development if the Soviet Union violated the 1962 agreement. When we have interrogated the Soviet Union through diplomatic channels they have assured us that no shipments of weapons to the Cubans have or will violate the terms of the 1962 agreement.

We will monitor their compliance with this agreement very carefully, which we have been doing in the past, both as to the quality of weapons sent there and the quantity of weapons sent there to be sure that there is no offensive threat to the United States possible from Cuba.

I might add that we have no evidence at all, no allegation, that atomic weapons are present in Cuba.

Iran

Q: Mr. President, is there any reason that you feel that the Shah is justifiably in trouble with his people?

P: Well, I think the Shah understands the situation in Iran very clearly and the reasons for some of the problems that he has experienced recently. He has moved forcefully and aggressively in changing some of the ancient religious customs of Iran, for instance, and some of the more conservative or traditional religious leaders deplore this change substantially. Others of the Iranian citizens who are in the middle class who have a new prosperity brought about by enhanced oil prices and extra income coming into the country, I think, feel that they ought to have a greater share of the voice in determining the affairs of Iran. Others believe that the democratization of Iran ought to proceed more quickly.

The Shah, as you know, has offered the opposition groups a place in a coalition government. They have rejected that offer and demand more complete removal from the Shah of his authority.

We trust the Shah to maintain stability in Iran, to continue with the democratization process, and also to continue with the progressive change in the Iranian social and economic structure. But I don't think either I or any other national leader could ever claim we have never made a mistake or have never misunderstood the attitudes of our people. We have confidence in the Shah, we support him and his efforts to change Iran in a constructive way, moving toward democracy and social progress, and we have confidence in the Iranian people to make the ultimate judgments about their own government.

We do not have any intention of interfering in the internal affairs of Iran and we do not approve any other nation interfering in the internal affairs of Iran.

Oil Pricing

Q: The General Accounting Office is currently working on a report to Congress criticizing the Department of Energy intensely for failing to follow through with enforcing some pricing regulations on oil, and in particular failing to follow up on some oil fraud situations in Texas that GAO says the Department of Energy was aware of two or three years ago.

What do you think about that, and what do you intend to do to increase the Department of Energy's enforcing actions?

P: I am not familiar with the particular late development that you described, if it is a late development. I know that in the past, earlier this year, on several occasions the Department of Energy has taken very strong action to require some of the oil companies to repay consumers or to pay actual fines when they have violated the laws of the American Government. My own position is probably predictable to you. I will do everything I can to enforce the law and to assure that any Members of my Cabinet or any agency enforce it also. But I am not familiar with the specific allegation that you described.

Q: If I could follow up, the General Accounting Office report is supposed to come out sometime in December. This is the new report which is going to say that the Department of Energy has consistently failed to respond to these previous reports.

P: Well, I would obviously want them to comply completely with the law and do it very rapidly.

Federal Employment

Q: Mr. President, I was looking at the employment figures for the Federal Government. It looks like there are 6,000 more employees now than when you took office, and depending on how you look at it, it looks like it is a net increase in Government agencies. I don't mean advisory commissions, but government agencies. Now, what has happened to your program to streamline the Government?

P: I think we have streamlined it considerably. I would like to go out of office having had no increase in the total Federal employment in spite of the natural and inevitable growth in services delivered to the American people. Some of the mandated programs that I asked Congress to approve by law are expanded by the Congress in a proper way, but more than I would originally have proposed, and sometimes a program is put forward by the Congress that I did not advocate, that I accept sometimes reluctantly, sometimes with enthusiasm. But I think that we have made the Government much more efficient.

The new move toward Civil Service reform is a good example of that potential progress in the future. It is a new law that has just gone into effect.

In addition to that, we have put forward five or six reorganization plans, all of which have been approved overwhelmingly by the Congress.

So my expectation, and my goal, is to complete my own service as President with substantially-enhanced delivery of service to the American people, and with no increase in the total employment of the Federal Government.

Intelligence Agencies

Q: Mr. President, when you came to office, there was a lot of criticism of the intelligence agencies about the methods they were using, and now since the Iran thing there is a good deal of criticism, it seems, about their evaluation.

How concerned were you about the intelligence evaluations in Iran, and could you give us a general comment about what you think the state of the intelligence arts is today?

P: I have said several times that one of the pleasant surprises of my own Administration has been the high quality of work done by the intelligence community. When I interrogate them about a specific intelligence item or when I get general assessments of intelligence matters, I have been very pleased with the quality of their work.

Recently, however, I have been concerned that the trend that was established about 15 years ago to get intelligence from electronic means might have been overemphasized sometimes to the detriment of the assessment of the intelligence derived, and also the intelligence derived through normal political channels, not secret intelligence, sometimes just the assessment of public information that is known in different countries around the world.

And recently I wrote a note — which is my custom; I write several every day — to the National Security Council, the State Department and the CIA leaders, and asked them to get together with others and see how we could improve the quality of our assessment program, and also particularly political assessments.

Since I have been in office, we have substantially modified the order of priorities addressed by the intelligence community in its totality. When I became President, I was concerned during the first few months, that quite often the intelligence community itself set its own priorities.

As a supplier of intelligence information, I felt that the customers, the ones who receive the intelligence information, including the Defense Department, myself and others, ought to be the ones to say, "This is what we consider to be most important." That effort has been completed, and it is now working very well.

So to summarize, there is still some progress to be made. I was pleased with the intelligence community's work when I first came into office, and it has been improved since I became President.

FRANK CORMIER (AP): Thank you, Mr. President.

THE PRESIDENT: Thank you, Frank, very much. Thank you, everybody. ∎

December 12, 1978

Following is the transcript of President Carter's Dec. 12 news conference, his 41st since taking office.

THE PRESIDENT: Good morning, everybody.

Please be seated. Thank you.

I do not have an opening statement, so Ms. Thomas?

SALT

Q: Mr. President, can you confirm reports that a tentative agreement has been reached on SALT with the Soviets, that you may meet at the summit with Brezhnev in January, and also, if these are true, can you say what caused the breakthrough?

P: We have made good progress on SALT. I can't say that we have reached agreement. A statement will be made later on today by the State Department and by the Soviets simultaneously about a possible meeting of the Foreign Ministers.

I think that there has been steady progress made in the last almost two years. I can't recall any time when there was a retrogression or a pause in the commitment to reach a SALT agreement.

Our positions have been clear. We have harmony, I believe, among the Defense Department, State Department and the White House on what should be the United States' position. If the Soviets are adequately forthcoming, we will have an agreement without further delay. If they are not forthcoming, then we will continue to negotiate.

Summit Meeting

Q: How about the summit?

P: I think as we approach a time when we are sure that the items have been resolved that are still under negotiation, at that time we will have a summit meeting and at that summit meeting we will discuss not only concluding the SALT agreement officially, but also have a broad agenda of other items that are of mutual interest to us and the Soviet Union.

Decontrolling Gas Prices

Q: Mr. President, do you lean toward or against a decontrolling of gasoline prices at this time of high inflation? It is a two-edged sword, I guess.

P: It is, and it is one that I haven't yet decided upon. When I presented my comprehensive energy plan to the Congress in April of 1977, inflation, although important, was not the preeminent issue in my mind.

The Secretary of Energy, my own advisors in the White House, and Alfred Kahn, who is responsible for the anti-inflation program, are now assessing all the ramifications of the pricing of gasoline and, of course, the Congress will be involved in the decision, also. But I have not yet reached a decision about what the Administration's position will be.

Middle East - 1

Q: Mr. President, the other day you took a very serious view of Israel and Egypt going past the 17th of this month without concluding a treaty, as the date they themselves set for it. With five days left, what is your belief, or hunch, as to whether they will meet that deadline; and do you still think it is sort of a "now or never" proposition?

P: I don't think it is now or never. And you very accurately described this deadline date as one established by Israel and Egypt in the most solemn commitment at Camp David.

Secretary Vance reports to me, from Cairo, good progress having been made between him and President Sadat. He has not begun further negotiations with the Israelis yet because of Mrs. Meir's funeral. He will return to Egypt, try to conclude his discussions with President Sadat, and then go back to Israel for discussions with the Israelis.

I consider the deadline date to be quite important. If the Egyptians and Israelis cannot keep a commitment on a three-month conclusion of a peace treaty when they themselves are the only two nations involved, I, serving as a mediator in the process, then I think it would be very difficult for them to expect the terms of the treaty they are negotiating to be carried out with assurance. It sets a very bad precedent for Israel and Egypt not to reach a conclusion.

I think the differences that presently divide Israel and Egypt are minor, certainly compared to the resolution of major differences in the past. And I believe that President Sadat has reconfirmed his intention, his commitment, to Secretary Vance to conclude the negotiations without further delay.

My hope is, and my expectation is, that the Israelis will have the same attitude.

National Anthem

Q: Mr. President, this may sound like a frivolous question, but I hope you won't think so. But the National Anthem is played at every trashy football game and baseball game and wrestling match and boxing. Don't you think that downgrades it quite a bit to do that incessantly?

P: That is not any more frivolous a question than I have gotten in the past. (Laughter)

I think it is a very good question. I personally don't think that frequent playing of the National Anthem downplays its importance. No matter how often I hear the National Anthem, I am always stirred within myself toward more intense feelings of patriotism and a realization of what our Nation stands for. And I think for audiences at sports events to hear the National Anthem played is good and not contrary to the influence the National Anthem has on all of us.

Year in Review

Q: Mr. President, at year's end, how do you assess the last 11 months, the pluses and minuses as you see them, the hits and the errors and, particularly, would you speak a little bit about the errors?

P: As a completely non-biased analyst, I would say that the pluses far outweigh the minuses. I think any analysis of the accomplishments of the 95th Congress, including those made by the news media representatives here, have been positive, that the accomplishments were substantial, much greater in the final stages of the Congress session than had been anticipated earlier in the year.

We have still got a lot of unfulfilled expectations and hopes. We have not successfully addressd the question of inflation. It has been greater during the second half of the year than we had anticipated. We have been pleasantly surprised at maintaining the higher and higher level of employment, preventing the unemployment rate from going up. Last year we had 660,000 new jobs created in America in spite of some slowing down in the national economy, which was expected.

In international affairs, our country has injected itself, I think wisely, into regional disputes where we have no control over the outcome. But we have added our good services, in some instances with almost no immediate prospect of success. My own reputation has been at stake and that of our country.

In Nicaragua, I think instead of having violent and massive bloodshed we now have the parties negotiating directly with one another for the first time on the terms of plebiscite and whether or not there should be general amnesty. In Namibia we are making some good progress, I believe. The South Africans have now accepted the terms set up by the Secretary General of the United Nations. We are waiting for SWAPO to respond.* Cyprus, very minimal but steadily increasing prospects. Mideast, you are well acquainted with that.

I think that on SALT and other major international items we have made steady progress. So in balance, I am pleased with the last 11 months and don't underestimate the difficulties still facing us.

Social Goals

Q: Wouldn't you say that your inability to move faster towards your social goals that you spelled out during the campaign and since, wouldn't you call that a distinct minus?

P: No. I wouldn't. I think we have made excellent progress in social goals. I

In fact, SWAPO accepts the relevant United Nations resolutions on Namibia. The President's intention was to call for their continued support. The United States is waiting for South Africa to indicate in definitive terms its acceptance of the proposal and a date for the arrival of the United Nations transition assistance group. [Footnote to White House transcript.]

have just commented on the fact that we have had large numbers of new Americans at work. We have had a net increase of about 7 million in the number of jobs held by Americans. We have reduced the unemployment rate a full 2 percent. We have had a 25 percent increase in the net income of farmers. We have increased exports there. We have had a stabilization of the American dollar, which was surprisingly effective.

We also, of course, recognized a continuing problem that has been of greater importance lately for inflation. So I think, in balance, the performance has been positive; although we still have very great problems ahead of us.

Midterm Convention

Q: Mr. President, the Democratic Party just spent what seems to some people an enormous amount of money to hold a mini-convention. I just wonder, some people are already saying perhaps the money would have been better spent in Congressional campaigns or Senatorial campaigns. Do you think that was worth the money, and how do you feel about midterm conventions in general?

P: For the first time in — I think more than ten years, the Democratic National Committee this year did make substantial contributions to the campaigns of Congressional candidates. This was a step in the right direction.

This midterm conference was mandated by the 1976 Convention. There was no way I could circumvent that mandate. I personally did not favor the midterm conference when it was decided upon in 1976. I was pleasantly surprised. I think, in balance, the conference was worth the money.

My understanding is that additional funds have been raised in Memphis and in other places to adequately pay for the cost of the convention.

I believe it is very important for me, as a President, and also as head of the Democratic Party, to have my success and failures assessed objectively and openly by Democrats representing the grass roots of our Party around the Nation. I think that was done in a very forthcoming way. I have observed the deliberations, participated in them with a great deal of interest, and I think in general the policies of my Administration were endorsed.

The one single issue concerning budget matters which was highly disputed, and on which the more liberal members of the Party concentrated their efforts, showed that my policies were endorsed by, I think, more than 60 percent. So I am very pleased with it. And I don't think there was anyone who went to the conference who couldn't say in its closing hours that they had an adequate opportunity to express their views, either supportive of me or contrary to what I have done.

So I feel very pleased about it.

National Health Insurance

Q: Mr. President, to what extent do you feel bound, or influenced, by the resolution passed by the midterm conference on calling for enactment of national health insurance in the next Congress, and specifically, will you seek to have comprehensive legislation passed in the next Congress to take effective phases, or will you go at it one piece of legislation at a time?

P: The midterm conference decision was compatible with the 1976 Convention decisions on the Democratic Party platform concerning comprehensive health care. I favor that campaign commitment, and the platform commitment. There are differences about how to implement a national health care system.

Under any circumstances, those policies espoused by Senator Kennedy, those policies espoused by me, the first major implementation, or financial assessment for that purpose, would be made in 1983. It is necessarily a slow process. I think it is better done step by step, recognizing the ultimate goal and moving as we can afford it, and as we can implement it in a very carefully conceived, methodical way, bringing on board the Congress, and also bringing on board for support the American people, and the different interest groups involved.

So I think that the policy expressed by the midterm conference was compatible with my own, and that is what I intend to carry out.

View of Oil Industry

Q: Mr. President, this goes to your general attitude with the oil industry. Last week, consumer advocate Clarence Ditlow blocked the multi-million dollar price increases in unleaded gasoline by your Administration; said you were ignoring the aspect of destroying catalytic converters.

There has been a major increase in home heating fuel at a time when there is a glut of home heating fuel. Particularly here in the Northeast, we have had a very mild winter. It looks like some very high-level, deep-sixing of criminal actions against oil companies in Texas is going on at the Energy Administration, going on for more than a year now.

And lastly, your Justice Department's testimony from the Antitrust Division going along with oil industry acquisition of uranium companies, solar development companies, and coal companies — all of these were decisions that seemed to be opposed to what you promised as a candidate. Could you give us a general view? Have you changed your view to the oil industry since becoming President?

P: No. I have not changed my views at all. We want to have the principles of the National Energy Plan carried out effectively. The Congress has now given us legislative authority to carry out 60, 65 percent of what I did propose. Any violation by the oil companies of regulations or law will be persecuted — prosecuted enthusiastically by me, by the Justice Department, and also by the Department of Energy. And, obviously, we are very deeply dedicated to the enforcement of the antitrust laws. I am concerned also about the growing investment by the oil companies in competitive areas of energy supply. I expressed this during my own campaign and I still feel very strongly about this. I think that the Congress itself is now prepared to move more effectively to modify the law when necessary to minimize abuse. But I don't consider my Administration at all reticent about carrying out the policies that I espoused during the campaign when I ran for President, and I certainly don't consider them to be reticent at all in enforcing the law.

Second Term

Q: Mr. President, a yes or no question, and then, if I may, a follow-up.

In your own mind, have you decided yet whether or not you will seek a second term?

P: Yes. (Laughter)

Q: You know my follow-up question. When will you share it with us and the American people?

P: Later. (Laughter)

Q: Later means —

P: It means later.

Inflation Fight

Q: Mr. President, your anti-inflation fighter, Mr. Kahn, yesterday suggested that one way to fight inflation would be to have organized consumer boycotts against firms which violate your wage-price guidelines and another suggestion he made was that the government might consider reducing or withholding Federal revenue sharing money to cities, or States, where officials in those cities and States violate the wage guidelines. I was wondering, first of all, would you support a reduction of Federal revenue sharing money to a city or State which didn't observe or which violated your wage-price guidelines, and how do you feel generally about the government backing consumer boycotts?

P: I don't personally favor any organized boycotts. I think that the posture of prudent purchaser is one that applies to me as President and also ought to apply to the average consumer who is buying retail items and who should be conversant with the relative compliance of suppliers with our wage and price guidelines, the price guidelines in this instance.

As far as withholding revenue sharing funds, I think this would be illegal under the present law. We have had very good response from governors and mayors in applying the same policies of a prudent purchaser so that the mayor, for instance, would be restrained against buying items from companies which patently violate the price guidelines. And we are encouraging mayors to take this action, and governors as well.

I might say that we encourage them

with very good results, very good successes. But as far as withholding revenue sharing funds, this would require an Act of Congress and it is not possible under the present law.

Q: Could you reduce Federal revenue-sharing funds to a state which didn't comply?

P: No, we could not do that under the present law.

Trade Restrictions

Q: Mr. President, we seem to be headed for a record trade deficit this year, at a time when a major new market for U.S. exports is opening in Communist China.

P: Yes.

Q: There are a number of restrictions in U.S. trade laws which inhibit our trading with communist countries, some aspects of the Export-Import Bank Act, the Jackson-Vanik Amendment to the 1974 Trade Act.

My question is, do you intend to try to change and remove some of those restrictions next year?

P: We are constantly assessing the advisability of maintaining administrative restraints.

Of course, we have to put trade in a proper perspective. We cannot assess trade itself completely separated from our overall relationships with communist countries, particularly those who are potential adversaries of ours, like the Soviet Union.

We want to have increased trade with the Soviet Union and with the People's Republic of China. I think the statistics will show that recently we have had increasing trade with both those countries, compared to last year, or several years ago.

If we, in the future, have normal relationships with China, diplomatic relationships, this would open up increased opportunities for trade with those people.

In this present time, short of diplomatic relations, we still have major trade missions going to China, Chinese trade missions coming to our country. And I think that this is bearing good results.

We have one more point, and that is security restraints. If there is a sale of high technology items to the Soviet Union, or the People's Republic of China proposed, then not only do the Commerce Department and the State Department and the National Security Council assess this, but I refer it to the Defense Department as well, to be sure that we are not deliberately, or inadvertently giving to those countries a means by which their military capabilities would be greatly escalated. This would be contrary to the existing law. But within the bounds of those restraints, we are attempting to improve our relationships with the People's Republic of China, and with the Soviet Union. And in the process, as part of a stream of increased interrelationships, improved relationships, enhanced trade.

Middle East - 2

Q: Mr. President, to follow up the earlier question on the Middle East, you

said last week that if Prime Minister Begin and President Sadat had been able to negotiate together on some of these questions over the past few weeks, that there would not have been some of the problems that have arisen. My question is, if all else fails, would you consider calling the two leaders back to Camp David, or some other place to negotiate directly with you to resolve this matter?

P: Let me say that I don't have any present plans to do that. If all else failed — and I felt that we could get together again — I would not hesitate to do so. But I don't envision that being — I don't envision that taking place.

Democratic Party Divisions

Q: Mr. President, if I may follow up on the question raised by Mr. Schieffer and Mr. Hurd.* Do you sense, Mr. President, that there is a widening schism in the Democratic Party between yourself and Senator Kennedy, who emphasized in Memphis the need for finishing the great agenda of the Democratic Party as he put it, and do you have any plans to try to conciliate your differences with him, or with the labor leaders, who have generally opposed your economic policies?

P: First of all, I don't consider there is a schism, a growing schism in the Democratic Party at all. And as a general principle, and almost entirely, Senator Kennedy and I communicate well, we have a good relationship. We espouse the same ultimate goals. We have some differences which are expected on exactly how to achieve those goals.

I have a unique perspective in this country as President. I have to look at a much broader range of issues than does Senator Kennedy.

He is extremely interested, for instance, in the comprehensive health program, having devoted several years of his legislative life to that position.

Also, I think it is accurate to say that Senator Kennedy represents a family within the Democratic Party which is revered because of his two brothers, and the contribution of his family to our Party. There is a special aura of appreciation to him that is personified because of the position of his family in our Nation, and in our Party.

This makes him a spokesman, not only in his own right, but also over a much broader and expected constituency. I recognize it, and I have no objection to that. I was with Senator Kennedy the night after the Democratic Conference adjourned, I think on Monday (Sunday) night. And the following morning in a non-related way, the Office of Management and Budget, Jim McIntyre and my own Domestic Adviser, Stu Eizenstat, met with Senator Kennedy and his staff to try to resolve differences.

The differences are minor. So I think this is a healthy situation to have within

---

* *The reporter meant to say Ted Knap of the Scripps-Howard News Service. [Footnote to the White House transcript.]*

the Democratic Party. And I think that the Congress will be the ultimate judge of whether my budget, as proposed, is fair and balanced and adequate. I have not changed my goals whatsoever. The Democratic Conference endorsed those goals, either unanimously, or with a 60 percent margin on the most controversial of the issues. I am going to have an adequate defense. I am going to meet our obligations to our allies around the country and I am going to cut the budget deficit down below $30 billion, and I am going to do the best I can to meet the social needs of our Nation. I am committed to that. That is what I am going to do. And I have no aversion to an open and public debate because I think my positions are sound.

But the differences between me and Senator Kennedy are very minor.

Iran

Q: Mr. President, what will be the domestic and international effect if the Shah fails to maintain power in Iran?

P: I fully expect the Shah to maintain power in Iran and for the present problems in Iran to be resolved, although there have been certainly deplorable instances of bloodshed which we would certainly want to avoid, or see avoided.

I think the predictions of doom and disaster that came from some sources have certainly not been realized at all. The Shah has our support and he also has our confidence.

We have no intention of interfering in the internal affairs of Iran and we have no intention of permitting others to interfere in the internal affairs of Iran. The difficult situation there has been exacerbated by uncontrolled statements made from foreign nations that encourage blood baths and violence. This is something that really is deplorable and I would hope would cease after this holy season passes.

I think it is good to point out that the Iranian people for 2,500 years, perhaps as long as almost any nation on earth, have had the ability for stable, self-government. There have been changes in the government, yes, sometimes violence, but they have a history of an ability to govern themselves and because of that and other factors which I have just described, I think the situation in Iran will be resolved successfully.

Oil Price Rise

Q: Mr. President, to what extent are you concerned over the prospect of the OPEC nations raising the price of oil this weekend — reports are it will be in the neighborhood of 5 percent — the impacts it will have on inflation, and do you contemplate any future actions to curb imports?

P: Most of our problems with the adverse trade balances can be attributed to oil imports, although we have other problems as well. I certainly hope that the OPEC nations will decide not to raise the

price of oil. If they do, I hope it would be minimal.

We have tried to convince them that this is in the best interests of the world economy and also in the best interests of the OPEC nations themselves, to have a stable world economy with minimum inflation in the future. We are trying to set a good example in our own Nation, both in controlling inflation and also in stabilizing the value of the dollar on which the price of oil is based.

The countries in the OPEC nations have suffered somewhat, because for a time the dollar value was going down very rapidly. It has recovered since the first of November. So I would hope, first of all, to repeat myself, that there will be no increase in the price of oil. If they must increase the price of oil, I think it ought to be minimal for their own benefit and for the benefit of the world.

Urban Aid

Q: Mr. President, at the Memphis Convention some of the mayors expressed concern over the possibility of sharp reductions in employment programs like the CETA program and also they expressed concern over the possible lack of support, not by you particularly, but by Congress, for programs like the revenue sharing program which is very important to the cities.

Do you foresee, keeping in mind you haven't made your final budget decision, sharp reductions in either the CETA program or in revenue sharing which is devoted to the cities?

P: It depends on what you mean by sharp reductions. I have to say that there will be some tightening of the budget in almost every aspect of American life. There will be some programs that will be expanded; others will be basically kept at the same level. The decisions have not yet been made. I am conversant with the problems of the cities. I don't think any Administration has ever had a closer consultative relationship with the mayors than our own has had.

In the evolution of our urban policy earlier this year, the Mayors were full partners in the process, along with Governors and others, and local officials.

So I can't say. The revenue sharing legislation is a multi-year authorization and we support the carrying out of the revenue sharing at its present level until this present law expires.

I can't foreclose the possibility it might be modified in the future. My own attitude has always been that with a given amount for revenue sharing, that a greater portion of it should go to the cities and local governments than to the States. That is one modification in the revenue sharing laws that I would espouse. But the exact level of the CETA programs and other job programs will have to be decided in the next couple of weeks, and I personally favor as much as possible keeping job opportunities open for Americans.

MR. FRANK CORMIER (AP): Thank you, Mr. President.

THE PRESIDENT: Thank you, Frank. ∎

June 26, 1978

(Continued from p. 111-A)

Capital Gains Tax—2

Q: Mr. President, to get back to the opening statement on capital gains tax policy, as you know, Mr. President, the House Ways and Means Committee is considering the so-called compromise proposal advanced by Congressman Jones of Oklahoma which would set capital gains, I believe, at a 35 percent maximum rate and also eliminate the so-called alternative tax.

My question is, is the Jones compromise equally unacceptable as the Steiger proposal to you?

P: When I referred to the Steiger Amendment or proposal, I was also referring to the Jones proposal, which is a version of the Steiger Amendment. Both these proposals apply basically to the desire of some Members of the Congress to remove part of the income of very wealthy taxpayers from the minimum tax.

A few years ago, the Congress very wisely said that if there were loopholes or provisions in the tax law that let a wealthy person avoid paying any tax, they would at least have to pay some tax under the new minimum tax laws. And the Steiger Amendment and the Jones Amendment, part of it, refers to that basic principle. I disagree with the Steiger and Jones proposal.

Ms. Woodruff.

Q: If these proposals, if these plans, the Steiger bill and the Jones bill, are as onerous as you suggest, then why have so many Members of Congress, including so many Democrats, come around in support of it?

P: We don't have any clear indication of that. They do have enough support to cause me concern. My guess is that when the Congress becomes acquainted with which taxpayers in our country benefit, that is the very wealthy taxpayers, and how they give no relief to the average and middle-income families, my guess is that the Congress will reject this proposal.

Q: Mr. President, are you satisfied that your tax cut and your tax reform plan were sufficiently fair for middle-income taxpayers?

P: Yes. I think they were eminently fair and my preference, of course, is that my original proposal would be adopted. My guess is that the Congress will not adopt my tax reform proposals in their entirety.

White House Guests

Q: Mr. President, since you have extended White House hospitality to a variety of people, including jazz musicians and prizefighters, could you tell us why you haven't invited Alexander Solzhenitsyn or, in another category, Howard Jarvis or, in another category, your fellow Southern Baptist Convention speaker, Anita Bryant, or do you approve of -— disapprove of the positions of these people?

P: I don't have any inclination now to say whether I approve or disapprove of what they do. I am sure they have all done things of which I do approve and they probably have all done things of which I disapprove. But there are —

Q: You wouldn't subscribe to original sin, then. (Laughter)

P: There are 220 million people in America and there is a limit to how many we can invite. (Laughter) But we will continue our invitations in the future, maybe somedays get around to those whom you offer as a possibility.

Q: Anita Bryant said to the Southern Baptist Convention that Midge Costanza came down and intruded herself into the Dade County ordinance struggle.

Was that at your direction or was that Midge's kind of spontaneity?

P: I didn't know that she went to Dade County. If she did, it was not at my direction.

National Health Program

Q: Mr. President, given the seriousness of the inflation problem, do you still plan to offer a comprehensive national health program and if so, when? What is your current thinking on that problem?

P: Within the next few days I will direct the Secretary of HEW to comply with principles that I outlined to him in the preparation of a national health proposal. The implementation of it, and the passage of it by Congress before it is implemented, will have to accommodate budget constraints and the attitude of both the Congress and the American people.

I do favor a comprehensive health proposal. Now at this time, the high inflation rate and the very tight budget constraints would not permit immediate implementation of it. It might take many years before the final plan is completely put into effect.

After I give these instructions to Mr. Califano, then he will be consulting with Members of the Congress who are particularly interested and will be consulting with governors and interest groups like the hospital administrators, doctors and so forth, to work out not only the specifics of the proposal, but also the rough time schedule that we would follow in their implementation.

MR. FRANK CORMIER (AP): Thank you, Mr. President.

THE PRESIDENT: Thank you, Mr. Cormier. ∎

Carter Speech on Panama Canal

Following is the prepared text of President Carter's Feb. 1, 1978, televised address on the Panama Canal treaties, as released by the White House.

Seventy-five years ago, our nation signed a treaty which gave us rights to build a canal across Panama to take the historic step of joining the Atlantic and Pacific Oceans. The results of the agreement have been a great benefit to ourselves and to other nations throughout the world who navigate the high seas.

The building of the canal was one of the greatest engineering feats of history. Although massive in concept and construction it is relatively simple in design and has been reliable and efficient in operation. We Americans are justly and deeply proud of this great achievement.

The canal also has been a source of pride and benefit to the people of Panama but a cause of some continuing discontent. Because we have controlled a 10-mile-wide strip of land across the heart of their country and because they considered the original terms of the agreement to be unfair, the people of Panama have never been satisfied with the treaty. It was drafted here in our country and was not signed by any Panamanian. Our own Secretary of State who did sign the original treaty said it was "vastly advantageous to the United States and...not so advantageous to Panama."

In 1964, after consulting with former Presidents Truman and Eisenhower, President Johnson committed our nation to work toward a new treaty with the Republic of Panama. Last summer, after 14 years of negotiations under two Democratic Presidents and two Republican Presidents, we reached and signed an agreement that is fair and beneficial to both countries. The United States Senate will soon be debating whether these treaties should be ratified.

National Security Protected

Throughout the negotiations, we were determined that our national security interests would be protected; that the canal would always be open, neutral and available to ships of all nations; that in time of need or emergency our ships would have the right to go to the head of the line for priority passage through the canal; and that our military forces would have the permanent right to defend the canal if it should ever be in danger.

The new treaties meet all of these requirements. Let me outline the terms of the agreement. There are two treaties—one covering the rest of this century and the other guaranteeing the safety, openness and neutrality of the canal after the year 1999 when Panama will be in charge of its operation.

For the rest of the century we will operate the canal through a nine-person board of directors. Five members will be from the United States, and four from Panama. Within the area of the present Canal Zone, we have the right to select whatever lands and waters our military and civilian forces need to maintain, operate and defend the canal.

About 75 per cent of those who now maintain and operate the canal are Panamanians; over the next 22 years as we manage the canal together, this percentage will increase. The Americans who work on the canal will continue to have their rights of employment, promotion and retirement carefully protected.

Sharing of Fees

We will share with Panama some of the fees paid by shippers who use the canal. As in the past, the canal should continue to be self-supporting.

This is not a partisan issue. The treaties are strongly backed by President Gerald Ford and by former Secretaries of State Dean Rusk and Henry Kissinger. They are endorsed by our business and professional leaders, and especially by those who recognize the benefits of good will and trade with other nations in this hemisphere. They are endorsed by the Senate Democratic Leader, Robert Byrd, and by Republican Leader Howard Baker, and overwhelmingly by the Senate Foreign Relations Committee, which this week moved us closer to ratification by approving the treaties, although with some recommended changes which we do not feel are needed.

And the treaties are supported enthusiastically by every member of the Joint Chiefs of Staff, Gen. George Brown, the Chairman; Gen. Bernard Rogers, Chief of Staff of the Army; Adm. James Holloway, Chief of Naval Operations; Gen. David Jones, Chief of Staff of the Air Force, and Gen. Lewis Wilson, Commandant of the Marine Corps—responsible men whose profession is the defense of this nation and the preservation of our security.

Support in Latin America

The treaties also have overwhelming support throughout Latin America, but predictably they are opposed abroad by some who are unfriendly to the United States and who would like to see disorder in Panama and a disruption of our political, economic and military ties with our friends in Central and South America and in the Caribbean.

I know that the treaties also have been opposed by many Americans. Much of that opposition is based on misunderstanding and misinformation. I have found that when the full terms of the agreement are known, most people are convinced that the national interests of our country will be served best by ratifying the treaties.

Tonight I want you to hear the facts. I want to answer the most serious questions, and tell you why I feel the Panama Canal treaties should be approved. The most important reason—the only reason—to ratify the treaties is that they are in the highest national interests of the United States, and will strengthen our position in the world. Our security interests will be stronger. Our trade opportunities will be improved. We will demonstrate that as a large and powerful country, we are able to deal fairly and honorably with a proud but smaller sovereign nation. We will honor our commitment to those engaged in world commerce that the Panama Canal will be open and available for use by their ships—at a reasonable and competitive cost—both now and in the future.

Answers to Some Questions

Let me answer specifically the most common questions about the treaties:

Will our Nation have the right to protect and defend the canal against any armed attack or threat to the security of the canal or of ships going through it?

The answer is yes, and is contained in both treaties and also in the statement of understanding between the leaders of our two nations.

The first treaty says: "The United States of America and the Republic of Panama commit themselves to protect and defend the Panama Canal. Each party shall act, in accordance with its constitutional process, to meet the danger resulting from an armed attack or other actions which threaten the security of the Panama Canal or of ships transiting it."

The neutrality treaty says: "The United States of America and the Republic of Panama agree to maintain the regime of neutrality established in this treaty, which shall be maintained in order that the canal shall remain permanently neutral."

The statement of understanding says: "Under [the neutrality treaty] Panama and the United States have a responsibility to assure that the Panama Canal will remain open and secure to ships of all nations. The correct interpretation of this principle is that each of the two countries shall, in accordance with their respective constitutional processes, defend the canal against any threat to the regime of neutrality, and consequently will have a right to act against any aggression or threat directed against the canal or against the peaceful transit of vessels through the canal."

It is obvious that we can take whatever military action is necessary to make sure that the canal always remains open and safe.

Panamanian Integrity

Of course, this does not give the United States any right to intervene in the internal affairs of Panama, nor would our military actions ever be directed against the territorial integrity or political independence of Panama.

Military experts agree that even with the Panamanian Armed Forces joined with us as brothers against a common enemy, it would take a large number of American troops to ward off a heavy attack. I would not hesitate to deploy whatever armed forces are necessary to defend the canal, and I have no doubt that even in sustained combat we would be successful. But there is a much better option than sending our sons and grandsons to fight in the jungles of Panama.

We would serve our interests better by implementing the new treaties, an action that would help to avoid any attack on the Panama Canal.

What we want is the permanent right to use the canal and we can defend this right through these treaties—through real cooperation with Panama. The citizens of Panama and their Government have already shown their support of this new partnership, and a protocol to the neutrality treaty will be signed by many other nations, thereby showing their strong approval.

The new treaties will naturally change Panama from a passive and sometimes deeply resentful bystander into an active and interested partner whose vital interests will be served by a well-operated canal. This agreement leads to cooperation, not confrontations between our country and Panama.

Another question is: "Why should we give away the Panama Canal Zone?" As many people say, "We bought it, we paid for it, it's ours."

I must repeat a very important point: We do not own the Panama Canal Zone—we have never had sovereignty over it. We have only had the right to use it.

The Canal Zone cannot be compared with United States territory. We bought Alaska from the Russians, and no one has ever doubted that we own it. We bought the Louisiana Territories from France, and it is an integral part of the United States.

Never Owned Canal Zone

From the beginning we have made an annual payment to Panama to use their land. You do not pay rent on your own land. The Canal Zone has always been Panamanian territory. The U.S. Supreme Court and previous American Presidents have repeatedly acknowledged the sovereignty of Panama over the Canal Zone.

We have never needed to own the Panama Canal Zone, any more than we need to own a 10-mile wide strip of land through Canada when we build an international gas pipeline.

The new treaties give us what we do need—not ownership of the canal, but the right to use it and to protect it. As the chairman of the Joint Chiefs of Staff has said: "The strategic value of the canal lies in its use."

There is another question: Can our Naval ships, in time of need or emergency, get through the canal immediately instead of waiting in line?

The treaties answer that clearly by guaranteeing that our ships will always have expeditious transit through the canal. To make sure that there could be no possible disagreement about what these words mean, the joint statement says that expeditious transit, and I quote, "is intended to assure the transit of such vessels through the canal as quickly as possible, without any impediment, with expedited treatment, and in case of need or emergency, to go to the head of the line of vessels in order to transit the canal rapidly."

Will Help U.S. Influence

Will the treaties affect our standing in Latin America—will they create a so-called "power vacuum," which our enemies might fill?

They will do just the opposite. The treaties will increase our nation's influence in this hemisphere, will help to reduce any mistrust and disagreement, and will remove a major source of anti-American feeling.

The new agreement has already provided vivid proof to the people of this hemisphere that a new era of friendship and cooperation is beginning, and that what they regard as the last remnant of alleged American colonialism is being removed.

Last fall I met individually with the leaders of 18 countries in this hemisphere. Between the United States and Latin America there is already a new sense of equality, a new sense of trust and mutual respect that exists because of the Panama Canal treaties. This opens up a fine opportunity for us, in good will, trade, jobs, exports, and political cooperation.

If the treaties should be rejected, this would all be lost, and disappointment and despair among our good neighbors and traditional friends would be severe.

In the peaceful struggle against alien ideologies like Communism, these treaties are a step in the right direction. Nothing could strengthen our competitors and adversaries in this hemisphere more than for us to reject this agreement.

What if a new sea-level canal should be needed in the future?

This question has been studied over and over throughout this century, from before the canal was built up through the last few years. Every study has reached the same conclusion: that the best place to build a sea-level canal is in Panama.

The treaties say that if we want to build such a canal, we will build it in Panama—and if any canal is to be built in Panama, we will have the right to participate in the project.

This is a clear benefit to us, for it insures that 10 or 20 years from now, no unfriendly but wealthy power will be able to purchase the right to build a sea-level canal, bypass the existing canal, perhaps leaving that other nation in control of the only usable waterway through the isthmus.

Payments to Come Out of Tolls

Are we paying Panama to take the Canal? We are not. Under the new treaties payments to Panama will come from tolls paid by ships which use the canal.

What about the present and future stability and the capability of the Panamanian Government? Do the people themselves support the new agreement?

Panama and her people have been our historical allies and friends. The present leader of Panama has been in office for more than nine years, and he heads a stable government which has encouraged the development of free enterprise in Panama. Democratic elections will be held this August to choose the members of the Panamanian Assembly, who will in turn elect a President and a Vice President by majority vote.

In the past, regimes have changed in Panama—but for 75 years no Panamanian Government has ever wanted to close the canal. Panama wants the canal open and neutral—perhaps even more than we do. The canal's continued operation is very important to us, but it is much more than that to Panama.

To Panama, it is crucial. Much of her economy flows directly or indirectly from the canal. Panama would be no more likely to neglect or close the canal than we would be to close the interstate highways.

In an open and free referendum last October which was monitored by the United Nations, the people of Panama gave the new treaty their support.

The major threat to the canal comes not from any government of Panama, but from misguided persons who may try to fan the flames of dissatisfaction with the terms of the old treaty.

There is a final question, about the deeper meaning of the treaties themselves—to us and to Panama.

Recently I discussed the treaties with David McCullough, author of "The Path Between the Seas," the great history of the Panama Canal. He believes that the canal is something that we built and have looked after these many years; it is "ours" in that sense, which is very different from just ownership.

'Deep and Elemental Feelings'

So when we talk of the canal, whether we are old, young, for or against the treaties we are talking about the very deep and elemental feelings about our own strength.

Still, we Americans want a more humane and stable world. We believe in good will and fairness, as well as strength. This agreement with Panama is something we want because we know it is right. This is not merely the surest way to protect and save the canal; it is the strong, positive act of a people who are still confident, still creative, still great.

This new partnership can become a source of national pride and self-respect in much the same way as building the canal 75 years ago. It is the spirit in which we act that is so very important.

Theodore Roosevelt, who was President when America built the canal, saw history itself as a force, and the history of our own time and the changes it has brought would not be lost on him. He knew that change was inevitable and necessary. Change is growth. A true conservative, he once remarked, puts his faith in the future.

But if Theodore Roosevelt were to endorse the treaties, as I am quite sure he would, it would be mainly because he could see the decision as one by which we are demonstrating the kind of great power we wish to be.

"We cannot avoid meeting great issues," Roosevelt said. "All that we can determine for ourselves is whether we shall meet them well or ill."

The Panama Canal is a vast, heroic expression of that age-old desire to bridge the divide and bring people closer together. This is what the treaties are all about.

We can sense what Roosevelt called "the lift toward nobler things which marks a great and generous people."

In this historic decision he would join us in our pride for being a great and generous people, with the national strength and wisdom to do what is right for us and fair to others.

Thank you very much. ∎

Defense Policy

Following is the White House transcript of President Carter's March 17, 1978, speech at Wake Forest University, Winston-Salem, N.C., in which the president spoke on national security.

Thank you very much. It is good to be here.

As someone who comes from a great tobacco-producing state, it is an honor for me to be here in the capital of the greatest tobacco state in the world. (Applause) What you do here means a lot to Georgia. And we have always found the people in Winston-Salem and throughout North Carolina share with us common purposes, a common heritage, and a common future. You have always received me with open arms. You expressed your confidence in me during the campaign for President. And I am indeed honored to come here to Wake Forest, to Winston-Salem, and North Carolina, our neighbor state, to make a speech of major importance.

It is a pleasure to be with your great Senator, Bob Morgan, who cast a courageous vote yesterday, and who is extremely knowledgeable about the subject that I will talk about. He is on the Armed Forces Committee, as you know, the Armed Services Committee is responsible for our nation's defense. He is on the special committee, a highly selective committee on our nation's intelligence, and he has been one of the staunch protectors of our nation and is a great man and a great statesman.

Bob, I am very glad to be with you. (Applause)

It is also good to renew my friendship with your great Governor, Jim Hunt. I first met him before he was Governor and before I was President. We formed an instant personal friendship and his leadership of your State has brought credit to you and the admiration of the rest of the nation. And I am particularly grateful to be here with Steve Neal. (Applause)

The first time I came here was to join with him in his campaign in 1974, when the prospects were not very bright. But because of the confidence in him, expressed by the people of the Fifth District, he was successful.

He has now assumed a leadership position in the Congress. He is a man, also, who believes in the strong defense of our country. His voting record proves this. In addition, he is on the Science and Technology Committee, which is responsible for advancing our purposes in the future. And he is honored by being the Chairman of that portion of the Banking and Finance Committee responsible for international trade. This means a great deal to us because the exporting of our products and the protection of our textile industry, our tobacco industry, our farm products, is very crucial and Steve has now worked himself up to a seniority position so he can be selective now and in the future.

I would like to also acknowledge the presence of two of the members of my Cabinet, Secretary of Defense Harold Brown, and your own Juanita Kreps, Secretary of Commerce. (Applause)

To Georgia and to North Carolina, the most important, perhaps, member in the Congress is the Chairman of the Senate Agriculture Committee. He takes care of tobacco farmers; he takes care of peanut farmers, important to both Georgia and North Carolina, and I am very honored to have with us my own United States Senator, Herman Talmadge. (Applause)

I won't acknowledge the presence of every distinguished guest here today, but I would like to say I am pleased that several of North Carolina's great Members of Congress have chosen to come to honor me by their presence, Charlie Whitley, Richardson Preyer, Bill Hefner, and Lamar Gudger. Would you stand up? (Applause)

Charlie, I believe that you and Bob Morgan are alumni of Wake Forest. Is that not correct? I know Wake Forest people are glad to have you back.

Well, I would like to say that this is a remarkably great honor for me. This is a great college, and it is a time in our nation's history when we need to stop and assess our past, our present, and our future.

I have noticed the statistics in North Carolina that show that under my own Administration, because of your work, not mine, there has been remarkable economic progress.

In the state of North Carolina, the unemployment rate, for instance, last year, dropped 2.3 percent. You now have an extraordinarily low rate of only 4.5 percent. This shows not only that our nation is strong, but the North Carolina people want to work and when they are given a chance, they do work. And I thank you for that. (Applause)

Military Heritage

One hundred ninety-eight years ago, in the southern part of your State, 400 North Carolina militiamen took up arms in our own war of independence. Against a force of 1,300 British soldiers, the North Carolinians prevailed — and their battle at Ramsour's Mill became a step on the road to victory at Yorktown one year later.

Your ancestors in North Carolina and mine in Georgia and their neighbors throughout the 15 Colonies earned our freedom in combat. That is a sacrifice which Americans have had to make time and time again in our Nation's history. We have learned that strength is the final protector of liberty.

This is a commitment and a sacrifice that I understand well, for the tradition of military service has been running deep for generations in my own family. My first ancestor to live in Georgia, James Carter, who moved there from North Carolina, fought in the Revolution. My father was a First Lieutenant in the Army in World War I. My oldest son volunteered to go to Vietnam. And I spent 11 years of my life as a professional military officer in the United States Navy. This is typical of American families.

Down through the generations, the purposes of our armed forces have always been the same, no matter what generation it was: to defend our security when it is threatened and through demonstrated strength, to reduce the chances that we will have to fight again.

These words of John Kennedy will still guide our actions, and I quote him, "The purpose of our arms is peace, not war — to make certain that they will never have to be used."

That purpose is unchanged. But the world has been changing and our responses as a Nation must change with it.

This morning I would like to talk to you about our national security — where we now stand, what new circumstances we face, and what we are going to do in the future.

Dispelling Myths

Let me deal at the beginning with some myths. One myth is that this country somehow is pulling back from protecting its interests and its friends around the world. That is not the case, as will be explained and demonstrated in our actions as a Nation.

Another myth is that our defense budget is too burdensome, and consumes an undue part of our Federal revenues. National defense is, of course, a large and important item of expenditures, but it represents only about five percent of our gross national product, and about a quarter of our current Federal budget. It also is a mistake to believe that our country's defense spending is mainly for intercontinental missiles or nuclear weapons. Only about ten percent of our defense budget goes for strategic forces or for nuclear deterrence. More than 50 percent is simply to pay for and support the services of the men and women in our armed forces.

Finally, some believe that because we do possess nuclear weapons of great destructive power, that we need do nothing more to guarantee our Nation's security.

Unfortunately, it is not that simple. Our potential adversaries have now built up massive forces armed with conventional weapons — tanks, aircraft, infantry, mechanized units.

These forces could be used for political blackmail, and they could threaten our vital interests unless we and our allies and friends have our own military strength and conventional forces as a counterbalance.

Of course, our national security rests on more than just military power. It depends partly on the productive capacity of our factories and our farms, on an adequate supply of natural resources with which God has blessed us, on an economic system which values human freedom above centralized control, on the creative ideas of our best minds, on the hard work, cohesion, moral strength and determination of the American people, and on the friendship of our neighbors to the north and south.

Our security depends on strong bonds with our allies, and on whether other nations seek to live in peace and refrain from trying to dominate those who live around them.

But adequate and capable military forces are still an essential element of our national security. We, like our ancestors, have the obligation to maintain strength equal to the challenges of the world in which we live, and we Americans will continue to do so. (Applause)

World Changes

Let us review briefly how national security issues have changed over the past decade or two.

The world has grown both more complex and more interdependent. There is now a division among the Communist powers; the old colonial empires have fallen, and many new nations have risen in their place; old ideological labels have lost some of their meaning. There have also been changes in the military balance among nations. Over the past 20 years, the military forces of the Soviets have grown substantially, both in absolute numbers and relative to our own.

There also has been an ominous inclination on the part of the Soviet Union to use its military power — to intervene in local conflicts with advisors, with equipment, and with full logistical support and encouragement for mercenaries from other Communist countries, as we can observe today in Africa.

This increase in Soviet military power has been going on for a long time. Discounting inflation, since 1960, Soviet military spending has doubled, rising steadily in real terms by three or four percent a year, while our own military budget is actually lower now than it was in 1960.

The Soviets, who traditionally were not a significant naval power, now rank number two in world naval forces.

In its balanced strategic nuclear capability, the United States retains important advantages. But over the past decade, the steady Soviet buildup has achieved functional equivalence in strategic forces with the United States.

These changes demand that we maintain adequate responses — diplomatic, military and economic; and we will. (Applause)

As President and as Commander-in-Chief, I am responsible, along with the Congress, for modernizing, expanding and improving our armed forces whenever our national security requires it. We have recently completed a major reassessment of our national defense strategy. And out of this process have come some overall principles designed to preserve our national security during the years ahead.

Will Not Lose Superiority

We will match, together with our allies and friends, any threatening power through a combination of military forces, political efforts and economic programs. We will not allow any other nation to gain military superiority over us. (Applause)

We shall seek the cooperation of the Soviet Union and other nations in reducing areas of tension. We do not desire to intervene militarily in the internal domestic affairs of other countries, nor to aggravate regional conflicts. And we shall oppose intervention by others.

While assuring our own military capabilities, we shall seek security through dependable, verifiable arms control agreements wherever possible.

We shall use our great economic, technological and diplomatic advantages to defend our interests and to promote American values. We are prepared, for instance, to cooperate with the Soviet Union toward common social, scientific and economic goals — but if they fail to demonstrate in missile programs and other force levels or in the projection of Soviet or proxy forces into other land and continents, then popular support in the United States for such cooperation with the Soviets will certainly erode.

These principles mean that, even as we search for agreement in arms control, we will continue to modernize our strategic systems and to revitalize our conventional forces. And I have no doubt that the Congress shares my commitment in this respect.

We shall implement this policy that I have outlined so briefly in three different ways: By maintaining strategic nuclear balance, by working closely with our NATO allies to strengthen and modernize our defenses in Europe; and by maintaining and developing forces to counter any threats to our allies and friends in our vital interests in Asia, the Middle East, and other regions of the world.

Let me take up each of these three in turn.

Maintaining Nuclear Balance

Our first and most fundamental concern is to prevent nuclear war. (Applause) The horrors of nuclear conflict, and our desire to reduce the world's arsenals of fearsome nuclear weapons, do not free us from the need to analyze the situation objectively and to make sensible choices about our purposes and means.

Our strategic forces must be — and must be known to be — a match for the capabilities of the Soviets. They will never be able to use their nuclear forces to threaten, to coerce, or to blackmail us or our friends. (Applause)

Our continuing major effort in the SALT talks taking place every day in Geneva are one means toward a goal of strategic nuclear stability.

We and the Soviets have already reached agreement on some basic points, although still others remain to be resolved. We are making good progress. We are not looking for a one-sided advantage.

Before I sign any SALT agreement on behalf of the United States, I will make sure that it preserves the strategic balance, that we can independently verify Soviet compliance, and that we will be at least as strong relative to the Soviet Union as we would be without any agreement.

But in addition to the limits and reductions of a SALT II agreement, we must take other steps to protect the strategic balance. During the next decade, improvements in the Soviet missiles can make our land-based missile forces and silos increasingly vulnerable to a Soviet first strike. Such an attack would amount to national suicide for the Soviet Union. But however remote, it is a threat against which we must constantly be on guard.

We have a superb submarine fleet which is relatively invulnerable to attack when it is at sea, and we have under construction new Trident submarines and missiles which give our submarine ballistic missile force even greater range and security.

I have ordered rapid development and deployment of cruise missiles to reinforce the strategic value of our bombers. We are working on the M-X intercontinental ballistic missile and a Trident II submarine-launched ballistic missile to give us more options to respond to Soviet strategic deployments. If it becomes necessary to guarantee the clear invulnerability of our strategic deterrent, I shall not hesitate to take actions for full-scale development and deployment of these systems.

Our strategic defense forces are a triad — land-based missiles, sea-based missiles and air-breathing systems such as bombers and cruise missiles. Through the plans I have described, all three legs of this triad will be modernized and improved. Each will retain the ability, on its own, to impose devastating retaliation upon an aggressor.

Working With NATO Allies

For thirty years and more we have been committed to the defense of Europe, bound by the knowledge that Western Europe security is vital to our own. We continue to cooperate with our NATO allies in a strategy for flexible response, combining conventional forces and nuclear forces so that no aggressor can threaten the territory of Europe or its freedom which in the past we have fought together to defend.

For several years we and our allies have been trying to negotiate mutual and balanced reductions in military forces in Europe with the Soviets and with the Warsaw Pact nations who are their allies. But in the meantime, the Soviets have continued to increase and to modernize their forces beyond a level necessary for defense. In the face of this excessive Soviet buildup, we and our NATO allies have had to take important steps to cope with short-term vulnerabilities and respond to long-term threats. We are significantly strengthening U.S. forces stationed in Western Europe and improving our ability to speed additional ground and air forces to the defense of Europe in a time of crisis.

Our European allies, who supply the major portion of NATO's conventional combat strength, are also improving their readiness and their reinforcement capabilities and their antitank defenses. The heads of the NATO governments will be here in our country attending a summit meeting in May, where we will address a long-term defense program which will expand and integrate more closely allied defense plans.

Protecting U.S. Interests

For many years, the United States has been a major world power. Our longstanding concerns encompass our own security interests and those of our allies and friends far beyond our own shores and Europe.

We have important historical responsibilities to enhance peace in East Asia, in the Middle East, in the Persian Gulf, and throughout our own hemisphere. Our preference in all these areas is to turn first to international agreements that reduce the overall level of arms and minimize the threat of conflict. But we have the will, and we will also maintain the capacity, to honor our commitments and to protect our interests in those critical areas.

In the Pacific, our effective security is enhanced by mutual defense treaties with our allies and by our friendship and cooperation with other Pacific nations.

Japan and South Korea, closely linked with the United States, are located geographically where the vital interests of great powers converge. It is imperative that Northeast Asia remain stable. We will maintain and even enhance our military strength in this area, improving our air strength, and reducing our ground forces, as the South Korean army continues to modernize and to increase its own capabilities.

In the Middle East and the region of the Indian Ocean, we seek permanent peace and stability. The economic health and well being of the United States, Western Europe, Japan, depend upon continued access to the oil from the Persian Gulf.

In all these situations, the primary responsibility for preserving peace and military stability rests with the countries of the region. We shall continue to work with our friends and allies to strengthen their ability to prevent threats to their interests and to ours.

In addition, however, we will maintain forces of our own which can be called upon, if necessary, to support mutual defense efforts. The Secretary of Defense at my direction is improving and will maintain quickly deployable forces — air, land and sea — to defend our interests throughout the world.

Arms control agreements are a major goal as instruments of our national security, but this will be possible only if we maintain appropriate military force levels. Reaching balanced, verifiable agreements with our adversaries can limit the cost of security and reduce the risk of war. But even then, we must — and we will — proceed efficiently with whatever arms programs our own security requires.

When I leave this auditorium, I shall be going to visit with the crew aboard one of our most modern nuclear powered aircraft carriers in the Atlantic Ocean. The men and women of our own armed forces remain committed as able professionals and as patriotic Americans, to our common defense. They must stand constantly ready to fight, in the hope that through strength combat will be prevented. We as Americans will always support them in their courageous vigil. (Applause)

'No Cause for Pessimism'

This has been a serious and a sober talk, but there is no cause for pessimism. We face a challenge and we will do whatever is necessary to meet it. We will preserve and protect our country and continue to promote and to maintain peace around the world.

This means that we shall have to continue to support strong and efficient military forces.

For most of human history, people have wished vainly that freedom and the flowering of the human spirit, which freedom nourishes, did not finally have to depend upon the force of arms. We, like our forebears, live in a time when those who would destroy liberty are restrained less by their respect for freedom itself than by their knowledge that those of us who cherish freedom are strong.

We are a great Nation made up of talented people. We can readily afford the necessary costs of our military forces, as well as an increased level, if needed, to prevent any adversary from destabilizing the peace of the world. The money we spend on defense is not wasted any more than is the cost of maintaining a police force in a local community to keep the peace. This investment purchases our freedom to fulfill the worthy goals of our Nation.

Southerners, whose ancestors a hundred years ago knew the horrors of a homeland devastated by war, are particularly determined that war shall never come to us again. All Americans understand the basic lesson of history: that we need to be resolute and able to protect ourselves, to prevent threats and domination by others.

No matter how peaceful and secure and easy the circumstances of our lives now seem, we have no guarantee that the blessings will endure. That is why we will always maintain the strength which, God willing, we shall never need to use.

Thank you very much. (Applause) ▌

Anti-Inflation Speech-1

Following is the prepared text of President Carter's April 11, 1978, speech to the American Society of Newspaper Editors, in which the president outlined his program to control inflation.

During the last 15 months we in the United States have made good progress in sustaining growth and creating jobs. Four-and-a-half million more people are at work today than fifteen months ago. The unemployment rate has fallen from nearly 8 percent to a little more than 6 percent. Average household income, after adjustment for both taxes and inflation, is 5 percent higher now than a year ago. Business profits in the second half of 1977 were 15 percent higher than one year before, and during that time the inflation rate was held to a reasonable and predictable level.

But too many Americans — particularly young people and members of minority groups — are still without jobs. I am determined to sustain our economy's progress toward high employment and rising real income, with both existing programs and with new, carefully targeted incentives to encourage private business to hire the hard-core unemployed.

We have other economic problems which cause us continuing deep concern.

Our nation's economic health can be protected only if we can cope with the two developments that now threaten it most seriously — the high level of oil imports and the increasing rate of inflation.

These two problems both imperil our economic recovery and threaten the strength of the dollar, and they must be controlled.

The steps that we will take are part of a wider international effort by the major industrial nations to promote world recovery in 1978. In this effort, each country has a role to play — with the U.S. maintaining its growth while attacking inflation and limiting oil imports, other countries achieving their growth targets, and all countries avoiding protectionism and providing greater aid to developing countries. In the hope that this concerted approach will make a large contribution to world recovery, I joined the leaders of six other nations yesterday in announcing that we will meet on July 16 and 17 in Bonn to press ahead with our common efforts.

But the first requirement is effective action within each nation.

Excessive Oil Imports

The primary reason for our problems with the balance of trade and the decreasing value of the dollar is no mystery. Ten years ago we were paying roughly $2 billion for imported oil. This year oil imports will cost us more than $45 billion.

Our energy problems are no longer theoretical or potential. They are an active threat to the economic well-being of our people.

Of all the major countries in the world the United States is the only one without a national energy policy, and because the Congress has not acted, other nations have begun to doubt our will. Holders of dollars throughout the world have interpreted our failure to act as a sign of economic weakness, and these views have been directly translated into a decreasing value of our currency.

The falling dollar in international monetary markets makes inflation worse here at home. It raises the price of goods we import, and this makes it easier for domestic producers to raise their own prices as well.

That is why we must have meaningful energy legislation without further delay. Our security depends on it, and our economy demands it. If Congress does not act, then oil imports will have to be limited by administrative action under present law, which is not the most desirable solution. One way or the other, oil imports must be reduced.

Recently our healthy and sustained economic growth has exceeded that of most other nations who are our major trading partners, so we have been better able to buy their goods than they have to buy ours.

Our standard of living and our ability to grow depend on the raw materials and goods we import from other countries. Therefore, to prevent further serious trade imbalances, we need to export more agricultural products and other goods and services to pay for our purchases abroad.

A Cabinet-level task force, chaired by the Secretary of Commerce, will develop additional measures to promote exports, and will report back to me within 60 days.

Now I will discuss the steps we must take to protect our national economic growth and the jobs and prosperity of our people from the threat of growing inflation.

'No Easy Answers'

Conserving energy, increasing efficiency and productivity, eliminating waste, reducing oil imports and expanding our exports will help to fight inflation; but making that fight a success will require firm government policies and full private cooperation.

The inflation we are suffering today began many years ago and was aggravated in 1973 and 1974 by a quadrupling of OPEC oil prices, widespread crop shortages, Soviet grain purchases, substantial devaluation of the dollar, and a worldwide industrial boom that led to double digit inflation in the United States and around the world. It now has become embedded in the very tissue of our economy. It has resisted the most severe recession in a generation. It persists because all of us — business and labor, farmers and consumers — are caught on a treadmill that none can stop alone. Each group tries to raise its income to keep up with present and anticipated rising costs; eventually we all lose the inflation battle together.

There are no easy answers. We will not solve inflation by increasing unemployment. We will not impose wage and price controls. We will work with measures that avoid both extremes.

Our first and most direct efforts are within government itself. Where government contributes to inflation, that contribution must be lessened; where government expenditures are too high, that spending must be reduced; where government imposes an inflationary burden on business, labor, and consumers, those burdens must be lightened; wherever government can set an example of restraint and efficiency, it must do so.

The budget I have proposed for the next fiscal year is both tight and capable of meeting the nation's most pressing needs. The prospective deficit in that budget is as large as we can afford without compromising our hopes for balanced economic growth and a declining inflation rate. As always, pressures are developing on all sides to increase spending and enlarge that deficit.

Potential outlay increases in the 1979 budget which are now being considered by Congressional committees would add between $9 billion and $13 billion to spending levels next year. The price of some of these politically attractive programs would escalate rapidly in future years. I am especially concerned about tuition tax credits, highway and urban transit programs, postal service financing, farm legislation, and defense spending.

By every means at my disposal, I will resist those pressures and protect the integrity of the budget.

Indeed, as opportunities arise, we must work to reduce the budget deficit, and to ensure that beyond 1979 the deficit declines steadily and moves us toward a balanced budget. I will work closely with the Congress and, if necessary, will exercise my veto authority to keep the 1979 budget deficit at or below the limits I have proposed.

The Federal government must also act directly to moderate inflation.

Two months ago I proposed that in each industry and sector of the economy wage and price increases this year be voluntarily held significantly below the average increase for the two preceding years — an important principle of deceleration.

Ceiling on Federal Pay Raise

I am determined to take the lead in breaking the wage and price spiral by holding Federal pay increases down. Last year, federal white collar salaries rose by more than seven percent. I intend to propose a limit of about 5.5 percent this year, thereby setting an example for labor and industry to moderate prices and wage increases. This year I will also freeze the pay of all Executive appointees and members of my senior staff. I believe that those who are most privileged in our nation — including other executives in government and in private companies — should set a similar example of restraint.

State and local governments employ every seventh worker in our nation and I have sent letters to every Governor and to the Mayors of our larger cities asking that they follow the federal example and hold down their pay increases. I have also asked that if those governments plan to reduce taxes they first consider lowering sales taxes, which add directly to the consumer's burden.

The Federal government will take several other steps to reduce inflation:

● All Executive Branch agencies will avoid or reduce the purchase of goods or services whose prices are rising rapidly, unless by so doing we would seriously jeopardize our national security or create serious unemployment. I am also asking that all new or renegotiated Federal contracts which contain price escalation clauses should reflect the principle of deceleration.

● We must cut the inflationary costs which private industry bears as a result of government regulations.

Last month I directed Executive regulatory agencies under my control to minimize the adverse economic consequences of their actions. I am determined to eliminate unnecessary regulations and to ensure that future regulations do not impose unnecessary costs on the American economy. Our efforts to reorganize the Federal bureaucracy and to streamline the Civil Service will help us put the government's house in order.

I support "sunset" legislation to ensure that we review these regulatory programs every few years, and eliminate or change those that have become outdated.

I also urge Congressional budget committees to report regularly to the Congress on the inflationary effect of pending legislation, much as the Council of Economic Advisors and the Council on Wage and Price Stability now report to me.

● The combined actions of my Administration and the Civil Aeronautics Board have already led to substantial cuts in some airline passenger fares. Despite the opposition of private interests, the airline regulatory reform legislation must be enacted this year. We are also re-examining excessive Federal regulation of the trucking industry, an effort which may result in increased efficiency while reducing freight transportation costs and retail prices.

In addition, I am asking the independent regulatory agencies to try to reduce inflation when they review rate changes, and to explore regulatory changes that can make the regulated industries more efficient.

● Last fall, major new legislation was passed which will improve economic conditions for farm families, and we have announced additional administrative action to raise farm income this year.

Unfortunately, the Senate has just passed a bill that would raise food prices by 3 percent and the overall cost-of-living by .4 percent, shatter confidence in the crucial export markets for America's farm products, and cripple American farm families through increased costs. It is bad for farmers, bad for consumers, and bad for our nation.

I will veto any farm legislation, beyond what I have already recommended, that would lead to higher food prices or budget expenditures.

● Housing construction rates have been at a high level and costs have risen rapidly, partly because of sharp increases in the price of raw materials such as lumber. Since lumber accounts for one-fourth of the total cost of a new house, we can obtain some relief by increasing production and using our existing lumber output more efficiently. Therefore, I have instructed the Departments of Agriculture and Interior, the Council on Environmental Quality, and my economic advisors, to report to me within 30 days on the best ways to sustain expanded timber harvests from Federal, State and private lands, and other means of increasing lumber yields in ways that would be environmentally acceptable,

economically efficient and consistent with sound budget policy.

● Daily hospital costs have jumped from $15 in 1950 to over $200 today, and physicians' fees have risen 75 percent faster than other consumer prices. It is very important that Congress act now on the proposed Hospital Cost Containment Bill as the most effective step we can take toward reasonable hospital prices. Failure of Congress to act on the Hospital Cost Containment legislation will cost the taxpayer more than $18 billion in needless government spending over the next five years.

Together with the airline deregulation bill, this is one of the two most important measures the Congress can pass to prevent inflation.

These measures have so far been delayed by the opposition of powerful lobbying groups. I will continue to give this legislation my full support, and I call on the leaders of Congress to do the same.

Industry, Labor Cooperation Needed

Such government actions as I have discussed today can be important steps toward controlling inflation. But it is a myth that the government itself can stop inflation. Success or failure in this overall effort will largely be determined by the actions of the private sector of the economy.

I expect industry and labor to keep price, wage and salary increases significantly below the average rate for the last two years. Those who set medical, legal and other professional fees, college tuition rates, insurance premiums and other service charges must also join in. This will not be easy. But the example of Federal action must be matched. Inflation cannot be solved by placing the burden of fighting it only on a few.

The Council on Wage and Price Stability recently began a series of meetings with representatives of business and of labor in major industries such as steel, automobiles, aluminum, paper, railroads, food processing, communications, lumber and the postal services. In consultation with the private parties the Council will identify the rate at which prices, wages and other costs have been rising in recent years, the outlook for the year ahead and the steps that can be taken to reduce inflation.

Let me be blunt about this point. I am asking American workers to follow the example of Federal workers and accept a lower rate of wage increase. In return, they have a right to expect a comparable restraint in price increases for the goods and services they buy. Our national interest simply cannot withstand unreasonble increases in prices and wages. It is my responsibility to speak out firmly and clearly when the welfare of our people is at stake.

Members of my Administration have already discussed this deceleration program with a number of leaders of labor, business and industry. They have promised

their cooperation. Later I expect to meet with business and labor leaders to discuss contributions that they can make to help slow the rate of inflation. One of the most important contributions they can make is to show that restraint applies to everyone — not just the men and women on the assembly line, but also the managers in the executive suites. Just as I will freeze the pay of the top executives in the Federal government, the American people will expect similar restraint from the leaders of American business and labor.

I am determined to devote the power of my office toward the objective of reduced inflation. Our approach must be flexible enough to account for the variations in our complex economy — but it must be comprehensive enough to cover most of the activities of our economy.

In the long run, we should develop special programs to deal with sectors of the economy where government actions have the greatest potential for reducing inflation. These include housing, medical care, food, transportation, energy and the primary metals industries. The members of my Cabinet will work individually and with the Council on Wage and Price Stability to develop and to announce early action to reduce inflation within their own areas of responsibility.

Strauss 'Inflation Counselor'

To accomplish our deceleration goals in the private sector, I am asking my Special Trade Representative, Robert Strauss, to take on additional duties as a Special Counselor on Inflation. He will work with me, with Treasury Secretary Blumenthal, my chief financial spokesman, with Charlie Schultze, the Chairman of the Council on Wage and Price Stability and its Executive Director, Barry Bosworth. He will have specific authority to speak for me in the public interest, and will be a member of the Steering Committee of the Economic Policy Group under the chairmanship of Secretary Blumenthal.

Reducing the inflation rate will not be easy and it will not come overnight. We must admit to ourselves that we will never cope successfully with challenge until we face some unpleasant facts about our problems, about the solutions and about ourselves.

The problems of this generation are, in a way, more difficult than those of a generation before. We face no sharply focused crisis or threat which might make us forget our differences and rally to the defense of the common good.

We all want something to be done about our problems — except when the solutions affect us. We want to conserve energy, but not to change our wasteful habits. We favor sacrifice, as long as others go first. We want to abolish tax loopholes — unless it's our loophole. We denounce special interests, except for our own.

No Act of Congress, no program of our government, no order of my own can bring out the quality that we need: to change from the preoccupation with self that can cripple our national will, to a willingness to acknowledge and to sacrifice for the common good.

As the nation prepared for the challenge of war, Walter Lippmann addressed these words to our nation forty years ago:

"You took the good things for granted," he said. "Now you must earn them again. It is written: for every right that you cherish, you have a duty which you must fulfill. For every hope that you entertain, you have a task you must perform. For every good that you wish could happen . . . you will have to sacrifice your comfort and ease. There is nothing for nothing any longer."

These words of admonition apply to us now. ∎

Carter on Lawyers

Following is the White House transcript of President Carter's speech, as delivered, to the Los Angeles Bar Association on May 4, 1978:

Governor Brown, Mayor Bradley, President Williams, President-Elect Taylor, distinguished members of the Los Angeles County Bar, ladies and gentlemen:

For the last half an hour, I have been sitting in a room nearby listening to the report on the background of this tremendous organization and also listening to the report on the future of the organization. And I have been thrilled with your past accomplishments and I have been touched by some of the struggles that you have experienced in your own history.

I congratulate you on your 100th Anniversary.

I would like to begin my speech with a quote from a book published in 1852.

"Jarndyce and Jarndyce drones on. This scarecrow of a suit has, in the course of time, become so complicated that no man alive knows what it means — innumerable children have been born into the case; innumerable old people have died out of it; whole families have inherited legendary hatreds with the suit — there are not three Jarndyces left upon the earth, perhaps since old Tom Jarndyce in despair blew his brains out at a coffee house in Chancery, but Jarndyce and Jarndyce still drags its dreary length before the court."

This quotation comes from the novel "Bleak House," and although Charles Dickens, who by the way was a court reporter himself, was writing about a chancery suit in London long ago, he could have been writing about a modern anti-trust suit in Federal Court. His subject was the same that should preoccupy you and me, lawyers, mayors, governors and the President of the United States; that is, insuring that our legal system serves the ends of justice without delay.

I am not a lawyer, but there is no question that has concerned me more throughout my adult life than that of human justice — striving to alleviate the inequalities, the unfairness, the chance differences of fortune that exist among people and to help ensure that all people possess the basic material and political rights that they need for full participation in the life of our society.

I grew up in a community in Georgia that often did not provide simple justice for a majority of our citizens because of the divisions of privilege between those who owned land and property, and those who did not, the divisions of power between those who controlled the political system and those who were controlled by it, the wall of discrimination that separated blacks and whites.

As a Governor and as a President, I have learned that, as Reinhold Niebuhr said, "It is the sad duty of politics to establish justice in a sinful world." I am trying now as your President to carry our Nation's message of basic justice and human rights to other nations.

But I know that we cannot speak of human rights in other countries unless we are going to do our utmost to protect the rights of our own people here at home.

Excessive Delays, Litigation

Let me tell you about some of the things that concern me.

On the last day of the Administration of Lyndon Johnson, the government filed an anti-trust suit against a major computer company. Nine years have passed; three new presidential administrations have taken office; hundreds of millions of dollars have been spent on legal fees. But still the trial is not nearly over, and it has been speculated that the judge who has supervised it for the last nine years may die or retire before the trial is completed, in which case it would start all over again. Generations of computers have come and gone, there is not a single computer now being sold that was being sold when the case began — but still the case goes on.

I am worried about a legal system in which expensive talent on both sides produces interminable delay — especially when delay itself can often mean victory for one side.

Justice should not be forced to obey the timetables of those who seek to avoid it.

As a public official, I have inspected many prisons and I know that nearly all inmates are drawn from the ranks of the powerless and the poor. A child of privilege frequently receives the benefit of the doubt; a child of poverty seldom does.

In many courts, plea bargaining serves the convenience of the judge and the lawyers, not the ends of justice, because the courts simply lack the time to give everyone a fair trial.

We have the heaviest concentration of lawyers on earth — one for every 500 Americans: three times as many as are in

England; four times as many as are in West Germany; twenty-one times as many as there are in Japan. We have more litigation; but I am not sure that we have more justice. No resources of talent and training in our own society, even including the medical care, is more wastefully or unfairly distributed than legal skills.

Ninety percent of our lawyers serve ten percent of our people. We are over-lawyered, and under-represented.

Excessive litigation and legal featherbedding are encouraged. Non-contested divorces become major legal confrontations in many states. Complete title searches on the same property are unnecessarily repeated with each sale. Routine automobile accidents, the cases clog our courts while no-fault automobile insurance is opposed.

The number of medical malpractice suits skyrockets. Mahatma Gandhi, who himself was a very successful lawyer, said of his profession, and I quote, "Lawyers will as a rule advance quarrels rather than repress them." We do not serve justice when we encourage disputes in our society, rather than resolving them.

In my own region of the country, perhaps even yours as well, lawyers of great influence and prestige led the fight against civil rights and economic justice. They were paid lavish fees by their states and heaped with honors for their efforts. They knew all the maneuvers, and for too long they kept the promises of the Constitution of the United States from coming true.

The basic right to vote, to hold a job, to own a home, to be informed of one's legal rights when arrested, to have legal counsel if an indigent — these rights have been denied for generations, in our country, and are being recently won only after intense struggle.

I think about these things when I come to speak with you. What I think about most, however, is the enormous potential for good within an aroused legal profession, and how often that potential has not been and is not used. More than any other nation on earth, ours was created out of respect for the law. We had the first written Constitution — it is the oldest; we proclaimed ours a government of laws, not of men; we put our faith in interpretations of the laws to resolve our most basic disputes.

None of us would change our system of laws and justice for any other in the world. From the beginning, it made the citizens the masters of the state, and not the other way around, and it has extended increasing protection to the poor and the victims of discrimination.

It is because of the enormous power of the law, and of the position of great influence and privilege which lawyers occupy within our society, that lawyers bear such a heavy obligation to serve the ends of true justice, and through dynamic effort, individually and collectively through organizations such as this, search for those ends of justice. I know that you understand these obligations.

During the last generation, many of our most important advances toward racial integration and protection of our people against government and its abuse have been made through the courts.

Four Challenges

I heard the comments a few minutes ago about Chief Justice Earl Warren who has been an inspiration to all of us who serve in government. But let me mention briefly four challenges that we should face in order to improve justice in America.

First, in making criminal justice fairer, faster, more sensible, and more certain; second, in holding the law to the highest standards of impartiality, honesty, and fairness; third, in ensuring that access to the legal systems does not depend on political influence or economic power, and fourth, in reducing our over-reliance on litigation, and speeding up those cases that are litigated.

Fairer Criminal Justice. Our starting point in ensuring justice is to reduce crime through measures that are effective and fair.

There was encouraging progress in this direction last year, when the volume of crime fell for the first time in many years by four percent below the previous year's level. It is a welcome development, but it does not change the urgent need to control crime. States and local governments must take the lead in this effort, but the federal government must do its part.

We should streamline the Federal Criminal Code, which now contains many provisions which overlap, duplicate one another, are inconsistent and need upgrading. With the leadership of Senator Eastland and Senator Kennedy and the late Senator McClellan, a twelve-year effort recently culminated in the Senate passage of this new comprehensive criminal code. I hope the House will pass it this year without delay.

We are working with congressional leaders to reorganize the Law Enforcement Assistance Agency, to gear our funding system to our most pressing needs, and to provide better support for state and local governments, and to concentrate our help on improving the criminal justice system and reducing crime. I will propose a consolidation and a reorganization of many of the functions now performed by more than 110 different federal agencies that have direct responsibility for law enforcement.

We can reduce the tremendous overload on our criminal justice system by removing such crimes as drunkenness, and vagrancy from the courts, thereby freeing the courts to deal with serious offenses and enabling us to treat these social illnesses in ways that offer a greater hope of success than conviction and incarceration.

I am supporting uniform sentencing standards for federal offenses, which will make the punishment for crimes more rational and fair and will help ensure that the rich and the poor are treated alike, no matter what court might convict them.

Powerful white-collar criminals cheat consumers of millions of dollars; public officials who abuse their high rank damage the integrity of our nation in profound and long-lasting ways. But too often these big-shot crooks escape the full consequences of their acts. Justice must be blind to rank, power and position. The Justice Department is now undertaking a major new effort on white-collar crime.

I have directed the Justice Department also to review our prison policy alternatives to incarceration, such as station house citations, supervised release, work-release programs and other community-based facilities.

I urge all judges and all lawyers to use your enormous influence to make these efforts a success.

Adherence to Standards. Our second challenge is to see that our legal system lives up to its noblest tradition of honesty and impartiality, so that all people stand equal before the bar of justice.

One of the most important steps that we can take is to restore public confidence in our system of justice, to assure that government decisions are thoroughly impartial, and that personal interests and influence have no part. I have required all major appointees of mine, as a condition of accepting office, to disclose their personal financial interests. I have also required them to pledge that, after their term of public service is over, they would forego all contacts with their former agency in government for one year.

Last year I proposed legislation to make these standards a permanent part of the American law. In its current form, this ethics legislation would extend similar standards to the Legislative and Judicial Branches of our government. It has already passed the Senate and cleared the Rules Committee in the House and is ready for floor action without delay.

Last week the House passed a bill I supported requiring those organizations which do significant lobbying of Congress to disclose their activities to the public. Although lobbying is a constitutionally protected activity, the American people have a right to know what major forces are affecting the legislative process. It is time now for the Senate to follow the lead of the House and pass a lobby reform bill.

Law enforcement agencies must set a clear example for their respect for the law. Recently, as the number of undocumented aliens has grown, there has been a disturbing trend particularly in your part of the country toward routine police harassment of our Mexican-American families. I know that your own bar association has studied this problem.

Last month, the Justice Department intervened in a harassment case in Texas where three policemen had been convicted for the death of a Mexican-American prisoner. In filing for a review of the one-year jail terms given to the convicted men, the Justice Department said, and I quote,

"The public perception of inequality and the belief that the life of a Mexican-American citizen has little value can only do damage to respect for the laws and belief in justice." (Applause)

This kind of harassment must stop, and my administration, working with you, will do what it can to see that it does. Moreover, we have submitted legislation to Congress now which will stop the flow of illegal immigration while fully protecting the rights of our Hispanic citizens.

When I was Governor of Georgia, I appointed judges on the basis of merit alone. And one of my first acts as President was to create a nominating commission to recommend candidates to me for all appointments as Federal Circuit Judges. I am pleased that many Senators, including those from California, have now set up similar commissions at the District Court level.

The passage of the Omnibus Judgeship Act, now pending in a House-Senate Conference Committee, will provide a test for the concept of merit selection. The conferees have recently agreed that the President should set "standards and guidelines" governing the selection of District Judges, and I intend to use this authority to encourage establishment of more merit panels and to open the selection process.

The passage of this act — which will create 152 Federal judgeships — offers a unique opportunity to make our judiciary more fully representative of our population. We have an abominable record to date. Of the 525 Federal judges, only 20 are black or Hispanic, and only six, about one percent, are women.

While the Federal Bench in Southern California has become more representative, this is not true elsewhere in the nation. My Executive Order on the Circuit Court Nominating Commission specifically requires special efforts to identify qualified minority and female candidates.

During too many of the struggles for equal justice, just in the lifetimes of you and me — the questions of one-man, one-vote, voting rights for blacks, representation for indigent clients, and others — much of the organized bar sat on the sidelines or actually opposed these efforts. In today's struggle for women's rights, the passage of the Equal Rights Amendment — (Applause) — and the full participation of women and minorities at all levels of society, I hope that lawyers throughout the country will follow the actions that your bar association has already taken here in Los Angeles County.

Remove Economic Barriers. The third challenge is suggested by the American Bar Association's theme for this year "Access to Justice." Too often the amount of justice that a person gets depends on the amount of money that he or she can pay. Access to justice must not depend on economic status, and it must not be thwarted by arbitrary procedural rules.

Overcoming these procedural barriers means that groups with distinct interests to defend — in civil rights, economic questions, environmental causes and so forth — must be able to defend them fully. We are supporting efforts to broaden the use of class action, and to expand the definitions of standing to sue. My administration supports bills before Congress that would empower citizens to participate in the proceedings of federal agencies — a right that has too often been reserved for the large and the powerful corporations which have the legal resources to express their view forcefully.

We must remove the economic barriers to justice. When a poor family is cheated by a merchant, unfairly threatened with eviction, falsely accused of a crime, it can very rarely take advantage of the skilled legal talent at reasonable rates.

In the City of New York there are 35,-000 lawyers — one for every 200 citizens. But only a handful of these lawyers are available for service to the city's poor — one lawyer for every 5,000 poor people. That is why we have now expanded the Legal Services Corporation; in fiscal year 1979, its budget will be more than twice as large as it was when my administration took office about a year ago. (Applause)

But you know and I know that legal help is often beyond the reach of most of the middle class Americans as well. Here, too, I believe that the bar has an obligation to accommodate those with modest incomes. Free and open competition is the best way to bring legal services within the reach of average citizens. Another solution, which my administration supports, is the expansion of pre-paid legal plans, legal clinics, and other low cost alternatives, such as those pioneered by the United Auto Workers.

The Neighborhood Justice Center near here in Venice and Marvista is a good example of what we are trying to do.

I also ask that lawyers join the effort to stop inflation by following the example we have asked of — (applause) — of following the example that we have asked of every other group in our society and join in decelerating the rise in legal fees. This morning new inflation figures were published in Washington that caused me grave concern. How can we, the privileged members of American society, call upon the working people, the men and women of our country, to make a financial sacrifice to deal with inflation unless attorneys, doctors, accountants and other professionals, Presidents, assume the same responsibility to assist in our efforts to keep a lid on inflation?

One of the greatest failings of the organized bar in the past century since the American Bar Association was founded is that it has fought innovations. When greater competition has come to the legal profession, when no-fault systems have been adopted, when lawyers have begun to advertise or compete — in short, when the profession has accommodated the interests of the public — it has done so only when forced to.

Constructive work is now under way and as the second century of the Bar Association begins, the people of this country are beginning to see leadership from the members of the bar.

Reduce Litigation. But as we make litigation more accessible, our fourth challenge is to make the adversary system less necessary for the daily lives of most Americans — and more difficult when it must be used. By resorting to litigation at the drop of a hat, by regarding the adversary system as an end in itself, we have made justice more cumbersome, more expensive and less equal than it ought to be.

This is a phenomenon more and more widely recognized — I know — among members of the bar.

One answer is to be sure that other pathways to justice do exist.

Many suggestions have already been made for making litigation less necessary, and my administration will work with you and other members of the bar to implement them.

In the great number of cases there is no sound reason for a lawyer to be involved in land transfers or title searches. Simplified procedures and use of modern computer technology can save consumers needless legal fees.

We must eliminate from our judicial system cases which can be resolved in other ways. No-fault automobile insurance systems, adopted by many states, are a step in the right direction; national standards for no-fault will have a much greater impact. We support no-fault divorce laws, like those passed when I was Governor of Georgia and the ones passed here in California, that can reduce litigation that is unnecessary and also the bitterness that litigation brings. We must look for ways to reduce the tremendous burden of medical malpractice costs.

Delays in our courts because of the excessive litigation are matched by the interminable delays in many federal regulatory agencies.

In trying to solve society's problems, our regulators have proposed unnecessarily detailed specifications, and written regulations in the kind of gobbledygook that could employ a generation of law school graduates just to interpret them. (Applause)

I have pledged to reduce this regulatory burden for the first time on American citizens and we have taken some steps toward change. A few weeks ago, I signed an Executive Order that will be carried out which requires the heads of departments and agencies personally to approve the regulatory agendas of their organizations; that regulations be signed by the one who wrote them; that regulations be gone over rigorously — (Applause) — in "sunset" reviews to terminate them when they have served their purpose; that they be simply written; and that they are the most cost effective rules possible to devise.

Where the free marketplace can do a better job than regulations — as in the set-

ting of airline fares — I will work hard to deregulate that industry, and to encourage free and effective competition.

The Senate has passed a superb airline deregulation bill. I predict that next week it will come out of the House subcommittee and we expect success on the floor of the House.

We must also find a way to remove the vested interests in over-litigation and delay. Last year, corporations spent $24 billion on legal services — 12 times as much as we spent on all federal, state and local courts combined. We must ask whether this is the right way or the best way to conserve our legal resources or to ensure justice.

We are reviewing suggestions for reducing litigation, including more arbitration, greater reliance on small claims courts and experiments with alternative systems for resolving disputes, such as the experimental arbitration systems now in existence in San Francisco, and in Philadelphia, and in other parts of our country.

But even with all of these steps, much litigation will of course still be necessary. There are a variety of steps that can be taken together to make necessary litigation more efficient and to reduce unnecessary delays.

I support legislation now in Congress to expand the functions and the jurisdiction of federal magistrates, to reduce the burden on federal judges.

I support a speedy appeals act to reduce the delay between sentencing and appeal; and I have directed Attorney General Bell to study whether we can also apply strict time limits to civil trials and to regulatory proceedings.

Timeless Responsibility

Those of us — Presidents and lawyers — who enjoy privilege, power and influence in our society can be called to a harsh account for the ways we are using this power. Our hierarchy of privilege in this nation, based not on birth but on social and economic status, tends to insulate some of us from the problems faced by the average American. The natural tendency for all of us is to ignore what does not touch us directly. The natural temptation when dealing with the law is to assure that whatever is legal is just.

But if our nation is to thrive, if we are to fulfill the vision and promise of our founding fathers, if we are truly to serve the ends of justice, we must look beyond these comfortable insulations of privilege.

I have too much respect for the potential of the law to believe that this leadership is not possible from you.

I hope that lawyers throughout the country will take up the challenges I have made today. I know you understand the responsibility to serve justice. You have dedicated your very lives to this task.

This responsibility is older than our Constitution, older than the Bill of Rights, older even than the tradition of the common law.

It comes from the roots of our western heritage, with the prophet Amos, who said, "Let justice roll down like waters, and righteousness like an ever-flowing stream."

Thank you very much. ∎

Comments on Doctors

The following comments by President Carter on doctors and the medical profession were excerpted from his statements May 5, 1978, at a "town meeting" in Spokane, Wash. The remarks followed by one day Carter's speech about the legal profession.

. . . I know that doctors care very seriously about their patients. But when you let doctors organize into the American Medical Association, their interest is to protect the interests, not of patients, but of doctors. And they have been the major obstacle to progress in our country in having a better health care system in years gone by.

So I look upon myself as a spokesman for the client and the medical patient and the student in a classroom, the elderly person, the mentally ill person. And I think this sense that I am that person would be the greatest achievement that I could derive for myself on the domestic scene. . . .

Q: Mr. President, my name is Kathy Coffee. I know what I want to say, first of all, is really unprofessional and un — what am I trying to say? — not really related, but I think you are really cute. I do. (Laughter)

P: You are the first questioner that has made me blush. (Laughter)

Q: Now I would like to ask my question. If you are going to reduce the government interference in the lives of the American people as you said, why then are you pushing for a national health care plan which will only increase our income tax, and increase our national debt, just as it has in England and Sweden? Thank you.

P: Thank you. If that was the result of a national health plan, just to increase the burden on the American people financially, I of course would never consider it. Beginning with President Truman's Administration, there has been a growing interest and desire among the American people to have a more far-reaching or comprehensive health plan for our nation.

There would be several emphases in the new plan that don't presently exist and I will just mention a few of them.

One is the prevention of disease, and not just a commitment to treat an affliction or disease, after it occurs in the human body. Fifteen months ago the immunization program for children, for instance, had almost been completely forgotten. Now with our new CHAPS Program, so-called, we are trying to test people at an early age, four or five years old, to see what defects they have, immunize them against prospective diseases for a change as did occur in my childhood, perhaps in yours,

and make sure that the emphasis is on prevention.

The second thing we want to do is let Americans prepay through a routine monthly payment, for instance, for this kind of care and not just depend upon a concerted and very expensive care after they become ill.

We need to get away from the commitment of medical doctors, hospital administrators, even patients, to go into a hospital for treatment when they could get adequate treatment in an outpatient clinic. As you know, many hospital insurance policies won't pay off unless you are admitted to the hospital as a patient.

Obviously, this is more convenient for the doctors perhaps. It is much more profitable for those who own, operate hospitals. You are quite often given services or treatment that you don't need and of course it makes the expense of hospital care in our country far greater per person than any other nation on earth, including Sweden, Canada, England, where they do have a more comprehensive health care program. . . .

We have seen in recent years an unbelievable explosion in health care costs. Last year, for instance, the hospital costs went up in our country 16 percent. The inflation rate went up about 6 percent. This has been typical of the last few years....

We now spend about $600 or $700 — I am not sure of the exact figure — for every man, woman and child in this country for health care and we don't nearly have the best health care in the world. . . . ∎

Criticizes Bureaucracy

Following are excerpts from the prepared text of a speech President Carter distributed, but did not read, to the Illinois state legislature on May 26, 1978:

. . .After a year-and-a-half, I am still frustrated by the federal bureaucracy. There are few levers a President can pull to bring immediate action. There are too many agencies, doing too many things, overlapping too often, coordinating too rarely, wasting too much money — and doing too little to solve real problems.

Our federal budget will soon reach a half-trillion dollars. That's higher than the budget of any other nation; it's higher than the total national product of all but a few; it's higher than any of us want it to be — but it often fails to get the job done, because of the senseless hodgepodge of Federal programs.

There are, for example, at least 75 agencies and 164,000 Federal employees in police or investigative work. Many of them duplicate or overlap state and local law enforcement efforts unnecessarily. . . .

When private citizens seek the simplest form of help from their government, too often they get only long waits, unanswered letters, complicated forms, referrals to other agencies and plain inaction.

For example, a welfare widow with two children may have to deal with eleven different Federal agencies for services. If there is an old or disabled person in the family, there are even more agencies to see. All told, there are more than 100 Federal human services program, administered by 10 different departments and agencies.

Overlapping

If state or local governments seek help, they may not fare much better.

While many of our cities and towns are in deep economic trouble, the Federal effort to aid them is shackled by this bureaucratic burden. To aid community economic development, for example, there are:

• over eleven different business-assistance programs in more than ten agencies;

• 46 sewage-related programs in five departments, two independent agencies, and eight regional commissions;

• at least 77 different housing programs in 15 different agencies;

• 60 transportation grant programs in the Department of Transportation and 25 other agencies;

• and 24 programs administered by ten agencies for employment and training.

These confused programs give states and cities a difficult choice. They can accept the share of Federal funds that come through this twisted pipeline, or they can invest some of their precious money to hire advisors and lobbyists....

We are attempting to overhaul the way government regulations are set, to make sure that they accomplish their objectives in the least burdensome way....

But even this beginning will fail if I do not enlist your help, and the help of your citizens.

For there is powerful resistance to any change in the status quo.

There is in Washington an iron triangle of bureaucracy, congressional committees and well-organized special interests who can mobilize strong opposition to the reforms we need. When the great majority of our people would benefit from change — such as Civil Service reform — and only a small minority is opposed, it is often only the voice of the minority that is heard.

As John Kennedy said:

"As every generation has had to disenthrall itself from an inheritance of truisms and stereotypes, so in our time we must move . . . to a new, difficult but essential confrontation with reality. . . . We cannot understand and attack our contemporary problems . . . if we are bound by traditional labels and worn-out slogans."

I believe strongly in our ability to solve problems together....

I only ask that you help me develop the kind of Federal government capable of fulfilling its responsibilities.... ∎

Carter's NATO Speech

President Carter pledged to leaders of the North Atlantic Treaty Organization May 31, 1978, that the United States will use nuclear weapons if necessary to protect European allies against a Soviet attack. Following is a transcript of the president's remarks at the Washington, D.C., NATO briefing:

Thank you, Mr. Secretary General.

These briefings illustrate the magnitude of the challenges we face. They do not justify alarm, but they should strengthen our resolve.

When I took office 16 months ago, I reviewed the condition of U.S. defenses. I found them strong, although needing improvement. In particular, I concluded that the United States should give top priority to Europe, especially the conventional defenses needed in the initial stages of a conflict.

I reached this conclusion for two reasons. First, the Warsaw Pact countries, especially the Soviet Union, have steadily expanded and modernized their conventional forces beyond any legitimate requirement for defense. They are now able to attack with large armored forces more rapidly than we previously believed. Second, although U.S. nuclear forces remain strong and are fundamental to deterrence, the long-recognized role of conventional forces in deterrence of war is increasingly important.

As a result, I directed the Secretary of Defense to strengthen initial conventional defense capacity in Europe. Of course, such efforts would amount to little unless accompanied by improvements in the conventional capacity of our NATO allies. European NATO countries, not the United States, provide the bulk of our military forces in Europe. Also, the competing demands of our free societies limit the portion of our resources we can use for defense. Therefore, we must coordinate our defense planning to make the best use of these limited resources.

From our discussions in London last year, I know that you share my view of the challenges we face. The answers we have developed together are impressive. We are all making significant real increases in our defense budgets. We are strengthening our national forces — and we will do more. Finally, we have designed a bold Long-Term Defense Program to pull together a more effective collective defense during the years ahead.

Nuclear Forces

As we improve our conventional defenses, we must remember that the strength of our strategic and theater nuclear forces is also necessary for deterrence and defense. These forces are — and will be — fully adequate. Arms control can make deterrence more stable and perhaps less burdensome — but it will not, in the foreseeable future, eliminate the need for nuclear forces.

For years, the Alliance has relied principally on American strategic forces for deterring nuclear attack on Europe. This coupling of American strategic forces to Europe is critical, for it means that an attack on Europe would have the full consequences of an attack on the United States. Let there be no misunderstanding. The United States is prepared to use *all* the forces necessary for the defense of the NATO area.

As an Alliance, we must continue to review our nuclear deterrence needs in light of developments in Soviet nuclear and conventional forces. As one result of the Long-Term Defense Program, the Nuclear Planning Group is examining in detail the modernizing of our theater nuclear forces, including the question of long-range nuclear systems. We need also to consider jointly the relation of long-range theater nuclear systems to arms control.

This will require considering the full scope of political and military issues, and being sure that we maintain the coupling of American strategic forces to the defense of Europe. As we examine this together, I assure you that the United States will protect the options before us as the SALT II negotiations move toward completion.

Conventional Forces

Let me now turn to conventional forces — the bulk of the Long-Term Defense Program. After all, our largest expenditures are for conventional, not nuclear, forces.

We must prepare to fight more effectively together as an Alliance. We must markedly improve our ability to work together on the battlefield. We should overcome unnecessary duplication in our national programs, thus buying more security for the same money.

That is what the Long-Term Defense Program is all about. It is an unprecedented attempt by NATO to look across a longer span of years than ever before. It seeks a more cooperative course, as the only sensible way to improve our defenses without unnecessary increases in defense spending. It lays out specific measures of Alliance cooperation. It is the blueprint we need, and we must carry it out vigorously.

Of course, each of us depends on legislative approval for particular programs and projects within the Long-Term Defense Program. Because we lead democracies, we cannot bind our people by fiat. We can, however, pledge to do what is necessary to secure this approval and make this program work.

The United States is already responding to many Long-Term Defense Program recommendations, particularly in the field of reinforcement. And the recommendations will receive the highest priority in our own national defense programming. In short, we will do our part in adapting or modifying U.S. programs to support the NATO Long-Term Defense Program. I am confident that you will take similar action.

Follow-Through

Finally, I want to mention the one remaining unresolved aspect of the Long-Term Defense Program. Although the program calls for new and unprecedented Alliance cooperation, no procedures have yet been devised for ensuring that it is carried out. We must avoid bold programs heartily endorsed — then largely ignored. The Report before us directs the Secretary General to present for national review what changes are essential for vigorous follow-through.

Both the NATO Task Forces and we Americans have made several specific proposals to this end. For example, we favor explicitly recognizing NATO's new focus on logistics. One way is to create a new Assistant Secretary General for Logistics. We also favor clear assignment of responsibility for each program to one NATO body. Where appropriate, we would prefer a major NATO command. But I do not ask that you discuss our proposals today. Instead, I ask that all Alliance leaders here today join me in calling for vigorous follow-through of the program.

In conclusion, let me state that we confront a unique opportunity to bring our national defense programs closer together. The result will be a more effective defense. The consequences will be greater security for our people. It is our responsibility not to let this opportunity pass. ∎

Annapolis Speech

Following is The New York Times *transcript of President Carter's speech June 7, 1978, to the graduating class at the U.S. Naval Academy, Annapolis, Md.:*

Admiral McKee, Governor Lee, distinguished guests, members of the graduating class and friends:

We do have many distinguished guests here today. I invited my old boss, Adm. Hyman Rickover, to come and join us. He sent word back that he would, of course, comply with my order as commander in chief, but he thought his work for the Navy in Washington was more important than listening to my speech. I was not surprised.

I am glad to be back for the Naval Academy graduation, although I return with a different rank.

I remember that 32 years ago I had the same experience that most of you are sharing today. I was not a midshipman officer. Most of you are not officers. I was thinking more about leave and marriage than I was about world events or a distant future. I would guess there are some among you who would feel the same.

I was quite disappointed with my first appointment. We drew lots for assignments and I had requested a new destroyer in the Pacific. I was assigned to the oldest ship in the Atlantic, the *U.S.S. Wyoming*, which was so dilapidated that because of safety purposes it was not permitted to come into Norfolk harbor alongside a pier, but had to anchor in isolation in Hampton Roads.

We had a distinguished speaker, Adm. Chester Nimitz, as will be the case with you, I don't remember a word he said.

My one hope was that the graduation services would be brief. As will be the case with you, I was disappointed. And I have to confess to you in confidence that at the time I did not expect to come back here later for the career which I eventually chose.

Seven years later I reluctantly left the Navy. But I can say in retrospect the Naval Academy and my service in the U.S. Navy was good preparation for the career which I eventually chose.

I congratulate the members of the Class of 1978. Although your education from the perspective of an older person has just begun, you have laid the foundation for a career that can be as rewarding and as challenging as any in the world.

Role of Modern Naval Officers

As officers in the modern Navy you will be actors in a worldwide political and military drama. You will be called upon not only to master the technicalities of military science and military leadership but also to have a sensitive understanding of the international community within which the Navy operates.

Today I want to discuss one of the most important aspects of that international context — the relationship between the world's two greatest powers, the United States of America and the Soviet Union.

We must realize that for a very long time our relationship with the Soviet Union will be competitive. That competition is to be constructive if we are successful. Instead it could be dangerous and politically disastrous.

Then our relationship must be cooperative as well. We must avoid excessive swings in the public mood in our country from euphoria, when things are going well, to despair, when they are not; from an exaggerated sense of compatibility with the Soviet Union to open expression of hostility.

Detente Termed Central to Peace

Detente between our two countries is central to world peace. It is important for the world, for the American public and for you as future leaders of the Navy to understand its complex and sensitive nature.

The word detente can be simplistically defined as the easing of tension between nations. The word is in practice, however, further defined by experience as those nations evolve new means by which they can live with each other in peace. To be stable, to be supported by the American people and to be a basis for widening the scope of cooperation, detente must be broadly defined and truly reciprocal.

Both nations must exercise restraint in troubled areas and in troubled times. Both must honor meticulously those agreements which have already been reached to widen cooperation, naturally, and mutually limit nuclear arms production, permit the free movement of people and expression of ideas and to protect human rights.

Neither of us should entertain the notion that military supremacy can be attained or that transient military advantage can be politically exploited.

Our principal goal is to help shape a world which is more responsive to the desire of people everywhere for economic well-being, social justice, political self-determination and basic human rights. We seek a world of peace but such a world must accommodate diversity — social, political and ideological. Only then can there be a genuine cooperation among nations and among cultures.

We desire to dominate no one. We will continue to widen our cooperation with the positive new forces in the world. We want to increase our collaboration with the Soviet Union, but also with the emerging nations, with the nations of Eastern Europe and with the People's Republic of China.

We are particularly dedicated to genuine self-determination and majority rule in those areas of the world where these goals have not yet been attained.

Advantages of Cooperation

Our long-term objectives must be to convince the Soviet Union of the advantages of cooperation and of the cost of disruptive behavior.

We remember that the United States and the Soviet Union were allies in the Second World War. One of the great historical accomplishments of the U.S. Navy was to guide and protect the tremendous shipments of armament and supplies from our country to Murmansk and to other Soviet ports in support of a joint effort to meet the Nazi threat.

In the agony of that massive conflict, 20 million Soviet lives were lost. Millions more who live in the Soviet Union still recall the horror and the hunger of that time. I'm convinced that the people of the Soviet Union want peace. I cannot believe that they could possibly want war.

Through the years our nation has sought accommodation with the Soviet Union, as demonstrated by the Austrian Peace Treaty, the Quadripartite Agreement concerning Berlin, the termination of nuclear testing in the atmosphere, joint scientific explorations in space, trade agreements, the antiballistic missile treaty, the interim agreement on strategic offensive armaments and the limited test-ban agreement.

Efforts on Arms Treaty Continue

Efforts still continue with negotiations toward a SALT II agreement, a comprehensive test ban against nuclear explosives, reductions in conventional arms transfers to other countries, the prohibition against attack on satellites in space, an agreement to stabilize the level of force deployment in the Indian Ocean, and increased trade and scientific and cultural exchange.

We must be willing to explore such avenues of cooperation despite the basic issues which divide us. The risks of nuclear war alone propel us in this direction.

The numbers and destructive potential of nuclear weapons has been increasing at an alarming rate. That is why a SALT agreement, which enhances the security of both nations, is of fundamental importance.

We and the Soviet Union are negotiating in good faith almost every day because we both know that a failure to succeed would precipitate a resumption of a massive nuclear arms race.

I'm glad to report to you today that the prospects for a SALT II agreement are good.

Beyond this major effort, improved trade and technological and cultural exchange are among the immediate benefits of cooperation between our two countries. However, these efforts to cooperate do not erase the significant differences between us.

What are these differences? To the Soviet Union, detente seems to mean a continuing aggressive struggle for political advantage and increased influence in a variety of ways. The Soviet Union apparently sees military power and military assistance as the best means of expanding their influence abroad. Obviously, areas of instability in the world provide a tempting target for this effort. And all too often they seem ready to exploit any such opportunity.

As became apparent in Korea, in Angola, and also, as you know, in Ethiopia more recently, the Soviets prefer to use proxy forces to achieve their purposes.

Buildup Is Considered Excessive

To other nations throughout the world, the Soviets' military buildup appears to be excessive far beyond any legitimate requirements to defend themselves or to defend their allies. For more than 15 years they have maintained this program of military growth, investing almost 15 percent of their total gross national product in armaments, and this sustained growth continues.

The abuse of basic human rights in their own country, in violation of the agreement which was reached at Helsinki, has earned them the condemnation of people everywhere who love freedom. By their actions they have demonstrated that the Soviet system cannot tolerate freely expressed ideas or notions of loyal opposition and the free movement of people. The Soviet Union attempts to export a totalitarian and repressive form of government resulting in a closed society.

Some of these characteristics and goals create problems for the Soviet Union. Outside their tightly controlled bloc, the Soviet Union has difficult political relations with other nations. Their cultural bonds with others are few and frayed. Their form of government is becoming increasingly unattractive to other nations so that even Marxist-Leninist groups no longer look on the Soviet Union as a model to be imitated.

Many countries are becoming very concerned that the nonaligned movement is being subverted by Cuba, which is obviously closely aligned with the Soviet Union and dependent upon the Soviets for economic sustenance and for military and political guidance and direction.

Although the Soviet Union has the second largest economic system in the world, its growth is slowing greatly and its standard of living does not compare favorably with that of other nations at the same equivalent stage of economic development.

Soviet Agricultural Lag

Agricultural production still remains a serious problem for the Soviet Union so that in times of average or certainly adverse conditions for crop production, they must turn to us or turn to other nations for food supplies.

We in our country are in a much more favorable position. Our industrial base and our productivity are unmatched. Our scientific and technological capability is superior to all others. Our alliances with other free nations are strong and growing stronger, and our military capability is now and will be second to none.

In contrast to the Soviet Union, we are surrounded by friendly neighbors and wide seas. Our social structure is stable and cohesive and our foreign policy enjoys bipartisan public support, which gives it continuity. We are also strong because of what we stand for as a nation — the realistic chance for every person to build a better life, protection by both law and custom from arbitrary exercise of government power, the right of every individual to speak out, to participate fully in government and to share political power.

U.S. Social System Praised

Our philosophy is based on personal freedom, the most powerful of all ideas, and our democratic way of life warrants the admiration and emulation by other people throughout the world.

Our work for human rights makes us part of an international tide growing in force. We are strengthened by being part of it.

Our growing economic strength is also a major political factor, a potential influence for the benefit of others.

Our gross national product exceeds that of all nine nations combined in the European Economic Community and it is twice as great as that of the Soviet Union.

Additionally we are now learning how to use our resources more wisely, creating a

new harmony between our people and our environment.

Our analysis of American military strength also furnishes a basis for confidence. We know that neither the United States nor the Soviet Union can launch a nuclear assault on the other without suffering a devastating counterattack which could destroy the aggressor nation.

Missile Strength Compared

Although the Soviet Union has more missile launchers, greater throw-weight and more continental air defense capabilities, the United States has more warheads, generally greater accuracy, more heavy bombers, a more balanced nuclear force, better missile submarines and superior antisubmarine warfare capabilities.

A successful SALT II agreement will give both nations equal but lower ceilings on missile launchers and also on missiles with multiple warheads.

We envision in SALT III an even greater mutual reduction in nuclear weapons. With essential nuclear equivalents, relative conventional force strength has now become more important. The fact is that the military capability of the United States and its allies is adequate to meet any forseeable threat. It is possible that each side tends to exaggerate the military capability of the other.

Accurate analyses are important as a basis for making decisions for the future. False or excessive estimates of Soviet strength or American weakness contribute to the effectiveness of the Soviet propaganda effort.

For example, recently, alarming news reports of the military budget proposals for the U.S. Navy ignored the fact that we have the highest defense budget in history and the largest portion of this will go to the Navy.

You men are joining a long tradition of superior leadership, seamanship and ship design. And I am confident that the U.S. Navy has no peer nor equal on the high seas today, and you, I and others will always keep the Navy strong.

Let there be no doubt about our present and future strength. This brief assessment, which I have just made, shows that we need not be overly concerned about our ability to compete and to compete successfully. Certainly there is no cause for alarm. The healthy self-criticism and the free debate which are essential in a democracy should never be confused with weakness or despair or lack of purpose.

U.S. Foreign Policy

What are the principal elements of American foreign policy to the Soviet Union? Let me outline them very briefly:

We will continue to maintain equivalent nuclear strength because we believe that, in the absence of worldwide nuclear disarmament, such equivalency is the least threatening and the most stable situation for the world.

We will maintain a prudent and sustained level of military spending keyed to a stronger NATO, more mobile forces and undiminished presence in the Pacific.

We and our allies must and will be able to meet any forseeable challenge to our security from either strategic nuclear forces or from conventional forces.

America has the capability to honor this commitment without excessive sacrifice on the part of our citizens and that commitment to military strength will be honored.

Looking beyond our alliances we will support worldwide and regional organizations which are dedicated to enhancing international peace, like the United Nations, the Organization of American States and the Organization for African Unity.

Attitudes on African Issue

In Africa we and our African friends want to see a continent that is free of the dominance of outside powers, free of the bitterness of racial injustice, free of conflict and free of the burdens of poverty and hunger and disease.

We are convinced that the best way to work toward these objectives is through affirmative policies that recognize African realities and that recognize African aspirations.

The persistent and increasing military involvement of the Soviet Union and Cuba in Africa could deny this hopeful vision.

We are deeply concerned about the threat to regional peace and to the autonomy of countries within which these foreign troops seem permanently to be stationed. That is why I have spoken out on this subject today and that is why I and the American people will support African efforts to contain such intrusions as we have done recently in Zaire.

I urge again that all other powers join us in emphasizing works of peace rather than the weapons of war.

Wider Exchange With Soviets Sought

In their assistance to Africa, let the Soviet Union now join us in seeking a peaceful and a speech transition to majority rule in Rhodesia and in Namibia. Let us see efforts to resolve peacefully the disputes in Eritrea and in Angola. Let us all work not to divide and to seek domination in Africa but to help those nations to fulfill their great potential.

We will seek peace, better communication and understanding, cultural and scientific exchange and increased trade with the Soviet Union and with other nations.

We will attempt to prevent the proliferation of nuclear weapons among those nations not now having this capability. We will continue to negotiate constructively and persistently for a fair strategic arms limitation agreement.

We know that no ideological victories can be won by either side by the use of nuclear weapons. We have no desire to link the negotiation for a SALT agreement with other competitive relationships nor to impose other special conditions on the process.

In a democratic society, however, where public opinion is an integral factor in the shaping and implementation of foreign policy, we do recognize that tensions, sharp disputes or threats to peace will complicate the quest for a successful agreement.

This is not a matter of our preference but a simple recognition of fact. The Soviet Union can choose either confrontation or cooperation. The United States is adequately prepared to meet either choice. We would prefer cooperation through a detente that increasingly involves similar restraints for both sides, similar readiness to resolve disputes by negotiation and not by violence, similar willingness to compete peacefully and not militarily.

Anything less than that is likely to undermine detente and this is why I hope that no one will underestimate the concerns which I have expressed today.

A competition without restraint and without shared rules will escalate into graver tensions and our relationship as a whole with the Soviet Union will suffer.

I do not wish this to happen and I do not believe that Mr. Brezhnev desires it. And this is why it is time for us to speak frankly and to face the problem squarely by a combination of adequate American strength, of quiet self-restraint in the use of it, of a refusal to believe in the inevitability of war and of a patient and persistent development of all the peaceful alternatives we hope eventually to lead international society into a more stable, more peaceful and a more hopeful future.

Role to Be Played by Midshipmen

You and I leave here today to do our common duty, protecting our nation's vital interests by peaceful means if possible, by resolute action if necessary. We go forth sobered by these responsibilities but confident of our strength. We go forth knowing that our nation's goal, peace, security, liberty for ourselves and for others, will determine our future and that we together can prevail.

To attain these goals, our nation will require exactly those qualities of courage, self-sacrifice, idealism and self-discipline which you as midshipmen have learned here at Annapolis as well. That is why your nation expects so much of you and that is why you have so much to give.

I leave you now with my congratulations and with a prayer to God that both you and I will prove worthy of the task that is before us and the nation which we have sworn to serve. ▌

Health Plan Order

Following is President Carter's July 29 letter directing Secretary of Health, Education and Welfare Joseph A. Califano Jr. to draft a health

plan to be submitted to Congress in 1979:

July 29, 1978
Presidential Directive/DPS-3
TO: **The Secretary of Health, Education and Welfare**
SUBJECT: **National Health Plan**

I have consistently expressed my support for the goal of a universal, comprehensive national health plan to contain skyrocketing health costs and to provide all Americans with coverage for basic health services and with protection from catastrophic expenses.

Such a plan would be the cornerstone of a broader national health policy designed to improve the health of Americans by reducing environmental and occupational hazards and encouraging health enhancing personal behavior, as well as by improving the effectiveness of our medical care system.

The current health care system has significant defects which must be remedied:

● The health care system is highly inflationary. Spending in the health care industry — the nation's third largest industry — has been rising at an annual rate of 12% with little improvement in the health of Americans. These expenditures cannot be successfully contained under current health delivery and financing methods, which produce unnecessary hospitalization, over-reliance on expensive technology and inadequate preventive care.

● At least 20 million Americans have no health insurance.

● Another 65 million Americans face potential bankruptcy because they lack insurance protecting them against catastrophic medical expenses.

● Health resources are unevenly distributed across the country resulting in significant gaps in vital medical services for many residents of rural and inner city areas.

In pursuing the goal of a comprehensive national health plan, I also wish to draw on the strengths of the American health care system:

● American health care professionals and hospitals are among the finest in the world and deliver dedicated, high quality medical care.

● A growing number of Americans have private health insurance. American business increasingly is paying for health coverage for its employees.

● Various government programs have provided an opportunity for millions of elderly, poor and geographically isolated Americans to obtain quality health care.

In past months you and other members of my Administration have been exploring the most effective means of fulfilling my commitment to a comprehensive national health plan. You have considered a broad range of options. However, before I submit legislation to the Congress, I want to be certain that the plan is consistent

with our efforts to control inflation in the health care sector and the general economy. Before you send me final recommendations for a national health plan, you should analyze the issues of cost control and health system reform in greater depth. The American people would not accept, and I will not propose, any health care plan which is inflationary.

At the same time, the American people must recognize that if we fail to act, health expenditures will continue to soar. In 1977, health expenditures were $162 billion; they are expected to reach $320 billion by 1983. A comprehensive national health plan will provide a critical opportunity to mount a national effort to bring the system under control.

I am directing you to address these concerns as you proceed to develop in greater detail a national health plan for the American people. The plan must improve the health care system, and combat inflation by controlling spiralling health care costs. To achieve these objectives, the plan, when fully implemented, should conform to the following principles.

1. The plan should assure that all Americans have comprehensive health care coverage, including protection against catastrophic medical expenses.

2. The plan should make quality health care available to all Americans. It should seek to eliminate those aspects of the current health system that often cause the poor to receive substandard care.

3. The plan should assure that all Americans have freedom of choice in the selection of physicians, hospitals, and health delivery systems.

4. The plan must support our efforts to control inflation in the economy by reducing unnecessary health care spending. The plan should include aggressive cost containment measures and should also strengthen competitive forces in the health care sector.

5. The plan should be designed so that additional public and private expenditures for improved health benefits and coverage will be substantially offset by savings from greater efficiency in the health care system.

6. The plan will involve no additional federal spending until FY 1983, because of tight fiscal constraints and the need for careful planning and implementation. Thereafter, the plan should be phased in gradually. As the plan moves from phase to phase, consideration should be given to such factors as the economic and administrative experience under prior phases. The experience of other government programs, in which expenditures far exceeded initial projections, must not be repeated.

The plan should be financed through multiple sources, including government funding and contributions from employers and employees. Careful consideration should be given to the other demands on government budgets, the existing tax burdens on the American people, and the ability of many consumers to share a moderate portion of the cost of their care.

8. The plan should include a significant role for the private insurance industry, with appropriate government regulation.

9. The plan should provide resources and develop payment methods to promote such major reforms in delivering health care services as substantially increasing the availability of ambulatory and preventive services, attracting personnel to underserved rural and urban areas, and encouraging the use of prepaid health plans.

10. The plan should assure consumer representation throughout its operation.

I am directing you to develop a tentative plan as soon as possible which embodies these principles and which will serve as the basis for in-depth consultation with the Congress, State and local officials, interest groups, and consumer representatives. You should then provide me with detailed recommendations so that I can make final decisions on the legislation I will submit to the Congress next year. To respond fully to my economic and budgetary concerns, you should develop alternative methods for phased implementation of the plan.

Jimmy Carter ∎

Camp David Remarks

Following is the White House transcript of remarks Sept. 17, 1978, between President Carter, Israeli Prime Minister Menachem Begin and Egyptian President Anwar Sadat at the conclusion of the Camp David summit meeting:

President Carter

When we first arrived at Camp David, the first thing upon which we agreed was to ask the people of the world to pray that our negotiations would be successful. Those prayers have been answered far beyond any expectations. We are privileged to witness tonight a significant achievement in the cause of peace, an achievement none thought possible a year ago, or even a month ago, an achievement that reflects the courage and wisdom of these two leaders.

Through 13 long days at Camp David, we have seen them display determination and vision and flexibility which was needed to make this agreement come to pass. All of us owe them our gratitude and respect. They know that they will always have my personal admiration.

There are still great difficulties that remain and many hard issues to be settled. The questions that have brought warfare and bitterness to the Middle East for the last 30 years will not be settled overnight. But we should all recognize the substantial achievements that have been made.

One of the agreements that President Sadat and Prime Minister Begin are sign-

ing tonight is entitled, "A Framework For Peace in the Middle East." (Applause)

This framework concerns the principles and some specifics in the most substantive way which will govern a comprehensive peace settlement. It deals specifically with the future of the West Bank and Gaza, and the need to resolve the Palestinian problem in all its aspects. The framework document proposes a five-year transitional period in the West Bank and Gaza during which the Israeli military government will be withdrawn and a self-governing authority will be elected with full autonomy.

It also provides for Israeli forces to remain in specified locations during this period to protect Israel's security.

The Palestinians will have the right to participate in the determination of their own future, in negotiations which will resolve the final status of the West Bank and Gaza, and then to produce an Israeli-Jordanian peace treaty.

These negotiations will be based on all the provisions and all the principles of the United Nations Security Council Resolution 242. And it provides that Israel may live in peace within secure and recognized borders.

This great aspiration of Israel has been certified without constraint with the greatest degree of enthusiasm by President Sadat, the leader of one of the greatest nations on earth. (Applause)

The other document is entitled, "Framework For the Conclusion of a Peace Treaty," between Egypt and Israel.

It provides for the full exercise of Egyptian sovereignty over the Sinai. It calls for the full withdrawal of Israeli forces from the Sinai; and after an interim withdrawal which will be accomplished very quickly, the establishment of normal, peaceful relations between the two countries, including diplomatic relations. (Applause)

Together with accompanying letters, which we will make public tomorrow, these two Camp David agreements provide the basis for progress and peace throughout the Middle East.

There is one issue on which agreement has not been reached. Egypt states that the agreement to remove Israeli settlements from Egyptian territory is a prerequisite to a peace treaty. Israel states that the issue of Israeli settlements should be resolved during the peace negotiations. That is a substantial difference.

Within the next two weeks, the Knesset will decide on the issue of these settlements.

Tomorrow night, I will go before the Congress to explain these agreements more fully, and to talk about their implications for the United States, and for the world. For the moment, and in closing, I want to speak more personally about my admiration for all of those who have taken part in this process, and my hope that the promise of this moment will be fulfilled.

During the last two weeks the members of all three delegations have spent endless hours, day and night, talking, negotiating, grappling with problems that have divided their people for 30 years. Whenever there was a danger that human energy would fail, or patience would be exhausted, or good will would run out — and there were such moments — these two leaders and the able advisers in all delegations found the resources within them to keep the chances for peace alive.

Well, the long days at Camp David are over. But many months of difficult negotiations still lie ahead.

I hope that the foresight and the wisdom that have made this session a success will guide these leaders and the leaders of all nations as they continue the process toward peace.

Thank you very much. (Applause)

President Sadat

Dear President Carter, in this historic moment, I would like to express to you my heartfelt congratulations and appreciation. For long days and nights, you devoted your time and energy to the pursuit of peace. You have been most courageous when you took the gigantic step of convening this meeting. The challenge was great, and the risks were high, but so was your determination.

You made a commitment to be a full partner in the peace process. I am happy to say that you have honored your commitment.

The signing of the framework for the comprehensive peace settlement has a significance far beyond the event. It signals the emergence of a new peace initiative with the American nation in the heart of the entire process.

In the weeks ahead, important decisions have to be made if we are to proceed on the road to peace. We have to reaffirm the faith of the Palestinian people in the ideal of peace.

The continuation of your active role is indispensable. We need your help and the support of the American people. Let me seize this opportunity to thank each and every American for his genuine interest in the cause of people in the Middle East.

Dear friend, we came to Camp David with all the good will and faith we possessed, and we left Camp David a few minutes ago with a renewed sense of hope and inspiration. We are looking forward to the days ahead with an added determination to pursue the noble goal of peace.

Your able assistants spared no effort to bring out this happy conclusion. We appreciate the spirit and dedication. Our hosts at Camp David and the State of Maryland were most generous and hospitable. To each one of them and to all those who are watching this great event, I say thank you.

Let us join in a prayer to God Almighty to guide our path. Let us pledge to make the spirit of Camp David a new chapter in the history of our nation.

Thank you, Mr. President. (Applause)

Prime Minister Begin

Mr. President of the United States, Mr. President of the Arab Republic of Egypt, ladies and gentlemen: The Camp David conference should be renamed. It was the Jimmy Carter Conference. (Applause)

The President took an initiative most imaginative in our time and brought President Sadat and myself and our colleagues and friends and advisers together under one roof. In itself it was a great achievement.

The President took a great risk on himself and did it with great civil courage, and it was a famous French field commander who said that it is much more difficult to show civil courage than military courage.

And the President worked. As far as my historic experience is concerned, I think that he worked harder than our forefathers did in Egypt, building the pyramids. (Laughter, applause)

Yes, indeed, he worked day and night, and so did we — (laughter) —

THE PRESIDENT: Amen.

PRIME MINISTER BEGIN: Day and night. We used to go to bed at Camp David between 3:00 and 4:00 o'clock in the morning, arise, as we are used to since our boyhood, at 5:00 or 6:00, and continue working.

The President showed interest in every section, every paragraph, every sentence, every word, every letter — (laughter) — of the framework agreements.

We had some difficult moments, as usually, there are some crises in negotiations; as usually, somebody gives a hint that perhaps he would like to pick up and go home. (Laughter) It is all usual. But ultimately, ladies and gentlemen, the President of the United States won the day. And peace now celebrates victory for the nations of Egypt and Israel and for all mankind.

Mr. President, we, the Israelis, thank you from the bottom of our hearts for all you have done for the sake of peace, for which we prayed and yearned more than 30 years. The Jewish people suffered much, too much. And, therefore, peace to us is a striving, coming innermost from our heart and soul.

Now when I came here to the Camp David conference, I said perhaps as a result of our work, one day people will, in every corner of the world, be able to say "Habemus pacem" in the spirit of these days. Can we say so tonight? Not yet. We still have to go the road until my friend President Sadat and I sign the peace treaties.

We promised each other that we shall do so within three months.

Mr. President, tonight, at this celebration of the great historic event, let us promise each other that we shall do it

earlier than within three months. (Laughter, applause)

Mr. President, you inscribed your name forever in the history of two ancient civilized peoples, the people of Egypt and the people of Israel.

Thank you, Mr. President.

THE PRESIDENT: Thank you very much. (Applause)

PRIME MINISTER BEGIN: I would like to say a few words about my friend, President Sadat. We met for the first time in our lives last November in Jerusalem. He came to us as a guest, a former enemy, and during our first meeting, we became friends.

In the Jewish teachings, there is a tradition that the greatest achievement of a human being is to turn his enemy into a friend, and this we do in reciprocity. Since then, we had some difficult days. (Laughter) I am not going now to tell you the saga of those days. Everything belongs to the past. Today, I visited President Sadat in his cabin because in Camp David you don't have houses, you only have cabins. (Laughter) He then came to visit me. We shook hands. And, thank God, we again could have said to each other, "You are my friend." (Applause)

And, indeed, we shall go on working and understanding, and with friendship and with good will. We will still have problems to solve. Camp David proved that any problem can be solved, if there is good will and understanding and some wisdom.

May I thank my own colleagues and friends, the Foreign Minister, the Finance Minister; Professor Barak who was the Attorney General. Now he is going to be His Honor, the Justice of the Supreme Court, the Israeli Brandeis and Dr. Rosenne and our wonderful Ambassador to the United States, Mr. Simcha Dinitz, and all our friends, because without them, that achievement wouldn't have been possible.

I express my thanks to all the members of the American delegation, headed by the Secretary of State, a man whom we love and respect. So I express my thanks to all the members of the Egyptian delegation who worked so hard together with us, headed by Deputy Prime Minister, Mr. Touhamy, for all they have done to achieve this moment. It is a great moment in the history of our nations and indeed of mankind.

I looked for a precedent; I didn't find it. It was a unique conference, perhaps one of the most important since the Vienna Conference in the 19th century; perhaps.

Now, ladies and gentlemen, allow me to turn to my own people from the White House in my own native tongue.

(Brief remarks in Hebrew)

Thank you, ladies and gentlemen. (Applause)

President Carter

The first document that we will sign is entitled, "A Framework For Peace in the Middle East Agreed at Camp David," and

the text of these two documents will be released tomorrow. The documents will be signed by President Sadat and Prime Minister Begin. It will be witnessed by me.

We have to exchange three documents that we will all sign three times for this one.

I might say that the first document is quite comprehensive in nature, encompassing a framework by which Israel can later negotiate peace treaties between herself and Lebanon, Syria, Jordan, as well as the outline of this document that we will now sign.

As you will later see, in studying the documents, it also provides for the realization of the hopes and dreams of the people who live in the West Bank and Gaza Strip and will assure Israel peace in the generations ahead.

This second document is the one relating to a framework for a peace treaty between Egypt and Israel. This is the document that calls for the completion of the peace treaty negotiations within three months. I have noticed the challenge extended by these two gentlemen to each other. They will complete within three months — I might say that this document encompasses almost all of the issues between the two countries and resolves those issues. A few lines remain to be drawn on maps and the question of the settlements is to be resolved. Other than that, most of the major issues are resolved already in this document.

We will now sign this document as well.

(Signing of document.)

THE PRESIDENT: Thank you very much. (Applause) ∎

Speech on Middle East

Following is the prepared text of President Carter's Sept. 18, 1978, address to Congress:

It has been more than 2,000 years since there was peace between Egypt and a free Jewish nation. If our present expectations are realized, this year we shall see such peace.

I would like to give tribute to the two men who have made this impossible dream now become a real possibility — the two great national leaders with whom I have met for the last two weeks at Camp David — President Anwar Sadat and Prime Minister Menachem Begin. At Camp David we sought a peace which is not only of vital importance to their own two nations, but to all the people of the Middle East — to all the people of the United States — indeed, to the rest of the world as well.

The world prayed for the success of our efforts, and those prayers have been answered.

I have come here tonight to discuss what these strong leaders have accomplished — and what it means for all of us.

The United States has had no choice but to be concerned about the Middle East, and to use our influence and efforts to advance the cause of peace. For the last 30 years, through four wars, the people of this troubled region have paid a terrible price in suffering, division, hatred and bloodshed. No two nations have suffered more than Israel and Egypt. But the dangers and the costs of conflict in this region for our nation have been great as well. We have longstanding friendships with the nations and people of the region, and profound moral commitments which are deeply rooted in our values as a people.

'Vital to Our Nation'

The strategic location of these countries and the resources they possess mean that events in the Middle East directly affect people everywhere. We and our friends could not be indifferent if a hostile power were to establish domination there. In few areas of the world is there a greater risk that a local conflict could spread among other nations and then erupt into confrontation between the superpowers. Our people have come to understand that unfamiliar names — Sinai, Aqaba, Sharm el Sheikh, Ras en Naqb, Gaza, the West Bank of the Jordan — can have a direct and immediate bearing on our well-being as a nation and our hope for a peaceful world.

That is why we cannot be idle bystanders, why we have been full partners in the search for peace, and why it is so vital to our nation that these meetings have been a success.

Through the long years of conflict, four main issues have divided the parties.

One is the nature of peace — whether peace will mean simply that the guns are silenced, the bombs stop falling and the tanks cease to roll, or whether it will mean that the nations of the Middle East can deal with each other as neighbors and equals, with the full range of diplomatic, cultural, economic and human relations between them. The Camp David agreement has defined such relationships for Israel and her neighbors.

The second main issue is providing for the security of all the parties involved, including Israel, so that none of them need fear attack or military threats from any other. When implemented, the Camp David agreement will provide for such security.

Third is the question of an agreement on secure and recognized boundaries, the end of military occupation, and the granting of self-government or return to other nations of territories occupied by Israel during the 1967 conflict.

The Camp David agreement provides for the realization of these goals.

And finally, there is the painful human question of the fate of the Palestinians who live or who have lived in this disputed region. The Camp David agreement guarantees that the Palestinian people may participate in the resolution of the Palestinian problem in all its aspects.

Over the last 18 months there has been progress on some of these issues. Egypt and

Israel came close to agreeing about the first issue — the nature of peace. They saw that the second and third — withdrawal and security — were intimately connected. But fundamental divisions remained in other areas — about the fate of the Palestinians, the future of the West Bank and Gaza, and the future of Israeli settlements in occupied Arab territories.

Sadat Initiative

We all remember the hopes for peace that were inspired by President Sadat's visit to Jerusalem last November, by the warm response of Prime Minister Begin and the Israeli people and by the mutual promise that there would be no more war. Those hopes were sustained when Prime Minister Begin reciprocated by visiting Ismailia on Christmas Day.

That progress continued, at a slower and slower rate, through the early part of this year, but by early summer the negotiations had come to a standstill once again. It was this stalemate and the prospect of an even worse future that prompted me to invite both President Sadat and Prime Minister Begin to meet me at Camp David.

It is impossible to overstate the courage of these two men, or the foresight they have shown. Only through high ideals, through compromises of words and not of principle, and through a willingness to look deep into the human heart and to understand one another, can progress ever be made.

That is what these men and their wise and diligent advisers have done during these last 13 days.

When this conference began, I said that the prospects for success were remote. Enormous barriers of ancient history, nationalism and suspicion would have to be overcome if we were to meet our objectives.

But President Sadat and Prime Minister Begin have overcome those barriers, exceeded those expectations, and signed two agreements that hold out the possibility of resolving issues that history had taught us could not be resolved.

'Framework for Peace'

The first of the two documents is entitled "A Framework for Peace in the Middle East Agreed at Camp David." It deals with comprehensive settlement between Israel and all her neighbors, as well as the difficult question of the Palestinian people and the future of the West Bank and Gaza.

The agreement provides a basis for the resolution of issues involving the West Bank and Gaza over the next five years. It outlines a process of change which is in keeping with Arab hopes, while also respecting Israel's vital security interests. The Israeli military government over those areas will be withdrawn and will be replaced with a self-government with full autonomy. Israeli forces will also be withdrawn and redeployed into specified locations to

protect Israel's security. The Palestinians will further participate in determining their own future through talks in which elected representatives of the inhabitants of the West Bank and Gaza will negotiate with Egypt, Israel and Jordan to determine the final status of the West Bank and Gaza.

Israel has agreed that the legitimate rights of the Palestinian people will be recognized. After the signing of this framework and during the negotiations concerning Palestinian self-government, no new Israeli settlements will be established in this area. The issue of future settlements will be decided among the negotiating parties.

The final status of the West Bank and Gaza will be decided by the end of the five-year transitional period, as part of a negotiation which will also produce a peace treaty between Israel and Jordan. These negotiations will be based on all the provisions and principles of U.N. Security Council Resolution 242. The agreement on the final status of these areas will be submitted to a vote by the representatives of the inhabitants of the West Bank and Gaza, and they will have the right, for the first time in their history, to decide how they will govern themselves. We also believe there should be a just settlement of the problems of displaced persons and refugees, which takes into account appropriate U.N. resolutions.

Finally, this document also outlines a variety of security arrangements to reinforce peace between Israel and its neighbors.

This is, indeed, a comprehensive and fair framework for peace in the Middle East.

'Framework for Treaty'

The second agreement is entitled "A Framework for the Conclusion of a Peace Treaty Between Egypt and Israel." It returns to Egypt the full exercise of its sovereignty over the Sinai peninsula and establishes several security zones for the protection of all parties. It also provides that Egypt will extend full diplomatic recognition to Israel at the time Israel withdraws her armed forces from most of the Sinai, which will take place between three and nine months after the conclusion of the peace treaty. The treaty is to be fully negotiated and signed no later than three months from now. Prime Minister Begin and President Sadat have now challenged each other to conclude the treaty even earlier. This will be a wonderful Christmas present for the world. Complete withdrawal of all Israeli forces will take place no more than three years after the treaty has been signed.

While both parties are in complete agreement on the goals I have just described, there is one issue on which agreement has not been reached. Egypt states that agreement to remove Israeli settlements from Egyptian territory is a prerequisite to a peace treaty. Israel states that the issue of the Israeli settlements should be resolved during the peace negotiations. Within two weeks the Knesset [Israeli parliament] will decide on the issue of the settlements. Our own government's position on this issue is well-known and has been consistent. It is my strong hope that the question of Israeli settlements on Egyptian territory will not be the final obstacle to peace.

None of us should underestimate the historic importance of what has been done. This is the first time that an Arab and an Israeli leader have signed a comprehensive framework for peace. It contains the seeds of a time when the Middle East, with all its vast potential, may be a land of human richness and fulfillment, rather than of bitterness and conflict. No region of the world has greater natural and human resources — and nowhere have they been more heavily weighed down by hatred and war. These agreements hold out the real possibility that this burden might be lifted.

Obstacles Remain

But we must also not forget the magnitude of the obstacles that remain. The summit exceeded our expectations — but we know that it left many difficult issues still to be resolved. These issues will require careful negotiation in the months to come.

The Egyptian and Israeli people must recognize the tangible benefits that peace will bring, and support the decisions their leaders have made so that a secure and peaceful future can be achieved. The American public must also offer its full support to those who have difficult decisions still to make.

What lies ahead for all of us is to recognize the statesmanship that President Sadat and Prime Minister Begin have shown and to invite others to follow their example. I have already invited the other leaders of the Arab world to help sustain progress toward a comprehensive peace.

We must also join in an effort to bring to an end the conflict and terrible suffering in Lebanon. We need to consult closely with the Arab leaders, and I am pleased to say that King Hussein of Jordan and King Khalid of Saudi Arabia have now agreed to receive Secretary [of State Cyrus R.] Vance, who will be leaving tomorrow to explain to them the terms of the Camp David agreement and to secure their support for the realization of the new hopes and dreams of the people of the Middle East.

For many years, the Middle East has been a textbook for pessimism, a demonstration that diplomatic ingenuity was no match for intractable human conflicts. Today we are privileged to see the chance for one of the bright moments in human history — a chance that may open the way to peace. We have a chance for peace because these two brave leaders found within themselves the willingness to work together to seek a lasting peace; for that, I hope you will share my prayer of thanks and my hope that the promise of this moment shall be fully realized.

The prayers at Camp David were the same as those of the shepherd King David who prayed in the 85th Psalm:

Wilt thou not revive us again that thy people may rejoice in thee?
I will hear what God the Lord will speak: for he will speak peace unto his people, and to his saints: but let them not turn again to folly. ∎

Anti-Inflation Speech - 2

Following is the text of President Carter's Oct. 24, 1978, nationally televised speech in which he outlined his program to combat inflation.

Good evening.

I want to have a frank talk with you tonight about our most serious domestic problem. That problem is inflation. Inflation can threaten all the economic gains we have made, and it can stand in the way of what we want to achieve in the future.

This has been a long-time threat.

For the last ten years, the annual inflation rate in the United States has averaged 6.5 percent, and during the three years before my inauguration, it had increased to an average of 8 percent.

Inflation has, therefore, been a serious problem for me ever since I became president. We have tried to control it, but we have not been successful. It is time for all of us to make a greater and a more coordinated effort.

If inflation gets worse, several things will happen. Your purchasing power will continue to decline, and most of the burden will fall on those who can least afford it. Our national productivity will suffer. The value of our dollar will continue to fall in world trade.

We have made good progress in putting our people back to work over the past 21 months. We have created more than 6 million new jobs for American workers. We have reduced the unemployment rate by about 25 percent, and we will continue our efforts to reduce unemployment further, especially among our young people and minorities.

But I must tell you tonight that inflation threatens this progress. If we do not get inflation under control, we will not be able to reduce unemployment further, and we may even slide backward.

No Simple Solution

I do not have all the answers. Nobody does.

Perhaps there is no complete and adequate answer, but I want to let you know that fighting inflation will be a central preoccupation of mine during the months ahead, and I want to arouse our Nation to join me in this effort.

There are two simplistic and familiar answers which are sometimes proposed — simple, familiar, and too extreme. One of these answers is to impose a complicated scheme of Federal government wage and price controls on our entire free economic system.

The other is a deliberate recession, which would throw millions of people out of work.

Both of these extreme proposals would not work and they must be rejected.

I have spent many hours in the last few months reviewing with my own advisors and with a number of outside experts every proposal, every suggestion, every possibility for eliminating inflation.

If there is one thing I have learned beyond any doubt, it is that there is no single solution for inflation.

What we have, instead, is a number of partial remedies. Some of them will help, others may not. But we have no choice but to use the best approaches we have — and to maintain a constant search for additional steps which may be effective.

I want to discuss with you tonight some of the approaches we have been able to develop. They involve action by government, business, labor and every other sector of our economy. Some of these factors are under my control as president — especially government actions — and I will insist that the government does its part of the job.

But whether our efforts are successful will finally depend on you as much as on me. Your decisions — made every day at your service station or your grocery store, in your business, in your union meetings — will determine our nation's answer to inflation as much as decisions made here in the White House or by the Congress on Capitol Hill.

I cannot guarantee that our joint effort will succeed. In fact, it is almost certain not to succeed if success means quick or dramatic changes. Every free government on earth is wrestling with this problem of inflation, and every one of them knows that a long-term disease requires long-term treatment. It is up to us to make the improvements we can, even at the risk of partial failure, rather than to ensure failure by not trying at all.

Government Must Set Example

I will concentrate my efforts within the government. We know that government is not the only cause of inflation. But it is one of the causes, and government does set an example. Therefore, it must take the lead in fiscal restraint.

We are going to hold down government spending, reduce the budget deficit, and eliminate government waste.

We will slash federal hiring and cut the federal work force.

We will eliminate needless regulations.

We will bring more competition back to our economy.

And we will oppose any further reduction in federal income taxes until we have convincing prospects that inflation will be controlled.

Let me explain what each one of these steps means.

The federal deficit is too high. Our people are simply sick and tired of wasteful federal spending and the inflation it brings with it.

We have already had some success. We have brought the deficit down by one-third since I ran for president — from more than $66 billion in fiscal year 1976, to about $40 billion in fiscal year 1979 — a reduction of more than $25 billion in the federal deficit in just three years.

It will keep going down. Next year with tough restraints on federal spending and moderate economic growth in prospect, I plan to reduce the budget deficit to less than one-half what it was when I ran for office — to $30 billion or less.

The government has been spending too great a portion of what our Nation produces. During my campaign I promised to cut the government's share of our total national spending from 23 percent, which it was then, to 21 percent in fiscal year 1981.

We now plan to meet that goal one year earlier.

Reducing the deficit will require difficult and unpleasant decisions.

We must face a time of national austerity. Hard choices are necessary if we want to avoid consequences that are even worse.

I intend to make those hard choices. I have already vetoed bills that would undermine our fight against inflation, and the Congress has sustained those vetoes. I know that the Congress will continue to cooperate in the effort to meet our needs in responsible, non-inflationary ways.

Will Use Veto

I will use the administrative and the budgetary powers of my office, including the veto, if necessary, to keep our Nation firmly on the path of fiscal restraint.

Restraint involves tax policy as well as spending decisions. Tax reduction has never been more politically popular than it is today. But if future tax cuts are made rashly, with no eye on the budget deficits, they will hurt us all by causing more inflation.

There are tax cuts which could directly lower costs and prices and help in the fight against inflation. I may consider ways to reduce those particular taxes while still cutting the budget deficit, but until we have a convincing prospect of controlling inflation, I will oppose any further reductions in federal income taxes.

To keep the government a manageable size, I am ordering tonight a reduction in federal hiring. This order will mean a reduction of more than 20,000 in the number of permanent federal employees already budgeted for this fiscal year and will cut the total size of the federal work force.

I have already placed a 5.5 percent cap on the pay increase for federal employees, and federal executive officers are receiving no pay increases at all.

It is not enough just to control government deficits, spending and hiring. We must also control the costs of government regulations.

In recent years, Congress has passed a number of landmark statutes to improve social and environmental conditions. We must and we will continue progress toward protecting the health and safety of the American people.

But we must also realize that everything has a price — and that consumers eventually pick up the tab. Where regulations are essential, they must be efficient. Where they fight inflation, they should be encouraged. Where they are unnecessary, they should be removed.

Reduced Regulation

Early this year, I directed federal agencies to eliminate unnecessary regulations and to analyze the costs and benefits of new ones. Today, for instance, the Occupational Safety and Health Administration, sometimes called OSHA, eliminated nearly 1,000 unnecessary regulations.

Now we can build on this progress.

I have directed a council of my regulatory departments and agencies to coordinate their regulations, to prevent overlapping and duplication.

Most important, the council will develop a unified calendar of planned major regulations. The calendar will give us, for the first time, a comprehensive list of regulations the federal government is proposing, with their costs and objectives.

As president, I will personally use my authority to ensure that regulations are issued only when needed and that they meet their goals at the lowest possible cost.

We are also cutting away the regulatory thicket that has grown up around us, and giving our competitive free enterprise system a chance to grow up in its place.

Last year we gave the airline industry a fresh shot of competition. Regulations were removed. Free market forces drove prices down, record numbers of passengers traveled — and profits went up. Our new airline deregulation bill will make these benefits permanent. For the first time in decades, we have actually deregulated a major industry.

Next year, we will work with Congress to bring more competition to others, such as the railroad and trucking industries.

Of all our weapons against inflation, competition is the most powerful. Without real competition, prices and wages go up — even when demand is going down.

We must therefore work to allow more competition wherever possible so that powerful groups — government, business, labor — must think twice before abusing their economic power.

We will redouble our efforts to put competition back into the American free enterprise system.

Another reason for inflation is the slowdown in productivity growth. More efficient production is essential if we are to control inflation, make American goods more competitive in world markets, add new jobs, and increase the real incomes of our people.

We have made a start toward improving productivity. The tax bill just passed by the Congress includes many of the investment incentives that I recommended last January. Federal support for research and development will continue to increase, especially for basic research. We will coordinate and strengthen federal programs that support productivity improvements throughout our economy.

Inflation in the Essentials

Our Government efforts will attack the inflation that hurts most — inflation in the essentials: Food, housing, and medical care.

We will continue to use our agricultural policies to sustain farm production, to maintain stable prices, and to keep inflation down.

Rising interest rates have always accompanied inflation. They add further to the costs of business expansion and to what consumers must pay when they buy houses and other consumer items.

The burden of controlling inflation cannot be left to monetary policy alone, which must deal with the problem through tight restrictions on money and credit that push interest rates up.

I will work for a balanced, concerted, and sustained program under which tight budget restraint, private wage and price moderation, and responsible monetary policy support each other.

If successful, we should expect lower inflation and lower interest rates for consumers and businesses alike.

As for medical care, where costs have gone up much faster than the general inflation rate, the most important step we can take is to pass a strong bill to control hospital costs. This year, the Senate passed one. Next year, I will try again, and I believe the whole Congress will act to hold down hospital costs — if your own Members of Congress hear from you.

Between now and January, when the new Congress convenes, I will be preparing a package of specific legislative proposals to help fight inflation.

The government will do its part, but in a country like ours, government cannot do the job alone.

In the end, the success or failure of this effort will also rest on whether the private sector will accept — and act on — the voluntary wage and price standards I am announcing tonight.

'Standards Are Fair'

These standards are fair. They are standards that everyone can follow. If we do follow them, they will slow prices down

— so that wages will not have to chase prices just to stay even.

And they point the way toward an eventual cure for inflation, by removing the pressures that cause it in the first place.

In the last ten years, in our attempts to protect ourselves from inflation, we have developed attitudes and habits that actually keep inflation going once it has begun. Most companies raise their prices because they expect costs to rise.

Unions call for large wage settlements because they expect inflation to continue. Because we expect it to happen, it does happen, and once it is started, wages and prices chase each other up and up.

It is like a crowd standing at a football stadium. No one can see any better than when everyone is sitting down — but no one is willing to be the first to sit down.

Except for our lowest paid workers, I am asking all employees in this country to limit total wage increases to a maximum of 7 percent per year. From tonight on, every contract signed and every pay raise granted should meet this standard.

My price limitation will be equally strict. Our basic target for economy-wide price increases is 5.75 percent. To reach this goal, I am tonight setting a standard for each firm in the Nation to hold its price increases at least one-half of one percentage point below what they averaged during 1976 and 1977.

Of course, we have to take into account binding commitments already in effect, which will prevent an absolute adherence to these standards.

But this price standard is much lower than this year's inflation rate — and more important, it is less than the standard for wage increases. That difference is accounted for by rising productivity — and it will allow the income of America's workers to stay ahead of inflation.

This is a standard for everyone to follow — everyone. As far as I am concerned, every business, every union, every professional group, every individual in this country, has no excuse not to adhere to these standards. If we meet these standards, the real buying power of your paycheck will rise.

The difficulty with a voluntary program is that workers fear that if they cooperate with the standards while others do not, then they will suffer if inflation continues.

Rebate Program

To deal with this concern, I will ask the Congress next January to enact a program that workers who observe the standards would be eligible for a tax rebate if the inflation rate is more than 7 percent. In other words, they would have a real wage insurance policy against inflation which might be caused by others.

This will give our workers an additional incentive to observe the program — and

will remove their only legitimate reason not to cooperate.

Because this is not a mandatory control plan, I cannot stop an irresponsible corporation from raising its prices, or a selfish group of employees from using its power to demand excessive wages. But then if that happens, the government will respond — using the tools of government authority and public opinion.

Soon after they raise prices or demand pay increases that are excessive, the company or the union will feel the pressure that the public can exert, through new competition to drive prices down, or removal of government protections and privileges which they now enjoy.

We will also make better use of the $80 billion worth of purchases the government makes from private industry each year. We must be prudent buyers. If costs rise too fast, we can delay those purchases as your family would — or switch to another supplier. We may not buy a fleet of cars this year, for example, if cars cost too much, or we may channel our purchases to suppliers who have observed our wage and price standards rather than to buy from those who have not.

We will require firms that supply goods and services to the government to certify their compliance with the wage and price standards. We will make every effort, within legal limits, to deny government contracts to companies that fail to meet our wage and price standards.

We will use our buying power more effectively — to make price restraint and competition a reality.

The government now extends economic privileges to many parts of the private economy — special franchises, protected wages and prices, subsidies, protection from foreign competition. If wages or prices rise too fast in some industry, we will take that as a sign that those privileges are no longer needed — and that this protection should be removed.

We will make sure that no part of our economy is able to use its special privilege or its concentrated power to victimize the rest of us.

Public Cooperation Needed

This approach I have outlined will not end inflation. It simply improves our chances of making it better rather than worse.

To summarize the plan I am announcing tonight:

We will cut the budget deficit.

We will slash federal hiring and reduce the federal work force.

We will restrain federal pay.

We will delay further tax cuts.

We will remove needless regulations.

We will use federal policy to encourage more competition. We will set specific standards for both wages and prices throughout the economy. We will use all the powers at our disposal to make this program work. And we will submit new

anti-inflation proposals to the Congress next January, including the real wage insurance proposal I have discussed tonight.

I have said many times that these steps will be tough — and they are. But I also said they will be fair — and they are. They apply equally to all groups. They give all of us an equal chance to move ahead.

And these proposals, which give us a chance, also deserve a chance. If tomorrow, or next week, or next month, you ridicule them, ignore them, pick them apart before they have a chance to work, then you will have reduced their chance of succeeding.

These steps can work, but that will take time, and you are the ones who can give them that time. If there is one thing I am asking of every American tonight, it is to give this plan a chance to work — a chance to work for us.

You can help give it that chance by using your influence.

Business and labor must know that you will not tolerate irresponsible price and wage increases. Your elected officials must know how you feel as they make difficult choices.

Too often the only voices they hear are those of special interests, supporting their own narrow cause. If you want government officials to cut inflation, you have to make sure that they hear your voice.

I have heard you with unmistakable clarity.

Nearly 40 years ago, when the world watched to see whether his nation would survive, Winston Churchill defied those who thought Britain would fall to the Nazi threat. Churchill replied by asking his countrymen, "What kind of people do they think we are?"

There are those today who say that a free economy cannot cope with inflation, and that we have lost our ability to act as a nation rather than as a collection of special interests. And I reply, "What kind of people do they think we are?"

I believe that our people, our economic system, and our government are equal to this task. I hope that you will prove me right.

Thank you, and good night. ∎

Details of Program

The White House distributed the following "fact sheet" Oct. 24 to help provide details of President Carter's anti-inflation program:

Federal Government Actions

The federal government alone cannot solve the inflation problem, but it must take the lead. The administration will do everything in its power to ensure that its actions are consistent with the objectives of the anti-inflation program.

Budgetary Policy

● Substantial progress has been made in reducing the rate of unemployment. But further progress in reducing unemployment will depend on our success in reducing the rate of inflation. The budget that will be submitted in January will give top priority to moderating inflation. To achieve that goal the president will:

—Put a tight rein on the growth of federal spending. He has pledged to cut the share of Gross National Product accounted for by federal spending from 23 percent in FY 1976 to about 21 percent in FY 1980, one year ahead of his previously announced schedule.

—Reduce the federal deficit. In fiscal year 1976, the federal deficit was $66 billion. In just three years, by 1979, the deficit will be cut to below $40 billion. In the 1980 budget, the deficit will be reduced still further — to less than one-half the 1976 deficit.

• In order to contribute to these goals, the president has imposed severe limits on the hiring of federal employees. Effective immediately, for an indefinite period, federal agencies will be permitted to fill only one out of two vacancies as they occur.

Regulatory Policy

• Programs to protect the environment and the health and safety of workers and consumers are vital. But the achievement of these critical objectives should not place unnecessary burdens on the economy. Regulatory agencies are now required to analyze major new regulations to identify and compare benefits and costs. In addition, the president has:

—Directed the formation of a Regulatory Council. This council will include all regulatory departments and agencies. The council will have the important task of coordinating duplicative and overlapping regulations, in concert with the Office of Management and Budget's efforts to enforce the regulatory-process Executive Order 12044.

—Directed the new Regulatory Council to develop a unified *calendar* of major regulations. The calendar will provide, for the first time, a comprehensive list of major regulations to be proposed by the various agencies of the federal government. This calendar will facilitate a comprehensive and consistent approach to the evaluation of costs and benefits of proposed regulations. The council will help to ensure that regulatory objectives are achieved at the lowest possible cost.

—Pledged to use his authority to ensure that regulations are issued only when necessary and that they achieve their goals at the lowest possible cost.

—Directed each Executive branch regulatory agency to include additional regulations that have a major economic impact in the "sunset" reviews that are required by E.O. 12044.

Private Sector Actions

Success of this anti-inflation effort will depend upon the cooperation of the private sector. To this end, the president has set forth explicit numerical standards of behavior for pay and prices in the year ahead.

Pay Standard

• Annual increases in wages and private fringe benefits should not exceed *7 percent*.

—Workers earning less than $4.00 per hour will be exempt as well as wage contracts already signed.

—In new collective bargaining situations, a contract in which wage and fringe benefit increases average no more than 7 percent annually over the life of the contract will be consistent with the standard. In evaluating a contract for consistency with the standard, cost-of-living clauses will be evaluated using a 6 percent per year rate of price inflation over the life of the contract.

—No more than an 8 percent pay increase should be included in the first year of a multi-year contract.

—Increases above the standard will be acceptable to the extent that they reflect changes in work rules and practices that show demonstrable productivity improvements.

—The standard does *not* apply to individual workers. The standard applies to *average* pay increases for *groups* of workers. Firms will be expected to divide their work force into three categories:

(a) management employees, (b) groups of employees covered by separate collectively bargained contracts, and (c) all other employees.

Price Standard

• Individual firms are expected to limit their price increases over the next year to *one-half of one percentage point* below their average annual rate of price increase during 1976-77.

—If wage-rate increases for a firm decelerate by more than one-half percentage point from the 1976-77 base period, greater deceleration in prices will be required in order to ensure that savings are reflected in prices.

—The standard does not apply to specific products, but to a firm's overall average price.

—Firms unable to meet the one-half percent deceleration standard due to *unavoidable* cost increases must demonstrate, as an alternative, that their before-tax profit margins are no higher than in the best two of the last three years.

Objectives for the Program

• The pay and price standards have been developed to be consistent with one another.

—The deceleration standard for prices can be related to the wage standard by adding 0.5 percentage point to the 7 percent wage standard to reflect scheduled increases in legislatively mandated payroll costs and deducting 1.75 percentage points for productivity growth. The result is a 5.75 percent economy-wide rate of increase in unit labor costs. If firms reduce their average price increases by the price standard — that is, if they reduce their average price increase by one-half percentage point below the average rate of price increase in 1976-77 — the result would be a 5.75 percent increase in prices of nonfood commodities and services. The pay and price standards are thus consistent with one another.

—Because of the allowances necessary to deal with a complex economy — such as the treatment of wage contracts already signed and the existence of some uncontrollable cost increases — widespread observance of the standards would lead to an overall rate of inflation of 6 to 6.5 percent in the year ahead, well below the rate of inflation in 1978 to date.

Real Wage Insurance

• The president will recommend to the Congress a program of "real wage insurance." Under this program, workers who are members of groups that meet the pay standard would receive a tax rebate if the rate of inflation in the year ahead exceeds 7 percent. The program will be developed for submission to the Congress in January. Although final decisions remain to be made, the broad outlines of the program are as follows:

—The amount of the rebate would be equal to the difference between the actual rate of inflation and 7 percent, multiplied by an individual worker's pay, up to some reasonable limit.

—Workers who are members of groups that meet the 7 percent pay limitation would be eligible for the real wage insurance.

—The rebate would be paid *only* if the rate of inflation in the year ahead actually exceeds 7 percent.

Incentives for Compliance

The administration will interpret wage and price increases above the standards as indications of inflationary conditions, such as shortages, excessive market power, or shelter from competition. Thus, increases in excess of the standards will trigger actions by the government such as:

—Reexamining various restrictions on imports and, where possible and appropriate, relaxing them.

—Asking regulatory agencies to review rate levels and other rules in light of the standards for wages and prices.

—Seeking modification in those regulations that set minimum levels for prices or wages in specific situations.

Government Purchases

• The federal government itself is a major purchaser of goods and services. By channeling its procurement to those firms whose price and wage decisions meet the standards, it can realize long-term savings in its procurement budget and simultaneously take the lead in fighting inflation.

—To the extent consistent with legal requirements and ensuring national security, the president will direct government agencies to limit purchases to those firms observing the pay and price standards.

—After January 1, the government will require firms awarded contracts in excess of $5 million to certify that they are observing the standards.

—This program will be administered by the Office of Federal Procurement Policy (OFPP) of the OMB.

—Specific procedures to carry out this policy will be announced soon by OFPP and by The Council on Wage and Price Stability (CWPS).

Monitoring

• The Council on Wage and Price Stability will be expanded by about 100 persons to monitor the adherence to the wage and price standards by firms and employee groups.

—CWPS has the authority to obtain, where necessary, required information on prices, profits and wage rates. It will publicly identify areas of the economy and firms that are not complying with the standards.

—In addition CWPS will monitor on a regular basis wage and price developments of individual firms whose annual sales exceed $500 million. It will also monitor individually all major collective bargaining settlements. ∎

Carter to City Officials

Following is the White House text of President Carter's Nov. 27 speech to the League of Cities 1978 meeting in St. Louis, Mo.

Thank you very much. President Tom Moody, thank you for that introduction; my good friend, soon to be President, John Rousakis, Vice President Jessie Rattley, President Bill McNichols; a great help to me and all of you, I am sure, Alan Beals; Governor Teasdale, Senator Hatch, Senator Jake Garn, former Mayor of Salt Lake City, and who would have been perhaps almost surely President of this organization had he not been elected to the U.S. Senate; members of the board, members of the National League of Cities:

I spent this last weekend at Camp David with 30 relatives, and I am very grateful to escape — (Laughter) — and to come and join you in a wonderful city. I received the congratulations and interest of my own family. Amy said that when I got to St. Louis I would find not only a beautiful city but one of the finest zoos in the world. My brother Billy pointed out that there is one of the largest breweries in the world here. (Laughter and applause) I had other comments from different members of

my family. So I want to thank you for inviting me.

It is very good to see so many old friends and to come to this delightful community to share with you my thoughts about American cities.

But in any discussion of where we have been, where we are, and what we must do to conserve the greatness of our cities, we must also deal with our number one economic problem, and that is inflation. I admired the strength and the viability of our cities when I was a boy growing up in Southwest Georgia. I first experienced it as a child when I went from Archery to Plains and then a little later to our county seat of Americus and eventually to the metropolis of Atlanta.

After I was elected President, I began to realize more vividly the problems of our cities. Shortly after the election, two men knocked on my door. I went outside. It was Mayor Abraham Beame and Governor Carey. I asked them what they needed. They said, "We need a loan guarantee of $1,650,000,000.00 and two bus tickets back to New York." (Laughter)

We have, I think, come a long way since then. And I am in a somewhat better position both to appreciate and to help the dynamic cities of our Nation since I have become President. I want you to help me and me to help you build and conserve cities that are bright, vital, filled with life and filled with enterprise.

Close Cooperation

That requires, as you know, a close cooperation between cities, counties, states, the Federal Government, private citizens, and our own free enterprise system.

Essential to this partnership is a long-term commitment of efficient federal aid to cities.

This is how you and I have worked together already in the last 22 months. After my election in 1976, I met with the Board of the League of Cities. I learned then that your most urgent need was for a comprehensive local public works program.

You asked for $3 billion. At my urging, the Congress added $4 billion to the local public works programs.

We started the Urban Development Action Grant, the UDAG program. The **result has been a net gain** of more than 6 million new jobs since I was elected.

More important, our cooperation has resulted in the evolution of our Nation's first comprehensive urban policy — a goal of the National League of Cities for 21 years — a policy of action, not default, to enhance the quality of American cities.

I have already initiated much of that program administratively. Following your advice, we made more than 100 changes to existing federal programs, and I have issued four Executive Orders to make those programs more effective.

Stopping Job Losses

My first order reversed the disturbing

trend of moving federal jobs and facilities out of cities into the suburbs.

I directed the General Services Administration to make every effort to locate new federal facilities and jobs in central cities.

As an example, the Old Post Office Building here in St. Louis is being renovated for federal offices under this program. Its first level, incidentally, will include restaurants and shops to help draw people downtown.

In talking to the Mayor on the way in from the airport, we also discussed a vital UDAG program for this central city; $150 million, matching UDAG grants, on roughly a ten-to-one basis.

We need your help and your initiative to enhance the value of these policies and these programs.

Another Executive Order directed a greater share of federal purchases to bidders from high unemployment areas.

A third Executive Order established an urban impact process for any major new federal initiative. This was a direct result of the National League of Cities' long effort to dramatize the often unforeseen effects of new federal programs in our cities.

The fourth order established an interagency coordinating committee to target, to package and to coordinate federal assistance to cities.

We also reordered the priorities of the Economic Development Administration. When I took office, only 15 percent of EDA funds went to cities. This year half, one-half of EDA funds will go to cities.

I directed the Federal Environmental Protection Agency to change the priorities of its multibillion dollar waste treatment programs. The new emphasis will be to rehabilitate older systems in disrepair — instead of encouraging urban sprawl with new construction.

We also submitted to Congress 19 bills as the legislative program of our urban policy that you helped to evolve. It was a tough fight, still going on, but we have already won enactment of 13 of those bills. Of course, you deserve much of this credit.

We reauthorized the CETA program. There will be an estimated 660,000 jobs. We toughened requirements in CETA to eliminate fraud and abuse and to ensure that only genuinely disadvantaged workers get those jobs. And we added incentives for businesses which hire and train those same workers.

We passed a targeted employment tax credit for businesses which hire jobless young people. We also included in the tax code a credit for rehabilitation of older industrial and commercial buildings. These were the first major reforms of the tax code explicitly to help businesses and individuals stay in the cities and not move out.

The new Surface Transportation Act, which Brock Adams is discussing with you more thoroughly at this convention, will now let us plan and build balanced transportation system.

We worked to secure the New York City loan guarantee, and initiated other measures that underscore my commitment to cities.

And we added a new emphasis throughout our urban programs to help rebuild the private economic base of our cities. I want to convince everyone that it is good business to invest in the cities.

I am proud of these accomplishments. (Applause) I am proud of these accomplishments and you should be proud, too. I certainly couldn't have done it without you. The Congress has responded well. It is just a good beginning for a new and continuing partnership.

I want you to know that my commitment to this partnership remains firm. Together, our progress will continue. I will not step back from this job as long as I hold office. (Applause)

Attack on Inflation

I am also determined to alleviate another program that now affects cities and every American more deeply than any other economic problem. That is inflation.

I don't need to tell you how inflation affects our cities. You can see it every week on purchasing invoices, on utility bills, higher salaries, constantly increasing budget costs of the same items. Inflation eats into maintenance and capital funds, and with restricted budgets, your streets, buildings and parks fall into greater disrepair.

The same thing happens throughout our economy. Consumers put off needed purchases. Businesses tend to postpone modernization. Our factories age a few more years. For every year of this, we become much less productive.

In other words, inflation jeopardizes the economic progress we have made since the recession of 1974-1975 — including the fragile recovery of our troubled cities. It means that federal dollars sent to cities buy less. General revenue sharing, for example, has sent about $6.2 billion each year to states and cities since 1972.

But by next year its purchasing power will have dropped one-third.

Cities badly need these dollars. And the Federal Government cannot replace all such major losses to inflation. Plainly, the future of our cities is at stake in our fight against inflation. And just as plainly, the people whom we serve, you and I, want something done. They will not accept Federal and local government indifference about inflation. I have no doubt that the American people want the Federal Government to act. They want greater efficiency, less waste, less corruption. They want restraints on government spending and government taxing.

Those are demands that I cannot — and will not — disregard. Last month I announced a tough program to fight inflation. I chose a course that is politically difficult. But I intend to hold to it.

Fiscal 1980 Budget

The 1980 fiscal year budget will be very, very tight. I have pledged to submit a 1980 budget with a deficit of $30 billion or less. That is much less than one-half the deficit of fiscal year 1976 when I was running for office.

It will not be an easy task, but I intend to do this without starving useful programs. I will not make wholesale, arbitrary spending cuts. We are simply going line by line, item by item, through the budget to limit or to cut those things we cannot afford.

For the cities, the impact will be clear. We will do as much as we can within the necessarily severe limits. We can and we will propose new programs like the National Development Bank.

We will take into account explosive growth in rapidly growing areas that bring about serious problems, as well as we take into account the problems of areas which are in distress.

But there will be little money for new initiatives next year. It will be an austere budget. However, I promise that the cities will bear no more and no less than a fair share of budget restraint.

My responsibility as President to the people of the United States is to demonstrate clearly, when the budget is presented to the Congress, that there is a sound and fair and equitable balance as we meet the needs of urban Americans and rural Americans, to provide for an education, jobs, defense, domestic programs and for our international programs. All will be examined very closely. All will be examined very closely. And I can assure you that the budget will be fair.

Streamline City Aid

We will continue to streamline federal aid to cities. When I ran for President, I pledged to make urban programs more efficient, more responsive, simpler and more targeted, and to be evolved and administered in closer cooperation with you, the local officials of our country. I am carrying out that pledge to the best of my ability.

I know from personal experience that federal programs often cost the state and local governments too much. And frankly, that is still true today.

For example, for the small town of Junior, West Virginia, it took seven years, $1.7 million and five different federal agencies to build a required sewer and treatment system.

I know that we can do better. That is why my urban policy emphasizes less processing time, less overhead costs, less paperwork, and better coordination with you and with state officials. (Applause)

OSHA, for instance, has eliminated hundreds, even thousands, of unnecessary regulations. HEW is eliminating, simplifying or consolidating about 60 percent of its nearly 1,400 planning requirements. EPA is doing the same with over half of its 300 planning requirements. We are doing that throughout the Government.

We need your continued help. You should point out specifically those planning requirements, those reporting requirements that you consider to be unnecessary, too

complicated or required too frequently. We can also expect to benefit from our review of new federal regulations for their cost impact. I am going to use my power as President to stop cold any new regulation that ignores its impact on costs to cities and states. (Applause)

I urge you to contact Jack Watson on my staff directly, or me, if necessary, to point out where this commitment might tend to be violated. We will stop it immediately, if you will let us know. (Applause)

State, Local Cooperation

But, I also expect State Government and you, the local government officials, to do your part. We have long known the inflationary impact of state or local regulations that restrict competition and raise costs.

Much of the inflation in housing, for example, comes from outmoded building codes. Productivity in building construction in the last 10 years has actually gone down, almost two percent each year. We will look to the cities and the counties to encourage local construction companies and unions to attack the problem of productivity directly, to re-examine the cost-inflating work practices and the possibility of adopting new technologies that will combat rising costs. We will look to the localities to attack directly high real estate transaction costs. Similarly, the states and localities must attack other restraints on competition, both governmental and private.

These include the use of licensing to restrict entry into occupations and eliminate competition, restrictions by private groups on advertising of prices by their members, insurance regulations that hold premium costs up, public utility rate structures that fail to encourage conservation and so promote the unnecessary installation of costly additional capacity.

In the next few weeks I will be calling on state and local officials and working closely with you when necessary to revise regulations of businesses to increase competition and reduce costs and to follow restrained, prudent tax and spending policies.

In this fight, all sectors have a role. I have taken painful action at the federal level already by reducing federal spending, putting a cap on federal employment, putting a cap on federal salaries, vetoing popular legislation, and performing a tough cost analysis benefit of new regulations. The most important things that cities can do to fight inflation is to make sure that all goods and services which you procure come only from suppliers who will certify that they are in compliance with federal wage and price guidelines.

The second is for cities themselves to abide by our wage and price standards in negotiating contracts and in setting your own fees. This will not only help hold down costs but set an example for private firms and others in your own localities. I call on you today to follow the guidelines in these two important areas. But these steps alone will not be enough.

Building Foundation

Let me repeat what I said earlier. The 1980 budget will be very, very tight. It will disappoint those who do not take inflation seriously. It will disappoint those who expect protection from inflation while someone else bears the burden. It will disappoint those who think only of next year and not the next decade. And it will disappoint those who excpect constantly-expanding federal aid and a constantly-expanding number of federal programs and agencies.

We must control inflation. We must bring it down. We must stop it from interfering with our lives, our aspirations and our hopes for the future.

That is why I need your understanding and your cooperation and your help to solve this problem once and for all. If we fail to control inflation, we face a deeply troubled future. We would erode the commitment of the American public to helping cities, to helping the poor, to helping the elderly, the jobless, the sick and the weak. That is a prospect we dare not face.

But as we are successful and bring down inflation, with a concerted effort, we can look back on these years with the satisfaction that we built a solid foundation that kept our country prosperous, compassionate and strong.

That will take an unprecedented effort by us all in the next few years. It will take imagination. It will require initiative; a close attention paid to local and unique circumstances. It will require sacrifice. And it will take the patience to realize that we cannot afford everything that we want now.

I believe strongly that we have the will to solve this problem of inflation in America. I believe strongly that the people are ready to make the necessary sacrifices, if only Government provides the leadership and the example.

I ask only that you help me in this task — that we as partners might end any drift and indecision and lead our cities and our country toward a brighter, more prosperous and a more secure future.

With your help, we will not fail.

Thank you very much. (Applause) ∎

China Relations Text

Following is the text of President Carter's Dec. 15, 1978, address announcing establishment of diplomatic relations between the United States and the People's Republic of China.

Good evening.

I would like to read a joint communique which is being simultaneously issued in Peking at this very moment by the leaders of the People's Republic of China:

"Joint Communique on the Establishment of Diplomatic Relations Between the United States of America and the People's Republic of China, January 1, 1979

"The United States of America and the People's Republic of China have agreed to recognize each other and to establish diplomatic relations as of January 1st, 1979.

"The United States recognizes the Government of the People's Republic of China as the sole legal government of China. Within this context, the people of the United States will maintain cultural, commercial and other unofficial relations with the people of Taiwan.

"The United States of America and the People's Republic of China reaffirm the principles agreed on by the two sides in the Shanghai Communique of 1972 and emphasize once again that:

"—Both sides wish to reduce the danger of international military conflict.

"—Neither should seek hegemony — that is a dominance of one nation over the other — in the Asia-Pacific region or in any other region of the world and each is opposed to efforts by any other country or group of countries to establish such hegemony.

"—Neither is prepared to negotiate on behalf of any other third party or to enter into agreements or understandings with the other directed at other states.

"—The Government of the United States of America acknowledges the Chinese position that there is but one China and Taiwan is part of China.

"—Both believe that normalization of Sino-American relations is not only in the interest of the Chinese and American peoples but also contributes to the cause of peace in Asia and in the world.

"—The United States of America and the People's Republic of China will exchange Ambassadors and establish embassies on March 1, 1979."

Yesterday, our country and the People's Republic of China reached this final historic agreement.

On January 1, 1979, a little more than two weeks from now, our two governments will implement full normalization of diplomatic relations.

As a nation of gifted people who comprise about one-fourth of the total population of the earth, China plays, already, an important role in world affairs — a role that can only grow more important in the years ahead.

We do not undertake this important step for transient tactical or expedient reasons. In recognizing the People's Republic of China, that it is the single government of China, we are recognizing simple reality. But far more is involved in this decision than just recognition of a fact.

Before the estrangement of recent decades, the American and the Chinese people had a long history of friendship. We have already begun to rebuild some of those previous ties. Now, our rapidly expanding relationship requires the kind of structure that only full diplomatic relations will make possible.

The change that I am announcing tonight will be of great long-term benefit to the peoples of both our country and China and, I believe, to all peoples of the world.

Normalization — and the expanded commercial and cultural relations that it will bring — will contribute to the well-being of our own Nation, to our own national interest, and it will also enhance the stability of Asia.

These more positive relations with China can beneficially affect the world in which we live and the world in which our children will live.

We have already begun to inform our allies and other nations and the members of the Congress of the details of our intended action. But I wish also tonight to convey a special message to the people of Taiwan — I have already communicated with the leaders in Taiwan — with whom the American people have had and will have extensive, close and friendly relations.

This is important between our two peoples.

As the United States asserted in the Shanghai Communique of 1972, issued on President Nixon's historic visit, we will continue to have an interest in the peaceful resolution of the Taiwan issue.

I have paid special attention to ensuring that normalization of relations between our country and the People's Republic will not jeopardize the well-being of the people of Taiwan.

The people of our country will maintain our current commercial, cultural, trade and other relations with Taiwan through nongovernmental means. Many other countries in the world are already successfully doing this.

These decisions and these actions open a new and important chapter in our country's history, and also in world affairs.

To strengthen and to expedite the benefits of this new relationship between China and the United States, I am pleased to announce that Vice Premier Teng has accepted my invitation and will visit Washington at the end of January. His visit will give our governments the opportunity to consult with each other on global issues and to begin working together to enhance the cause of world peace.

These events are the final result of long and serious negotiations begun by President Nixon in 1972, and continued under the leadership of President Ford. The results bear witness to the steady, determined and bipartisan effort of our country to build a world in which peace will be the goal and the responsibility of all nations.

The normalization of relations between the United States and China has no other purpose than this — the advancement of peace.

It is in this spirit, at this season of peace, that I take special pride in sharing this good news with you tonight. ∎

Index

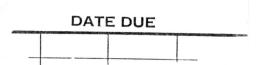

DATE DUE